German Philosophy Since Kant

ROYAL INSTITUTE OF PHILOSOPHY SUPPLEMENT: 44

EDITED BY

Anthony O'Hear

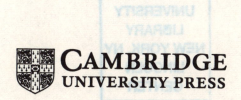

CAMBRIDGE
UNIVERSITY PRESS

PUBLISHED BY THE PRESS SYNDICATE OF THE UNIVERSITY OF CAMBRIDGE
The Pitt Building, Trumpington Street, Cambridge, CB2 1RP,
United Kingdom

CAMBRIDGE UNIVERSITY PRESS
The Edinburgh Building, Cambridge CB2 2RU, United Kingdom
40 West 20th Street, New York, NY 10011–4211, USA
10 Stamford Road, Oakleigh, Melbourne 3166, Australia

© The Royal Institute of Philosophy and the contributors 1999

Printed in the United Kingdom at the University Press, Cambridge
Typeset by Michael Heath Ltd, Reigate, Surrey

*A catalogue record for this book is available
from the British Library*

Library of Congress Cataloguing in Publication Data

German Philosophy since Kant/edited by Anthony O'Hear
     p. cm.—(Royal Institute of Philosophy supplement, ISSN
1358-2461 : 44)
     Includes index
     ISBN 0 521 66782 8 (pbk.)
     1. Philosophy, German—19th century. 2. Philosophy, German—
20th century. I. O'Hear, Anthony. II. Series.
B3181.G47 1999
193—dc21   99–35520
                                                              CIP

ISBN 0 521 66782 8 paperback
ISSN 1358-2461

Contents

Contents

Preface

The essays in this volume are based on the Royal Institute of Philosophy's annual lecture series for 1997–8. One underlying aim of the series was to show that German-speaking post-Kantian philosophers cannot be straightforwardly divided into those of an analytic bent and those of a metaphysical or idealist bent. The categories themselves will be anachronistic for many of the thinkers considered in this volume; in any case, hardly any admits of so simplistic a characterisation. As will be seen, themes and interests overlap and criss-cross in German philosophy throughout the two centuries since Kant, which may in itself cast doubt on the validity of any clear divide even to-day between 'analytic' and 'continental' philosophy.

In the main the essays are arranged in chronological order according to the philosophers considered, and the book concludes with two articles which take a longer view than those which concentrate on one, two or three figures.

In conclusion, I would like to thank all those who so generously contributed to both lecture series and book, especially Jürgen Habermas, whose contribution brings both to a fitting conclusion.

Anthony O'Hear

Notes on Contributors

Roger Hausheer, Lecturer in German, University of Bradford

Stephen Houlgate, Professor of Philosophy, University of Warwick

Christopher Janaway, Reader in Philosophy, Birkbeck College, London

David-Hillel Ruben, Professor of Philosophy, London School of Economics

Robert C. Solomon, Quincy Lee Centennial Professor, The University of Texas, Austin

Peter Simons, Professor of Philosophy University of Leeds

Hans-Johann Glock, Reader in Philosophy, University of Reading

Donald Gillies, Professor of Philosophy, King's College, London

David Bell, Professor of Philosophy, University of Sheffield

Stephen Priest, Senior Lecturer in Philosophy, University of Edinburgh

P. M. S. Hacker, Fellow of St John's College, Oxford

Thomas E. Uebel, Lecturer in Philosophy, University of Manchester

Michael Inwood, Fellow of Trinity College, Oxford

David E. Cooper, Professor of Philosophy, University of Durham

Jay Bernstein, Professor of Philosophy, Vanderbilt University

Friedel Weinert, Lecturer in Philosophy, University of Bradford

Andrew Bowie, Professor of Philosophy, Anglia Polytechnic University

Martin Seel, Professor of Philosophy, University of Giessen

Jürgen Habermas, Professor Emeritus at the Institute of Philosophy of the Johann Wolfgang Goethe University of Frankfurt.

Fichte and Schelling

ROGER HAUSHEER

I

Intellectual historians have often remarked that German thought from its earliest beginnings is marked by two major features that distinguish it from the greater part of the remainder of Western European thought. These are, first, the tendency to seek some kind of participatory relationship with nature and the universe conceived in quasi-animistic terms, which represents a kind of reversion to a much older, much more primitive way of conceiving the world and man's place in it, and has led to all kinds of mysticism. It is a strain in the history of German thought which has been brought out very clearly by Lévy-Bruhl[1] and others. In all its forms the essential core of this view consists in the thinker's desire to place himself in the position of the creator, to become in some sense privy to his master-plan and, by engaging the productive part of his own nature, thereby himself to enter into the great act of creation by a species of co-creation. The second defining characteristic is that of antinomianism, that is to say, a hatred of laws and rules as such. This usually went hand in hand with a distrust of traditional forms of logic and reasoning and, in the more extreme cases, of all conceptual thought. Above all, emphasis was laid upon the first hand experience of the inner life of one's own subjective moral and spiritual world with all its agony and struggle; and there was a corresponding aversion to all forms of generalising and bloodless abstract schemas. The language of these mystics was therefore often dark, turbid, and rhapsodic, dealing in vast imaginative images, in deeply suggestive symbols and obscure allegories, which were intended to capture or in some sense mimic or gesture towards the living creative energy which was the pulsating source of all things. The line of these great German mystics runs from Meister Eckhart through Seuse and Tauler to Paracelsus, Weigel and Böhme, down to the brothers Helmont, and on to Angelus Silesius in the Age of Leibniz. It is also, perhaps, worth noting in addition a certain depth and earnestness which characterises much German speculation: 'The German People', Moritz Heimann once remarked, 'treats things ideal not as a banner, like other peoples, but takes them several degrees more literally than

---

[1] Lucien Lévy-Bruhl, *L'Allemagne depuis Leibniz*. 1890.

Roger Hausheer

they do, with a corresponding frivolity where things real are concerned.'[2]

These successive waves of mystical antinomianism represent a kind of running battle against the universal cosmopolitan rationalist thought of the West – first against Aquinas and the scholastics, then against the secular rational humanism of the Renaissance, and then again, against the thinkers of the early German Enlightenment. What we have, in effect, is a series of irrationalist eruptions through the smooth and polished surface of Western European thought. One after another these successive waves battered the backbone of Western scientific and enlightened thought until, in a sense, it is finally cracked by the two thinkers I propose to consider here. For Fichte and Schelling exemplify this pattern in the most dramatic and revolutionary manner. Indeed, it is scarcely an exaggeration to say that it was they, above all, who between them opened the greatest chasm between the old rationalist universalist tradition stretching from Plato to Aquinas right down to Kant and the new unpredictable world of the nineteenth and twentieth centuries.

Yet the reputation of both, and especially that of Fichte, has suffered a curious fate. Neither has as yet received his full due in the history of ideas, even in Germany itself, but this goes quite particularly for the English-speaking world. Admittedly, both thinkers – and again this is particularly true of Fichte – are at times quite especially dark, contorted, and impenetrable; but this alone is not enough to account for their comparative neglect. Their real misfortune has been to be largely eclipsed by their successors, Hegel and Schopenhauer. Hegel, many features of whose thought, and especially the dialectic, are directly derived from Fichte, went out of his way to diminish him. And again, Schopenhauer, in the entirety of whose writings there is arguably not a single substantial idea that is not derived, directly or indirectly, from Fichte or Schelling, treated his philosophical benefactors with withering scorn. The standard histories of philosophy, in Germany and elsewhere, to the present day are built around a tacit acceptance of the view of their predecessors perpetrated by Hegel and Schopenhauer. If only as an act of historical justice, therefore, claims to precedence in generating some of the most powerful and fatefully formative ideas of the past two hundred years must be established in the case of Fichte and Schelling. They loosened the old landmarks once and for all. Indeed, they belong to, and very largely shape, a phase of thought in Germany stretching roughly from the 1770's to 1830 and beyond

[2] Moritz Heimann, quoted by Egon Friedell, *Kulturgeschichte der Neuzeit*, vol. I, p. 264.

2

which was prodigiously rich and revolutionary. To find historical parallels for the creative ferment in the Germany of this period, we must go to the fourth century BC in Greece, or to Renaissance Italy, or to the 18th century France of the great Enlightenment. It literally transformed everything, and gave birth to the modern world. Fichte and Schelling are major actors in this great drama.

II

They had two immediate harbingers of very unequal quality and character, who to no small degree may be said to have formed them, namely the *Sturm und Drang* movement in literature; and, above all, Kant in the sphere of philosophy proper.

In the 1770's a movement sprang up in Germany which had not seen its like before. It was essentially driven by youth and frustration. A whole generation of young men emerged in Germany especially at the universities whose social origins made any kind of advancement virtually impossible for them but whose creative energies were bursting to express themselves. Fired partly by the critical writings of Lessing and other disciples of the Enlightenment they called in question the social fabric of their era. But there were no natural channels for their pent up and balked energies. They therefore rapidly moved from social criticism to ever more extreme forms of exhibitionistic behaviour. Eventually their rejection of things became virtually universal so that it was not just social institutions that they sought to batter down but even nature herself. This was not least due to the fact that the relentless progress of the positive sciences, and particularly the current of ideas that flowed across from the French Enlightenment, was revealing a world indifferent and even hostile to man and human concerns. Nature was being steadily robbed of her ancient enchantments; animism, anthropomorphism, religious accounts of the universe and human existence, were being remorselessly swept aside by the levelling bulldozers of natural causality. The universe was coming to be seen as a vast monolithic slab, cold, funereal and grey, in which living men were trapped like veins in marble. This prison house of the spirit is memorably epitomised by the words of the young Goethe – one of the principal figures in the *Sturm und Drang* movement – when he spoke of Holbach's *Système de la Nature* as, I quote, 'frigid, Cimmerian, corpse-like, and grey'.[3] There was no longer a breath of life, colour or movement in the world.

[3] Goethe, *Dichtung und Wahrheit*, book II.

Roger Hausheer

It was against this terrifying vision of men walled up in a closed universe that the young rebels of the *Sturm und Drang*, Lenz, Klinger, Gerstenberg and Leisewitz, hurled some of their wildest cries of anguish and despair. It is perhaps worth noting in passing the remarkable similarity between the tortured, unstructured and violently rebellious screams of unbridled self-expression of these *Stürmer und Dränger* and later manifestations of what is essentially the same mood of suffocating terror and despair before the iron laws of nature so typical of German Expressionism in the twenties of our century. Indeed, I should like to observe in passing that it seems to me that altogether too little attention is paid to the *Sturm und Drang* movement by English Germanists, both for its own intrinsic interest, and for the premonitory relationship in which it stands to later literary and intellectual currents. For the young dramatists and poets of the *Sturm und Drang*, however irritatingly adolescent and immature they may often be, were after all, among the very first writers and – though one hesitates to call them this – thinkers in the Western tradition to rebel absolutely and quite consciously against all rules and laws as such. In so doing they helped to inaugurate an era which has still not closed. Rejection of unjust or irrational rules, laws, ethical codes, and rebellion against the norms of oppressive social and political institutions, or against the ordinances and decrees of tyrants, kings, conquerors and priests, is as old as humanity itself. But the idea that all rules, as they are rules – that is, address themselves to the abstract and general properties of things with no regard to what makes them living, concrete and unique – are bad as such, is utterly novel and upsetting.

But even this revolutionary step was not enough to appease the at once so destructive and so liberating passions of these turbulent young rebels. In their most uncompromising moods their literally world-shattering ambitions were even more sweeping, for they sought at times to batter down not only the rules and customs created by men, but to burst open the iron frame of causality governing nature itself. This attempt to prise the universe apart at its very hinges – to treat the granite building-blocks of the world as so much airy insubstantial stuff to be freely moulded by the infinite operations of their titanic creative wills – marks a hitherto unparalleled development in the history of European thought. Without warning an entire set of novel attitudes is frenziedly struck out on the anvil of cosmic despair. Against the inexorable machine of human convention and nature-ordained law, and ultimately reducing these to nought, the *Stürmer und Dränger* set up the poor, fragile, trapped, yet in the end utterly free and infinitely creative human self. Hence their worship of the lonely creative personality pitting his powers

4

against the most fearful odds, the heroic outsider whose reckless failure is vastly more noble than cautious philistine success; hence their cult of pure, unbridled self-expression, utterly unadulterated by any admixture of tame convention or respectable norms; hence, too, their faith in the capacity of genius (and, at times and to a degree, of all men) to project into the world their own wholly original, self-created forms – to generate values which are not copies of anything outside themselves, but which bear intrinsically some self-authenticating mark which men intuit and embrace by some species of direct recognition – as they recognise a face or a work of art – and not by measuring them against some publicly accredited objective yardstick. As we shall see in a moment, Fichte especially caught something of this wild, exuberant, rebellious *stürmisch* mood. Their ideas hung like great storm clouds in the air of Germany when Fichte embarked on his philosophical career.

The second great presence in the background of these two thinkers is of course that of Immanuel Kant. He stood at the absolute opposite pole from that of the *Kraftgenies* and *Kraftkerls* and turbulent and disordered young students of whom I have just spoken. He was in almost every way a product of the eighteenth century Enlightenment. He was totally averse to enthusiasm and exuberance of any kind and his criticisms of the excesses of self-expression indulged in by false genius, which we find in his *Critique of Judgement* and elsewhere in his writings, testify to the deep horror he felt for all forms of irrationalism and unbridled exhibitionism. He was a champion of calm methodical, rational method, and believed that orderliness in thought and action were prerequisites for any form of civilized life. Above all, he was greatly influenced and impressed by the empirical sciences of his time and believed in the search for universal principles and laws wherever these could be found. Yet for all this he is a kind of Janus figure in the history of modern thought: one face – cool, classical, marmoreal – calmly contemplates a two thousand year old tradition of rational thought; the other – mysterious, perplexed, and anguished – is turned towards a stormy and ambiguous future. Or, to vary the image, Kant stands with one foot firmly planted on eighteenth century soil; with the other, he has entered a quagmire, or, more aptly perhaps, is probing a bottomless abyss. Kant's work is much more than just a highly significant historical episode in a specialised area of human speculation, namely the evolution of German idealism. Rather, his thought marks a major revolutionary turning-point in the history of the human mind itself and its interpretation of its place in, and relationship to, the scheme of things. It has a universal sweep and application unparalleled in modern times. The radically creative,

5

formative powers of the human mind itself were established with scientific precision for the first time. It is a familiar story and I shall do no more than to sketch its outlines here tonight. As we all know, Kant was a trained mathematical physicist deeply versed in the theories of Newton. He was scandalised by the Babel of conflicting voices that he encountered in the sphere of philosophy and metaphysics. If universally accepted order is possible in Newtonian physics, he argued, then the same should also be possible for the humanly even more important realm of metaphysics. He therefore set out painstakingly and systematically to trace the bounds of all possible human thought. In the *Critique of Pure Reason*, where he investigated the prerequisites for our knowledge of the external world, that is to say of theoretical knowledge in general, he came to certain revolutionary conclusions. The forms of space, time, and the categories – substance, relation, causality, etc – are all deduced from the general universal structure of the knowing subject itself. These modes of perception and understanding therefore, do not inhere in the objective world itself but are in some sense imposed upon it by ourselves. In this way the formative, creative capacities of the mind are extended in an unprecedented, almost Promethean fashion. But at this point Kant now found himself in serious difficulties. For in so far as I, as a finite empirical being, possess a body which exists in nature and is subject to nature and natures laws, as these have been most accurately described by Newtonian physics, I do not possess freedom. As a denizen of the world of Kantian phenomena, I am wholly and exhaustively predictable in principle. Clearly, there is some kind of profound conflict here with the claims of freedom and morality. Kant attempts to address this problem in his second great critique, the *Critique of Practical Reason*. In this work he seeks to reinstate freedom, morality, God, and an immortal soul as postulates of the moral life. I cannot discover or prove these theoretically: I can only assert them by a free act of will. And to this end the fateful distinction between the empirical self and the noumenal self is made. As contrasted with my normal everyday finite self, my noumenal or higher self is raised clear of the causal treadmill. This has certain very far-reaching consequences for Kant's moral theory, and, as we shall see, for Fichte and what has come to be called the German concept of freedom.

But Kant's three critiques bring together a set of philosophical positions which, though they proved revolutionary in the history of thought, represent a highly unstable mixture of incompatible notions. Apart from the unresolved and perhaps unresolvable tension between the empirical and the noumenal self, at least two further features of Kant's philosophy show serious signs of defect.

Hegel once described Kants things-in-themselves as 'ghosts hovering at the portals of the Kantian philosophy'.[4] This is very apt because not only can we know nothing of these things-in-themselves, since they lie outside the sphere of phenomena, but also in some mysterious fashion Kant claims they are capable of some kind of causal influence upon us. But this is a contradiction of what Kant says about causality. Causality operates solely within the sphere of natural phenomena. To extend the category of causality, therefore, into the realm of things-in-themselves, is quite illicit.

And again, it has often been pointed out that Kant produced not one, but three systems, which lie uneasily side by side. They are not all deduced from one single originating principle, and they are not all perfectly compatible with each other in some neat logical fashion. The essential point we wish to stress here, however, is that with Kant a profound shift occurs in the conception of ethics: morality ceases to be grounded on knowledge or objective truth, as had been customary in western philosophy from its earliest beginnings, and now for the first time the force and quality of the will and of willing as having value in their own right is thrust to the fore. Since Kant had shown that knowledge can illuminate but a tiny portion of the world and is incapable of penetrating to the innermost essence of reality, so knowledge, theoretical reason, rational investigation was bound to be driven from the position of pre-eminence it traditionally enjoyed. Practical reason usurped its place. Not knowledge and intellect are the supreme human values but self-assertion and will.

III

Kant's immediate contemporaries were not slow to point to some of these inconsistencies and weaknesses. Among the most penetrating, logically effective, and constructively creative of these was Johann Gottlieb Fichte. But first let me say something briefly about him as a man and as a character. He has quite rightly been described as the Napoleon of German philosophy. He was renowned in his time and after for his indomitable, inflexible will, his utter contempt for anyone who dissented from his views and his tyrannical, overmastering personality generally in his dealings with others. In his life and in his works he displayed an ethical rigour second not even to that of Luther. He is, indeed, the German *Willensphilosoph* par excellence. The great Goethe once wrote of him: 'He was one of the most formidable personalities I have ever encountered, and in some higher

[4] Hegel, *Geschichte der Philosophie*, ed. Lasson, p. 73.

7

sense his views were beyond criticism; but how could he ever have kept in step with the world, which he viewed as his own free creation?[5] He came of very humble origins, was frequently baulked in the course of his development and saw life as consisting in the battering down, one after another, of an endless series of obstacles. He was born in 1764, the son of humble weavers and was soon picked out by the local baron for his quite extraordinary powers of memory and intelligence. He was very early on oppressed by the determinism of Spinoza. And for quite a lengthy period of his early manhood he languished hopelessly, as he thought, in the chains of an unbreakable fatalism. From this he was awoken abruptly by reading Kant's *Critique of Practical Reason*. He was asked by a student to teach him the philosophy of Kant and it was from this moment onwards that Fichte dated the transforming revelation that caused the scales to fall from his eyes. Suddenly his sense of despair lifted, for here he found to hand the means whereby he could cure the terrible conflict between heart and head which to him, as to the *Stürmer und Dränger* had seemed utterly intractable. And it was after a deep and thorough reading of the works of Kant that he proceeded to produce, in 1794, the first version of his *Wissenschaftslehre* which subsequently went through ten or more versions, but which at its core propounded one and the same vision.

Of Kant's problems with things-in-themselves Fichte made short work. He simply declared that there was no justification for postulating their existence at all, and proceeded to deduce the whole scheme of reality from the subjective self, the ego, *das reine Ich*. He thereby also found a solution to Kant's second major difficulty, that produced by the three largely independent or self-subsistent systems that he produced – the *Critique of Pure Reason*, the *Critique of Practical Reason* and the *Critique of Judgement*. For now, unlike Kant, Fichte believed that he had been able to penetrate to the original root of all forms of experience and to deduce them from that root. How exactly does he do this? He does it by demonstrating that what is absolutely primal and original is not thing-in-themselves but the self, the ego. This is the fundamental presupposition and prerequisite for each and every kind of experience. It alone makes experience as such possible. Since the entirety of human experience and human thought, everything that makes up the empirical realm of phenomena, is postulated in the ego and in the ego alone, it follows that the ego cannot be posited by anything other than itself. That is to say, the existence of the ego is in some sense its own product or deed and therefore not a fact – *eine Tatsache* – but an act – *eine*

[5] Goethe, *Dichtung und Wahrheit*, book 10.

8

Tathandlung. But why should the ego engage in this original act of creation? This is explained by Fichte through the fact that the ego or self, by its innermost nature, has an urge to be active, to produce; it is a nucleus of energy which naturally seeks expression through its own works. It follows, therefore, that the theoretical ego is based upon, and derived from, the practical ego, and not the other way about. The innermost essence of this practical ego is drive, will, striving. The existence of the ego then is not an assertion, but a demand, indeed an ethical demand; not an axiom, but a postulate; not a conclusion or an inference, but a decision, an act of will. Hence the first, not further reducible principle of Fichte's philosophy is: posit thyself! Without the self there is no objective world, no nature, no non-ego. So the second principle is: the ego posits a non-ego over against itself; and we have the situation then where the ego posits itself and its opposite. The theoretical ego posits an object – *einen Gegenstand* – in order that the practical ego should experience opposition – *einen Widerstand*. Thus arises a field for the exercise of free ethical action.

In short, the world is a product of the ego. The ego performs a series of acts, and thus arises what we call the external world. But these acts of the ego occur unconsciously. We – finite empirical human beings – know nothing of this creative activity. Our situation is rather like that of a man in a dream: just like dreams the objects of our ordinary experience occur to us as having an independent existence, yet nevertheless they are the product of our own minds and imaginations. This unconscious world-creating activity on the part of the ego Fichte calls 'unconscious production' (bewußtlose Produktion). The faculty whereby we carry this out is the imagination. Because such production is unconscious, the world appears to us as existing outside ourselves, as a non-ego, or object: that is, as something independent of ourselves as knowing subjects. But what we take for an object is really through and through the product of our own subjective creation. Here Fichte draws the arresting parallel with the activity of the creative artist which was to have such an influence on Schelling: 'Art', he says, 'makes the transcendental viewpoint the common one'.

The task Fichte sets himself in the *Wissenschaftslehre* – one which the transcendental philosopher alone can perform – is to raise the process which has hitherto been unconscious and instinctive into the clear light of day and render it conscious and rational. Thus by a long and highly complex series of constructive dialectical acts, which are often exceedingly intricate and obscure, he causes the world – myself and others, nature and the entire scheme of natural objects – to come into being before our very eyes. Let me quote *in extenso* a characteristic passage from his *The Vocation of Man*: 'Man does not consist of two independent and separate elements; he is absolutely one. All our thought is founded on our impulses; as a man's affections are, so is his knowledge ... I shall stand absolutely independent, thoroughly equipped and perfected through my own act and deed. The primitive source of all my other thought and of my life itself, that from which everything proceeds which can have and existence in me, for me, or through me, the innermost spirit of my spirit, – is no longer a foreign power, but it is, in the strictest possible sense, the product of my own will.' And again, 'I am wholly my own creation ... I accept that which nature announces; – but I do not accept it [i.e. the natural scientist's conception of the world] because I must; I accept it because I will.'[6]

Schleiermacher once asserted that Fichte's idealism had superseded and absorbed naive realism; our common everyday view of the world reveals itself on inspection to be incomplete and defective in ways that can be explained and rectified only by a deeper, more rigorous, more comprehensive account. The completed system of idealism – the *Wissenschaftslehre* – contains within itself, and can account fully for, the system of realism or empiricism; but not vice versa. This is the nub of Fichte's claim to priority for his system of philosophy over all others. This deep insight into what he believed to be the true relation between the human mind and the world it inhabits proved revolutionary.

I mentioned just now the German concept of freedom. It is when we come to look at how Fichte sought to resolve the tension we found in Kant between the finite empirical self and the transcendental noumenal self that this emerges most clearly. Scholars generally divide Fichte's thought into two main phases. When we look at his epistemology and metaphysics it is true that it begins with an individualistic and almost anarchistic ego, the isolated self, and this is the Fichte who is the proto-existentialist, who had a great impact on the Romantics such as Novalis, Tieck, and the Schlegels, and who is the source of what later came to be called romantic Titanism. This first phase then increasingly gives way to a collective and mystical, ontological approach to the nature of the self. Now it is no longer the isolated individual but it becomes God, the absolute, or history itself, or at times mankind, and finally, and most fatefully of all, the German nation or *Volk*. But in both phases the ceaselessly active subject – however defined – is the creator of the world. All this comes out most clearly in the development of Fichte's political thought. In this we are able to trace the strange story of the career

[6] Fichte, *Werke*, vol. II, p. 256.

of the German concept of liberty. It is a very strange and sinister story indeed.

His political thought developed in response to the demands of his philosophical system and to the vicissitudes of the German peoples during the Napoleonic period. His early writings in defence of the French Revolution, *Die Zurückforderung der Denkfreiheit von den Fürsten Europas* (demand for the return of free thought from Europe's princes) of 1793 and the *Beiträge*, also of 1793, rail against oppression and paternalism, and preach an extreme, almost anarchist individualism in the framework of a minimal contractual state. I quote: 'No man can be bound other than by himself.'[7] This is the Fichte who appealed deeply to Stirner, Bakunin and the anarchists, and after them to the existentialists.

Legal and moral constraints begin to loom larger in the *Grundlage des Naturrechts* (Treaties on natural law) of 1796, and the *Sittenlehre* (ethics) of 1798: the state must now actively promote the welfare of its citizens, and freedom becomes the right (and duty) to develop one's 'higher', rational self. Here it becomes quite clear that the state has become the vehicle for the transcendental self.

With *Der Geschlossene Handelsstaat* (the closed commercial state) of 1800, and *Die Grundzüge des gegenwärtigen Zeitalters* (characteristics of the present age) of 1806, state power is further enlarged and the ends of the state become identical with human life itself. Autarchy, rigidly centralised control of trade, tightly concerted collective action, turn society into an army on the march. 19th century German Socialists and Marxist political philosophers in the former GDR, not surprisingly, saw in this phase the remote origins of German state socialism.

We now come to the next phase, to Fichte's nationalism. German, and particularly Prussian, pride was deeply wounded by the German defeat at the hands of Napoleon in 1806. Fichte's *Reden an die Deutsche Nation* (addresses to the German Nation) of 1807 and 1808 contain the classic exposition of the doctrine of modern nationalism. The German nation, defined above all by language and an 'organic' collective character, will summon its untried spiritual forces and assume a civilising mission. By education and indoctrination the German will be brought to see that his nation is 'his own extended self',[8] in which he realises his 'higher' freedom and for which he must be permanently prepared to immolate his mere empirical self. At this stage the finite concrete empirical self is clearly merged with, and vanishes into, the collective self of the *Volk*.

[7] Ibid., VI, p. 12
[8] Ibid., VII, p. 274.

Fichte's last phase, which was marked by his reading of the writings of Machiavelli, which deeply impressed him, represents the doctrine of aggressive nationalist expansionism with a vengeance. His essay *Machiavelli* of 1807, and his political fragments of the years 1807 and 1813, expound the doctrines of pan-Germanism naked *Realpolitik,* and the individual's forcible submission to the higher insight of the leader. In relations between states, Fichte says, 'there is neither law nor right, but only the right of the stronger'; a nation has a natural propensity 'to incorporate in itself the entire human race'[9]; and in order to be welded into an effective nation the Germans need a coercive national pedagogue, a *Zwingherr zur Deutschheit.* 'Compulsion is itself a form of education'[10], the *Zwingherr* says; 'you will later understand the reasons for what I am doing now'[11]. Democratic numbers and common sense melt before him. 'No-one has rights against reason'. And he who possesses 'the highest understanding has the right to compel everyone to follow his insight.'[12] This paradoxical chain of developments has been a source of puzzlement to many. Its inner logic has been discussed by scholars such as F. S. C. Northrop, and most illuminatingly of all by Isaiah Berlin in his celebrated essay 'Two Concepts of Liberty'.

In the face of all this, we may or may not be surprised to learn that Fichte has been described with varying degrees of accuracy as an idealist, a liberal an anarchist and a modern Machiavelli. As a Christian, a pantheist, an atheist. An anti-semite, a nationalist, a chauvinist; a prophet of the politics of the masses, and a precursor of National Socialism. As the first exponent of the doctrine of the inspired leader as an artist in human materials. As the philosopher of Romanticism and the progenitor of depth psychology. As a socialist, a communist and a thinker with a secure place in the Marxist-Leninist pantheon. As a nihilist, and as a major forebear of existentialism, voluntarism, and philosophical pragmatism. Finally, as an aggressive imperialist and a peace-loving cosmopolitan. There can be no doubt that his dark works scattered the seeds of much that was later fully developed only in the nineteenth and twentieth centuries.

IV

Let me now come to the second of my philosophers, Friedrich Wilhelm Joseph von Schelling. He was an entirely different kind of

[9] Ibid., XI, p. 423.
[10] Ibid., VII, p. 574.
[11] Ibid., VII, p. 576.
[12] Ibid., VII, p. 578.

personality from Fichte. He came from a much more cultured and much more easy background. He was the son of a learned Lutheran pastor, was born in 1775 at Leonberg in Württemberg and died in high old age in Ragaz in Switzerland. He was from the start extraordinarily precocious, indeed something of a child prodigy. Where Fichte is all iron will, rigid dialectic, and ethical duty, unswayed and unswayable by the wishes of others, Schelling is the sensitive, aesthetic, artistic, responsive personality par excellence. Where Fichte pursued his course undeterred and uninfluenced by others, Schelling was constantly following the signals picked up by his infinitely receptive antennae. When he was only eighteen he published an essay on myths, and one of the last preoccupations at the end of his long life was precisely mythology.

This is not the place to enter into a detailed discussion of the various periods into which Schelling's work falls. His commentators are fond of dividing up his life as a productive philosopher into fairly clearly defined compartments. They distinguish an early period when Schelling was under the influence of Fichte's *Wissenschaftslehre*; and this in turn is succeeded by a period of aesthetic philosophy, a preoccupation with the innermost essence of art and artistic creativity; then comes the celebrated *Identitätsphilosophie*; and finally, after a long gap, the period of the philosophy of religion. But it seems to me that the view of Karl Jaspers and other scholars is essentially correct, namely that there was in Schelling a central generative core which at the very beginning threw forth all the seeds out of which later positions grow. All that follows represents a greater or lesser emphasis on this or that aspect of his thought, the growing into prominence or the gradual dwindling of this or that doctrine.

What then are the central Schellingian germs? First of all, Schelling held a peculiar view of the task of philosophy in his time. It was for him a return to what he called the 'great objects' of philosophy. These were to be attained, he said, by 'raising oneself above ordinary knowledge'. What are these objects? 'Essentially', he says, 'the objects of philosophy are none other than those of the other sciences, that it sees them in the light of higher relationships, and conceives their individual objects, e.g. the cosmos, the world of plants and animals, the state, world history, art – simply as members of one great organism which, out of the abyss of nature in which it is rooted, rears itself up into the world of spirits (Geisterwelt)'. On this definition philosophy, so far from being remote from, or even hostile to, the most recent discoveries and developments of empirical science, and historical scholarship, will on the contrary attempt to bring them out and evaluate them at their true worth: 'Only a

Roger Hausheer

philosophy that goes back to the deepest beginnings is adequate to them.'[13] This respect for the empirical sciences and the desire to see them come into their own in a larger framework, is something which Schelling interestingly enough shares with the later ideas of Bergson.

Secondly, Schelling is consistently adamant that such philosophy cannot be imposed from without, in conformity with an objective pattern, or in pursuit of some external goal. It is, he says, 'through and through a work of freedom. In each and everyone it is only that into which he himself has fashioned it.'[14] Philosophy rises to her fullest height, therefore, by responding to her own innermost necessity.[15] Freedom, for Schelling, is an intrinsic ingredient in our existential situation. He says: 'Man finds himself at the outset of his existence cast, as it were, into a torrent, whose motion is independent of him and which at first he suffers passively; nevertheless, he is not doomed merely to be swept and drawn along by the current like a dead object.'[16] What then should he do? Pursuit of selfish ends, pleasure, power, status, or material goods will not avail him. It is the place of the philosopher to understand and enter into the sense and purpose of the torrent, and so in tune with it, to merge with it and abet it. This sympathetic self-identification with the innermost drive, the intimate 'go' of things, is freedom. This is the proper element in which men live and move and communicate their being, the oxygen of human souls. 'The medium through which minds (Geister) understand one another is not the ambient air but: their common freedom, whose tiniest tremors reverberate right to the innermost recesses of the soul. Where the mind (Geist) of a man is not filled with the consciousness of freedom, all mental communion (geistige Verbindung) is broken, not just with others, but even with oneself; no wonder that he remains unintelligible just as much to himself as to others and exhausts himself in his fearful solitude with mere empty words, which find no friendly echo in his own or another's breast.'[17] Narrow and constricting views in philosophy entail an equally narrow language and vice versa. With those who 'apply to everything only a restricted range of formulae and standard phrases', true communication becomes impossible. Ultimately, it leads to the ravings of madmen.[18]

[13] Schelling, *Werke*, IX, p. 361.
[14] Ibid., II, p. 11.
[15] Ibid., VIII, p. 84.
[16] Ibid., XIII, p. 202.
[17] Ibid., I, p. 443.
[18] Ibid., II, p. 7.

Thirdly, philosophy as a product of freedom must spring from the will. In some sense it *is* will. 'Hence proof is only proof for those with a will to progress and press on with their thinking, not like geometrical proof which can compel even those of limited understanding, indeed fools.' In this, of course, Schelling is very close to Fichte's famous dictum, 'the kind of philosophy you choose depends on the kind of person you are.' Again, the parallel with later thinkers like Bergson or Sartre is clear. A disposition of the will cannot be brought about by a compelling proof. Schelling goes on: 'positive philosophy is the truly free philosophy; if you want nothing to do with it, you are free to leave it.'[19] 'A universally valid philosophy' – and by that he means a system based upon irresistible demonstrative proof – 'is an inglorious folly (ein ruhmloses Hirngespinst).'[20]

Early and late, Schelling never tires of repeating that will, action, is the source of philosophy. Action, not speculation, is the end of man. This is the young Schelling speaking: 'The first postulate of all philosophy is to act freely from within oneself (aus sich selbst). As little as the geometrician proves the lines he draws as the first postulate of geometry, just as little should the philosopher prove freedom.' When a man is fully engaged in an act of true creation, which is the paradigm of liberty for Schelling, his mind is directed upon nothing outside himself. If he stands aside even for one moment from his total absorption in pure creativity, and tries to reduce to theoretical terms the object of his practical activity, he frustrates his hidden but emerging purpose, and instead generates mere intellectual chimeras. What by definition lies beyond the categories of the understanding, the innermost essence of the world, yields itself only to the freedom of the creative will. Hence, paradoxically, it is precisely at that point where the philosopher first really comes into possession of his freedom, that the analytical understanding sees 'Nought else but that yawning Nothingness which it has no means of filling, and which leaves it conscious of nothing but its own mental bankruptcy (Gedankenlosigkeit).'[21] The view of the older Schelling is: by pure reason I may arrive at the idea of God, but not at God and reality themselves. Thought, which is purely contemplative, theoretical, can never penetrate to these; only will, creative action can. 'I crave what lies above being (Ich will das, was über dem Sein ist).' Driven by voluntary impulse, I am not satisfied with a God who is an abstract intellectual construct; I want the real thing. This is the source of what Schelling calls positive philosophy.[22]

[19] Ibid., XII, p. 132.
[20] Ibid., II, p. 11.
[21] Ibid., I, p. 243.
[22] Ibid., XI, p. 560ff.

Roger Hausheer

Philosophy before Schelling (and Fichte), and for the most part since, has generally aimed to be systematic, objective, rational, universally valid, susceptible of rational proof, etc. But confronted with a body of philosophical writing which is none of these (at least in the traditionally recognised sense), what does one do? Does one just reject it out of hand, as Brentano and Husserl did with Schelling? Schelling attempts to counter his critics in advance: 'Whoever attacks another man's philosophical system is basically attacking not just his understanding, but at the same time his will.'[23] Despite occasional equivocation, Schelling claims that this view does not lead to philosophical – nor indeed ethical – arbitrariness. If the will surges up from the depths, and is thus in some sense 'true', then it will possess an inner necessity. But by what hallmark we are to recognise its 'truth' is far from plain. In some not-further-analysable way it is self-authenticating. This is a difficulty that bedevils all philosophies of authenticity down to Bergson, Sartre, and beyond.

In the fourth place, philosophy as an essentially practical activity has ethical implications: Schelling says: 'The spirit of ethics and of philosophy is one and the same'. All divisions between theory and practice, therefore, are entirely illusory. So far from being a purely theoretical activity, metaphysics forms the living core of all genuine life, individual, communal, and religious. He says: 'A philosophy which is not already in its principle religion, we do not recognise as philosophy'.[24] In doing philosophy, we should be transformed and reborn. (How far, by the way, Schelling himself succumbed to the temptation to produce dead schematic abstractions and empty intellectual systems is another matter.) Every moment of our lives will burn with the intense fires of metaphysics. 'This gold of divine knowledge will not be found on the path of a supine tearfulness (tatenlose Tränen) and a vain (müssig) longing, but only in the flames of the spirit will it be won.'[25] There is a remarkable echo of all this in a letter written by Bergson to one of his contemporaries, where he uses exactly the same imagery, saying that a man who has attained philosophical insight, who truly understands intuition and the nature of what he calls *durée,* will lead a life every single aspect of which will be suffused with the flames of metaphysics. Until the metaphysical scales have fallen from our eyes, for both Schelling and Bergson, we have not really begun to live.

The immediacy, the first hand quality of genuine philosophical activity, is stressed again and again by Schelling: he says, 'Whoever

[23] Ibid., XII, p. 201.
[24] Ibid., V, p. 116.
[25] Ibid., VIII, p. 71.

16

feels and apprehends nothing real within and outside himself – whoever lives exclusively on concepts, and plays with concepts – for whom his very own existence is no more than a feeble thought (ein matter Gedanke) – how should he ever speak about reality?'.[26] And most unambiguously of all, he says: 'With mathematics, physics, natural history (I revere these sciences deeply), with poetry and art even, human affairs cannot be governed. True understanding of the world is furnished precisely by the right metaphysics, which for that reason alone has from time immemorial been called the queen of the sciences.'[27]

Fifthly, Schelling speaks at times as though philosophy is, and should be, accessible to every man, and certainly he believes in its capacity to transform all our social practices, yet at others he speaks as though the peculiar kind of metaphysical illumination he describes is available only to the happy few. Here again, he shares this equivocation with Bergson. There is in both of them in certain moods a tendency to sort the spiritual sheep from the goats. Both seem to say: all are called, few are chosen to follow the call.

In the sixth place, and closely connected with much of what has gone before, Schelling has quite distinctive views about the ways in which philosophy should be taught. Above all, philosophy is not a technique reducible to a finite set of concepts governed by clearly defined rules. What is in perpetual movement, vital, and constantly self-transforming, cannot be grasped by immobile concepts. Philosophy must be a 'bag of tricks (Kunststück) which only arouses our admiration for its author's wit.'[28] Again, compulsion is totally alien to it. 'Compulsion', he says, 'is only properly at home where it is a question of mere mechanical learning.'[29] By its very nature, philosophy cannot compel, only seek to secure a person's free conviction, 'for no man can believe for another, or be convinced for another'. Wherever philosophy is the victim of compulsion, he goes on, 'it resembles a captive eagle, whose true home, the rocky heights, is denied it.'[30] Philosophy then must first awaken and then purify in a man what he already possesses in his innermost being. In this sense it is negative, since it has nothing to give. Its task is 'to purify him of the contingencies that the body, the world of phenomena and the life of the senses have superadded upon him, and to lead him back to the original source (das Ursprüngliche).'[31] Finally, most do not

[26] Ibid., I, p. 353.
[27] Ibid., XIII, p. 27.
[28] Ibid., I, p. 293.
[29] Ibid., IX, p. 356.
[30] Ibid., IX, p. 358.
[31] Ibid., VI, p. 26.

study philosophy in order to become philosophers in their turn, but hasten, so illuminated by philosophical study, to take up 'sciences which enmesh directly with life.'[32]

V

I think by now I may have said enough about the general drift of these two thinkers for their relevance to a great deal that came after them to be apparent. Let me now, in conclusion, add a few brief words about all this. Anyone with even but a cursory knowledge of the writings of Husserl will be struck by some of the profound parallels with some of the things said by Fichte. Husserl's sharp distinction in his middle period between what he calls the 'natural stand-point' and what he calls the 'standpoint of transcendental phenomenology' bears a quite remarkable resemblance to Fichte's distinction between common empirical reality as experienced by all men and his own transcendental idealist genetic reconstruction of it. And much the same kind of parallel can be seen in what Husserl says of the nature of the ego, the transcendental self. Like Fichte, he asks us to observe any common object, say a chair, and then to observe ourselves observing that chair. It is just a matter here of concentrating on the observing subject rather than on the chair being observed. But this 'I' which we are now seeking to observe is what Husserl terms 'psychical subjectivity' and is the proper subject of empirical psychology. But behind this again, there is a deeper 'I', Husserl says, 'which for want of language we can only call "I myself"'.[33] This is transcendental subjectivity and it is one of the main topics of transcendental phenomenology. This is the hidden 'I' to which the psychical 'I' is present. By a process of stripping away it is possible to end up, after the most stringent reduction, with what Husserl calls the transcendental self This is, as it were, the nominative self as opposed to the accusative self – the self that can never grasp itself, the systematically elusive 'I'. Husserl's account of this transcendental ego and of its deeply constitutive role in the formation of the structure of reality profoundly resembles a great deal of what is said by Fichte.

So much for some of the more striking parallels between Husserl's thought and that of Fichte. When we turn to Sartre the parallels become more startling still. Sartre himself, of course, fully acknowledges the deep debt that he owes to Husserl; and others have pointed to the roots of his existentialism in thinkers as various

[32] Ibid., I, p. 417.
[33] Husserl, *Ideen zu einer reinen Phänomenologie*, p. 37.

as Hegel and Marx. Yet no-one so far as I know has traced the roots of existentialism to their Fichtean source. This is exceedingly puzzling when one considers the astonishing similarity between the central ideas and insights of these two thinkers, Fichte and Sartre; and also the fact that Sartre was deeply versed in the tradition of thought which is represented by German idealism and its related currents. Here, however, I shall be concerned not to discover any direct historical link between Fichte and Sartre, something which by the nature of things may no longer be recoverable, but simply with a bare presentation of the core ideas of Sartre's existentialism accompanied by a few comments on their strongly Fichtean associations. The most interesting of Sartre's works from this point of view is undoubtedly *L'Etre et le néant* which I suppose it is fair to say is the philosophical rock on which French existentialism is founded, though much valuable and highly concentrated light is also shed on it by his *L'existentialisme est un humanisme*. It is to a brief consideration of this work that I now turn.

Sartre's famous dictum that existence precedes essence is pure Fichte. The idea that first I surge into being as a nucleus of as yet unchannelled energy, and that I then proceed, by a series of choices, of free acts of will, to construct my essence (which is really no essence at all, since I can make and unmake it at will by an endless multiplicity of absolutely free acts), is a profoundly Fichtean thought. Man first exists, Sartre says, then defines himself. 'What do we mean by saying that existence precedes essence? We mean that man first of all exists, encounters himself, surges up in the world – and defines himself afterwards. ... Thus there is no human nature ... Man is nothing else but that which he makes of himself. That is the first principle of existentialism'.[34] Again, man is constantly hurling himself into the future, in pursuit of projects, but to these there is no finite end.

And again, the idea originated by Fichte, partly following Kant, that we are authors of our own values, finds its natural home among the existentialists. To quote Sartre again 'To choose between this or that is at the same time to affirm the value of that which is chosen'.[35] And: 'There is no determinism – man is free, man *is* freedom.'[36] I quote again 'There is no reality except in action ... man exists only in so far as he realises himself he is therefore nothing else but the sum of his actions, nothing else but what he makes his life to be'.[37] Before Fichte especially, this type of voluntarist discourse would

[34] Sartre, *L'existentisalisme est un humanisme*, pp. 21–2.
[35] Ibid., p. 25.
[36] Ibid., pp. 36–7.
[37] Ibid., p. 22.

have been literally inconceivable, after him it has helped to characterise an entire epoch.

I could go on quoting almost ad infinitum from the writings of
Sartre but let us now turn to a figure who is sometimes described as
the greatest of the French voluntarists, and whose works and ideas
manifest quite remarkable parallels with those of Schelling. I have
in mind Henri Bergson. The whole idea of an essentially spiritual
or mind-driven universe, where, properly conceived, matter itself is
truly intelligible only in the context of an intelligent creative divine
spirit is wholly Schellingian. Teleology and the life-drive, the *élan
vital,* and divine purpose are absolutely central concepts in
Bergson's anti-mechanistic and anti-chaotic world picture. This is
all pure Schelling. But it is in their common notion of intuition that
the two thinkers are most startlingly alike. Intuition was, as it were,
their leading battle-cry. Intuition, Bergson tells us, 'is that sympathy by means of which one transports oneself into the interior of an
object in order to coincide with that about it which is unique and
hence inexpressible. Analysis, on the contrary, is that operation
which reduces the object to elements with which we are already
familiar, that is to say elements which are common both to this
object and to others. Analysis, then, consists in expressing a thing as
a function of what it is not.'[38] And he goes on, in a very Schellingian
way, to contrast what he calls 'true empiricism' with 'false empiricism'. True empiricism has as its aim, 'to follow as closely as possible the original itself, to deepen its life, and by a kind of "spiritual
auscultation", to feel its soul pulsate. This true empiricism is true
metaphysics.'[39] Bergson, like Schelling, set out from a sharp
dichotomy between what is essentially human, immersed in time,
durée, and what is purely mechanical and external. But as time went
on he modified, somewhat, this stark contrast. In fact, what Bergson
had in mind when talking about intuition can perhaps be best
understood in the context of his cosmology and his theory of life.
For he comes increasingly to see that where the pure self, as it were,
casts a material shadow, so too all matter, in some sense participates
in spirit. And in creative evolution intuition is presented as being an
aspect of the universal *élan vital* or life drive which pervades the
entire universe and guides the evolutionary process. Indeed, it is
something in which even the minutest particles of matter participate. Schelling, too, underwent much the same kind of development. And Bergson strikes a profoundly Schellingian note when, in
speaking of the 'deep self' as contrasted with the 'superficial self',
which is mechanical, conventional, inauthentic, he says, 'We are free

[38] Bergson, *Introduction à la métaphysique,* p. 181.
[39] Ibid., p. 196.

when our acts emanate from the whole of our personality, when they express it, and when they have this kind of indefinable resemblance to it that we see sometimes between a work of art and the artist.'[40] We find all these Schellingian and Bergsonian themes recycled in a writer like Teilhard de Chardin and those who came under his influence.

Premonitory tremors of some of the most profoundly transforming political movements of the twentieth century also unmistakably radiate out from these two thinkers. When Hitler declaims in one of his speeches: 'Nothing in heaven or on earth can stand in the path of the German *Volk* and its freedom. A nation has an absolute right to expand to the full extent of its powers; it will be victor or vanquished, and will absorb and assimilate and batter down all before it; or it will be nothing.' And when a leading National Socialist said: 'The Führer alone has insight into the soul and the deepest evolving needs of the German nation from moment to moment; he alone in any given instance can issue the supreme commands. He is the source of the living law of the German *Volk*'; or again, when Heidegger declared in the thirties, 'The Führer himself and he alone is the present and future German reality and law.'[41] – it is, I think we can see, not too difficult to discover who helped, however remotely, to prepare the ground for all this. Let me again quote from the novel written by Goebbels, *Michael,* a truly awful literary performance, but exceedingly revealing for all that. Here we find one of the most sinister expressions of the Romantic aesthetic model applied to politics. The novel is built around a methodical rejection of the core values of Enlightenment Europe: reason, science, criticism, toleration, the existence of objective norms and values, the moral unity of the human race – all these are denied and systematically replaced by the values of will, heroic self-assertion, authenticity, and, finally, free self-immolation to the higher will of the artist-leader. Let me quote just a few passages: 'Today we are all expressionists. Men who want the world outside themselves to take the form of their life within themselves ... The expressionist world-feeling is explosive. It is an autocratic sensation of its own being.' Reproducing almost exactly the tones of the German *Sturm und Drang* of the 1770's, Michael cries: 'I can endure no longer this life among dead books. I must shape something. More than intellect works in us ... Intellect is lifeless. It cannot provide us with a sense of existence.' And finally, most sinister of all, because here the artist

[40] Bergson, *L'évolution créatrice*, p. 129.
[41] All these quotations are drawn from Walther Hofer (ed.), *Der Nationalsozialismus: Dokumente 1933–45.*

is transformed into the political leader whose artistic materials are human beings: 'The artist is distinguished from him who is not an artist by the fact that he can express that which he feels ... The statesman is also an artist. For him the people are that which a stone is for the sculptor. Leader and masses, that is exactly the same problem as painter and colour.'[42]

At the opposite political pole from all this, the Marxist doctrine of Praxis has a strongly Fichtean ring about it. For Marx, it is man's own active, creative essence which presents the world to him, as so much passive stuff to be worked upon and moulded; not the world as a causal originator which impinges on a wholly neutral receiver, as Locke and the empiricists would have it. Only by its impingement on the material world is human nature revealed to itself. This central Marxist notion, drawn no doubt by Marx himself from Hegel, scarcely antedates Fichte, indeed was virtually originated by him. There are entire passages in the writings of the early Marx where the echo of Fichte is unmistakable. The world for man is what Marx terms his 'gegenständliches Sein', his objective being, his 'materielles Leben', his material life. Only in the world, and through his unceasing action in and on the world, does man find himself, individually and collectively. The ultimate significance of the life of mankind lies in its capacity for collective self-creation through transforming labour: 'the entire so-called history of the world is nothing but the creation of man through human labour, nothing but the emergence of nature for man, so that he has the visible, irrefutable proof of his birth through himself, of the process of his creation.'[43] Here the absolute subject becomes something like the human race itself in its long historical Odyssey towards full rational adulthood in the final period of post-history. But all this leads ultimately not only to Marx, but on to the mystique of technological-industrial production, of impinging upon, transforming, and exploiting the world as an activity valuable in its own right and therefore to be pursued *per se*, even in the absence of any final goal. Thus we arrive at the pure nightmare of activism and decisionism for their own sakes.

Finally, it is not for nothing that historians of American pragmatism have suggested that Fichte is one of its most important, if most remote, sources. The whole pragmatist theory of truth, as we find it in William James, with its operational implications and its source in our ever evolving practical activities, is profoundly Fichtean. The notion that in cognition the will and not the intellect takes absolute

[42] Goebbels, *Michael*, 1929.
[43] Marx, *Economic and Philsophic Manuscripts of 1844*, p. 145.

primacy is very clearly stated by James when he says 'We need only in cold blood act as if the thing in question were real, and keep acting as if it were real, and it will infallibly end by growing into such a connection with our life that it will become real'.[44] His entire doctrine of postulation makes it abundantly clear that thought is everywhere inspired by will. To present Fichte as the first philosophical pragmatist, as it were, is indeed a bold claim, and one which I cannot possibly begin to defend here. But at the same time, it cannot be denied that what is perhaps the main feature of pragmatism, to be found in Peirce, James, and Dewey, and their followers – namely the element of dynamism – first comes to the fore in the philosophy of Fichte. Where classical European thinkers like Plato and Aristotle, Leibniz, Descartes, and even Kant, adopt the stand-point of a pure intelligence in contemplation of eternal verities, the attitude of a fixed perceiving subject set over against an objective and static reality of already structured facts, Fichte, and after him the pragmatists, see the human subject as an enquirer with certain practical needs and purposes, adapting itself to a changing environment, and thereby changing both itself and the world. Our ultimate concepts and categories, on this view, evolve out of practical human activities; they are therefore relative and ever-changing, and practice is prior to theory. There is no pre-formed, objective external reality (nature, things-in-themselves, etc) of whose immutable structure our contemplative theoretical knowledge is, as it were, a static transcription or model. Instead of a fixed, immutable, pre-categorical external nature, we are to imagine an ever-changing flux upon which men seek to impose their creative stamp. This is Fichtean indeed.

VI

It has not been possible in the space available to offer anything like a full and balanced account of the roots, genesis, character, and influence of the philosophical doctrines advanced by Fichte and Schelling, still less to engage in their critical evaluation. All I have been able to do, at best, is to point in the most sketchy manner to some of the central problems these two thinkers confronted and to which they sought to find solutions; to isolate some of the major themes each struck up and then abandoned to their independent careers and unpredictable variations at the hands of others; and to show how we begin in one world – that of Kant and the serene walled garden of the eighteenth century – and end in another that is transformed beyond recognition: our own chaotic century, torn and

[44] William James, *The Will to Believe*, p. 15.

violent, a vast luxuriant jungle, many, perhaps most, of whose fatefully contending growths have sprung from the seeds first scattered
by these two Prometheans of the spirit. If this is an accurate
description, then it pays a massive tribute to the sheer prodigality
and profundity of these two literally proleptic thinkers, Fichte and
Schelling, whom Karl Jaspers in a moment of visionary insight
somewhere describes as two great sentinels, standing in the gateway
to the future. If I am not much mistaken, this vivid image still
applies.

Hegel's Critique of Foundationalism in the 'Doctrine of Essence'

STEPHEN HOULGATE

I

It is a commonplace among certain recent philosophers that there is no such thing as the *essence* of anything. Nietzsche, for example, asserts that things have no essence of their own, because they are nothing but ceaselessly changing ways of acting on, and reacting to, other things.[1] Wittgenstein, famously, rejects the idea that there is an essence to language and thought – at least if we mean by that some *a priori* logical structure underlying our everyday utterances.[2] Finally, Richard Rorty urges that we 'abandon ... the notion of "essence" altogether', along with 'the notion that man's essence is to be a knower of essences'.[3]

It would be wrong to maintain that these writers understand the concept of essence in precisely the same way, or that they are all working towards the same philosophical goal. Nevertheless, they do share one aim in common: to undermine the idea that there is some deeper reality or identity *underlying* and *grounding* what we encounter in the world, what we say and what we do. That is to say, they may all be described as *anti-foundationalist* thinkers – thinkers who want us to attend to the specific processes and practices of nature and humanity without understanding them to be the product of some fundamental essence or 'absolute'[4].

One philosopher who is sometimes thought to appeal to just such an underlying essence or 'absolute' in his explanation of natural and historical development, and so to be an undisputed foundationalist, is G. W. F. Hegel (1770–1831). In *Capital*, for example, Marx describes Hegel in overtly foundationalist terms:

[1] Friedrich Nietzsche, *The Will to Power*, ed. W. Kaufmann, trans. W. Kaufmann and R. J. Hollingdale (New York: Vintage Books, 1968), §§556–8, 567. See also, Alexander Nehamas, *Nietzsche: Life as Literature* (Cambridge, MA: Harvard University Press, 1985), pp. 80–1.

[2] Ludwig Wittgenstein, *Philosophical Investigations* (Oxford: Blackwell, 1958), §§89, 92, 97.

[3] Richard Rorty, *Philosophy and the Mirror of Nature* (Oxford: Blackwell, 1980), pp. 361, 367.

[4] For a defence of the view that Nietzsche does not understand the will to power to be the 'underlying essence' of things, but rather their inner 'pathos', see Stephen Houlgate, *Hegel, Nietzsche and the Criticism of Metaphysics* (Cambridge: Cambridge University Press, 1986), pp. 66–7.

25

Stephen Houlgate

> To Hegel ... the process of thinking, which, under the name of 'the Idea', he even transforms into an independent subject, is the demiurgos of the real world, and the real world is only the external, phenomenal form of 'the Idea'.[5]

A similar interpretation of Hegel can be found in many other post-Hegelian writers (including Nietzsche). The exhortation to 'abandon the notion of essence' is thus interpreted by many today as the call to abandon Hegel – or at least a certain side of Hegel. Some avowed anti-foundationalists, such as Marx and Dewey, are of course profoundly indebted to Hegel, in particular to his emphasis on the historicity of human life. But it is clear that they are equally concerned to distance themselves from what they perceive to be Hegel's unfortunate foundationalism or essentialism. As Richard Rorty aptly puts it, 'Dewey, like Marx, wants Hegel *without the Absolute Spirit*'.[6]

Even sophisticated modern commentators, such as Charles Taylor, who see in Hegel a trenchant critic of 'reality-behind-appearance' dualism, find it hard to avoid slipping back into foundationalist vocabulary when characterising Hegel's own position. Taylor points out, quite rightly, that for Hegel 'the inner connectedness of things, or the totality, cannot lie behind but must be immanent to external reality'. Yet, when he reaches Hegel's analysis of the Concept (*Begriff*) in the *Science of Logic*, Taylor resorts to the very foundationalist vocabulary he has just shown Hegel to be criticising. For Taylor, the basic Hegelian ontological vision is thus:

> that the Concept *underlies* everything as the inner necessity which deploys the world, and that our conceptual knowledge is derivative from this. We are the vehicles whereby this *underlying* necessity comes to its equally necessary self-consciousness.[7]

What I wish to suggest in this essay is that this foundationalist interpretation of Hegel is in fact deeply mistaken. It is certainly true that Hegel understands nature and history to be rational processes which lead necessarily to human freedom and self-understanding. It is also clear that even this belief is too much for advocates of radical contingency, like Nietzsche and Rorty, to stomach.

[5] Karl Marx, *Selected Writings*, ed. D. McLellan (Oxford: Oxford University Press, 1977), p. 420.
[6] Richard Rorty, *Consequences of Pragmatism* (Minneapolis: University of Minnesota Press, 1982) pp. 46–7, my italics.
[7] Charles Taylor, *Hegel* (Cambridge: Cambridge University Press, 1975), pp. 287, 299, 300, my italics.

Yet, it is important to recognise that, for Hegel, reason does not constitute the *foundation* of change in the world: reason is not some principle or 'pre-existing "Idea"' (as Nietzsche calls it) that underlies nature or history and drives us forward to freedom.[8] Hegel's claim is that natural and historical change *itself* proves to be rational, and that rational ends are brought about by nothing other than observable natural processes and historical actions. In this sense, Hegel is not a foundationalist.

What is set out in the *Science of Logic*, therefore, is not an account of a rational principle or Idea that *precedes* being and *grounds* all natural and historical development; rather, the *Logic* sketches an initial, abstract picture of being *itself* as self-determining rationality. As Hegel shows in the later parts of his system, such rationality proves, on closer examination, not just to be rationality in the abstract, but to be the concrete process of nature and history. The understanding of being reached in the *Logic* thus turns out (once we get to the *Philosophy of Nature*) to be an underdetermination of what being is in truth: it tells us merely what being must *first* be understood to be. But, for Hegel, what we first understand being to be should not be mistaken for some underlying ground or foundation of being. When we see a person from afar, we first say that we see *someone*, and then, as we approach the person, we recognise that it is a man or a woman, a friend or a stranger, and so on. It would be absurd for us to say that being *someone* constitutes the foundation of the whole person or grounds whatever the person does. That is simply what the person is first thought to be. The same is true of Hegel's philosophical system. We first understand being (in the *Logic*) to be Idea or self-determining rationality, but (in the *Philosophy of Nature* and *Philosophy of Spirit*) we then recognise such rationality itself to exist as space, time, matter, and history. Pure self-determining rationality (or the Idea) does not serve as the underlying ground of nature, therefore, but is simply what rational nature (and history) is initially thought to be. As Hegel puts it in the *Phenomenology*, 'the *basis* or principle of the system is, in fact, only its *beginning*'.[9]

Now, it is true that at times Hegel does describe spirit, the Idea or the Concept in an apparently foundationalist way. In the *Science of Logic*, for example, he describes the transition from the concept of substance to that of 'Concept' or *Begriff* as the process whereby

[8] Nietzsche, *The Will to Power*, §515. See Houlgate, *Hegel, Nietzsche and the Criticism of Metaphysics*, p. 37.

[9] G. W. F. Hegel, *Phänomenologie des Geistes*, ed. E. Moldenhauer and K. M. Michel (Frankfurt: Suhrkamp Verlag, 1970) [*Theorie Werkausgabe*, vol. 3], p. 28; *Phenomenology of Spirit*, trans. A. V. Miller (Oxford: Oxford University Press, 1977), p. 14.

substance passes over 'into its *ground*'.[10] This is what allows writers like Marx and Taylor to interpret Hegel as they do. To my mind, however, Hegel's use of such vocabulary should not be taken to commit him to a fundamentally foundationalist view of the world. The clearest evidence that he is not a foundationalist is to be found in his analysis of the concept of 'essence' itself in the *Science of Logic*.

In the *Logic* Hegel argues that philosophical thought has to pass from the study of being in its immediacy – as simple *being* – to the study of being as it is *in truth* or *in essence*. He also argues that the essence of being inevitably seems to be something other than, and to underlie, being itself. This is due not to any hankering for foundations on our part, but to an intrinsic characteristic of the essence itself (a characteristic which we will examine later). Hegel maintains, however, that the very idea of essence also undermines this appearance and exposes it as an illusion. The essence of being thus turns out not to be something other than being or to underlie being after all, but rather to be what being itself is in truth. According to Hegel, then, there is no hidden *foundation* to being. Yet he does not take this view because, like Nietzsche or Rorty, he rejects the idea of essence as such. He takes this view because he believes that the concept of essence itself undermines the illusion (which it generates) that there is a foundation to being, and so prepares the way for the non-foundational insight that being is itself self-determining reason ('Concept' [*Begriff*] or 'Idea'). Hegel is an anti-foundationalist thinker, therefore, precisely because he endorses the concept of essence, but has a much subtler understanding of it than either Nietzsche or Rorty.

There is a considerable risk in trying to explain how Hegel understands the concept of essence. His analysis is very dense, very abstract, very complex, and may well seem utterly absurd to those unfamiliar with Hegel. A large part of the difficulty we face in understanding Hegel's conception of essence is due to the fact that he believes it to be defined more negatively than any other concept in the *Logic*. As Robert Pippin puts it, this means that Hegel's text 'often threatens to disintegrate under the opprobrious weight of the "nothings", "negations", "nonbeings", and "negatives"'.[11] For those who have little time anyway for what Schopenhauer calls Hegel's 'frantic word-combinations', this section of the *Logic* will undoubtedly try one's patience more than any other.[12] In my view, however,

[10] G. W. F. Hegel, *Wissenschaft der Logik*, ed. E. Moldenhauer and K. M. Michel, 2 vols. (Frankfurt: Suhrkamp Verlag, 1969) [*Theorie Werkausgabe*, vols. 5, 6], 2: 246; *Science of Logic*, trans. A. V. Miller (Atlantic Highlands, NJ: Humanities Press International, 1989), p. 577.

[11] Robert Pippin, *Hegel's Idealism. The Satisfactions of Self-Consciousness* (Cambridge: Cambridge University Press, 1989), p. 213.

it contains one of the subtlest accounts of the concept of essence that we have, and the risk involved in trying to understand it (and even more in trying to explain it in public) is eminently worth taking.

II

Hegel's project in the *Science of Logic* (1812–1816, 2nd edn, 1832) is twofold. On the one hand, its aim is logical: to identify the basic categories of thought. (In this sense, the *Logic* represents Hegel's alternative to Kant's 'Metaphysical Deduction' in the *Critique of Pure Reason*.) On the other hand, the aim of the *Logic* is ontological: to determine what it is to be. (In this sense, the *Logic* represents Hegel's alternative to Spinoza's *Ethics*.) Hegel believes these two aims can be met together, if we adopt a quasi-Cartesian approach to the categories, that is to say, if we suspend all our traditional assumptions about the categories and seek to derive them anew from the quite indeterminate concept of *being* as such. For by showing which categories are implicit in the very concept of being, we will be able to show all the different things that 'being' means; and to determine what it means to be – and so what it *is* to be – is precisely to do ontology. The first categories to be considered in the *Science of Logic* (in the 'doctrine of being') are those that are immediately entailed by the concept of being itself: categories such as 'reality', 'something', and 'quantity'. The initial ontological lesson of the *Logic* is thus that being is not just some utterly indeterminate condition, but that to be is to be *real*, to be *something*, to be *quantifiable*, and so on.

What becomes clear in the doctrine of being is that being in all its forms involves *immediacy*. Hegel understands the term 'immediacy' (*Unmittelbarkeit*) to mean three intimately related things. Negatively, being immediate means not being mediated (or produced) by something else. Positively, it means simply *being* what one is, simply *being* this. Positively, it also means simply being *oneself*, having an identity of one's *own*, simply being *this* (rather than *that*). In this latter sense, immediacy implies determinacy (*Bestimmtheit*).[13] Such immediacy is enjoyed not only by individual

[12] Arthur Schopenhauer, *The World as Will and Representation*, trans. E. F. J. Payne, 2 vols. (New York: Dover Publications, 1969), 1: xxiv.

[13] Hegel, *Wissenschaft der Logik*, 1: 68–9, 82, 116–18, 131; *Science of Logic*, pp. 69–70, 82, 109–11, 122. See also Dieter Henrich, 'Hegel's Logik der Reflexion. Neue Fassung', in *Die Wissenschaft der Logik und die Logik der Reflexion*, ed. D. Henrich (Bonn: Bouvier Verlag, 1978) [*Hegel-Studien*, Beiheft 18], p. 246.

things, but also by the constituent features of things, that is, by their qualities and magnitude (both extensive and intensive). Each thing is immediately what *it* is and not something else; similarly, the specific qualities and specific magnitude of a thing are immediately whatever they are. It is true, of course, that Hegel shows all such immediacy to be intrinsically related to, and connected with, other such immediacy. To be something is thus necessarily to stand in relation to other things, and the qualities of something always have a certain magnitude or degree. Nevertheless, such relations and interconnections hold between things or features of things that are *immediately* what they are: one thing relates to another thing as the specific thing that *it* is, and this specific quality has this particular magnitude.

Yet Hegel's analysis also shows that there is actually more to immediacy than meets the eye. In his discussion of what it is to be 'something', Hegel argues that the immediate identity of a thing – that which distinguishes it from other things – is itself influenced by other things to which it relates.[14] The sheer immediacy of a thing – the simple fact of its being *this* thing rather than something else – is thus not simply immediate after all, but is rather *mediated* 'immediacy'.

At the end of the doctrine of being, it then becomes clear that the immediate qualities and magnitude of a thing are not simply immediate, either. Something can certainly change its magnitude – become bigger or smaller – and still remain the thing that it is. Yet the qualities of a thing are not utterly indifferent to size or degree, for at a certain point a thing can get so big or so small, or so hot or so cold, that it undergoes qualitative change. Water, for example, is a fluid at moderate temperatures, but ceases to be a fluid and becomes ice or steam at low or high temperatures. The magnitude or degree of something thus actually plays a role in determining the character of that thing.[15]

But once it is recognised that changes in the magnitude or degree of something can bring about changes in the thing's quality, it becomes clear that neither quality nor quantity can continue to be regarded as simply immediate features of things. The qualities of

[14] Hegel, *Wissenschaft der Logik*, 1: 134; *Science of Logic*, p. 124: 'the determination is, as such, open to relationship to other'.
[15] G. W. F Hegel, *Enzyklopädie der philosophischen Wissenschaften (1830). Erster Teil: Die Wissenschaft der Logik*, ed. E. Moldenhauer and K. M. Michel (Frankfurt: Suhrkamp Verlag, 1970) [*Theorie Werkausgabe*, vol. 8], pp. 225–7 [§108 and Addition]); *The Encyclopaedia Logic*, trans. T. F. Geraets, W. F. Suchting and H. S. Harris (Indianapolis: Hackett Publishing Company, 1991), pp. 171–2.

something cannot be simply immediate, since they depend upon, and so are mediated by, the thing's size or temperature. Equally, the magnitude or temperature of something is not simply immediate either, since the size or temperature that a thing can reach whilst remaining what it is, depends upon, and so is mediated by, the qualitative make-up of *that* thing. Neither quality nor quantity is simply immediate, therefore, since (to quote from the *Encyclopaedia Logic*) 'each is only *through the mediation of* (*vermittels*) the other'.[16]

The conclusion reached at the end of the doctrine of being is thus deeply paradoxical: namely, that the immediacy characterising things – their being this or that, and having these qualities and this size – is not simple immediacy after all, because it is the result of *mediation*. This is not to say, however, that we may now do away with the idea of immediacy altogether. The lesson to be drawn from the doctrine of being, according to Hegel, is more complex than that. Things do exhibit immediacy, and must do so in so far as they are anything at all; but we now recognise that that very immediacy is not simple immediacy *in truth* or *in essence*. For Hegel, the doctrine of being thus leads directly into the doctrine of essence. The doctrine of being shows all being to be immediacy; the doctrine of essence then explores the ramifications of the insight that the essence of such immediate being is not immediacy itself, but mediation or *non-immediacy*.

This account of Hegel's derivation of the concept of essence has been far too brief and has neglected much of what Hegel has to say.[17] Nevertheless, the account does make three important features of that concept clear. First of all, the concept of essence has to be understood in relation to that of immediacy: for it only emerges when the immediacy of being proves not to be simple immediacy after all. The concept of essence thus cannot stand alone: we cannot talk of essence *tout court*, but only of the essence *of* something immediately given. Second, the concept of essence is not one from which we can start, but is by definition a thought that we must come to *after* having thought about what is immediately there before us. 'Essence issues from being', Hegel writes; 'hence it is not immediately in and for itself but is a result of that movement'.[18] Third, the

[16] Hegel, *Enzyklopädie der philosophischen Wissenschaften (1830). Erster Teil: Die Wissenschaft der Logik*, p. 229 [§111]; *The Encyclopaedia Logic*, p. 173.

[17] For a more detailed discussion of the transition from the doctrine of being to the doctrine of essence in Hegel's *Science of Logic*, see J. Biard et al., eds., *Introduction à la lecture de la Science de la Logique de Hegel. I. L'Etre* (Paris: Aubier, 1981), pp. 280–91.

[18] Hegel, *Wissenschaft der Logik*, 2: 17; *Science of Logic*, p. 393.

concept of essence is fundamentally *negative*. It is above all the thought of the *non*-immediacy at the heart of all immediate being, and as such it necessarily negates the idea of immediacy itself – at least initially.

According to Hegel, the negation of immediacy that is inherent in the very concept of essence takes two forms. First of all, it reduces immediacy to something merely *inessential*, then it reduces immediacy even further to mere *illusion*. We shall now look at each of these reductions in turn.

To understand why the very idea of essence causes us to regard immediacy as something inessential, we need to recall that the essence is initially conceived in simple and direct *contrast* to immediacy. Things do exhibit a certain immediacy as distinct things; but the essence of such things is not immediacy, indeed is sheer *non*-immediacy. To begin with, then, the essence is understood to be quite different from the simple immediacy of being, to be what Hegel calls the sheer *'negation* of the sphere of being as such.'[19]

According to Hegel, however, this initial understanding of essence invests essence itself – paradoxically – with an *immediacy* of its own. For it makes us think of the essence as being *this* rather than that, as having its own character and identity that is quite distinct from that of immediacy itself. In other words, it makes us think of the essence of things as *being* something other than their immediacy. As Hegel puts it, our initial understanding of essence makes us think of 'essence itself [as] *simply affirmative* [*seiendes*], immediate essence.'[20] Furthermore, this idea in turn requires us to think of the immediacy of things as being something other than their essence. But if immediacy is understood to *be* one thing and the essence is understood to *be* something else, then both are understood to belong to the sphere of being and to form part of what there *is*.

In Hegel's view, therefore, drawing an immediate contrast between the essence of being and the immediacy of being makes less of a difference to the way we understand the world than we might imagine: for we still conceive the object of thought to be *immediacy*. We distinguish the essence from simple immediacy, but we are forced by the immediacy of that very distinction to regard each as having '*a being, an immediacy*' of its own (*ein Sein, eine Unmittelbarkeit*).[21] The distinction we draw thus turns out to be between *being* that is of the essence and *being* that is merely immediate and so not of the essence. Being that is not of the essence,

---

[19] Hegel, *Wissenschaft der Logik*, 2: 18; *Science of Logic*, p. 394 (translation emended).

[20] Hegel, *Wissenschaft der Logik*, 2: 18; *Science of Logic*, p. 394

[21] Hegel, *Wissenschaft der Logik*, 2: 18; *Science of Logic*, p. 394.

Hegel says, is being that is *inessential* (*das Unwesentliche*), whereas being that is of the essence is being that is *essential* (*das Wesentliche*). The initial effect of introducing the concept of essence is thus not to force us to abandon the idea of immediacy altogether, but to force us to regard simple immediacy as something inessential. This is the first reduction or negation of immediacy brought about by the concept of essence.

The beginning of Hegel's doctrine of essence is abstract and terse, but his point is nevertheless clear: the introduction of the concept of essence initially does no more than divide being into two – into one kind of being that is inessential and contingent and another kind of being that is essential. Hegel does not state explicitly that what is essential is to be understood as the *foundation* of what is inessential, but it is clear that the two ideas are closely related. For the idea of an underlying foundation to things is merely a further refinement of the idea that inessential being points back to something more essential than itself. We can thus see why the essence of things should so often be conceived as their *foundation* by appreciating why the essence has initially to be understood as essential being.

For Hegel, the essence is conceived as *being* something other than immediacy – and so as essential being – because it is initially understood to be immediately *different* from immediacy itself. That is to say, it is initially understood *not* to be immediate being, but to be simple *non*-immediacy. Conceived in this way, essence is the simple *negation* of immediacy or, as Hegel puts it, is the '*first* negation' of being.[22] It is this, and this alone, that invests the essence with an immediate being or identity of its own and gives it 'determinacy' (*Bestimmtheit*) or distinctness. It is this alone, therefore, that turns the essence into something other than immediacy. The conception of essence as what is other than immediacy is thus not just an error, but is generated by an intrinsic feature of the very concept of essence itself: namely, that the essence is quite simply *not* immediate being. The source of the immediacy initially conferred on essence is thus the simplicity of that little word 'not'.[23]

To recapitulate: so far the essence of being has been contrasted with the immediacy of being – the essence of being has been understood *not* to be immediacy, but to be *something else* (namely, non-immediacy), and immediate being itself has been understood to be *something other* than the essence of things (namely, what is inessential). According to Hegel, however, in conceiving of imme-

---

[22] Hegel, *Wissenschaft der Logik*, 2: 19; *Science of Logic*, p. 395.
[23] See Henrich, 'Hegel's Logik der Reflexion. Neue Fassung', p. 236.

diacy and the essence in this way we are overlooking something very important: immediacy cannot actually *be* something distinct from, or other than, the essence of things, because what there is in essence is *all* that there truly is. The concept of essence thus requires us to revise the idea that immediacy is real but inessential, and to conceive of it in a new way.

The concept of essence, we recall, is the concept of the true character of immediacy *itself*; it arose when we discovered that immediacy is not simple immediacy after all, but is in truth non-immediacy. Hence the opening sentence of Hegel's doctrine of essence: 'the truth of *being* is *essence*'.[24] In truth, therefore, there is nothing to 'immediacy' *but* non-immediacy. But that means that *there is in fact no simply immediate being.* Immediacy thus cannot be understood to *be* something separate from the essence of things – to be inessential being – because it cannot have any *being* of its own at all. Yet, as we have seen, we may not simply dispense with the idea of immediacy altogether: the doctrine of being shows all being to be immediate and shows that we must encounter immediacy in so far as we encounter anything at all. How can these two conflicting claims be reconciled? The answer, in Hegel's view, is this: the simple immediacy which things exhibit, in so far as they are anything at all, but which in truth is not really there, must be understood to be an *illusion*. To be is to be immediate; but immediacy is in truth not immediacy after all. In essence, therefore, there is no immediacy. The immediacy which we encounter – indeed the whole sphere of being described in the doctrine of being – can thus only be what there *seems* to be. The second important effect of conceiving the essence of things to be non-immediacy is, consequently, to reduce the immediacy of things to mere seeming immediacy, to mere *Schein*. Focusing our attention on the essence of things does not just render immediate being inessential, it renders it utterly illusory.

III

Hegel's analysis of the concept of essence might appear at first sight to have little to do with the traditional understanding of that concept. No mention has yet been made of the difference between essence and existence, and nothing has been said about the unchanging character of the essence of things. The suspicion inevitably arises, therefore, that Hegel is not actually talking about the accepted concept of essence at all. Yet I believe that, despite his

---

[24] Hegel, *Wissenschaft der Logik*, 2: 13; *Science of Logic*, p. 389.

unusual language, Hegel is indeed explaining what is meant by the word 'essence'. If he initially neglects some of the features normally associated with the concept of 'essence', that is because he does not wish simply to take such features for granted at the outset, but prefers to build up his conception of essence from scratch. In Hegel's view, we should not just assume that the essence of things 'endures' or that it is identical with 'form' and so on, but should seek to discover whether such claims are true, starting from the *least* that the essence of things can possibly be.

As we have seen, the least that the essence can be is the *negation* of immediacy. This may strike some as a strange way to begin. But it surely overlaps with our deepest intuitions about 'essence'. For all Hegel is claiming is that thinking about the essence of things is at least thinking about what is *not* immediately given to us. 'When we say ... that all things have an essence', Hegel writes, 'what we mean is that they are *not* truly what they *immediately* show themselves to be (*daß sie wahrhaft* nicht *das sind, als was sie sich* unmittelbar *erweisen)*'.[25] To deny this minimal claim is surely to reject the very idea of essence altogether.

Hegel's further claims about essence are also considerably less remote from our normal understanding than his abstract account might lead one to believe. We often think of the essence of things as being something apart from their inessential qualities. We might say, for example, that what is important or essential about a person is his kindness, and that his occasional moments of unkindness towards us are really inessential or immaterial. Furthermore, we also recognise that, once we understand the essence of something to be what it *truly* is, we have to consider the immediate characteristics of the thing, that are at variance with that essence, to be what the thing merely *seems* to be. I might see someone in the street and find him rather ferocious. I might then come to recognise that he is not really ferocious at all, but that he is in truth very friendly. In the light of this thought that the man is actually a friendly person, I cannot but think that the ferocity, which I still see in him, is merely apparent.

Now, in the example I have just given, the man's apparent ferocity is contrasted with his true friendliness. It is not enough, however, simply to *contrast* his true and apparent character in this way: for the man *himself* seems to be ferocious. Since the man himself is, as it were, sheer friendliness, it must be his friendliness that appears to

---

[25] Hegel, *Enzyklopädie der philosophischen Wissenschaften (1830). Erster Teil: Die Wissenschaft der Logik*, p. 232 [§112 Addition]; *The Encyclopaedia Logic*, p. 176, my italics.

be ferocity. The man's seeming ferocity cannot simply be set over against his essential friendliness, therefore, because it is nothing but that which his essential friendliness itself seems to be. Or, to put it more abstractly, even though the essence of things differs from what things seem to be, it can only be their essence or true being itself that seems to be other than it is. In Hegel's words, seeming is thus nothing but the *'seeming of essence itself* (*der Schein des Wesens selbst*).[26] In the terms of Hegel's own analysis, we recall, what is illusory is simple immediacy. For Hegel, therefore, it is the essence itself – non-immediacy as such – that seems to be immediate being. If we think about it, this has to be the case: for if non-immediacy proves to be the truth of immediacy, then only non-immediacy can *seem* to be such immediacy in the first place.

We have seen that the concept of essence reduces immediacy to mere illusion. What we have now to recognise is that the concept of essence does not just negate and dissolve a sphere of immediacy that lies outside it. It negates a sphere of immediacy that is actually generated by essence and non-immediacy itself. We now need to consider precisely how non-immediacy can itself seem to be immediate being.

Note that the issue here is not how the essence can appear to have an immediacy of its own *over against* immediate being. That has already been explained: the essence appears to have that immediacy because it is initially understood as the simple negation of being. What Hegel now wishes to explain is how the essence can itself seem to be that very immediate being *from which* it is initially distinguished – how the essence can appear in the guise of simple immediate being *itself*. This appearance of immediacy on the part of essence clearly cannot stem from its being taken as the simple negation of being. Indeed, Hegel insists that it can only arise from the new form that essence is conceived to have once it is understood to reduce immediate being to mere illusion. According to Hegel, then, when the essence is understood to reduce being to mere illusion, it is *thereby* conceived as that which itself appears in the form of such illusory being. To appreciate why the essence itself appears to be immediate being, we need to consider how the concept of essence changes as it sets itself in relation, not just to what is inessential, but to what is illusory.

Hegel's new conception of essence is, however, not an easy one to comprehend: for he argues that essence has now to be understood as sheer *negativity* – as double negation, self-negating negation, negation that is *not* just simple negation. Essence itself seems to be sim-

[26] Hegel, *Wissenschaft der Logik*, 2: 22; *Science of Logic*, p. 398 (translation emended).

ple immediate being, therefore, because essence is negativity. It is at this point that the 'opprobrious weight' of the negatives, referred to by Pippin, is felt most acutely by readers of Hegel's text. Indeed, some – like Schopenhauer – may be tempted to think that Hegel is deliberately indulging in mind-befuddling word-play, or that he has taken leave of his philosophical senses altogether (assuming that he had any to begin with). It is important to recognise, however, that Hegel's new conception of essence is not the product of sinister intent or of madness. He is driven to conceive of essence as sheer negativity because he takes seriously what is implied by the concept of essence itself.

We know that the essence has initially to be conceived as the negation of immediacy, because the least that the essence can be is what is *not* immediately given; and we know that conceiving of essence in this way turns it into something separate from immediate being, into that being which is essential rather than inessential. It is also clear, however, that the essence cannot actually be something separate from immediacy, because it is the true character of immediate being *itself*: essence is the sheer non-immediacy that immediacy *itself* is in truth. This idea requires us to recognise that there is in fact nothing to 'immediacy itself' except non-immediacy. That means that there is no simple *immediacy* as such; and that in turn means that the immediacy we encounter must be an illusion. The idea that essence, or non-immediacy, is the true character of immediacy itself does not eliminate the very idea of immediacy, but renders all immediacy merely apparent.

Note now how the concept of essence has been altered in the process. If the essence, or non-immediacy, is the *truth* of immediacy, then it is not simply something separate from, or other than, immediacy; it is not simply the direct and immediate *negation* of immediacy. That is merely what essence initially seems to be. Essence remains the negation of immediacy, in so far as it is still defined as *non*-immediacy; but it is now to be conceived as the negation of immediacy that is *not* just immediacy's *negation* but immediacy's truth. In other words, the essence has now to be understood as the negation of simple negation or as 'absolute negativity'.[27] The very logic of the concept of essence itself, therefore, forces us to conceive of essence as negativity.

The manifold complexities of Hegel's concept of negativity have been explored with great clarity, subtlety and precise attention to detail by Dieter Henrich in his exemplary essay, 'Hegel's Logik der Reflexion'. My concern here is not to present a similarly detailed

[27] Hegel, *Wissenschaft der Logik*, 2: 19, 21; *Science of Logic*, pp. 395, 397.

account for the English-speaking reader. It is simply to highlight those features of negativity that are relevant to the specific task at hand: that of demonstrating that Hegel has a non-foundational concept of essence. It is to these that we now turn.

The most obvious thing to note about negativity is that it is much more radically non-immediate and negative than simple negation. Simple negation, for Hegel, is simply that: negation. It has an immediacy of its own and so, for that reason, can be understood to *be* something different from immediacy itself.[28] Negativity, on the other hand, lacks such simple immediacy. It is not simple, immediate negation, but self-*negating* negation – negation that recoils back upon itself and undermines the immediacy of simply *being* negation.

Yet Hegel argues that, paradoxically, such negativity itself takes the form of immediate being. This is due, not merely (as Nietzsche might argue) to the constraints of our language, but to a structural feature of negativity as such. Negativity takes the form of immediacy, in Hegel's view, because, as self-negating negation, it is purely *self-relating* negation. As such, it is wholly self-sufficient and is not mediated by anything else. It stands alone; it is, as Hegel puts it, 'equal' only to itself. Consequently, it is *immediately* itself: it is simply what it is. 'Negativity', Hegel writes, 'is negativity *per se*; it is its relation to itself and is thus in itself immediacy.'[29] Immediacy was initially conferred on essence because essence was taken to be the simple *negation* of immediate being. Essence now takes the form of immediate being as such because, as negativity, it is purely self-relating, purely *itself*.

Or, at least, that is how it appears. In truth, negativity cannot simply *be* what it is – cannot simply be *itself* – because it is self-*negating* negation or 'negative self-relation'. That is to say, it is the explicit activity of negating any simple immediacy that it appears to have. The 'immediacy' exhibited by negativity thus cannot be real *immediacy*, but can only be an 'effect' generated by self-negating (and so self-relating) negation. Simple 'immediacy', in other words, can only be an illusion projected by negativity: 'the immediacy is not simply affirmative (*seiend*), but is the purely mediated or reflected immediacy that is illusory being'.[30] We have seen that the essence initially *seems* to be something other than immediate being. Now we see that the essence *seems* to be that very immediate being itself.

Our ordinary intuition tells us that what there seems to be must be an illusion projected by what there is *in truth*. If a person is, as it

[28] Hegel, *Wissenschaft der Logik*, 1: 118; *Science of Logic*, p. 111.

[29] Hegel, *Wissenschaft der Logik*, 2: 22; *Science of Logic*, p. 398.

[30] Hegel, *Wissenschaft der Logik*, 2: 22; *Science of Logic*, p. 397.

were, nothing but friendliness, then his apparent ferocity must be a projection of his friendliness itself. Seeming can only be the seeming of essence. Hegel makes the same point by drawing attention to the inherently negative character of the essence. Essence must be understood as sheer negativity, because it is the negation of immediacy that is *not* just immediacy's simple negation. As sheer negativity (or as the 'second negation' of being), it is the utter dissolution of all simple immediacy: it reduces all immediacy to mere illusion and even negates the immediacy that initially attaches to essence itself as simple negation. Yet, as self-relating negation, sheer negativity exhibits an apparent simple immediacy of its own. This immediacy is merely *apparent*, however, because it is merely an illusory effect generated by self-*negating* negation. Essence as negativity thus seems – but only *seems* – to be simple immediate being. Consequently, simple immediacy is the illusion projected by essence itself; or, as Hegel puts it, seeming is the '*seeming of essence itself*'.[31]

The simple immediacy of being – which is described in detail in the doctrine of being – hereby suffers a third reduction. First, it was reduced to what is merely inessential. Then it was reduced to what is merely illusory. Now it has been reduced even further to an illusion projected by the essence itself. It is essence – and essence alone – that seems to be simple immediate being. It can only be essence, therefore, that creates the impression that there is a realm of simple immediacy made up of things with specific qualities and magnitude. Such immediate being thus really is nothing in itself, because it is merely the result of an unwitting trick played on us by essential negativity.

According to Hegel, however, the concept of essence implies a further – fourth – reduction of immediacy. This involves the elimination of the very distinction between essence and its own seeming. At the point we have now reached, essence is understood to generate the illusion of being simple immediacy itself (and so to generate the illusion of *there being* a realm of such immediacy). In conceiving of such apparent immediacy as mere illusion, however, we are still distinguishing between the essence itself and the illusion it projects: We are still understanding the essence *not* to be the simple immediacy that it *seems* to be. Hegel's next – and most radical – suggestion is that even this distinction is undermined by the sheer negativity and non-immediacy of essence. Hegel's reasoning here is clear. If we understand essence to be distinct from what it itself seems to be, then we continue to confer a simple immediacy on to essence: we posit the essence as being pure and simple negativity

[31] Hegel, *Wissenschaft der Logik*, 2: 22; *Science of Logic*, p. 398.

rather than (illusory) immediacy, and so give essence itself its own immediate identity over against what it merely seems to be. But in so doing, we fail to think of essence as negativity and *non-immediacy*. As Hegel writes:

> In the sphere of essence, we have first essence opposed to the unessential, then essence opposed to illusory being .... But both the unessential and illusory being, and also the difference of essence from them, derive solely from the fact that essence is at first taken as an *immediate* (*als ein* unmittelbares), not as it is in itself.[32]

In truth, as we know, essence only *seems* to be simple immediacy – whether it is understood as the 'simple' negation of being or as purely 'self-relating' negation. The conclusion we must draw, therefore, is that essence only seems to have an immediacy of its own beyond the simple immediacy it seems to be. This is the strikingly Nietzschean implication of Hegel's analysis of essence: the thought of essence as distinct from, or as underlying, what it seems to be, is itself merely the thought of what essence *seems to be*. Or, to put it another way, the idea that the essence of things can be distinguished from the illusion of immediacy that essence projects, is itself one of the illusions that essence projects.

In truth essence is not something underlying what it seems to be; it is not *that which* seems. It has no immediacy of its own that is distinct from its seeming. But if that is the case, then essence can be nothing but seeming as such. This, indeed, is the conclusion that Hegel finally comes to: essence, in truth, is nothing but *the very process of seeming*, 'the seeming of itself in itself' (*das Scheinen seiner in sich selbst*).[33] In essence, then, there is no simple immediacy, and there is no essence or foundation underlying the appearance of immediacy, either. All these is, is the process of seeming itself – the process whereby sheer negativity first seems to be immediacy, then seems to be distinct from its own seeming immediacy, and finally dissolves this distinction and reveals itself to be nothing but seeming as such.[34] In the terms of the example we gave earlier, if we say that the man is essentially friendly, but all we encounter directly is ferocity, then we must conclude that his 'friendliness' is in fact nothing but seeming to be ferocity.

The importance of Hegel's abstract analysis of essence should now be clear. For, on the one hand, Hegel has shown that the

[32] Hegel, *Wissenschaft der Logik*, 2: 23; *Science of Logic*, p. 399 (translation emended).
[33] Hegel, *Wissenschaft der Logik*, 2: 23; *Science of Logic*, p. 398 (translation emended).
[34] Hegel, *Wissenschaft der Logik*, 2: 22; *Science of Logic*, p. 398. For Henrich's subtle analysis of this process, see 'Hegel's Logik der Reflexion. Neue Fassung', pp. 256–60.

essence of things cannot be something *other than* or *underlying* what is inessential or what appears. Essence does not constitute the *foundation* of real or apparent being, because to think of it that way is to confer on it a simple immediacy which it cannot actually have. Yet, on the other hand, Hegel has explained why people might believe that the essence does constitute such a foundation: because the essence is precisely the process of *seeming* to be such a foundation. It is the process of seeming to be simple immediacy and of seeming to underlie any immediacy it seems to have.

Foundationalists and anti-foundationalists disagree about whether there is actually an underlying ground to things or not. But they agree that the term 'essence' means, amongst other things, just such an underlying ground. Hegel's distinctive contribution to the debate between these two groups is to argue that the term 'essence' does *not* mean such an underlying ground, but that – for essential reasons – it does seem to. From Hegel's point of view, therefore, foundationalists and anti-foundationalists are both taken in by the same illusion – an illusion projected, not merely by our own thought or language, but by essential negativity itself.

IV

So far we have conceived of the essence as negating all immediacy and reducing it to mere illusion. Essence negates immediacy to such a degree that it cannot even be thought as being *that which* seems to be immediate, but must be understood as the mere process of seeming as such, the process of negativity. Hegel argues, however, that the concept of essence does not negate *all* immediacy whatsoever. This is because, as the process of sheer seeming, essence has an immediacy of its own that is irreducible. Essence, after all, *is* the process of sheer seeming; it *is* sheer negativity. The previous immediacy exhibited by negativity proved to be illusory because it belied essence's inherently self-*negating* character: it invested negativity with a simple, immediate identity which, as sheer self-negation, it could not have (see pp. 37–39). The new immediacy exhibited by negativity, to which Hegel now draws attention, is different from this. It does not belie essence's self-negating character, but, on the contrary, is the immediacy negativity must have in so far as it is nothing but negativity, nothing but sheer seeming to be. Such immediacy is, Hegel says, the 'immediacy that *is* as pure mediation or absolute negativity'.[35] This immediacy is real, because essence cannot be anything less than sheer negativity and seeming.

At this point in the analysis, we begin to see that the essence does

[35] Hegel, *Wissenschaft der Logik*, 2: 23; *Science of Logic*, p. 399.

not just negate and reduce immediacy but is itself *constitutive* of immediate being. There is immediate being after all, therefore, because of the very nature of essence itself; negativity does not simply render all immediate being illusory, but actually makes immediate being necessary. Negativity, in other words, is now understood to be the true character or essence of real, *irreducible* immediacy. Later in the *Logic* Hegel will show that the immediacy constituted by negativity is to be understood as identity, existence, actuality and, ultimately, self-determining reason or the 'Idea'. It is here at the end of the section on 'seeming', however, that the profound reversal in our conception of the essence of things occurs: for it is here that we first see the essence play a positive – indeed, generative – role, rather than a purely negative one. Here, in other words, we first see negativity negate itself into positivity.[36]

But how can negativity constitute irreducible immediacy, if, as we have seen, it also reduces immediacy to mere illusion? Hegel's answer is clear. What proved to be illusory, and is still to be regarded as illusory, is *sheer* or *simple* immediacy. There is no *simple* immediacy, because, as we saw at the end of the doctrine of being, all such 'immediacy' is in truth mediated. The simple immediacy that consists in simply *being* what something is, is thus a mere illusion – an illusion projected by negativity itself. But we have now learned that this does not render immediacy as such illusory, because there is such a thing as *mediated immediacy* – immediacy that is constituted, and so mediated, by negativity. Indeed, according to Hegel, that is all there can actually be. 'There is nothing', he says, 'nothing in heaven or in nature or mind or anywhere else which does not equally contain both immediacy and mediation'.[37] As we have just noted, such mediated immediacy will prove to be identity, existence, actuality and, eventually, the Idea. The self-identical, existing, actual Idea is thus *in truth* all that there is, for Hegel.

Yet this sharp contrast between simple and mediated immediacy actually needs qualification. For it becomes clear during the further course of the doctrine of essence that simple immediacy is itself a necessary 'moment' or aspect of mediated immediacy.[38] In other

---

[36] Hegel, *Wissenschaft der Logik*, 2: 25; *Science of Logic*, p. 400.

[37] Hegel, *Wissenschaft der Logik*, 1: 66; *Science of Logic*, p. 68.

[38] See, for example, Hegel, *Wissenschaft der Logik*, 2: 202; *Science of Logic*, p. 542 (on '*immediate, unreflected* actuality'). For Hegel, therefore, the world of nature and history, which is the unfolding of reason or the Idea, must include a moment of irreducible, immediate *contingency*. On this, see Dieter Henrich, 'Hegels Theorie über den Zufall', in Dieter Henrich, *Hegel im Kontext*, (Frankfurt: Suhrkamp Verlag, 1967), pp. 157–86, and Stephen Houlgate, 'Necessity and Contingency in Hegel's *Science of Logic*', *The Owl of Minerva*, 27, 1 (Fall 1995): 37–49.

words, every existing or actual thing is itself *something* with *these* specific qualities and *this* specific magnitude. In so far as simple immediacy is understood to be part of mediated immediacy, and so to be mediated itself in its very simplicity, such immediacy is thus not illusory after all. It is only an illusion, in so far as it is taken by itself and conceived in complete abstraction from mediation as *utterly* simple immediacy. Up to now simple immediacy has been taken by itself in just this way. Consequently, it has been undermined, and eventually reduced to mere appearance, by the recognition that it is the product of mediation. In the further course of the doctrine of essence, however, simple immediacy will be restored to reality by being conceived as a moment of, and as a form of, mediated immediacy.

For Hegel, therefore, this pen does not just *seem* to be something of its own and to be quite separate from this piece of paper. The pen *is* something in its own right and it *is* quite separate from this piece of paper. Each is simply what it *is* and, in an obvious sense, is not created, produced or 'mediated' by the other. Each is thus simply *immediate*. But to say this is to tell only one part of the story: for it omits any reference to the negativity – in the shape of difference and form – which constitutes them *as* separate things, and it ignores the ways in which their character is determined by other things around them (for example, by the people that use them or by the temperature and humidity of the air). To think of each thing as simply being what it is, is thus not wrong, but it is severely to underdetermine them.

To recapitulate: the illusion is not that things are simply immediate, but that they simply are what they are *and nothing more* – that being is nothing but simple immediacy. It is this *utterly simple* immediacy that has been the subject of the successive reductions or negations we have traced during the course of this essay. The truth that emerges through Hegel's analysis is that things are indeed simply what they are, but that that is not all there is to be said about them – because such simple immediacy is merely one aspect of their *constituted, mediated* immediacy and existence.

With the idea that negativity is itself constitutive of all true immediacy, Hegel breaks definitively with dualism and foundationalism. He proves that the essence of things does not underlie being as its foundation, but is immanent in being, indeed is identical with being itself. Later in the *Logic* Hegel will show that negativity has to be understood as difference, form and, eventually, reason. In no case, however, does the ontological status of negativity change: it is always to be understood as constitutive of being itself. The ultimate message of Hegel's *Logic* is thus not that all being has a rational or dialectical *foundation*, but that being is itself rational and dialectical.

In the doctrine of the Concept – the third part of the *Logic* – Hegel provides his fullest account of the structure of constituted, rational being. There being is understood to consist in mechanical, chemical, organic, cognitive and practical processes. In the remaining parts of the doctrine of essence – which fall between the section which we have examined and the doctrine of the Concept – Hegel considers more general conceptions of constituted being, such as existence and actuality. But he also highlights the various ways in which negativity continues to appear to be something *underlying* being itself (for example, when it determines itself to be the *ground* of all being or the *substance* of things). Such an appearance is nothing but an illusion, in Hegel's view, and is shown to be such by closer analysis of what it is to be the 'ground' or 'substance' of things.[39] Nevertheless, it is an illusion that is necessarily projected by essential negativity itself. In my view the lasting significance of Hegel's whole doctrine of essence lies above all in this insight: that we are seduced into looking for the hidden ground of things, not just by the grammar of our language and the structure of our thought, but by the very nature of the world itself.[40]

Among those who succumb most readily to the seductive wiles of the world are some who charge Hegel himself with foundationalism. Deleuze, for example, rejects what he takes to be Hegel's view that there is a fundamental identity to things; but he himself maintains that 'all identities are ... produced as an optical "effect" by the more *profound* game of difference and repetition'.[41] Similarly, Marx criticises Hegel's alleged contention that history is governed by an underlying absolute; yet he himself claims that 'the sum total of ... relations of production constitutes ... the real *foundation*, on which rises a legal and political superstructure and to which correspond definite forms of social consciousness'.[42] Granted, the foundations to which Deleuze and Marx refer do not exhibit the identity, unity, and invariance commonly associated with the metaphysical concept of essence or ground; but they are nevertheless conceived as *underlying* what we encounter in some way. They are thus the products of a way of thinking that has been

[39] Hegel, *Wissenschaft der Logik*, 2: 122–3, 220; *Science of Logic*, pp. 477–8, 556.

[40] This might well be one significant difference between Hegel and Wittgenstein and one significant similarity between Hegel and Nietzsche.

[41] Gilles Deleuze, *Difference and Repetition*, trans. P. Patton (London: Athlone Press, 1994), p. xix, my italics.

[42] Marx, *Selected Writings*, p. 389, my italics.

taken in by – rather than seen through – the illusion generated by the very nature of things.

Hegel's position, by contrast, is radically anti-foundationalist. He seeks to understand not what (allegedly) 'grounds', 'underlies' or 'conditions' being, but what being *itself* is in truth. He is, in other words, an ontological rather than a (quasi-)transcendental thinker: one who looks to determine what is constitutive of being as such, rather than what is 'presupposed' by being, what 'makes objects possible', or what 'grants' being, as it were, 'from behind'. This I believe is what ultimately distinguishes Hegel from his German Idealist predecessors, such as Kant, Fichte and Schelling, and from many of his successors, such as Marx, Deleuze, Nietzsche, Heidegger and Derrida. None of these philosophers can be regarded as a straightforward, metaphysical foundationalist; indeed, as I indicated earlier, many are avowed anti-foundationalists. Any comparison of their thought with that of Hegel would thus have to pay very careful and subtle attention to the different ways in which they submit metaphysical foundationalism – the belief in a unified, identifiable, enduring ground of things – to critique or deconstruction. Nevertheless, such a comparative study would, I believe, show that they remain seduced by the illusion that immediacy points back to 'something' (or, rather, to some *non*-thing) more 'fundamental' than immediacy itself, and that, consequently, their thought falls short of Hegel's radical anti-foundationalism.

Hegel's doctrine of essence is by no means easy to follow. Even Hegel admits that it is the 'most difficult' part of the *Logic*.[43] To my mind, however, the doctrine of essence is essential reading for those who wish to understand Hegel properly. For it is here that we see why Hegel cannot be the philosopher of legend – the one for whom everything that occurs is but the appearance of an underlying, all-controlling absolute. It is also here that we discover why Hegel might nevertheless *seem* to be that legendary figure. In addition, the doctrine of essence provides a particularly fine example of Hegel at work subtly unfolding the sometimes surprising implications of concepts we thought we already understood – a 'method' he follows throughout his philosophy. Taking these three things together, it is tempting to say that it is in the doctrine of essence that we encounter the very *essence* of Hegel himself.

---

[43] Hegel, *Enzyklopädie der philosophischen Wissenschaften (1830). Erster Teil: Die Wissenschaft der Logik*, p. 236 [§114]; *The Encyclopaedia Logic*, p. 179.

Schopenhauer's Pessimism

CHRISTOPHER JANAWAY

Patrick Gardiner 1922–1997

This series of lectures was originally scheduled to include a talk on Schopenhauer by Patrick Gardiner. Sadly, Patrick died during the summer, and I was asked to stand in. Patrick must, I am sure, have been glad to see this series of talks on German Philosophy being put on by the Royal Institute, and he, probably more than anyone on the list, deserves to have been a part of it. Patrick Gardiner taught and wrote with unfailing integrity and quiet refinement in the Oxford of the 1950s, '60s, '70s and '80s, when the changing fashions in philosophy, and Oxford philosophy in particular, were quite remote from his own central interests. He went his own way, radically but quite undemonstratively. His book on Schopenhauer, originally published in 1963, was a beacon in the night as far as English-language publications on that philosopher are concerned. It is still a leader in the field, and I am pleased to say it has been re-issued just this year after being out of print for too long. Patrick worked in aesthetics, on Kant, and on the German Idealists, showing an expertise and a fondness for Fichte which now seem well ahead of their time. He also contributed well known books on Kierkegaard and on the philosophy of history. I am honoured to be invited as Patrick's replacement. He was a true pioneer, whom all of us working in these several fields that have now grown more fashionable and more populated should pause to salute.

Schopenhauer's Question

In Book Five of *The Gay Science* Nietzsche writes that 'unconditional and honest atheism' is 'the locus of Schopenhauer's whole integrity' and 'the *presupposition* of the way he poses his problem'. If we reject the 'meaning' Christianity assigns to the world, then, writes Nietzsche, '*Schopenhauer's* question immediately comes to us in a terrifying way: *Has existence any meaning at all*? (*Gay Science*, 357). Schopenhauer speaks of 'meaning' but more often uses the vocabulary of value. I shall take his question to be: What is the value of my being what I am? or What value does the existence of any of us have? For Schopenhauer, as Nietzsche implies, certain answers that were once thinkable on the assumption that each of us

47

was an immaterial substance or a pure, rational soul, or part of some supernatural design, are not available. We have to face the question of value as material, biological individuals; and Schopenhauer's response is that the value in such existence is not – cannot be – greater than the value non-existence would have had. Paradoxically, as he says, 'nothing else can be stated as the aim of our existence except the knowledge that it would be better for us not to exist' (*W2*, 605).[1] My guiding question is simply: How does Schopenhauer reach this predicament?

Will to life

Now Schopenhauer is clear that each of us is a material thing, and an organism. For all organisms, to exist is to strive towards some end or other, to be continually pointed in a direction. The direction or end that governs all others is the perpetuation of life: its maintenance in the material individual one is, and the generation of life in the form of offspring. As particular manifestations of *Wille zum Leben*, will to life, we tend towards survival and reproduction, and this sets the common form of our existence:

> the fundamental theme of all the many different acts of the will is the satisfaction of the needs inseparable from the body's existence in health; they have their expression in it, and can be reduced to the maintenance of the individual and propagation of the species. (*W1*, 326-7)

Because we live, we must strive. However the actual content of our striving may be elaborated, its form, set by the will to life, locates us always somewhere on a cycle of willing and attaining. Any determinate episode of willing comes to an end, but not willing itself. Nothing we achieve by willing could ever erase the will itself; as Schopenhauer says,

> its desires are unlimited, its claims inexhaustible, and every satisfied desire gives birth to a new one. No possible satisfaction in

[1] I use the following abbreviations for works by Schopenhauer: *W1, W2: The World as Will and Representation*, vols. 1 and 2; *P1, P2: Parerga and Paralipomena*, vols. 1 and 2. Translations are as follows, with minor modifications: *The World as Will and Representation*, trans. E. F. J. Payne (New York: Dover, 1969); *Parerga and Paralipomena*, trans. E. F. J. Payne (Oxford: Clarendon Press, 1974). An important divergence from Payne's translation should be noted: for *Wille zum Leben* I use 'will to life' where Payne has 'will-to-live'. I have substituted my preferred version even in citations which are otherwise from Payne's translation.

the world could suffice to still its craving, set a final goal to its demands, and fill the bottomless pit of its heart. (*W2*, 573)

Let us note two immediate points about this will which Schopenhauer says constitutes our essence. Firstly, although the will to life operates in conscious and rational life-forms, it is not essentially rational or conscious. The use of the term 'will' is thus misleading. Schopenhauer begins his discussion of willing with the pursuit of ends in human action. But he contrives to extend the same term to every instinctual or biological process, conceiving them as occurring because they fulfil some end for the organism or species. He does not incorporate all the features of human mental or conscious willing into his wider use of the term 'will'. Will manifests itself 'blindly' – i.e. without consciousness or mentality of any kind – in the vast majority of nature, including the human organism. So the will to life within me is not a quasi-mind, not a consciousness, not something working rationally towards purposes. It is the principle that organises me, this individual human being, just as it organises a snail or an oak tree, so that I tend towards being alive and propagating the species I belong to.

Secondly, life is an unchosen goal of our striving. Later we rationally choose to live – or perhaps embrace an allegiance to life by some less explicit process – but the will to life already inhabits us prior to any understanding or deliberation. In a sense the primary will to life 'in' me is not *my* will. Schopenhauer would rather say the will to life manifests itself as me (among other things). Georg Simmel puts it well in his classic lectures of 1907: 'I do not will by virtue of values and goals that are posited by reason, but I have goals because I will continuously and ceaselessly from the depth of my essence.'[2]

As an exercise in metaphysics Schopenhauer's notion of the will is notoriously problematic: he appears to claim that the metaphysical thing in itself underlies and expresses itself in every process in nature, indeed that it is the world; that it transcends space, time, and causality, that it is unknowable, and yet that we can securely attach to it the predicate 'will' which we understand from its application within the knowable phenomenal world. I shall not here discuss the difficulties that beset this account. However, we should clarify one further point about Schopenhauer's will, namely that it has no ultimate end or purpose to which it tends.

[2] Georg Simmel, *Schopenhauer and Nietzsche*, trans. Helmut Loiskandl, Deena Weinstein, and Michael Weinstein (Amherst, MA, 1986), p. 30.

> The will dispenses entirely with an ultimate aim and object. It always strives, because striving is its sole nature, to which no attained goal can put an end. Such striving is therefore incapable of final satisfaction; it can be checked only by hindrance, but in itself it goes on for ever. (*W1*, 308)

One consequence Schopenhauer draws is that there can be no absolute good. What is good is by definition, for Schopenhauer, what satisfies an end for which some part of reality strives, or towards which it naturally tends. An 'absolute good' or 'highest good, *summum bonum*' would be 'a final satisfaction of the will, after which no fresh willing would occur', but 'such a thing cannot be conceived. The will can just as little through some satisfaction cease to will always afresh, as time can end or begin; for the will there is no permanent fulfilment which completely and forever satisfies its craving'. (*W1*, 362). Willing continues in the world in perpetuity. But since absolute value could be possessed only by a state of affairs in which nothing more was willed, no state of affairs can ever possess absolute value – it would involve a contradiction to think otherwise. There is value only locally, relative to some occurrence or state of willing.

The argument from the ubiquity of suffering within the structure of willing

Schopenhauer's pessimism is not reducible to any single argument. Nevertheless I want to reconstruct one which relies on an intimate link between the human will and suffering. Suffering is defined by Schopenhauer as 'the will's hindrance through an obstacle placed between it and its temporary goal' (*W1*, 309), while the opposite state, '*satisfaction*, well-being, happiness' consists in the will's attainment of its temporary goal. Suffering, non-attainment of goals, will be a likely occurrence in the life of a being that wills. But this alone is hardly grounds for pronouncing that non-existence should be preferred to the life of a willing being. However, for Schopenhauer suffering is more than just one ingredient in such a life: it is a permeating and necessary feature of it. To see this let us consider the structure of willing in a schematic way (see figure 1). A being will strive towards some goal, X, and will either attain X or not attain X. The latter state, marked as c in the diagram, is a state of suffering. It seems there are just three subsequent possibilities once a goal is not attained. Having not attained a goal, I may continue to strive for it nevertheless. This is the route looping back to

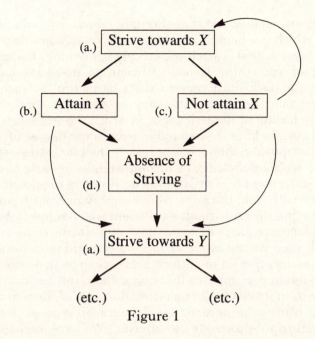

Figure 1

the original state of striving, which, repeated endlessly, is the nightmare of Tantalus and other mythical figures whom Schopenhauer is prone to mention:

> so long as our consciousness is filled by our will, so long as we are given up to the throng of desires with its constant hopes and fears, so long as we are the subject of willing, we never obtain lasting happiness or peace. … Thus the subject of willing is constantly lying on the revolving wheel of Ixion, is always drawing water in the sieve of the Danaids, and is the eternally thirsting Tantalus. (*W1*, 196)

Powerful though the symbolism of this route is for a pessimist, there are of course others: I may move on to another goal, or I may cease for a while to strive towards any goals. What we have next to establish is that, for Schopenhauer, both states *a* and *d* – both striving itself and the absence of striving – also constitute or presuppose forms of suffering.

On the first point Schopenhauer declares: 'all striving [*Streben*] springs from want or deficiency, from dissatisfaction with one's own state or condition, and is therefore suffering so long as it is not satisfied' (*W1*, 309). The assumption appears to be that a wholly self-sufficient state, a state of lacking nothing (or at least registering no lack), would continue in principle perpetually, without tending towards any change of state brought about by will. Thus any episode which is a being's striving for a goal assumes that the being is, or at least registers itself as, lacking something. Being aware of the lack of something is not sufficient to make me suffer. The awareness of lack must present itself as painful as such. A clear example would be a felt deficiency or incompleteness, such as a thirst or a feeling of homesickness, in which the awareness of something's being lacking is inseparable from some degree of suffering. (But I suppose Schopenhauer must include cases where one painfully feels a deficiency or incompleteness because one makes a rational judgement of a situation as detrimental to oneself. Thirst is a form of suffering, but so is recognising (while not feeling thirst) that one is in a desert without a sufficient water-supply.) At any rate, Schopenhauer requires us to suppose that whenever we strive after any goal, then we are aware of lacking something in some manner which amounts to pain or suffering. Hence to be in a state of type *a* in the diagram presupposes that one suffers. But because our ordinary life is, in its essence, a manifestation of will, there is no end in ordinary life to the occurrence of states of type *a*. So we must always return to some state of suffering. We have, perhaps, come a small step nearer to pessimism.

How plausible, though, is the claim that whenever we strive for a goal, the striving presupposes an awareness of lack which amounts to suffering? The American scholar David Cartwright[3] finds this point unconvincing, saying that having a desire does not entail being in misery. That is true. However, that is not what Schopenhauer alleges. Rather the claim is that every episode of *striving* entails *some degree* of painful lack or dissatisfaction. Let us look at this more closely. Firstly, does striving always presuppose an awareness of lack, or a dissatisfaction, of any kind? Cartwright suggests this is not always true for desiring: I may desire to retain my good health which I believe I have rather than lack, and with which I am satisfied. However, Schopenhauer's point (at least in the last quoted passage) was one about *Streben*, striving or trying. (i) Striving, I take it, must be episodic rather than dispositional, whereas the desires just mentioned may be construed as dispositions; and (ii) striving must aim at change in a way that desire need not. So the question we must ask is: When an episode of my behaviour is describable as my striving to retain good health – which by hypothesis I do not lack – must I be experiencing some 'dissatisfaction with my own state or condition'?

[3] David E. Cartwright, 'Schopenhauer on Suffering, Death, Guilt and the Consolation of Metaphysics' in *Schopenhauer: New Essays in Honor of his 200th Birthday*, ed. E. von der Luft (Lewiston, NY, 1988, pp. 51–66.

The answer, arguably, is Yes: part of what distinguishes striving from mere wanting is that I regard the prior state of affairs (the state of affairs minus my striving), as deficient in whatever it requires to ensure my goal. If I register the state of affairs minus my striving as involving no such deficiency, it arguably becomes unintelligible to describe me as striving or trying to retain my health.

Even if we allow that to strive for something presupposes some dissatisfaction, Cartwright makes another objection: such dissatisfaction commonly 'lacks the vital tone which is associated with misery' (Cartwright, p. 59). This is correct. But it misses the mark as regards Schopenhauer's argument. Schopenhauer does not hold that each episode of willing involves the subject in misery; rather that, as a presupposition of there occurring an episode of willing, dissatisfaction or painfully felt lack must be present in some degree. Misery is, let us say, some prolonged frustration of what is willed, or massive non-attainment of goals basic to well-being. Most lives contain some misery and some lives contain mostly misery, facts which Schopenhauer has not forgotten and of which he writes movingly. But his point here is that all lives, even those free of misery, inevitably contain numerous, if minuscule, dissatisfactions. Each occurrence of striving presupposes a state with some degree of negative value for the being that strives. Hence, if we are looking for positive value within life, we shall not find it at any of the states of type a.

But it is time we mentioned other parts of the picture. First, consider state d in the diagram. May we not hope that a lack of goals to strive for will indicate a lack of the feeling that anything is lacking – an absence of suffering, a respite that counterbalances states a and c? Here is Schopenhauer's answer:

> The basis of willing ... is need, lack, and hence pain, and by its very nature and origin [any animal] is therefore destined to pain. If, on the other hand, it lacks objects of willing, because it is at once deprived of them again by too easy a satisfaction, a fearful emptiness and boredom come over it; in other words, its being and its existence itself become an intolerable burden for it. Hence its life swings like a pendulum to and fro between pain and boredom, and these two are in fact its ultimate constituents. ($W1$, 312)

This is one of Schopenhauer's tragi-comic master-strokes. (Elsewhere he says: 'suppose the human race were removed to a Utopia where everything grew automatically and pigeons flew about ready roasted ... then people would die of boredom or hang themselves' ($P2$, 293).) The state of having nothing to strive for readily becomes one in which we suffer from not having anything whose lack we feel. We painfully miss the differently painful state of having something to strive for. The grip of pessimism tightens again. Either of the routes *a-c-a* contains only suffering. So now does route *a-c-d*. Routes *a-b-a* and *a-b-d* contain satisfaction, but only sandwiched between two forms of suffering. Satisfaction is thus never anything permanent, and always lapses again into painful lack or painful boredom. Schopenhauer expresses the situation thus:

> absolutely every human life continues to flow on between willing and attainment. Of its nature the wish is pain; attainment quickly begets satiety. The goal was only apparent; possession takes away its charm. The wish, the need, appears again on the scene under a new form; if it does not, then dreariness, emptiness, and boredom follow, the struggle against which is just as painful as is that against want. (*W1*, 314).

But why would such an existence be one we should prefer not to have? Such an attitude might intelligibly be occasioned by the complete shipwreck of all ones aims. But that is not the situation of every human being, as Schopenhauer wisely concedes:

> This is the life of almost all men; they will, they know what they will, and they strive after this with enough success to protect them from despair, and enough failure to preserve them from boredom and its consequences. (*W1*, 327)

If most lives are spiced with a sufficiently varied set of goals, and if, as they shuffle between the different forms of suffering, they come round to the state 'Attain X' sufficiently often – then it is still unclear why that is a kind of existence not to be chosen above non-existence.

But Schopenhauer has one more vital point to make:

> All satisfaction, or what is commonly called happiness, is really and essentially always *negative* only, and never positive ... the satisfaction or gratification can never be more than a deliverance from a pain, from a want ... Nothing can ever be gained but deliverance from suffering or desire; consequently, we are only in the same position as we were before this suffering or desire appeared. (*W1*, 319)

> We feel pain, not painlessness; care, but not freedom from care; fear, but not safety and security. We feel the desire as we feel hunger and thirst; but as soon as it has been satisfied, it is like the mouthful of food that has been taken and which ceases to exist for our feelings the moment it is swallowed. (*W2*, 575).

The thesis here – call it 'the negativity of satisfaction' – is that attainment of what one strives for is not accompanied by any positive feeling. Satisfaction is merely the temporary absence of suffering, which soon yields again to suffering. If this is true, then state b in my diagram can do little to counterbalance the sufferings which are presupposed at every other point. The conclusion that non-existence would have been preferable at least comes within sight: 'all life is suffering', as Schopenhauer helpfully puts it ($W1$, 310). Life is suffering of different kinds, plus some neutral stretches where suffering is briefly absent before a new suffering arrives.

Before looking at some objections to this desperate game of pinball, I shall note that Schopenhauer uses this last point – the negativity of satisfaction – to advance another extremely brief argument for his pessimistic conclusion, an argument which we may call 'the argument from the sheer existence of suffering':

> it is quite superfluous to dispute whether there is more good or evil in the world; for the mere existence of evil decides the matter, since evil can never be wiped off, and consequently can never be balanced, by the good that exists along with or after it.

> *Mille piacer' non vagliono un tormento.*[4]

> For that thousands have lived in happiness and joy would never do away with the anguish and death-agony of one individual; and just as little does my present well-being undo my previous sufferings. Were the evil in the world even a hundred times less than it is, its mere existence would still be sufficient to establish a truth that may be expressed in various ways ... namely that we have not to be pleased but rather sorry about the existence of the world; that its non-existence would be preferable to its existence; that it is something which at bottom ought not to be. ($W2$, 576)

This is the most extreme statement of pessimism: any suffering at all invalidates the whole world. But it is difficult to see why I should reject or think badly of existence merely on the grounds of its containing some suffering. It is true that no happiness I can attain expunges my sufferings. But then equally no suffering I undergo can remove, in one sense, whatever happiness there has been. So it seems perversely one-sided just to discount happiness. Schopenhauer's conviction that any suffering tips the balance against life depends crucially on the thesis of the negativity of satisfaction. With this as a premise it becomes conceivable how one could think no satisfaction or happiness can compensate for a single

4 'A thousand pleasures do not compensate for one pain', Petrarch.

suffering. But this premise must strike us as an unnecessarily pessimistic starting-point.

Objections

There are some clear objections to Schopenhauer's use of willing and suffering in these arguments. Firstly, he seems guilty of ignoring or stipulating away positive feelings that occur within the pattern of willing and attainment. As Simmel puts it, 'he should not … have overlooked the positive moment of happiness which differentiates it as a psychological fact from sleep and death, the two other states that end suffering' (Simmel, 64). Sleep and death stop my striving; but satisfaction, which Schopenhauer defines as the cessation of striving, is at least a different kind of cessation from that in sleep or death. The difference is not simply that in satisfaction I am conscious when my striving ceases, and in other cases not – at least sometimes there are positive feelings of satisfaction, and these cannot be argued away on any of the grounds Schopenhauer adduces: (i) that satisfaction or happiness is always relative to a prior dissatisfaction; (ii) that satisfaction is temporary and yields to further dissatisfactions; or (iii) that the sum of feelings of dissatisfaction is likely to be greater. None of these points entails that there are no positively felt satisfactions. So Schopenhauer can no longer claim that felt satisfaction must count for nothing in the balance against suffering. Life might still be worth living at least for what feelings of satisfaction it does contain.

A subtler point, also made by Simmel, is that Schopenhauer fails to recognise that there is felt happiness along the route from striving to attainment, but before its terminus. 'Expected happiness is truly experienced', notes Simmel, and the will's progress towards attainment is 'attended more by a pleasurable sensation than a painful one' (Simmel, 55–6). There is wisdom in these thoughts: we often feel positive enjoyment at the prospect of attaining what we actually lack, and the actions through which, while lacking it, we strive towards it, may also be pleasurable. So Schopenhauer's model of willing as movement from a wholly painful lack to its mere obliteration is unrealistic. Even states of unfulfilled striving cannot always be set down on the side of suffering pure and simple.

A final objection is to Schopenhauer's implicit notion of positive and negative value in general. An undefended assumption in his argument is a stark from of hedonism: something adds positive value to life if and only if it involves a felt pleasure, while something contributes negative value if and only if it involves a felt pain. So if a sequence of states from felt lack though striving to satisfaction contains no feelings of pleasure, but only feelings of suffering yielding to a neutral state in which those feelings are erased, then there could be no positive value in that sequence of states for the subject. But this is questionable in a number of obvious and familiar ways. Are felt pleasures and pains the sole bearers or contributors of value? Why do outcomes of our actions other than pleasures and pains count for nothing? Is there not a self-sufficient value in certain activities which are fundamental to our nature and well-being? So we can certainly question whether Schopenhauer is right to use any form of hedonic calculus at all – and when we combine this with our criticism of the negativity of satisfaction thesis, we see that Schopenhauer has done something quite bizarre: he has used as the test of value a hedonic calculus in which each felt pain accumulates points on the down side of life, but where the total figure for satisfaction is permanently set at zero. From here it seems too short a distance to pessimism – or no distance at all. If the good could be solely the felt satisfaction of attaining what is willed, but if no positive satisfaction is ever felt, then the good is nothing but a satisfaction we could never feel, and whatever could be good will always be valueless. To start from here would be an absurdity.

Still we are left with a relatively pessimistic description of things. A basic state of ours as living creatures, and one to which we must constantly return, is one of dissatisfaction or painful lack. The attainment of a goal never stops us slipping back into further states of dissatisfaction. And there is constantly the likelihood of prolonged or many-sided failure of attainment, turning dissatisfaction into misery, or over-attainment leading to wretched aimlessness. Because of our nature, which none of our strivings has the power to alter, some suffering is inevitable and great suffering is perfectly possible for any of us. I suppose this is somewhere near the truth. But what attitude should we adopt toward life if it is thus correctly described? Schopenhauer's view is that each suffering drains away some (or even all) of the potential value from life, which nothing can restore. But Nietzsche's attitude to the same description, which he arguably accepts, is diametrically opposed. In clear allusion to his 'teacher' Schopenhauer (as he calls him) Nietzsche asks whether suffering is an objection to life, and firmly answers No: it is a sign of strength and greatness of character to affirm one's sufferings as an integral and in some sense desirable element in one's life. We know that people who have endured more pain than the average may utter the sub-Nietzschean (if prosaic) thought 'I wouldn't change anything if I had my life over again' (Nietzsche adds 'an infinite number of times'). In a rough and ready way this suggests that people's lives can make sense to them partly because of their sufferings, not in spite of them. A pessimistic description of life is compatible with an affirmation of it.

Affirmation, denial, and the self

However, the issue does not end there. Schopenhauer's pessimism has, I believe, deeper foundations in his conception of the self. Consider the following two questions: (1) Would not suicide be the appropriate solution to the predicament Schopenhauer alleges we are in? (2) If we could live but in some sense become detached from willing, would that be another solution? To question (1) Schopenhauer answers No: suicide is not a solution – surprisingly perhaps. And he answers Yes to question (2), which might also seem odd, if we recall the pain attaching to boredom. Should not permanent detachment from all willing be a *longueur* in every sense?

But Schopenhauer's view here rests on a contrasting state, possible for at least some individuals, which he calls 'denial of the will', a state that releases them from striving and suffering altogether. On the other hand, someone who commits suicide fails to reach this state of release, and instead continues to affirm the will. Some explanations are required.

'The will to life ... must be denied if salvation is to be attained from an existence like ours' (*W1*, 405), Schopenhauer writes. He remarks ironically that denial of the will is the only state we might consider as candidate for 'highest good': if we wish to give that expression an emeritus position, then figuratively the *summum bonum* is

> the complete self-effacement and denial of the will, true will-lessness, which alone stills and silences for ever the craving of the will; which alone gives that contentment that cannot again be disturbed; which alone is world-redeeming. (W1, 362)

This would be, he acknowledges, 'self-denial or self-renunciation, *abnegatio sui ipsius*; for the real self is the will to life' (*W2*, 606). (The 'real self' or 'essence' as he often says.) So Schopenhauer advocates a radical and difficult cure: denial of, or loss of identification with, our essence. If the solution to pessimism lies in rejecting *one's real self*, then the justification for this must be that *being what one is* is not worthwhile.

Schopenhauer writes with impressive intensity about the temporary state of will-lessness to be found in aesthetic experience. And he recalls this experience in an attempt to convey the blessedness of prolonged will-lessness in 'denial of the will':

aesthetic pleasure consists, to a large extent, in the fact that, when we enter the state of pure contemplation, we are raised for the moment above all willing, above all desires and cares; we are, so to speak, rid of ourselves. We are no longer the individual that knows in the interest of its constant willing ... but the eternal subject of knowing purified of the will ... From this we can infer how blessed must be the life of a man whose will is silenced, not for a few moments, as in the enjoyment of the beautiful, but for ever, indeed completely extinguished, except for the last glimmering spark that maintains the body and is extinguished with it. Such a man who, after many bitter struggles with his own nature, has at last completely conquered, is then left only as pure knowing being ... Nothing can distress or alarm him any more; nothing can any longer move him; for he has cut all the thousand threads of willing which hold us bound to the world, and which as craving, fear, envy, and anger drag us here and there in constant pain. (*W1*, 390)

As I see it, a contrasting pair of higher-order evaluative attitudes has now entered the picture. One takes – explicitly or implicitly – some attitude of acquiescence or refusal towards one's existence as an organic embodiment of the will to life, caught in the cycle of willing and suffering. The ordinary person who registers wants and strives to compensate for them adopts an implicit second-order attitude of 'affirmation' towards the body in which they arise. I say implicit because this attitude is the natural, more or less unreflective state of human beings. Schopenhauer says: '*The affirmation of the will* is the persistent willing itself, undisturbed by any knowledge, as it fills the life of man in general ... instead of affirmation of the will, we can also say affirmation of the body.' (*W1*, 326–7). Humans in general pursue goals dependent on the needs of the bodily individual, but they also do something which other animals do not: *they regard this pursuit as the point of their existence*. Denial of the will is release from identification with the embodied individual one is.

Back to suicide. Schopenhauer's discussion of suicide is often found puzzling. For not only does he disapprove of it – why, if existence is never worth more than non-existence? – but his disapproval rests on the grounds that 'suicide is a phenomenon of the will's strong affirmation', and that the suicide 'by no means gives up the will to life' (*W1*, 398). The explanation is that the suicide is the ordinary person whose attitude concerning the point of life is unrevised, but whose actual life has not delivered enough of the outcomes which are considered – wrongly – to give it its point.

> The suicide wills life, and is dissatisfied merely with the conditions on which it has come to him. ... He wills life, wills the unchecked existence and affirmation of the body, but the combination of circumstances does not allow of these, and the result for him is great suffering. (*W1*, 398)

The assessment that leads to suicide faults the circumstances of the individual's actual life for failing to permit a sufficiently smooth transition from felt deficiency to its removal, or from striving to satisfaction. But Schopenhauer's point is that the person who makes this assessment still does so from a standpoint of identification with the individual: this person's attitude is that of 'willing the unchecked existence and affirmation of the body'. Because of this self-identification the suicide remains caught within the cycle of lacks and replenishments. But once suffering overwhelmingly gains the upper hand, this cycle seems to have let the individual down. 'Just because the suicide cannot cease willing, he ceases to live.' The suicide is no different in principle from any ordinary individual, in affirming the will to life. The hopelessness of the suicide, who has not 'conquered his own nature', is quite opposed to the state of denial of the will to life. Similarly, the will-lessness attained in this state cannot be equated with the aimlessness of boredom. The bored person still wrongly acquiesces in his or her bodily, striving existence and thinks that existence *can* gain value from goals pursued and needs satisfied. He or she suffers from the lack of goals because he or she continues – in what I have called a 'higher order' attitude – to affirm the pursuing and attaining of such goals as the locus of value.

Thus 'denial of the will' stands opposed to ordinary affirmation, to boredom, and to the view of the suicide. It does so by virtue of a re-orientation in one's self-identification. The self for Schopenhauer has unusual complexity. Each human individual is an organism that is part of the world of objects, but he or she is also the subject of knowledge: 'That which knows all things and is known by none is the *subject* ... Everyone finds himself as this subject, yet only so far as he knows, not in so far as he is an object of knowledge. But his body is already object' (*W1*, 5). What is this subject? It is not part of the spatio-temporal world, but the extensionless point from which experience of a spatio-temporal world is had, and which that experience presupposes, in the manner of Kant's transcendental unity of apperception. 'Subject' is not a kind of thing that occurs within the world. This subject which I am (or find myself as) is not the individual, which by definition is a spatio-temporal entity for Schopenhauer (space and time being the principle of individuation). Elsewhere Schopenhauer discusses the relationship between this subject or 'I' and the organic individual, saying that the 'I' is the 'focus of brain activity': objectively, states of the brain occur, but the 'I' is what the human organism 'finds itself as' *from the point of view of its own experience*. Since the organism is in turn a manifestation of the will to life, he is able to say this:

> This *knowing* and conscious 'I' is related to the will … as the image in the focus of a concave mirror is related to that mirror itself; and, like that image, it has only a conditioned, in fact, properly speaking, a merely apparent reality. Far from being the absolutely first thing (as, e.g., Fichte taught) it is at bottom tertiary, since it presupposes the organism, and the organism presupposes the will. (*W2*, 278)

We are accustomed to regarding this knowing 'I' as our real self, but in so doing we are in error: the real self is the will (*W2*, 239).

While rational thought and the subject's self-consciousness are instruments of the will to life and of the organism, they also give rise to a curious split in our self-conception. For this will to life can confront consciousness as something distinct from the thinking, knowing subject of consciousness. It is as if the motor which propels me, the *primum mobile* from which I am inseparable – indeed which is me – must present itself to me, the thinking, rational subject, as an agency alien to myself. Schopenhauer portrays the knowing subject as lacking autonomy *vis-à-vis* the will. That I am a being that wills life and must strive for other mediate goals, and hence must suffer, does not issue from *my* choices. Furthermore no contrivance of rationality, no episode of conscious willing, no steps I take, even when successful, can make it the case that the willing in me ceases. This means that it is not within our power whether or not we strive and are open to suffering. The self-conscious subject is a kind of victim of its underlying real self, the will to life. The life of willing in non-self-conscious animals has the same pattern as in human life (though it lacks some kinds of suffering for which conceptual thought is necessary: for instance, anxiety about the future, remorse about the past). But since they do not have this 'I' as a competing locus of self-hood, other animals cannot see themselves as victims of the will to life as humans can.

Schopenhauer says that our nature accounts for the 'inborn error' of thinking we exist in order to be happy: 'our whole being is only the paraphrase' of this error, 'indeed our body is its monogram' (*W2*, 634). The will to life is also what Christianity calls the 'natural man' (*W1*, 404–405). It is what we are that is the problem. The solution, then, is to reach a state in which one becomes indifferent

Christopher Janaway

to happiness and unhappiness, unattached to the body, not wedded to the furtherance of any goals which an individual willing being might pursue. The threat of suffering is neutralised if one stands in an attitude of renunciation towards the whole round of willing and attainment. One must still exist in order to take this attitude, and Schopenhauer's thought is that one can do so while identifying oneself wholly with the pure subject of knowledge, that fiction cast up by the organism, which yet we 'find ourselves to be'. Thus free from our allegiance to the individual, the body, we can have a kind of pure knowledge, which is had from the perspective of no place within the world, and stands no closer to the needs and goals of any one individual as opposed to others. Elsewhere Schopenhauer allies himself with Plato's view in the *Phaedo*, saying that the notion of liberating the soul from the body is better expressed as liberating oneself from the will (see *W2*, 608–9).

But the subject lacks autonomy even here: one cannot achieve this liberated state of will-lessness by an act of will. Just as the presence of the will to life in me does not result from my conscious choice or intention, so too the will to life – once more conceived as if a separate agency within me – must turn and abolish itself. There are two routes by which this may occur. One is that of overwhelming suffering. An individual may suffer so much that his or her will to life gives out spontaneously. The individual continues to exist, but in a state of detachment from living as an end, indifferent to the prospering or ruin of the individual he or she happens to be. The second and rarer route is that of an exceptional anti-egoistic vision, possessed by those whom Schopenhauer calls saints. The saint reaches an understanding that he or she is not fundamentally distinct from the world as a whole, that individuality itself is an illusion (cf. *W1*, 378–9). Descriptions of such insight are found, he reminds us, in a number of world religions.

Schopenhauer provides the paradigm of the stance Nietzsche calls resignationism, or no-saying or life-denial – while handing Nietzsche on a plate the claim that this is the uniting feature of Hinduism, Buddhism, Plato, and Christianity. For Nietzsche this is the controlling, degenerate, sick ideal against which we must make war. We might say: the pathos of Schopenhauer is that, revealing to us our 'true nature' in the will to life, he sees precisely this as what we must disown before our existence can claim to have value. But what is pathological in Schopenhauer – what Nietzsche diagnosed and understandably felt revulsion for – is Schopenhauer's view that my only hope lies in the withering away of my sense of individuality or in my suffering so severely that the will to life within me is broken. That these can be *hopes* at all is grotesque. That *only* these outcomes could give positive value to our existence, and to that of the whole world, is surely Schopenhauer's most pessimistic thought.

Karl Marx

DAVID-HILLEL RUBEN

Although it was, until recently, unfashionable in certain circles to say this, Marx was not a philosopher in any interesting sense. He was a social theorist. As social theory, I am thinking primarily of two areas (in all social theory, there is also a large body of empirical work, which I am not competent to comment upon): (a) the methodology of social inquiry, and its metaphysical presuppositions, and (b) normative philosophy (ethics and political theory).

Many social theorists are also philosophers: Hobbes, Locke, Hegel and Mill provide good examples. They articulate and develop a general philosophy, a metaphysics and an epistemology, and typically their social theory relies in essential ways on that general philosophy, or at any rate they believe that it does. There is a connection, for example, between Mill's empiricism, on the one hand, and, on the other, both his utilitarian philosophy, and the methodology of social science that he outlines in Book VI of his *A System of Logic*.

Marx also believed that his social theory depended on certain philosophical assumptions, but, unlike these aforementioned social theorists, he does not, for the most part, articulate or develop in any significant way the philosophy on which he believes his social theory depends. Rather, he uses, or 'raids', the philosophy of others for this underpinning of his social theory, and provides us with only aphorisms or terse summaries of it, scattered across his works.

I will not engage in lengthy exposition of Marx's views. I refer to them, but do not elaborate upon them. I will identify three important sources for his ideas: Hegel, classical Greek Philosophy and humanism, especially as expressed by the French revolution. I will not necessarily discuss these sources separately, since some of his ideas come from more than one source. Since the source for many of Hegel's own ideas was classical Greek thought, it is not always easy to tell whether Marx was influenced in a particular case by Hegel or by the Greeks, and even where Marx thought he knew which was the influence, his own self-understanding need not constitute the last word on the matter.

David-Hillel Ruben

I

There are three topics or areas I want to touch on, in discussing Marx's methodology of social inquiry and its metaphysical presuppositions: (1) individualism and holism; (2) the idea of historical change; and (3) Marx's metaphysics and epistemology.

1. There is a debate in the existing literature, much of it occasioned by Jon Elster,[1] about the compatibility or otherwise of Marx's apparently holistic ideas with ideas borrowed from an individualistic level of description, such as decision making, rationality, choices, preferences, desires, planning, action (or, in Marx's case, human labour), and the individual person. My understanding of Marx assumes that these two discourses, or sets of ideas, are compatible, and indeed that the latter ultimately lends support and credibility to the former, without reducing or in any way supplanting it. This is a theme which runs through much of what follows throughout my paper. (Perhaps my remark about the influence of humanism on Marx already suggests this.)

In thinking about Marx's views on these matters, there seem to be two strands of thought in Marx which one must acknowledge: an anti-individualist strand and an anti-Platonic one. On first inspection, the two strands are in some tension. If we take the anti-individualism seriously, we seem to reify social wholes, structures, and so on, and these seem to be abstract objects, very much like Platonic entities. On the other hand, if we take the anti-Platonising seriously, we seem to be back to individuals and their relations.

I believe that the two strands are consistent and can be reconciled. I interpret Marx's more holistic or sociological talk of social wholes, social structures, of the laws or tendencies of history, and so on as being grounded at the level of individuals and their interrelations. This does not make him what today we would call a 'methodological individualist', since there is no reductionist (or eliminativist) claim being advanced. Rather, it is that the individual level accounts for or supports the macrostructural features he claims to discover. The latter is made intelligible by the former. To think that the social or macrostructural is autonomous of the individual and has no need of such grounding would be Platonic; to think that, in the face of such grounding, the social can be replaced by what grounds it would be unacceptably (for Marx) individualistic.

Marx himself did not, and probably would not, have said of himself what I have said about him above. Marx was not entirely clear

[1] Elster raises these issues in many places, but see for example: Jon Elster, *Nuts and Bolts* (Cambridge University Press, 1989).

about this, and this unclarity arose for at least two reasons. First, unlike us, what Marx would have understood by 'individualism' signified either a methodological approach in political economy from which he wished to distance himself (he would have thought of Robinson Crusoe accounts of political economy as the allocation of scarce resources to meet an individual's needs[2]), or the objectionably egoistic philosophy of Max Stirner. Second, he seemed to think of the macrolevel or structural as potentially scientific, in contrast to the individual level of action, decisions and whatever, which he did not.

What I do say is that I cannot myself make ultimate sense of Marx's views, or reconcile the various strands in his thinking, without this somewhat individualistic underpinning to the social. Marx himself, when he reflects on his methodology, frequently makes observations that would support this view of what he is doing: 'The premises from which we begin are ... the real individuals, their activity, and the material conditions under which they live ....'.[3] Or: 'It is not "history" which uses men as a means of achieving – as if it were an individual person – *its* own ends. History is *nothing* but the activity of men in pursuit of their ends.'[4] Moreover, this way of understanding him does make sense of many of his specific ideas, for example his idea of alienation as apparent objectification of the powers of persons, and his Feuerbachian insistence on the 'economy' merely being a projection of what is human.

2. Marx held a theory about the nature of social change throughout history. On at least one occasion, he refers to the theory as 'the materialist conception of history', but does not himself make much of this label. Much of the content of historical materialism is well known and I will take it for granted. I do not propose to recount once again the various stages through which Marx thought societies might pass on their way to socialism.

The main point of the doctrine is that it is an account of social change. There are two cases: first, the change that occurs within a single society and second, the change that occurs across societies. In the first case, societies not only change but that change has a definite directionality to it; their productive forces grow and, finally

[2] Karl Marx, *General Introduction to the Grundrisse* in *A Contribution to the Critique of Political Economy*, ed. Maurice Dobb (London: Lawrence & Wishart, 1971), pp. 188–9.
[3] Marx and Engels, *The German Ideology* (Moscow: Progress Publishers, 1968), p. 31.
[4] Marx, *The Holy Family*; from *Marx Engels Gesamtausgabe* (MEGA), I/3, ed. D. Ryazanov, *et al*. (Frankfurt and Berlin, 1927), p. 265.

stagnate when further growth by those forces becomes impossible. After stagnation sets in, such societies transform their economic and social structures into something novel. For instance, the feudal system passes over into capitalism, a new social formation.

In the second case, there is, for Marx, a patterned development to history as a whole as well, even if particular societies might stagnate and fail to undergo further transformation. That development consists in the growth of the productive forces over time (or, from another angle, the growth and development of human labour), ending in their fullest realisation under socialism. In this overall sweep of things, there is no ultimate decay, although of course the development is not even, not without its setbacks and hiccups.

There are two salient features of this account: the importance it ascribes to change in human history, and the apparently nomic (lawlike) character of that change. Marx takes great pains to stress how nothing in society remains and is permanent; everything social and human changes, is unstable and fluid. He thought that writers who denied, or forgot, this had been captured by a false conception of social reality. He contrasts his method with that of other, earlier, social theorists, who might have postulated a fixed human nature or a fixed social form (capitalism, for example) that exists, albeit within a range of permissible variations, across all historical epochs. As far as the social world is concerned, Marx is Heraclitean. No one can step in the same social river twice.

Moreover, for Marx, the source of essential social change, the growth, stagnation, and transformation, is internal to the society itself. On Marx's view, there is an inner dynamic to a society, a 'logic' as his followers would say, which accounts for that change. For example, capitalist societies are driven, at one level, by the need to accumulate capital, and the dynamic of this process has a set trajectory. That trajectory leads to the self-destruction of the social form; in the case of capitalism, it leads to a falling rate of profit, overproduction, and hence to economic crises and the aforementioned stagnation.

This is a case, mentioned above, in which it is difficult to decide if Marx is writing only under the influence of Hegel or indirectly, perhaps even directly, under the influence of Aristotle's thought.[5] Both Hegel and Aristotle, in somewhat different ways, espoused a metaphysics of inner-impelled change. Both Aristotle and Hegel

[5] For a defence of the Aristotelian interpretation, see Scott Meikle, *Essentialism in the Thought of Karl Marx* (Open Court, 1985). The Aristotelian interpretation was advanced in the 1970s by Professor Heinz Lubacsz, of Essex University, in a short article in the *Times Higher Education Supplement*.

have teleological systems, in which things have their own telos, goal, or final end, towards which the change that befalls them advances, other, external influences being equal. Both use biological change as a paradigm for goal-directed change. The little acorn does not just change, but rather it grows into an oak tree. These two thinkers are philosophers of change par excellence, and Marx knew the work of both of them intimately.

Most post-Enlightenment philosophers, Hume, Hobbes, Berkeley, Descartes, have no difficulty in principle with the idea of change. However, the change they focus on is what is sometimes called 'transeunt', the change that befalls a thing that is introduced from the outside, by an external influence. A paradigm case of this is Hume's billiard ball being struck by another billiard ball. What they lack is the idea of immanent change, change directed by something's own nature, where the source or motor for change is inner or internal.

There is little doubt, I think, that Marx derives, as a matter of psychological fact, much of his view of social change from Hegel or Aristotle or both. What is less clear, I think, is whether Marx wished to adopt this general, metaphysical view of change as applying to the natural as well as the social world. The evidence is somewhat ambiguous. Although Marx applies this view of change to society, he neither applies it to all of nature nor disclaims that it can be so applied. In the main, it was left to Engels to do this, in work such as *The Dialectics of Nature*. I will say something more about this below.

Is such social change lawful, as the above would make it seem? Are there iron laws to history, or even merely lawful tendencies, both as to what happens within a social formation and what happens across history? To be sure, somehow Marx's writings encourage this idea. Rather than thinking of these as independent laws, we are, I think, more productively to think of them as generalisations grounded in, or explained by, certain features of human choice and decision making. (I am of course aware that Marx himself sometimes uses the word, 'law'; the question is what we are to understand by his use of that word.)

In the case of the development of the forces of production across history, Marx assumes that when confronted with the choice between old relations of production and reduced productive output on the one hand, and new productive relations with increased productive output on the other, humans will at the end of the day make the rational choice and opt for the latter. They, or anyway the majority in whose interests it is to so choose, become pro-growth advocates, and hence revolutionaries. This is no law that works in history

David-Hillel Ruben

behind the backs of humans, but merely an anticipation of what Marx thinks the (in most cases, unforeseen) consequences of their rational choices will be, in the circumstances he envisages.

But does this just push the question of scientific law back one stage? One might ask if Marx thought there were psychological laws that governed human decision making, choice. Perhaps there are historical laws or tendencies, underwritten by psychological ones. In truth, I see no evidence that Marx even asked himself this question. He does remark that men make history but not in circumstances of their own choosing. This line of thought is neutral on the question I have posed. Marx asserts what is undoubtedly true: there are necessary conditions for making certain choices, conditions which may be beyond the power of the choosers to control. But that by itself provides no hint of an answer to our question.

As for the change within a society, for example the law of accumulation, this too merely anticipates how capitalists will rationally decide to act, given the circumstances and constraints in which they find themselves. All things being equal, the capitalist who accumulates acts rationally, given his situation and the parameters within which he must make his choice. For Marx, societies and history itself move in the way that humans, usually without understanding the consequences of those choices, choose. The choices are sometimes confused, and the correct description of the choice situation may be opaque to the chooser, shrouded in ideological claptrap. But human choices they still are, nonetheless, and they account for the flow of social change. To think otherwise, to think that the inner logic to the change in and across society develops literally independently of human choice, is (as I have already said) to think in an alienated way.

This observation helps us with our first question, about the ubiquity of directional change. The particular sort of change that Marx finds in society, or across societies, has ultimately as its ground the choices and decisions of human actors. However extensive the change in the natural world may be, it has other sources, other explanations, about which Marx is silent. There is no legitimate extrapolation, in my view, from Marx's views on the nature and pattern of social change to what his views might have been about the nature and pattern of change in the natural world.

3. Action (praxis) is a special sort of change, namely a change brought about by an agent. (Some further refinements would be needed to get this right, but I will not pursue those refinements here.) Inquiry in the social sciences without inquiry into human action, its causes, consequences and meaning, would be patently absurd. Perhaps if any category is central to capturing human and

social reality within a philosophy, it is the category of agency, of action. It is an amazing fact, but fact it is nonetheless, that the category of physical agency almost disappears in post-Enlightenment philosophy.

In Locke, Berkeley, Hume and Kant, we do find the idea of mental action – the mind abstracts for Locke, the soul or spirit is the source of all agency for Berkeley, the mind can combine simple ideas into complex ones for Hume, the mind imposes the categories of the understanding on experience for Kant. Since these philosophers are either subjective idealist philosophers or have only a very attenuated notion of physical reality, they can at most offer some reductionist account of physical agency, in terms of mental agency and ideas.

For Marx, physical action or agency is an irreducible, ineliminable category. He makes physical activity, especially labour, work, central to his understanding of persons and society. This theme is salient in his 'Theses on Feuerbach'. Marx thought that the recovery of action, or 'praxis' as he, and subsequent Marxists so quaintly put it, was one of the most important advances of his own work.

We tend to distinguish between reductionist and eliminativist versions of a doctrine. For example, Berkeley was not an eliminativist idealist. He did not say that there were no such things as tables and chairs, that there were only ideas in minds. Rather, he was a reductionist idealist; he said that there were tables and chairs, but that all they are, are ideas in the mind. Only by utilising this distinction could Berkeley even attempt to portray himself as a defender of common sense.

Materialism offers the same alternatives. An eliminativist materialist would tell us that there is no social world, no action, no tables and chairs, only atoms, or matter, in motion. More plausibly, a reductive materialist says that there is a social world, there is action and agency, there are tables and chairs, but all they are, at bottom, are matter, or atoms, in motion.

Marx was not alive to the distinction between elimination and reduction, and it is no use pretending otherwise. (Nor was Lenin, when he wrote *Materialism and Empirio-Criticism*, as one can see by his mis-characterisation of Berkeley's position.) Marx saw materialism, or anyway all 'hitherto existing' varieties of materialism as eliminativist, and hence he would have thought of such materialism as denying the existence of human action, or anyway finding no metaphysical room in which to accommodate it.

Marx knew about the atomistic philosophy of Democritus and Epicurus, and indeed the latter formed the subject matter of his doctoral thesis. The atomistic philosophy of the Greeks was an early

71

form of materialist philosophy, and Marx was acquainted with latter forms of materialism as well, in Hobbes, in the French encyclopedists, especially Holbach, and in his immediate predecessor, Ludwig Feuerbach. All of these forms of materialism, for Marx, were inconsistent with accepting the reality of action, or the social world more generally, and so he could not possibly have been a materialist in the standard sense.

Confusingly, Marx contrasts his doctrine with 'hitherto existing materialism', suggesting that his own doctrine is a distinct variety of materialism. If by materialism is intended a metaphysical doctrine of the kind I have specified, nothing could be a less accurate description of Marx's views. It is clear, I think, that he rejects the atomist-Hobbesian-Holbachian metaphysical picture of reality. The world they imagine is too barren, too austere, for him. It does not include the social and human world which forms the centre of his intellectual attention. Marx's world is richer, more variegated, than any world that he can imagine the traditional materialist imagining.

Marx was, in contemporary terminology, a realist about the physical world. What he was anxious to reject was Hegelian idealism, the doctrine that everything that existed was essentially dependent on mind. The contradictory of idealism is not materialism, but (external-world) realism, the doctrine that there are objects, events, things, or whatever that are not mind-dependent in the Hegelian (or Berkleyian) sense.[6]

When Marx thinks of his doctrine as a form of materialism unlike previously existing versions of materialism, he is in fact espousing a realist and pluralist philosophy which holds both that there is a physical world essentially independent of the mind and also that there are parts of reality (the social, for example) which have their own integrity and can neither be eliminated nor reduced to the subject matter of physics.

Realism comes in a variety of versions, and I have attributed to Marx realism about the external world. Was he also a scientific realist, in the sense that he thought that the theoretical terms of mature scientific theory typically (attempt to) refer to real, but unobservable, entities, structures, or whatever in the world? To what, if anything, does 'capitalism' or 'capitalist societies' refer or designate? On this issue, there is reason to hesitate. Marx provides a discussion of this issue in a passage in his *Introduction to the Grundrisse*.[7] The passage in question is somewhat obscure, but the gist seems to be

[6] I have tried to defend this view of Marx in my *Marxism and Materialism* (Brighton: Harvester Press, 1979).

[7] Karl Marx, *General Introduction to the Grundrisse*, pp. 205–7.

that 'pure' theory consists of a set of abstractions, whose connection to reality is indirect and highly mediated. Theories in the natural sciences are often said to work in the same way, when they postulate perfectly elastic bodies, ideal gasses, or frictionless surfaces. Perhaps this understanding of abstracted theory is consistent with a properly interpreted scientific realism, but the point is only that due attention should be given to Marx's understanding about the nature of theory and how it might ultimately relate to the actual world, before ascribing scientific realism to him with any confidence.

If there is action, even physical action, then those beings who act have a mind, are conscious, possess a mental life with purposes, intentions, and so on. Marx certainly accepts this, as his remark about what makes human beings special presupposes: the human being 'raises his structure [what he intends to create] in imagination before he raises it in reality. At the end of every labour-process, we get a result that already existed in the imagination of the labourer at its commencement … he also realises a purpose of his own …'.[8] Any being that possesses the powers of imagination and purposive planning has a mind.

On the other hand, Marx was certainly no dualist. Of course, even dualists can recognise that, by interacting with the body, mind is causally dependent on body. Marx seems to have wanted to make mind more dependent on body than merely causally dependent, although he never defined the nature of the dependence he was supposing. In some sense, he wants to tie consciousness down, to rob it of its essential independence: 'Thought and being are indeed distinct but they also form a unity.'[9] Unity, I take it, whatever it means here, is meant to be stronger than causal interaction.

Marx's thoughts on the mind are consistent, and indeed make his view similar to contemporary positions in the philosophy of mind, that try to steer a path between reductive materialism (in the standard philosophical sense) and dualism. To borrow terminology and use it anachronistically, Marx held that consciousness, or the mind, supervened on the physical without being reducible to it.

There is a very secure sense of agency, and hence of self or inner directedness, in both Hegel and Aristotle. Hegel's agency was suspect, from Marx's point of view. It is the agency of Idea or ultimately the Deity. It is whatever sense can be given to agency by Absolute Idealism. Aristotle's realism, on the other hand, left Aristotle with a real physical world. Hence, there was for Aristotle

[8] Karl Marx, *Capital*, vol. I (Moscow: Progress Publishers, 1965), p. 178.
[9] From *The Economic and Philosophical Manuscripts of 1844*, and in *MEGA* I/3, pp. 116–17.

David-Hillel Ruben

genuinely physical action, the understanding of which was one of the tasks of philosophy. On this score, Marx is much closer to Aristotle than he is to Hegel. Marx's view is that what makes persons special, and sets them apart from the rest of nature, is their capacity for intentional action, action undertaken according to a plan.[10] It is this, and other, considerations that makes Marx value so highly the planned economy, as the expression of what is truly human. We will return to the importance of the centrality of action for Marx, in connection with his normative theory, in the section below.

A great deal of ink was spilt in trying to uncover Marx's theory of knowledge. Hegel rejected the correspondence theory of truth (and hence of knowledge), and some, like Leszek Kolakowski, have attempted to find, in the writings of the early Marx, a similar rejection of the 'classical' correspondence theory in favour of an idealist view on which reality is itself a human creation.[11] Much of this interpretation is built on the evidence of cute aphorisms in Marx's early work.

I find all such arguments uncompelling. Marx has little to say on these matters, and it takes some bending of quotes to show otherwise. Unlike Hegel, Aristotle is a defender of the 'classical' conception of truth: to say of what is, that it is, and to say of what is not that it is not, is to speak truly; to say of what is, that it is not, and of what is not, that it is, is to speak falsely. Since I believe the classical account of truth is vastly superior to Hegel's idealist account, and since nothing explicit in Marx forces either interpretation, I prefer to land Marx with the most plausible account, especially since that plausible account is consistent with his realist position and the Hegelian account is not. On this issue again, we find Marx closer to Aristotle than to Hegel.

II

In thinking about Marx's normative philosophy, the most important fact to remember is that Marx was, first and foremost, a true philosophical son of the Enlightenment. He shared its general philosophical humanism, but coupled it with a specific social critique which attempted to show under what social conditions its goals were genuinely achievable. One need not look for a particular individual who influenced him, although he does mention some by name. The impact of this humanism was visible all around him, and especially

[10] See text above and footnote 8.

[11] L. Kolakowski, 'Karl Marx and the Classical Definition of Truth', in *Marxism and Beyond*, trans. J. Z. Peel (London: Pall Mall Press, 1969), pp. 58–86.

in Trier, his birth city, close as it was to the French frontier. French revolutionary ideas were part of the air which he, and his immediate family, breathed.

Humanism is itself a rather vague body of propositions, but its guiding thread is the centrality and the importance of the human person, the need for humankind to be responsible and master of its own destiny. This humanist ideal runs through all of Marx's work, but is perhaps most apparent in the *Economic and Philosophical Manuscripts*. In the *Manuscripts*, Marx elaborates the idea that there are no gods responsible for man and his fate, that men have the power, given the right social circumstances, to be masters (and mistresses) of their social world, to take control of the social structures in which they exist. To be powerless in the face of one's own creations, or to falsely believe that one is powerless in this way, is what Marx called 'alienation'. The 'iron law of history' view, far from being Marx's own view, is itself an example of alienation.

As I said above, Marx says that what makes humankind unique, and sets it apart from any animal kind, is its ability to plan, the ability to raise in conception an idea and then to execute a series of tasks calculated to achieve that idea. For Marx, loss of control and mastery is the antithesis of planning. To be human is to plan. Although he does not use the words, what Marx is stressing is the centrality of practical deliberation to the human enterprise. Marx's view of man as the practical deliberator shares much in common with Aristotle's view of man in the *Nicomachean Ethics*.

Another aspect of Marx's own brand of humanism is his self-development or self-realisation theory. Such theories were rife at the time, thinkers as intellectually distant as Fichte and Mill providing examples. Hegel's theory itself can be seen as a self-realisation theory, where ultimately the Self to be realised is God. Marx's selfdevelopment theory asserts that the goal of each person is the fullest development of all of his latent powers and abilities, his human potential. When Marx speaks, in the *German Ideology*, of each person being a hunter in the morning, a fisherman in the afternoon, a cattle rearer in the evening, and a critical critic after dinner, he is proposing, in what he intends to be humorous fashion, the development of human potentiality in many different facets and directions for each person. He believed that the division of labour, for example, inhibited this desirable development. Marx believed that work, meaningful, creative work, was an ineliminable need of man. It is a need that capitalism, with its division of labour, does not answer. Part of what Marx understands by self-development is the developing of this creative capacity in all persons. Marx thought that such creative work would include both mental and physical elements.

David-Hillel Ruben

The novel twist, both in Marx's self-development theory and his view of man as rational planner and doer is that these ideals can only be achieved collectively: 'Only in community [with others has each] individual the means of cultivating his gifts in all directions; only in community, therefore, is personal freedom possible'.[12] The interconnection between persons within a community is a distinctively Hegelian idea.

In this way, the realisation of the moral goals of humankind, self-mastery and self-development, require more than the self; they require the collective effort of many individuals in the sorts of social circumstances conducive to these desiderata. Social and economic forces which defy human control and which inhibit the development of the individual are too strong for any individual, but not too strong for the joint efforts of the many. Planning is not just for the Aristotelian individual, but for Hegelian interrelated persons co-operating with one another and attaining desired ends that none could reach by himself. Not surprisingly for someone who so closely followed Hegel in these matters, Marx was a communitarian philosopher before the term was dreamt up.

The collective economy would do away with the division of labour, and thereby permit the encouragement of the multi-talented individual, do away with the market and thereby permit planning of the social output. Marx's idea of production planned to meet human need gives expression to this moral vision. Each person can work with others to tame the forces that humankind itself creates. The achievement of humanist ideals requires, according to Marx, the triumph of socialism, the collectively planned economy.

Because of his view that each person should contribute to planning as a social effort, there can be no doubt that Marx's ideal is a democratic one. Perhaps his belief that the State will ultimately wither away is naive, but it can leave us in no doubt about his theoretical commitment to a democratic vision, a vision in which there is no State power required to coerce individuals. The vision is also reinforced by his remarks on the Paris commune, in *The Civil War in France*, in which he praises direct or participatory over representative democracy. How is it possible, then, that such anti-democratic forces have taken his name in vain?

Marx says little about the transitional stage from contemporary society to full democracy, and what he does say misleads. His expression 'the Dictatorship of the Proletariat' is a term borrowed from Roman history and apt to mislead someone with modern ears. The theoretical gap in Marx's thinking about the transition was

[12] Marx and Engels, *The German Ideology*, p. 93.

76

filled in by others, who wrote in different circumstances and in ways of which Marx may well not have approved.

But there is a theoretical problem here worth considering. Social theorists often have to grapple with the tension between a final ethic and an interim ethic. To what extent is it plausible to think that these can differ? Can a revolutionary really use non-democratic means to achieve democratic ends?

Marx's political behaviour, and some of the things he says (and certainly many of the things some of his followers said very clearly), suggest non-democratic means to achieve democratic ends. This is always a position fraught with difficulty, and one might identify the seeds of the prevalence of anti-democratic tendencies within Marxism in this dilemma, a dilemma which Marx never wrote about and which he may not even have seen very clearly.

Marx's normative theory is implicit rather than explicit, and is a matter of some controversy, in part because Marx himself was confused about the issue of normativity. His disclaimers that there is any normative element in his critique and analysis of capitalism seem to derive from his distaste of *a priori* ethics, which he saw as groundless and open to unsupported speculation. He is thinking of Hegel, and perhaps of Kant as well, as examples of such ethical theorists from whom he wished to distance himself. For Marx, at least most of the time, there is an unbridgeable gap between scientific theory and normativity. He wished his critique of capitalism to rely only on the former and not the latter.

Had he been clearer about the possibility of a naturalistic system of ethics,[13] the ethical system that is undoubtedly latent in his thought might have been more fully acknowledged and elaborated. His normative theories of human self-development, and self-control, and the ethics they support, are implicit for the most part rather than explicit, but they are very much there nonetheless.

Marx's theory of just distribution is a matter of some scholarly and interpretative dispute.[14] Sometimes Marx seems to criticise the economic distribution under capitalism as unjust, as theft from the

[13] Can an ethic be fully grounded naturalistically, or is there always an ultimately normative principle that must reappear in any such grounds? This is an issue that is not specific to Marx, and that we need not deal with here. For this issue with specific reference to Marx's ideal of human nature, see Steven Lukes, 'Alienation and Anomie', in *Philosophy, Politics and Society*, third series, ed. Peter Laslett and W. G. Runciman, (Oxford: Blackwell, 1967), pp. 134–56.

[14] See for example the articles by A. Wood, Z. Husami, and others, in *Marx, Justice and History*, ed. Marshall Cohen, Thomas Nagel, and Tim Scanlon (Princeton University Press, 1980).

worker, and so on. At other times, he says that the distribution is fair, fairly arrived at by the sale of his labour power for a wage by the worker, although with distressing social consequences. I suspect that this confusion too arises from Marx's unwillingness to admit that there are any normative strands to his critique of capitalism, given the view he had of normativity.

On the other hand, when it is not a matter of his analysis of capitalism and where it leads, Marx does espouse quite explicitly alternative principles of economic distribution, one for the transitional period to full communism and another to operate under a fully communist society. The latter is the famous ability–need principle: from each according to his ability, to each according to his need.[15] Given Marx's view, which we have already discussed, that holds as an ideal the full self-development of each individual, it follows that Marx would wish to ensure that each person had the resources to achieve this. And since part of self-development is to be able to work creatively at the many things one is capable of, it follows that Marx would wish to ensure that each person has the opportunity to give of himself appropriately. The ability–need principle seems just what one might expect from him.

If humanism proposes that man is the measure of all things, then it is in this framework that we can understand Marx's Labour Theory of Value. According to Marx, only human labour power creates new value. Why should this be so? Some have suggested that machines, even animals, are capable of value creation, whereas Marx insists that machines and non-human animals can only transfer the value they have, given them by human labour in their creation or training, into the objects produced with their help. Marx's view relates to this humanistic perspective, which places humankind and only humankind on centre stage.

Marx makes many disparaging remarks about Liberty, Equality and Fraternity, the war cry of the Revolution. I understand these disparaging remarks not really as about the abstract ideals themselves, which I believe he shares, but about the possibility of their realisation within a capitalist framework. For Kant, it is a matter of principle to develop an ethical system without reference to the empirical world. In later German philosophers, Hegel and Feuerbach for example, in different ways the real world gets a (sometimes perfunctory) look-in, but it is only with Marx that there is a serious attempt to investigate the extent to which a certain sort of society is compatible with ethical goals and ideals.

On Marx's view, only under socialism could these ethical ideals become realised. Under socialism, freedom, as we have seen, has a

[15] See Karl Marx, *Critique of the Gotha Programme*.

social rather than only an individual meaning, and can only be realised therefore on a social scale. Equality, understood as giving each according to his need and not as strict equality regardless of circumstance, is the method of distribution of full communism. Fraternity, the true brotherhood (and sisterhood) of all persons, is the guiding principle of socialism. In short, only socialism could achieve the genuine goals of the French Revolution. Marx's ethic is an enlightenment ethic, with a hitherto undeveloped social dimension.

Nietzsche's Virtues: A Personal Inquiry

ROBERT C. SOLOMON

Give style to your character, a great and rare art.
Nietzsche, *Gay Science* (290)

What are we to make of Nietzsche? There has been an explosion of scholarship over the past twenty years, much of it revealing and insightful, a good deal of it controversial if not polemical. The controversy and polemics are for the most part straight from Nietzsche, of course, and the scholarly disputes over what he 'really' meant are rather innocuous and often academic compared with what Nietzsche meant (or might have meant) with his conscientiously inflammatory rhetoric and hyperbole. We have been treated to extended debates about Nietzsche's politics, his attacks on Christianity and morality, his famed notion of the *übermensch* and his less lampooned (but more edifying) doctrine of the 'eternal recurrence'. We have recently heard Nietzsche reinterpreted as an analytic philosopher, as a deconstructionist, as a feminist, even as a closet Christian and a liberal. Stephen Aschheim suggests in his recent book[1] that Nietzsche provides us with something like a Rorschach test, inviting readers with amazingly different commitments and ideologies to 'make their own Nietzsche' (as a *Times Literary Supplement* review bluntly put it). But there is another approach to Nietzsche, something quite different from interpreting him in terms of his various 'theses' and positions, unpacking his 'system' or repeating unhelpfully that he displayed no such coherence and consistency, something more than finding out 'who' Nietzsche is as opposed to what we have made out of him. The simplest way of getting at this alternative approach might be to ask, what Nietzsche would make of us? I grant that this is a bit cryptic, and it invites a variety of unflattering answers. But I think it is very much in the spirit of what he (and his spokesman Zarathustra) are all about. It is an intimately personal approach to Nietzsche, an approach that will, no doubt, be somewhat different for each and every one of us. But that, too, of course, is just what Nietzsche (and Zarathustra) would have demanded.

[1] Stephen Aschheim, *The Nietzsche Legacy in Germany, 1890–1990* (Berkeley: University of California Press, 1992).

Robert C. Solomon

Friedrich Nietzsche: historical figure, moral advisor

Despite his various complaints about being 'untimely', his self-conscious solitude and voluntary exile, and his often deprecating remarks about his philosophical and artistic predecessors (some of whom, we surmise, he had not read), Nietzsche fits neatly and profoundly into the philosophical and cultural history of Germany in the century following Kant. Much of his moral philosophy can be read as an attack on Kant's influential ethics, and his epistemology, fragmentary as it is, can be viewed in the context of nineteenth century experimentalism, positivism and the philosophy of science. His relationship with Wagner, of course, was one of the pivotal issues of both his own career and the history of German cultural aesthetics, but all of this I leave to my distinguished colleague Michael Tanner to elaborate in elegant detail. My aim here is rather to treat Nietzsche – as I think he often intended to be treated himself – as something of a contemporary, not a nineteenth century philosopher in Germany but a moral philosopher with a great deal to say to us, a 'moral advisor', if you will, a description Nietzsche no doubt would have despised. But given the considerable body of recent literature that denies to Nietzsche any such status – indeed, denies to him *any* substantive assertions or prescriptions whatever, not to mention the still enduring portrait of Nietzsche as a jack-booted amoral monster – I believe that an understanding of Nietzsche as a benign and quite thoroughly moral prescriptivist – not quite to say a 'moralist' – might be quite enlightening as well as therapeutic.

Nietzsche did not see himself as just another philosopher, social or culture critic, analyst or diagnostician. Nietzsche intended to change lives, a somewhat arrogant pretence according to a great many distinguished philosophers today.[2] But let me give you a very personal example. It has to do with Nietzsche's doctrine of eternal recurrence, the thesis that whatever happens, whatever we do, whatever we suffer, has and will repeat itself (in sequence) an innumerable number of times. Despite the few passages and short *schrift* Nietzsche gives to this thesis, an enormous amount of ink has been spilled or bubbled out of computer printers concerning its meaning. As a physical hypothesis, I am rather willing to dismiss the thesis out of hand as a combination of out-dated physics and too-casual calculation. (Afterall, those were only 'notes'.[3]) As a serious ethical

[2] See, for example, Bernard Williams review and critique of Martha Nussbaum's *Therapy of Desire*, her analysis and praise of the Stoics precisely in terms of their providing such 'moral advice'.

[3] Collected and printed in *The Will to Power*, trans. and ed., Walter Kaufmann (New York: Random House, 1969). The status of Nietzsche's

proposal, say, along the lines of Kant's 'Categorical Imperative', it is readily obvious that Nietzsche's 'test' is too subjective and personal while Kant intends his ethics to be thoroughly objective (that is, rational and impersonal). Moreover, its says nothing whatever about the *content* of one's life, its ambitions, pleasures and pains, achievements and failures, much less about the person, except, of course, for his or her (momentary) attitude toward that content. As a subjective or psychological thought-experiment (*Gedanken-versuch*), there may be much to be said and debated (for instance, the scope of the 'moments' to be affirmed in the light of the thesis), but I find little reason to lean toward one or another such interpretation on the basis of the barebones sketch in Nietzsche's texts. And yet, when I first read and heard about the doctrine of eternal recurrence, while auditing Frithjof Bergmann's 'Philosophy in Literature' class at the University of Michigan several decades ago, it provided me with the philosophical resolve to take a close look at my life (I was an unhappy first year medical student at the time), apply what I then clearly conceived to be the personal 'test' of the idea of recurrence, and fifteen minutes later (more or less) I resigned from the medical school and entered into a life of philosophy, a decision I have never regretted.

Now, it might be the case that my life has been based on a misunderstanding of Nietzsche, a somewhat cruel suggestion but, nevertheless, one to which my response would certainly be the Vonnegutian retort, 'so it goes'. I do not know exactly what Nietzsche had in mind by what Bernd Magnus has nicely called his 'Existential Imperative', but the idea of eternal recurrence certainly has had a dramatic effect, on me at least. I actually tend to doubt that Nietzsche had anything very precise in mind, despite his occasional enthusiasm and now the precision of several recent, excellent commentaries about eternal return.[4] I certainly doubt that he ever

---

unpublished notes (*Nachlass*) has been exhaustively debated and no doubt commented upon by virtually every commentator on Nietzsche. The best policy, it seems to me, is to trust Nietzsche's notes only when they are confirmed by (and thus reiterate, occasionally in more striking language) Nietzsche's published statements. In the case of external recurrence as a physical hypothesis, no such statements exist are to be found.

[4] For example, the Magnus book already mentioned, *Nietzsche's Existential Imperative* (Indiana University Press, 1978) Alexander Nehamas, *Nietzsche: Life as Literature* (Cambridge, MA: Harvard University Press, 1985), Kathleen M. Higgins, *Nietzsche's Zarathustra* (Philadelphia: Temple University Press, 1987), Julian Young, *Nietzsche's Theory of Art* (Cambridge University Press, 1992), Maudemarie Clark, *Nietzsche on Truth and Philosophy* (Cambridge University Press, 1990).

Robert C. Solomon

conceived of the idea of eternal recurrence as a device to precipitate an end to wrong-headed professional career ambitions. I am confident, however, that what did interest him was (in some very qualified sense) the transformation of his readers by way of his writings, through intensive self-scrutiny, the pun-ful 'going under' (undergoing) that pervades the early fragments of *Zarathustra*. In that case – in my case – he certainly succeeded.

There is a substantial body of writing in his many books which can only be understood, I would argue, as what might be called 'moral advice'. To be sure, it is often oracular advice, as mischievously equivocal and ironic as those ancient voices that sent kings (and philosophers) to their deaths (and worse). But it has been strongly suggested, by Bernd Magnus and Alexander Nehamas, for example, that Nietzsche had nothing of the sort to offer. Indeed, it can readily be shown on the basis of any number of his texts that he rejected the very idea of moral advice on the ground that one must 'find one's own way'. Such an insistence permeates *Zarathustra*: 'If you would go high, use your own legs', for example.[5] One might say that Nietzsche, like Socrates, did not believe that 'virtue could be taught'. Any view to the contrary, that philosophy cannot only stimulate but in some sense teach virtue, is to make Nietzsche out to be 'some sort of sublime philosophical Ann Landers', as Magnus has rather unkindly put it.[6] And yet, that is precisely the Nietzsche whom I want to explore here.

The above quote from *Zarathustra*, for instance, 'If you would go high, use your own legs', can be interpreted as a rejection of advice, but it can also be construed as itself a piece of advice, indeed one of many versions of Nietzsche's most pervasive words of advice, 'become who you are'.[7] It is my contention that Nietzsche's works are filled with such advice, not along the lines of 'don't lie' and 'change your underwear daily', perhaps, but rather by way of being purposively provocative, provoking self-scrutiny in specific directions and along certain dimensions, not to mention his many little lessons and suggestions about such matters as love, friendship, diet and weightier matters such as war and gossip. A quick glance at *Daybreak* or *Human-All-to-Human*, for instance, reveals hundreds of such titbits as 'The best means of coming to the aid of people who suffer greatly from embarrassment and of calming them down

[5] Friedrich Nietzsche, *Thus Spoke Zarathustra*, trans by R. J. Hollingdale (Harmondsworth: Penguin, 1973), IV §10.

[6] Magnus, Stewart and Miller, *Nietzsche's Case* (New York: Routledge, 1995) with reference to Maudemarie Clark's (excellent) discussion of a similar thesis.

[7] As has often been noted, the phrase comes from Pindar.

is to single them out for praise'.[8] That is advice, plain and simple, though perhaps more appropriate to Judith Martin ('Miss Manners') than Ann Landers. We should hardly call it 'sublime'.

Often, Nietzsche's advice has to be scooped out of a context in which it is not clearly asserted. For example, in the first two books of *Zarathustra*, Nietzsche's (Zarathustra's) views are often posed in the form of questions, quotations or by way of his reactions to the usually odd or grotesque characters he meets along the way. For instance:

> Yet Zarathustra did not come to say to all these liars and fools:
> 'What do you know of virtue? What *could* you know of virtue?'
> Rather, that you, my friends, might grow weary of the old words you have learned from the fools and liars.
> Weary of the words: reward, retribution, punishment and revenge in justice.
> Weary of saying: what makes an act good is that it is unselfish.
> Oh, my friends, that your self be in your deed as the mother is in her child – let that be your word concerning virtue![9]

This is a rich condensation of a number of central Nietzschean themes, and it is hard to see how they could be construed as other than the giving of (profound) moral advice. But there is no simple imperative to be found here, indeed, it is not at all clear who is being addressed (who are the 'friends' – the same liars and fools, or are we the friends – or the liars and fools?). Indeed, it is not at all clear what sort of utterance follows the 'rather'. This much is clear: much of the message is negative, 'words to be weary of', though the point is not just about 'words' to be sure. And yet, the imagery is undeniably positive. It is an incitement to *virtue*. (And one might note here, as elsewhere, Nietzsche's use of an unusually saccharine philosophical metaphor, the maternal metaphor.[10]) Nietzsche's advice is often embedded in sarcasm, encased in the words of an imaginary or projected speaker ('You will be quick to insist that …'). It is often expressed in exaggerated or opaque metaphors ('that your self be in your deed as the mother is in her child'). It is sometimes hidden in a long historical or sociological description. (I would read virtually the whole of *On the Genealogy of Morals* this way, for example.) Some post-modern readers, like those earlier twentieth-century readers who declared Nietzsche 'the great destroyer', insist that Nietzsche 'has nothing to say', that is, nothing instructive much less impera-

[8] Friedrich Nietzsche, *Human, All Too Human*, trans by R. J. Hollingdale (Cambridge University Press, 1986), §301.
[9] Nietzsche, *Zarathustra* II 'On the Virtuous'.
[10] Kelly Oliver, *Womanizing Nietzsche* (New York: Routledge, 1995).

tive, nothing remotely by way of advice, much less a 'moral [normative] theory'. Indeed, it is now a matter of routine for philosophers to compare Nietzsche's strident criticism with 'deconstruction', suggesting that neither Nietzsche nor deconstruction presents (or can, by its own lights, present) any such thesis. I would say this is wrong on at least two counts, since both deconstructionists and Nietzsche are capable of making and make many more moral commitments.[11] I will not defend the former here, nor would I encourage the already tired comparison between them. But to say Nietzsche's writing is descriptive, purely destructive or merely non-assertive 'play' is surely indefensible.

Nietzsche (like Socrates) gave 'moral advice'. It was what he was all about. His whole philosophy, too, is aimed at provoking self-examination and self 'undergoing', to 'know thyself', to cultivate the virtues and, ultimately, to 'become who you are'. Nevertheless, like Socrates, Nietzsche's criticisms are far more trenchant than the concrete implications of his moral advice. (Socrates' constant reminders – as he devastates his interlocutors' arguments – that we should always cultivate our virtues and care for our souls hardly entails any specific behaviour, indeed, including his own.) To make matters more difficult, any account of Nietzsche's philosophy, even a 'personal' one, must make allowances for the multiple inconsistencies in his texts, including his inconsistencies in giving advice and refusing to do so. (Again, the comparison with Socrates, or rather with Plato's various dialogues, is obvious, but this is already wearing a bit thin.[12]) But this does not mean that Nietzsche had nothing of the sort to say. Rather, he had too much of the sort to say, or, rather, he didn't have it all straight in his own mind, or, at least, he changed his mind, sometimes within the frame of a single work. There's lots of advice, too much advice, too many different hints, winks, suggestions and arguments, often competing and allowing very different interpretations. Perhaps it is true, as Aschheim's sobering study of Nietzsche's reception reminds us, that we all 'make our own Nietzsche', whether by design or by mistake, no matter how good and careful the scholarship, no matter how

[11] This is certainly true of Jacques Derrida, who recently has emerged from his own web of obscurantism to make it amply clear that deconstruction as he practices it is rich with 'political' implications (see, e.g., his recent *The Specter of Marx* (New York: Routledge, 1994) and Gayatri Chakravorty Spivak (introduction to her translation of Jacques Derrida's *Of Grammatology* (Baltimore: Johns Hopkins University Press, 1976), who has always made her political commitments (if not her prose) quite explicit.

[12] Not that the topic itself is thin. See Nehamas on Nietzsche and Socrates in *The Art of Living* (Berkeley: University of California Press, 1998).

thorough the reading. Perhaps there is no 'real Nietzsche'. And, of course, one can always add the now standard Nietzschean disclaimer, 'this too is only an interpretation'. But isn't that often just another bit of post-modern hypocrisy, a deflection of any possible disagreement and a disavowal of any responsibility? The Nietzschean question that should follow and then be pursued, however, is 'but what, then, does that interpretation do for you? What will it make of you?' That is a personal, even intrusive question that is too rarely, if ever, approached in the voluminous and too often impersonal Nietzsche literature.

Nietzsche's Ethical Imperative: 'Become Who You Are!'

Man's character is his fate. Heraclitus

'Become who you are!' Nietzsche says to us, again and again. What does that mean? It seems to presume a theory (or, at any rate, a conception) of the self, a self that is (in some sense) already present, as potential, as not only a possibility but something of an obligation. It presents itself as an ethic, a series of 'oughts', even if those oughts are in everyone's case individually determined. It is also, despite its tautology-like appearance, an aggressive attack on a multitude of popular ethical pretensions. Nietzsche's targets include 'the improvers of mankind', those who would ignore or deny actual human natures in pursuit of (usually impossible) ideals or models, moralists who would oppose 'principles of practical reason' to the natural inclinations, educators who would strait-jacket children and young people into the banal, conformist images of 'the good citizen', and Christians, especially, who insist on the importance of a future 'other-worldly' existence at the expense of our 'this-worldly' one, the importance of one's inner soul-pellet as opposed to the rich wholeness of one's life. But 'become who you are' also implies and demands an 'examined life', a life subjected to scrutiny and reflection along with the rejection of many of the values accepted unthinkingly by *hoi poloi*, and their replacement with new ones. It thus becomes, despite its seeming banality, a radical imperative.

In what follows, I might seem to be trying to contribute to that pretentious Nietzschean effort called the 'revaluation of values'.[13] I am not sure, especially in Nietzschean terms, what this would mean. The attempt sounds as if it aspires to step *outside* of all values – outside of every 'perspective' – to value all values, or to value 'value'

[13] The phrase is a title briefly considered by Nietzsche for his last several works, but he wisely rejected it, I presume because even he found it too pretentious.

Robert C. Solomon

itself. This is nonsense, and it is doubly nonsense on a Nietzschean reading. Indeed, I have often questioned even Nietzsche's seemingly more perspectival (but no more modest) insistence that we 'create new values', invent a new perspective. But it is by no means clear that what Nietzsche encourages is anything 'new'. Indeed, the values he defends are in general very old – pre-Christian, pagan, often heroic virtues (though these were deeply woven into the fabric of nineteenth-century romantic culture as well). He defends courage, honesty, courtesy. Hardly 'new values'! (And if he did invent a new value, how would we recognise it? How would we evaluate it?) What Nietzsche does, I think I can say somewhat safely, is to defend a conception of ethics that has not (and had not) been adequately appreciated, either in contemporary ethics or in nineteenth-century German philosophy. In its current clumsy but readily handy phrase, this conception is 'virtue ethics', a view of ethics that focuses not on rational rules or principles, not on utility or the public good, not on social contracts or individual rights but on *personal character*.[14] And in defending this concept of the virtues, he defends several virtues that are at odds with current moral norms, and no doubt they were much more so when he first presented them.

Nietzsche was not, whatever else he may have been, 'sublime'. He was often subtle – indeed, much too much so – but he was the most brutally and often rudely moralistic of philosophers. He despised, he disdained, he was repulsed and disgusted. Such visceral metaphors permeate his philosophy. Perhaps it is the continuing exclusion of such visceral notions from the eviscerated vocabulary of ethics and morals that persuades more well-mannered moralists that Nietzsche is not interested in ethics.[15] To be disgusted, after all, is much more than merely 'disapproving', and, from a rational point of view, much less. Perhaps it is because of the playful prevalence of more disgusting visceral (especially genital and excretory) imagery in recent post-modernist writing[16] that Nietzsche's current readers

[14] The interpretation of Nietzsche's philosophy as an ethics of virtue has been prosecuted at length by Lester Hunt in his *Nietzsche and the Origins of Virtue* (Routledge, 1991). I first defended this interpretation in 'A More Severe Morality: Nietzsche's Affirmative Ethics' in *Nietzsche as affirmative thinker*: papers presented at the Fifth Jerusalem Philosophical Encounter, ed. Y. Yovel, 1983 (Dordrecht: M. Nijhoff, 1986), reprinted in *From Hegel to Existentialism* (New York: Oxford, 1988).

[15] William Miller has suggested that disgust is the most basic moral emotion. See his *The Anatomy of Disgust* (Cambridge, MA: Harvard University Press, 1996).

[16] E.g. Arthur Kroker to take one example of many, in *The Postmodern Scene: Excremental Culture and Hyper-aesthetics* (New York: St. Martin's Press, 1986).

are dulled to those far from playful responses in Nietzsche. Nietzsche called himself an 'immoralist' (although it is doubtful that he ever did anything truly immoral in his life), and his rejection of what was typically called 'morality' was certainly caustic and contemptuous. Judao-Christian morality and even the ethics of Socrates he declared 'decadent' at best. Kant's second *Critique* and *Metaphysics of Morals* he considered something of a subtle 'joke', and utilitarianism was simply 'vulgar'. But, today, the direction of ethics has shifted away from the Kantian rational willing subject (which Nietzsche clearly rejected) and the utilitarian attention to hedonistic consequences ('Man does not live for pleasure, only the Englishman does'.). What has taken their place is renewed attention to the character and integrity of the individual, his or her *virtues*. What is ultimately good, according to this viewpoint, is a good person, a person with good character, a person with the right virtues. (Even Kant and Mill have been brought into the act.[17]) Thus the central questions of ethics become – what kind of character? which virtues? How, in other words, would Nietzsche have wanted us? (Let's skip over the unflattering reply that we are merely Nietzschean clowns, precisely the pupils that horrified Zarathustra, and Nietzsche would not have 'wanted us' in any sense at all.)

That is the question that I want to approach here, 'how would Nietzsche want us?' The answer, as I have indicated, should be couched in terms of the virtues, those traits of personal character that are particularly admirable. But admirable to whom? And according to what standard? It is not as if Nietzsche gave us a simple prescription or 'list' of virtues nor does there seem to be any single pattern to the multitude of virtues he praises (a good night's sleep, keeping our friends, being strong, do not universalise but 'legislate values'). And then there are the familiar dead-ends: I do not expect much of anything from Zarathustra's attention-getting concept of the *übermensch*, nor will I try to squeeze more meaning than I have already suggested from the also much-discussed idea of eternal recurrence or the rather unfortunate and greatly overplayed notion of the 'will to power'. But between those much-talked about phantoms in Nietzsche's philosophy, there is a great deal of material to be drawn in particular from what I would consider the more 'morally absorbed' books of Nietzsche's 'middle' creative period,

---

[17] Kant has been turned into an 'agent-based' virtue ethicist, for example, by Steve Darwall (see his *The British Moralists and the Internal 'Ought' 1640–1740* (Cambridge University Press, 1995). John Stuart Mill betrays his Aristotelian secrets in chapter V of *Utilitarianism* (Indiannapolis: Hackett Publishing Company, 1979).

that is, from *Human-all-to-Human* and *Daybreak* to *Beyond Good and Evil* and the *Genealogy*. The theses I will be employing are rarely so exciting as the (empty) promise of the *übermensch*, but they constitute, taken together, a recognisable if not entirely consistent philosophy of life, a philosophy of virtue that might best be summarised in the good advice 'to give style to one's character'.

Quite the contrary to viewing Nietzsche as an iconoclastic immoralist, I think that we would be well advised to see him as part of a long ethical tradition. Aristotle, in particular, developed what is now called a 'virtue ethics' twenty-five hundred years ago, before the antithetical views of Christianity, Kant and the utilitarians were around to provide a dramatic contrast. Aristotle's *Nicomachean Ethics* is essentially a theory of virtue. A theory of just those traits and habits must be cultivated to make one a 'flourishing (*eudaimon*) person' and have a good character. As everyone knows, Aristotle defined the virtues as states of character that were 'the mean between the extremes'. Aristotle further offered us a neat little list of virtues as well as this supposedly precise criterion (never mind that the list and the criterion do not fit together, giving the whole project an overtone of the *ad hoc.*). But the entire *Ethics* is essentially the fleshing out of this list (Courage, Temperance, Liberality, Magnificence, Pride, Good temperament, Friendliness, Truthfulness, Wittiness, Shame [a 'quasi-virtue'], Justice and the various virtues of practical reasoning and intellectual life). Aquinas, too, gave us a series of formulaic neo-Aristotelian lists (in particular the lists of Cardinal Sins and Virtues, e.g., prudence, fortitude, temperance, justice), and, just to make sure we do not get overly ethnocentric, Confucius and the Upanishads, on the other side of the world, had their more or less concise conceptions of the virtues as well. There was a time, it seems, when virtue ethics was about the only game in town. (A qualified exception was the ancient Hebrews, whose tribal ethics was a fascinating combination of virtue and The Law, thus setting up the scenario that Nietzsche so polemically exploits in his *Genealogy*.)

Nietzsche himself offers us two short lists, one in *Daybreak* 556 (honesty, courage, generosity, politeness), the other in *Beyond Good & Evil* 284 (courage, insight, sympathy, solitude). We should not be surprised that they are not consistent (with each other or with what he says elsewhere in his work) and it is hardly clear how serious he may have been. He further insists that the virtues should not be 'named' (for that would make them 'common') and he several times insists that each of us has 'unique' virtues, which would make any discussion of the 'right' or 'best' virtues seemingly impossible. Nevertheless, there is more than enough in Nietzsche's various musings, polemics, pronouncements and attacks on the character of others to convince me that the project has significance, both practical and philosophical. Nietzsche provokes in us an image of ourselves, often a most unflattering image, in order to prompt us to reconsider ourselves. Or, sometimes it is an image for which we have been searching (as in the adolescent fascination with the *übermensch*), perhaps without knowing it. As Nietzsche often points out, our ignorance of our own ideals may well be based on the fact that we so often seek others' virtues and not our own.

Philosophy *Ad Hominem*: exemplary virtues (and vices)

A person of superior *de* [virtue] does not get *de*,
That is why he has *de*.

A person of inferior *de* cannot get *de*,
That is why he has no *de*.

> *Tao Te Ching*

Each of us has his or her own virtues. That claim is evident in Nietzsche, although the sense of 'own-ness' (as unique, as individuating or as merely 'had' by that person) is not altogether clear. Much of what we are looking for, nevertheless, may be found in Nietzsche's critical and sometimes scathing portrayals of other philosophers. I think that it is a mistake to assume that virtues and vices are opposites (as all of those neat lists made by tea-shop moralists might imply), but nevertheless, Nietzsche's condemnations of others (or of whole cultures or schools of thought) can give us considerable insight into what he found valued and what he did not. It is not unimportant that much of Nietzsche's philosophy consists of attacks on others, attacks on them personally, *ad hominem*, so to speak, rather than critical comments on their works or ideas as such. Nietzsche famously insisted that a philosopher should be, above all, an example. This already marks a return to ancient 'heroic' ethics, which is exemplary rather than rule-governed or action-guiding. Ethics, on this archaic model, might be simply summarised as 'be like him'![18] Examples, accordingly, provide the basis of much of Nietzsche's moral philosophy.

The positive examples are comparatively few and far between. The most prominent is Goethe, who is lavishly praised for 'creating himself' and making himself 'into a whole man'. Even Goethe,

[18] I owe this insight into the nature of early Greek morality to Julius Moravscik.

Robert C. Solomon

however is subject to Nietzsche's sharp pen. There are some positive words about Schopenhauer, Wagner, Socrates, even Jesus, but they are often drowned out in a chorus of subsequent criticism. Even heroes turn out to be 'human-all-too-human'. There are occasional good words about Emerson, Heine and Dostoevsky, to name a few, but the personal details are scant at best. Perhaps such writers – for they are virtually all writers – enjoyed the anonymity and safety of distance because Nietzsche never knew – or never bothered to know – much about them. Nietzsche often praises himself (more on that later) but regarding himself too that praise is typically undermined by ridicule.

The negative examples, on the other hand, are to found throughout the Nietzschean corpus. 'In his relation to the state', writes Nietzsche, 'Kant was not great'. He adds, 'German decadence as philosophy', 'the final exhaustion of life', 'the Chinaman from Køningsberg'.[19]) Socrates, of course, is a continuous target for ridicule, from the fact that he was 'ugly' (for a Greek, already a 'refutation') to the fact that he (personally) 'turned reason into a tyrant'.[20] Euripides gets a drubbing early on, the church fathers get their worst later. The English are a favourite butt for Nietzsche's wisecracks, second, perhaps, only to the Germans. 'There is too much beer in the German intellect', he observes.[21] Morality was the product of servile and herd-like thinking, the morality of slaves, an expression of *ressentiment*.[22] Priests betray a spectrum of vices, from hypocrisy to cruelty and philosophers (in general) seem to suffer from a variety of personal infirmities, self-deception and self-denial. (A few years later, Freud would diagnose his own view of the neuroses of philosophers. Taking the German romantics as his examples, he diagnosed a form of *Weltschmerz*. Today, given the methods in favour, he would probably render a diagnosis of anal compulsiveness.) One can only imagine what harsh words Nietzsche would add to the contemporary 'Heidegger Crisis', Heidegger's hardly heroic stance *vis-à-vis* National Socialism.[23] Indeed, one would like to hear his views on some of the movers and shakers of the American Philosophical Association. But, anyway,

[19] Friedrich Nietzsche, *The Antichrist* in *The Portable Nietzsche*, trans and ed. by Walter Kaufmann (New York: Viking, 1954), §11.

[20] Friedrich Nietzsche, *Twilight of the Idols* in *The Portable Nietzsche*, trans and ed. by Walter Kaufmann (New York: Viking, 1954), 'The Problem of Socrates', §3.

[21] Nietzsche, *Twilight* 'Germans', §2.

[22] Friedrich Nietzsche, *On the Genealogy of Morals,* trans by Walter Kaufmann and R. J. Hollingdale (New York: Vintage, 1967), Book I, §10.

[23] Hans Sluga, *Heidegger's Crisis* (Cambridge, MA: Harvard University Press, 1994).

the point is that Nietzsche is readily willing to find fault with his fellows, and from these faults we can infer (with caution) some virtues.[24]

Philosophy is not just a realm of ideas detached from and only contingently connected to their promulgators, their world, their culture, their context and their character. The *character* of a philosopher, although certainly not the whole story, is certainly part of what is to be understood, indeed, much more influential than most philosophers are willing to believe. Ideas may have a life of their own, but the impact and influence of ideas has a great deal to do with the position and personality of the promulgator. To be sure, biography can be overdone, but tales and gossip about some still-living Oxbridge philosophers, for example, still circulate freely, long after their actual works have become all but irrelevant. We should not be surprised that the biography of, say, Ludwig Wittgenstein has virtually eclipsed his philosophy. The philosophy may, indeed, still invite scrutiny, but the character, that tortured, over-heated personality, those gestures, the Betty Grable compulsion, those hang-ups, now that is a real example of a philosopher. (How much time does Ray Monk, the most illustrious of Wittgenstein's biographers, spend on his actual ideas?[25]) Recent biographies of Jean-Paul Sartre have all but fled in terror from the task of trying to comprehend or even summarise his ideas in their description of the long flow of fights and friendships, alliances and daliances that now constitute the *being* of 'Jean-Paul Sartre'. Contemporary academic theorists have already become classic comedy, even if the names have been changed to protect from lawsuits, thanks to novelists like David Lodge and Malcolm Bradbury. Long after 'deconstruction' has been packed away in the mausoleum of worn-out philosophical jargon, the pretensions of its protagonists will live on as illustrative personal foibles.

Nietzsche took *ad hominem* arguments very seriously, which is why, one might argue, he is fair game for them in return. He placed both Socrates and Jesus under such intense scrutiny not so much because of their teachings as such but because of their spectacular roles as characters in the development of Western thought, roles which, we can say with some confidence, Nietzsche greatly emulated and envied.[26] Thus he peppered his works with a heavy dose of

[24] Again, the opposite of vice is not a virtue. Gossiping is a vice. Not gossiping is not a virtue. Indeed, one might argue, it is itself another type of vice.

[25] Ray Monk, *Ludwig Wittgenstein: The Duty of Genius* (New York: Free Press, 1990).

[26] No one is more pithy on this point than Nehamas, who works out the Nietzsche-Socrates connection in great detail.

Robert C. Solomon

ad hominem arguments which, in his hands at least, were not a
species of 'informal fallacy' but a sharp diagnostic tool. (How many
of the 'informal fallacies' are, at least sometimes, perfectly proper as
well as persuasive arguments, e.g., the fallacy of 'appeals to emotion'?) An *ad hominem* question asks: 'Who was this person (or who
were these people) and why did they believe and insist on that? Yes,
they say this, but what were their virtues and what were their vices?'
Indeed, for all of the emphasis Nietzsche seems to put on 'values',
we should at least ask whether values are rather secondary in his
philosophy, secondary, that is, to the virtues of the characters who
have them. Thus Socrates can be understood. Kant was found out.
The Germans are fair game. 'Every great philosophy', Nietzsche
concludes (in *Beyond Good and Evil*), 'is nothing but' the personal
confession of its author and a kind of involuntary and unconscious
memoir.[27]

So considered, what philosophers, which peoples, could possibly
live up to their own ideas as a living exemplar of the philosophy
they preach? Socrates? (A mixed evaluation at best.[28]) David
Hume? (Depends on your politics.[29]) Kant? (Unlikely.[30])
Schopenhauer? (![31]) Heidegger? (apparently the very antithesis[32])
Wittgenstein? (Can you measure a role model from his scores of
imitators?[33]) Bertrand Russell? (What does it suggest about the self-
awareness of a man who, while riding along on a bicycle, 'suddenly'
realises that he does not love his wife?[34]) Jean-Paul Sartre? (Why did

---

[27] Friedrich Nietzsche, *Beyond Good and Evil*, trans by Walter
Kaufmann. (New York: Vintage, 1966).

[28] Gregory Vlastos would certainly disagree. But for a brilliant semi-schol-
arly reply see I. F. Stone's *Trial of Socrates*. (Boston: Little, Brown, 1988).

[29] Alasdair MacIntyre, in *Whose Justice? Which Rationality?* (Notre
Dame, IN: University of Notre Dame Press, 1988) is far from praising of
his Scots countryman.

[30] Heine's account of a clockwork Kant, for instance, may make the man
charming but hardly a hero. (*Religion and Philosophy in Germany*, trans by
John Snodgrass.) (Boston: Beacon Press, 1959).

[31] One does not have to believe Bertrand Russell here, but Schopenhauer's
grumpy hedonism is indeed at odds with the pessimism of his philosophy.
Nietzsche is much more insightful than Russell on this matter, needless to
say. Whereas Russell simply dismissed Schopenhauer, Nietzsche had once
idolised him. Accordingly, Nietzsche is also, at times, more scathing.

[32] But see, for a more subtle account, Hans Sluga's admirable *Heidegger's
Crisis* (op. cit.).

[33] The Monk book makes perfectly clear the unenviable sense in which
Wittgenstein was an exemplar of his philosophy, a philosophy of tortured self-
doubts (rather than the mere gestures which are taken up by his students).

[34] Russell, *My Autobiography* (Boston: Little Brown, 1967–1969).

he stop his account of his life at puberty, to have the story continued uncensored by his often ill-treated life-time companion
Simone?[35]) W. V. O. Quine (Have you read his biography?[36]) More
likely examples are Dietrich Bonhoeffer and Giordano Bruno, who,
like Socrates, literally gave their lives. Does it have to be so dramatic? What about Kierkegaard, who in some sense practised what he
preached (if only by preaching what he practised), or the partly
apocryphal Pyrrho, who is said to have survived his own scepticism
(until the age of ninety) only by the grace of his students? There are
the Stoics, especially Seneca and Marcus Aurelius, and the latter-
day stoic Spinoza. And, more often than one would think, there is
the latter-day college philosophy professor, a real Mr (or just as likely, Ms) Chips, whose visions and ambitions are much more modest
but, nevertheless, consonant with their daily behaviour. Then,
again, is consistency always a virtue, inconsistency always a vice?
Must a philosopher live in accordance with his or her philosophy,
and what follows if he or she does not?

Nietzsche *ad hominem*: Nietzsche as a paragon of virtue

> The inner struggle with his pathologically delicate soul, overflow-
> ing with pity, was what led him to preach, 'be hard'!, and to look up
> with admiration at those Renaissance men of violence who had
> walked stolidly over corpses to reach their goal.
>
> *Marie von Bradke*
> (who knew Nietzsche in Sils Maria, Summer 1886)

One can make too much of biography, and with Nietzsche this is all
too tempting, particularly by those who would like to simply dismiss him. (I am thinking, for example, of Ben-Ami Scharfstein's
interesting but wholly reductive portrait of Nietzsche.[37]) But, of
course, Nietzsche, in an obvious sense, 'asks for it'. He is not one of
those evaporating (sometimes said to be 'dead') post-modernist
authors that Barthes and Foucault talk about. Unlike Malcom
Bradbury's ludicrous example of that phenomenon (*Mesonge*), disappearing altogether and leaving his works quite literally without an
author, Nietzsche is always 'in your face', not only present in person
but reminding us just *who he is*.

---

[35] Sartre, *Les mots (The Words)*. Translated by Bernard Frechtman
(Greenwich, CT: Fawcett, 1966).

[36] W. V. O. Quine, *The Time of My Life: An Autobiography* (Cambridge,
MA: MIT Press, 1985).

[37] Ben-Ami Scharfstein, *The Philosophers: Their Lives and the Nature of
Their Thought* (Oxford: Basil Blackwell, 1980).

Robert C. Solomon

Accordingly, one can and probably should take Nietzsche himself as a philosophical example.[38] It is not at all clear that he would come off at all well. He was lonely, desperate, occasionally embarrassing in his behaviour not to mention some of his published writings. He was incompetent to the point of self-humiliation with women, this great 'seducer'.[39] He participated in no great friendships and had no memorable (or even plausible) love affairs. He did no great deeds. Unlike his imaginary *alter ego* Zarathustra and his one time mentor Wagner, he addressed no crowds, turned no heads, confronted no enemies. Like his near-contemporary in Copenhagen, Søren Kierkegaard, he did not have much of a life. For Kierkegaard, it was the 'inner life', 'passionate inwardness' that counted. But, we should certainly ask, can virtues be entirely 'internal', even 'private'? In what sense is a rich inner life an admirable life, a virtuous life? In Kierkegaard's case, at least this seems plausible. But not for Nietzsche.

For Nietzsche, a rich inner life could hardly be sufficient. His warrior and earth-shattering ('dynamite') metaphors cannot plausibly be restricted to thoughts and jottings, and what Kierkegaard called 'subjectivity' was hardly his favoured domain. Nietzsche's philosophy is a heroic philosophy, and, if you did not know him, a philosophy of action. But the sad truth is that it degenerates into an almost self-help philosophy of health. Two of the favourite quotes among *hoi poloi* who have barely read him are, 'that which does not kill (overcome) me makes me stronger' and 'live dangerously!' The first, of course, is nonsense. That which does not kill me most likely leaves me debilitated. And the second? Nietzsche was sickly all of his life. The celebration of 'health' as a philosophical ideal, by a chronically unhealthy philosopher, is pathetic, at best. And Nietzsche died badly, indeed, he was perhaps the worst imaginable counter-example to his own wise instruction, 'die at the right time'. He lingered in a virtually vegetative state for a full decade, cared for by a sister whose views he despised and who ultimately used him to publicly defend those views. He railed throughout his career against pity, that pathetic emotion which, according to those who knew him, was one of the most prominent features of his own personality.[40] (His

---

[38] Here is an example of a typical anti-Nietzsche ad hominem argument, from a logic textbook, no less: 'Don't waste your time studying the philosophy of Nietzsche. Not only was he an atheist but he ended his days in an insane asylum'. (William H. Halverson *A Concise Introduction to Philosophy* (New York: Random House, 1967) p. 58.

[39] Dionysus, as Nietzsche well knew, was also considered the great seducer (e.g. Euripides *Bacchus*).

[40] Cf. the Marie von Bradke quote at the beginning of this section, 'his pathologically delicate soul, overflowing with pity', (op. cit.).

final gesture on behalf of animal welfare deserves sincere appreciation.) As an example, Nietzsche is more plausibly viewed as a play of opposites, like Rousseau, whose advice might be best understood as, 'let us admire people most *unlike* myself'.

Nietzsche's life, insofar as it serves as an example at all, is an example of a tortured and unhappy spirit who managed, through his genius and through his suffering, to produce a magnificent corpus of writings. Thus Alexander Nehamas, in one of the most ingenious philosophico–biographical reconstructions since Plato set his sights on his teacher's career, gives us good reason to ignore the 'miserable little man' named 'Nietzsche' and accept instead the *persona* he created, namely Nietzsche.[41] One might counter by insisting that 'life isn't literature',[42] but I now think that this blunt contrast glosses over not only the fascinating intimacy between Nietzsche and 'Nietzsche' but also clouds over some of the most fascinating features of the notion of 'character' and, thus the nature of both personal identity and *ad hominem* arguments in philosophy.

Briefly stated, that intimacy has to do with the complex interaction between a person's thoughts, plans, emotions and self-conception and what one might (problematically) identify with the bald 'facts' about a person's behaviour, accomplishments, comments and history. I am concerned here with the familiar distinction in Jean-Paul Sartre between 'facticity' and 'transcendence' (without getting into the exponential complications of what he calls 'being-for-others'). The problem is that how we 'read' a person's behaviour and the narrative of that history depends to a large extent on the person's intentions, ambitions and ideals. In Nietzsche's case, the 'events' his life were so minimal and his intentions, ambitions and ideals were so grand that it is a mistake, as well as unfair, to interpret either without continuous reference to the other. In other words, what I am trying to do is to clear a path between overly *ad hominem* Scharfstein-style psychoanalytic reductionism and Arthur Danto's old 'Nietzsche as Philosopher' thesis (which Danto himself has retracted[43]). The relationship between Nietzsche and

<hr />

[41] Alexander Nehamas, *Nietzsche: Life as Literature* (Cambridge, MA: Harvard University Press, 1985).

[42] See my comment on Nehamas, 'Nietzsche and Nehamas's Nietzsche', *International Studies in Philosophy* (Nietzsche issue) Vol. xxi, no. 2 (Summer, 1989).

[43] Danto, *Nietzsche as Philosopher* (New York: Macmillan, 1963). I do not mean to deny for a moment of course, that Danto's book was one of the most important events in recent Nietzsche scholarship. Following Walter Kaufmann's equally important de-Nazification of Nietzsche a few

Robert C. Solomon

'Nietzsche' raises all sorts of tantalising questions, such as whether good fortune – e.g. the good fortune or good health is indeed (as Aristotle simply presumed) a presupposition of the virtuous, *eudamimon* life or whether (as in Kant) it is morally irrelevant. But the question of virtue, and the philosopher as example, is first of all to be sought in the writing itself. The mistake is thinking that *ad hominem* arguments ought to look at the personal character *instead of* the writing, and this, certainly, is an even bigger mistake than its converse. It is the philosopher-in-the-philosophy that ought to be our point of focus. The virtues of the philosopher are those that are evident in the philosophy.[44]

Like many philosophers (Plato, Rousseau and Marx come to mind), Nietzsche created an ideal world – or in his case an identity – dramatically different from the world of his experience. That vision becomes, in an important Sartrian sense, an essential part of the identity of the philosopher. Thus there is another interpretation of the view that a philosopher should be an example, with somewhat less dramatic requirements. One need not be a world historical figure. One need not be a hero or happy. One must not be a hypocrite, of course, and this alone would eliminate a considerable number of would-be philosophers, including, especially, a rather large number of philosophy professors. We judge a philosopher – and not only his or her ideas – by what he or she says, even ironically (especially ironically). Pleas for 'playfulness' will not get you off the hook. In writing, in case anyone ever doubted it, one betrays oneself – pseudonyms, sarcasm, dialogue or scholarly form notwithstanding. Nietzsche's character, in other words, cannot be detached from his writings. Nietzsche and 'Nietzsche' cannot so

---

years earlier, Danto captured Nietzsche's ideas in a form that made Nietzsche 'respectable' in the then overwhelmingly analytic world of American professional philosophy. His recognition of the limits of this approach can be found in several places, among them his presidential address to the American Philosophical Association in 1983 ('Philosophy as/and/of Literature', reprinted in *The Philosophical Disenfranchisement of Art* New York: Columbia University Press, 1986) and in his essay 'Some Remarks on the Genealogy of Morals' in Higgins and Solomon, *Reading Nietzsche* (New York: Oxford University Press, 1988).

[44] It is the demand for integration of philosopher and philosophy that distinguishes philosophy from most other disciplines, and it is what makes it so odd when we meet 'philosophers' (almost always philosophy professors) who keep their philosophical interests wholly compartmentalised and isolated from the rest of their lives – no matter how exciting or boring, no matter how admirable or loathsome. This is also what drives the 'Heidegger crisis'. (See Sluga, op. cit.).

easily be distinguished, nor separated for the purpose of criticism and interpretation.[45]

Nietzsche's virtues: Nietzsche's 'List'

What are the Nietzschean virtues? I would not pretend to be able to isolate a small number of virtues, such as Nietzsche himself (twice) does in those two short lists (honesty, courage, generosity and politeness and courage, insight, sympathy, and solitude[46]), and one certainly must further distinguish between those virtues Nietzsche preached and those he exemplified in his writing. But preaching is itself an indication of a person's character, and disdainful preaching, prophetic preaching, ironic preaching, may be quite distinct and quite relevant to the question whom [the preacher] is. A philosopher who ponderously insists on being careful and serious, let us repeat, careful and serious, careful and serious, and is extremely careful to say this any number of times, quite seriously, surely shows us something important not only about his or her thesis (which will insist on caution and seriousness) but about this (most cautious and serious) person as well. So, too, when Nietzsche tells us, with multiple exclamation points and italics, with frequent references to the classics and theology, with rhetorical questions and harsh insults, that Christian morality is a 'slave' morality, we rightfully conclude not only that he does not think particularly well of Christian morality but also that he endorses and represents this intentionally offensive, polemical style. The perspectival view of history that Nietzsche employs also indicates a distinctive personality, who clearly emerges from that particular style of presentation. And if we find many variations of styles in Nietzsche (as when one reads a handwritten letter in which the style changes with each line or sentence), this, too, indicates something quite illuminating about character. (Ask any handwriting analyst.) Nietzsche's virtues are to be found not only in what he says but in how he says it.

What is a virtue? This, as what follows, is properly postponed for a much more ambitious work, but let us just say for the moment (what is trivially agreed by most virtue theorists) that a virtue is an

---

[45] Here I backtrack from my objection to Nehamas's reconstruction of Nietzsche as 'Nietzsche' in his *Nietzsche: Life as Literature* and my 'Nietzsche and Nehamas's Nietzsche'. (*op. cit.*) The issue now seems to me much more complicated.

[46] Friedrich Nietzsche, *Daybreak: Thoughts on the Prejudices of Morality*. Translated by R. J. Hollingdale (Cambridge University Press, 1982), §556, Nietzsche, *Beyond Good and Evil* §284.

admirable or desirable state of character. In fact, this says very little (and what it says can be challenged). But even accepting such a claim, virtues might be interpreted as interpersonally derived (as when Hume suggests that they are 'pleasing' to self and others), or they might be taken to be (in a sense to be refined) good in themselves (as in Michael Slote's 'agent-based' virtue ethics[47]) or they might be action tendencies that are aimed toward an independently justified set of values (e.g., Christine Swanton's 'value-centred' virtue ethics[48]). One might tie the virtues to specific cultures (as Alasadair MacIntyre, for example, suggests[49]) or there might be 'non-relative virtues' (as Martha Nussbaum argues in a fairly well-known paper and elsewhere[50]). One might complicate matters by insisting that Chinese (e.g., Confucian) conceptions of ethics are not to be simply assimilated to, say, Aristotle's conception of the virtues, despite some obvious but possibly superficial similarities (e.g., the doctrine of the mean), and one might, of course, argue that there is not a single dimension to the virtues any more than there is a single 'moral' dimension of an act. But all of this for later. For now, I would like to just suggest a not at all simple list of more and less plausible candidates for a catalogue of 'Nietzsche's virtues'. I offer these in three groups, first, what I call 'traditional' virtues, those that might well appear on almost any respectable list of virtues. Second a set of peculiarly 'Nietzschean' virtues, although this list is hardly without its internal conflicts and contradictions. Finally, a 'problematic' list, a mismatched set of Nietzschean virtues that require far more discussion and analysis.

To begin with, a somewhat traditional list (that is, pretty much in accord with Aristotle):

COURAGE
HONESTY
TEMPERANCE
HONOUR/INTEGRITY
JUSTICE
PRIDE (*megalopsychos*)
COURTESY
FRIENDSHIP
GENEROSITY

[47] Michael Slote, *From Morality to Virtue* (New York: Oxford University Press, 1992).

[48] Christine Swanton 'Profiles of the Virtues' (unpublished paper).

[49] Alasdair MacIntyre, *After Virtue* (Notre Dame University Press, 1981).

[50] Martha Nussbaum, 'Non-Relative Virtue' in French *et al.*, *Ethics and Character: Midwest Studies XIII* (Notre Dame University Press, 1988).

All of these require some commentary, for it should not be assumed that what Nietzsche means by these virtue names is what other philosophers mean by them. For example, I will suggest that courage, for Nietzsche, refers not so much to overcoming fear (the standard account) or even having 'just the right amount' of fear (the overly quantitative Aristotelian account), and it certainly does not mean (the pathological conception of courage) having *no* fear. Rather, as in so many of his conceptions of virtue, Nietzsche has a model of 'over-flowing', in the case of courage, I would suggest, overflowing with assertiveness, overwhelming (rather than the bland 'overcoming') fear. One imagines one of Homer's Greek heroes, surging with patriotism, warrior gusto, machismo (or whatever) who, driven by that motive, charges through whatever fear is surely there. So, too, the most inspired artist or philosopher pursues his or her ideas despite the dangers of failure and ridicule or, perhaps worse, being utterly ignored.[51]

Consider an example that would have been dear to both Aristotle and Nietzsche, the scene of Achilles revenge in *The Iliad*.[52] Achilles, enraged by the death of his friend Patroclus, crashes on to the battlefield outside of Troy with vengeance ('justice') on his mind. There is no fear. There is no room for fear in the midst of all of that well-directed murderous fury. To call Achilles 'courageous', in such a state, would seem rather an understatement, if not absurd. Our own understanding of courage may or may not be in line with Aristotle, that is, courage as the amount of resistance or fear that it has to overcome. But if we view the scene as Nietzsche (and Homer) did, fear and courage are not complementary but rather opposed, and it is Achilles who is courageous, not the poor soldier with the shaking knees who 'forces himself' to stand his ground. (The word 'brave' once carried with it this meaning, except insofar as it has also been infected with the Aristotelian understanding of 'courage'.) Courage, in other words, is not overcoming emotion (namely, fear). It is itself constituted by overwhelming and yet skillfully directed overflowing of emotion, which incorporates rather than excludes

[51] But cf. Nietzsche, *Daybreak* §277 on the 'hot and cold virtues'.

[52] Homer, *The Iliad*, xv. 348–512, Aristotle *Nicomachean Ethics* Trans. W. D. Ross (London: Oxford University Press, 1925), Book III, Ch. 8 (1116). Ross points out that the quotation more likely resembles Agamemnon than Hector (op. cit. p. 68), but cf. Aristotle (ibid. 1117) where he considers: 'passion is sometimes reckoned as courage ... for passion above all things is eager to rush on danger ... Hence Homer's "put strength into his passion"'. Aristotle goes on to say that men who act from passion are not truly brave but more akin to beasts. They do not act 'for honor's sake nor as the rule directs'. (ibid.) Nevertheless, he adds, 'they have something akin to courage'.

Robert C. Solomon

ones sense of honour, which because of its keen focus is too easily interpreted as calm. It is the power, efficiency and effectiveness of the passion, not this only apparent calm, that is its virtue.

One can give the same sort of analysis of generosity (which in *Zarathustra* is called the 'gift-giving virtue'). It is not mere giving, nor the habit of giving. Consider generosity in the context of one current charity demand which insists 'give 'til it hurts!' One can imagine the donor, struggling against the pain of his or her own miserliness, weighing the burden of conscience against the bottle of Chateau le Poeuf that is on sale at the wine store down the street. Finally, generosity overcomes resistance, and the virtue is admirably displayed. *But*, notice, first of all, that the more one has to struggle to give, the less virtuous one is. Thus Aristotle insists that, with all virtues, their performance is actually pleasurable, not painful, and this itself is a test of one's virtuousness. Suppose, however, that one's generosity consisted of what one might simply call ones 'overflowing' nature. This is the way, I hear, that Mick Jagger behaves on tour. Having more money than he (or anyone) could know how to spend, Jagger simply allows it to flow freely, somewhat indiscriminately, to recipients and causes both just and frivolous. Now this abandon and lack of concern, one might argue, is true generosity, not the struggle against personal deprivation but an indifference that can only come with great wealth. So, too, the other virtues emerge as 'overflow' of a great-souled spirit, of one who has an abundance. To object that the virtues are not this, but rather the sense of duty in contrast to self-interest and personal need, is to fall back into what Nietzsche would consider a pathetic model of the virtues, the model that emerges in Kant and in Christianity, where it is the poor and not the rich in spirit who become the focus. Aristotle, writing for the aristocracy, would have fallen somewhere in between. But, indeed, what constitutes a Nietzschean virtue is first of all a kind of fullness, a sense of oneself on top of the world. One need not get hung up on money, prestige and power to adopt such an ethic. Nietzsche himself, impoverished, passed over by his intellectual peers and poor in health, might serve as just such an example. Indeed, even temperance (the most tempting counter example to this account) represents a kind of fullness, a sense of buoyant self-discipline. Consider Nietzsche's many *Californische* comments on diet, good health and creative well-being.

Nietzsche's virtues are not proper 'balance' or 'means between the extremes'. A virtue is an excess, and overwhelming, an overflowing. It is not merely withstanding or enduring (as in all of those made-for-TV movies about 'heroes' and 'heroines' who suffer through horrible diseases). This is only a sketch, of course, but it is a model that I think Nietzsche endorses throughout his philosophy, from *Birth of Tragedy* to *Ecce Homo*, as opposed to the more 'rational' models of the virtues one finds, for example, in most philosophers and moralists. So, too, it is easy to understand generosity not as a mere overcoming of miserliness but as a quite literal overflowing. One might think of honesty as an 'overflowing' of the truth or, more cautiously, one's most heartfelt opinions. This is obviously much more than Aristotle's 'truthfulness', and it is radically different from any prohibition against lying that might be derived from the 'categorical imperative'. Telling the truth is not so much an obligation as it is a powerful 'inclination'. And needless to say, it has little to do with the 'greatest good for the greatest number'.

Reading Nietzsche's letters (not to mention his embarrassing marriage proposals) we also get the sense that his conception of friendship was far from a calm amiability. It was rather an explosion of desperate affection. (No one, except perhaps Hume, insisted that the virtues were easy to live with.) Integrity is a virtue (or a way of integrating the virtues) that is highly prized by Nietzsche, for example, in his elaborate praise of Goethe.[53] Pride requires special attention as one of the traditionally controversial virtues, one of the 'seven deadly sins' in Christianity but something more like 'self-respect' in heroic society. (Thus David Hume, a self-proclaimed 'pagan', took pride to be a virtue as opposed to its 'Monkish' opposite, humility.) Nietzsche talks about pride as an ultimate motive, e.g., in *Daybreak* 32, where he analyses pride as the basis of morality and asks, in closing, whether a new understanding of morality (*viz.* his own) will require 'more pride? A new pride?'.

Justice, finally, requires considerable attention as well. Today, few philosophers would consider justice to be a personal virtue, as Plato and Aristotle did (even given the much broader meaning that *diké* had in Greek). Bernard Williams, for example, has argued explicitly against it, and most other philosophers seem simply oblivious (or contemptuous) of the possibility. Justice is a rational scheme, a virtue of societies, not individuals. But justice for Nietzsche is very much a personal virtue, not a virtue of proportion (as in Aristotle) nor even 'giving each his due' (as in Plato), although Nietzsche often makes comments that could be so construed. For one thing, Nietzsche seems far less concerned with 'distributive' justice than either the ancient or contemporary philosophers. In fact, his philosophy is virtually devoid of any suggestions – much less a theory – concerning the equitable distribution of material goods and honours in distributive justice. But he is greatly concerned with what is

---

[53] Michael Tanner, *Nietzsche* (Oxford University Press, 1994).

sometimes called 'retributive' justice, that is, essentially, the problems of punishment. In short, Nietzsche is against punishment. He finds it demeaning, essentially based on resentment, a sign of weakness, a traditional form of decrepitude. This may surprise those who are particularly struck by Nietzsche's frequent discussion – sometimes bordering on an excuse if not a justification – of cruelty. But justice for Nietzsche – which is tightly tied to the equally problematic concept of mercy – is first of all the overcoming of the desire to punish, not the usual interpretation of that virtue, to be sure.

Second, I want to suggest a list of distinctively 'Nietzschean' virtues:

EXUBERANCE
'STYLE'
'DEPTH'
DYNAMISM
RISK
FATALISM (*AMOR FATI*)
PLAYFULNESS
AESTHETICISM
SOLITUDE

Exuberance, I would want to argue, is not only a virtue in itself (in contrast to such traditional virtues as *apatheia* and *ataraxia* – 'peace of mind') but the core of virtually all of Nietzsche's virtues. Overflowing, according to this view, is a metaphor that is derivative of Nietzsche's celebration of energy, very much in line, not coincidentally, with the new conception of physics that had become very much in vogue toward the end of the nineteenth century. Exuberance is hardly the same as 'effervescence', needless to say, and Nietzsche would have nothing but utter contempt for those personalities that, particularly in the United States, are characterised as 'bubbly' or 'outgoing'. Like most virtues, exuberance cannot be taken out of context, that is, the context of the other virtues (however true it may be to say that everyone has his or her own [set of] virtues). Nietzsche denies that the virtues 'fit' together in any unified way – a direct rejection of one of Aristotle's most perplexing theses. The virtue of exuberance, in particular, depends upon what it is that is 'overflowing'. (One can think of all sorts of unacceptable candidates.) It also depends on the discipline with which it is expressed, or, one might say, the style of its expression. Except that I'm also tempted to say that style, for Nietzsche, is exuberance (though not the other way round).

Style, rightly represented as in some sense the heart of

Nietzsche's 'new' values, should also be conceived as the expression of exuberance. Style is not just a way of 'dressing' oneself, a way of 'coming on'. It reflects an essential 'inner' drive, sometimes expressed by Nietzsche in terms of the instincts, an obvious carry-over of Schopenhauer's biologism (but without the metaphysical baggage of 'the Will'). Thus the metaphors of 'depth' that permeate Nietzsche's writings (that is, when he is not being sarcastic, referring to a phony profundity), and the virtue of playfulness, which should not be understood in the current rather anaemic sense of intellectual self-indulgence (hardly unknown in Nietzsche) but in terms of the rich, buoyant enthusiasm of a child. (The child metaphor in Zarathustra's 'Three Metamorphoses', I would suggest, represents not so much newness as this exuberant playfulness. Nietzsche was not a fan of innocence as such.) Style, on Nietzsche's account, involves careful cultivation and experience (although, in some sense, it is the development or realisation of an already existing inner template of the virtues).

Aestheticism is a virtue that is certainly most pronounced in Nietzsche's early works, but I think that it would be a mistake to conclude (with Nietzsche, in one of his [unpublished] prefaces to *HATH*, in 1886) that he rejected this perspective (along with metaphysics). What he rejected, I believe, was Schopenhauer's pessimism, and along with this his metaphysics of the Will (obviously, incompletely) and his view that art provides a unique escape from the meaninglessness of life. But the ideal of beauty is one that Nietzsche (like Plato) held on to far more obstinately than most philosophers. He talks about beauty (and its antithesis, the ugly) in all sorts of different ways. Indeed, one would not go wrong in suggesting that it remains one of the primary non-moral evaluative categories of his philosophy. But aestheticism, too, requires cultivation and experience. Nietzsche continually praises the aesthetic virtues of refinement and taste (and uses startling metaphors to suggest their absence). To see the world as beautiful, despite suffering, even because of suffering, remains one of his explicit aspirations throughout his philosophy. His attack on Socrates as 'ugly', by contrast, goes hand in hand with Socrates' attempted 'escape' through reason.

Finally, it is worth at least a note to point out Nietzsche's repeated emphasis on solitude (and not only by way of Zarathustra's example). The virtues are often conceived (e.g., by Aristotle, Hume and MacIntyre) as social functions. In Nietzsche, I want to suggest, they are better understood in an extremely individual context. Indeed, many of his traditional virtues (e.g., courtesy) rather painfully reflect the *necessity* of acting properly in the presence of other people. Most of Nietzsche's distinctive virtues, by contrast, are exemplified in solitude, and, sometimes, only in solitude. This is true, I would suggest, even of virtues that might more usually be taken as obviously social virtues. The image of a dancing Zarathustra, for example, is not set in a ballroom. The virtues exemplified by dancing are, to the contrary, very much the virtues of a hermit, dancing alone. (Of course, it is not clear that Zarathustra ever actually dances. He rather praises dancing, talks about dancing, and 'walks like a dancer'. Nevertheless, one can safely assume that, were he to dance, he would not be dancing the tango.)

It is, perhaps, one of the most personally troublesome problems of Nietzsche's philosophy, this continuous suggestion (and sometimes more than that) of a deep misanthropy. 'Hatred' of humanity and being 'weary of man' are not only *other* people's symptoms of decadence and sickness. Nietzsche betrays them all too frequently. But, then, his account of the virtues, like his example, Zarathustra, shows an uncomfortable bias towards the solitary. Perhaps this is what appeals to a good many of Nietzsche's most admiring followers, but I hesitate to follow them. 'Herd'-like behaviour is possible in isolated individuals as well as in mobs and what are usually called (in non-Nietzschean contexts) 'communities'. Indeed, that is where it becomes least a virtue, free of what Nietzsche sometimes refers to as custom and tradition, free, in other words, to follow a path that is least one's own under the illusion that one is following nothing but 'oneself'.

Finally, there are the problematic virtues. The problem is not their frequency of mention in Nietzsche but their status as virtues, for various reasons:

HEALTH
STRENGTH
'PRESENCE'
'THE FEMININE'
'HARDNESS'
EGOISM
EXISTENTIALISM

Health, of course, is one of the pervasive themes of Nietzsche's philosophy (not to mention his personal life). The question, of course, is whether good health can sensibly be called a virtue. (I take it that this question turns, in part, on the degree to which one believes that he or she is responsible for one's good health, and, even then, the health itself might well be understood as the result of certain virtues rather than constitutive of them.) Strength, too, is a pervasive theme, but the same sorts of questions apply. This is made more confused, of course, by some of Nietzsche's comments about 'natural' strength, as in his brilliant but discomforting lambs and eagles parable in the *Genealogy*. And then there are Nietzsche's obsessive references to the will to power. It is not at all clear to what extent strength and the will to power are correlated, and Nietzsche presents all sorts of conflicting views about this. His suggestion that 'increase in power' is the ultimate motivation (for all things, not to mention his sometimes quoted note to the effect that everything is *nothing but* the will to power) makes it somewhat unclear to what extent we are talking about a state of character in any sense. Nevertheless, if strength is taken to be a virtue (and we have not even broached the question, what is strength?), it is clear enough why Nietzsche would take it to be such, given his repeated accusations of 'weakness' in virtually everything he opposes. The contrast to Christianity ('the meek shall inherit the earth') is obvious, but the virtue of strength presents us with far more problems than answers.

'Presence', of course, makes no sense except as an interpersonal phenomenon.[54] (Nietzsche is certainly not consistent in this.) But he does seem to admire those with that *je'ne sais qua* that we all recognise in certain people who command (not just 'attract') attention. He suggests that Zarathustra has it, despite his failure to command much attention on his entrance to the marketplace. Goethe certainly had it, but here, again, there are difficult questions about whether or not 'presence' can be cultivated and, before that, a more basic reopening of the question, what is a virtue? Indeed, if health, strength and presence are considered virtues (and not just 'excellences') then perhaps the whole discussion of the virtues, as carried on since Aristotle, has to be reconsidered.

The idea of 'the feminine' as a virtue involves much more discussion than I can possibly afford here, but it is a suggestion that I think is often overshadowed by the (unfortunate) emphasis on Nietzsche's well-known misogynist comments. His 'hardness', too, is, I think, typically misunderstood, typically as part of his dubious campaign against compassion and pity (*Midleid*). I think a better interpretation would involve only Nietzsche's exaggerated (but not unGerman) emphasis on self-discipline. (A Buddhist proverb: "if a man were to conquer in battle a thousand times a thousand men, and another conquer one, himself, he indeed is the greatest of conquerors". *Dhammapada*.[55]) Egoism, too, is a theme that requires a

[54] cf Robert Nozick on people with an 'aura' (emphatically not the New Age sense) in his *Philosophical Explanations* (Cambridge, MA: Harvard University Press, 1981).

[55] Quoted in Freny Mistry, *Nietzsche and Buddhism* (Berlin: De Gruyter, 1981), p. 3.

long discussion. Suffice it to say that, for Nietzsche, it is not a vice but a virtue, but it must be egoism properly understood, not 'selfishness'[56] and not mere self-aggrandisement. 'Existentialism', finally, refers to the complex sense in which Nietzsche properly belongs to that group of philosophers with whom he so often taught, for whom non-self-deceptive individual choice is an essential ingredient in 'authentic' existence. But Nietzsche expresses more than his share of skepticism about many of the conceptual presuppositions of autonomy and free choice, not to mention the complications he adds to the idea of self-deception. How this important conflict can be resolved must, again, wait for a more protracted study, as must the further elaboration of the theses suggested here.[57]

---

[56] As in Ayn Rand's derivative 'virtue of selfishness' (in *The Virtue of Selfishness*, New York: American Library, 1964).

[57] This piece will appear in slightly different form in a book edited by Richard Schacht, also for Cambridge University Press, of essays on Nietzsche for Nietzsche's 150th birthday.

Bolzano, Brentano and Meinong: Three Austrian Realists

PETER SIMONS

Rudolf Haller zur Emeritierung in Freundschaft gewidmet

Introduction

The architect and publicist of the Vienna Circle Otto Neurath pointed out in the 1930s that the course taken by philosophy in the Habsburg Empire and the rump Republic of Austria differed markedly from that in the rest of the German-speaking world. Philosophy in Austria had, as he put it, spared itself the Kantian interlude. Until the temporary extinction of Austria in 1938 her philosophers, like her artists, musicians and writers, produced a disproportionately large amount of high quality creations. In philosophy this work was characterised by a rejection of all forms of idealism, an emphasis on psychological and linguistic analysis, respect for empirical science, a general mistrust of philosophical speculation, and stylistically by an eschewal of profound-sounding obscurity in favour of plain clarity of exposition and thought. Neurath's thesis was seconded and extended by Rudolf Haller, so that Barry Smith has termed the thesis of the distinctness of Austrian against German philosophy the Neurath–Haller Thesis.

In the late 1920s Gilbert Ryle offered a lecture course at Oxford University entitled 'Bolzano, Brentano, Meinong and Husserl: Four Austrian Realists'. The course was soon dubbed 'Ryle's three Austrian mountain railway stations and a parlour game', or just 'The Mountain Railway'. Ryle rightly identified the anti-Kantian realism of these thinkers as an important common feature, though Husserl, the naturalised Prussian, was less unwavering than the

This is not a paper with scholarly footnotes so I must thank those from whose knowledge I have gratefully profited over the years and which is summarised here. They are Wilhelm Baumgartner, Jan Berg, Johannes Brandl, Roderick Chisholm, Evelyn Dölling, Reinhard Fabian, Reinhard Grossmann, Rudolf Haller, Wolfgang Künne, Wolfe Mays, Edgar Morscher, Kevin Mulligan, Dieter Münch, Richard Routley, and Barry Smith. I also thank Anthony O'Hear for inviting me to give the view from the Danube.

others. This paper offers picture postcard views of the three unequivocally Austrian stops on the railway. Each of the philosophers I shall mention more than merits a paper to himself, but it is gratifying that it is now widely recognised that special mention should be made of the 'other Austrians' (other than Wittgenstein, that is). Of German-language philosophers other than Frege, these three come closest to being 'analytic' in their approach, whether the analysis is logico-semantic (as in Bolzano) or predominantly psychological (as in Brentano and Meinong).

For each philosopher I shall first give a little biography, as they all had interesting lives, then say something about their main views and contributions to philosophy as I see them. I add a brief personal evaluation of their prospects and relative merits. This is followed by a chronology and a select bibliography for each of the three. My chief aim is to encourage anyone whose interest is aroused in any of the three philosophers to go and look at their work, even if you do not read German: the rewards are well worth the trouble.

Bernard Bolzano (1781–1848)

Bernard Bolzano was born in Prague in the year Kant's first *Critique* was published, and he died there in the revolutionary year, which also saw the birth of the great logician Frege. Comparisons with Kant and Frege could cover a fair part of Bolzano's philosophy, since many of his views are reactions to (mainly against) Kant, while the positions he adopted are often uncannily similar to those of Frege, more than half a century later.

Bolzano was the son of an art dealer whose parents had emigrated from Como to Prague. His native language was German. He attended school and university in Prague and showed early all-round brilliance, but opted, against the wishes of his family, to train as a Roman Catholic priest. He was at first plagued by religious doubts, but persuaded himself of the worth and truth of Catholicism by an ethical argument.

Despite his personal mildness, Bolzano's firmly held beliefs made him a figure of political controversy. In the 1800s the Holy Roman Emperor Francis II (soon plain Emperor Francis I of Austria) was alarmed by the revolutionary ideas emanating from France, and to help contain these he instituted in the Austrian universities special catechistic chairs whose holders were to help turn out right-thinking Christians and obedient citizens. The chair in Prague went, not without opposition, to the young Bolzano, in the same few weeks in 1805 in which he obtained his doctorate and took higher orders.

The chair, later made a professorship, required the incumbent not only to teach theology and other subjects, but also every Sunday and holiday to deliver a sermon or exhortation to the compulsorily assembled students of the university. Bolzano's exhortations were meticulously prepared and soon very popular, as they were politically, socially and racially liberal and tolerant, quite the opposite of what the court and church expected and wanted.

Bolzano's early writings are mainly on the foundations of mathematics. The most notable is an 1817 essay on the intermediate value theorem, *Purely analytical proof of the theorem that between any two values which have opposite results there lies at least one root of the equation.* Bolzano insisted that number theory and analysis needed to be purged of all alien concepts such as those of space, motion and change, and that proofs in mathematics should be logically rigorous. He was the first to insist on this and his work set the tone for developments from Cauchy to Frege.

Bolzano's heavy teaching duties, his conscientiousness and frequent poor health combined to ensure that he published little else in this period beyond a selection of his sermons. But his religious and political views were finding enemies. Bolzano's ethics were utilitarian, developed, surprisingly, without acquaintance with the British sources. He based his argument for religion, in particular Christian religion, and in particular Roman Catholicism, on the argument that belief in the doctrines and practice of the principles of that church were more conducive to the general good than any other set of beliefs concerned with ultimate things.

Bolzano's views did not fit with the restorative and repressive spirit of Metternichian Austria, and his criticism of and refusal to use the prescribed theology textbook by one Jacob Frint proved a mistake, for Frint had influential friends at the Imperial Court. In 1819 Bolzano was summarily dismissed from his position and forbidden to publish. An internal church investigation of Bolzano's doctrines, the 'Bolzano Trial', dragged on for six years. He was eventually cleared of charges of heresy but could neither teach nor preach nor celebrate mass. This political and religious persecution turned out to be in part a blessing, because it gave him at last the time for research, without which we would not have the great works he produced. It did mean though that he had little chance to exercise direct influence on the thought of his time: his views were published anonymously or under the names of his pupils.

Bolzano did not suffer personally: an extremely ascetic person, his needs were modest, and he spent the rest of his life living either with his brother, a Prague merchant, or with the family of Anne Hoffman, a friend and admirer with a house in the country where

Bolzano spent his summers. In the 1830s censorship restrictions were relaxed and Bolzano was allowed to publish works without political content. In 1834 there appeared the four-volume *Textbook of the Science of Religion* and in 1837, also in four volumes, Bolzano's justly most famous work *Theory of Science*, which, despite its title, is a comprehensive and radically reforming treatise on logic. Bolzano's last years were spent working again on the philosophy of mathematics, but the major work *The Theory of Magnitude* was unfinished at his death. Bolzano lived to see and welcome the liberal revolution of 1848, and he intervened publicly for calm. After his death a short book of excerpts from his philosophy of mathematics appeared under the title *The Paradoxes of the Infinite*. Unlike his blockbuster treatises (which even Bolzano admitted were too long for most readers) this was widely read and influential, contributing via Dedekind and Cantor to the beginnings of set theory.

After his death Bolzano's extensive *Nachlass* went to his former pupil Robert Zimmermann, Professor of Philosophy in Vienna, but Zimmermann had turned away from Bolzano's ideas and did nothing with them; they remained buried among his own papers until he died in 1898. Thus the opportunity was lost to make Bolzano posthumously as influential as he deserved to be. Various efforts to publish Bolzano's literary remains and re-edit his works were made from the 1890s onwards, and in the 1930s several pieces appeared in Prague, including the broadly communist utopia *On the Best State*. It was not until the 1970s that plans for a *Complete Edition* got under way. This edition is now about half-way through and its editor-in-chief Jan Berg estimates that all being well it will be completed between 2030 and 2050. From this fact we may gain some impression of Bolzano's fecundity.

Bolzano's philosophy is notable for its clarity and for his reliance on logical argument. This, his monadological metaphysics and his many-sidedness helped to earn him his sobriquet of 'the Bohemian Leibniz'. Bolzano's stalking horse was Kant, whom he respected as an important philosopher but with whom he disagreed on many fundamental matters. A follower, Franz Přihonský, collected his critical discussions of Kant into a volume entitled *New Anti-Kant*. So Neurath's epithet about Austrian philosophy being spared Kant is wrong: Bolzano took Kant very seriously, but disagreed with him.

The most characteristic doctrine of Bolzano's philosophy is his semantic Platonism, which anticipates that of Frege. Bolzano distinguished mental judgements and linguistic sentences (*Sätze*) from what he called *Sätze an sich*, which I shall call 'propositions'. Likewise he distinguished mental ideas (*Vorstellungen*) and linguistic names from *Vorstellungen an sich*, which I shall call 'concepts'. The *an sich* entities, propositions and concepts, are abstract and timeless: they are the meanings of linguistic expressions and the contents of significative mental acts. Bolzano had an argument against scepticism which he thought proved the existence of true propositions. Suppose there were no truths. Then the proposition that there are no truths would be a truth, so by *reductio* there is at least one truth. Since any proposition p is distinct from (though equivalent to) the proposition that it is true that p, it follows for Bolzano that there are infinitely many truths, and these are all abstract propositions (in themselves). Some years later Dedekind produced a similar (and similarly flawed) argument to try and show the existence of an infinite set. It is important that for Bolzano false propositions have the same ontological status as true ones, and objectless concepts have the same status as concepts under which objects fall.

This Third Realm of the in-itself is brilliantly wielded by Bolzano to define and explain truth and falsity, logical truth and logical falsity, logical consequence, compatibility, derivability, analyticity, logical analyticity, probability, degrees of derivability and probabilistic inference. His definition of logical consequence differs little from that of Tarski, which it anticipated by about a century, and his theory of logical truth anticipates that of Quine. In logic it seems to have been Bolzano's fate to have invented wheels that others more famously reinvented after him. Had his views been widely known and available in readable texts in or shortly after his lifetime, I estimate that the advance of logic would have been accelerated by at least thirty, perhaps even fifty years. Where he falls short of Frege is that he does not have the concept of a formal system, where axioms are laid down and theorems follow by precisely defined syntactic rules of inference. Bolzano on the other hand prefers to work throughout with semantic concepts. The most important of these is the idea of *variation*. If we take a proposition and consider some logical part of it, whether a concept or another proposition, then we can consider what happens when we allow this part to vary and consider the range of its possible variants. For example if we take the proposition *John loves Mary* then we could replace *John* by *Fred, Harry, Elisabeth* etc., usually providing only that the name replacing *John* always denotes, and consider various properties of the class of variants so obtained. It is amazing how many different logico-semantic concepts Bolzano can define using this one idea. In one respect though he remains old-fashioned and Leibnizian, namely in his affection for the subject–predicate form of propositions. The basic form of proposition for Bolzano is *A has b,*

Peter Simons

where *A* is the subject-concept and *b* is an abstract name for a predicate-concept, e.g., instead of *This is red* he would say *This has redness*. He even thought that every proposition could be tortured into this form. Our recent relational example would be *John has love for Mary*. Two philosophically interesting concepts are truth and existence. For *It is true that it rains in Spain* Bolzano has *The proposition that it rains in Spain has truth* and for *Tigers exist* he has *The concept of tiger has objectuality,* meaning that at least one thing falls under it. The latter analysis will evoke memories of Kant and Frege: like them Bolzano considers existence a second-level concept. Even non-existence has subject–predicate form: *There are no unicorns* becomes *The concept of unicorn has objectlessness.*

Metaphysically Bolzano was an atomist and monadist, his monads, unlike those of Leibniz, having a physical location. Taking the idea of atoms as physical points seriously led him into an odd theory of contact. At a point on its surface a physical body may have an atom (and so be closed there) or lack an atom (or be open there). Consider now two non-overlapping bodies in contact at a certain point. If they were both open there they would fail to be in contact there, since there would be a spatial point between them that neither occupies. If they were both closed there they could not be in contact without sharing a point, in which case they would overlap. Hence contact can only take place where one body is open and the other is closed. Bolzano's chief metaphysical work was *Athanasia, or Reasons for the Immortality of the Soul*. Here he took the standard view that the soul is a monad and hence indestructible. The book contains an ontology of substance and accidents, which he calls *adherences*.

In ethics, Bolzano was a hedonist utilitarian, though without direct knowledge of the British sources: as predecessors he mentions only minor German thinkers. His formulation of the Utility Principle, which he splendidly calls The Supreme Moral Law, is much more precise than anything before Sidgwick, whose views incidentally resemble his in several ways. One formulation is *Do only among all the alternatives available to you that action which most promotes good of the whole, no matter in which parts*. His attempt to prove the principle is less successful, relying on a naive ethical cognitivism and a questionable classification of mental states. But at least he does try to prove it.

Bolzano's philosophy of religion is orthodox in content but novel and argued in form. His cosmological argument for the existence of an unconditionally existing being is in my view logically valid and metaphysically sound, but like other cosmological arguments it is not backed by a convincing proof that the object whose existence is thereby established is God.

In the philosophy of mathematics he has a position close to logicism, and the complex theory of collections (*Inbegriffe*), including numbers as a special abstract kind of collection, served to stimulate the growth of set theory, though it is in many ways much richer than set theory. In other areas such as aesthetics and physics Bolzano showed himself to be never less than well-informed and astute. He was a keen supporter in Prague of the young physicist Christian Doppler, after whom the Doppler Effect is named.

Taken all together Bolzano's achievements mark him in my view as the greatest philosopher of the nineteenth century, bar none. No one else matches his Leibnizian polymathy of such uniformly high quality. Other thinkers of the century were more incisive, e.g., Frege in logic, or more inventive, e.g., Gauss in mathematics, or more revolutionary, e.g., Darwin in biology. But Bolzano has that *balance* and system that constitutes a great synoptic thinker, and his work has a wonderful limpid clarity. He is far from infallible, and he can be at times dully pedantic, but it is nothing less than a scandal that he and his work are still regularly omitted from university courses teaching nineteenth-century philosophy, that so little of his work is translated into English, and that there is no good introductory textbook in any language, even his own.

Franz Brentano (1838–1917)

Franz Brentano was born in the Rhineland into a famous German literary family. After studying at various German universities he completed his doctorate in Berlin and his doctoral dissertation *On the Several Senses of Being in Aristotle* (1862) later became the work which interested the theology student Martin Heidegger in philosophy. Brentano's preoccupation with Aristotle, whom he considered his 'only real teacher', lasted a lifetime. Even the posthumously published *Theory of Categories,* which is quite critical of Aristotle, takes him as its foil.

Following the wishes of his religious mother, Brentano took holy orders. In 1866 he obtained his Habilitation at the University of Würzburg with a written dissertation and a series of theses publicly disputed. The famous fourth thesis states that the true method of philosophy is none other than that of the natural sciences. Brentano's defence of his theses was so impressive that he convinced a casually observing student, Carl Stumpf, to turn to philosophy: Stumpf went on to become an influential philosopher and psychologist in his own right. The dissertation, on a topic set by the examiners, was Schelling's philosophy, no doubt much to

Brentano's chagrin, since he always considered German idealism as a nadir of philosophy.

In his early years Brentano, who was tall, striking and rhetorically gifted, was a rather glamourous representative of the Catholic revival in Germany, regarded by Catholics as their most promising intellectual. His return to Aristotle as a source of inspiration contributed to the growth of neo-scholasticism in Europe. Brentano's post at Würzburg was linked to his religious calling and he was mistrusted by anti-clerical elements. When in 1869–70 it became clear that Pope Pius IX intended to have the First Vatican Council adopt the neo-Ultramontane doctrine of papal infallibility, German bishops opposed to the doctrine got Brentano to write a position paper against it. The opposition was unsuccessful, and this, together with Brentano's own increasing religious doubts, put him in a difficult position, as his reservations began to leak out. Brentano postponed leaving the church until 1873, after the death of his mother, by which time his position in Würzburg had become untenable, as he was now holding his position under false pretences and was mistrusted by the Catholic party as well. He postponed a decision by taking leave and travelling to Britain, whose philosophers he much admired, visiting Herbert Spencer in London. He was working on a large treatise of psychology which he called his 'passport out of Würzburg'. Continuation and completion of this was interrupted by smallpox, from which Brentano spent several months recovering. He was appointed, with the support of Zimmermann and Lotze, to the vacant Chair of Philosophy at the Imperial-Royal capital city, Vienna. In this year, 1874, the first two books of a planned six of *Psychology from an Empirical Standpoint* were published, and secured his international reputation. It was his first, but also his last major book. Brentano plunged into the life of late Habsburg Vienna, was lionized by students and salon hostesses alike. Usually dressed in black despite being no longer a priest, he was an exotic and charismatic figure, and at last his considerable didactic qualities could find a fit audience. The time he gave to his students and the social round kept him from publishing, for which he had in any case little relish. Brentano was, in terms of the talents he fostered and the public response to his teaching, perhaps the most successful philosophy teacher in history. The list of his students reads like a Who's Who of late nineteenth-century Central European philosophy: Anton Marty, Carl Stumpf, Thomas Masaryk, Alexius Meinong, Christian von Ehrenfels, Edmund Husserl and Kasimir Twardowski are the most famous. His lectures on Practical Philosophy regularly overflowed with hundreds of students, for one of whom, the young Sigmund Freud, Brentano found some money by engaging him to translate minor works of John Stuart Mill for Theodor Gomperz's German edition. As well as Masaryk, the founder of Czechoslovakia, the ranks of Brentano's students also included a later German Chancellor, Count Georg von Hertling.

In 1880 Brentano fell in love with Ida Lieben, and proposed marriage. An Austrian law seemed to forbid ex-priests from marrying. The case was not legally clear, but to save time and effort Brentano resigned his post, which required him to be an Austrian citizen, travelled with his bride to Leipzig, took Saxon citizenship, married, and returned, fully expecting reinstatement. But his act had displeased the Emperor Francis Joseph, who refused to sign. Thereafter, despite annual unanimous petitions by the Philosophical Faculty in Vienna, Brentano was to remain mere *Privatdozent* with no salaried position. He held out for fifteen years, but after the death of his wife he bitterly quit Austria for Florence. As had happened with Bolzano, the pettiness, short-sightedness and rigidity of the Court resulted in Austria being deprived of the talents of a great philosopher. Although as a teacher Brentano enjoyed a continuing popularity, now spiced with scandal, he was debarred from supervising dissertations and of exercising the administrative power he would have liked to wield for the advancement of philosophy. This may not have been such a bad thing, as his correspondence with Marty shows him to have been partial and opinionated, so he might well have been, as Rudolf Haller once suggested to me, 'a terrible tyrant'.

Brentano's first marriage produced a son Johann, known in the family as Gio, who became a lecturer in chemistry at Manchester and later professor in New York, where he was known as John. It was through Gio, now buried with his father in the family grave in Aschaffenburg, that Brentano's papers came to America, where they now repose in the Houghton Library in Harvard under the control of the Franz Brentano Foundation, whose President is the foremost living Brentano specialist Roderick M. Chisholm.

Brentano's eyesight deteriorated and he was left blind after unsuccessful cataract operations in 1903. His last works were all dictated. He left Italy in 1915 as war with Austria became probable, and like Lenin he settled in Zurich, where unlike Lenin he died in 1917. His writings were edited by two former students of Marty from Prague, Oskar Kraus and Alfred Kastil. Their devotion to Brentano and his ideas was fanatically intolerant, but they laid the foundations for the wide range of Brentano's works now available, helped until 1938 by generous grants from the Czechoslovak state.

By now over twenty books by Brentano have been published in

Peter Simons

German, and the editors have done sterling work in getting the manuscripts into publishable form. Nevertheless the state of some of Brentano's published and unpublished works is, by the high standards of international textual scholarship, frankly rather a mess. It bears a similarity to the situation of Wittgenstein, which is, I believe, not accidental. Brentano recognised his own inability to turn his best thoughts into books and was happy to delegate the task to others, commending to his followers the creative editing of Bentham's works as a model of how to proceed. This involved making compilations on a topic from different sets of notes and dictations, often of different periods and with inconsistencies, and presenting the whole as if it were a treatise by the master. The Bentham–Brentano model must have been impressed on the young Brentanian Rush Rhees when he visited Kastil in Innsbruck in the early 1930s, and probably influenced the manner of dealing with Wittgenstein's literary remains.

Although Brentano generally regarded himself as at heart a metaphysician, his work then and subsequently has always been dominated by the *Psychology*. He is rightly celebrated as the person who reintroduced the Aristotelian–Scholastic notion of *intentio* back into the study of the mind. Brentano's inspiration was Aristotle's theory of perception in *De anima*, though his terminology of intentional inexistence was medieval. For the history of the work and its position in his output may I refer to my Introduction to the reprinted English translation. Alongside Aristotle the work shows influences of Descartes, Comte and the British empiricists. The theory of intentionality presented in the *Psychology* is much less modern and less plausible than almost all recent commentary would have it, and was in any case not where Brentano's main interest lay. Intentionality simply served to demarcate mental phenomena from physical, in Book One, but the main aim was a classification of the mental, outlined in Book Two. Books Three to Five were to have dealt in detail with the three main classes of presentations, judgements and feelings, with the final book considering the metaphysics: mind–body and the immortality of the soul. Brentano's shifting views, recently documented in English with Benito Müller's translation of *Descriptive Psychology,* a work from the transitional 1890s, made the original plan obsolete. The role of an *a priori,* philosophical or descriptive psychology, methodologically prior to empirical–experimental genetic psychology, foreshadowed and influenced Husserl's notion of phenomenology, and Brentano's Comtean methodological *epochē* of desisting from controversial metaphysical statements in favour of an examination of the phenomena likewise presaged Husserl's more ponderous phenomenological reductions.

Bolzano, Brentano and Meinong: Three Austrian Realists

Brentano's other work covers most areas of philosophy, notably ethics, where he upheld a form of *a priori* intuitionism much admired by G. E. Moore, the philosophy of religion, metaphysics, philosophy of language, deductive and inductive logic, and the history of philosophy. I shall mention just two areas. In his logic lectures from 1866 onwards (a compilation published 1956) Brentano rejected the subject-predicate analysis of simple judgements and proposed instead (for which he apparently secured written assent from Mill) that all judgements are logical compounds of positive and negative existential judgements. For example the universal judgement *All men are mortal* becomes the negative existential *There are no immortal men.* On this basis Brentano radically simplified the inference rules of deductive logic. While unlike de Morgan, Frege and others he does not go beyond logic's traditional scope by recognising relations, within its bounds his reformed-term logic is simple, elegant and easily teachable. Some of his ideas in logic influenced the young Husserl. Unfortunately Brentano took against mathematical logic, which he wrongly associated exclusively with Hamilton's confused doctrine of the quantification of the predicate. His inductive logic, which takes up by far the greater part of his logic lectures, remains unresearched to this day.

In the history of philosophy Brentano propounded an interesting theory of the development of philosophy (1894). Unlike all others, it is cyclical, with philosophy going through four phases of advance and decline, from (1) a high theoretical phase, descending through (2) a practical, (3) a sceptical and finally (4) a mystical–dogmatic phase, to rise again like a phoenix with a new theoretical phase. The cycle had been around three times up until the nineteenth century, and Brentano obviously saw himself as spearheading a new fourth cycle. His many interesting texts on the history of philosophy take this scheme as their framework. Like all simplifications, it is an inexact fit, and it seems to break down irretrievably in the twentieth-century cacophony.

In his last years Brentano lost none of his intellectual vitality. Whereas in the 1880s and 1890s his views are often fluid and difficult to pin down exactly, with the new century they became more fixed and radical. He upheld a dualist nominalist *reism*, according to which only things exist, there being no properties, relations, states of affairs, events, abstract objects or anything else other than concrete individual things. All doctrines suggesting the contrary are to be demolished by a *Sprachkritik* exposing such talk as fictitious (though often usefully so). The two kinds of simple things or substance are souls and portions of space. All qualitative determinations of substances result in complex things called accidents, which have their substances as their sole parts but which enrich the substances. Alongside this austere ontology Brentano develops interesting and often strikingly modern accounts of predication, continua, truth, fictions, relative determinations and much more.

Brentano's philosophy stands the test of time less well than Bolzano's. His writings are often unclear on and at critical points, and it was perhaps more his rhetorical brilliance, personal charisma and genuine sense of mission which account for his public and professional success than the clarity or soundness of his views. His major pupils all, on maturity, deviated to a greater or lesser extent from his views. Nevertheless he remains one of the outstanding philosophers of the last two hundred years, and an examination of the titles of his major works listed below will show the breadth of his concerns. Like all Austrians, he consciously eschewed 'system', associating it with German idealism, yet his works are more wide-ranging and systematic than he would readily admit.

Alexius Meinong (1853–1920)

Brentano's most wayward and probably least favourite pupil was Alexius Meinong. Born the son of a military administrator, with a brother who later engineered Alpine railways, Meinong was schooled in Vienna and studied history at the university there, first encountering philosophy as a compulsory examination subject. He tried to criticise Kant without using secondary literature: this stubborn independence was to remain his hallmark. Like other bright young men he came to Brentano's notice and fell under his spell, but Brentano's ambition to turn him into a tame historian of philosophy badly misfired, for Meinong was an indifferent historian but a dedicated and independent-minded pursuer of problems. His early studies of Locke and Hume aroused his love for and affinity with British empiricism and prompted his distaste for Kant, a leaning which flew then and afterwards in the face of German philosophical opinion and fashion. In his early writings Meinong pursued ontological themes, espousing a moderate conceptualism about universals and becoming interested in relations.

In 1882 after only four years as a *Privatdozent* in Vienna, Meinong was invited to become *professor extraordinarius* at Graz, where he remained for the rest of his life. An important reason for this voluntary confinement to an Austrian provincial city, despite offers from Kiel and later Vienna, was Meinong's functional blindness from an early age, movingly and at times amusingly recounted in Evelyn Dölling's forthcoming biography. Meinong strove desperately but in vain to conceal his handicap from the world, never wearing spectacles or carrying a stick, fearing quite unreasonably that if discovered he might be dismissed. His students, friends and family (he married in 1882) good-naturedly colluded in the pretence and rarely if ever called it by name; his bulky bearded figure was avoided by the carriage and later car drivers of Graz. He contrived to run until 1916 an experimental psychology laboratory where experiments on vision were conducted. Meinong always delivered his lectures extempore and never travelled to conferences, and his works were written on a specially modified American Remington typewriter obtained via Thomas Masaryk, so his *Nachlass* presented no editorial problems.

Meinong's early work is mainly concerned with psychology, ethics and the theory of value. While still in Vienna he carried out rudimentary experimental demonstrations, paid for out of his own money. Had Brentano still been a professor after 1880 and had he managed to convince the miserly Austrian ministry of education to part with enough money, there is little doubt that Brentano would have founded a psychology laboratory in Vienna to rival that of Wundt in Leipzig. As it was, laboratory and institute had to wait until 1894, when the ministry finally coughed up for Graz, after endless wheedling by Meinong in the excruciatingly tortured officialese that passed (and still passes) for German in Austrian officialdom. By that time Austria had lost the psychology race and Graz was condemned to remain a relative psychological backwater by comparison with Leipzig, Berlin, Würzburg and Cornell. The Graz School of Psychology produced only one experimental psychologist of genius, Vittorio Benussi, the author of the Graz production theory of Gestalt perception. Benussi's nationality impeded his progress: though he eventually founded an Italian school of experimental psychology in Padua, he was depressive and took his own life at an early age. The most talented theoretical psychologist of the school, Stephan Witasek, whom Meinong groomed as his successor, also died as a young man in 1915. Most of Meinong's original apparatus is incidentally still in working order and is proudly preserved by the Psychology Department in Graz.

Among Meinong's own psychological interests were, apart from typological classification (he predictably disagreed with Brentano's taxonomy) such visual phenomena as colour and the rotation of objects, the methodology of measurement in psychology (work which was admired by Russell) and Gestalt qualities, which name was invented by his own friend and former student Christian von Ehrenfels, while Meinong himself preferred the name 'objects of higher order'.

Peter Simons

Meinong's insistent supplications to Vienna resulted in 1897 in the establishment of full degree and postgraduate study in Philosophy and resulting departmental status in Graz: prior to that Philosophy was taught only as a service subject.

Meinong's ethical theory is interesting. As a student in Vienna Meinong heard Carl Menger's first lectures on economic value, and his own ideas were in part an attempt to extend Menger's ideas beyond the economic sphere. Like Brentano he based value theory on psychology, but whereas Brentano placed emotions, desires and volitions in a single class, Meinong did not, and grounded value on feelings alone. Ehrenfels by contrast preferred desires as his psychological basis. Ehrenfels wrote a large book on value theory and ethics, a reaction to Meinong's early Vienna lectures, preceding Meinong's own *Psychological-Ethical Studies in Value Theory* of 1897. The debate between Meinong and Ehrenfels on the question of the basis of valuing is uncharacteristic of its time and country in its constructive good humour. This early work is largely subjectivistic, but Meinong leaned increasingly towards value-realism, and by the end of his life, supported by his reflections on the war, Meinong espoused objectively real or *unpersonal* values in two ontological classes, dignitatives and desideratives, towards which our subjective attitudes of feeling and wanting respectively are directed as external objects. Meinong continued to write on the philosophy of value until his death; a new large ethics book was largely complete and appeared in 1921. His preoccupation with the laws of valuation led in 1926 to the first attempt at a deontic logic by his student and successor Ernst Mally.

Meinong accepted Brentano's thesis of the intentionality of the mental but modified it in a realistic direction, distinguishing, like Twardowski, between the content and object of a mental act; indeed this distinction had been pointed out in 1890 by Meinong and Höfler as an ambiguity in the notion of *object*. Like Twardowski and unlike Husserl, Meinong regarded it as necessary that a mental act of whatever kind always have an object as well as a content, and in those cases where nothing exists which is targeted by the act, Meinong followed Twardowski in accepting a non-existent item as the object. It is from this use of the accusative term 'object [sc. of an act]' that Meinong derives the term 'theory of objects' which he preferred to such – as he thought, existentially loaded – terms as 'metaphysics' and 'ontology'. Both of these, and especially the former, suffered from a prejudice, rampant among materialists and nominalists, but present to some degree in most philosophers, the 'prejudice in favour of the actual', i.e., an unsupported preference for the spatiotemporally situated or real object.

Bolzano, Brentano and Meinong: Three Austrian Realists

Ontological questions always interested Meinong, from his early preoccupation with universals, especially relations, through his interest in Gestalt or higher-order objects and complexes. But object theory as a distinct discipline and forming the nucleus of his philosophical endeavour dominate only late in his career, from about 1899 until his death in 1920.

The first major work in object theory, initially prompted by considerations of the psychology of play and make-believe, is *On Assumptions* of 1902. What Meinong calls an assumption is roughly any intellectual act regarding what might be the case (nowadays called a 'propositional attitude') that falls short of a firm conviction or judgement. Only while working on this area did Meinong realise that he needed an ontology of the *objects* of assumptions and judgements, which objects he called *objectives,* preferring not to use Stumpfs term *Sachverhalt* (state of affairs), which he thought was loaded in favour of the true. Objectives combine some of the behaviour of propositions and other characteristics of states of affairs. Like propositions, they are there for all judgements and assumptions, including false ones, but like states of affairs their existential status is different for truth than for falsity: the objective of a true judgement or assumption, while not spatiotemporally real, still *subsists* or obtains (*besteht*), while the objective of a false judgement or assumption does not even have this kind of being.

The property of objectives corresponding to the truth of judgements Meinong calls *factuality*, the property corresponding to falsity *unfactuality*. He reserves 'true' for objectives which are both factual and apprehended by someone; 'false' is similarly restricted. For an objective, to be factual is to subsist, to be unfactual is to not subsist: there is an existential distinction between them. Objectives about an object do not have that entity as part, for an objective can at best subsist, whereas many objects can also be spatiotemporally actual or real. If *Graz is in Austria* had Graz as part, then it would be a subsistent with a real part, and if *Sherlock Holmes is not real* had Sherlock Holmes as part, it would have an object as part which does not exist at all. Both cases are absurd, thinks Meinong, so what an objective is about is not part of it.

Object theory received its programmatic statement in the 1904 essay 'The Theory of Objects'. This appeared in a volume by the Graz School commemorating ten years of the Psychology Laboratory and contained essays on object theory by Rudolf Ameseder and Ernst Mally. Meinong's earlier work was enthusiastically reviewed by Russell in a three-part article for *Mind,* a journal which Meinong himself had regularly reviewed for German speakers in the 1880s. Russell had presumably hoped that

Peter Simons

Meinong's theory of impossible objects would offer some help on the solution of the logical paradoxes, but he was disappointed there. It was Meinong's painstaking method that Russell admired. Russell could not accept non-existent objects like the round square, or unfactual objectives: he avoided them initially by adopting Frege's distinction between sense and reference for definite descriptions, and saying that false propositions do exist. (Russell wrongly identified Meinong's objectives with his and Moore's propositions.) In 1905 Russell rejected Frege too: 'On denoting' is a battle on two fronts, one against non-existent objects, one against sense. Russell's initial sympathy gave way to increasing criticism of Meinong, whom he accused (wrongly) of believing in contradictions. Although the dismissal of Meinong in *Introduction to Mathematical Philosophy* is curt and unfair, in the unpublished 1913 manuscript *Theory of Knowledge* Russell still discussed Meinong's views extensively, accurately and with some sympathy.

Through Russell, some ideas of Meinong became well known in the English speaking world and through the efforts of Findlay, Chisholm and others it has gradually become possible to get a fair picture of object theory, its strengths and weaknesses. Meinong's work is the best documented in English of our three Austrian realists. *On Assumptions* and *On Emotional Presentation*, where Meinong discusses paradoxical objects like Russell's set, have been translated. Findlay's commentary, based on a 1933 dissertation completed with guidance from Mally in Graz, is one of the finest commentaries of one philosopher on another that there is. It accurately summarises and compresses Meinong's often long-winded prose. Meinong's punctiliousness and his refusal to be hurried have been compared more than once with similar characteristics in G. E. Moore.

Of Meinong's lesser-known works one may mention his generally neglected epistemology, which with its theory of conjectural evidence and his assertion that the existence of the world is not logically but conjecturally certain, deserves more than a cursory glance. A mere curiosity, on the other hand, is his attempt to give an *a priori* proof of universal causality.

His most unfortunately neglected work is also his longest and perhaps his best. *On Possibility and Probability*, over 700 pages, was published in 1915 with support from the Austrian Academy of Sciences, who had elected Meinong as a member. Meinong understands the term 'probability', like 'truth', as a partly epistemological notion, and the second half of the book investigates the phenomenology and laws of our experiences of estimating, surmising, and inducing. The ontological aspect Meinong calls 'possibility', and he distinguishes between straightforward or ungraded possibility, which he calls 'unincreasable', and graded or 'increasable' possibility, which is another name for objective probability. An objective is ungradedly possible if it has a probability greater than 0. Though inconsistent in detail, Meinong's theory of modality is an attractive realistic alternative to possible world theories.

Between objectives which are factual (degree of possibility = 1) and those which are unfactual (degree of possibility = 0) Meinong now interpolates those with intermediate degrees of possibility, which he calls *subfactual*. Since all actually existing objects are fully determinate, all objectives about them have possibility either 1 or 0, so the subjects of subfactual objectives have to be *incomplete* non-existent objects. The degree of possibility of a subfactual objective about an incomplete object is determined by the statistics of real, complete objects in which the incomplete object is *implected*, that is, which have all the characteristics of the incomplete one (and more of their own besides). Suppose that 27% of all hotels in England have a TV in every room. Then the objective *The English hotel has a TV in every room* is subfactual with a degree of possibility of 0·27. Probability applies to real, complete objects via that applying to incomplete objects implected in them. Necessity on the other hand is not a kind of superfactuality or heightened factuality, but occurs when the factuality of an objective is part of the inherent nature of its subject. Meinong says that necessity is *inhesive* factuality, contingency is inhesive subfactuality and impossibility is inhesive unfactuality. He believes that no real object exists of necessity. There is no mention of God or Religion in Meinong's philosophy.

Meinong's theory of subfactual objectives embodies many-valued semantics and it is no accident that a visitor to Graz in 1908–9 when Meinong was working on incomplete objects was the young Jan Łukasiewicz, who went on to develop many-valued logic.

Meinong's theory of objects outside being, his most notorious view, is generally rejected, usually with little argument, yet it occupies a novel and cardinal position in the abstract geography of metaphysical theories. The obsessive concentration on inconsistent objects like the round square, stemming from Russell's own obsession with contradiction, has obscured the more undramatic idea of incomplete objects, which can be turned to application not just in theories of modality, but also in fiction, mathematics and perhaps even in the strange world of quantum physics.

Prospects and Evaluation

What does the future hold for the reputations of these three Austrian philosophers? Meinong's works are, barring one or two incidentals, all published and accessible in German, and there is little hidden, although there are areas of his work that need more study from a modern point of view. A biography will appear this year. His position in the philosophy of his time is I think fairly well understood and will not change much.

Because of the intentionality thesis, Brentano's importance is recognised in modern analytic philosophy, and through Chisholm and others he has attracted a fair degree of scholarly interest. But a fully informed evaluation of Brentano will take much longer, because although much of his work is published in German and more is available in English than of the others, because of the state of his *Nachlass* a comprehensive view of his development will take time to emerge: the difficulties of chronicling and assessing his shifts and changes of mind are considerable and many of the texts are unedited. Until this is done, the place and rank of this, the most influential of our three philosophers, will remain only provisionally determined.

Bolzano's work will in due course be wholly accessible in print and should present relatively few problems of interpretation. I foresee a steadily growing reputation, but whether he comes to his just recognition will depend on attracting sufficiently many interested and talented commentators. The most promising centre of Bolzano studies is currently Hamburg, where a number of young enthusiasts have gathered around Wolfgang Künne.

Of the three philosophers I have mentioned, Bolzano is without doubt the most considerable. Meinong's theories are in the end unacceptably extreme and Brentano's work is often unclear in its implications, though both say things which are of much value to present-day discussions. On the other hand, whether one agrees with his semantic Platonism or not, Bolzano's views are up to the highest standards of contemporary discussion and in their clarity above much of it. His correspondence with Ferdinand Exner has been called the first text of modern analytical philosophy. Most work has to date concentrated on his logic and semantics, but his ethics, political philosophy, philosophy of religion and philosophy of mathematics all deserve greater exposure. *The Complete Edition* will serve as a definitive textual basis, but it is very expensive, and we badly need cheap study texts in English and German to complement it, and a good introduction to Bolzano in English. We also need to revise our histories of nineteenth-century philosophy to take adequate account of its greatest representative.

Bolzano Chronology

5 October 1781	Born in Prague as fourth of 12 children
1791–1796	Attendance at Piarist Gymnasium in Prague
1796–1799	Preliminary Study of Philosophy, Mathematics and Physics at Charles University (Prague)
1799–1800	'Year for Thought' Further Mathematics and Physics
1800–1804	Study of Theology at Prague University
1804	*Treatment of Several Subjects of Elementary Geometry*
7 April 1805	Takes Holy Orders
17 April 1805	Doctor of Theology
19 April 1805	Takes Chair of Religious Theory
2 December 1805	**Battle of Austerlitz. Austria defeated by Napoleon**
23 September 1806	Ordinary (Full) Professor
1810	*Contributions to a Better Founded Presentation of Mathematics*
1813	First Book of *Edifying Sermons*
1813–1815	Ill with (non-tubercular) hæmoptysis
1815	Ordinary Member, Royal Bohemian Society of Sciences
1815	**Congress of Vienna and Final Defeat of Napoleon**
1816	*The Binomial Theorem ... More Exactly Proved than Hitherto*
1817	*Purely analytical proof of the theorem that between any two values which have opposite results there lies at least one root of the equation*
1818/1819	Dean of the Faculty of Philosophy
1819	Director, Royal Bohemian Society
1819	**Carlsbad Decrees**
24 December 1819	Dismissal order signed by Emperor
20 January 1820	Dismissal effective
1823	Meets Anna Hoffman
31 December 1825	End of ecclesiastical 'trial'
1827	*Athanasia or Reasons for the Immortality of the Soul* (anonymous)
1830	Moves to Těchobuz to live with Hoffmans
1831	*A suggestion for improving several institutions for the poor*
1834	*Views of a liberal Catholic theologian on the relationship between Church and State*
1834	*Textbook of the Science of Religion* (4 volumes)
1837	*Theory of Science* (4 volumes)
1838	*Athanasia* with author's name
1841	Final illness of Anna Hoffman: return to Prague

Peter Simons

1841–1848	Lives with brother
1843	Director, Royal Bohemian Society
March 1848	**Revolution in Prague**
18 December 1848	Bolzano dies of pneumonic paralysis in Prague
1849	*What is Philosophy?*
1850–1852	*Edifying Sermons* Volumes 2–4
1851	*The Paradoxes of the Infinite*
1914–1915	*Works of Bernard Bolzano* (Höfler) (Vols 1–2 of *Theory of Science* only)
1930	*Theory of Functions*
1931	*Theory of Numbers*
1932	*On the Best State*
1935	*Correspondence with F. Exner*
1969	Vol. 1 *Complete Edition* (Biography by Eduard Winter)
1972	Bibliography and Editorial Principles of *Complete Edition*
1975–	*Introduction to the Theory of Magnitudes* begins *Complete Edition* proper
1991	Founding of Internationale Bernard-Bolzano-Gesellschaft (Salzburg)
1992–	*Beiträge zur Bolzano-Forschung*

Brentano chronology

16 January 1838	Born in Marienberg near Boppard on the Rhine
1838	Father expelled from Prussia, settles in Aschaffenburg, Franconia
1856	Completes schooling at Royal Bavarian Gymnasium
1856–1857	Study in Munich
1858	Study in Würzburg
1858–1859	Study in Berlin (Aristotle under Trendelenburg)
1859–1860	Study in Münster (Medieval Aristotelians under Clemens)
1861	Death of father, Christian Brentano
17 July 1862	Doctor of Philosophy, University of Tübingen (in absentia)
	On the Several Senses of Being in Aristotle
6 August 1864	Ordination
14–15 July 1866	Public defence of *Habilitation* at Würzburg University
1866	**Six Weeks' War between Prussia and Austria**
1867	*The Psychology of Aristotle, in Particular his Theory of nous poietikos*
1869	'Auguste Comte and the Positive Philosophy'

1870	Position paper against papal infallibility
1872	Trip to England, meets Spencer
13 May 1872	Appointment as Extraordinary Professor, Würzburg
24 March 1873	Resigns chair, priesthood and post
11 April 1873	Leaves the church
Summer 1873	Travels in England and France
22 January 1874	Appointment as Ordinary Professor in Vienna
May 1874	*Psychology from an Empirical Standpoint* Books I–II
Summer 1874	Smallpox
1879	*New Puzzles by Aenigmatias*
1880	Resigns professorship
16 September 1880	Marries Ida Lieben in Leipzig
1887	Buys house at Schönbühel an der Donau
1888	Birth of son Johann Christian Michael (Gio, John)
1889	*On the Origins of Ethical Knowledge*
1893	*On the Future of Philosophy*
1894	*The Four Phases of Philosophy and its Present State*
1895	*My Last Wishes for Austria*
April 1895	Moves to Florence
1897	Marries Emilie Ruprecht
1902	English translation of *Origins,* reviewed by Moore
1903	Unsuccessful eye operations leave Brentano blind
1907	*Investigations of Sensory Psychology*
1911	*Aristotle and his World View*
	Aristotle's Theory of the Origin of the Human Mind
	On the Classification of Mental Phenomena (= *Psychology* Book II)
1915	Move to Switzerland
1915	**Italy declares war on Austria**
17 March 1917	Dies in Zurich
1924	*Psychology* 2nd edition
1925	*Essay on Knowledge*
1928	*Sensory and Noetic Consciousness (= Psychology* Book III)
1929	*On the Existence of God*
1930	*Truth and Evidence*
1933	*Theory of Categories*
1952	*Foundation and Construction of Ethics*
	The Turn from the Nonreal
1956	*The Theory of Correct Judgement*
1959	*Foundations of Aesthetics*
1973	English translations of *Psychology, Construction*
1976	*Philosophical Investigations of Space, Time and the Continuum*
1982	*Descriptive Psychology*
1988–	*Brentano Studien*

Peter Simons

Meinong Chronology

17 July 1853	Born in Lvov, sixth child of Major-General Anton Meinong
1862–1870	Student at Vienna Academic Gymnasium
1870	Death of Anton Meinong
1870–1874	Student at the University of Vienna
1874	Meinong meets Brentano
	Doctor of Philosophy, Dissertation *Arnold of Brescia*
1878	*Habilitation* Vienna: *Hume Studies I* (On nominalism)
1878–1882	*Privatdozent,* University of Vienna
1880	First experimental demonstrations in Psychology
1882	Appointed Extraordinary Professor, University of Graz
	Hume Studies II (On relations)
1885	*On Philosophical Science and its Propadeutics* [with Alois Höfler]
1889	Appointed Ordinary Professor, Graz
	Marries Doris Buchholz
1890	*Logic* [co-authored with Höfler]
1894	Founding of Psychology Laboratory in Graz
	Psychologico-Ethical Investigations of Value Theory
1896	'On the Significance of Weber's Law'
1897	Founding of Philosophy Seminar in Graz
1899	'On Objects of Higher Order'
1902	*On Assumptions*
1903	'Comments on the Colour Solid and the Law of Mixtures'
1904–1907	Correspondence with Russell
1904	'The Theory of Objects'
	Russell, 'Meinong's Theory of Complexes and Assumptions'
1906	*On the Experiential Foundations of Our Knowledge*
1910	*On Assumptions* 2nd edition
1911	'For Psychology and Against Psychologism in Value Theory'
1913	*Collected Writings I-II* (edited by his students for his 60th birthday)
1914	Elected Member of the Imperial-Royal Academy of Sciences
	Declines Chair of Philosophy in Vienna
June-August 1914	**Sarajevo Assassinations; First World War begins**
1915	*On Possibility and Probability*
1917	*On Emotional Presentation*
1918	*On the Demonstration of the General Causal Law*

27 November 1920	Dies in Graz
1923	*Foundations of General Value Theory*
1965	*Philosophers' Letters*
1968–1978	*Alexius Meinong Complete Edition*
1999	Biography (Evelyn Dölling)

Annotated Select Bibliography

This is a preliminary guide to the sources and some of the secondary literature. I have divided it by philosopher and type except for the collections at the beginning.

GENERAL WORKS AND COLLECTIONS

Chisholm, R. M., ed., *Realism and the Background of Phenomenology* (Atascadero: Ridgeview Press, 1981). Originally published in 1960, this contains excerpts of Brentano and Meinong with other realists.

Nyiri, J. C., ed., *From Bolzano to Wittgenstein: The Tradition of Austrian Philosophy* (Vienna: Hölder-Pichler-Tempsky, 1986). Covers the Austrian tradition in general.

Simons, P. M. *Philosophy and Logic in Central Europe from Bolzano to Tarski* (Dordrecht: Kluwer, 1992). Several essays on background and our protagonists as well as others.

Smith, B. *Austrian Philosophy: The Legacy of Franz Brentano* (Chicago: Open Court, 1994). Originally separate essays but now smoothed together. The nearest to a monograph. Starts with Brentano.

Bolzano

COMPLETE EDITION

Bernard-Bolzano Gesamtausgabe. Stuttgart: Frommann-Holzboog. Founded by Eduard Winter, current editor-in-chief Jan Berg. There are five series: E: Editorial Principles and Bibliography; 1: Published Works; 2: Posthumous Writings; 3: Correspondence; 4: Documents (Biography, Iconography). Expected date of completion c. 2030. This is the definitive text and is marvellously produced, but it is expensive. The typographical and bracketing system of the *Nachlass* works (2) makes it possible to reconstruct the original text without making the trip to Prague.

INDIVIDUAL WORKS IN MODERN PRINTINGS

Paradoxien des Unendlichen (Hamburg: Meiner, 1975).

Bernard Bolzano's Grundlegung der Logik. Selections by F. Kambartel from *Wissenschaftslehre I–II*. (Hamburg: Meiner, ²1978).

A new selection from the *Wissenschaftslehre* by W. Künne is in preparation, as is a reprint of *Neuer Anti-Kant,* ed. F. Přihonský (St. Augustin: Academia, forthcoming)

ENGLISH TRANSLATIONS

The Paradoxes of the Infinite, trans. D. A. Steele (London: Routledge & Kegan Paul, 1950).

Peter Simons

The Theory of Science, Selected and translated by R. George; (Oxford: Blackwell, 1972).
Theory of Science, Selected and edited by J. Berg, translated by B. Terrell, (Dordrecht: Reidel, 1973).

SECONDARY LITERATURE
Most secondary literature is in German. The only general introduction to Bolzano in English is
Wedberg, A. *A History of Philosophy, vol. III From Bolzano to Wittgenstein* (Oxford: Clarendon, 1984), ch. II.
A very nice general introduction is
J. Berg and E. Morscher, 'Bernard Bolzano – der österreichische Philosoph', in *International Bibliography of Austrian Philosophy for 1974/75* (Amsterdam: Rodopi, 1986), pp. 15–65.
Berg. J., *Bolzanos's logic* (Stockholm: Almqvist & Wiksell, 1962). A classic monograph.
Sebestik, J. *Logique et mathématique chez Bernard Bolzano* (Paris: Vrin, 1992). Very comprehensive.
Philosophia Naturalis, 24, 4 (1987) is devoted to Bolzano. Mixed English and German.
Beiträge zur Bolzano-Forschung (Sankt Augustin: Academia Verlag). This series started in 1992 and in early 1998 numbered 8 small monographs; 2–4 appear annually, mostly in German.

BRENTANO
For reasons explained in the text Brentano's works are editorially complex. There is as yet no Brentano Critical Edition though one is in planning with Meiner Verlag. Correspondence and university lectures on metaphysics will lead the way.

INDIVIDUAL WORKS IN MODERN PRINTING
There are over 20 works, mainly published by Meiner Verlag in their *Philosophische Bibliothek* series. These go back to the work done before the war in Prague and Innsbruck by Kraus and Kastil. Here are some of the most important with dates of the most recent reprints. Unless otherwise stated the imprint is Hamburg: Meiner. Starred works are untranslated, for the others the translations are given below.

Von der mannigfachen Bedeutung des Seienden nach Aristoteles (Hildesheim: Olms, 1984). Brentano's doctoral dissertation, still highly readable.
Die Psychologie des Aristoteles, insbesondere seine Lehre vom nous poietikos (Darmstadt: Wissenschaftliche Buchgesellschaft, 1967). Brentano's *Habilitationsschrift* and the first appearance of intentional inexistence.
Psychologie vom empirischen Standpunkt, 2nd edn, ed. and annotated by O. Kraus, 1973.
Vom sinnlichen und noetischen Bewußtsein, ed. O. Kraus, 1974. Based on material originally intended for Book II of the *Psychologie*.

Deskriptive Psychologie, ed R. M. Chisholm and W. Baumgartner, 1982. Later psychology lectures.

**Untersuchungen zur Sinnespsychologie*, ed. R. M. Chisholm and R. Fabian, 1979.

**Zur Lehre vom richtigen Urteil*, ed. F. Mayer-Hillebrand (Bern: Franke, 1956).

Wahrheit und Evidenz, ed. O. Kraus, 1974. Essays and lectures documenting Brentano's move from a correspondence to an evidence theory of truth.

Vom Ursprung sittlicher Erkenntnis, ed. O. Kraus, 1969. Expanded from a lecture in Vienna, a short statement of Brentano's ethical views, which captured Moore's admiration when first translated in 1902.

Grundlegung und Aufbau der Ethik, ed. F. Mayer-Hillebrand, 1952. Based on Brentano's popular Vienna lecture course on practical philosophy.

Kategorienlehre, ed. A. Kastril, 1974. A compilation of late writings on ontology.

Philosophische Untersuchungen zu Raum, Zeit und Kontinuum, ed. and annotated by A. Kastil, ed. and introduced by S. Korner and R. M. Chisholm, 1976.

**Die vier Phasen der Philosophie und ihr augenblicklicher Stand*, 1968. Brentano's cyclic account of the history of philosophy. Also contains 'Auguste Comte und die positive Philosophie' of 1869.

**Die Abkehr vom Nichtrealen* ed. F. Mayer-Hillebrand, 1977. Papers and correspondence with Anton Marty setting out Brentano's opposition to abstract entities.

Vom Dasein Gottes 1968. Lectures from Würzburg and Vienna 1868–1891. Contains Brentano's proof from design for the existence of God.

**Uber Ernst Machs 'Erkenntnis und Irrtum'*, ed. R. M. Chisholm and J. C. Marek (Amsterdam: Rodopi, 1988). Contains Brentano's dictations and other notes about Mach, and the Brentano–Mach correspondence.

ENGLISH TRANSLATIONS

On the Several Senses of Being in Aristotle, trans. R. George (Berkeley: University of California Press, 1975).

The Psychology of Aristotle, trans. R. George (Berkeley: University of California Press, 1977).

Psychology from an Empirical Standpoint, trans. A. C. Rancurello, D. B. Terrell and L. L. McAlister (London: Routledge, 1995).

Sensory and Noetic Consciousness, trans. L. L. McAlister (London: Routledge & Kegan Paul, 1981).

Descriptive Psychology, trans. B. Müller (London: Routledge, 1995).

The True and the Evident, trans. R. M. Chisholm (London: Routledge & Kegan Paul, 1961).

The Origins of Our Knowledge of Right and Wrong, trans. R. M. Chisholm and E. H. Schneewind (London: Routledge & Kegan Paul, 1969).

The Theories of Categories, trans. R. M. Chisholm and N. Guterman (The Hague: Nijhoff, 1981).

Philosophical Investigations on Space, Time and the Continuum, trans. B. Smith (London: Croom Helm, 1988).

On the Existence of God, trans. S. F. Krantz (The Hague: Nijhoff, 1987).

Peter Simons

SECONDARY LITERATURE
The doyen of Brentano experts and commentators is Roderick Chisholm, who has also been very active in editing and translating.

Chisholm, R. M. *Brentano and Meinong Studies* (Amsterdam: Rodopi).
—— *Brentano on Intrinsic Value* (Cambridge University Press, 1986).

A reliable precis of Brentano's later views by an adherent and editor is:

Kastil, A. *Die Philosophie Franz Brentanos. Eine Einführung in seine Lehre* (Bern: Francke, 1951).

Collections include:
Chisholm, R. M. and Haller, R., eds, *Die Philosophie Franz Brentanos* (Amsterdam: Rodopi, 1978) (= *Grazer Philosophische Studien* 5). Conference papers: mixed English and German.
McAlister, L. L. ed., *The Philosophy of Brentano* (London: Duckworth, 1976). A useful collection including personal reminiscences by Kraus, Stumpf and Husserl.
Brentano Studien is a yearbook first published in 1988. Most articles are in German or English.

Meinong

COMPLETE EDITION
Alexius Meinong Gesamtausgabe, ed. R. Haller, R. Kindiger, R. M. Chisholm and R. Fabian. In seven volumes and an *Ergänzungsband* containing papers from the *Nachlass*. Graz: Akademische Druck- u. Verlagsanstalt, 1968–78.

CORRESPONDENCE
Philosophenbriefe, ed. R. Kindinger. Graz: Akademischer Druck- u. Verlagsanstalt, 1965. A selection of Meinong's correspondence with philosophers including Russell.
Alexius Meinong und Guido Adler: Eine Freundschaft in Briefen, edited and introduced by G. J. Eder (Amsterdam: Rodopi, 1995). The musicologist Adler studied with Meinong in Vienna and they remained friends until Meinong's death: the 266 letters cover the years 1877–1920, filling in much biographical and cultural detail. Astonishingly for us, the two friends always called each other 'Sie'.

MODERN PRINTING
The only pieces of Meinong's work cheaply available are:
Über Gegenstandstheorie – Selbstdarstellung, ed. J. M. Werle (Hamburg; Meiner, 1988). Meinong's 1904 programme for object theory and the little autobiography he wrote in his last year.

ENGLISH TRANSLATION
'The Theory of Objects', in *Realism and the Background of Phenomenolgy*, trans. R. M. Chisholm, pp. 76–117.

On Emotional Presentation, trans. M.-L. Schubert-Kalsi (Evanston: Northwestern University Press, 1972).

On Objects of Higher Order and Husserl's Phenomenology, ed. and trans. M.-L. Schubert-Kalsi (The Hague: Nijhoff, 1978). Contains a translation of the higher-order objects article and Meinong's telegraphic criticisms of Husserl's *Ideas*.

On Assumptions, trans. J. Heanue (Berkeley: University of California Press, 1983).

SECONDARY LITERATURE

Dölling, E. *Wahrheit suchen und Wahrheit bekennen*, Alexius Meinong: *Skizze seines Lebens*. (Amsterdam: Rodopi, forthcoming). Fascinating account of Meinong's life and especially how he coped with blindness.

Findlay, J. N. *Meinong's Theory of Objects and Values* (Oxford: Clarendon Press, 1963). The indispensable guide.

Grossmann, R. *Meinong* (London: Routledge & Kegan Paul, 1974). Stresses the transition from Meinong's early ontological economy to his later big ontology.

Lambert, K. *Meinong and the Principle of Independence* (Cambridge University Press, 1983). Examination by a contemporary logician of the key proposition of object theory that how a thing is is independent of whether it exists.

Lindenfeld, D. *The Transformation of Positivism: Alexius Meinong and European Thought, 1880–1920* (Berkeley: University of California Press). Stresses Meinong's Pan-Germanic political views as well as his general position in the thought of the time.

Russell, B. 'Meinong's Theory of Complexes and Assumptions', in *Essays in Analysis*, ed. D. Lackey (London: Allen & Unwin, 1973), pp. 21–76. Russell's longest, most accurate and most appreciative piece on Meinong, reprinted here with two more critical reviews.

Russell, B. *Introduction to Mathematical Philosophy* (London: Allen & Unwin, 1919).

Russell, B. *Theory of Knowledge. The 1913 manuscript,* ed. E. R. Eames (London: Allen & Unwin, 1984).

Schubert-Kalsi, M.-L. *Meinong's Theory of Knowledge* (Dordrecht: Nijhoff, 1987). Based on her Graz dissertation.

COLLECTIONS

Haller, R., ed. *Jenseits von Sein und Nichstein. Beiträge zur Meinong-Forschung*. Graz: Akademische Druck- u. Verlagsanstalt. A very useful collection, mainly in German. Together with Chisholm, Rudolf Haller has been most instrumental in reviving and reprinting Meinong's writings and bringing them to wider attention.

Haller, R., ed. *Meinong and the Theory of Objects* (Amsterdam: Rodopi, 1995) (= *Grazer Philosophische Studien* 50. Commemorating 20 years of *GPS*, 50 volumes, and 75 years after Meinong's death, the 627 pages contain articles by almost everyone alive having anything to do with Meinong and his ideas. Some German, but now mainly English.

Peter Simons

Bibliography

Psychologie und Philosophie der Grazer Schule, compiled by M. and W. G. Stock, *International Bibliography of Austrian Philosophy* (Amsterdam: Rodopi, 1990). A monster volume of 968 pages on Meinong and his Graz School.

Vorsprung durch Logik: The German Analytic Tradition

HANS-JOHANN GLOCK

Introduction: analytic Germans and surprisingly analytic Germans

Although at present analytic philosophy is practiced mainly in the English-speaking world, it is to a considerable part the invention of German speakers. Its emergence owes much to Russell, Moore, and American Pragmatism, but even more to Frege, Wittgenstein, and the logical positivists of the Vienna Circle. No one would think of analytic philosophy as a specifically Anglophone phenomenon, if the Nazis had not driven many of its pioneers out of central Europe.

So there are analytic Germans. It is nevertheless controversial to speak of a German analytic tradition. For it may seem that Frege, Wittgenstein, and the Vienna Circle stand radically apart from the mainstream of Germanophone philosophy. (Wedberg 1984, chapter I; Coffa 1991, 1–4). In so far as they belong to a tradition at all, the story goes, it is that of anglophone analytic philosophy, which received either these thinkers or at least their ideas with open arms. The German and Austrian origins of Frege, Wittgenstein, and the Vienna Circle are, it appears, merely an unfortunate coincidence, just like the origins of Händel, Freud, Einstein, the House of Windsor, or the christmas tree.

In this paper I want to undermine this image and to make out a tentative case for the existence of a German analytic tradition.[1] I shall argue that, in addition to the analytic Germans, there are the surprisingly analytic Germans, namely Leibniz, Kant, and certain neo-Kantians. Moreover, together with the usual suspects, these form a distinctively analytic tradition within German philosophy. They also form a distinctively German tradition within analytic philosophy, an anti-naturalist input which contrasts sharply with the

---

[1] A different position is held, e.g., by Smith (1994), who contrasts a level-headed Austrian tradition close to British empiricism with an obscurantist German tradition going back to Kant. But even if one leaves aside the close institutional connections between the two academic cultures, the figures of Frege, Carnap, Hempel, and Reichenbach and the important Kantian influences on Wittgenstein's work point in the direction I pursue here.

empiricism that dominates the mainstream of anglophone philosophy.

By German philosophy, I mean Germanophone philosophy, philosophy that was originally published in German. In effect, this is the philosophy of Germany and the Habsburg empire, and, to a lesser degree, of those other parts of northern and central Europe which, till 1945, were academically oriented towards the German-speaking world. By a tradition, I do not mean a self-professed school like the Vienna Circle, or even one identified by adversaries, but a loose and diverse intellectual movement. However, this does not undermine my claim. Even in the English-speaking world, the term 'analytic philosophy' rarely refers to that kind of school. When it caught on – in the fifties – its denotata were already very diverse.

The term 'analytic philosophy' poses greater problems. Some, like Michael Dummett, define analytic philosophy narrowly, by reference to a particular doctrine. In Dummett's case, it is the doctrine that an analysis of thought can and must be given by an analysis of language. But such definitions tend to exclude paradigmatic analytic philosophers. Dummett's own definition, for example, does not fit either Moore or Russell, because it ignores the difference between their projects of logical and conceptual analysis on the one hand, and the linguistic turn inaugurated by Wittgenstein's *Tractatus* on the other (Dummett 1993, chapters 2, 12–13; cp. Sluga 1997, Monk 1997, Hacker 1997, Glock 1997b).

Others, like Føllesdal, define analytic philosophy as a general attitude towards philosophical problems, in his case that of being 'very strongly concerned with argument and justification' (1997, 7). But such definitions tend to make the bulk of philosophy analytic; indeed, they exclude only prophets or sages like Pascal and Nietzsche. Ever since Socrates, the attempt to tackle fundamental questions by way of reasoned argument has been regarded as one of the distinguishing features of philosophy as such, e.g., *vis-à-vis* religion or political rhetoric, not as the hallmark of a particular philosophical movement.

Yet others, like Ray Monk (1997; see also Hacker 1997, 56) take the term 'analytic' literally, namely as referring to a decomposition of complex phenomena into simpler constituents. What distinguishes modern analytic philosophy from the ham-fisted mental analysis of the British empiricists is that it employs sophisticated logical techniques to identify the structures and components of propositions. But although this proposal is more in keeping with the commonly recognised extension of the term 'analytic philosophy' than the previous two, it can be faulted on this count. Both the later Wittgenstein and Oxford linguistic philosophy deny that propositions have ultimate components or even a definite structure; and in theory, although not in practice, the same might be said of Quineans. For Wittgenstein and Oxford philosophy, analysis means the description of the rule-governed use of expressions, and of their connections with other expressions by way of implication, presupposition, and exclusion. Peter Strawson has coined the label 'connective analysis' for this kind of procedure (1992, chapter 2); but as he himself points out, the term 'analysis' is misleading in so far as this procedure is no longer analogous to chemical analysis.

Finally, analytic philosophy can be understood genetically, as a historical sequence of individuals and schools that influenced, and engaged in debate with, each other, without sharing any single doctrine, problem, or method. This is the approach taken by Peter Hacker (1997) and Hans Sluga (1997). Thus Sluga writes:

> Following common practice, I take analytic philosophy here as originating in the work of Frege, Russell, Moore, and Wittgenstein, as encompassing the logical empiricism of the Vienna Circle, English ordinary language philosophy of the post-war period, American mainstream philosophy of recent decades, as well as their worldwide affiliates and descendents. (1997, 16n)

I am sympathetic to this historical conception of analytic philosophy. Moreover, I think that Sluga's list indeed conforms to common practice. But I am keen to add to it those Germanophone influences on Frege, Wittgenstein, and the Vienna Circle which have contributed, however indirectly, to the distinctive analytic tradition that I detect in German philosophy, namely Leibniz, Kant, and some neo-Kantians. For this revisionist purpose, I need to go beyond the historical conception. It is not enough, moreover, to point to German philosophers that influenced individual analytic philosophers; otherwise one would have to include, e.g., Hegel, Schopenhauer, and Marx. What I need are general features, whether doctrinal, thematic, or methodological, which unite my additions to the core list.

To this end I shall argue that my surprisingly analytic Germans share with the analytic Germans, and with the core of analytic philosophy more generally, certain Kantian ideas concerning the non-empirical nature of philosophy (section I). Next I turn to the task of establishing that the surprisingly analytic Germans actually influenced the analytic Germans. Having discussed Kantian ideas in Wittgenstein elsewhere (Glock 1997a and 1999), I shall focus on Frege. Sections II and III discuss the relationship between Frege and Kant. I shall argue that Kant's *a priori/a posteriori* and analytic/synthetic distinctions set the agenda for Frege, but that the two are separated by Frege's rejection of transcendental idealism and Kant's rejection of Platonism. Section IV turns to Frege's connection with neo-Kantianism. It rejects some alleged influences on matters of detail while confirming that Frege's anti-naturalism (rationalism, anti-psychologism, anti-geneticism) is part of a Kantian tradition. In the conclusion I argue that the Kantian influence on Frege has been overlooked partly because Kant inspired not just the anti-psychologism of the German analytic tradition but also psychologistic and idealistic modes of thought which the latter combated. I end by returning to the contrast between the naturalistic heritage analytic philosophy imbibed from empiricism and the anti-naturalistic legacy of the German analytic tradition.

I Kant's analytic legacy

The features which unite the analytic Germans and the surprisingly analytic Germans all stem from a Kantian preoccupation. From Kant to the end of the twentieth century, one concern has united the otherwise diverse traditions of German philosophy, namely the question whether philosophy can preserve a distinct role in view of the progress of the empirical sciences (see Schnädelbach 1983). Moreover, unlike their American colleagues, on the one hand, and their French colleagues, on the other, German philosophers have tended to resist the attempt to reduce philosophy either to the natural sciences or to a branch of *belles lettres* unrestrained by academic standards of truth or rationality.

This question about the nature of philosophy was linked to a second one, namely whether logic, mathematics, and philosophy are *a priori*. If philosophy is to be a cognitive discipline, yet distinct from the empirical sciences, this is because, like logic and mathematics, it aspires to knowledge of a non-empirical kind. This question immediately leads on to the third, namely whether there are non-empirical preconditions of experience. If logic, mathematics, and philosophy are indeed *a priori*, that special status needs to be explained. One explanation is the kind of Platonism favoured by Frege: logic and mathematics are *a priori* because they deal with entities (numbers, concepts, thoughts, truth-values) beyond the physical realm. Another explanation is provided by what I have called Kant's reflective turn (Glock 1997a). Philosophy is immune to confirmation or refutation by empirical evidence (observation or experiment) not because it deals with abstract entities beyond the empirical world, but because it is a second-order discipline which reflects on the non-empirical preconditions of empirical knowledge, logical or epistemological structures that antecede matters of empirical truth or falsity.

Both positions agree that philosophy (logic and epistemology) is neither a branch of science, nor a branch of *belles lettres*. Philosophy is *a priori*; and it is *a priori* because it deals with issues that lie beyond the scope of natural science. This idea separates the analytic German tradition from two other important movements. The intellectual scene in nineteenth-century Germany was successively dominated by three trends:

1800–1831   German idealism, which regards philosophy as a super-science;

1831–1865   Naturalism, which reduces philosophy to empirical science;

1865–1900   neo-Kantianism, which rehabilitates philosophy as a second-order discipline.[2]

The German idealists were ultra-rationalists. They held that *all* knowledge is *a priori*, because philosophy can deduce even apparently contingent claims from first principles. The naturalists – Vogt, Moleschott, Büchner, Czolbe – were physiologists by training, who treated the collapse of German idealism as a sign of the bankruptcy of all metaphysical speculation and *a priori* reasoning.[3] They held that all knowledge is *a posteriori*, because the allegedly *a priori* disciplines can either be reduced to empirical disciplines like psychology or physiology – this was their preferred line on logic and mathematics – or be rejected as illusory – their favourite treatment of philosophy.

For all their violent differences, the German idealists and the naturalists were united in propounding a monolithic conception of knowledge as either wholly *a priori* or wholly empirical. By contrast, the German analytic tradition retained Kant's dichotomy between *a priori* and *a posteriori* knowledge. Of course, this dichotomy is rejected by post-Quinean American philosophy, which is certainly part of the analytic tradition as commonly conceived. Still, before

---

[2] Around 1800 Kant became too frail to curb the ravings of his would-be follower Fichte; in 1831 Hegel died, thus accelerating the demise of German idealism; in 1865, Otto Liebmann published his influential *Kant und die Epigonen*, which provided neo-Kantianism with its war-cry 'Back to Kant!'. See Sluga 1980, chs. I–II; Schnädelbach 1983.

[3] It should be noted that the term 'naturalism', which we associate with Quine, was not coined by the American pragmatists (Santayana, Dewey), as has been suggested by Danto (1967), but goes back at least to these German physiological naturalists. Thus Czolbe, the most philosophical of them, referred to his work as a 'system of naturalism' (1855, 233–4).

Quine the majority of analytic philosophers, including the Anglophones, were united by the conviction that their activity was distinct not only from that of the poet, but also from that of the scientist.

Moreover, there are four other features which unite my designated analyticians to hard core analytic philosophy, Quineans included. One is that they took a keen interest in the empirical science of their day. Although they resisted the dissolution of philosophy into empirical science, they insisted that philosophy must take notice of science. Some historians of analytic philosophy have suggested that Kantian philosophy was pursued in isolation from developments in the special sciences (Wedberg 1984, 1–2; Coffa 1991, 22). This is mere prejudice. One group of neo-Kantians was constituted by eminent scientists such as Helmholtz, Hertz, and Boltzmann. Moreover, from Kant to Cassirer, the neo-Kantians tended to know more about the science of their day – both natural and social – than contemporary analytic philosophers tend to know about present-day science.

This is no coincidence. Kant's reflective turn implies that philosophy provides, among other things, an account of the non-empirical preconditions of empirical science. This idea was not only taken up by the philosopher-scientists, it was the core inspiration behind the Marburg school of neo-Kantianism founded by Cohen. For Cohen, philosophy starts out with 'the fact of science'; it is nothing other than the meta-theory of the natural sciences. And when the natural sciences were revolutionised by the theory of relativity, the Marburg school followed suit through the works of Natorp *Die Logischen Grundlagen der exakten Wissenschaften* of 1910, long before any analytic treatment of special relativity) and Cassirer's *Zur Einsteinschen Relativitätstheorie* (1921). Indeed, there is only a single step from the idea that philosophy is the meta-theory of science to Carnap's slogan that philosophy is the 'logic of science' (1937, 279), especially since the meta-theory of the Marburg school was explicitly conceived as a combination of logic and methodology, that step being the linguistic turn of the *Tractatus* according to which logic is to be understood by reference to language.

This brings us to a third feature which ties my German candidates to hard-core analytic philosophy, namely their emphasis on logic. Indeed, logocentrism has been an important but largely unappreciated characteristic of mainstream German philosophy from Leibniz (see Sluga 1980, 10–12) to the early Husserl and the Marburg school. While Descartes and the empiricists from Bacon to Hume disparaged logic, Leibniz assigned a central role to it both in his methodology and in his metaphysics. He protested against

Vorsprung durch Logik: The German Analytic Tradition

Descartes, that clarity and distinctness is a wholly subjective criterion of truth, which needs to be replaced by an objective, logical one. This *Vorsprung durch Logik* was passed on to later German philosophers through Wolff. Whereas the French and the British relied on purely subjective phenomena like the clarity and distinctness of ideas or the vividness of sense-impressions, the Germans tried to erect philosophy on the basis of objective logical principles. Even the speculative systems of German idealism evolved around the logical laws canonised by Leibniz (identity, non-contradiction, and sufficient reason). According to Hegel, for example, logic rather than metaphysics constitutes the beginning of all science.

Kant gave logocentrism a new twist by distinguishing between 'general' or 'formal logic', a term he coined (Trendelenburg 1870, 35), and 'transcendental logic'. Formal logic consists of analytic *a priori* truths because it 'deals with nothing but the pure form of thought' and abstracts from the objects of knowledge. By contrast, transcendental logic 'concerns itself with the laws of understanding and of reason solely in so far as they relate *a priori* to objects'. That is to say, it accounts for the *synthetic a priori truths* of metaphysics. Moreover, it does so by spelling out the preconditions of thinking about objects. Transcendental logic is 'a logic of truth' (1998, A 63/B 87; unless otherwise specified, all references to Kant are to the *Critique of Pure Reason*). No knowledge can contradict it 'without loosing all content, that is, all relation to any object, and therefore all truth'. Conformity with transcendental logic does not guarantee that a judgement is true, but only that it is in the running for truth, because it refers to objects or reality.

Analytic philosophers have frequently attacked Kant for confusing logic with metaphysics, epistemology, and psychology (e.g., Kneale and Kneale 1984, 355). But this ignores several points. First, in one of its guises, transcendental logic is simply a kind of philosophical logic. It is concerned with conceptual connections which lie beyond the scope of formal logic, because they are connected with concepts other than the logical constants. In contemporary terminology, formal logic seeks to establish logical truths, transcendental logic and philosophical logic seek to establish analytic truths proper, usually of a non-trivial kind that Kant himself regarded as synthetic. To be sure, whereas contemporary philosophical logic tends to confine itself to semantic notions such as meaning and reference, Kant's transcendental logic deals with epistemological and metaphysical notions (experience, self-consciousness, object). But that distinction is both topical rather than methodological and vague, as the examples of truth and existence show.

Moreover, in connecting logic to epistemology and metaphysics, Kant was setting a precedent that perfectly respectable analytic philosophers like Wittgenstein, the logical positivists, Quine, Strawson, and Dummett were to follow. In fact, the idea of a transcendental logic investigating the preconditions of thinking about objects is a direct precursor to the 'logic of representation' in Wittgenstein's *Tractatus*, which deals with the preconditions for the possibility of symbolic representation (6.13, 4.015) and thereby puts the relation between language and reality at the core of analytic philosophy. Finally, Kant himself already insisted adamantly on the purity of *formal* logic.

> If some modern philosophers have thought to enlarge [logic], by introducing *psychological* chapters on the different faculties of knowledge ... *metaphysical* chapters on the origin of knowledge or the different kinds of certainty according to the differences in the objects ... or *anthropological* chapters on prejudices, their causes and remedies, this could only arise from their ignorance of the peculiar nature of logical science ... . The limits of logic are quite precisely determined: it is a science concerned solely with the exhaustive exposition and strict proof of the formal rules of all thought. (B VIII).

This passage also indicates a fourth feature which ties the surprisingly analytic Germans to core analytic philosophy, namely their anti-psychologism. For the German naturalists, psychology rather than logic or metaphysics is the fundamental science (Czolbe 1855, 8). Moreover, following Mill (1973, 245–6), they insisted that logic is a branch of psychology, and that the laws of logic are ultimately empirical generalisations based on induction. Unlike the British empiricists, they conceived of psychology and experience in materialist, indeed physiological terms, namely as concerning movements of the nervous system.

This proto-Quinean picture was sharply rejected by the German analytic tradition. Kant, the neo-Kantians, Frege, Wittgenstein, and the Vienna Circle all maintain that logic and epistemology are autonomous, distinct not just from psychology, but also from other natural sciences such as physiology. Moreover, as part of the dualistic epistemology inherited from Kant, they resist any attempt to reduce logical propositions to empirical ones.

Accordingly, the analytic Germans and the surprisingly analytic Germans concur on these five points:

a dichotomy between *a priori* and *a posteriori* knowledge;
an *a prioristic* conception of philosophy;

philosophy is closely connected to science without being reducible to it;

logocentrism: logic plays a central role to philosophy;

anti-psychologism: logic and epistemology cannot be reduced to psychology.

In the remainder of this paper I want to show that the surprisingly analytic Germans actually influenced the first of the analytic Germans – Frege – along these lines. Given the influence of Frege on Wittgenstein and of Wittgenstein on the Vienna Circle, this provides us with a respectable historical family tree.

II Frege and Kant: *a priori/a posteriori* and analytic/synthetic

Until recently Frege's relation to his contemporaries and predecessors has been either ignored or misdescribed. For example, Michael Dummett conjectured that Frege might have been the realist knight who slew the dragon of Hegelian idealism (1973, 683). That might have been a splendid idea, were it not for two facts. First, in 1848, the year of Frege's birth, Hegelianism was already as dead as a dodo. Second, unlike Berkeley, German idealism does not reduce the world to mental episodes, it merely insists that reality is intelligible because it is the manifestation of a divine spirit or rational principle. It is far from obvious that Frege's arguments against psychologistic idealism have any bearing on this position.

Eventually, historical consciousness caught up with Frege studies, making them at once more scholarly and more scholastic. The main watershed has been the work of Hans Sluga. Sluga claimed first in a series of articles that Frege was a transcendental idealist, and later in his book *Frege* of 1980 that he was strongly influenced by Kant and Lotze. Dummett responded in characteristically robust manner, insisting that the alleged similarities are superficial and concluding: 'Frege's philosophy looks forward, not backward: the fruitful comparisons are with later ideas, not with earlier ones' (1981, xviii; see 1991, vii).

In my view, Dummett has refuted the suggestion that Frege was a transcendental idealist, but not the idea of a more general Kantian heritage. Frege's debt to the Southwest school has been confirmed through subsequent research by Sluga and Gottfried Gabriel. First, however, I shall turn to Frege's relation to Kant himself, which has been misdescribed not just by Dummett, but also by some of those who regard Frege as a Kantian thinker.

Unlike his relation to the Neo-Kantians, this is not a matter of speculation, since Frege was at pains to state it explicitly wherever he thought it relevant. In §89 of *The Foundations of Arithmetic*, having rejected Kant's view that without sensibility no object could be given to us, he goes on:

> I have no wish to incur the reproach of picking petty quarrels with a genius to whom we must all look up with grateful awe; I feel bound, therefore, to call attention to the extent of my agreement with him, which far exceeds any disagreement. To touch upon what is immediately relevant, I consider Kant did great service in drawing the distinction between synthetic and analytic judgements. In calling the truths of geometry synthetic and *a priori*, he revealed their true essence ... If Kant was wrong about arithmetic, this does not seriously detract, in my opinion, from the value of his work. His concern was that there are such things as synthetic judgements *a priori*; whether they are to be found in geometry only, or in arithmetic as well, is of less importance. (1953; unless otherwise specified, all references to Frege are to this text).

Dummett has called these remarks 'disingenuous' and 'pious', and insists that the points of agreement constitute 'rather a thin crop' (1991, 23; 1981, 463). However as Sluga has pointed out (1997, 20n), there is no evidence to suggest that Frege's admiration was insincere (unless one feels that admiring a philosopher is incompatible with disagreeing with him). What is true is that *Foundations* was explicitly written with a view to attract the attention of philosophers to Frege's logicist programme (Pref.). He may well have felt that emphasising the Kantian connections (both positive and negative) would facilitate this. But of course this does not entail that he invented such connections; indeed such a course of action would obviously have been inimical to his goal.

In any event, Frege's admiration had much sounder reasons than academic fashion. After all, it was Kant who raised the question to which Frege devoted almost his entire career, namely of clarifying the logical and epistemological status of mathematical propositions. Moreover, in our passage Frege makes clear that he regards both the analytic/synthetic distinction and the question of whether there are synthetic *a priori* judgements as important to a fruitful discussion of that problem. This echoes Kant's assessment according to which the analytic/synthetic distinction is an essential prerequisite of any critique of pure reason.

One might protest that Frege never used the analytic/synthetic distinction after *Foundations*. But, as Dummett himself has pointed out (1918, 11, 378), the same can be said about his context-principle and his invocation of criteria of identity. Unless there is evidence to suppose that later views conflict with these earlier views, there is no reason to suppose that Frege abandoned them; and in the case of the analytic/synthetic distinction there is no such evidence. The fact that it recedes into the background is easily explained. The basic contention of *Foundations* is that arithmetic is analytic rather than synthetic, i.e., derivable from logical axioms and definitions alone. But once the logicist project is thus explained the emphasis shifts to the more demanding task of effecting this derivation.

Accordingly, Dummett's suggestion that the points of agreement professed by Frege constitute rather a thin crop is rather an astonishing one. For these points amount to nothing less than that Frege

inherited his master-problem from Kant;

tackled that problem using Kant's conceptual framework;

reached the same result as Kant in one of the cases considered – geometry – while describing the disagreement over arithmetic as less important.

How much closer could one philosophical revolutionary get to another?

Dummett would dispute the last two points. According to him Frege uses Kantian terminology, but in a non-Kantian fashion. Frege himself states that he does not wish 'to assign a new sense' to the *a priori/a posteriori* and analytic/synthetic distinctions, but 'only to hit off what earlier writers, and Kant in particular, have intended' (§3n). Dummett begs to differ:

just as Frege's explanation of 'analytic' differs from Kant's, so does his explanation of '*a priori*'. According to Frege, the characterisation of a truth as analytic, synthetic *a priori* or *a posteriori* relates to the ultimate justification for holding it to be true (*Grundlagen*, §3); not the actual ground we may have for believing it, but the type of justification that is to be found. (1981, 463; see 1991, 23)

The passage Dummett invokes runs as follows:

Now these distinctions between *a priori* and *a posteriori*, synthetic and analytic, concern, as I see it, not the content of the judgement but the justification for making the judgement (*Berechtigung zur Urteilsfällung*). Where there is no such justification, the possibility of drawing the distinctions vanishes. An *a priori* error is thus as complete a nonsense as, say, a blue concept. When a proposition is called *a posteriori* or analytic in my sense, this is not

> a judgement about the conditions, psychological, physiological and physical, which have made it possible to form the content of the proposition in our consciousness ... rather, it is a judgement about what the justification for holding the proposition ultimately rests on.

It is not clear whether Frege uses 'content' (*Inhalt*) here in his customary sense, according to which the content of a proposition is that feature of it which bears on the logical validity of arguments in which it occurs. But contrary to Dummett, the two points he makes using the contrast between content and justification are in line with Kant. Firstly, the distinctions are confined to truths: neither Kant nor Frege allow such a thing as an *a priori* or analytic falsehood. Secondly, the distinctions do not concern the manner in which beliefs are acquired, but the manner in which they can be justified.

Dummett is demonstrably wrong in suggesting that Kant's distinction between *a priori* and *a posteriori* concerns the content of our beliefs or the empirical conditions of their acquisition rather than their justification. Not only is Kant's distinction an explicitly epistemological one, it differs from the rationalist distinction between innate and adventitious ideas precisely because it distinguishes between the non-empirical and the empirical by reference to the justification of beliefs rather than to the way they are acquired.

> There can be no doubt that all our knowledge begins with experience ... In the order of time, therefore we have no knowledge antecedent to experience, and with experience all our knowledge begins. But though all our knowledge begins with experience, it does not follow that it all arises (*entspringt*) out of experience. ... This, then, is a question which at least calls for closer examination, and does not allow of any off-hand answers: – whether there is any knowledge that is thus independent of experience and even of all impressions of the senses. Such knowledge is entitled *a priori*, and distinguished from empirical knowledge, which has its sources *a posteriori*, that is, in experience. (B 1–3)

What makes a true belief either *a priori* or *a posteriori* according to Kant is precisely not the way we acquire it, but the justification we have for it. The same anti-genetic point is made by his distinction between the question of how we acquire a certain kind of experience or belief (*quaestio facti*) and the question of what the logical and epistemological status of that experience or belief is (*quaestio iuris*) (A 84–5/B 116–17). It also underlies the very conception of Kant's project, which evolves around a distinction between transcendental philosophy, on the one hand, and 'empirical psychology', notably

Locke's 'physiology of the human understanding' on the other (A ix; 1953, §21a). Finally, as these distinctions make patently obvious, the *a priori/a posteriori* distinction depends not on what Dummett calls the 'actual ground' individuals may have for holding the belief, but on the kind of ground that *can* be given, the way it can be verified, what the logical positivists later called the method of verification. To use the neo-Kantian distinction which ultimately derives from this seminal passage (see §IV), *a priori* knowledge is independent of experience not as regards its *genesis*, but as regards its *validity*.

Dummett seems on firmer ground concerning the analytic/synthetic distinction. According to Frege, both the *a priori* and the analytic status of a proposition turns on the 'primordial truths' (*Urwahrheiten*) featuring in its proof.

> If, in carrying out this process, we come only on general logical laws and on definitions, then the truth is an analytic one ... If, however, it is impossible to give the proof without making use of truths which are not of a general logical nature, but belong to the sphere of some special science, then the proposition is a synthetic one. For a truth to be *a posteriori*, its proof must be impossible without appeal to facts, that is to unprovable truths without generality, which contain assertions about particular objects. If, on the other hand, it is possible to construct the proof entirely from general laws, which themselves neither admit of nor require proof[4], then the truth is *a priori*. (§3)

A truth is *a priori* precisely if it is provable from general laws without appeal to particular facts; an *a priori* truth is *analytic* precisely if the general laws and definitions from which it is provable are laws of *logic*; and a law is a law of *logic* precisely if it is universally applicable and not restricted to a particular discipline.

These definitions become clearer through the reasons Frege gives for regarding arithmetic but not geometry as analytic (§§13–14). Geometry is *a priori* because its theorems are provable from general laws (the Euclidean axioms) without any appeal to particular figures or bodies. But it is not analytic, because its axioms involve spatial concepts, and these do not apply to all disciplines. Conceptual thought is not confined to what we can intuit, and hence to what is spatial. This is why some axioms of Euclidean geometry can be denied without self-contradiction. And this in turn 'shows that the axioms of geometry are independent of one another and of the primitive laws of logic and consequently are synthetic'. By contrast, arithmetic truths are analytic, since their

---

[4] As Dummett (1993, 24n) points out, this phrase echoes Lotze 'truths that neither need nor are capable of proof' (*Metaphysik*, §1).

proof relies on logic alone, which means that rejecting them is self-contradictory.

Frege's reason for treating geometry as synthetic *a priori* is reminiscent of Kant's notion of an impure *a priori* judgement (B 3–5), namely one which can be known without recourse to reason, but which contains concepts that are derived from experience and hence not universal. Frege also joins Kant in treating the generality of a proposition as a hallmark of its *a priori* status. However, unlike Kant, he fails to specify that this generality must be 'strict', i.e., of a non-contingent or non-inductive kind. In this respect Kant has the edge over Frege. As Wittgenstein later pointed out, generality is neither sufficient nor necessary for *a priori* status (1961, 6.1231f.). 'All matter is subject to gravity' is general, but not *a priori*, while 'Either it rains or it does not rain' is *a priori*, but not general.

As regards analyticity, there are important differences. Frege rightly complained that Kant underestimates the value of analytic judgements because his definition is 'too narrow' since it is restricted to judgements of the subject-predicate form (§88). This objection applies to Kant's initial explanation, according to which analytic judgements are those in which the predicate is implicitly contained in the concept of the subject (A 8). There is another well-known objection to this explanation, which owes something to Frege's anti-psychologism. The notion of containment is hopelessly metaphorical. Worse still, the way in which Kant uses it conflates psychological and logical questions. It seems that whether a judgement is analytic turns on whether in thinking the subject-concept people think the predicate. Thus Kant argues that '$7 + 5 = 12$' cannot be analytic, because in thinking its subject-concept – 'The sum of 7 and 5' we do not yet think the predicate – 'equals 12', and, for this reason, denies the existence of non-obvious analytic truths in arithmetic. However, as Frege and later Wittgenstein have taught us, what goes through peoples' minds is irrelevant for the logical status of their beliefs (1996 [1893], Pref.). For example, the judgement that all Tories are extended is analytic by Kant's lights (A 7–8/B 11–12). But when people think of the Tories, or even all Tories, they do not, by and large, think of their being extended.

Dummett concludes that Frege's *a priori/a posteriori* and analytic synthetic distinctions are fundamentally different from Kant's, and hence that their agreements on the *a priori* nature of arithmetic and the synthetic *a priori* nature of geometry is mainly verbal (1981, 464–75; 1991, 131). But this does not follow. For Frege recognised that Kant also provided a second explanation of analytical truth which is much closer to his own (§§3, 88, 90). According to this explanation, analytical judgements are true solely in virtue of the 'principle of contradiction', i.e., their negation is self-contradictory, whereas for synthetic propositions an additional support is necessary (B 11, B 14, A 151–2/B 190–1, A 598/B 626; 1953, §2). This explanation avoids the forementioned disadvantages. It is not necessarily confined to subject/predicate judgements (although the passage explains the principle of contradiction in a restricted way); it does not rely either implicitly or explicity on mental goings-on; and although Kant himself stubbornly denied that analytic propositions could extend our knowledge (A 8/B 12), it makes room for *non-obvious* analytic truths, since such proofs can be far from trivial.

Kant's second explanation also militates against Dummett's suggestion that for Kant analyticity is a matter of logic rather than epistemology, since it refers solely to the content of a judgement rather than to its justification.

> Judgements of experience, as such, are one and all synthetic. For it would be absurd to found an analytic judgement on experience. Since, in framing the judgement, I must not go outside my concept, there is *no need to appeal to the testimony of experience in its support* (B 11; my emph.).

> ... if the judgement is analytic ... its truth *can always be adequately known* in accordance with the principle of contradiction. (B 190; my emph.; similarly 1953, §2b)

Kant here explains the analyticity of a judgement by reference to the *kind of justification* that can be given for it. An analytic judgement is one which can be verified solely by examining its constituent concepts, whereas synthetic judgements must be verified by referring to something beyond the judgement – 'a third thing (X)', as Kant puts it, in terms which assume that the judgement itself consists of subject and predicate (A 8/B 12). What's more, the justification which characterises analytic judgements is precisely of the kind envisaged by Frege's own definition. Analytic judgements cannot be verified by reference to experience or reality, but only by establishing that the conceptual connections between its components make its denial a contradiction, i.e., by appeal to a paradigmatic logical law. The point of Kant's notion of analyticity is that the logical status of a judgement is intimately tied to how it can be verified. Frege himself was aware of this, since he glosses Kant's claim that geometry is synthetic *a priori* as the claim that pure intuition is 'the *ultimate ground* of our knowledge of such judgements' (§12, my emphasis).

One might protest that the passages from Kant do not provide a definition of analyticity, but merely specify consequences of a judgement being analytic. But the second one, at any rate, does not specify criteria of analyticity in the sense in which generality and necessity are criteria of *a prioricity*. For it is entitled 'The Highest Principle of all Analytic Judgements'.

One might further protest that even if Kantian analyticity has implications for the justification of a judgement, it is mainly a matter of its content. This is correct in that the *Prolegomena* (§2) declare analyticity to be a matter of content rather than form. But what Kant has in mind here is form as captured by his table of judgements: analytic judgements do not constitute a separate class according to their quantity, quality, or relation. Kant also emphasises that the principle of contradiction 'holds of knowledge, merely as knowledge in general, irrespective of its content' (A 151/B 190); and the same goes for the analytic judgements that owe their truth to it. Their status has got nothing to do with the content of the judgement – what kind of objects it is about – but depends exclusively on the conceptual connections between its components. These connections are not confined to what modern logic calls purely formal connections, because Kant's definition covers analytic truths in the narrow sense ('All bachelors are unmarried') no less than logical truths like 'All unmarried men are unmarried'. However, Kant does not operate with the modern notion of logical constants, and hence does not distinguish between logical connections involving logical constants and logical connections involving other concepts. Hence, analytical truths are a matter of logical form in the following sense: they combine concepts in such a way that all the factual references cancel out.

III Frege and Kant: geometry and the copernican revolution

If I am right, the agreements between Kant and Frege are not merely verbal. For both, calling mathematics *a priori* indicates a rejection of the empiricist position according to which mathematical truths can be reduced to well-confirmed empirical generalisations. For both, calling a judgement synthetic indicates in the first instance a negative point: it is not analytic, i.e., its truth cannot be derived from logical laws like that of contradiction alone.

From this perspective it is unsurprising that Frege's account of geometry evolves around two Kantian claims:

> geometry is synthetic *a priori*, neither reducible to experience nor to logic.

> geometry is based on non-empirical features of spatial intuition.

Vorsprung durch Logik: The German Analytic Tradition

At the very beginning of his career, Frege claimed that the axioms of geometry 'derive their validity from the nature of our intuitive faculty' and that 'geometry refers to intuition (*Anschauung*) as the source of its axioms' (1984, 1 57). In §12 of *Foundations* he suggests that synthetic *a priori* knowledge must rest on pure intuition; in §13 he states that the general propositions of geometry are derived from intuition; and in §89 he praises Kant for having revealed the 'true essence' of geometrical truths by calling them synthetic *a priori*.

Sluga initially concluded that Frege accepted Kant's transcendental idealism, according to which space and its contents are mere appearances and do not exist apart from cognition. In response, Dummett (1981, 469) has rightly pointed out that in the one place in which Frege explicity discusses Kant's view of the ideality of space, he disowns it.

> According to Kant, space belongs to appearances. It could be possible that to other rational creatures it presents itself completely differently. Indeed, we cannot even know whether it appears the same to two human beings; for we cannot place the spatial intuition of the one next to that of the other, to compare the two. And yet, something objective is contained in this; everybody recognises the same geometrical axioms. ... Objective here is the law governed, conceptual, judgeable, what can be expressed in words. The purely intuitive cannot be communicated. (§26)

Frege here seems to accept that intuitions are subjective and incommunicable while insisting that geometrical axioms are not. In view of the forementioned passages, however, this suggests not only that Sluga was wrong, but also that Frege's position is incoherent. In my view that conclusion can be avoided by distinguishing four different Kantian claims about space

(A) Space-occupants are mere appearances

(B) Space is an *a priori* intuition

(C) Space is a form of intuition

(D) Spatial knowledge involves intuition.

Frege's position can be rendered coherent if it is interpreted as rejecting (A) and (B) while accepting a version of (C) and (D).

According to (A), the spatial objects we experience are appearances rather than things in themselves. But according to Kant's definition of transcendental idealism, appearances are 'mere representations' (*bloße Vorstellungen*) (A 369). Furthermore, representations are 'inner modifications of the mind'. Although they have 'some mysterious kind of objective reality', the latter consists not in their representing a mind-independent object, but in the fact that they are governed by the categories (A 197/B 242, see A 33–4/B 50–1). Taken together, the two passages imply that what we experience (chairs, rivers, stones), namely appearances, are mere representations of unknowable things in themselves. Some contemporary Kantians have tried hard to detect a different position. Even if that is possible, however, Frege seems to have adopted a more straightforward reading. On that reading, (A) is incompatible with Frege's devastating objection to idealism and psychologism, namely that our judgements are, by and large, not about inner mental phenomena, mind, but about mind-independent objects.

By the same token, Frege cannot accept (B). Kantian intuitions are types of representations (A 319/B 376), and therefore private mental items that cannot be communicated or compared between individuals. That is why basing geometry on intuitions seems to endanger its intersubjective nature. By contrast, one thing Frege seems to find attractive in Kant is (D), the idea that our geometrical *knowledge* of space rests on intuition. Proofs in geometry require a special source of knowledge – intuition – which is connected to sensibility and thereby to the presentation of particular figures in space.

This leads on to (C). Kant's claim that space is the form of outer intuition amounts to the idea that geometrical laws express preconditions of outer perception. This is in line with *Foundations* (§14), according to which they must hold of anything which we perceive or imagine in space. Such a view is at odds with regarding geometrical laws as objective in the strong sense of being independent of human cognition. But it is compatible with the view that space-occupants are mind-independent, and that the laws we use for describing their spatial properties are intersubjective in that they hold for all creatures like us. Interestingly, this may be close to the conception of objectivity in *Foundations*. What is objective is independent of the sensations in the minds of individuals, but not 'independent of reason; – for what are things independent of reason? To answer that would be as much as to judge without judging, or to wash the fur without wetting it' (§26). If reason here includes the non-empirical and non-individual aspects of perception, as it does in the title *The Critique of Pure Reason*, we have roughly Kant's position.[5]

---

[5] Frege contrasts reason with 'our sensing, intuiting and imagining ... all construction of inner images out of memories of earlier sensations'. But the final gloss suggests that what he had in mind is the subjective nature of indi-

It is equally interesting, however, that Frege abandoned this Kantian conception of objectivity as intersubjectivity. He later argued that the objectivity and necessity of logic is not just incompatible with its subject matter – thoughts and their structure – being private ideas in the minds of individuals, but requires that this subject consist of abstract entities in a realm beyond space and time. He thus moves from a rejection of psychologism to a positive acceptance of Platonism. Many commentators who have detected Kantian elements in Frege have denied this (e.g., Sluga 1980, ch. IV). But on this issue they are wrong and Dummett is right. Although Frege's position is sophisticated, it falls squarely within the Platonist camp. Frege's insistence that it does not make sense to locate numbers (or ideas) in space does not amount to Platonism (§61). But his conclusion that they are therefore non-spatial objects, and that, like truth-values, senses, etc. they have 'existence' in a third realm, certainly does. For Frege, logic deals with a 'domain' (*Gebiet*) of entities which are 'non-actual', that is non-spatial, atemporal and imperceptible ('non-sensible'), yet 'objective'. He later characterised this region as a 'third realm' (*drittes Reich*) which contrasts with the 'first realm' of ideas (the mind), and the 'second realm' of material objects. Finally, he mused about the mysterious process by which the mind can get in touch with thoughts, which are one kind of denizen of this realm (1996 [1893], Pref.; 1953, §§26, 85, 93; 1979, 145–8, 1984, 351–72; see Glock 1996/7).

Like Frege, Kant tried to do justice to the objectivity of *a priori* judgements. But he tried to account for the special status of *all a priori* truths without recourse to Platonism, a position which he constantly rejected because he confined knowledge to possible experience. Analytic truths are, in effect, conceptual truths and involve no reference to anything beyond the judgement, and *a fortiori* no reference to abstract entities. But Kant also developed an account of how certain *a priori* propositions can be synthetic, tell us something about the world, which does not appeal to a Platonic third realm.

Any synthetic judgement must refer to something beyond the judgement itself. But this something is never an abstract entity. In the case of *a posteriori* judgements it is an empirical intuition, in the case of *a priori* synthetic judgements in mathematics it is a pure intuition (space or time) and in the case of *a priori* synthetic judge-

---

vidual sensations, not a contrast between reason and sensation, which leaves open the possibility that the intersubjective preconditions of perception are part of what he means by reason. Dummett (1981, 510) maintains that Frege cannot have regarded non-logical laws as presuppositions of perception since he denied this for the logical laws, but this is at odds with Frege's reflections on the difference between arithmetic and geometry in §14.

ments in metaphysics it is a concept, namely the concept of 'possible experience' (A 155–7/B 194–6, A 184/B 227–8, A 216–17/ B 263–4, A221–2/B 269, A 238–9/B 298, A 259/B 315, A 719–37/ B 747–65, A 782–3, B 810–11). But, like any other concept, that concept is not an abstract entity – as it would be for Frege. To say that metaphysical propositions are borne out by the concept of a possible experience is precisely to say that their special status rests not on the fact that they refer to immutable abstract entities, but on the fact that they express preconditions for the possibility of experiencing and referring to ordinary, material objects. For example, we experience objects as located in space and time, and as subject to casual laws. According to Kant these are not empirical facts about human nature, but *necessary* features of experience, which at the same time *define* what it is to be an *object* of experience. There is a difference between experiences and their objects, and the content of experience is contingent. But according to Kant, there are also necessary or structural features of experience, and these determine the necessary or essential features of the *objects* of experience.

IV Frege and Neo-Kantianism

Sluga has maintained that the main influences on Frege 'were no doubt Kant and Leibniz, Lotze and Herbart' (1980, 40). Against this, Dummett has protested that he is much closer to the Austrian realists and (proto-) phenomenologists Bolzano, Brentano, Meinong, and Husserl than to neo-Kantian idealists. There is some justice in this remark. But it overlooks two important facts.

Firstly, for better or worse, Frege was more exposed to the influence of Neo-Kantianism than to that of the Austrian school. The only member of that tradition that he had contact with was Husserl. And while the received story of Frege's influence on Husserl's renounciation of psychologism may be exaggerated, there is no evidence for a substantial influence in the reverse direction. Secondly, idealism was not a characteristic feature of Neo-Kantianism. In fact, Neo-Kantianism presented itself as an alternative both to German idealism and to the empiricism and materialism of the physiological naturalists. Even Kant's transcendental idealism was not a universal feature of Neo-Kantianism. The Marburg school, for example, pursued Kant's transcendental philosophy not as a psychologistic theory about how the mind creates nature, but as an attempt to explicate the presuppositions of empirical science.

Recent research by Gabriel (1986) and Sluga (1997) leaves no doubt that a significant part of Frege's *philosophical* background was constituted by neo-Kantians influenced by Hermann Lotze. Among these were Otto Liebmann whose *Kant und die Epigonen* had officially launched Neo-Kantianism with the war-cry 'Back to Kant', Wilhelm Windelband and Heinrich Rickert. The latter two were the leading members of the Southwest German School of neo-Kantianism. Liebmann, for his part, was Frege's colleague at Jena from 1882 onwards.

What we know for certain is that Frege

(i)   attended Lotze's lectures (albeit only on the philosophy of religion);

(ii) was referred to as a 'pupil of Lotze', e.g. by his colleague Bruno Bauch;

(iii) referred to Lotze's theory of judgement;

(iv) read Liebmann's *Zur Analysis der Wirklichkeit* at a time when he wrote *Foundations*.

However, it is less clear what he actually took from these sources, especially since his main background was *not* in philosophy but in mathematics. Sluga had originally claimed that Frege's early theory of judgement was the 'Kantian theory in the version that Lotze had given it' (1980, 192–45). In response, Dummett unearthed the first real evidence that Frege had read Lotze's *Logik*, namely his '17 Kernsätze zur Logik' (1979, 174–5; see Dummett 1981, 523). These reveal that Frege was critical of Lotze's idea that there are two thoughts in every judgement, the combination of ideas and an auxiliary thought which affirms this combination. Nevertheless, there are important analogies of a more general kind between Frege's theory of judgement and that of some neo-Kantian thinkers.

Most importantly, the latter distinguished between the act of judging – what Frege calls a judgement – and the content of the judgement – what Frege calls a judgeable content or thought. Sluga suggests that Kant himself already drew such a distinction (1980, 36). But although such a distinction is in line with Kant's anti-psychologism, I know of no passage in which he actually draws it. By contrast, he frequently treats judgements as mental phenomena. On the other hand, Kant did anticipate what is now known as the 'Frege-point', namely the insight that the assertive force is not associated with the copula, and for roughly the same reasons, namely that judgements with a copula can occur in conditional judgements without being asserted (1973, sct. 1A note; 1992, §30).

Frege maintained that the distinction between a judgement and its content was entirely his own. But whether or not he picked it up from someone else, he was anticipated not just by Bolzano, but also by neo-Kantians.[6] Thus Sigwart (1873) distinguished between 'the living act of thinking' and the ideas to which the act is directed. Windelband distinguished between the 'assessment' (*Beurteilung*) and the judgement, and also claims that this distinction goes back to Lotze (1921, I/30, 32n1). Rickert, finally tried to motivate the distinction between the act of judgement and the judgement by proposing an argument subsequently adopted by Frege. Every assertion of the form 'The sun is shining' can be transformed into a question "Is the sun shining? Yes', which is supposed to show that one and the same judgement or judgeable content can be the object of different kinds of acts (1904, 98–101).

Gabriel has made an additional claim, namely that Frege borrowed the notion of a truth-value from Windelband and Rickert. Both had a general theory of the contrast between fact and values. Prominent among values is that of truth.

> The laws of logic hold for us only on the assumption of the purpose (*Zweck*) of truth; it is the general validity, i.e. the value, of seeking recognition by everyone which distinguishes the logical forms of thought from the other associations that take place within processes governed by natural law. (1921, II/73)

Elsewhere, Windelband calls this value a 'truth-value' (*Wahrheitswert*):

> All sentences making knowledge claims are combinations of ideas whose truth-value has been determined by affirmation or negation. (1921, I/32)

In other words, the act of judging is a transition from the judgement (Frege's judgeable content or thought) to the truth-value. This idea was subsequently elaborated by Rickert (Sluga 1997, 222–3). Unlike Windelband but like Frege, Rickert admits a second truth-value–falsity. According to Rickert, in every judgement a value is affirmed, i.e., truth or falsity, which attaches timelessly to the content of the judgement. Truth and falsity are values in the strictest sense of the word, which is why we must take a positive or negative stand to judgeable contents that have these values. The objects of knowledge, therefore, are not things in the world of facts, but truth itself conceived as a positive value. Rickert also suggested that the

[6] That he might have been aware of this fact is suggested by 'Ueber den Zweck der Begriffsschrift', where he defends himself against the charge of having confused the act of judgement from the judgeable content, a charge that was no doubt fuelled by his new terminology in which 'judgement' designates what other authors regarded as the act of judgement.

truth-value True might be conceived as the totality of judgements that have a positive value, a suggestion which has parallels in Frege's *Grundgesetze der Arithmetik*.

Finally, Rickert is close to Frege in his Platonist leanings. He accepts Kant's account of the sensible world of science. But he insists, against Kant and with Frege, that there is also an intelligible world of non-sensuous objects that we know not by perception but by understanding (*Verstehen*).

The parallels are indeed striking. But before we conclude that Frege engaged in plagiarism of gigantic proportions, the following points should be borne in mind. First, although it is probable that Frege read some Windelband and Rickert, there is no evidence that he actually did. Second, it is unlikely that Frege hit on the notion of a truth-value as a result of reading Windelband or Rickert. His whole logic was based on a generalisation of mathematical function-theory, and the idea of a function is that of a mapping of arguments on to values.

Gabriel recognises this point, but insists that it cannot be the whole story, since truth-values (e.g. the True which is the value of the function *x conquered Gaul* for the argument Caesar) can also be arguments of other functions, namely the truth-functions (e.g., the function expressed by $\Phi \wedge \Psi$). But this response is feeble. The mathematical notion of a function from which Frege starts out in 'Funktion und Begriff' allows for precisely the same thing. Numbers are the values of numerical functions like $f(x) = x^2$, but they are also their arguments. Moreover, in certain cases argument and value are identical: for the argument 1, for example the forementioned function has the value 1.

At the same time, Gabriel is right to point out that in one passage from 'Sinn und Bedeutung', Frege introduces the notion of a truth-value in a quasi-teleological fashion reminiscent of Windelband. Frege here makes out the following case for holding that sentences do not just have a sense – the thought they express – but a meaning – a truth-value.

> The fact that we concern ourselves at all about the meaning of the part of a sentence indicates that we generally expect and recognise a meaning for the sentence itself. The thought loses value for us as soon as we recognise that one of its parts lacks meaning. We are therefore justified in not being satisfied with the sense of a sentence, and in inquiring also as to its meaning. But now, why do we want every proper name to have not only a sense, but also a meaning? Why is the thought not enough for us? Because, and to the extent that, we are concerned with its truth-value. (1984, 163)

Gabriel concludes that Frege took truth-values to be the meanings of sentences because of the following line of thought: it is their truth or falsehood which determines the value of sentences, and the meaning (*Bedeutung*) of a sentence is its significance, that which is important about it, i.e., its value or purpose.

Even if this line of argument played a role for Frege, however, the most important connection between him and the Lotzean neo-Kantians is of a more strategic kind, namely their rejection of psychologism in the name of logicism. Sluga has suggested that Frege's logicism was inspired by Lotze. But while there is plenty of evidence for the mathematical root of logicism – notably the need for more rigorous methods of proof and the rapprochement between logic and mathematics – the evidence for Lotze's input is thin.

When we turn to Liebmann, however, the results are more palpable. He characterises the relation between logic, geometry, and mathematics essentially in line with §§14 and 26 of *Foundations of Arithmetic*. Geometry is subjective in the sense of only possessing 'intuitive necessity' (*Anschaungs-Notwendigkeit*), i.e., it holds true only for creatures with perceptual capacities like ours. By contrast, logic and arithmetic possess 'logical necessity': they govern all thought because to reject them is self-contradictory. Liebmann also anticipated the famous passage in *Grundgesetze* according to which rejecting the laws of logic would amount to 'a hitherto unknown form of madness' (1996 [1893], XVI; Liebmann 1880, 77, 79, 253).

Nevertheless, such matters of detail are less important than either the project of logicism, which Frege himself traces back to Leibniz, or the revolutionary new logic he developed to pursue it. However, there is an important parallel here between Frege and neo-Kantianism. The term logicism was originally used not for the specific programme of reducing mathematics to logic, but more generally as a contrast to psychologism, notably by proponents of the latter like Wundt and Nelson (see Gabriel 1980).

Psychologism is a conception of the nature of logic. It maintains that the logical 'laws of thought' describe how human beings (by and large) think, their basic mental operations, and are determined by the nature of the human mind. Whereas psychologism reduces human knowledge to mental processes to be studied empirically, logicism insists on the autonomy of logic, and of questions of justification more generally. Just as psychologism is aligned with empiricism and naturalism, logicism is aligned with rationalism. As regards this more general notion of logicism, Frege was not in agreement with neo-Kantianism as such, since many writers that belong to neo-Kantianism in the wider sense, notably Fries and Nelson, were proponents of psychologism. But he was very much in agreement with the neo-Kantianism inspired by Lotze, which was fervently opposed to psychologism.

Moreover, in both the Lotzeans and Frege the rejection of psychologism goes hand in hand with a rejection of empiricism and materialism. They reject the empiricist thesis that all knowledge is based on induction, on the grounds that without some general truths, at the very least the principle of induction itself, induction from particular observations could not get off the ground (Lotze 1874, §330; Liebmann 1880, 208; Windelband 1921, II/107; Frege 1953, §3n, 4n).

This rejection of empiricism is combined with a very important distinction which goes back to Kant himself, namely that between the genesis of our beliefs and their validity. Empiricism is right in so far as all our knowledge is acquired as a result of experience, but wrong to conclude that the validity of all our knowledge depends on experience. The distinction was first drawn by Lotze (1874, 316ff.) and used by subsequent neo-Kantians, notably Windelband (1921, I/24). One of its functions is to demarcate the task of philosophy. While being (*Sein*) and genesis (*Genese*) are investigated by empirical science, investigating the validity of knowledge claims is the prerogative of philosophy (logic, epistemology). Neither Liebmann nor Frege use the terms 'genesis' and 'validity', but they both distinguish between psychological questions about how we acquire knowledge, and the epistemological question of what justifies these laws. Indeed, Liebmann anticipates Frege's related distinction between psychological laws of holding to be true which are descriptive, and logical laws of truth, which are normative (Liebmann 1880, 251, 546; Frege 1996 [1893], Pref.; 1953, §105n).

In the same anti-genetic and anti-psychologistic vein, both attack the attempts by physiological materialists to reduce thought to neurophysiological phenomena. Both refer in particular to Moleschott's infamous slogan 'No thoughts without phosphates.' Liebmann's reaction: 'And what have proteins, calcium and phosphate in the brain to do with logic?' (1880, 531). Similarly, Frege observes how absurd it is to analyse thoughts by reference to the amount of phosphate in the brain, once one realises that the laws of thought are the laws of logic. And he reminds us of the difference between the conditions for holding a belief and the conditions for its truth, lest we think that the proof of Pythagoras' theorem might have to mention the phosphate content of our brain (1953, Intr.; 1979, 5).

V Concluding thoughts on naturalism

I hope to have shown that Kant and neo-Kantianism influenced Frege's anti-naturalism, his opposition to empiricism, materialism, geneticism, and psychologism. Dummett is demonstrably wrong in claiming that 'it was Frege who first perceived ... the irrelevance of genetic questions' (1973, 676). Even the general logicism which Frege shares with some neo-Kantians goes back to Kant himself. Their conception of the nature of logic is closer than is usually realised, largely because they both accept many traditional assumptions (Kant 1998, B 76–9/A 52–4; 1992, Intr., sct.I; Frege 1893, VXIff; 1979, 2–3, 149, 122):

(i) Logic is concerned with the rules or laws of thought (*Regeln/Gesetze des Denkens*)
(ii) These laws are normative rather than descriptive. Unlike the laws of psychology, they do not describe how people actually think, but prescribe how they ought to think if they are to judge 'rightly';
(iii) logical laws are 'topic neutral': they govern all thought, whatever its 'object'.

Nevertheless, Dummett's reluctance to align Frege with Kant is not wholly unfounded. Sluga disparages Dummett's association of Kant and psychologism as based on 'obscure reasons' (1980, 53). To be sure, Kant not only founded modern anti-geneticism, the Refutation of Idealism provides a vigorous argument against idealism. Alas, his own transcendental idealism is not only committed to an obscure version of representationalism, it also involves a transcendental psychologism. We have seen how Kant explains synthetic *a priori* judgements as those which express necessary features of experience. One gloss of this idea is that these features are conceptual; they reflect concepts like that of experience and related epistemic concepts (sct. III).

But that gloss is belied by passages in which transcendental idealism is presented as a psychological or genetic doctrine: 'we can know *a priori* of things only what we ourselves have put into them' (B XVIII). Necessary preconditions of experience are features to which the objects of experience have to conform because they are imposed on them by our cognitive apparatus in the course of processing 'sensations', the material component of our experience. Hence they hold only for appearances, but not for the things in themselves which cause our experiences by 'affecting' our cognitive apparatus (see, e.g., A 19–20/B 34).

Kant's transcendental psychology is one of the main sources of nineteenth-century psychologistic logic (another one being associationist and introspectionist psychology), because it provides one model of how the mind can underpin necessary propositions. In fact, psychologism came in two versions (see Baker and Hacker 1984, 28–9). Both explained logical laws by reference to subjective mental goings-on. According to the naturalistic version, the structures and operations of the mind are contingent on human nature and to be investigated by empirical psychology (Erdmann, Moleschott). According to the Kantian version, they are necessary features, to be investigated by a transcendental psychology. In this vein Sir William Hamilton writes:

> in so far as a form of thought is necessary, this form must be determined or necessitated by the nature of the thinking subject itself; for if it were determined by anything external to the mind, then would it not be a necessary but merely a contingent determination. The first condition, therefore, of the necessity of a form of thought is, that it is subjectively, not objectively determined. (1860, 24–5)

This sounds absurd to the modern reader, because the anti-psychologism of the German analytic tradition has accustomed us to think of necessity as incompatible with mental subjectivity. But it makes perfect sense within the framework of Kant's transcendental idealism. The necessary features of thought must derive from the subject of knowledge, because the input from reality is always a matter of brute contingent fact.

Even in his psychologistic moments, however, Kant remained opposed to naturalism. This anti-naturalism is the most important common ground between Frege and Kantianism, and the one which is central to the German analytic tradition presented here. But this common ground is not liable to make either Kantianism or Frege look more fashionable in the current philosophical climate. In the USA in particular, it seems that no book in philosophy of mind can be published that does not start with a profession that the author is a naturalist.

At this juncture it is important to distinguish different types of naturalism. Metaphilosophical naturalism reduces philosophy and logic to a branch of natural science. Epistemological naturalism maintains that there is no knowledge outside of natural science. Ontological naturalism insists that there is no realm other than the physical, and hence that all casual explanation refers to natural events.

Kant, Frege, and the Neo-Kantians reject all of these versions. They strongly distinguish between philosophy (logic, epistemology) and natural sciences, notably psychology; they insist that logic and epistemology can provide knowledge of the content and validity of our beliefs which is independent of scientific knowledge of the origins of our belief. And they admit realms beyond the casual order of physical and mental nature, whether it be Kant's noumena or

163

Hans-Johann Glock

Frege's third realm. I am sympathetic to ontological naturalism. Although I have not argued for this claim here, reference to things in themselves, the transcendental workings of the mind, or the third realm is a case of mystery-mongering. A truly convincing anti-naturalism should therefore avoid both Kant's transcendental idealism and Frege's Platonism. But, on the other two issues, I think that they are right and current fashion is wrong. *A priori* conceptual questions cannot be reduced to empirical factual ones. In particular, the attempt to solve logical and epistemological problems by scientific investigations into the casual genesis of our beliefs either ignores the issues or amounts to the kind of genetic fallacy Frege and Kantianism warned against.

For this reason I should like to end with C. D. Broad, himself a Kantian of sorts, who once remarked 'All good fallacies go to America when they die, and rise again as the latest discoveries of the local professors' (1930, 55). These days they rise again as "scientific" discoveries of the local naturalists. It may be a bit disappointing to conclude a paper on the German analytic tradition with the quip of a Cambridge philosopher. But for all their numerous merits, German philosophers just aren't that funny![7]

References

Baker, G. and Hacker, P. M. S. *Language, Sense and Nonsense* (Oxford: Blackwell, 1984).
Carnap, R. *The Logical Syntax of Language* (London: Routledge & Kegan Paul, 1937).
Coffa, A. *The Semantic Tradition* (Cambridge University Press, 1991).
Czolbe, H. *Neue Darstellung des Sensualismus* (Leipzig, 1855).
Danto, A. 'Naturalism', in P. Edwards (ed), *The Encyclopedia of Philosophy* (New York: Macmillan, 1967).
Dummett, M. A. E. *Frege: Philosophy of Language* (London: Duckworth, 1973).
—— *The Interpretation of Frege's Philosophy* (London: Duckworth, 1981).
—— *Frege and other Philosophers* (Oxford: Oxford University Press, 1991).
—— *The Origins of Analytic Philosophy* (London: Duckworth, 1993).
Føllesdal, D. 'Analytic Philosophy: what is it and why should one engage in it', in H. J. Glock (ed), *The Rise of Analytic Philosophy* (Oxford: Blackwell, 1997).
Frege, G. *The Foundations of Arithmetic*, trans. J. L. Austin (Oxford, 1953 [1. edn. 1884]).

[7] Work on this paper was supported by a Fellowship from the Alexander von Humboldt-Foundation for which I am grateful.

—— *Grundgesetze der Arithmetik*, Vol. I (Hildesheim: Olms, 1996 [1. edn. 1893]).

—— *Posthumous Writings* (Oxford: Blackwell, 1979 [1. edn. 1969]).

—— *Collected Papers* (Oxford: Blackwell, 1984).

Gabriel, G. 'Logizismus', in *Historisches Wörterbuch der Philosophie*, Vol. V (1980).

—— 'Frege als Neukantianer', *Kanstudien* 77 (1986).

Glock, H. J. 'Kant and Wittgenstein: Philosophy, Necessity and Representation', *International Journal of Philosophical Studies*, 5 (1997a).

—— 'Philosophy, Thought and Language', in J. Preston (ed.), *Thought and Language* (Cambridge University Press, 1997b).

—— Review Article of *Frege* by Anthony Kenny, *Grazer Philosophische Studien*, **52**.

—— 'Schopenhauer and Wittgenstein: Language as Representation and Will, R. C. Janaway (ed.), *The Cambridge Companion to Schopenhauer* (New York: Cambridge University Press, 1999).

Hacker, P. M. S. 'The Rise of Twentieth Century Analytic Philosophy', in H. J. Glock (ed.), *The Rise of Analytic Philosophy* (Oxford: Blackwell, 1997).

Hamilton, W. *Lectures on Metaphysics and Logic*, Vol. III (Edinburgh & London: Blackwood, 1860).

Kant, I. *Prolegomena to any future Metaphysics*, trans. P. G. Lucas (Manchester University Press, 1953 [1. edn. 1783]).

—— *On a Discovery according to which any New Critique of Pure Reason has been made Superfluous by an Earlier One*, trans. H. Allison (Baltimore: John Hopkins University Press, 1973 [1. edn. 1790]).

—— 'The Jäsche Logic' in *Lectures on Logic*, trans. J. M. Young (Cambridge University Press, 1992).

—— *The Critique of Pure Reason*, trans. P. Guyer and A. Woods. (Cambridge University Press, 1998 [1. edn. 1781 and 1787]).

Kneale, W. and Kneale, M. *The Development of Logic* (Oxford: Clarendon, 1984).

Liebmann, O. *Zur Analysis der Wirklichkeit* (Strsßburg, 1880 [1. edn. 1876]).

Lotze, R. H. *Logik* (Leipzig, 1874).

Mill, J. S. *An Examination of Sir William Hamilton's Philosophy* (New York, 1973).

Monk, R. 'Was Russell an Analytic Philosopher?', in H. J. Glock (ed.), *The Rise of Analytic Philosophy* (Oxford: Blackwell, 1997).

Natorp, P. *Die Logischen Grundlagen der Exakten Wissenschaften* (Leipzig: Tenbner, 1910).

Rickert, H. *Der Gegenstand der Erkenntnis* (Freiburg, 1904 [1. edn. 1892]).

Sigwart, C. *Logik*, Vol. I (Tübingen: Mohr, 1873).

Schnädelbach, H. *Philosophy in Germany 1831–1933* (Cambridge University Press, 1984).

Sluga, H. *Frege* (London: Routledge, 1980). 'Frege on Meaning', in H. J. Glock (ed.), *The Rise of Analytic Philosophy* (Oxford: Blackwell, 1997).

Hans-Johann Glock

Smith, B. *Austrian Philosophy* (La Salle: Open Court, 1994).

Strawson, P. F. *Analysis and Metaphysics* (Oxford: Oxford University Press, 1992).

Trendelenburg, A. *Logische Untersuchungen*, Vol. I, (Leipzig, 1870).

Wedberg, A. *A History of Philosophy*, Vol. III, (Oxford: Clarendon Press, 1984).

Windelband, W. *Präludien* (Tübingen: Mohr, 1921 [1. edn. 1884]).

Wittgenstein, L. *Tractatus Logico-Philosophicus* (London: Routledge & Kegan Paul, 1961 [1. edn. 1922]).

German Philosophy of Mathematics from Gauss to Hilbert

DONALD GILLIES*

1 Introduction

Suppose we were to ask some students of philosophy to imagine a typical book of classical German philosophy and describe its general style and character, how might they reply? I suspect that they would answer somewhat as follows. The book would be long and heavy, it would be written in a complicated style which employed only very abstract terms, and it would be extremely difficult to understand. At all events a description of this kind does indeed fit many famous works of German philosophy. Let us take for example Hegel's *Phenomenology of Spirit* of 1807. The 1977 English translation published by Oxford has 591 pages, and as for style here is a typical passage:

> Self-consciousness found the Thing to be like itself, and itself to be like a Thing; i.e., it is aware that it is *in itself* the objectively real world. It is no longer the *immediate* certainty of being all reality, but a certainty for which the immediate in general has the form of something superseded, so that the *objectivity* of the immediate still has only the value of something superficial, its inner being and essence being self-consciousness itself. The object, to which it is positively related, is therefore a self-consciousness. It is in the form of thinghood, i.e. it is *independent*; but it is certain that this independent object is for it not something alien, and thus it knows that it is *in principle* recognized by the object. It is Spirit which, in the duplication of its self-consciousness and in the independence of both, has the certainty of its unity with itself. This certainty has now to be raised to the level of truth; what holds good for it *in principle*, and in its inner certainty, has to enter into its consciousness and become *explicit* for it. (p. 211)

Now of course it is by no means necessary that philosophy should

* I am most grateful to Max Albert, Herbert Breger, David Corfield, Ladislav Kvasz, and Volker Peckhaus who read an earlier draft of this paper, and made very helpful comments, many of which have been incorporated into the present version.

Donald Gillies

be written in this way. Many acknowledged masterpieces of philosophy are short in length and written in a clear and often charming literary style. Examples would be Plato's early dialogues, Descartes' *Meditations*, or Hume's *Enquiry concerning the Human Understanding*. There have consequently been a number of theories as to why classical German philosophy has the character just described. It is sometimes claimed that a love of obscure metaphysical theorising is a feature of the German character, or again that the complexities of German grammar lead to a convoluted style. I am sceptical of such theories, however, and will next present some arguments against them.

Let me begin by observing that by no means all great German philosophers write in the manner of Hegel. There is indeed a famous German philosopher whose works have almost exactly the opposite characteristics. His most important work is only 130 pages long in the currently standard English edition, while all his specifically philosophical writing put together would probably be shorter than a single tome by Hegel. Moreover his works as well as being concise are very clear, witty, and full of literary brilliance. I am sure that by now you have guessed that I am referring to Frege, and his *The Foundations of Arithmetic*. Let me sharpen the contrast with Hegel by quoting a short passage from this work. It should be explained that Frege uses the word 'idea' in the usual ordinary language sense as referring to part of the contents of the mind of a particular individual. He then argues against the view that number is an idea as follows:

> If number two were an idea, then it would have straight away to be private to me only. Another man's idea is, *ex vi termini*, another idea. We should then have it might be many millions of twos on our hands. We should have to speak of my two and your two, of one two and all twos. If we accept latent or unconscious ideas, we should have unconscious twos among them, which would then return subsequently to consciousness. As new generations of children grew up, new generations of twos would continually be being born, and in the course of millenia these might evolve, for all we could tell, to such a pitch that two of them would make five. (1884, p. 37)

How are we to explain the obvious differences between Frege's philosophical writings and those of Hegel and many other German idealistic philosophers? The explanation is in my view quite simple. Frege was trained as a mathematician, not as a philosopher. Though he obviously read a great deal of philosophy, his undergraduate degree and doctorate were both in mathematics, and his job was as a lecturer in a mathematics department. The difference between Hegel and Frege is nothing other than the difference between the German philosophical tradition[1] and the German mathematical tradition in the period c. 1800 to c. 1935. Let me now say a little about these two traditions.

Kant (1724–1804) was the founder of the German philosophical tradition, and it was he who broke with the tradition of writing clearly which had dominated philosophy from Descartes to this time. He also introduced the long and complicated philosophical tome with the publication of his *Critique of Pure Reason*. His followers among the philosophers took up these innovations and developed them further. Gauss whose life (1777–1855) partly overlapped with that of Kant was the founder of the German mathematical tradition, but his ideas about writing and style were very different. Gauss was always very reluctant to publish anything, and adopted as his motto *pauca sed matura* – few but ripe. His published works were short and highly polished. His successors in the great German mathematical tradition adopted the same style. Mathematics is usually hard to follow, but, nonetheless, there can be considerable difference in the clarity with which mathematical results are presented. I have found that the mathematical works which are easiest to follow were nearly all produced by German mathematicians in the period from Gauss to Hilbert. This was brought home to me when I was trying to learn Cantor's transfinite set theory. After struggling with a number of modern textbooks, I turned to Cantor's original exposition, and found it to be a model of clarity in comparison with later expositions.

My conclusion is that the characteristics of philosophical writing depend more on an intellectual tradition than on such factors as national character or language. Indeed in the same nation two distinct intellectual traditions with quite different characteristics can co-exist. This was the case in Germany in the period we are dealing with. In the next section I will give an overview of German philosophy of mathematics during this time, and argue that it was influenced more by the mathematical tradition than by that of philosophy.

[1] In speaking here of the German philosophical tradition I am thinking mainly of German Idealism. Volker Peckhaus has pointed out, however, that this is misleading in that there were other currents in German philosophy of the period such as Herbart's empiricism, neo-Kantianism, and Husserl's phenomenology. I will allude to these other trends from time to time in what follows – mainly in order to qualify some of my generalisations.

Donald Gillies

2 Overview of philosophy of mathematics in Germany from Gauss to Hilbert

German philosophy of mathematics in this period was without doubt strongly influenced by Kant, who after all presented a detailed philosophical account of arithmetic and geometry. Indeed most of the leading philosophers of mathematics take Kant as their starting point. However their attitude towards Kant is often ambiguous, and usually the emphasis is more on criticizing and rejecting some of Kant's views than on accepting and developing a Kantian position. Frege is a good illustration of this. In *The Foundations of Arithmetic* he refers to Kant as (1884, p. 101): 'a genius to whom we must all look up with grateful awe'. Yet in §5 of the same work (1884, pp. 5–7) he criticises Kant's view of arithmetic in a crushing, indeed dismissive, fashion.

Although the German philosophers of mathematics take Kant as their starting point it is a striking fact that they almost never discuss, or even mention, any of Kant's successors in the German idealist tradition. German philosophers of mathematics of this period practically never make any use of the ideas of Hegel, Fichte, Schopenhauer, etc. There is indeed one curious exception to this general rule, and this is none other than Karl Marx. Marx did not study any advanced mathematics as a university student, but, when he was working on *Capital* he taught himself differential and integral calculus, presumably thinking that these might be useful in developing his economic theory. As it turned out he did not produce a mathematical version of his economics, but he did write some essays on the foundations of the calculus which have now been published as *The Mathematical Manuscripts*. Marx was undoubtedly influenced by Hegel who discusses the calculus in his *Science of Logic* (book 1, section 2, chapter II. See particularly 1812–16, pp. 256–320). Marx's investigations are not without interest but suffer from the following flaw. Marx discusses the calculus in its 18th century dy/dx form, and did not know of the new ϵ, δ, approach being developed at the time by Weierstrass and other German mathematicians. So much of what he says is rendered obsolete by subsequent mathematical developments.

Still more curiously a philosophical programme not dissimilar from Marx's was attempted at one stage of his career by Bertrand Russell, who presumably knew nothing of Marx's work on this subject.[2] Russell's first book on philosophy of mathematics, his (1897)

[2] The first excerpts from Marx's *The Mathematical Manuscripts* were published in Russian translation in 1933. They were not published in full and in the original German until 1968. For further details see Kennedy (1977).

An Essay on the Foundations of Geometry adopted a Kantian position. However Hegel was still the dominant philosophical influence in Cambridge at that time, and Russell next attempted a Hegelian approach to mathematics. As he says himself in *My Philosophical Development*.

> However, there was worse to follow. My theory of geometry was mainly Kantian, but after this I plunged into efforts at Hegelian dialectic. I wrote a paper 'On the Relations of Number and Quantity' which is unadulterated Hegel. (1959, p. 40)

Russell goes on to quote extensively from this paper. A few lines will suffice for our purposes:

> On the first hypothesis, we shall see that extensive quantities are rendered contradictory by their divisibility, and must be taken as really indivisible, and so intensive. But intensive quantity too, it will appear, must, if it be an intrinsic property of intensive quantities, be also a mere relation between them. The hypothesis that quantity is a category giving an intrinsic property will therefore have to be rejected. The hypothesis that quantity is a datum in sense will also be found to lead to contradictions.

Russell then comments on this former Hegelian approach of his as follows:

> Although Couturat described this article as 'ce petit chef d'œuvre de dialectique subtile', it seems to me now nothing but unmitigated rubbish. (1959, p. 41)

Now the surprising thing is that, when he made this Hegelian attempt at a philosophy of mathematics, Russell, like Marx before him did not know of Weierstrass' ϵ, δ approach to calculus. Weierstrass' new approach to the foundations of the calculus became well known to German mathematicians as a result of Weierstrass' lectures at the University of Berlin in the 1860s. Russell completed the Cambridge mathematical tripos in May 1893 being placed 7th Wrangler, and yet there appears to have been no mention of Weierstrass' new methods in the course. Not for the first (and perhaps not for the last) time, it seems that English intellectuals were suffering from a bout of insularity and ignoring advances which had been made in Continental Europe.

According to Monk (1996, p. 113), Russell first heard of Weierstrass on a visit to America in 1896. The information came from two mathematicians Frank Morley and James Harkness who had been originally trained in Cambridge, but had gone on later to discover Weierstrass. In 1898, Morley and Harkness published a textbook *An Introduction to the Theory of Analytic Functions* in which they adopted the ϵ, δ methods. Russell studied this book carefully, and it was thus that he learned of Weierstrass' approach. This seems to have been one of the principal reasons for his abandoning Hegel. Yet the study of Hegel may have had a lasting influence on Russell. It could have made him particularly sensitive to contradictions, and hence prepared the way for his discovery of his own contradiction.[3]

After this digression which has taken us to London and Cambridge, let us now return to Germany. A second generalisation about philosophy of mathematics in Germany in the period from Gauss to Hilbert is that it was done almost exclusively by mathematicians with philosophical interests, but doing mathematical research and working in mathematics departments.[4] As a result their research in philosophy of mathematics was largely driven by problems arising out of current mathematical practice. Once again we can observe that this is not the only way in which philosophy of mathematics can be done. Another style is illustrated by contemporary philosophy of mathematics in the analytic tradition. This is mainly concerned with general philosophical questions about the ontology and epistemology of sets and numbers such as the following: Do numbers exist, and, if so, in what sense? How can we know truths about numbers? – and so on. Papers written in this style may mention results from elementary arithmetic or results from mathematical logic (mainly proved before 1940), but they almost never contain a reference to any current mathematical research programme.[5] For this reason this type of philosophy of mathematics

[3] This at any rate is the thesis of Moore and Garciadiego in their very interesting article of 1981. They write: 'Russell began to search for paradoxes in mathematics much earlier than is usually recognised. His predisposition to invent such paradoxes had its roots in the philosophical antinomies of Kant and Hegel, both of whom deeply influenced his early development as a philosopher' (p. 324).

[4] As Ladislav Kvasz pointed out to me, there are a number of exceptions to this rule. Edmond Husserl (1858–1938) is the most striking, but several neo-Kantians also wrote on the philosophy of mathematics – for example Hermann Cohen (1842–1918), Paul Natorp (1854–1924), and Ernst Cassirer (1874–1945). These qualifications to my thesis should be borne in mind in what follows.

[5] The papers by Benacerraf, Dummett, and Putnam in Benacerraf and Putnam (1983) (all first published between 1967 and 1977) are good examples of this type of philosophy. We can mention Field (1980) as well, while Wittgenstein (1956) also falls under the same general description. Generally speaking this style of philosophy of mathematics has been the dominant trend in English speaking countries since around 1960. For a general survey see Chihara (1990), and also my review of his book, Gillies (1992).

has been aptly described by Zheng as 'philosophy of mathematics for philosophers'.[6] In contrast, German philosophy of mathematics from Gauss to Hilbert could be described as 'philosophy of mathematics for mathematicians'. Popper is well known for approving of philosophy of the second rather than first type. He writes:

> The degeneration of philosophical schools is in its turn the consequence of the belief that one can philosophise without being compelled to turn to *problems which arise outside philosophy* – in mathematics, for example, or in cosmology, or in politics, or in religion, or in social life. In other words my first thesis is this. *Genuine philosophical problems are always rooted in urgent problems outside philosophy, and they die if these roots decay.* (1963, pp. 71–2).

Since German philosophy of mathematics was driven by problems which arose outside philosophy in mathematics, we can classify the main developments by the mathematical results which gave rise to them. Following this principle, we can distinguish three main philosophical views which will be discussed in the remaining three sections of the paper. In section 3, I will argue that the discovery of non-Euclidean geometry gave rise to an empiricist philosophy of mathematics which was applied to geometry, even if not to arithmetic. In section 4, I will trace a path which led from the arithmetisation of analysis by Cantor and Dedekind (itself the result of Weierstrass' ϵ, δ approach to analysis) to logicism in the philosophy of mathematics. Finally in section 5, I will argue that the development of a plurality of systems of geometry in the period following the discovery of non-Euclidean geometry was the main factor in the rise of formalism in the philosophy of mathematics.[7]

---

[6] See Zheng, *The Revolution in Philosophy of Mathematics*, Forthcoming, Zheng also stresses that there is another approach in contemporary philosophy of mathematics which originates with Lakatos (1963–4). This alternative paradigm stresses the historical development of mathematics, and is more in touch with contemporary developments in mathematics, particularly the changes in mathematics which are occurring because of the development of computer science.

[7] Volker Peckhaus pointed out that the development of the new algebras by the Grassmanns (both Hermann and his brother Robert), Hankel, and Schröder also had important implications for philosophy. For their importance in the development of logic, see Peckhaus (1997, pp. 50–4). Michael Wright also stressed in a comment on the paper that account should be taken of the philosophical importance of Hermann Grassmann's *Ausdehnungslehre* of 1844.

Donald Gillies

3 The discovery of non-Euclidean geometry and empiricism in the philosophy of mathematics

There were two principal stages in the discovery of non-Euclidean geometry. The first of these resulted in the development of hyperbolic (or Bolyai–Lobachevsky) geometry. The main figures involved were Gauss (who never published his results), Lobachevsky whose first publication on the subject was in 1826, and Bolyai who first published in 1832–3. The results of Bolyai and Lobachevsky did not become known to anyone outside a very small circle until the late 1860s.

Now it is obvious that the discovery of non-Euclidean geometry had profound philosophical consequences. Previous to this discovery it was thought that Euclidean geometry was the only possible geometry, and *a fortiori* the true geometry of space. All its theorems could be deduced from a few axioms generally held to be self-evidently correct. Thus Euclidean geometry did appear to be knowledge of the world which could be acquired *a priori,* and so Kant's view of Euclidean geometry as synthetic *a priori* must have seemed eminently reasonable. As soon, however, as it was recognised that an alternative non-Euclidean geometry was possible, the question naturally presented itself as to whether the true geometry of space might not, after all, be non-Euclidean rather than Euclidean. This question could apparently only be answered by observation and measurement, thus making the foundations of geometry empirical rather than *a priori*. This consequence of his discovery was clear to Gauss who wrote to Olbers in 1817

> I am becoming more and more convinced that the necessity of our geometry cannot be proved, at least not by human reason nor for human reason. Perhaps in another life we will be able to obtain insight into the nature of space, which is now unattainable. Until then we must place geometry not in the same class with arithmetic, which is purely *a priori*, but with mechanics. (quoted from Kline, 1972, p. 872)

It is worth noting that Gauss restricts his empiricism about mathematics to geometry, and continues to regard arithmetic as *a priori*.

The next step in the discovery of non-Euclidean geometry was taken by Riemann, a student of Gauss'. This resulted in the development of elliptic or Riemannian geometry. Riemann presented his new ideas in his famous lecture: 'Über die Hypothesen, welche der Geometrie zu Grunde liegen' (On the Hypotheses which lie at the Foundations of Geometry) delivered as a qualifying lecture (*Habilitationsvortrag*) for the title of *Privatdozent* to the faculty at

Göttingen on 10 June 1854. It was not however published until 1868 following Riemann's early death, and did not become widely known until after that date.

Riemann took as his starting point Gauss' investigations of the geometry of curved surfaces, which Gauss had published in 1827. Gauss had considered the geometry of figures on a curved surface, such as figures drawn on the surface of a sphere or ellipsoid. One application which Gauss had in mind was to figures on the Earth's surface. Throughout his investigations, Gauss had always taken the curved surface to be imbedded in a space of higher dimension. So, for example, he would consider the surface of a sphere in ordinary Euclidean three-dimensional space. Riemann's innovation was to consider the surface as a space in its own right with its own intrinsic geometry, and hence to leave out of consideration the question of whether this space was imbedded in a space of higher dimension.[8]

To arrive at his general conception of geometry, Riemann begins by introducing the concept of an *n*-dimensional continuous manifold. This is more general than the ordinary concept of geometrical space since there are other instances of continuous manifolds. Riemann mentions (1854, p. 413) the manifold of colours as an example. A point in an *n*-dimensional continuous manifold is given by *n* determinations of magnitude, but these do not suffice to fix the metric of the manifold which can be imposed in many different ways. These considerations lead Riemann to his empiricism regarding geometry since it becomes a matter of experience to determine the metric of our actual space. In his empiricism Riemann is of course influenced again by Gauss, but he also says that he made use of some philosophical investigations of Herbart. This is how Riemann himself summarises his general point of view

> I have proposed to myself at first the problem of constructing the concept of a multiply extended magnitude out of general notions of quantity. From this it will result that a multiply extended magnitude is susceptible of various metric relations and that space accordingly constitutes only a particular case of a triply extended magnitude. A necessary sequel of this is that the propositions of geometry are not derivable from general concepts of quantity, but that those properties by which space is distinguished from other conceivable triply extended magnitudes can be gathered only from experience. There arises from this the problem of searching

[8] As David Corfield pointed out to me, Gauss' mathematical work prepared the way for Riemann's insight. Gauss in fact realised, through the use of intrinsic co-ordinates on the surface, that curvature was intrinsic, i.e., independent of the embedding. This is his *Theorema Egregium*.

out the simplest facts by which the metric relations of space can be determined, a problem which in the nature of things is not quite definite; for several systems of simple facts can be stated which would suffice for determining the metric relations of space; the most important for present purposes is that laid down for foundations by Euclid. These facts are, like all facts, not necessary but of a merely empirical certainty; they are hypotheses; one may therefore inquire into their probability, which is truly very great within the bounds of observation, and thereafter decide concerning the admissibility of protracting them outside the limits of observations, not only toward the immeasurably large, but also toward the immeasurably small. (1854, pp. 411–12)

There are a number of points which can be made about this passage. To begin with Riemann argues that since the propositions of geometry are not derivable from general concepts of quantity because one needs to add a specific metric, the truth of these propositions can only be gathered from experience. He does not however comment on the epistemological origin of propositions about quantity. It is possible that he regarded these as *a priori* in character, so that the empirical character of geometry only arose from the problem of choosing the metric. Such a position would accord well with Gauss' statement that arithmetic is purely *a priori,* since general concepts of quantity might be thought of as belonging to arithmetic. However since Riemann is not explicit on this point, we cannot be sure what his position was. The title of Riemann's lecture is itself an implicit criticism of Kant, since Riemann's point is that *hypotheses* (which may be empirically confirmed or disconfirmed) and *not a priori truths* lie at the foundation of geometry. This point is made more explicit in the passage just quoted, since Riemann claims that the Euclidean assumptions are 'not necessary but of a merely empirical certainty', and that since 'they are hypotheses', 'one may therefore inquire into their probability'. Riemann regards this probability as very high for what falls within the bounds of observation, but still regards it as possible that the Euclidean assumptions might break down 'toward the immeasurably large' or 'toward the immeasurably small'.

The introduction by Einstein of the general theory of relativity in 1915 and its subsequent confirmation by observation showed that the Euclidean assumptions do break down 'toward the immeasurably large' and that physical space is Riemannian with variable curvature rather than Euclidean. Curiously enough, however, Riemann himself thought that the Euclidean assumptions were more likely to break down 'toward the immeasurably small' than 'toward the immeasurably large'. Indeed he says:

> Questions concerning the immeasurably large are, for the explanation of Nature, useless questions. Quite otherwise is it however with questions concerning the immeasurably small. Knowledge of the causal connection of phenomena is based essentially upon the precision with which we follow them down into the infinitely small. (1854, pp. 423–4)

And goes on to say a little later in the paper

> Now however the empirical notions on which spatial measurements are based appear to lose their validity when applied to the indefinitely small, namely the concept of a fixed body and that of a light-ray; accordingly it is entirely conceivable that in the indefinitely small the spatial relations of size are not in accord with the postulates of geometry, and one would indeed be forced to this assumption as soon as it would permit a simpler explanation of the phenomena. (1854, p. 424)

As an empiricist, Riemann does not think that his investigations into the foundations of geometry will determine what is the true geometry of space. That is a question for physics to decide. However he thinks that his investigations may help the physicist by suggesting alternatives to the Euclidean assumptions. As he himself says:

> A decision upon these questions can be found only by starting from the structure of phenomena that has been approved in experience hitherto, for which Newton laid the foundation, and by modifying this structure gradually under the compulsion of facts which it cannot explain. Such investigations as start out, like this present one, from general notions, can promote only the purpose that this task shall not be hindered by too restricted conceptions, and that progress in perceiving the connection of things shall not be obstructed by the prejudices of tradition. (1854, p. 425)

Riemann's new geometry and his empiricist philosophy of geometry did indeed help the progress of physics by giving physicists new possibilities to explore, and by removing the prejudices of tradition which might have led them to overlook these possibilities. If everyone had accepted Kant's view that Euclidean geometry is synthetic *a priori*, this would certainly have blocked the developments which led to the general theory of relativity.

Riemann was by no means the only German thinker to adopt the empiricist philosophy of geometry. Helmholtz published a number of works defending empiricism in geometry from 1866 on. His works after 1868 were influenced by Riemann's lecture which was published that year, but he seems to have worked out many of his ideas independently. Erdmann published a lengthy exposition and defence of the Riemann–Helmholtz position in 1877. I will not, however, give a detailed account of these developments here,[9] but rather turn to another philosophy of mathematics and this time an *a priorist* one, namely logicism. In the next section I will give a brief account of how this philosophy originated, and how it developed.

4 The arithmetisation of analysis and logicism in the philosophy of mathematics

In the nineteenth century logicism was the theory that arithmetic (or the theory of the natural numbers) could be reduced to logic. The first published works to advocate this philosophy were Frege's 1884 and Dedekind's 1888. Frege and Dedekind worked out their rather different versions of logicism independently.[10] Frege states in 1884 (§91, p. 103) that he invented his concept writing or *Begriffischrift* in order to carry out his logicist programme for arithmetic. Now the *Begriffischrift* was published in 1879, and this suggests that Frege started developing his logicist philosophy in the mid 1870s. Very likely Dedekind began at about the same time. This prompts the question as to why an interest in the foundations of arithmetic should have sprung up at that time. Nor is it difficult to find what is at least a partial answer. The logicism of Frege and Dedekind is a natural extension of developments in analysis and its foundations which had culminated in the early 1870s in what is

[9] A good account of the philosophical views on geometry of Helmholtz and Erdmann is to be found in Russell (1897, pp. 76–97). Herbert Breger drew my attention to another interesting discussion of empiricism in the philosophy of mathematics at about this time. This is summarised, largely in Breger's own words, below. It occurs in Paul du Bois-Reymond's *Allgemeine Funktionentheorie* of 1882. In this book there is a dialogue between an idealist and an empiricist on philosophy of magnitude, limit, and function. The empiricist says that the idealist makes an assumption of an exact measure, but this does not exist according to the empiricist. He continues that all reliable knowledge starts from perception. In an empiricist mathematics, axioms are not appropriate. The idealist thinks of a straight line as something completely exact, but the empiricist says that although the idea of a straight line can be made more and more perfect, it will never be completely straight. Paul du Bois-Reymond just gives the dialogue, and does not decide between the two positions.

[10] The differences between Frege's logicism and that of Dedekind are discussed in Gillies (1982). See particularly chapters 8–10, pp. 50–70.

known as the arithmetisation of analysis. I will now review briefly these developments.

Between 1820 and 1860 there occurred what is known as 'the revolution in rigour' in which the approach to analysis using infinitesimals dx, dy was replaced by the ϵ, δ method.[11] This change was not motivated simply by the desire for greater mathematical rigour, but also by changes and developments within analysis itself. The most important of these was the study of Fourier series. Fourier series are trigonometric series of the general form

$$\frac{a_0}{2} + \sum_{n=1}^{\infty} a_n \cos nx + b_n \sin nx$$

The study of trigonometric series had begun in the eighteenth century, and Fourier tried to use such series to solve the partial differential equations of heat flow in a series of articles beginning in 1807, and culminating in his *Théorie analytique de la chaleur* of 1822. The general idea is to express an arbitrary function $f(x)$ on a bounded interval as a Fourier series of the above form. Suppose we do this for $f(x)=x$ in the interval $(-\pi, \pi)$. The corresponding Fourier series gives the function $f(x)=x$ in the interval $(-\pi, \pi)$, but outside this interval we have a periodic continuation of this function ($g(x)$ say) as shown in figure 1.

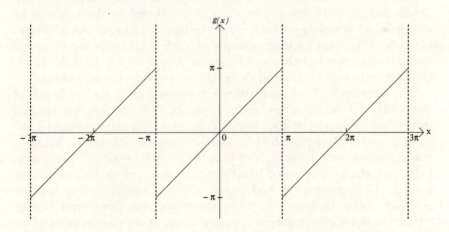

Figure 1.

[11] Two interesting articles about the revolution in rigour are Lakatos (1966), and Dauben (1992).

In other words we are led naturally to a function which is discontinuous in the modern sense. Moreover Cauchy had 'proved' in his *Cours d'Analyse* of 1821 that any convergent series of continuous functions always has a continuous limit function (see Lakatos, 1966, p. 45). Yet the function illustrated in figure 1 is the limit of a convergent series of continuous functions (the cosine and sine functions), but it is discontinuous. To clear up these problems the mathematicians of the time had to give more precise definitions of such concepts as continuity, convergence to a limit, differentiability, integrability, etc. This was eventually achieved in Weierstrass' work.

In Germany the study of Fourier series was continued by Dirichlet who had met Fourier in Paris in the years 1822–1825, and by Riemann who studied for a while in Berlin under Dirichlet. This study produced many more surprises. Such were the rigours of the German university system at the time that to qualify as a *Privatdozent* (an unpaid position) Riemann had not only to give a qualifying lecture (his *Habilitationsvortag* on the foundations of geometry), but also write a qualifying thesis. For this *Habilitationsschrift* (also of 1854), Riemann chose the topic of the Representability of a Function by a Trigonometric Series. In this work he developed his theory of integration to deal with the integrals which are needed for Fourier series. He also gave an example of a function which is continuous everywhere, but fails to have a derivative infinitely often in every arbitrarily small interval. In the 1860s and early 1870s this result was improved by the creation of examples of functions which were continuous but nowhere differentiable. The most famous example of such a function was given by Weierstrass in a lecture to the Berlin Academy on 18 July 1872. Significantly it is a function defined by a trigonometrical series.[12]

The development of such strange functions arose naturally out of the study of Fourier series, and it brought about a complete change in the basic concept of function. Previous to the separation of continuity and differentiability, it had seemed reasonable to identify real numbers with lengths, and to infer the properties of real numbers from the properties of lengths which geometrical intuition suggested. This procedure had been followed more or less unconsciously. Euler had even in 1734 identified functions with curves whose parts are either defined by a formula, or are curves drawn free hand (cf. Kline, 1972, p. 505). Now a continuous curve drawn free hand will always be intuitively differentiable except at a finite

[12] As Ladislav Kvasz pointed out to me the first continuous but nowhere differentiable function was described by Bolzano around 1830 in his *Funktionenlehre*. This book was not, however, published until long after 1870, and did not influence the course of events just described.

number of points. If we are to deal with functions which are continuous but nowhere differentiable therefore, 'curves drawn free hand' and 'geometrical intuition' are not adequate.

It is not therefore surprising that around 1860 a movement grew up to arithmetise analysis – that is to purge analysis of any dependence on geometrical concepts, and to base it on purely arithmetical concepts. Dedekind is one of the key figures in this movement, and in the preface to his 1872 he explains his motives very clearly. He recounts that, in the autumn of 1858, as professor at the Polytechnic School in Zürich, he had for the first time to lecture on the elements of differential calculus. He goes on

> In discussing the notion of the approach of a variable magnitude to a fixed limiting value, and especially in proving the theorem that every magnitude which grows continually, but not beyond all limits, must certainly approach a limiting value, I had recourse to geometric evidences. Even now such resort to geometric intuition in a first presentation of the differential calculus, I regard as exceedingly useful, from the didactic standpoint, and indeed indispensable, if one does not wish to lose too much time. But that this form of introduction into the differential calculus can make no claim to being scientific, no one will deny. For myself this feeling of dissatisfaction was so overpowering that I made the fixed resolve to keep meditating on the question till I should find a purely arithmetic and perfectly rigorous foundation for the principles of infinitesimal analysis. (1872, pp. 1–2)

From an historical point of view the strange feature of this passage is Dedekind affirmation without argument that a 'recourse to geometric evidences ... can make no claim to being scientific', and that this is something which 'no one will deny'. What makes this attitude curious is that geometry was for so many centuries regarded as the most perfect of the sciences. Yet Dedekind's mistrust of geometrical considerations is perfectly comprehensible if we take account of the mathematical context in which he was working. Dedekind was a friend of Riemann's and indeed edited Riemann's papers after the latter's early death. He would certainly have known of Riemann's results of 1854 on non-Euclidean geometry and on functions which are continuous but fail to have derivatives infinitely often in every arbitrarily small interval. This is sufficient to explain his conviction that the use of geometric intuition was unsatisfactory and his 'fixed resolve to keep meditating on the question till I should find a purely arithmetic and perfectly rigorous foundation for the principles of infinitesimal analysis'. Dedekind was not alone in setting himself this goal, and his efforts

Donald Gillies

and those of others resulted in the arithmetisation of analysis, whose general character I must next explain.

The arithmetisation of analysis consisted essentially of the definition of real numbers in terms of rational numbers. It can be dated to around 1870. Definitions of real numbers in terms of rational numbers were published by Méray in 1869, and by Cantor, Dedekind and Heine in 1872. Weierstrass had earlier (in the 1860s) expounded a theory of real numbers in his lectures at Berlin. The definitions which became best known were those of Dedekind and Cantor.[13]

Now once real numbers had been defined in terms of rational numbers, it was an easy matter to define rational numbers in terms of integers and integers in terms of the natural numbers $\{0, 1, 2, ... n, ...\}$. As complex numbers could be defined in terms of real numbers, it thus appeared as if the study of any kind of number in mathematics really reduced to the study of natural numbers. This is the sense of the claim that analysis had been arithmetised. With the advantage of hindsight, we can question whether this had really been achieved. The various definitions of real number were all in terms of infinite sets of rational numbers. Thus analysis had not been reduced simply to the theory of natural numbers, but to the theory of natural numbers together with the theory of infinite sets.

It is easy to see why this was overlooked at the time. The notion of set must have appeared in the 1870s to be straightforward and unproblematic. Indeed Dedekind regarded 'set' (or in his terminology 'system') as a basic notion of logic. Only after Cantor had developed the theory of infinite sets, and the paradoxes of set theory had emerged, did it become clear that set theory is highly problematic and anything but straightforward. From a contemporary point of view, then, some question marks hangs over the arithmetisation of analysis. Dedekind and the others certainly succeeded in eliminating geometrical considerations from the foundations of analysis, but only at the expense of introducing part of the theory of infinite sets. It could be argued, moreover, that the notion of infinite set is as doubtful as, if not more doubtful than, the geometrical notions which it replaced.

This, however, is a later point of view. In the 1870s it certainly seemed that analysis had been successfully reduced to the theory of natural numbers. The obvious next step in constructing a firm foundation for mathematics would be to provide a satisfactory foundation for the theory of natural numbers. Thus there is a natural transition from the arithmetisation of analysis in the early 1870s to publications on the foundations of arithmetic in the 1880s.

[13] For an account of Cantor's definition of real number, see Dauben (1979, pp. 37–40).

The link here is obvious as far as Dedekind is concerned. His first work on the foundations, his 1872 *Continuity and Irrational Numbers,* is on the arithmetisation of analysis, while his second work on the foundations of mathematics, his 1888, *Was sind und was sollen die Zahlen?,* deals with the foundations of the theory of natural numbers.

Frege (1848–1925) was 17 years younger than Dedekind (1831–1916). The arithmetisation of analysis had just been completed when he started his research career, and it was thus natural for him to concentrate on the foundations of arithmetic. Frege himself summarises the mathematical developments I have just described at the beginning of his *The Foundations of Arithmetic.* He writes:

> The concepts of function, of continuity, of limit and of infinity have been shown to stand in need of sharper definition. Negative and irrational numbers, which had long since been admitted into science, have had to submit to a closer scrutiny of their credentials.
>
> Proceeding along these lies, we are bound eventually to come to the concept of Number and to the simplest propositions holding of positive whole numbers, which form the foundation of the whole of arithmetic. (1884, pp. 1–2)

From all this it is clear that the logicist philosophy of mathematics arose naturally from developments within mathematics itself. This is an important point to stress, but it is also important to qualify it by another consideration. Logicism, as a philosophy of mathematics, is of course part of philosophy, and was therefore, naturally enough, influenced by philosophical problems. Frege makes clear his involvement in philosophy in a passage which follows shortly after the one just quoted. He writes:

> Philosophical motives too have prompted me to enquiries of this kind. The answers to the questions raised about the nature of arithmetical truths – are they *a priori* or *a posteriori*? synthetic or analytic? – must lie in this same direction. (1884, p. 3)

The philosophical problems which Frege mentions here are fundamental to Kant's philosophy, and Frege goes on to discuss Kant's views on mathematics in detail – disagreeing with him as regards arithmetic, but agreeing as regards geometry.

Frege is also very much concerned with another philosophical position, one with which he disagrees very strongly. This of course is *empiricism.* Frege goes as far as to say in his introduction that his views are likely to appeal least to philosophers of an empiricist persuasion. He writes of the results of his book:

Donald Gillies

Their reception by philosophers will be varied, depending on each philosopher's own position; but presumably those empiricists who recognise induction as the sole original process of inference (and even that as a process not actually of inference but of habituation) will like them least. (1884, pp. x–xi)

Moreover *The Foundations of Arithmetic* contains Frege's famous criticism of John Stuart Mill's empiricist philosophy of arithmetic. Our earlier discussion shows that this attack on Mill has perhaps a hidden reference to the situation in German philosophy of mathematics where empiricism was a powerful tendency. We have seen that Riemann, Helmholtz, and Erdmann all gave empiricist accounts of geometry. If these had been combined with a Millian empiricist account of arithmetic (perhaps in a developed form), a comprehensive empiricist philosophy of mathematics might have resulted. Frege, however, was a firm believer in the *a priori* character of mathematics, and was consequently determined to put an end to this empiricist trend in philosophy of mathematics. He even defends Kant's account of Euclidean geometry in the face of the discovery of non-Euclidean geometry (Frege, 1884, §14, pp. 20–1 and §89, pp. 101–2). He is not satisfied with Kant's account of arithmetic, but sees his logicist view as providing a more satisfactory but still *a priori* account.

In view of all this it is somewhat ironical that the first philosophers to admire Frege's work, namely Bertrand Russell and the Vienna Circle, were empiricists. However the situation is not as strange as it might seem at first sight. Both Russell and the Vienna Circle advocated a new form of empiricism according to which mathematics was reducible to logic, and hence true in virtue of the meaning of the words it contained, while the rest of scientific knowledge had an empirical justification.

The logicisms of both Frege and Dedekind were shown to be wrong by the discovery of the paradoxes, particularly Russell's paradox. Russell wrote to Frege on 16 June 1902 giving details of his paradox which showed that Frege's system of logic was inconsistent. Dedekind too in Theorem 60 of *Was sind und was sollen die Zahlen?* (1888, p. 62) had assumed a form of the principle of comprehension from which Russell's paradox follows (cf. Gillies, 1982, pp. 58 and 90–3). But of course the efforts of these two thinkers were far from wasted. *Was sind und was sollen die Zahlen?* was an important source for Zermelo's later axiomatisation of set theory;[14] while Frege brought about a revolution in logic, and, indeed, in his *Begriffsschrift* of 1879 introduced the concepts of formal language

[14] For details see Gillies, (1982, pp. 52–58).

and formal system for the first time. Thus the work of Dedekind and Frege is an important influence on the next philosophy of mathematics which we shall consider – Hilbert's formalism.

Hilbert, however, as we shall see in the next section, was influenced not only by work on the foundations of arithmetic, but also by developments in geometry. Indeed Hilbert's formalism provides a unified philosophy of mathematics covering both arithmetic and geometry which had been treated separately by Gauss, Riemann, and Frege. I will now examine some of the geometrical background to Hilbert's philosophy of mathematics.

5. The development of a plurality of systems of geometry and formalism in the philosophy of mathematics

For centuries Euclidean geometry had been regarded as the only possible system of geometry. However the emergence of an alternative system of geometry (Bolyai–Lobachevsky geometry) in the first half of the nineteenth century was the prelude to a remarkable proliferation of different systems of geometry in the second half of the nineteenth century. While at the beginning of the nineteenth century there had been just one system of geometry by the end there were dozens. This development of a plurality of systems of geometry is an essential part of the background to Hilbert's formalist philosophy of mathematics, and I will now try to sketch briefly how it came about.

Among the different systems of geometry, projective geometry played an important rôle. It might be objected that projective geometry was hardly new since it had been studied by Desargues and Pascal in the seventeenth century, and by Brianchon, Carnot, Gergonne, and Poncelet at the end of the eighteenth and beginning of the nineteenth century. However these earlier researchers had seen projective geometry simply as a part of Euclidean geometry. It was only gradually realised that projective geometry deals essentially with a proper subset of the properties of figures treated by Euclidean geometry. Thus projective geometry deals with relations of incidence between points, lines and conics (which are preserved under projection), but not with distances between points (which are not preserved under projection). This line of thought suggests a new perspective, namely that it might be possible to develop projective geometry without appealing to specifically Euclidean notions such as distance and congruence. This would turn projective geometry into a system of geometry independent of the Euclidean, and perhaps more fundamental.

Donald Gillies

The first to attempt such a treatment was von Staudt in his *Geometrie der Lage* (Geometry of Position) of 1847. Von Staudt tried to assign co-ordinates to points in the plane using only projective notions, and not employing the Euclidean concepts of distance and angle. Given such a system of numerical but non-metrical co-ordinates, Laguerre showed in 1853 how angle could be defined, while Cayley in his famous 'Sixth Memoir on Quantics' of 1859 showed how both distance and angle could be defined. The interesting thing here was that different definitions of distance and angle yielded different geometries, and, in particular, non-Euclidean as well as Euclidean geometries could be obtained in this way. Klein developed these ideas of Cayley, and used them to give consistency proofs of non-Euclidean geometries relative to Euclidean. It is worth noting that Klein's consistency proofs of 1871 and 1873, and the earlier one of Beltrami (1867) are the first example in the history of mathematics of a consistency proof for a whole mathematical system. Here is the origin of Hilbert's later demand that a consistency proof be provided for every branch of mathematics. (Klein incidentally was Hilbert's fellow professor of mathematics at Göttingen from Hilbert's appointment in 1895 till Klein's retirement in 1917.)

Klein is also responsible for the justly famous *Erlanger Programm* which sought to classify various geometries such as projective, Euclidean and non-Euclidean using ideas from group theory. What is significant here is a shift of interest from the object-level to the meta-level. Previously mathematicians had focused on proving new theorems within a particular system of geometry – for example Euclidean or projective. Now there was a move towards investigating different systems of geometry as wholes; examining, for example, whether they were consistent and how they were related to each other. This new point of view stimulated mathematicians in the 1880s to try to produce better axiomatisations of the different systems of geometry. Such axiomatisations could exhibit better the relationships between the various geometries, and also generate new geometries through changes in the axioms in the way in which Bolyai–Lobachevsky geometry had been developed from Euclidean geometry by changing the parallel axiom.

The first important attempt to improve existing axiomatisations of geometry was Moritz Pasch's *Vorlesungen über neuere Geometrie* (Lectures on recent Geometry). The first edition of this work appeared in 1882 just two years' before Frege's *Foundations of Arithmetic* – showing that foundational studies were in the air at that time. Pasch criticised Euclid for having tried to define everything. In particular, Euclid defined a point as that which has no parts, and a straight line as that which lies evenly among its points. Pasch objected that these definitions play no part in the subsequent deductions, and that they define point and straight line in terms of the more obscure notions of 'part' and 'lying evenly'. Pasch argued that the chain of definitions must come to an end, and that we must therefore begin with some undefined notions. He believed that, among others, the notions of 'point', 'line', and 'plane' should be taken as primitive or undefined for geometry. The axioms of geometry themselves then give an implicit definition of the primitive terms. Hilbert took over this approach from Pasch.

Pasch also criticised Euclid for relying on geometrical intuition, i.e., on results which appear immediately obvious when the diagram is drawn. For Pasch, however, the theorems should follow logically from the axioms, and no covert appeal to diagrams should occur in the proofs. Consider for example three points A, B, C on a line. Euclid takes as obvious the notion of B *lying between* A and C, but Pasch introduces a special set of axioms for this notion. Here again Hilbert follows Pasch.

Let us now turn to Hilbert's famous book: *Foundations of Geometry*. The first edition of this was published in 1899. By the time of Hilbert's death in 1943 six further editions had appeared, and, subsequently, 8th, 9th and 10th editions have been published. This book has been very influential in many directions, and also contains some of the main ideas of Hilbert's later formalist philosophy of mathematics.

Perhaps the most significant feature of the book is that Hilbert, having formulated his axioms in chapter I proceeds immediately in chapter II to investigate their consistency and independence. Here we see the shift from the object-level to the meta-level which of course is absent in Euclid's original treatment of geometry. If an axiom is shown to be independent its negation leads to a new system of geometry. For example Hilbert formulates what he calls Archimedes' Axiom as follows (1899, p. 26):

V, I (**Axiom of measure or Archimedes' Axiom**). *If AB and CD are any segments then there exists a number n such that n segments CD constructed contiguously from A, along the ray from A through B, will pass beyond the point B.*

Later (1899, §12, p. 41), Hilbert shows the independence of this axiom from the preceding axioms I–IV. A geometry in which axiom V, 1 fails to hold is called a non-Archimedean geometry. Such geometries were investigated by Dehn, a follower of Hilbert, and they turned out to have rather curious properties.

Hilbert's work on the foundations of geometry supplied many of the ideas of his later formalist philosophy of mathematics. We can mention in particular the following:

(1) the idea that a mathematical theory should be presented as a formal axiomatic system;
(2) the idea that such a formal system should begin with primitive notions which are not explicitly defined, but only implicitly defined by the axioms;

(Hilbert recognised that the axioms do not necessarily determine the meaning of the primitive notions completely, and thus allow these notions to have a number of different interpretations. However he regarded this as an advantage not a disadvantage since it enables the same formal theory to be used in a number of different situations.)

(3) the idea that the formal axiom systems of mathematics should themselves become the objects of 'meta-mathematical' investigation, and, in particular, should be proved to be consistent.

In the years 1900–1904, Hilbert started work on extending these formalist ideas from geometry to arithmetic. He had to assist him the works of Frege and Dedekind already discussed, and Peano's axiomatisation of arithmetic. The notion of a formal system had been developed by Frege and Peano, and Hilbert took this over, but at the same time rejected the logicism of Frege and Dedekind. As he says in his 1904 paper:

Arithmetic is often considered to be a part of logic, and the traditional fundamental logical notions are usually presupposed when it is a question of establishing a foundation for arithmetic. If we observe attentively, however, we realise that in the traditional exposition of the laws of logic certain fundamental arithmetic notions are already used, for example, the notion of set and, to some extent, also that of number. Thus we find ourselves turning in a circle, and that is why a partly simultaneous development of the laws of logic and of arithmetic is required if paradoxes are to be avoided. (p. 131)

Hilbert goes on to expound his system of primitive, finitary, intuitive arithmetic, and uses it to prove consistent an axiom system for a simple fragment of formal arithmetic. This formal axiom system contains essentially axioms of equality together with three of Peano's five axioms.

Here then we have in outline all the main features of Hilbert's later philosophy of mathematics. Yet, apart from his article *Axiomatisches Denken of* 1918, Hilbert did not publish anything further on the foundations of mathematics until 1922. In this period of 18 years, Hilbert was largely occupied with researches into Integral Equations (1902–1912) and Physics (1910–1912). When he took up the problem of foundations in earnest again, a further development had strengthened his general outlook. This was the axiomatisation of set theory.

Zermelo produced a set of axioms for set theory in 1908. He was working with Hilbert at Göttingen, and was obviously influenced by Hilbert's *Foundations of Geometry,* as we can see by comparing passages from Hilbert's classic with passages from Zermelo's 1908 paper. Thus Hilbert writes

> Consider three distinct sets of objects. Let the objects of the **first** set be *called points* ... of the **second** set be called *lines* ... of the **third** set be called *planes* ... The points, lines and planes are considered to have certain mutual relations and these relations are denoted by words like '**lie**', '**between**', '**congruent**'. (1899, p. 3)

Compare this with the beginning of §1 in Zermelo's 1908 paper:

> Set theory is concerned with a *domain* **B** of individuals, which we shall call simply *objects* and among which are the *sets.* ... Certain *fundamental relations* of the form $a \in b$ obtain between the objects of the domain **B**. (p. 201)

There were some weaknesses in Zermelo's 1908 axiomatisation of set theory, but these were corrected in 1922 by Fraenkel and Skolem who suggested independently at the same time that Zermelo's Axiom of Separation (or Subsets) should be eliminated, and a new axiom) – the Axiom of Replacement – used instead. The new ZSF (Zermelo–Skolem–Fraenkel) set theory was much more powerful, and, in particular, provided a framework within which the whole of Cantorian set theory could be developed.

This success set the stage for Hilbert's formalist philosophy. The various branches of mathematics, whether geometry, arithmetic, logic, or set theory, could all in this view be presented as axiomatic formal systems. To provide each branch with a foundation, all that was needed was to give a consistency proof for the corresponding formal system. For this purpose use had to be made of something which was not a formal system, but which had an indubitable character. This was intuitive, finitary arithmetic. We can see how this conception of mathematics arose naturally from preceding developments from the time of the discovery of non-Euclidean geometry. Yet the conception contained much that was revolutionary as well.[15] It had the great advantage of providing a uniform account of the

---

[15] For an interesting analysis of the more revolutionary aspects of Hilbert's ideas see Breger (1992).

whole of mathematics, geometry as well as logic and arithmetic. The only problem with this elegant and comprehensive account of mathematics was that it would soon run into difficulties created by Gödel's incompleteness theorems of 1931.

6 Some concluding remarks

Let us now look back at philosophy of mathematics from Gauss to Hilbert, this time concentrating exclusively on the main figures, and, in contrast to the account in the main part of the paper, considering developments from a purely philosophical point of view. The background is Kant's theory that both arithmetic and geometry were synthetic *a priori* and based on intuition. This was challenged by Riemann who proposed an empiricist account of geometry, but did not comment on arithmetic. Probably, following his teacher Gauss, he still regarded arithmetic as *a priori*. The analysis of arithmetic was taken up by Dedekind and Frege who developed different versions of the logicist thesis that arithmetic was reducible to logic and so *a priori*. Frege's work was distinguished by two important characteristics. One was his aversion to empiricist accounts of mathematics which led to his sharp criticisms of Mill, and his defence of Kant's view of geometry as synthetic *a priori*. Although Frege rejected Kant's theory of arithmetic, his alternative logicist view still made arithmetic *a priori*. A second very important feature of Frege's work was that he developed his logic formally, creating in his *Begriffsschrift* the first example of a fully formalised system. The discovery of Russell's paradox showed that the versions of logicism advocated by Dedekind and Frege were incorrect. Hilbert responded to this situation by abandoning Frege's logicism, but retaining and extending his concept of formal system. The whole of mathematics became for Hilbert a set of axiomatised formal systems. Thus Hilbert gave for the first time since Kant a unified account of mathematics covering both arithmetic and geometry. Hilbert also retained Kant's idea of founding mathematics on intuition, but he applied this at the meta-level rather than the object-level. Each formal system of mathematics had to be proved consistent using only a system of finitary arithmetic which was based on Kantian intuition.

If the main trends of philosophy of mathematics are presented in this fashion, the resulting internal, philosophical account is remarkably coherent. Nevertheless, as I have shown earlier, these philosophical developments were strongly driven by developments within mathematics itself. The philosophical influences came from

Kant, empiricism, and the project of formal logic, itself a project on the interface between philosophy and mathematics. There was no influence from Hegel and other post-Kantian systems of German idealist philosophy. Nor do we find any attempt to resuscitate the link between mathematics and politics for which Plato argues in *The Republic*. Such a link is only even considered in some obscure works on the calculus by Marx, and in the still unpublished 'secret political diary' of Frege.

This last point can be generalised by pointing out that the aim of philosophy of mathematics in this period after Kant is simply to provide an account of mathematics, and not to form part of a more general philosophical system. This is in sharp contrast to Kant himself whose philosophy of mathematics was only the starting point of a philosophical system designed to give an account of the whole of human knowledge, of metaphysics, and of ethics and aesthetics. It is only in the works of Russell, the early Wittgenstein, and the Vienna Circle that the philosophy of mathematics becomes once again the cornerstone of a whole philosophical edifice. Naturally these thinkers, in contrast to Kant, were able to draw on all the advances which we have considered in this paper.

References

P. Benacerraf and H. Putnam eds. *Philosophy of Mathematics. Selected Readings*, 2nd edn (Cambridge University Press, 1983).

H. Breger, 'A Restoration that failed: Paul Finsler's Theory of Sets', in *Revolutions in Mathematics*, ed. D. Gillies (Oxford University Press, 1992), pp. 249–64.

C. S. Chihara, *Constructibility and Mathematical Existence* (Oxford: Clarendon Press, 1990).

J. W. Dauben, *Georg Cantor. His Mathematics and Philosophy of the Infinite* (Cambridge, MA: Harvard University Press, 1979).

J. W. Dauben, 'Revolutions revisited', in *Revolutions in Mathematics*, ed. D. Gillies (Oxford University Press, 1992), pp. 72–82.

R. Dedekind, *Continuity and Irrational Numbers* (1872). English translation in *Essays on the Theory of Numbers* (Dover, 1963).

R. Dedekind, *Was sind und was sollen die Zahlen?* (1888). English translation in *Essays on the Theory of Numbers* (Dover, 1963).

H. H. Field, *Science without Numbers* (Oxford: Blackwell, 1980).

G. Frege, *Begriffsschrift, Eine der arithmetischen nachgebildete Formelsprache des reinen Denkens* (1879). English translation in Jean van Heijenoort, ed., *From Frege to Gödel: A Source Book in Mathematical Logic, 1879–1931* (Cambridge, MA: Harvard University Press, 1967), pp. 1–82.

G. Frege, *The Foundations of Arithmetic: A Logico-Mathematical Enquiry into the Concept of Numbers* (1884). English translation by J. L. Austin (Blackwell, 1968).

D. A. Gillies, *Frege, Dedekind, and Peano on the Foundations of Arithmetic* (Van Gorcum, 1982).

D. A. Gillies, 'Review of Chihara', *British Journal for the Philosophy of Science*, **43**, (1990), pp 263–78.

G. W. F. Hegel, *Phenomenology of Spirit* (*1807*) (Oxford: Clarendon Press, 1977).

G. W. F. Hegel, *Science of Logic*, Vols I and II, (1812–16), (Allen and Unwin, 1929).

D. Hilbert, *Foundations of Geometry* (1899). English translation of the 10th edn (Open Court, 1971).

D. Hilbert, *On the Foundations of Logic and Arithmetic* (1904). English translation in Jean van Heijenoort, ed., *From Frege to Gödel: A Source Book in Mathematical Logic, 1879–1931* (Harvard University Press, 1967), pp. 129–38.

H. C. Kennedy, 'Karl Marx and the Foundations of Differential Calculus', *Historia Mathematica*, **4**(3) (1977), pp. 303–18.

M. Kline, *Mathematical Thought from Ancient to Modern Times* (Oxford University Press, 1972).

I. Lakatos, *Proofs and Refutations* (Cambridge University Press, 1963–4).

I. Lakatos, (1966), *Cauchy and the Continuum*, in J. Worrall and G. Currie (eds), *Imre Lakatos. Philosophical Papers*. Vol. II (Cambridge University Press, 1978), pp. 43–60.

K. Marx, *The Mathematical Manuscripts* (c. 1881). English translation (New Park Publications, 1983).

R. Monk, *Bertrand Russell* (Jonathan Cape, 1996).

G. H. Moore and A. Garciadiego, 'Burali–Forti's Paradox: A Reappraisal of Its Origins', *Historia Mathematica*, **8**(3) (1981), pp. 319–50.

V. Peckhaus, 'The Way of Logic into Mathematics', *Theoria–Segunda Época*, **12**(1), pp. 39–64.

K. R. Popper, *Conjectures and Refutations* (Routledge and Kegan Paul, 1963).

B. Riemann, 'On the Hypotheses which lie at the Foundations of Geometry' (1854). English translation in D. E. Smith ed., *A Source Book in Mathematics*, Vol. II (Dover, 1959), pp. 411–25.

B. Russell, *An Essay on the Foundations of Geometry* (1897) (Routledge, Reprint, 1996).

B. Russell, *My Philosophical Development* (1959) (Allen and Unwin, 1969).

L. Wittgenstein, *Remarks on the Foundations of Mathematics* (Blackwell, 1956).

E. Zermelo, 'Investigations in the Foundations of Set Theory I', (1908). English translation in Jean van Heijenoort, ed., *From Frege to Gödel: A Source Book in Mathematical Logic, 1879–1931* (Harvard University Press, 1967), pp. 199–215.

Y. Zheng, *The Revolution in Philosophy of Mathematics* (Forthcoming).

The Revolution of Moore and Russell: A Very British Coup?

DAVID BELL

I

The question I shall attempt to address in what follows is an essentially historical one, namely: Why did analytic philosophy emerge first in Cambridge, in the hands of G. E. Moore and Bertrand Russell, and as a direct consequence of their revolutionary rejection of the philosophical tenets that form the basis of British Idealism? And the answer that I shall try to defend is: it didn't. That is to say, the 'analytic' doctrines and methods which Moore and Russell embraced in the very last years of the nineteenth century were not revolutionary, did not emerge first in Cambridge, were the creation of neither Russell nor Moore and cannot be explained by appeal to facts concerning British Idealism. The adoption of the doctrines and methods which characterised the earliest manifestations of British analytic philosophy are to be explained neither by reference to anything specifically *British,* nor by appeal to anything unproblematically *philosophical*. Or so I shall argue.

In taking this line I am, of course, intending to dissent from a very widespread and deeply entrenched view, the most detailed and authoritative defence of which forms the content of Peter Hylton's book *Russell, Idealism and the Emergence of Analytic Philosophy*.[1] Because his presentation of the case is, precisely, so detailed and authoritative, I shall tend to take it as exemplary. The view in question has, however, been endorsed by many other commentators, including, it must be said, both Russell and Moore themselves. This, for example, is how Russell typically came to describe the events with which we are concerned:

> It was towards the end of 1898 that Moore and I rebelled against both Kant and Hegel. Moore led the way, but I followed closely in his footsteps. I think the first published account of the new philosophy was Moore's article in *Mind* on 'The Nature of Judgement' ... I felt ... a great liberation, as if I had escaped from a hot house onto a wind swept headland ... In the first exuberance

[1] P. Hylton, *Russell, Idealism and the Emergence of Analytic Philosophy* (Oxford: Clarendon Press, 1990).

of liberation, I became a naive realist and rejoiced in the thought that grass really is green.[2]

Elsewhere Russell wrote:

I was at this time [1898] beginning to emerge from the bath of German idealism in which I had been plunged by McTaggart and Stout. I was very much assisted in this process by Moore. ... It was an intense excitement, after having supposed the sensible world unreal, to be able to believe again that there really are such things as tables and chairs.[3]

And a final example of Russell's reminiscences:

[Moore] took the lead in rebellion, and I followed, with a sense of emancipation. ... With a sense of escaping from prison we allowed ourselves to think that grass is green, [and] that the sun and stars would exist if no one was aware of them. ... The world, which had been thin and logical, suddenly became rich and varied.[4]

These reminiscences, we might note in passing, were written between 45 and 60 years after the occurrence of the events they purport to describe – and perhaps it is simply that great distance that has lent so much enchantment – not to say distortion – to the scene.

Be that as it may, there is now widespread, virtually unanimous agreement that analytic philosophy originated in Cambridge at the turn of the century, as a consequence of the revolt by G. E. Moore and Bertrand Russell against the prevailing idealism of such teachers and contemporaries as Bradley, McTaggart, Ward, and Stout.[5] This, it would seem, was indeed a *very* British coup. It was – so the claim goes – a revolt against British Idealism, in the name of British realism and common sense, by two British philosophers. It was only subsequently, with the arrival of Wittgenstein in Cambridge, the

---

[2] B. Russell, *My Philosophical Development* (London: George Allen & Unwin, 1954), pp. 42, 62.

[3] B. Russell, *Autobiography* (London: George Allen & Unwin, 1967), pp. 134–5.

[4] B. Russell, 'My Mental Development', in *The Philosophy of Bertrand Russell* P. Schilpp (ed.), (Evanston, Illinois: The Library of Living Philosophers), 1946. p. 12.

[5] See, e.g., B. Aune, 'Metaphysics of Analytic Philosophy' in *Handbook of Metaphysics and Ontology* (eds) H. Burkhardt and B. Smith. (Munich: Philosophia Verlag, 1991), vol. II, p. 539. A. J. Ayer, *Russell and Moore: The Analytical Heritage* (London: Macmillan, 1971), p. 141. T. Baldwin, *G. E. Moore* (London: Routledge, 1990), pp. 1–2. M. A. E. Dummett, *Ursprünge der analytischen Philosophie* (Frankfurt: Suhrkamp Verlag, 1988), p. 7.

The Revolution of Moore and Russell: A Very British Coup?

gradual assimilation of Frege's thought, and the emergence of the positivists in Vienna, that the analytic tradition became susceptible to significant non-British influence, or came to include any major non-British developments. In conformity with this picture, for example, Peter Hylton, in charting the antecedents and early development of analytic philosophy, finds very little to take him outside Cambridge. Indeed, there is little need to leave Trinity College, where we find, Moore, Russell, Ward, McTaggart, Broad, Whitehead, and, later, Wittgenstein. Stout, however, was at St John's College, Cambridge; and occasional trips to Oxford are necessary in order to incorporate Green and Bradley into the narrative.

This, then, is the picture of events which I wish to subvert – or rather, it is the picture *the usual significance of which* I intend to contest. The historical events themselves are, of course, not at issue. In order to make this clear, let me mention two claims inherent in the received view that strike me as undeniably true, but unilluminating. The first claim is a matter of mere chronology: Russell and Moore were initially attracted to certain forms of idealism current in Britain in the 1880s[6]. At a later date, around 1899/1900, they came to reject some of their earlier idealistic commitments. This is certainly true. The second claim – equally true, and equally unproblematic – is that the rejection of certain idealist doctrines was a necessary condition of the subsequent adoption of a number of distinctively analytic theories and methods. This, however, is trivially true, and amounts to no more than the assertion that if Moore and Russell were consistently to adopt a realistic and atomistic standpoint, then it was necessary for them to relinquish their early idealism and holism.

With these trivial truths out of the way, we can now ask. What were the forces at work in shaping the form in which analytic philosophy first emerged? What exactly was the role played in this context by British Idealism? And if, as I shall suggest, that role is small, then we need to ask: What were the relevant factors in the intellectual environment in terms of which we can come to understand the emergence of the 'new philosophy' of Russell and Moore?

II

First, some scene-setting is in order. I shall proceed by trying to characterise, in the most general of terms, the relevant intellectual

[6] I shall have nothing to say about the works of Moore and Russell in the period before 1899. For details see, e.g., P. Hylton, *Russell, Idealism and the Emergence of Analytic Philosophy*, pp. 72–101 and 117–21; and N. Griffin, *Russell's Idealist Apprenticeship* (Oxford: Clarendon Press, 1991), passim.

David Bell

environment in western Europe in the last quarter of the nineteenth
century, then in Britain and particularly in Cambridge and finally
with specific regard to the influences at work on the new philosophy
of Moore and Russell. Given the present constrains on length, however, this can only be done in a preliminary and impressionistic way,
and I apologise in advance for the dogmatism and superficiality
which inevitably result from using such a big brush.

The last decade of the last century – when Russell and Moore
were submerging themselves in, and then emerging from, 'the bath
of idealism' – was on the whole a period of intellectual consolida-
tion, during which the revolutionary programmes of the 1870s were
implemented, and their consequences explored.

The 1870s was a remarkable decade, and particularly so in the
German-speaking world. In 1872 Weierstrass, Cantor, and
Dedekind published revolutionary works that were to inaugurate a
new era in number theory and analysis. In the same year both Klein
and Riemann published works that revolutionised Geometry, and
Mach published his influential work on the conservation of energy.
Two years later, in 1874, Wilhelm Wundt's *Grundzüge der physiolo-
gischen Psychologie* appeared, as did Brentano's *Psychologie vom
empirischen Standpunkt*. And five years later, in 1879, Frege published his *Begriffsschrift*. What we witness here is the virtually
simultaneous emergence of a number of new disciplines, or at least
of old disciplines in what is, for the first time, a recognisably modern, contemporary form. In addition to the new logic, the new
geometry, and the new mathematics of the infinite, the works of
Wundt and Brentano heralded the emergence of psychology as a
discipline in its own right. This latter phenomenon will turn out to
be a significant factor in understanding Moore and Russell's new
philosophy, so I shall say a little more about it.

Both as an academic subject, and as an institutionally acknowledged discipline, psychology first distinguished itself from philosophy, on the one hand, and from medicine and physiology on the
other, in Germany, where it took two dominant forms. The pio-
neering work of Fechner and Helmholtz culminated in the establishment, under Wundt, of a massively influential tradition of
experimental psychology. In 1879 Wundt established the first psychological laboratory in Leipzig, and within a few years his students
and disciples followed suit in universities across Germany, and in
America. The other, no less influential tradition was that of the
Deskriptive Psychologie of Franz Brentano. Brentano's students
included Husserl, Freud, Meinong, Stumpf, Twardowski, and
Ehrenfels; and his importance for phenomenology, empirical psychology, gestalt theory, and philosophy of mind was vast.

The Revolution of Moore and Russell: A Very British Coup?

It is important to recognise, however, that although the emergence of psychology as an autonomous discipline began in Germany during the 1870s, the process was not completed for another 30 or 40 years in Germany – and it took much longer in Britain. Nevertheless, throughout the last quarter of the nineteenth century psychology was a discipline capable of generating a great deal of intellectual excitement, and of attracting many of the leading physicists, philosophers, physiologists, and theologians. And yet, of course, at this time there were no 'psychologists' as such. Fechner, for example, studied medicine, taught mathematics and physics, and published works on aesthetics and theology – as well as engaging in influential experiments on the measurement of sensation. Helmholtz, likewise, trained in medicine, transferred to fundamental physics and mathematics, while also pursuing research in optics, the psychology of visual perception, and much else besides. Wundt, often regarded as the first experimental psychologist properly so-called, nevertheless occupied a chair of philosophy, had studied medicine, physiology, and physics, and wrote works on logic, ethics, and the history of ideas, as well as on his own monumental *System der Philosophie*.

III

To what extent did these developments impinge on British academic life? How susceptible were those in Cambridge, Oxford, London and elsewhere to the new arithmetic, the new geometry, the new logic, and the new psychology? The answer – in the most general of terms – is that many *individuals* in Britain were fully apprised of events on the continent, were excited by them, and engaged in active debate with their continental colleagues. But at the same time there was considerable indifference, and often indeed antipathy, to the new ideas on the part of *institutions*, and especially on the part of the older universities. When Russell studied mathematics at Cambridge, for example, the discipline was in a parlous state – outmoded, parochial, and superficial. He dismissed the teaching he received there as 'definitely bad'.[7] Russell, however, kept a careful list of the books he was reading. And his reading matter between 1894–1897, that is, during his idealist period, included works by Riemann, Frishauf, Killing, Klein, Erdmann, Lobatchewski, Helmholtz, Gauss, Grassmann, Mansion, Bonnel, Lachelas, and others on geometry; works by Cantor, Couturat, Dedekind, Weierstrass, Durege, and others on number theory, Heymans,

[7] B. Russell. *My Philosophical Development*, p. 37.

David Bell

Mach, Helmholtz, Neumann, Hertz, and others on physics. James, Lotze, Stumpf, Meinong, Herbart, and others on philosophy and psychology.

The young Russell was not merely reading, however, but writing too. In his early years as a philosopher he published studies of Heymans, Meinong, Couturat, Frege, Bergson, and Poincaré. The first of his four studies of Meinong was in 1899, the last as late as 1907. Moreover, Russell's engagement with continental thinkers was not restricted to mathematics and philosophy. At the age of 26, for example, he knew enough contemporary psychology to write an authoritative review of Meinong's treatment of the Weber–Fechner law concerning the relations between changes in stimuli and changes in the corresponding extensive and intensive sensations.

Perhaps, it might be thought, Russell was an exception. Given his dissatisfaction with mathematics in Cambridge, perhaps it is no surprise that he looked abroad, to Germany. Perhaps, too, Russell was unusual in speaking almost perfect German and excellent French – so that he *could* look abroad for stimulation. But Russell was not the exception. To see this we need to examine the British response to the new developments in psychology.

As an autonomous, respectable discipline, experimental psychology emerged in Britain some thirty years after it had done so in Germany. Something of the attitude of British institutions to this new discipline is indicated by the reaction of Cambridge University Senate to an application by James Ward and John Venn for a grant to establish a psychological laboratory.[8] This was in 1877, and the application was turned down because 'it would insult religion by putting the human soul in a pair of scales'. Their application was again rejected in 1882, and yet again in 1886. It was not until 1891, a full fourteen years after the original application, that a room in the Physiology Department was made available for psychological experiments. In some places this hostile attitude to psychology died hard. It was not until as late as *1936*, for example, that the introduction of experimental psychology was permitted in Oxford University – almost 60 years after Wundt's laboratory was established in Leipzig.

Although institutions were slow to acknowledge the discipline of psychology, individual philosophers, mathematicians, psychologists, and scientists in Britain clearly found contemporary developments in continental Europe challenging and exciting, and did all within their power to keep abreast of them. The journal *Mind*, for example, was established in 1876 by the psychologist Alexander

[8] When we look beneath the covers of early psychology in Britain, we do indeed find some interesting bedfellows.

The Revolution of Moore and Russell: A Very British Coup?

Bain, as a 'Quarterly Review of Psychology and Philosophy'. It aimed specifically 'at making English readers acquainted with the progress of philosophical thought in other countries.'[9] And in this it succeeded admirably. The first issue contains articles on Wundt and physiological psychology in Germany, on Lotze's metaphysics; and on Fechner; and it contains articles *by* Wundt and Helmholtz. In addition, the first issue contains a lengthy critical study of Brentano's *Psychology from an Empirical Standpoint*, as well as of works by Czolbe, Hermann, and Frauenstädt. There are brief notices of some 46 new books, of which over half are German or French.

The rejection of insularity and parochialism by the first editor, Croom Robertson was endorsed whole heartedly by his successor, George Stout. Thus, for instance, in the 1899 issue of *Mind* that contains G. E. Moore's first 'analytic' publication, 'The Nature of Judgment', we find substantial critical studies of just four books: Friedrich Jodel: *Lehrbuch der Psychologie*; Paulin Malapert: *Les Éléments du Caractère*; Alexius Meinong: *Über die Bedeutung des Weberschen Gesetzes* [written by Russell]; and Hans Cornelius: *Psychologie als Ehfahrungswissenschaft* [written by Stout]. In addition there are brief notices of seven works published in French, German, or Italian, and useful abstracts of some 16 other journals of psychology and philosophy. Of these journals three are American, five are French, and eight are German. None is British.

In Britain, and as we will see, especially in Cambridge and Oxford, the lack of any institutional framework or support for the study of psychology had, I think, two noticeable effects. One was, predictably, that philosophers and would-be psychologists went abroad to study and train. The other was that the Brentanian, rather than the Wundtian tradition came to dominate in the older universities.

With respect to the first point: Before leaving for America, Titchener spent two years with Wundt in Leipzig, Spearman obtained his doctorate with Wundt, and studied also in Berlin, Würzburg, and Göttingen, Sully was with Lotze in Göttingen and Helmholtz in Berlin, McDougal studied under G. E. Müller in Göttingen; Croom Robertson, the first editor of *Mind*, had spent time studying in Heidelberg, Paris, Göttingen, and Berlin, and Samuel Alexander spent a year working in Hugo Münsterberg's laboratory in Freiburg. Many of these philosopher-psychologists subsequently went on to establish their own psychological laboratories in London, Aberdeen, St Andrews, and elsewhere. And, like so many of their contemporaries and teachers, both Russell and Moore went to study in Germany – in Berlin and Tübingen respectively.

The second consequence of the hostility to experimental psy-

[9] Croom Robertson's 'Editorial', *Mind*, vol 1 (1876), p. 2.

David Bell

chology by the older British universities was to drive the Wundtians elsewhere, and to leave the alternative, Brentanian approach as the most attractive and viable for those that remained. After all, one didn't need a laboratory to be a Brentanian – and that approach brought with it none of the financial (or indeed theological) costs which some British Universities found so exorbitant. We can perhaps best see some of the consequences of this process of selection if we turn to look specifically at the intellectual environment of Moore and Russell in Cambridge.

IV

Two of the teachers singled out by both Moore and Russell as having had the greatest influence on them were James Ward and George Stout – two figures whose names are today most often linked with those of Bradley and McTaggart as minor 'Neo-Hegelians' or 'British Idealists'. It is often assumed, therefore, that any contact with them or their works would have affected Russell and Moore exclusively in regard to either their adoption of, or their reaction against, such idealism.[10] My own view is that Ward's contribution was not primarily philosophical at all, and that Stout, despite the very high esteem in which he held Bradley, was not in fact an idealist of any kind. Be that as it may – their respective metaphysical orientations are simply irrelevant to the considerations that I wish to bring out at this point. As metaphysicians it may well be the case that works by Stout and Ward are today largely unread, and have been without significant influence. The proper place to locate their importance is, rather, in the discipline of psychology. Ward's massive (virtually book-length) article entitled 'Psychology' in the ninth edition of the *Encyclopaedia Britannica* (1885) is an extraordinarily erudite and well-informed survey of the subject. It is generally regarded as a major turning point in the development of the discipline in Britain.[11] Stout's books on psychology were standard

[10] Again, Russell himself may be in part responsible for this dismissive response. In *My Philosophical Development*, for instance, Stout is mentioned only once, and dismissed as 'a Hegelian'. Ward too is dispatched in peremptory fashion as 'a Kantian' (p.38).

[11] Incidentally, Ward had himself spent a number of years studying psychology in Germany, in both Göttingen and Berlin. It was Ward who eventually persuaded Moore and Russell to study abroad. And it was Ward, moreover, who first introduced Russell to Meinong, Poincaré, Cantor, and Frege (he gave Russell a copy of Frege's *Begriffsschrift* in 1896, though Russell failed to perceive its significance for at least another 4 or 5 years). See N. Griffin, *Russell's Idealist Apprenticeship*, pp.35–45.

texts for almost half a century: the fifth edition of his *Manual of Psychology*, for example, was issued 40 years after the first. For present purposes, however, it is not Stout's *Manual of Psychology* that is of interest, but his other major work, the (interestingly entitled) *Analytical Psychology* of 1896.[12] This work is in fact one of a handful that Moore admits to having read 'with a good deal of attention', and which dealt with subjects 'on which I had thought a great deal and thought as hard as I could.'[13]

Historically, the significance of Stout's *Analytical Psychology* is, I think, this: it was the most accurate and detailed presentation in English of Brentano's contributions to psychology. The phrase 'Analytical Psychology' just is Stout's translation of Brentano's *'Deskriptive Psychologie'* – which is the name of the discipline to which *Psychology from an Empirical Standpoint* is devoted.[14] And the translation is a good one, for Brentano's 'descriptive' procedures are analytic in the most literal sense: they are based exclusively on the whole/part decomposition of complex phenomena into their mental and physical components. Although there are a number of specific points on which Stout takes issue with Brentano, regarded as a whole *Analytical Psychology* is essentially a presentation, for an English audience, of the doctrines which had appeared some 22 years earlier in *Psychology from an Empirical Standpoint*.

Now the claim I am going to try to substantiate is this: that we can gain an historical understanding of the form in which analytic philosophy emerged in Moore's early writings,[15] on the basis of an understanding of the appropriate context – a context in which analytical psychology is the single most significant factor. To this end,

[12] G. F. Stout, *Analytical Psychology* (London: Sonnenschein, 1896).

[13] G. E. Moore, 'An Autobiography', in *The Philosophy of G. E. Moore*, (ed.) P. A. Schilpp, (Evanston and Chicago: The Library of Living Philosophers, Inc, Northwestern University), p. 29

[14] F. Brentano, *Psychologie vom empirischen Standpunkt* (Leipzig: Dunker & Humblot, 1874). Trans. by A. C. Rancurello *et al.*, as *Psychology from an Empirical Standpoint* (London: Routledge & Kegan Paul, 1973).

[15] By Moore's early writings I mean especially 'The Nature of Judgment', *Mind*, vol. 8 (1899), pp. 176–93; 'Review of Russell's *An Essay on the Foundations of Geometry*', *Mind* vol. 8 (1899) pp. 397–405; 'Experience and Empiricism', *Proceedings of the Aristotelian Society*, vol. 3 (1902–1903), pp. 80–95; 'The Refutation of Idealism', *Mind*, vol. 12 (1903), pp. 433–53; *Principia Ethica* (Cambridge University Press, 1903), 'Review of Franz Brentano's *The Origin of the Knowledge of Right and Wrong*', *International Journal of Ethics*, vol. 14 (1903), pp. 115–33; and 'The Subject Matter of Psychology', *Proceedings of the Aristotelian Society*, vol. 10 (1909–1910), pp. 36–62.

let me first try to provide a brief overview of the main and most characteristic elements comprising Moore's early philosophy between, say, 1899 and 1903. We can then try to establish the influences at work on them.

V

Moore's earliest publications contain numerous passages of an essentially negative, critical or *ad hoc* nature, in which he is merely concerned to attack specific doctrines – or more usually, the specific verbal formulations of doctrines – to be found in the works of Bradley, Kant, Russell, Sidgwick, Mill, Brentano, and others. His arguments in such contexts are often uninterestingly *ad hominem*, and on the whole I will ignore them. On the other hand, when Moore is engaged in either defending his own views, or in diagnosing what is wrong with large-scale philosophical alternatives to those views, we find a most impressive homogeneity. In these contexts, that is, Moore has a single framework which in turn determines his terminology, his methods, his presuppositions, and his substantial conclusions. The framework is straightforwardly mereological: Moore's early philosophical investigations are conducted entirely in terms of the analysis of complex wholes into the component parts that make them up. Whole/part decomposition is the machinery which yields his theories of analysis, definition, concepts, judgement, intentionality, existence, identity, knowledge, and value. It constitutes his realism and his atomism. And it provides the ammunition with which he attacks idealism, empiricism, psychologism, internal relations, the naturalistic fallacy, scepticism, and much else besides.

Moore's whole/part theory embodies three basic principles. The first is now generally referred to as the *principle of mereological essentialism*,[16] and states that a whole is internally related to its component parts. In other words, if x is a part of W, then W is necessarily such that it has x as a part. As Hylton points out, this is the *only* internal relation that was acknowledged by Moore at this time.[17] The second principle is methodological – we might call it the *principle of mereological adequacy*. It states that all forms of complexity (and hence all forms of analysis) involve only whole/part and part/part relations. And, thirdly, at least until 1902, Moore also sub-

[16] The phrase was coined by Chisholm. See, R. M. Chisholm, *Brentano and Intrinsic Value* (Cambridge University Press, 1988), p. 15.

[17] P. Hylton, *Russell, Idealism and the Emergence of Analytic Philosophy*, p.143.

scribed to a strong *principle of mereological atomism*, namely, that in any complex whole the parts are detachable: each part could exist independently of any whole in which it happens to participate. Moore took this to be tantamount to a denial of the existence of 'organic wholes', in which the existence, the identity, or the nature of a thing is dependent on some whole in which it occurs as a part.

Now, taken separately, none of these principles is weak; taken together, however, they commit one to a highly idiosyncratic – some would say downright bizarre – set of doctrines and procedures. Take for instance the principle of mereological adequacy, according to which any explanatory analysis of a complex phenomenon must proceed by identifying the parts that occur within it. In Moore's words: 'A thing becomes intelligible first when it is analysed into its [components]'.[18] The highly restrictive import of this principle becomes clearer if we note that it rules out all forms of functional explanation, and any recognition of any irreducible functional phenomena. (I am using the notion of a function here in a broadly Fregean sense, as that which can yield a value for one or more entities as its arguments.) So, from within a Moorean perspective, such relations as those between a class and its members, between an object and its properties, between a relation and its terms, between a sense and its reference, between a mental act and its object and between general concepts and propositional wholes – all such relations, if they are to be acknowledged at all, must be construed in purely mereological terms. And we do indeed find Moore claiming, for example, that an object is just a whole made up of its properties, where the properties and the object are entities of the same type, likewise a relation is a self-subsistent entity belonging to the same type as its terms. Propositions are indistinguishable in type from the concepts that comprise them – in other words, there is no intrinsic difference between a propositional whole and a complex concept. Mental acts have objects, but they must do so immediately, without the mediating role of sense or content.

The principle of mereological atomism – namely that no part of a whole depends for its existence or nature on its participation in that or in any other whole – delivers as an immediate consequence the following two theses. First, it yields the thesis that there are no internal relations. (Clearly, if an internal relation is one which, in Bradley's words, 'essentially penetrates the being of its terms, and, in this sense, is Intrinsical',[19] then, the principle of mereological atomism simply rules out any such possibility). Second, it straight-

[18] G .E. Moore, 'The Nature of Judgment', p. 182.

[19] F. H. Bradley, *Appearance and Reality* (Oxford: Clarendon Press, 1959), p. 347.

forwardly implies that in the complex phenomenon which is consciousness-of-an-object, the object depends in no way on the existence of any consciousness there may be of it. This is the case,
moreover, for objects of any kind, including sensations, perceptions,
concepts, propositions, and the like. Whatever we are aware of, in
other words, would exist, exactly as it is, in a world that contained
no consciousness. This, quite simply, is Moore's realism; and it
comprises the sole ground for his refutation of idealism. Both are
merely specific applications of a general mereological principle.

Although epistemic notions do not occur explicitly in the above
three mereological principles, it is not hard to identify the epistemological pressures they create. For example, if all philosophical
explanation and understanding is a product of analysis, that is, of
the identification of the ultimately simple parts which together
comprise a problematic whole, then it follows that there can be no
philosophical explanation and no articulable understanding of partless elements. And it is a short step from here to an insistence that
such simple elements must comprise what Moore calls 'the ultimate
data', or 'the given'. For they are what must be accepted as the irreducible basis for all genuine explanation.[20] Now within the context
determined by Moore's mereological principles, there is only one
epistemic relation in which one *can* stand to such a partless whole:
there must be awareness of it; it must be given immediately and
directly (and not, as we have seen, via any mediating content or
sense); and it must be given in its entirety (it can not be present
'partially', given that it does not have any parts). Moore's name for
this relation was 'intuition', Russell called it 'acquaintance', and
Brentano's term was 'presentation' (*Vorstellung*).

A further consequence of Moore's mereological approach is an
impetus towards the adoption of a form of platonic realism, which
typically expresses itself in a distinction between things that are
actual or which exist in time and/or space, and those which have
being or which *are*. The pressure here is simple to identify: explanation within classical whole/part theory is not ontologically neutral, for there can not *be* an entity that is made up of parts that simply *are not there*. Commitment to a given whole brings with it commitment to whatever items analysis of it may reveal. Now if, with
Moore, we take consciousness-of-an-object to be a complex entity

[20] Compare Russell's stark assertion: 'An idea which can be defined, or a
proposition which can be proved, is only of subordinate philosophical
interest. The emphasis should be laid on the indefinable and indemonstra-
ble, and here no method is available save intuition.' B. Russell, *A Critical
Exposition of the Philosophy of Leibniz* (London: George Allen & Unwin,
1900/1975), p. 171.

containing both consciousness and the object as its parts, then clearly we are committed to there being the object that the consciousness is of. Equally clearly, however, we can think of Golden Mountains, winged horses, and countless other things which do not exist, as well as of numbers, possibilities, concepts and the like which do not exist in time or space. This tension can be resolved by the introduction of a second, broader ontological category to which absolutely everything belongs, including those things which do not exist in time or space. This form of resolution was adopted by Moore, and also by Russell, Brentano, and Meinong.[21]

Within the restricted explanatory space allowed by Moore's whole/part principles, there is no place for a pair of distinctions which (to say the very least) others have found useful. One distinction is that between, on the one hand, the objects of sensory states, such as impressions, sensations, sense data, perceptions and the like, and, on the other hand, the objects of intellectual acts, like concepts, ideas, thoughts and propositions. If one thinks of all states of consciousness as possessing the same fundamental form, and more specifically, as possessing an object of the same type, then *that* type of object will be equally appropriate in perception or conception, in sensation or thought. For Moore, when I have a perception or sensation of blue, there is a single, unchanging entity (*blue*) to which I am also related when I have the concept blue, and to which I am also related when I have the thought that blue exists. There are no differences here in the object, nor in the intentional relation I have to it. The differences are 'merely psychological'. According to Moore, the single kind to which everything belongs is that of the *concept*: everything whatsoever, whether it exists of not, and whether or not there is consciousness of it, is a concept. For want of a better label, I shall call this Moore's doctrine of sensory/intellectual collapse.

The second problematic distinction within a whole/part framework is that between what is irreducibly singular or particular, on the one hand, and what is essentially general, universal or attributive on the other. The distinction is problematic, indeed, because one of its terms resists mereological analysis. The adoption of an exclusively whole/part framework, in other words, inevitably tends to favour the particular and the individual, at the expense of whatever is general or attributive. As Moore says, for him 'A concept is

[21] Compare Russell's famous affirmation of ontological commitment: '*Being* is that which belongs to every conceivable term, to every possible object of thought – in short to everything that can possibly occur in any proposition, true or false, and to all such propositions themselves. ... Numbers, the Homeric gods, relations, chimeras and four-dimensional spaces all have being ...'. B. Russell, *Principles of Mathematics*, p. 449.

not in any intelligible sense an 'adjective'. ... For we must, if we are to be consistent, describe what appears to be most substantive as no more than a collection of such adjectives.'[22] In other words, the world and everything in it must be explained without the invocation of anything irreducibly attributive, relational, general, functional, unsaturated, or universal. We can call this Moore's *particularism*.[23]

VI

I have tried to outline all the main elements of 'the new philosophy' which Moore embraced in his publications between 1899 and 1902, encompassing Moore's methodology, ontology, epistemology, philosophy of mind and ethics. I have stressed the importance of whole/part theory, the analytic method, atomism, realism, platonism, particularism and sensory/intellectual collapse, as well as of specific theses concerning intentionality, reference, self-evidence, judgement and acquaintance. The point I wish to make now is a simple one: with a single exception, every one of these methods, principles, concepts, and doctrines is to be found in the works of Brentano. They would, moreover, have been available to Moore, either directly, or via contact with Ward and Stout, or via the pages of *Mind*, say, or of Stout's *Analytical Psychology*.

The only major issue on which Moore differed from Brentano concerns what I have called the principle of mereological atomism. Moore believed at this time that there were no 'organic wholes', or 'internal relations' and that any part of a complex whole could exist

[22] G. E. Moore, 'The Nature of Judgment', pp. 192–93.
[23] I shall say nothing here about Moore's ethics, except to note that he subscribed to the following theses:

(1). There is just one primitive ethical concept, in terms of which all other ethical concepts can be defined.
(2). The concept in question is that of intrinsic value, or good as an end in itself.
(3). This property is entirely objective, and ethical judgements of goodness are either correct or incorrect.
(4). The property of goodness is a non-natural property, in other words it is not the case that 'it has existed, does exist, or will exist in time'.
(5). The fundamental principles of ethics are self-evident, that is, the evidence for them is given in immediate intuition.
(6). There are a plurality of goods, amongst which the most important are the 'higher' goods of knowledge and the aesthetic satisfaction we take in the contemplation of genuinely beautiful things.

All of these theses are to be found in Brentano's ethical writings.

independently of its occurrence in that, or in any other whole. Brentano, by contrast, distinguished between independent and dependent parts, and characterised an organic whole as one all of whose parts are dependent on it. Now, as we have seen, Moore's extreme mereological atomism, when applied to the analysis of conscious acts and states, yields the thesis that intentional objects are independent of any consciousness there may be of them.[24] Brentano, on the other hand, believed that consciousness was an organic whole, and that consequently the intentional object was always a dependent part of that whole. This is certainly a significant difference between Moore and Brentano; but it should not obscure how profound the similarities between them are, even on this issue.[25] For both Brentano and Moore, consciousness of an object is a complex whole which contains the object as a proper part. They differ only in construing the whole in question as, respectively, an organic as against a merely aggregative unity. By 1903, however, Moore had himself come to reject the principle of mereological atomism, and to accept the existence of organic wholes'.[26] At that point his Brentanianism was complete.[27]

VII

Where does this leave us? And, in particular, how does it help us to come to terms with the origins and development of British analytic philosophy?

[24] I have little doubt that Moore inherited this doctrine from Stout, who disagreed with Brentano on precisely this point, and who wrote: 'We may, I think, confidently affirm that the *object* of thought is never a *content* [i.e., a part] of our finite consciousness.' G. F. Stout, *Analytical Psychology*, p. 45.

[25] And neither should we think that on this issue Moore differed significantly from other Brentanians. As Coffa rightly observes, *all* of Brentano's most notable followers accepted that 'the object that is the target of the intentional act is not a mere component of the act, but must enjoy a mind-independent form of being.' (J. A. Coffa, *The Semantic Tradition from Kant to Carnap* [Cambridge University Press, 1991], p. 86). In this respect Moore's modification of Brentano's original theory of intentionality was no different from, say, Husserl's, Meinong's, Höfler's, Twardowski's or, as we have seen, Stout's.

[26] With massive (but of course unintentional) irony, Moore's major criticism of Brentano is precisely that he does not acknowledge organic wholes. See G. E. Moore, *Principia Ethica*, p. xi, and 'Review of Brentano', pp. 117ff.

[27] Moore's Brentanianism lasted a long time. His article 'The Subject Matter of Psychology' appeared in 1910, and is Brentanian throughout.

David Bell

Clearly that tradition *began* with the rejection, first by Moore and then by Russell, of the idealism prevalent in Cambridge at the end of the century. But that fact is, I think, incapable of providing any explanation of the form which the 'new philosophy' then took, or of the ways in which it subsequently developed. The widespread opinion to the contrary gains its plausibility, I suspect, from a tacit reliance on two anachronistic assumptions. The first is that intellectual life in Britain, and especially in Cambridge, was as insular and inward-looking at the turn of the century as it became after the second world war, and as it still indeed remains today. The second anachronistic assumption is that at that time the disciplines of mathematics, psychology, physics and philosophy were as distinct and independent as they were later to become. With these two assumptions in place, it is almost inevitable that one should look to developments in the *philosophical* context, above all in *Cambridge*, in order to identify the forces at work in shaping the early metaphysics and epistemology of Russell and Moore. If we discard these assumptions, however, then a quite different picture emerges.

Moore, I have suggested, is best seen as the major, though by no means the first, British participant in an existing debate whose other participants included Ward, Stout, Russell, Meinong, Stumpf, Husserl, Twardowski and Brentano. Many of the terms and goals of this debate originated in Germany, during the 1870s, in the attempts by philosophers, physiologists, theologians and others to come to terms with, and contribute to, the emergence of psychology as a discipline in its own right. Russell, too, during the period between 1899 and 1903 is best seen as engaging with issues and innovations associated, on the one hand, with the logico-mathematical works of Dedekind, Schröder, Cantor, Klein, Riemann, Helmholtz, Bolzano, Peano, and Frege, amongst others, and on the other hand, with the contributions to psychology and philosophy made by Brentano, Meinong, Ward, Stout, Fechner, Helmholtz and, of course, Moore. And if this is right, then the role of British Idealism – indeed of any specifically *British* factors – in the genesis of the analytic tradition is small indeed .[28, 29]

[28] Although he gives no grounds for it, Michael Dummett's verdict on the contributions of Russell and Moore is similar: 'Important as Russell and Moore both were, neither was the, or even *a* source of analytical philosophy.' M. A. E. Dummett, *Origins of Analytical Philosophy* (London: Duckworth, 1993), p. ix.

[29] For their helpful comments on the material contained in early drafts of this paper, I would like to thank Michael Dummett, Andy Hamilton, Bill Hart, Peter Hylton, Kevin Mulligan, Mike Rosen, Mark Sacks, John Skorupski and Peter Sullivan.

Husserl's Concept of Being: From Phenomenology to Metaphysics

STEPHEN PRIEST

Western philosophy since Kant has been essentially operating with-in a Kantian anti-metaphysical paradigm. German-language philos-ophy, and *a fortiori* Husserl's phenomenology, is no exception to this.[1] Here I argue that despite his putative eschewal of metaphysics in the phenomenological reduction or *epoché* Husserl deploys an ontological, even fundamental ontological, vocabulary and may be read as a metaphysician *malgre lui*. To the extent to which this inter-pretation is viable, one escape route from the critical paradigm would seem to be opened up.

Individual and real being

Husserl alters what he calls the ordinary concept of reality to facil-itate a distinction between two kinds of being:

> the ordinary concept of reality needs a fundamental limitation according to which a difference between real being and individual being (temporal being simpliciter) must be established (*Ideas* I, p. xxi)[2]

[1] I argue this in *The Critical Paradigm: Modern Philosophy's Kantian Assumptions* (forthcoming). There is no philosophical, historical or geo-graphical basis for the still fashionable distinction between 'analytical' and 'modern continental' philosophy. If we use 'analytical philosophy' as a name for all of Frege's philosophy, Logical Atomism, Logical Positivism and Linguistic Analysis then we should note that each of these movements is German or Austrian in its modern genesis. In brief, analytical philoso-phy is a sub-species of continental philosophy. Of course this is not to deny the conspicuous stylistic and methodological differences between each of the movements just mentioned and betweeen Phenomenology, Existentialism, Structuralism and Post-structuralism. Nevertheless, all of these movements operate within the set of Kantian assumptions that I am calling 'the critical paradigm'.

[2] All references to *Ideas* I are to Edmund Husserl *Ideas Pertaining to a Pure Phenomenology and to a Phenomenological Philosophy:* First Book trans. F. Kersten (The Hague: Martinus Nijhoff, 1982).

It is not yet clear what the sense of 'real' is ordinarily or in Husserl's amended use but it is clear that the extension of 'real' is being restricted. Ordinarily, or pre-phenomenologically, one might be inclined to regard ordinary spatio-temporal particulars as real, perhaps as the paradigm case of reality, but Husserl is inviting us to give up this assumption. The limitation of 'real' he is talking about is, then, at least a limitation of scope or extension.

What is this distinction between real being and individual being? Husserl says individual being is:

> factually existing spatiotemporally. (*Ideas* I, §2)

So if something is an individual being it is spatio-temporal and it is a fact that it exists. Husserl does not mean by this that it is analytic or part of the concept of an individual being that it exists. Quite the contrary, because he says:

> Individual existence of every sort is, quite universally speaking, '*contingent*'. It is thus; in respect of its essence it could be otherwise. (*Ideas* I, §2)

So in the case of any individual being it is not a necessary truth that that being exists and it is not a necessary truth that it is the thing it is. Although this conjunctive disclaimer marks a difference between real beings and individual beings it would seem only stipulatively constitutive of that distinction. This is because it does not seem incoherent, even if unlikely to be right, to hold that something that is not real necessarily exists and conversely, that something that is real contingently exists. For example, someone might hold that numbers necessarily exist (for example on the ground that they exist in every possible world) but hold that they are not real (perhaps because they are abstract objects) . On the other hand, someone who held to the 'ordinary' view, against Husserl, that spatio-temporal particulars are real might nonetheless agree with him that they exist contingently and could be other than they are. Because Husserl has no argument against these suggestions he has done no more than assert that the class of individual beings is part of the class of contingent beings. He has not yet shown that contingency is essential to irreality or that necessity is essential to reality.

Husserl glosses over a problem when he says that any individual being *in respect of its essence* could be otherwise. We can make sense of the idea of a spatio-temporal particular gaining or losing properties so long as we think of these properties as *not* essential to it. There seems to be a difficulty in saying that something could lose any or all of its *essential* properties. This is partly the conceptual point that something's essential properties are precisely the ones it could not lack yet still be or be the thing it is. It is also the more metaphysically threatening point that something's possibly lacking all its essential properties and possibly acquiring a new set does not seem to be any kind of possibility at all. This is because 'it' cannot retain a reference through the putative transition. This is obvious if we ask *what* could lose all its essential properties and possibly acquire a new set. No answer would seem to be possible, even in principle. Husserl in fact does not need this strong claim about the essences of spatio-temporal particulars for the rest of his phenomenology so he should just drop it. Then we have: an individual being has some contingent properties.

What kind of modal notion is being invoked by Husserl in his use of this distinction between contingency and necessity? A modest clarification is offered when he says:

> But the sense of this contingency, which is called factualness, is limited in that it is correlative to a *necessity*. (*Ideas* I, §2)

I take it contingency *is limited* by necessity because if something is contingent it is not necessary and if something is necessary it is not contingent. Formally: $\lozenge -P \rightarrow -\square P$ and $\square P \rightarrow -\lozenge -P$. I take it contingency is *correlative* because necessity and contingency are interdefinable: $\square P \leftrightarrow -\lozenge -P$ and $\lozenge P \leftrightarrow -\square P$. Husserl's endorsement of these formal relations tells nothing however about the *content* of the modality he has in mind.

A clue is given when he calls the contingency of individual beings 'factualness' and contrasts it with '*eidetic necessity*' (*Ideas* I, §2). It is essential to Husserl's phenomenology that pure essences may be intuited: *what* something is may be studied independently *of whether* it is. Through the imaginative process of eidetic variation hierarchies of dependencies may be established. For example, redness is founded or grounded on extension and so on. These dependencies are not *factual* because they obtain whether or not there are any red objects or any extended objects. The dependencies are necessary dependencies but the factual existence of objects is a contingent existence.

Although this tells us a little more about Husserl's modal notions it leaves the fundamental philosophical problem about modality unsolved: saying exactly what new information is added to 'If x is red then x is extended' by prefacing that whole sentence with the necessity operator. Saying that this would add that if x is red x cannot not be extended just shifts the problem of the unanalysed modal notion on to 'can'. It is hard to see how modality can be analysed in non-modal terms. Suppose someone wished to maintain that the world is all that is the case. It is hard to see what extra information is provided about a portion of the world when it is claimed that it is not only the case but could not not be the case or although the case might have not been the case.

To summarise so far, Husserl draws a distinction between real being and individual being. Real being is a realm of eidetic necessity but individual being is a realm of spatio-temporal contingency. If this distinction sounds familiar it is probably because it sounds so thoroughly Platonic. Husserl himself however positively insists that this is not the case. This is because essences may have spatio-temporal location. *Prima facie* this blurs the distinction he has just drawn because it would seem that *malgre lui* essences as well as individual beings have what he calls 'actual (veritable) being' (*Ideas* I, §22). Husserl's difficulty is perhaps not so acute as might appear because the spatio-temporal location of essences differs in crucial respects from the spatio-temporal location of individual beings. Notably an essence can be in *different places at the same time* but an individual being can only be in one place at one time. For example, Husserl thinks that *redness* may exist simultaneously in this coloured surface, in that coloured surface. Against Husserl, we could claim that this allows essences 'actual (veritable) being' (*Ideas* I, §22): the redness *exists* (rather than there being no redness), the redness is *actual* because redness can exist now, and redness is *veritable* because the redness is truly here and truly there. In favour of Husserl we may construe 'actual (veritable) being' as a narrow empirical concept. A *token* of redness may be directly presented to perceptual consciousness but redness may only be detected by the abstractive process of imaginative variation. This would be to use an epistemological criterion, or as Husserl would prefer, a phenomenological criterion to distinguish tokens of red from redness, or individuals from essences.

Absolute being

Individual being is not only to be distinguished from real being, but from what Husserl calls 'absolute being'. Absolute being is *consciousness* or, perhaps better, absolute being is the kind of being that consciousness is or has. By 'consciousness' here we must not understand consciousness as the ordinary empirical awareness exercised on a day to day basis, but that consciousness as 'reduced' by the phenomenological reduction or *epoché*. As Husserl puts it:

> The realm of transcendental consciousness as the realm of what is, in a determinable sense, 'absolute' being, has been provided [for] us by the phenomenological reductions (*Ideas* I, §76)

We are offered here a criterion for distinguishing individual being from absolute being. Individual being falls by the *epoché*. It is subject to that phenomenological suspension of belief or putting into parentheses of the natural attitude that entails a methodological agnosticism about the existence of the empirical world. One's own consciousness survives the *epoché* and so falls on the side of absolute being, even though one's empirical self and the existence of one's own body is phenomenologically suspended. Although I indubitably am, and am indubitably conscious, I am no longer a human being.

Why does Husserl call consciousness as opened up by the *epoché* 'absolute being'? In one sense of 'absolute' something is absolute if it depends upon nothing else, but other things, perhaps everything, depend on it. We can see the second of these dependencies in this:

> It is the primal category of all being (or in our terminology, the primal region), the one in which all other regions of being are rooted, to which, according to their *essence,* they are relative and on which they are all essentially dependent. (*Ideas* I, §76)

It is controversial to what degree Husserl's transcendental idealism is a kind of idealism but because Husserl is describing the constitution of objects after the *epoché* it would be a gross misconstrual of this passage to take it to express a quasi-Berkeleyan empirical idealism. By 'rooted' here Husserl means 'phenomenologically rooted' and by 'dependent' he means 'phenomenologically dependent'. To explore this rootedness or dependency further would require analysis of Husserl's doctrine of the transcendental constitution of objects. For the moment we may just note that the empirical world is not 'absolute' because it depends on consciousness and one ground for holding that consciousness is absolute has been adduced by saying the empirical world depends on it. Although the being of consciousness is not suspended through the *epoché*, the *epoché* entails:

> the possibility of non-being of everything physically transcendent. (Ideas I, §49)

We can see the lack of dependence of consciousness on the empirical world in this:

> *while the being of consciousness,* of any stream of mental processes whatever, *would indeed be necessarily modified by an annihilation of the world of physical things its own existence would not be touched.* (*Ideas* I, §49)

So, if there were no empirical world the being of consciousness would be modified but its existence would not be touched. This means which mental processes obtain would be affected by the disappearance of the empirical world but consciousness as a whole would survive this disappearance. For example, a mental process which falls under the description 'the knowledge that such and such is the case' or 'the true belief that such and such is the case' or 'the veridical perception of that such and such' would not fall under those descriptions if their putative objects in the empirical world did not exist. Husserl is enough of an externalist to realise that those mental processes would not be just *those* states in the absence of their objects in the external world. This is what it means to say 'the being of consciousness, of any stream of mental processes whatever, would indeed be necessarily modified'.

On the other hand, consciousness' 'own existence would not be touched' because phenomenologically, or *from the inside,* consciousness is unaffected by the *epoché*. Husserl is enough of an internalist to realise that from within its own resources consciousness has no check on the veridical or non-veridical nature of its own mental states. Using 'real' in its 'ordinary' sense and not in its gradually constructed phenomenological sense Husserl validly infers from his claims so far:

> consequently no real being, no being which is presented and legitimated in consciousness by appearances, is necessary to the being of consciousness itself. (*Ideas* I, §49)

Phenomenologically it is as though if the empirical world were to be annihilated consciousness would survive.

We now have a new criterion for distinguishing between absolute and individual being. Absolute being sustains a measure of internalism about consciousness. Individual being sustains a measure of externalism. If we ask at exactly what point internalism about the mental becomes false and externalism becomes true, then Husserl's *noesis/noema* distinction falls wholly on the internalist side of the distinction as does the transcendental ego. The whole of the world of the natural attitude falls on the externalist side of the distinction.

Husserl talks about consciousness as 'immanental being', and says that immanental being is absolute being because it needs no *thing* in order to exist:

> *Immanental being is therefore indubitably absolute being in the sense that by essential necessity immanental being nulla 're' indiget ad existendum. (Ideas* I, §49)

The empirical world of physical objects is 'transcendent' because it is not exhausted by the consciousness of it. It is not part of absolute being precisely because it depends upon consciousness for its own constitution as a world:

> In contradistinction, the world of transcendent 'res' is entirely referred to consciousness and, more particularly, not to some logically conceived consciousness but to actual consciousness. (Ideas I, §49)

Husserl considers an objection to the whole project of the phenomenological reduction. He worries that it might be inconceivable, contradictory or meaningless:

> is it still conceivable and not rather a countersense that the corresponding transcendent world does not exist? (Ideas I, §49)

It is not incoherent to deny the existence of the external world because no contradiction is entailed by the claim: 'There is no external world.' Husserl's epoché is not a denial of the existence of the external world. It is agnosticism about that, but even that agnosticism requires the coherence of the supposition that there be no external world because it requires the coherence of the second conjunct of 'It is possible that there is an external world and it is possible that there is no external world.'

There is a further worry. Husserl talks about consciousness in relation to the corresponding transcendent world. Does it make sense to affirm the existence of an immanent world while entertaining the possible non-existence of a transcendent world? Arguably it does. If Husserl were involved in making the ontological denial that there is a transcendent world then there would be no clear or obvious sense in which consciousness could be called 'immanent'. It would be rather like the claim that something is up even though nothing is was or could be 'down'. However, Husserl is only employing the heuristic device of supposing that there might not be a transcendent world. The concept of a transcendent world used to do this would seem to provide 'immanent' with the requisite semantic contrast.

The answer to Husserl's question then is that it is conceivable that there is an immanent world but no transcendent world.

Husserl tries to mark a further distinction between absolute being and individual being, or real being in the ordinary sense of 'real' when he says:

> consciousness (mental process) and real being are anything but coordinate kinds of being, which dwell peacefully side by side and occasionally become 'related to' or 'connected with' one another. (Ideas I, §49)

Once shorn of metaphorical content it is not clear that this passage expresses very much. We can at least say that Husserl is trying to dispel the idea that phenomenologically we are presented with consciousness and the external world in the same kind of way: as for example we might be presented with two physical objects through the same sensory modalities. The phenomenological differences between the ways of accessing absolute being and individual being are so radically distinct as to be partly constitutive of the distinction between these two kinds of being. Individual being is accessed by *perceiving* it. Absolute being is accessed by *being* it.

Is Husserl therefore committed to the view that 'being' is equivocal, that there are different senses of 'being'? Certainly, the sense and reference of 'absolute being' is not the sense and reference of 'individual being' but Husserl recognises that there is a primordial sense of being that they share. He sometimes calls this 'existence'. For example he says:

> An immanental or absolute being and a transcendent being are, of course, both called 'existent'. (*Ideas* I, §49)

This means that what falls under the description 'absolute being', consciousness, and what falls under the description 'transcendent being', the empirical world, both exist. They are rather than are not.

This suggests that Husserl does not think 'being' equivocal. There are different kinds of being in the sense that part of what is is truly called 'immanent' and 'absolute' and part of what is is truly called 'empirical' and 'transcendent' but these two portions of what is do not differ in respect of *being*. In so far as they both are they are identical.

I turn now to a fresh way in which Husserl draws the distinction between absolute being and individual being. He says that on the one hand there is:

> an adumbrated being, not capable of ever becoming given absolutely, merely accidental and relative

and, on the other hand, there is:

> a necessary and absolute being, essentially incapable of becoming given by virtue of adumbration and appearances. (*Ideas* I, §49)

What does this distinction amount to? An *adumbrated* being is an object that is perceptually presented through phenomenological profiles or perspectives rather than all at once. Husserl thinks that *physical objects* are preceptually presented in this way. A non-adumbrated being is not presented through profiles or perspectives but is presented all at once. Husserl thinks *feelings* and other mental states are presented in this way. Crucially adumbrated beings admit of an appearance/reality distinction but non-adumbrated beings admit of no appearance/reality distinction.

This is a new way of marking the distinction between absolute being and individual being because no absolute being admits of an appearance/reality distinction and any individual being admits of an appearance/reality distinction. Husserl speaks of the:

> Merely Phenomenal Being of Something transcendent, [and the] Absolute Being of Something Immanent. (*Ideas* I, §44)

Phenomenal being is *appearing to be*. Appearing to be is consistent with appearing veridically to be but does not logically entail it. Although states of consciousness in a sense appear: they are available to phenomenological reflection once the field of transcendental subjectivity is opened by the *epoché*, they do not appear in the way that empirical objects appear. Empirical objects are transcendentally constituted by intentional acts and it is this fact of constitution that leaves room for an appearance/reality distinction. Appearing to be presupposes appearing to *someone* or *something or other* so Husserl talks of:

> the being of something transcendent, understood as being for an ego. (*Ideas* I, §44)

Consciousness is an absolute being because it does not appear to anything in this rather perspectival way.

The examples Husserl adduces in support of this distinction are rather contentious. He thinks that feelings do not admit of an appearance reality distinction but the tone of a violin does. Here is Husserl on feelings:

> A mental process of feeling is not adumbrated. If I look at it, I have something absolute; it has no sides that could be presented sometimes in one mode and sometimes in another. (*Ideas* I, §44)

Husserl has to be right that there is an enormous phenomenological difference between the way a feeling is presented and, say, a physical object is presented. In the case of a physical object I may be visually presented with one or more sides but not all of them at once. I may tour the physical object if it is not too large or remote, pick it up if it is not too heavy, crack it open if it is not too resilient and so on. There is a clear non-idealist sense in which one's knowledge of the physical object is 'constructed' out of one's various experiences of it. Although the whole of it is not directly presented at any one time, I take it to be a whole object that is presented through my perspectives on it.

Now, nothing quite like this seems to be true of the ways in which I am conscious of my own feelings. Clearly, they have no physical sides, back, front, and so on. It makes no literal sense to tour them, pick then up and so on. However, what is far less clear is whether these phenomenological contrasts justify Husserl's claim that my feelings admit of no appearance/reality distinction. This seems not to be right.

Construed prior to the phenomenological *epoché*, to the extent to which my feelings are dispositions or take objects in the external world their internal phenomenology is no infallible guide to what they are. I might feel something phenomenologically similar to love that is only infatuation and might make empirical mistakes about the identity of the person I feel this for. Even construed internalistically after the *epoché* it is not clear that there is no logical room for mistakes about the phenomenology of my feelings. If it seems to me that I am in love it follows from this that it seems to me that I am in love but this tautological entailment tells us nothing about incorrigibility. If I say 'I believe I am in love', it does not follow that I am in love. This is because I may be caused to believe that I am in love by something other than being in love. Someone might have *persuaded* me for example. I leave aside the Freudian and the neurological possibilities that the phenomenology of a state might not be revelatory of the reality of the state.

For all these reasons Husserl might not be right about mental states even internalistically construed to say:

I see when I look at it [it] is there, with its qualities, its intensity, etc., absolutely (*Ideas* I, §44)

There are also reasons for blurring the distinction in the opposite direction, even if less persuasive ones. He thinks an episode or object in the external world always and everywhere admits of an appearance/reality distinction. Here he gives the example of a violin tone:

A violin tone, in contrast, with its objective identity, is given by adumbration, changing its mode of appearance. (*Ideas* I, §44)

Clearly, if a tone alters over time and its changes are only directly empirically detectable, it is necessary to hear the tone over all that time to become acquainted with all of it. Although this seems right, it hardly marks a contrast with one's feelings which could equally change over time. A tone at a time is given just as incorrigibly or corrigibly as a feeling at a time. If anything at all is given incorrigibly it would seem to be *phenomenological content at a time* and if this is right, it is right whether this contributes to understanding the contents of consciousness or the contents of the external world.

Husserl provides us with a more secure contrast between the absolute being of consciousness and the transcendent or individual being of the external world when he says:

> the sort of being which belongs to the mental process is such that the latter is essentially capable of being perceived in reflection. The physical thing is also essentially *capable of being perceive*d. (*Ideas* I, §45)

So the contents of consciousness but not the contents of the external world may be perceived in *reflection*. By 'reflection' Husserl means the special kind of scrutiny of consciousness by consciousness facilitated when the field of transcendental subjectivity is opened up by the *epoché*. (He does not mean ordinary empirical introspection. If he meant 'reflection' in its broad ordinary sense it is not clear that he would be right. I can after all *reflect* upon episodes that have occurred in the external world, for example if I remember them.) Using his phenomenological sense of 'reflection' his claim is stipulatively right because reflection is consciousness's awareness of its own contents after the *epoché*. Husserl cannot however use this as an independent criterion for demarcating what belongs to consciousness from what does not because the concept of consciousness is already being invoked.

Husserl develops in more detail the idea that consciousness could exist even if nothing else existed. This ground for calling consciousness 'an absolute being' is logically similar to some quasi-Aristotelian grounds for calling something a substance:

> consciousness considered in its 'purity' must be held to be a *self-contained complex of being,* a complex of absolute being into which nothing can penetrate and out of which nothing can slip, to which nothing is spatiotemporally external and which cannot be within any spatiotemporal[ly] (sic) complex, which cannot be affected by any physical thing and cannot exercise causation upon any physical thing. (*Ideas* I, §49)

It perhaps should be reiterated that Husserl is making a set of phenomenological claims not a set of ontological claims here. He is describing how consciousness *appears* after the *epoché* not claiming how it is metaphysically. Nonetheless, it appears to be a substance. Consciousness after the *epoché* is given to itself *as though* it could exist even if nothing else existed. The immunity of consciousness to physical causes is reminiscent of Leibniz's claim that those substances called 'monads' have no windows through which anything could enter or go out.

Phenomenologically this seems to be right. Indeed, it is the fact that consciousness may be given to itself as though it could exist even if nothing else existed that makes solipsism thinkable. *Why* consciousness may be given to itself in this way seems to me an unsolved and difficult philosophical problem.

Suppose then, that Husserl is right that consciousness is phenomenologically given as a *self-contained complex of being*. This would seem not to warrant the conclusion that consciousness *is* an absolute being. If we accept that something is absolute if it depends upon nothing else for its existence then Husserl would seem only entitled to the conclusion that consciousness is given as if it is an absolute being.

Husserl talks about 'the whole spatiotemporal world' as '*a merely intentional being*' and says it has 'the merely secondary sense of a being *for* a consciousness' (*Ideas* I, §49). This raises a question faced by all kinds of transcendental idealism, including Kant's and Husserl's. Is there conceptual room to talk about a world that is not *our* world? Husserl, and in a way, Kant, think there is no such room. Necessarily, what we take to be reality is reality as it appears to us. Husserl says:

It is a being posited by consciousness in its experiences

and, perhaps rashly

beyond that it is nothing. (*Ideas* I, §49)

How can he know that there is nothing to the world except what we can in principle know of it? *Prima facie,* this would seem to be a negative metaphysical existential claim that outstrips the self-imposed limits of his own phenomenology. To appreciate Husserl's claim we need to realise that he is talking about what is *given*. He is demarcating what is given as being opposed to what is believed to be or, more fundamentally, posited. The distinction is a phenomenological one between presence and absence, or the presentation of what is present and the presentation of absence, not a distinction between the known and the unknown.

The metaphysics of absolute being

Husserl, I suggest, in his use of 'absolute being' is unwittingly describing *the inside of the soul*. If we gather together the phenomenological facts about consciousness that Husserl has adduced these are sufficient for consciousness being a soul in a pre-Kantian metaphysical sense. The soul of pre-Kantian metaphysics is not physical, it is what one's own existence consists in and it is a naturally immortal substance.

Husserl's absolute being or reduced consciousness survives the *epoché* and so survives the suspension of everything physical, so it is not physical. It is but it is not composed of matter.[3] *Pace* Husserl's attempted metaphysical agnosticism, Husserl's absolute being is at least *naturally* immortal because its existence is not threatened by the suspension of the natural attitude. It is given as though it is a substance and so in that minimal phenomenological sense, it does not depend on the empirical world. Although that empirical psycho-physical human being who I am falls by the *epoché*, I none the less survive the *epoché*. This, I conjecture, is not as Husserl supposes because I am a transcendental ego, but because I am a soul. The soul *qua* absolute being survives the phenomenological 'reduction' of the empirical world. The field of transcendental subjectivity is to be *identified* with the soul. Husserl was indeed right when he used to say that he had 'discovered' transcendental subjectivity but he misunderstood what he discovered. Instead of discovering the region for a new science he was rediscovering the subject of an old theology.

Husserl's absolute being is that subjectivity without objectivity called 'transcendental subjectivity' which is necessary for the presentation of an objective world. It exhibits what Sartre calls 'absolute interiority'. Phenomenologically, it is an inside without an outside.[4]

I maintain, then, that these are metaphysical facts about the soul, not only phenomenological facts about transcendental subjectivity. Admittedly, there is no valid *logical* inference from something's appearance to itself as a substance to its being a substance. It is not

---

[3] Husserl underestimates the spatial properties of consciousness after the *epoché*, although his use of metaphors such as 'transcendental field' suggests a quasi-spatiality. My considered view is that the soul is space: the subjectively orientated space that contains one's experiences. It follows from this picture that the body is in the soul. The soul is not in the body as traditionally conceived. It also follows *pace* Descartes that the soul is directly acquainted with its own interiority. For more of phenomenology's unacknowledged metaphysical consequences see Stephen Priest *Merleau-Ponty* (London: Routledge, 1988), chapter XV.

[4] For Sartre's use of 'absolute interiority' see his *The Transcendence of the Ego* trans. Forrest Williams and Robert Kirkpatrick (New York: Farrar, Straus and Giroux, 1958). Sartre thinks consciousness is a 'non-substantial absolute' (p. 42) which is inconsistent with my view that consciousness is the soul. Sartre's critique of Husserl in *The Transcendence of the Ego* is pivotal in the transition from 'pure' transcendental phenomenology to existential phenomenology. I evaluate the logic of Sartre's arguments against Husserl in *The Subject in Question: Sartre's Critique of Husserl in The Transcendence of the Ego* (Routledge, London, 1999).

Stephen Priest

incoherent to suppose that some putative substance in fact depends for its existence on something that is hidden from it. However, one extremely plausible metaphysical explanation for something's appearing to be a substance is that it is a substance. In Husserl's transcendental phenomenology transcendental subjectivity *grounds* the objective world. The onus is on the non-Husserlian metaphysical sceptic to show that transcendental subjectivity itself is grounded in some reality not open to phenomenological description.

Because Husserl is using the vocabulary of *being* he may be legitimately construed as engaging in a kind of fundamental ontology. Of course he does not offer an analytic of Dasein or a detailed inquiry into the ontological primordiality of temporality. Nevertheless at the level of *being* he is doing metaphysics *malgre lui;* engaging in metaphysical ontology recognisably similar to that of the closing pages of *Being and Time* or *Phenomenology of Spirit*. Every time Husserl uses the word 'being' we can *see though* the still psychologistic essentialism of his phenomenology to the metaphysical ontology underneath.

I conjecture, then, that absolute being is the soul. This is an unrecognised ontological presupposition of Husserl's transcendental phenomenology. Far from phenomenology being primordial with regard to metaphysics, metaphysics is primordial with regard to phenomenology. Within the critical paradigm, metaphysics seems *extravagant;* as though something extra and superfluous is being added to what we know. I suggest instead that what we know presupposes the unknown.

Transcendental phenomenology rewritten as the metaphysics it tacitly implies provides at least one escape route from the critical paradigm: an escape *via* the soul.

Frege and the Later Wittgenstein

P. M. S. HACKER

Preliminaries

In the preface to the *Tractatus* Wittgenstein acknowledged 'Frege's great works' as one of the two primary stimulations for his thoughts. Throughout his life he admired Frege both as a great thinker and as a great stylist. This much is indisputable. What is disputable is how he viewed his own philosophical work in relation to Frege's and, equally, how we should view his work in this respect. Some followers of Frege are inclined to think that Wittgenstein's work builds on or complements that of Frege. If that were true it would be plausible to suppose that the joint legacy of these two great philosophers can provide a coherent foundation for our own endeavours. But it is debatable whether their fundamental ideas can be synthesized thus. The philosophy of Wittgenstein, both early and late, is propounded to a very large extent in opposition to Frege's. They can no more be mixed than oil and water – or so I shall argue.

Frege's logical works did indeed stimulate the young Wittgenstein's thoughts. His formalization of the propositional and predicate calculi was the most momentous advance in formal logic since Aristotle. In many ways it, together with Russell's and Whitehead's *Principia*, set the agenda for twentieth-century philosophy of logic and for modern philosophical reflection on the relation between logical calculi, thought and language. For given the power of the new calculus of logic to formalize arguments which had been beyond the scope of previous systems of logic and to display their validity (or invalidity), the moot philosophical question was: what does the new logic signify? What does it show us about the nature of thought, or language, or of the world?

Frege argued that his new logic freed thought 'from that which only the nature of the linguistic means of expression attaches to it' (BS, Preface). For:

> It cannot be the task of logic to investigate language and determine what is contained in a linguistic expression. Someone who wants to learn logic from language is like an adult who wants to learn how to think from a child. When men created language,

I am indebted to Dr Hanoch Ben-Yami for his comments on an earlier draft of this paper.

> they were at a stage of childish pictorial thinking. Languages are not made so as to match logic's ruler. (PMC, 67f.)

The subject matter of logic is the nature of thoughts (the contents of judgements) and their logical relations. Thoughts, according to Frege, are abstract entities, expressible in, but independent of, language. It is thoughts that can be true or false, and logic is 'the science of the most general laws of truth' (PW, 128). The propositions of logic *are* the laws of truth – laws which govern all thoughts, irrespective of their specific subject matter. Like the laws of the special sciences, the laws of logic describe what is the case – they describe the truth-functional relationships involved in valid reasoning. What is distinctive about them is their absolute generality and topic neutrality. All propositions of logic are generalisations – what *we* would now call 'generalisations of tautologies', particular tautologies such as 'Either it is raining or it is not raining' being thought of as applications or instances of the general laws of logic, derivable from them by universal instantiation. The laws of logic, in this sense, are valid for any thoughts whatsoever, irrespective of their subject matter. It is because of this that they are *also* perfectly general laws of thought – not descriptive psychological laws of thinking, but normative laws of how one *ought* to think if one is to preserve truth in reasoning concerning any domain whatsoever. The relation of the descriptive laws of truth (the laws of logic) to the normative laws of thinking is similar to the relation between laws of physics and technical rules which specify how to achieve certain ends, e.g., build bridges or aeroplanes. Of course, since language is a vehicle for the expression of thoughts, language must model itself upon what happens at the level of thought, hence scrutiny of the linguistic expression of thoughts has its place in logical investigation – it is, as it were, a bridge from the perceptible to the imperceptible (PW, 259). Nevertheless, 'we should not overlook the deep gulf that yet separates the level of language from that of thought, and which imposes certain limits on the mutual correspondence of the two levels' (ibid.). Language is full of logical imperfections which make logical investigations especially difficult, but 'Fortunately as a result of our logical work we have acquired a yardstick by which we are apprised of these defects' (PW, 266). The yardstick is Frege's concept-script, conceived as a logically perfect language – ideally suited for proof-theoretic purposes in the exact sciences. Frege did not conceive of his logical system as a description of the underlying depth-grammar of any, let alone every, possible language. On the contrary: natural languages are logically defective, but concept-script is a logically perfect language which accurately mirrors the logical forms and structures of thoughts.

It was against this conception of logic that Wittgenstein set his face from the beginning of his philosophical work in 1912 until the end of his life. The *Tractatus* is to a large extent a dialogue with Frege and Russell. They were the greatest philosophers of his day, and they had advanced logic beyond anything achieved by their predecessors. Nevertheless, he thought that they had misunderstood the nature of their invention – the new logical calculus, misconstrued its relation to language and thought, and, indeed, misunderstood the nature of logic itself. As far as the relation between logic and natural languages is concerned, he parted company from his two predecessors straight away. Sentences of natural language in use express thoughts, i.e., have a sense, and if so then they are in good logical order, even though the forms of natural languages may not disclose their underlying logical forms. For there can be no halfway house between sense and nonsense, and if a sentence in use expresses a sense, it expresses a sense perfectly. Logic is a condition of sense, so the sentences of natural language – the expressions of thoughts in the medium of natural language – are in good logical order. This conception of logic and language marks a gulf between Wittgenstein and Frege and Russell. One consequence of it is that he approaches the philosophical problems of logic from a completely different perspective from theirs. On this matter, he never changed his mind. But whereas in the *Tractatus* he adjusted his conception of language, its role and deep structure, to his conception of logic, in his later philosophy he liberalised his conception of logic to fit the contours of natural language and its use.

The *Tractatus* is Wittgenstein's most extensive confrontation with the philosophy of Frege.[1] He criticized Frege's conception of the sense of a sentence (what we understand when we understand an utterance) as a mode of presentation of an object. The sense of a sentence, e.g., 'Fa', is, according to Frege, the mode in which its meaning – a truth-value – is presented as the value of a function, namely the function $F\xi$, for an argument, namely a. Wittgenstein found this conception wanting and replaced it by a completely different one, construing the sense of a sentence as its agreement and disagreement with possibilities of existence and non-existence of a state of affairs. He criticized Frege's conception of a sentence as having a meaning, i.e., as the name of a truth-value which is its meaning, arguing that there is a categorial difference between sen-

---

[1] I have discussed Wittgenstein's *Tractatus* criticisms of Frege in 'Frege and the Early Wittgenstein' (forthcoming). Here I merely summarize his conclusions.

tences and names. He held that Frege had misunderstood the essential nature of the proposition, which is not bivalency, let alone the mere possibility of bivalency – as Frege held, but bipolarity. It is of the nature of a proposition to be capable of being true *and* capable of being false, and it must be the one or the other. Frege's account of sense, the young Wittgenstein argued, failed to meet the requirement that sense be independent of the facts. For, according to Frege, if a proposition 'Fa' is true, then it presents the True as the value of the function $F\xi$ for the argument a. But had the world been different, had it not been the case that Fa, then 'Fa' would have been false, i.e., its sense would have been the mode in which it presents the False as the value of the function $F\xi$ for the argument a, and the function would accordingly be different. However, Wittgenstein argued, a proposition – a sentence in its projective relation to reality, what we understand when we understand what is said – must have the same sense no matter how the facts might be or might have been.

Not only was Frege's account of sense and meaning inadequate, but so too was his account of judgement and assertion. His formal theory of assertion in *The Basic Laws of Arithmetic* was defective, for according to Frege's stipulations, the symbol for the content of an assertion is required to be a symbol that, on the one hand, expresses a thought (which is to be asserted) and, on the other hand, cannot by itself be used to assert anything – it merely names a truth-value. But it is not coherent to suppose that there might be a symbol which expresses a thought but which *cannot* by itself be used to make an assertion, or that there might be a symbol that says something true and yet *can only* be used to make an assertion. The defects in Frege's account of assertion, in Wittgenstein's view, ramify further. For while Frege connected the notion of a proposition or thought with the ideas of truth and falsehood, a proposition being construed as the sense of a sentence which presents the True or the False as its meaning, he represented these two objects as coordinate, neither having any special priority over the other. But, Wittgenstein remonstrated, truth has priority. For a proposition depicts how things are if it is true. Its sense is the possible state of affairs that obtains if it is true. Negation is an operation on a proposition which reverses its sense. Hence it presupposes the determination of what is the case if it is true.

Frege's failure to apprehend correctly the relation of the proposition and its truth-value and hence too the nature of negation is, Wittgenstein argued, an aspect of a more general flaw – namely of construing the logical connectives as functions, i.e., as a concept (in the case of negation) or as relations (in the case of the binary connectives) between truth-values that are the meanings of sentences. In Wittgenstein's view, the logical connectives are not function-names and do not represent any entities at all, let alone concepts or relations. Rather they signify truth-operations on propositions. They can all be reduced to the single operation of joint negation, from which all truth-functions of any set of elementary propositions can be generated. The propositions of logic, i.e., tautologies, are a limiting case of truth-operations upon a set of elementary propositions. They are not, *pace* Frege, characterized by their generality but by their necessity, by the fact that they are unconditionally true – true no matter what the assignment of truth-values to their constituent elementary propositions. The proposition that it is either raining or not raining is no less a proposition of logic than the generalisation that if anything that is F is G, and if anything that is G is H, then anything that is F is H. Moreover, the generalisation of a tautology, such as $(p)(p v \sim p)$, is not a genuine proposition at all, but a formal statement about the formal concept of a proposition, viz. that any proposition is either true or false. But the necessary truth of tautologies is purchased at the price of their vacuity, for they say nothing at all, since they exclude no possibility. Hence they are, technically speaking senseless, they have zero sense. If so, then they are not about anything and do not describe anything – and logic is not a science with a subject matter. So Frege's conception of logic as the general science of the laws of truth is misconceived. And if that is so, then his conception of logic as also being a normative science of the laws of thought is equally misguided. So his conception of the relation of the propositions of logic to thinking and reasoning is likewise awry.

Wittgenstein saw matters differently. The propositions of logic are limiting cases of propositions with a sense – they say nothing and describe nothing. Although they are tautologies which, one and all, say nothing, each distinct logical proposition is internally related to, and displays, a distinct general form of valid inference. So called laws of thought are not related to the tautologies of logic as technical (means/ends) rules are related to regularities (laws) of nature. Indeed, at this stage in the development of his thinking, Wittgenstein held rules of inference to be redundant, in as much as they attempt to justify internal relations between propositions. But it makes no sense to seek for a justification of what cannot be otherwise. In a perspicuous notation, such as the T/F notation he invented in the *Tractatus*, the internal relations between propositions are literally shown by their representation. Furthermore, Frege's conception of the science of logic as an axiomatic science akin to geometry, in which indefinitely many truths can be derived from axioms that are self-evident, is likewise awry. For the axioms of an axiomatized system of logic must be logical propositions no less than the theorems. Hence they are tautologies no less than the theorems. So there are no 'privileged' propositions in logic which are more fundamental than others. For all logical truths stand on the same level – they are all true under every possible circumstance, and they all say the same thing, namely nothing. Whether or not they are self-evident is irrelevant to their status as propositions of logic. For being self-evident, unlike being tautologous, is not a criterion of a proposition of logic at all.

It should be evident from this synoptic survey of Wittgenstein's early criticisms of Frege's philosophy of logic that he conceived of himself not as building on it, but as demolishing it and replacing it by a sound conception of the nature of logic.

Wittgenstein's transitional period

Between 1929 and 1932 Wittgenstein's philosophy underwent radical transformation. He repudiated the linchpin of the *Tractatus*, namely the logical independence of the elementary proposition. For he became aware of the insolubility of the problem of determinate exclusion within the framework of the logic of the *Tractatus*. Colour exclusion, e.g., the fact that A is red all over implies that it is not green, or yellow, etc., is but a special case of logical relations determined not by truth-functional combinations of elementary propositions, but by the *content* of elementary propositions. If that is so, then the logic of the *Tractatus* requires radical rethinking. For the idea that all logical relations are generated by operations upon logically independent elementary propositions was pivotal for the *Tractatus* conception of logic. The thought that every possible truth-function of a set of elementary propositions is already given with the set of propositions in question collapses. That idea depended on the bipolarity of the proposition, for 'p is false' = 'not-p', and the possibility of joint assertion of a pair of propositions is given with the possibility of their successive assertion. If negation and conjunction are given, then so too is joint negation, and if joint negation is given, then so too are all the truth-functions. By the operation of joint negation, 2^n truth-combinations can be constructed for any set of n elementary propositions, given that they are logically independent. For with that proviso, no combination is excluded by the content of the relevant elementary propositions. But if they are not independent, as 'A is red' and 'A is green' are evidently not, that does not hold – for the TT line in any truth table for combinations of propositions ascribing different determinates of the same determinable to an object must be excluded as possessing greater logical multiplicity than that of which the facts admit. Similar flaws infected the *Tractatus* account of the quantifiers.[2]

With the collapse of these pivotal *Tractatus* ideas much else disintegrated too (e.g., the metaphysics and ontology of logical atomism, the conception of a meaning-endowing connection between language and reality, the account of the intentionality of thought and language which was given by the picture theory of representation). This is not my present concern. The moot question is whether Wittgenstein's attitude towards Frege's philosophy changed significantly.

It seems to me that it did not. Most of his criticisms of Frege stand firm independently of his own (defective) constructive account in the *Tractatus*. For most of them do not depend for their correctness upon the metaphysics of symbolism or the ontology of logical atomism which marred Wittgenstein's account of logic in that book. The detailed technical criticisms of the philosophical apparatus of Frege's logical system are by and large not repeated in Wittgenstein's later writings, but taken for granted. So, for example, he does not repeat his criticisms of Frege's conception of sense – although it is interesting that in one notebook (MS, 105, 130f.) he observed that Frege's conception of sense and meaning might indeed be applied to tautologies and contradictions. Frege's conception of sense has no intelligible application to empirical propositions but only to logical truths, i.e., only to those propositions which, according to Wittgenstein's conception of sense, are senseless.[3] Similarly, Wittgenstein does not repeat in detail his criticisms of Frege's conception of the logical connectives as names of concepts or relations, although he continued to insist that the logical connectives do not stand for anything and that logical propositions are not about relations or indeed about anything else. He continued to argue that the propositions of logic are vacuous, say nothing – and, by implication, that Frege's idea that they have a sense *in the sense in which empirical propositions do* and that different logical propositions have *different* senses, is misconceived. Rather, logical propositions all have the same sense, namely none. And he still emphasised that any appeal to intuition to justify the propositions of

[2] For a more detailed discussion, see G.P. Baker, *Wittgenstein, Frege and the Vienna Circle* (Oxford: Blackwell, 1988). pp. 116–25.
[3] In MS, 161, 55 he observed that he was inclined to invoke Frege's notion of sense in application to mathematical propositions. Both remarks implicitly confirm his earlier criticisms of the Fregean conception of sense for the central case of the empirical proposition.

logic as resting on self-evident axioms is misguided. In his lectures, he repeated points he took himself to have established in the *Tractatus*, for example that

> one can discard the idea Russell and Frege had that logic is a science of certain objects – propositions, functions, the logical constants – and that logic is like a natural science such as zoology and talks about these objects as zoology talks of certain animals. Like a natural science, it could supposedly discover certain relations. ... But logic is a calculus, and in it one can make inventions but not discoveries. (AWL, 138f.)

He reiterated one of his earliest insights, namely that 'Logic must turn out to be of a *totally* different kind than any other science' (letter to Russell, 22.6.1912) – indeed, not a science at all. In his later philosophy, this idea had to be cut loose from its *Tractatus* underpinnings.[4] But it already fundamentally differentiated his conception of logic from Frege's, who thought that the propositions of logic are not categorially distinct from all other propositions. Their hallmark, in Frege's view, is generality – they express genuine thoughts, as do the propositions of any other science, and their arrangement in an axiomatic system does not differ in principle from an axiomatization of the laws of mechanics or geometry. Logic is the science of the general laws of truth, and its subject matter is the truth of thoughts and their logical relations, no matter what their content. On the falsity of this conception Wittgenstein never changed his mind.

Re-evaluation of what Wittgenstein had accepted from Frege

If Wittgenstein by and large conceived of himself as having settled his accounts with Frege in the *Tractatus*, what can we hope to find by way of criticisms of Frege in his later work (excluding his philosophy of mathematics)? There are three kinds of consideration which might be explored. First, although the *Tractatus* was highly critical of Frege, there were some respects in which Wittgenstein accepted, in whole or in part, some Fregean principles. After 1929, he came to reconsider these. His self-criticism is often, by implication, also a criticism of Frege. Second, as he came to revise the

[4] To use Wittgenstein's own *Blue Book* metaphor, 'Some of the greatest achievements in philosophy could only be compared with taking up some books which seemed to belong together, and putting them on different shelves; nothing more being final about their positions than that they no longer lie side by side' (BB, 44f.).

Tractatus conception of logic, he sometimes explicitly and sometimes implicitly reformulated his differences with Frege, probing
deeper than hitherto. Finally, it is possible to compare his later philosophy with Frege's at a global level. Various comparisons are possible, and in the compass of this lecture only one can be essayed.
Their philosophies will be compared with respect to Augustine's
picture of language.[5]

Among the things which the young Wittgenstein did accept from
Frege, with or without modification and with or without a similar
rationale, are (1) a methodological commitment to anti-psychologism in philosophical analysis; (2) the functional structure of
propositions; and (3) the topic neutrality of the logical operators.
On each of these he was led to rethink his position.[6]

1. *Anti-psychologism* Frege's anti-psychologist polemic against
Erdmann and Husserl was motivated by the desire to ensure the
objectivity of the laws of truth and the objective validity of the normative laws of thought. These had been jeopardized by the psycho-
logicians, who held that the laws of logic describe the ways in which
we are constrained to think by the nature of our minds. But the laws
of logic are not laws of psychology. Not psychologism, but realism,
or more specifically Platonism, is the key to a correct understanding
of logic. In Frege's view, this had an important methodological
corollary. If the laws of truth are objective laws concerning a mind-
independent subject matter, then psychological considerations of
how human beings think and reason must be excluded from the philosophy of logic. Hence although thoughts and the truth-functional relations of their truth values are the proper subject matter of the
science of logic and thoughts are what we understand when we
'grasp' a truth, the investigation of understanding belongs to psychology. To be sure, 'this process [of grasping a thought] is perhaps

---

[5] It is noteworthy that Frege's brief foray into epistemology in 'The
Thought' (as well as in some remarks on ideas, colour perception and subjective experience in *The Foundations of Arithmetic* and in the preface to
the *Basic Laws*) is implicitly and by intimation criticized in the private language arguments (cf. PI, §273, in which the phrase 'uns Allen
Gegenüberstehendes' is quoted from *Basic Laws*, preface p. xviii (see P. M.
S. Hacker, *Wittgenstein: Meaning and Mind* (Oxford: Blackwell, 1990),
Exegesis, §273)). Frege was committed to the two fundamental misconceptions that lie at the root of the galaxy of confusions that Wittgenstein
assails, namely the epistemic privacy of experience and the privacy of
ownership of experience. This will not be discussed here.

[6] Other important points of convergence between the *Tractatus* and
Frege are (i) the context principle, and (ii) the requirement of determinacy of sense. These will not be discussed in this paper.

the most mysterious of all. But just because it is mental in character we do not need to concern ourselves with it in logic' ('Logic', PW, 145).

In the *Tractatus*, Wittgenstein denied that logic is a science with a subject matter of its own, *a fortiori* rejected Frege's Platonist conception of the laws of truth. Logic is not a (Platonist) body of doctrine, 'but a mirror-image of the world' (TLP, 6.13). This 'transcendental', essentialist but not Platonist, conception of logic was no less committed than Frege's to the objectivity and mind-independence of the truths of logic, and hence to the rejection of psychologism. Consequently, Wittgenstein argued (parallel to, but not in agreement with, Frege) that his 'study of sign-language' must not get 'entangled in unessential psychological investigations' (TLP, 4.1121).[7] So he too excluded from philosophical consideration any investigation of the nature of understanding.

With the transformation of his philosophy in the early 1930s, Wittgenstein came to realise that anti-psychologism in logic does not justify the exclusion of philosophical investigation into the concepts of thinking, meaning something and understanding. Indeed, the examination of these concepts is essential for a correct account of the concept of the meaning of an expression. Like Frege, Wittgenstein, in the *Tractatus*, had misused the concept of meaning or *Bedeutung*. *That* conception of meaning, he declared, is now obsolete, and the use of the expression should be restricted to such phrases as 'This expression means the same as that' or 'That expression has no meaning'. The meaning of an expression is what is explained by an explanation of its meaning, and we should look to the manifold forms of explanations of meaning in our linguistic practices in order to become clear about the concept of meaning. Similarly, the meaning of an expression is the correlate of understanding, for it is what we understand when we understand an utterance, what we know when we know the meaning of a word. So an investigation of understanding is directly relevant to the clarification of the concept of meaning. One criterion of understanding is giving an explanation of what an expression in use means. An explanation of meaning in effect provides a rule for the use of an expres-

[7] Frege did not conceive of his logical investigations as being a 'study of sign-language', but rather a study of thoughts and their logical relations conducted by the use of a sign-language, preferably the ideal sign-language of his concept-script. By contrast, according to Wittgenstein, 'It is the peculiar mark of logical propositions that one can recognize that they are true from the symbol alone' (TLP, 6.113), that 'If we know the logical syntax of any sign-language, then we have already been given all the propositions of logic' (TLP, 6.124).

sion – a standard of correct use. Hence another criterion of understanding an expression is using it correctly, i.e., using it in accordance with the customarily accepted rules for its use. And a third criterion is responding appropriately to its use. Understanding is not a mental state of entertaining or 'grasping' an abstract entity, nor is it a process of meaning something by the words one utters or of interpreting the words one hears in accord with a theory of meaning. Rather, it is mastery of a technique of use, hence akin to an ability, not to a state or process. It is an ability exhibited in using an expression correctly, giving explanations of what is meant by an expression, and in responding appropriately to the use of an expression in an utterance. The meanings of words are not entities correlated with the words by 'a method of projection' (as had been argued in the *Tractatus*) or by the abstract machinery of 'senses' (modes of presentation of a meaning – as Frege had argued). To know what a word means is not to 'grasp' an abstract entity, a sense, which is associated with the word, nor to know what entity a word stands for, but rather to know its use. The meaning of an expression is best conceived as its use, i.e., the manner in which it is to be, and normally is, used.

It is no coincidence that the opening chapters of the 'Big Typescript' are concerned with the investigation of understanding, meaning and explanation, for it is this which signals the transformation in Wittgenstein's conception of language and representation. For the thought that a speaker might know or understand what an expression which he uses correctly means, but be altogether incapable of saying what he means by it is incoherent. And if what he means by it does not coincide with what it means (in context), then he was misusing it. If a speaker cannot, in some way or other, say what he means by an expression he has used, then we would be entitled to conclude that he does not understand what he has said in using it and was speaking without understanding. But if this is correct, then what counts as a correct explanation of meaning must be liberalised. And since a correct explanation of meaning is a rule for the use of the word in question, the conception of a rule for the use of a word must be taken in a far more homely manner than philosophers from Plato onwards have done. It is misguided to suppose, as Frege did, that mankind has been using number-words since time immemorial without knowing what they mean and had to wait upon Frege to be told that the number-word 'one' means 'the number which belongs to the concept "identical with 0"' (FA, §77). And it must be equally misconceived to suppose that Frege's explanation constitutes the essential rule for the use of the word 'one', for most English speakers who use this number-word would be incapable of understanding Frege's explanation and hence incapable of following the rule which it expresses and of justifying their use of this word, from case to case, by reference to it. In fact, one can give ostensive definitions of the initial terms of the series of integers[8] and such explanations are perfectly correct. 'The definition of the number two, "That is called 'two'" – pointing to two nuts – is perfectly exact' (PI, §28).

Wittgenstein's realisation of the error of assuming that anti-psychologism licenses the neglect of a philosophical investigation of understanding and his consequent exploration of understanding and its relation to meaning led him to part company with Frege over a host of ramifying issues. First, the idea that only a *Merkmal* definition in terms of necessary and sufficient conditions of application is a genuine explanation of meaning is chimerical. We must recognise numerous legitimate forms of explanation, including ostensive definition, explanation by a series of examples, by paraphrase or contrastive paraphrase, and so on. Hence, second, the Fregean requirement that an explanation must determine for any object whether or not it falls under the concept in question must be mistaken – irrespective of whether it is or is not appropriate for proof-theoretic purposes in mathematics. For a perfectly decent explanation of a family-resemblance concept by reference to a series of examples together with a similarity rider does not do that and many other licit explanations of meaning do not do so either. Yet explanations by examples are 'decent signs, not rubbish or hocus-pocus' (PG, 273)[9] and ostensive definitions are perfectly proper explanations of what certain words mean – they are not descriptions (as Russell and Wittgenstein had thought) but rules, standards of correct use. Hence, third, Frege's thought that when it comes to simple expressions that cannot be defined by analytic definition, the best we can do is 'to lead the reader or hearer by means of hints to understand the words as intended' misconstrues the character of the so called 'hints' and obscures the fact that explanations of meaning by examples or by ostensive definition constitute rules for the use of a word no less than analytic definitions. Finally, since understanding an expression is not a matter of 'grasping' an abstract entity, since the rules for the use of an expression are given by the humdrum explanations of meaning that play a manifest role in our lin-

[8] One might distinguish here between 'visual number' and 'inductive number' (cf. PLP, 105).

[9] To be sure, there are many other reasons which Wittgenstein explored for faulting the Fregean and *Tractatus* demand for determinacy of sense. For detailed discussion, see G. P. Baker and P. M. S. Hacker, *Wittgenstein: Understanding and Meaning* (Oxford: Blackwell, 1980), pp. 367–85.

guistic practices of explaining, justifying, criticizing uses of words and since there can be no such thing as following, as opposed to acting in accordance with, a rule of language with which one is unacquainted or which one does not understand, there can be no such thing as hidden rules awaiting discovery – such as the definitions of number words which Frege produced or the hidden logical syntax of language which the *Tractatus* supposed would be disclosed by analysis. Hence too, it must be mistaken to suppose that the rules for the use of an expression follow from the nature of what the expression signifies – as Frege supposed,[10] or ineffably and necessarily mirror the essence of what the expression means – as the *Tractatus* had argued. The rules of grammar are not answerable to the language-independent essence of things, rather they constitute it (PI, §§371, 373).

2. *Function/argument depth structure* Although it is evident that in the *Tractatus* Wittgenstein's understanding of function-theoretic analysis of propositions differed from Frege's,[11] and although he did not think that Frege's and Russell's logical systems – by contrast with natural languages – were *ideal languages*, it is clear that he thought that they approximated an ideal *notation* which would, as Frege supposed, reflect the logical forms of what is represented. Unlike Frege, he thought that the depth-structure of *any* possible language has a function-theoretic form. However, with the transformation of his views in the early 1930s, he came to think that the very

[10] Frege, in his polemic against formalists in arithmetic argued that mathematics is no mere game with signs, in which the rules for the use of signs may be arbitrarily stipulated. The mathematician is not concerned with numerals but with the numbers that are their meanings. Hence it is not the case that 'the numerals are contentless marks, which are used according to arbitrary rules. Rather, the rules follow necessarily from the meaning of the signs.' (BLA, ii, §158.) Wittgenstein characterized this as 'the meaning-body conception' and criticized it extensively (see G. P. Baker and P. M. S. Hacker, *Wittgenstein: Rules, Grammar and Necessity* (Oxford: Blackwell, 1985), pp. 312–17.

[11] Unlike Frege, he did not think that the value of a first-level concept for an object as argument is a truth-value. Nor did he think that the quantifiers are correctly construed as second-level functions taking first-level functions as arguments and mapping them on to truth-values – they are logical operations on elementary *propositions* (not functions whose arguments are first-level *concepts*) and the sense of a generalisation is a function of the *senses* of the elementary propositions in question. And he did not think that the sense of a sentence, what we understand when we understand an utterance, is the mode of presentation of its meaning as the value of a function for an argument.

idea that a natural language has a concealed depth structure is misconceived. To be sure, he continued to think that the surface grammatical forms of natural languages are profoundly misleading, but not because they conceal a hidden, underlying logical syntax that shows the logical forms of the facts, but rather because they deceptively suggest a uniformity of use where there is a diversity.

The resultant awareness of the diversity of use of sentences similar in grammatical form, a diversity manifest *inter alia* in the 'multitude of familiar paths leading off in different directions' (PI, §534) from such sentences, led Wittgenstein to reassess his attitude to the function-theoretic calculus introduced by Frege and Russell. Far from approximating a logically ideal *notation* which reveals the logical forms of thought and/or reality, it is merely a calculus, which has no special privileges. To be sure, it makes some things clearer, makes perspicuous some distinctions that are obscured by the forms of natural languages, e.g., differences between A, B, and C's being red and being three, or between A's flourishing and A's existing. To that extent, it may be a useful object of comparison for natural languages – making clear that a different notation is possible, and that such a notation may reveal on its surface features which become evident in natural language only through a painstaking description of use. But no less than natural languages, and indeed no less than the calculus of syllogistic, the predicate calculus obscures logical differences. It treats fundamentally different concepts as if they were similar, representing them in the symbolism by signs of the same form – governed by the same rules. In his lectures he observed:

> All this symbolism comes from ordinary language. It could have been written in English or German, except for a few dodges, like brackets and dots. – It's all right as far as it goes. But apart from that, it doesn't clear anything up. In fact, it makes confusions. I do not mean that it is valueless. But it does not show the *point* of anything; it leaves everything as it is. It makes language a *trifle* more explicit, leaving all the confusions. (LFM, 264)

I shall select from his remarks three salient issues.

(i) Frege's distinction between objects and concepts (first-level functions) distorts no less than the subject/predicate distinction in ordinary grammar, indeed, it is, in certain respects, the same distinction (PG, 205).[12] It is no coincidence that his calculus became known as 'the predicate calculus'. For Frege's object is in effect a

[12] Wittgenstein does not qualify his remark thus. But in other respects Frege's distinction is obviously not the same one. No one, prior to Frege, would have called 'If ξ is F, then if ς is G, ξ is H' 'a predicate' or 'the

thing (or perhaps a *sublimation* of our ordinary concept of a thing) – the subject of predication, and his concept is a property (or a sublimation of our ordinary concept of a property). Hence he would treat 'A is red' and 'Red is a colour' as having the same form; and he would represent 'Jack is taller than Jill' and 'Red is darker than pink' in the same way; 'I have a pain', 'He has a pain', and 'A has a penny' would all be represented in the form '*Fa*'. But this altogether obliterates the logical differences between such sentences and obscures their radically different roles. 'Jack is taller than Jill' is an empirical proposition, whereas 'Red is darker than pink' is the expression of a rule constitutive of the concepts expressed by its constituent terms. The negation of the former makes sense, whereas the negation of the latter is nonsense. 'I have a pain' is typically used as an expression of pain, and does not accept the epistemic prefixes (such as 'I doubt whether', 'I think but am not sure that', 'I wonder whether') which the description 'He has a pain' does. 'Having a penny' signifies a relation of ownership, whereas 'having a pain' does not. And so on.

(ii) Frege's notation fails to distinguish sortal nouns from adjectives, representing both by undifferentiated predicate-letters. The resultant distortion becomes evident in quantified propositions. In natural language we have the form 'There is a ... with such and such properties', where the gap can be filled with such expressions as

expression of a concept', or have held that the expression 'ξ is a law' is a form of words which signifies the concept of law. Our concept of a concept is not that of a function from objects to truth values, and much of what Frege says about what he calls 'a concept' makes no sense if predicated of what we call 'concepts'. Since for Frege a concept is a function, the relation between a concept and an object that falls (or does not fall) under it is *internal*, for it is an intrinsic feature of any function that it takes a particular value (e.g., the True) for a given argument. But according to our concept of a concept, a singular empirical judgement states that an *external* relation holds between an object and a concept. An invariant concept might have different extensions in different possible circumstances and different concepts might as a matter of fact have the same extension. Frege required that every concept be defined for every possible object as argument, whereas we countenance vague concepts. Frege would take the expression 'a round square' to signify an empty concept, like 'a unicorn', whereas we would claim that it expresses no concept at all but is a meaningless form of words. And so on. Similarly, Frege's concept of an object extends our ordinary, imprecise concept of an object far beyond anything we would countenance. On his account, the simultaneous occurrence of a court case and a lunar eclipse is an object. But his liberality is not correlated with any sharp criterion for what is and what is not an object in his technical sense of the term.

'book from my library' or 'chair in my room', etc. Here we identify an object of a certain kind and ascribe a property to it and think of the substance thus identified as the bearer of the property (PG, 205). But the form of the predicate calculus sublimates this form into 'There is an x which ...' (PG, 265; LFM, 167). So a sentence such as 'A man is in the quad' or 'There is a red circle in the square' is represented by 'There is an x which is a man and is in the quad', or 'There is an x such that x is a circle and is red and is in the square'. But what is the x that is a man? What has the property of being a circle? The model of *bearer of property* disintegrates here: 'man', 'circle', etc. are not names of properties of a substratum (PR, 120). We may say that the circle has the property of being red, but not that there is something which has the properties of being a circle and being red – for we have no idea *what* thing is being referred to. We can say 'In this circle there are only crosses', but to represent this sentence by the form 'For all x, if x is in the circle, then x is a cross' is nonsense – for what on earth might the x be? It might be all sorts of thing – chalk marks, figures I have just drawn, pieces of wood and so on. But any such elucidation would itself immediately be represented by an additional predicate letter in this notation. Of course, one can stipulate that the 'x' in '$\exists x$' means 'circle in the square', in which case '$(\exists x)(Fx)$' makes sense (i.e., 'There is a circle in the square that is red'); but then '$(\exists x)$' and '$\sim(\exists x)$' should be well formed propositions (i.e., 'There is (or: is not) a circle in the square'), but in the calculus they are not (PG, 266). One can say that there are only two men who have climbed a certain mountain, but not that there are only two things which are circles in this square (*what* things?), let alone that there is no object which has the property of being a circle in this square without being circle A or circle B. 'Nothing is to be gained by forcing the proposition "There are two circles in the square" into that form; it only helps to conceal that we haven't cleared up the grammar of the proposition' (PG, 265). In short, 'Fx' must be an *external description* of x (PG, 207) and that is not provided for in the notation of the new logic.

(iii) The formation-rules for the Fregean (and Russellian) predicate calculus presuppose that if '$(x)(Fx)$' or '$(\exists x)(Fx)$' makes sense, then so too do '$(x)(\sim Fx)$', '$\sim(\exists x)(Fx)$', '$\sim(x)(Fx)$' and '$(\exists x)(\sim Fx)$'. In other words, the quantifiers are topic neutral. But this again is a distortion of thought and language. For our quantifiers are not topic neutral. It makes sense to say that there is a circle in the square, but none to say that all circles are in the square; it makes sense to say 'A wrote down a cardinal number' but not 'A wrote down all cardinal numbers'; it makes sense to say that some of the rules can be broken some of the time, but not to say that all of the rules can be broken all of the time; and so on.

The Fregean idea that the function-theoretic structure is 'founded deep in the nature of things' (FC, 31) is misconceived, projecting a feature of a particular mode of representation on to reality. And so too is the *Tractatus* idea that every possible language has a function-theoretic depth-structure. The function-theoretic form of representation of the predicate calculus distorts our thought and its linguistic expression no less than the subject/predicate form of traditional syllogistic. There is no mechanical short cut to the elucidation of the logic of our language – one must describe the uses of expressions in particular cases.

3. *The topic neutrality of the logical connectives* Just as the quantifiers are not topic neutral, so too, Wittgenstein came to realise, the logical connectives are not topic neutral either. His original reasons for having thought them to be so had been different from Frege's. Frege had conceived of the connectives as names of functions from truth-values to truth-values. Wittgenstein had conceived of them as operations on elementary propositions, indifferent to the content of the propositions upon which they operate. But with his realisation of the possibility of logical relations that are determined by the content of propositions which contain no logical connective, namely determinate exclusion, it became evident that the connectives are not indifferent to the content of the propositions to which they are affixed. It makes no sense to conjoin the proposition that A is red with the proposition that A is green, for it makes no sense to say that A is simultaneously both red and green. If A is one metre long, it follows that it is not also two metres long.

A fourth point merits mention, even though it is never explicitly brought to bear on Frege. At the heart of the *Tractatus* is the thought that there is such a thing as the general propositional form – 'Thus and so is how things stand' – shared by anything that can be deemed to be a proposition. This idea was pivotal to the doctrine that every proposition can be generated by truth-functional operations upon elementary propositions. Frege too cleaved to a (different) conception of the general propositional form – the presentation of a truth-value as the value of a function for an argument. After 1930 Wittgenstein repudiated the whole idea. The concept of a proposition is a family-resemblance concept and it does not have the unity which he had earlier envisaged. In the *Tractatus* he had wrongly excluded propositions of arithmetic, of ethics, aesthetics and religion, as well as the formal (metaphysical) propositions of the *Tractatus* itself from the category of well-formed propositions. They are neither bipolar, nor degenerate senseless propositions – so they are condemned as nonsense, attempts to say what can only be

P. M. S. Hacker

shown. By implication, he also condemned Frege for treating them all as genuine propositions with a sense, as he condemned him for treating the senseless propositions of logic and the propositions of arithmetic as having a sense.

The realisation that the concept of a proposition lacks the formal unity he had ascribed to it did not rehabilitate Frege's vision. On the contrary. For if Frege had been castigated for failing to see that logical and arithmetical propositions (not to mention ethical or metaphysical ones) are categorially different from empirical propositions with a sense, Wittgenstein's realisation that there is far *greater* diversity within the family of propositions than he had originally thought signalled even greater flaws in Frege's conception. The greatest mistake of the philosophers of his day, Wittgenstein remarked in 1938, was to focus upon the forms of expressions rather than upon their uses (LA, 2). Clearly, Frege was unimpressed by the grammatical forms of expression in natural language; rather, he *imposed* a single set of function-theoretic forms upon all expressions of thought, in total disregard of the different uses and roles of propositions that are uniformly represented in function-theoretic notation. But the family of what we call 'propositions' is diverse. Thus, for example, among members of the family one must recognise *grammatical propositions* such as 'Red is a colour' or 'One is a number', which are expressions of rules for the use of the constituent terms in the misleading guise of factual propositions. But if so, then the negation of a grammatical proposition is neither a grammatical proposition nor a falsehood. 'Red is a colour' expresses the rule that anything that can be said to be red can also be said to be coloured. But 'Red is not a colour', although it is the negation of a (grammatical) proposition, is mere nonsense – being neither a rule for the use of 'red' and 'colour', nor a true or false empirical proposition. Similarly, the negation of a mathematical proposition is not like the negation of an empirical proposition. Whereas the negation of a true empirical proposition is a false empirical proposition, i.e., a proposition which does not correspond to the facts, does not correctly describe how things are, the negation of a true mathematical proposition is not a proposition which fails to correspond to the mathematical facts, which does not correctly describe how things are 'in the realm of numbers'. Rather it stigmatizes a proposition which has the form of a mathematical proposition as not having the standard role of mathematical propositions, viz. as licensing the transformation of empirical propositions in accordance with the rule expressed by the true mathematical proposition – even though it may have a role *within* mathematics, e.g., in indirect proofs. 'True' and 'false' in mathematics correspond to *valid* and *invalid* in the

240

transformation of empirical propositions about the relevant magnitudes of things. So what results from the negation of a proposition depends upon the role of the proposition negated. Similarly, the propositions of ethics, aesthetics or religion, propositions of geometry, first- and third-person present tense psychological propositions, propositions of our 'world-picture', and so forth, all display forms which conceal their distinctive uses and conceptual involvements. In short, there can be no swifter path to confusion than to impose a single form upon all propositions and then take the chosen form of representation as a guide to philosophical elucidation – which is precisely what Frege did.

Rethinking the role of the propositions of logic

Wittgenstein continued to think that the propositions of the calculus of logic are degenerate senseless propositions. But he ceased to think that they flow from the essential nature of the elementary proposition as such or that they are mirror images of the logical structure of the world. It was true that each distinct proposition of logic is internally related to – and shows – a form of valid inference but wrong to claim that rules of inference are neither necessary nor possible. On the contrary, internal relations are reflections of grammatical rules which determine how expressions are to be used. Rules of inference are grammatical rules and they are constitutive of the senses of the logical operators. The tautologies of logic are not rules of grammar, but *that* a certain proposition *is a tautology*, i.e., that a certain well-formed proposition says nothing, that it is so constructed that all content is cancelled out, *can* be said to be a rule. '$(x)(Fx)\supset Fa$' is a tautology, and to recognise it as a tautology, i.e., to recognise that this implication is true come what may, *is* to recognise the rule of inference '$(x)(Fx)$' $\vdash$ 'Fa'. To fail to recognise this tautology is a criterion of not understanding the quantifier, of not grasping the rule for its use.

This transformation in Wittgenstein's thinking strengthened his criticisms of Frege's conception of the relation between the propositions of logic and the laws of thought. Frege, as noted above, held the latter to be related to the former as technical rules concerning how best to achieve certain goals, e.g., build bridges or aeroplanes, are related to the laws of physics. Wittgenstein had repudiated that conception in the *Tractatus*. But now he elaborated further. Frege argued that the laws of truth are distinct from any psychological laws of taking-to-be-true. 'Every object is identical with itself', he claimed, is a law of truth. 'It is impossible for us to acknowledge an object as being different from itself' is a psychological law of human beings' taking-to-be-true (BLA, i, preface p. xvii). But 'this impossibility of our rejecting the law in question hinders us not at all in supposing beings who do reject it' (ibid.). If such beings whose laws of thought flatly contradicted ours, leading to contrary results in practice, were to be found, then Frege would say, 'we have here a hitherto unknown type of madness' (BLA, i, preface p. xvi). But, Wittgenstein remonstrated, he never said what this type of madness would be like (RFM, 95).

What was Wittgenstein driving at in this obscure riposte? Frege represents the impossibility of our thinking contrary to the law of identity as a psychological impossibility. But it is no such thing. If it were a psychological impossibility, one might try to think thus, as one might try to run a mile in three minutes. But, Wittgenstein notes, when I look at my lamp and say: 'This lamp is different from itself', nothing stirs. It is not that I see that it is false, I can't do anything with it at all (RFM, 89). It is not too difficult, but impossible – because there is nothing to think. The impossibility is akin to the impossibility of checkmating in draughts. The 'laws of truth' are not descriptions of relations between thoughts or truth-values, but vacuous tautologies, internally related to inference rules. These are not technical rules, but grammatical rules which are *constitutive* of the meanings of the logical operators. They partially define what we *call* 'thinking', 'inferring', 'reasoning'. Hence Frege was wrong to concede that the 'impossibility' of our rejecting a law of thought 'hinders us not at all in supposing beings who do reject it', and mistaken to think that if there are such beings, we are right and they are wrong. Had he tried to describe the 'hitherto unknown type of madness', he would have seen that what he was describing was not a case of inferring, reasoning or thinking, but something else (cf. LFM, 203f.). The laws of logic

> show: how human beings think, and also *what* human beings call 'thinking'. ...
>
> The propositions of logic are 'laws of thought', 'because they bring out the essence of human thinking' – to put it more correctly: because they bring out, or show, the essence, the technique, of thinking. They show what thinking is and also show kinds of thinking. (RFM, 89f.)[13]

[13] To be sure, Wittgenstein recognised the intelligibility of alternative forms of thought – within limits. But the limits are indeterminate, as indeterminate as our concepts of thinking, inferring, and calculating. Nevertheless, they are not arbitrary but circumscribed 'by natural limits corresponding to the body of what can be called the role of thinking and inferring in our life' (RFM, 80).

Frege and the Augustinian picture of language

The *Philosophical Investigations* opens with a quotation from the autobiography of St Augustine in which he adumbrates the manner in which he takes himself to have learnt language as a child. From this unselfconscious description, Wittgenstein precipitated a number of theses which, he thought, with sophisticated qualifications and refinements, inform numerous philosophical accounts of the nature of language. For present purposes, the relevant theses are two. First, that (after due logical parsing or analysis) every significant expression that contributes to the determination of the sense of a sentence has a meaning, which is the entity it stands for. So the essential function of words is to stand for a meaning in the context of a sentence. Second, sentences are combinations of words the essential function of which is to describe. These two components of the Augustinian picture constitute a *leitmotif* of the *Philosophical Investigations*, and indeed of much of Wittgenstein's philosophy of mathematics. If one takes for granted this conception of sub-sentential expressions, one will think that the central questions to be asked are not: What is the use of such and such an expression? What is its role? What need does it meet in discourse? – but rather: What kind of entity does it stand for? What is the mechanism whereby it represents the entity it stands for? Does it adequately reflect the essential nature of the meaning it represents? If one thinks that the essential function of sentences is to describe, the pivotal differences between sentences will turn on *what* exactly it is that they describe. What do arithmetical propositions describe? Do geometrical propositions describe ideal shapes? Or the properties of space? Or the way the human mind is constrained to apprehend the data of sense? Do psychological propositions describe behaviour or mental states, processes and events? Do first-person psychological propositions describe the same phenomena as third-person ones? What is described by imperative and interrogative sentences? And so on. Wittgenstein's aim was to turn philosophers away from the unthinking temptation to succumb to the charms of the Augustinian picture, to abandon these misguided questions and to replace them with more fruitful questions which do not presuppose that the essential function of words is to stand for entities or of sentences to describe something.[14]

---

[14] For detailed discussion of the Augustinian picture as Wittgenstein conceived it, see G. P. Baker and P. M. S. Hacker, *Wittgenstein: Understanding and Meaning* (Oxford: Blackwell, 1980), pp. 33–59 and *Wittgenstein: Rules, Grammar and Necessity* (Oxford: Blackwell, 1985), pp. 3–24.

P. M. S. Hacker

In *Wittgenstein: Understanding and Meaning*, Gordon Baker and I argued that Wittgenstein, in expounding Augustine's picture of language, had Frege, Russell and the *Tractatus* in his target area. Their philosophies lay within the field of force of these misguided presuppositions, despite the sophisticated overlay of distinctions between surface and depth grammar, between subject/predicate parsing and alternative function/argument forms of decomposition, between sense and meaning, and between unanalysed and fully analysed sentences. Professor P. T. Geach has written that what he heard about Frege from Wittgenstein's lips makes him confident that this interpretation is perverse,[15] although he does not recount what it was that he heard from Wittgenstein's lips. Elsewhere Geach has claimed that it is easy to show that Frege was so far from thinking that every word named an object or function, he did not ascribe even a meaning to every expression, whether in ordinary language or in his symbolism. For Frege expressly denies that quantified phrases like 'some man' have a meaning in ordinary language or that bound variables have a meaning in his symbolism.[16]

To be sure, Wittgenstein did not even intimate that Frege cleaved to the Augustinian picture in its naïve, pre-theoretical form – indeed, it is not clear that *anyone* has. Certainly Augustine himself did not do so in his philosophical writings. But this fact does not derogate from its importance, let alone show that Wittgenstein was ill advised to begin his masterwork with this quotation. So we must answer the question of why he did so. It would be wildly implausible to suppose that he began his major book by delineating a theory which no one has ever held. In fact, Augustine's picture of language is not a theory, but an *Urbild* which moulds the form of different theories – with endless possible refinements and qualifications. Of course Frege did not think that 'some man' in the sentence 'Some man is rich' has a meaning, since it does not form a logically significant unit contributing to the sense of the sentence of which it is a part. But properly parsed, each significant expression *does* have a meaning; e.g., if parsed 'For some *x*' and 'if *x* is a man, then *x* is rich', the first expression (called 'a second-level concept-word') has as its meaning a second-level function and the second (called 'a first-level concept-word') has as its meaning a concept. *Pari passu*, a bound variable in concept-script does not have a meaning but the quantifier has a meaning, and the 'indicating' variable is to be treated as a feature of the name which has a first-level concept as its

[15] P. T. Geach, ed., *Wittgenstein's Lectures on Philosophical Psychology 1946–7* (Hemel Hempstead: Harvester Wheatsheaf, 1988), preface p. xiv.
[16] P. T. Geach, 'Wittgenstein on Names', in J.-M. Terricabras ed., *A Wittgenstein Symposium* (Amsterdam: Rodopi, 1993), pp. 72f.

meaning. As Frege wrote in the preface to *The Basic Laws*, 'every well-formed name must have a meaning' (BLA, i, xii), but a complex name may contain signs which indicate but do not have a meaning, viz. variables. A well-formed name is either a proper name which has an object as its meaning, or a concept-word such as 'Fξ' or 'if Fξ, then Gξ', which has a first-level concept as its meaning, or an n-level concept-word, which has an n-level function as its meaning, or a sentence which has a truth-value as its meaning, and so forth. To be sure, an expression has a meaning only in the context of a sentence, and how the sentence is to be parsed into names which stand for meanings depends, in the case of some kinds of sentences, upon our mode of apprehension (*Auffassungsweise*). A sign of concept-script which does not have a meaning, yet is not part of a name, is the judgement-stroke, which 'contains the act of assertion' (BLA, i, §6); similarly, the double-stroke of definition has no meaning. With these provisos (and others), Frege's conception of the functioning of any symbolism for the expression of thoughts perspicuously lies within the force-field of the Augustinian proto-picture (*Urbild*).

Similarly, Frege thought that the essential function of sentences is to describe. Sentences concerning physical objects describe phenomena in the 'physical world'. Psychological sentences describe psychological phenomena in the 'mental world'. Logical and arithmetical sentences describe relations between abstract objects in the 'third world'. Geometrical sentences describe the synthetic *a priori* properties of space. Frege therefore converges upon the Augustinian paradigm (although here too there are exceptions – as with all other philosophers, including Russell and the young Wittgenstein). But it is a cardinal error in philosophy to treat these different classes of sentences as having a uniform role, as differentiated only by *what* they describe – for many do not *describe* anything.

How did Wittgenstein see matters? Simplifying somewhat, he held that the propositions of logic are senseless tautologies which say nothing, that the propositions of arithmetic form a body of rules for the transformation of empirical propositions about magnitudes or quantities, etc., and that the propositions of geometry are norms of representation for the description of spatial relations and forms. Many first-person psychological propositions in the present tense are not descriptions at all, but *expressions* of what we think of as 'the inner', whereas third-person ones are descriptions. And so on. Where Frege by and large saw uniformity of function, Wittgenstein saw diversity; where Frege discerned common logical forms in regimented structures, Wittgenstein detected endless multiplicity manifest in use rather than form; where Frege identified fields for the advancement of science, Wittgenstein identified a multitude of cases for philosophical, therapeutic, treatment – for the dispelling of illusion.

Frege, like so many of the greatest of philosophers, such as Plato, Descartes or Spinoza, was a spinner of wonderful webs of illusion. Wittgenstein was the paradigmatic destroyer of philosophical illusion. Their philosophies can no more *fruitfully* be put to work together than Lachesis and Atropos.

Abbreviations

1 *Works by Frege*

BLA, i – *The Basic Laws of Arithmetic: Exposition of the System,* vol. I, trans. and ed. M. Furth (Berkeley: University of California Press, 1964).

BLA, ii – *The Basic Laws of Arithmetic*, vol. II.

BS – *Begriffsschrift, eine der arithmetischen nachgebildete Formelsprache des reinen Denkens* (Halle: L. Norbert, 1879); *Conceptual Notation, a formula language of pure thought modelled upon the formula language of arithmetic*, in *G. Frege, Conceptual Notation and related articles*, trans. and ed. T. W. Bynum (Oxford: Clarendon Press, 1972).

FA – *The Foundations of Arithmetic,* trans. J. L. Austin, 2nd rev. edn. (Oxford: Blackwell, 1959).

FC – 'Function and Concept', repr. in *Collected Papers on Mathematics, Logic, and Philosophy*, ed. B. McGuinness (Oxford: Blackwell, 1984) with original page reference.

PMC – *Philosophical and Mathematical Correspondence,* ed. G. Gabriel, H. Hermes, F. Kambartel, C. Thiel, and A. Veraart, trans. H. Kaal (Oxford: Blackwell, 1980).

PW – *Posthumous Writings*, ed. H. Hermes, F. Kambartel, F. Kaulbach, trans. P. Long, R. White, (Oxford: Blackwell, 1979).

2 *Works by Wittgenstein*

AWL – *Wittgenstein's Lectures, Cambridge 1932–35*, ed. A. Ambrose (Oxford: Blackwell, 1979).

BB – *The Blue and Brown Books* (Oxford: Blackwell, 1958).

LA – *Lectures and Conversations on Aesthetics, Psychology and Religious Beliefs*, ed. C. Barrett (Oxford: Blackwell, 1970).

LFM – *Wittgenstein's Lectures on the Foundations of Mathematics, Cambridge 1939*, ed. C. Diamond (Hassocks, Sussex: Harvester, 1976).

MS – Manuscripts in the Wittgenstein *Nachlass*, referred to by Von Wright number.

PG – *Philosophical Grammar*, ed. R. Rhees, trans. A. J. P. Kenny (Oxford: Blackwell, 1974).

PI – *Philosophical Investigations*, ed. G. E. M. Anscombe and R. Rhees, trans. G. E. M. Anscombe, 2nd edn (Oxford: Blackwell, 1958).

PR – *Philosophical Remarks*, ed. R. Rhees, trans. R. Hargreaves and R. White (Oxford: Blackwell, 1975).

RFM – *Remarks on the Foundations of Mathematics*, ed. G. H. von Wright, R. Rhees, G. E. M. Anscombe, rev. edn (Oxford: Blackwell, 1978).

TLP – *Tractatus Logico-Philosophicus*, trans. D. F. Pears and B. F. McGuinness (London: Routledge and Kegan Paul, 1961).

3 *Others*

PLP – *The Principles of Linguistic Philosophy*, F. Waismann, ed. R. Harré (London: Macmillan, 1965).

Otto Neurath, the Vienna Circle and the Austrian Tradition

THOMAS E. UEBEL

It is one of the distinctive claims of Neurath, though not of the Vienna Circle generally, that the Vienna Circle's philosophy was not really German philosophy at all. The relation is, if Neurath is to be trusted, anything but straight-forward. To understand it, not only must some effort be expended on specifying Neurath's claim, but also on delineating the different party-lines within the Vienna Circle.

Some might, of course, be tempted to dismiss the claim as just another cranky idea of the *enfant terrible* of logical empiricism, but I shall not do so. Neurath's admittedly problematic claim is too important to dismiss. My thesis here is that Neurath's claim holds the key for recovering, as it were, *Neurath's* Vienna Circle. Developing this thesis in turn helps, first, to deepen the appreciation of the heterogeneity of the Vienna Circle and, second, to provide a valuable vantage point on the pre-history of the Vienna Circle. Moreover, it provides an example of the multi-layered historicity of early analytic philosophy. The philosophy of the Vienna Circle was neither simply a logicised version of British empiricism nor even just an admixture of that and Neokantian elements: still other influences need to be recognised.

In place of detailed excavation, which will be provided elsewhere, I am concerned to bring out the more general interest that my thesis possesses. I will first present an overview of the Vienna Circle as a whole, then focus on Neurath specifically and then return to delineate certain divisions within the Circle. So prepared I will then turn to the problematic relation of Neurath's Vienna Circle to German philosophy.

1 The Vienna Circle was a group of philosophers and scientists who met periodically for discussions in Vienna from 1923 to about 1938. Centred around the philosopher Moritz Schlick, it included – to name but the main players – the mathematician Hans Hahn, the physicist Philipp Frank, the social scientist Otto Neurath, the logician Rudolf Carnap, the philosopher Viktor Kraft, and Schlick's students Herbert Feigl and Friedrich Waismann, and counted the mathematicians Kurt Gödel and Karl Menger and the historian Edgar Zilsel among its associates.

Thomas E. Uebel

As is well-known, the Circle proposed a controversial conception of scientific philosophy. By means of an empiricist criterion of cognitive significance the Circle divided all meaningful inquiry into empirical and logical ones and declared metaphysics to be meaningless. Characteristically, its manifesto *The Scientific World-conception. The Vienna Circle* declared war on so-called 'school-philosophy'. At the same time its authors (Carnap, Hahn and Neurath) promised to 'fulfil a demand of the day: ... to fashion intellectual tools for everyday life, [not only] for the life of the scholar but also for the daily life of all those who in some way join in working at the conscious re-shaping of life.' (Carnap, Hahn and Neurath 1929 [1973, 305]) In a word, the Vienna Circle believed that one was in the grip of a mistaken image of knowledge and of science (to use Yehuda Elkana's term). And at least the authors of the manifesto, if not the entire Circle, believed that being possessed by this mistaken image of knowledge had consequences that went far beyond matters of scholarship and research, and associated their philosophy with movements like *Neue Sachlichkeit*, even socialism. (As a first indication of the division in the Circle it may be noted that the latter association scandalised Schlick, who in turn dismissed the expressly anti-philosophical stance, with which Neurath laced his promotions of the scientific world-conception, as unserious posturing, which upset Neurath.)

The Circle's activities were originally confined to Schlick's *Privatseminar* until 1929 (the two academic years, 1924–1926, were spent on reading Wittgenstein's *Tractatus* line by line). In 1929, however, Carnap, Hahn and Neurath issued the manifesto, Schlick and Frank began publishing a series of philosophical monographs ('*Schriften zur wissenschaftlichen Weltauffassung*') and the entire group started collaborating with the Berlin 'Society of Empirical Philosophy' (including Hans Reichenbach, Kurt Grelling and C. G. Hempel) in organising international conferences and editing the journal *Erkenntnis*. Major individual works of roughly this period include Carnap's *Aufbau* (*The Logical Structure of the World*, 1928) and *Logical Syntax of Language* (1934), Frank's *The Causal Law and its Limits* (1932), Neurath's *Empirical Sociology* (1931) and Schlick's 'Form and Content' lectures (1932), as well as strings of important journal articles. On the face of it, their work was strictly academic and concerned with working out a tenable version of empiricism, a version whose borrowings from conventionalism were to help avoid both simplistic inductivism and idealism and whose logicisation, as it were, was to account for the formal sciences as Mill never could. Nonetheless, we may see in their active participation in the Viennese adult education movement, within and without the Ernst Mach Society, a reflection of wider concerns.

250

Otto Neurath, the Vienna Circle and the Austrian Tradition

Soon the Circle was drawn into the unfolding tragedy that is the Central European history of the first half of this century and against which they tried to uphold enlightenment values. Neurath was driven into exile in Holland in the spring of 1934, Schlick was murdered by an ex-student in the summer of 1936, Carnap left for America later that year, to be followed by Frank in 1938, when also Waismann emigrated to England (where Neurath escaped to after the German invasion of Holland). With Feigl in America since 1930 and Hahn having suddenly died in the summer of 1934 (from unpolitical causes), the Vienna Circle – like many of the other intellectual and artistic circles that made the Vienna of the inter-war years an extraordinarily rich environment – was virtually extinct in Vienna itself from the *Anschluss* onwards[1].

The death and dispersion in exile of key members from 1934 onwards did not mean the extinction of Vienna Circle philosophy however. Through the subsequent work of foreign visitors (A. J. Ayer, E. Nagel, W. V. O. Quine, to name just three) and emigré members and collaborators (especially Carnap, Feigl, Reichenbach and Hempel), so-called 'logical positivism' or 'logical empiricism' strongly influenced the development of analytic philosophy. Constituting the 'received view' in the philosophy of science in the 1950s and 1960s, logical empiricism is now widely perceived to have been overthrown by the external critiques of Toulmin, Feyerabend and Kuhn as, in short, unduly formalist and ahistorical. To this it may be added that Quine's celebrated attack on the two dogmas of empiricism helped transform the 'received view' also from within (Hempel being an early sympathiser).

With logical positivism officially 'dead' since the late 1960s (and so no longer a threat to current practitioners), the Vienna Circle and Reichenbach's Berlin group have of late enjoyed a renewed interest from historians of analytical philosophy. These historians contend that, contrary to the popular misconceptions, early logical empiricism deserves as much study as Frege, Russell, Moore, Wittgenstein, Ramsey and the French conventionalists Poincaré and Duhem. Of course, very few if any of these historians would wish to promote a revival of logical positivism; their motive is rather the suspicion that the actual mistakes in that philosophy have still not been properly understood. Not surprisingly, just how some of these supposed mistakes (e.g. Carnap's definition of analyticity in *Logical Syntax* (1934) ought to be understood is a topic of lively discussion

[1] Only a small group around Kraft and von Juhos continued to meet very much in private. From their (still marginalised) post-World War II discussion group emerged Paul Feyerabend who went on to post-doctoral work with Popper, whom Kraft had mentored in the 1920s.

among them. Still, if there is one thing they all agree on it is this: there is a much greater variety of doctrines and heterogeneity of research interests in logical positivism generally, and the Vienna Circle in particular, than either have traditionally been credited with.[2]

2 And this brings me to Neurath. It seems fair to say that it is he who held the most surprises in store for recent students of the Vienna Circle. Neurath most strikingly contradicts the common stereotype of the logical positivists. Far from being merely the organisational motor (the 'big locomotive', as Carnap once called him) of the Circle's internationalisation in the Unity-of-Science movement of the 1930s and 1940s, Neurath has emerged as a philosopher of quite striking originality. Moreover, already in the Circle itself Neurath argued against the failings attested to logical positivism by its external critics, criticising the trend towards seemingly purely logically oriented formal inquires and the neglect of the social and historical dimension of science. Similarly, Neurath anticipated the turn towards naturalism, commonly associated with Quine's later internal critique, albeit along different lines than Quine. (It is little wonder then that Neurath has become something of a cult hero for post-positivists.)[3]

A number of questions arise here. First, systematic ones like: what precisely were Neurath's own views on, say, epistemology, and what relation do they stand in to contemporary discussions? Not wishing to repeat too much what I said on these issues on other occasions, I will only touch on them here – enough, I hope, to indicate the trend of his anti-foundationalism.[4] But there are also more historical questions that arise from the case of Neurath. First, how was it possible that Neurath's unorthodox version of logical positivism disappeared from view until the recent rediscovery? One reason is Neurath's early death in 1945 which prevented him from promoting what already then had become a minority view in the by then fully internationalised movement of logical empiricism. Another is his rather discursive and impromptu style and the contrapuntal nature of his interventions in ongoing debates. This means that his

---

[2] There is to date no single volume in English that covers the entire Vienna Circle and the Berlin group from the perspective of recent scholarship. Spohn (1991), Uebel (1991b), Bell and Vossenkuhl (1992), Sarkar (1992), Stadler (1993), Giere and Richardson (1996) and Nemeth and Stadler (1996) provide representative essays and Coffa (1991) a monumental early work in the field. A traditional place to start on the Circle remains Ayer (1959).

[3] See, eg., Zolo (1989) and Carwright, Cat, Fleck and Uebel (1996).

[4] See Uebel (1991a) and (1996b).

remarks require extensive contextualisation still before their systematic reconstruction can be begun. Another, perhaps even more interesting historical question is what prompted Neurath to develop his unorthodox version of Vienna Circle philosophy in the first place. I will return to this presently.

Before that, however, I briefly outline the plot of Neurath's philosophy. His central theme was the absence of epistemic foundations and the irreducible contextuality of knowledge and justification. The continuity of this theme is illustrated by his frequent employment of the metaphor which subsequently Quine made common coin: we are like sailors who have to repair their boat on the open sea, without ever being able to pull into dry dock. Neurath first used this simile in 1913 in a long journal article on the methodology of economics; he re-employed it in 1921 in the course of his critique of Spengler's *Decline of the West*, then in 1932 in the protocol sentence debate with Carnap and Schlick, again in 1937 in the course of promoting the project of the International Encyclopeadia of Unified Science, and finally in 1944 in conclusion of his last monograph on the methodology of social science, having just (re-)issued the call for a reflexive theory of science, or, as one commentator calls it, a 'reflexive epistemology'.[5] Throughout, it is to be noted, the boat metaphor also expresses a certain constructivist impulse. Knowledge is gained and justification assessed by tools which we ourselves have created.

Like his colleagues in the Vienna Circle – and, it has to be added, like a few of the 'school philosophers' he opposed (Cassirer springs to mind) – Neurath sought to comprehend the upheavals in the scientific understanding of the world which the preceding turn of the century and the first decade thereafter had initiated. Neurath explored ways of overcoming the dilemma of foundationalism or relativism, which only grew more intense as the twentieth century grew older, but whose roots – and whose pseudo-solutions which waylaid progress all along – he had (or had thought to have) discerned early on. Neurath's distinctive answer consisted in exploring a guiding idea which may be put as that of 'controllable rationality'. Neurath took the old Enlightenment idea of scientific knowledge as liberator from the reign of dogma and prejudice and sought to import it from the domain of the natural sciences, the natural world, to that of the social sciences, the social world. (This is not to say, of course, that Neurath believed that science could tell us what 'ought to be done'.) What allowed science to serve as liberator was its empirical method, its reliance on intersubjective evidence and the

[5] The story of Neurath's boat is told in Uebel 1996a, the phrase 'reflexive epistemology' is due to Zolo (1989).

Thomas E. Uebel

adjudication of theory acceptable in its light. This method, so Neurath, was not simply given to us but had been historically developed. The task that he saw facing him was to investigate the conditions under which it was possible, in science, to exercise something like 'conceptual responsibility by collective management'.

The later Neurath (and Carnap joined him on this point) was something of a constructivist therefore, but not a constructivist on the object level, but on the metalevel of epistemological reflection. Scientific knowledge (of nature or society) does not simply 'flow from its subject matter', as he already urged in his revealing review of Carnap's *Aufbau* (1928 [1981, 296]). Importantly, it was not the objects but the standards of cognition that were to some degree socially constructed. Neurath's sketches of a non-reductive physicalism and a non-dogmatic scientific 'encyclopedism' – his alternative to the orthodox hierarchical model of the unity of science may be deemed a version of the patchwork conception[6] – stressed not only the hypothetical nature of science but also its creative aspect. Always, however, he saw it as a creation that was negotiated in the collective of scientists so as to answer to criteria of acceptance both internal and external to science itself, criteria which in turn were not pre-given but arrived at in collective work and reflection.

3 That such a view contradicts the stereotype of the logical positivists as epistemologically foundationalist empiricists hardly needs pointing out. As it happens, I think that stereotype is mistaken also in the case of other major members of the Vienna Circle, including even Schlick, but it is clear that some were more radically anti-foundationalist than others.[7] So let me turn to classifying the different factions within the Circle.

The material at hand suggests the following divisions and terminology. Let the well-known Vienna Circle of the inter-war years around Moritz Schlick be called 'Vienna Circle proper' or 'Schlick's Circle' and let the name 'later Vienna Circle' designate the association of members of the Schlick Circle in their dispersion in exile. Then let the term of art 'left Vienna Circle' designate a subformation in the Schlick Circle and the later Vienna Circle. This left Vienna Circle comprised Neurath, Hahn, Frank and Carnap and is placed particularly in opposition to the wing around Schlick and Waismann. Despite the moniker, it is not political ideology that accounts for the philosophical difference between Schlick's faction and the left wing (though the distinction along those lines held true), but rather their respective attitudes towards Wittgenstein, in

[6] See Cartwright and Cat (1996).
[7] See Uebel (1996c).

254

particular his strictures on metalinguistic discourse. As the end of the *Tractatus* so strikingly tells us, talk about meaning is strictly speaking meaningless itself. That such a view would bar the type of metatheoretical constructivism that engages in language and conceptual tool construction, as envisaged by Neurath and Carnap, should be apparent. Given their metatheoretical constructivism, the left wing's opposition to Wittgenstein is not hard to understand. (We may leave open whether Wittgenstein's view leads back to metaphysics, as Neurath alleged.)

Finally, let the name 'first Vienna Circle', designate the members of the left Vienna Circle minus Carnap, that is, Hahn, Frank and Neurath, in their role as members of a discussion group in Vienna, roughly from 1907 to 1912, and in their loose association until the end of the World War II.[8] It is this first Vienna Circle that is of great importance for evaluating Neurath's claim concerning the distinctness of the Vienna Circle from German philosophy.

To approach this issue somewhat obliquely and to examine an example of its problematic relevance, consider Carnap. Carnap was in no small measure indebted to German Neokantianism at the start of his career, but soon came to shed this influence so that already his *Aufbau* of 1928 represents as much of a break with that tradition as it does with that of foundationalist empiricism. In place of Rickerts, Cassirer's and Bauch's psychologised transcendental logic, Carnap employed the logic of Frege and Russell to delineate the conceptual and logical framework which made scientific objectivity possible. It was his resolute rejection of the *synthetic a priori* that aligned Carnap with the empiricists, not his supposed attempt to exhibit, in rational reconstruction, the empirical well-foundedness of science.[9] Both the anti-foundationalism and the rejection of the *synthetic a priori*, of course, are more forcefully expressed and particularly striking in his *Logical Syntax*. There Carnap likened logic itself to the Neurathian boat: we have to construct even our logics on the open sea – without foundational certainties (1934 [1937, p. xv]). With Carnap then, Vienna Circle philosophy was by no means unaffected by German philosophy. (Given that Carnap, like Schlick, was German, this should not be too surprising.) Yet with Carnap we can also see how one Vienna Circle philosophy increasingly came to differentiate itself from the German tradition.

We may wonder whether Carnap's development reflects the workings of the distinct tradition to which Neurath chose to associate the Vienna Circle, namely the tradition of Austrian philosophy.

[8] See Frank (1949a) and Haller (1985).
[9] See Friedman (1992) and Richardson (1997).

Thomas E. Uebel

Note that I am saying 'reflect', for Carnap always remained very much his own man (as can be shown by reference to his changing positions in his protocol sentence debate with Neurath).[10] The convergence of their views would seem to be more of a case of an intellectual affinity between Carnap and the ex-members of the first Vienna Circle working itself out. The interesting question of which the case of Carnap and his association with ex-members of the first Vienna Circle on the left wing gives rise, is rather whether, in the current climate of rediscovering Kantian themes in analytical philosophy, it might not be timely again to stress also its anti-Kantian roots – if, that is, we see something of value in tracing genealogies in the first place.

To be specific to the case at hand: Just as it would be a mistake to continue to view the Vienna Circle in the ahistorical fashion, with which analytical philosophy tends to regard itself, and consider it in abstraction from the German-language philosophy of its time – and so to neglect the importance which Neokantianism undoubtedly possessed for the Circle – so it would be a mistake to fail to note that not all German-language philosophy of importance to the Circle was German philosophy in the Neokantian sense. For it is precisely from the other tradition that the original Viennese core of the left Vienna Circle – the first Vienna Circle – imbibed their *ab initio* objectivist and anti-idealist orientation towards philosophy, indeed their *ab initio* anti-Kantian stance, just as it is to that other tradition that they owe their proclivity to pursue philosophical questions by means of *Sprachkritik*, the critique of language. It is precisely their rootedness in that Austrian tradition – commonly defined by its objectivist, empiricist and linguistically critical perspective – that helps to explain the distinctive radicalism of Neurath's Vienna Circle. (Moreover, once we have specified which particular part of that Austrian tradition the first Vienna Circle is most closely associated with, we can go on to claim that even the phenomenon of the Vienna Circle proper finds a partial explanation thereby: it was very much due to the efforts of Hans Hahn, a member of the first Vienna Circle, that Schlick was called to Mach's old chair in 1922.)

In specifying that 'other' tradition, it would be no news at all simply to refer to Ernst Mach, already known as the virtual patron saint of the Vienna Circle. The point is that Mach himself is to be regarded as part of a larger tradition. That, of course, constitutes precisely Neurath's thesis of a distinct Austrian tradition reaching back to Bolzano, a thesis that has been revitalised in our day by Rudolf Haller.[11] So the point is rather this: Neurath was correct to

[10] On the protocol sentence debate see Uebel (1992).
[11] See, eg., Haller (1986).

discern a distinctively Austrian tradition and he also was correct to associate not only, as it were, *his* Vienna Circle with it, but also – considering that arguably Wittgenstein too belongs to the Austrian tradition – the Schlick Circle as a whole. For the reasons indicated above, however, Neurath is wrong to assert that Austrian philosophy *wholly* 'saved itself from Kantian interlude' (1936a [1981, 676]), if we count the Vienna Circle as a whole into the Austrian tradition.

So let me suggest acceptance of the Neurath–Haller thesis as neither claiming that Austrian philosophy developed without any influence from German philosophy, nor that all philosophy done in the Habsburg empire or the first Austrian republic was Austrian in the relevant sense. Then the Neurath–Haller thesis provides us with a vantage point from which to approach the puzzling 'anomaly' that Neurath represents: an anti-foundationalist pragmatist who still rolled the drums for 'logical empiricism' (Neurath actually preferred this term to 'logical positivism') when that movement already showed signs of becoming a new, as Neurath put it, '*Metaphysica modo logico demonstrata*' (1936a [1981, 701]).

4 Listeners and readers of Peter Simons' lecture in this series will have noted that my theme links up with his, but may wonder about the precise relation between our theses.[12] Simons also defends the Neurath–Haller thesis that there is a distinct tradition of Austrian philosophy. Within this framework he introduces Bernard Bolzano, Franz Brentano and Alexius Meinong and drew lines to Kazimir Twardowski and his school in Lvov: Lukasiewics, Lesniewski, Kotarbinski. From the Polish logicians, amongst whose second generation Alfred Tarski features prominently, of course, it is less than a stone's throw to analytical philosophy of logic and metaphysics – they already practiced it themselves. So a developmental line can be drawn from Bolzano to contemporary analytic philosophy – the opposite in many people's eyes of the German philosophy that credits Kant and Hegel as its founders.

Now the Vienna Circle is also rightly credited, together with Frege, Russell and Wittgenstein, as one of the sources of contemporary analytic philosophy. The Circle's influence pertains primarily to philosophy of science, also philosophy of logic. Notoriously, however, they inveighed against what they called 'metaphysics' and so exhibited a different intellectual proclivity from that of the Polish heirs of Bolzano. So the question arises whether it is correct to associate the Vienna Circle with the lines of Austrian philosophy focused upon by Simons.

---

[12] See Simons in this volume.

Thomas E. Uebel

Here we must already note a twist to the Neurath thesis that was emphasised by Haller. Haller distinguishes two strands in the Austrian tradition, the Bolzano, Brentano, Twardowski and Meinong line and the line of Mach, Boltzmann and the Vienna Circle. This sharpens our question: would it be correct to associate the Vienna Circle with the tradition of Austrian philosophy going back to Bolzano? Or, sharper still: was Neurath correct when he remarked in a discussion at the 8th International Congress of Philosophy in Prague in 1934 that '[i]t does not seem to be an accident that a man like Bolzano belongs to our predecessors' (1936b, p. 157)? In other words, was Neurath mistaken when he associated the Vienna Circle with the Austrian tradition he correctly linked back to Bolzano?

My answer is 'no'. What is at issue, rather, is the precise location of the connecting link of the first Vienna Circle with the Austrian tradition. As it happens, all we have to do to locate it is to follow Neurath's own hints. In his expansive historical sketch (which remains untranslated into English so far) he wrote:

> Let us note that in Austria[–Hungary] the anti-Kantian and Leibnizian Herbartianism was well regarded ... since Kantianism was viewed as an effluence of the French Revolution. It is not difficult to see why the state and the Church on the one hand favoured anti-Kantianism, but on the other hand feared the new scientismn, even though they contributed to its progress. Bolzano, author of *The Theory of Science* and *The Paradoxes of Infinity* and other important works, whose importance is appreciated only today [1936], was partly supported [by the authorities] and partly persecuted. ...
>
> The speed with which logical analysis came to predominate [in Austria–Hungary] is remarkable. ... There was a systematic effort to link the particularity of Austrian culture [, its basically empiricist outlook,] grounded on logic, with certain pre-Kantian tendencies of a utilitarian and empiricist nature and thereby to avoid the Kantian interlude. One example: the *Ordinarius* in Vienna was the Herbartian Robert Zimmermann, who was taught exact and mathematical thinking still by Bolzano himself. ... already Zimmermann had a discernible influence on our present period.... Brentano worked in Vienna more in a logical and critical vein than in a metaphysical. ... Notably Meinong too, whose theory of objects always proved stimulating for partisans of logical empiricism, continued Brentantan lines of inquiry. His student Mally works on logic. Also continuing Bretanean lines is Twardowski (Lvov), who has awakened interest in the problems of modern logic in Poland ...

Otto Neurath, the Vienna Circle and the Austrian Tradition

In Vienna itself the logical efforts of the Brentano school were developed further by a man, who supported the beginnings of the Viennese school [sic!] at the beginning of the twentieth century by introducing discussions of the foundations of physics: Alois Höfler. ... He was for a long time the editor of the 'Publications of the Philosophical Society of the University of Vienna'; they show the enthusiasm with which at that time the problems were discussed which later on were to occupy the Vienna school. ... the most decidedly empiricist standpoint was represented by Mach. ... The anti-metaphysical outlook, which Mach promoted in Vienna, did not remain his alone. In contrast to the development in Germany, an entire generation went over to positivism, utilitarianism and empiricism. (1936a [1981, pp. 688–91]).

Now you may wonder whether Neurath's historiography is to be trusted. In a longer work currently in preparation for publication I have followed up Neurath's hints and found them to be deeply revealing indeed.

For our purposes here note first the expression 'Vienna school': it is the Vienna Circle that is referred to thereby. Note second whom Neurath points to as their most immediate link with that Austrian tradition: Alois Höfler. Now Höfler can indeed be shown to be the central link between the first Vienna Circle and the Austrian tradition.[13] Moreover, by focusing on his activities we can specify the aspect and the phase of the Austrian tradition that was of specific importance to the Vienna Circle. Four points are pertinent here.

Consider first the series 'Publications of the Philosophical Society of the University of Vienna'. That Society was founded in 1888 and was headed by Höfler for numerous years at various times between then and his death in 1921. In 1899 the Society published an anthology, edited by Höfler, *Vorreden und Einleitungen zu klassischen Werken der Mechanik* (Prefaces and Introductions to Classical Works of Mechanics), which featured, besides texts of Galilei, Newton, D'Alambert and Lagrange, also Kirchhoff, Hertz and Helmholtz. In 1900, there followed Höfler's own *Studien zur gegenwärtigen Philosophie der Mechanik* (Studies in the Contemporary Philosophy of Mechanics) as a free-standing critical commentary, as it were, on and afterword to Höfler's new edition of Kant's *Metaphysische Anfangsgründe der Naturwissenschaft* (Metaphysical

---

[13] Hints to this effect can be found in Haller (1993), Blackmore (1995) and Stadler (1997). The Höfler connection is developed in detail in Uebel (forthcoming), chapter 4, the results of which are summarised below (albeit it without the unwieldly apparatus of citations). See Reininger (1938) for the activities of the Philosophical Society.

Thomas E. Uebel

Groundings of Natural Science), also published by the Society. Höfler's commentary discussed Kant's topics from the perspective of the state of scientific and philosophical play in 1900. Many of the numerous, sometimes bi-weekly meetings of the Philosophical Society in the following decade and still later dealt with the themes of Höfler's anthology and his Kant commentary. This focus on philosophy of science is reflected also in the *Yearbooks* which the Society published from 1902 until 1916, though it was by no means the only area of interest to members of the Philosophical Society as a whole.

The second point to note is that the Philosophical Society also provided the first public forum for the members of the first Vienna Circle. Remember, Hahn, Frank and Neurath were young scientists. It was in the Philosophical Society that they first ventured into philosophy of science. When they did so, they had already proven themselves promising practitioners of their own fields.[14] Between 1906 to the end of World War I, Hahn, Frank and Neurath lectured and led discussion evenings 17 times in the Philosophical Society; five of their lectures were published in the *Yearbooks* of the Society. After World War I, Hahn and Neurath lecturered or moderated discussions another ten times. Their participation stopped, however, in 1927: that year the Philosophical Society became the local chapter of the Kant-Society. It is surely no accident that in the following year, Neurath and Hahn were active in the formation of the Ernst Mach Society, which consciously sought a broader audience for their by then maturing 'scientific world-conception'.

Yet another aspect of Höfler's activities is to be noted for our purposes (point three). After Zimmermann's death in 1899, Höfler

---

[14] By 1905 was a freshly habilitated mathematician who had just spent the two previous years as a post-doctural fellow in Göttingen with Klein, Hilbert and Zermelo and had begun to make significant contributions to the calculus of variations and the theory of functions. In 1906 Neurath gained his doctorate *summa cum laude* in political economy under Eduard Meyer and Gustav Schmoller in Berlin and returned to Vienna, participating amongst other things in the research seminar of Böhm-Bawerk (and contributing to his journal). (He had to wait for his habilitation in Heidelberg until 1917 and promptly lost it in 1919 for political reasons). In 1909 Frank, who had gained his doctorate still under Boltzmann and spent a year studying in Göttingen with Minkowski, habilitated with a study of 'The Role of the Principle of Relativity in the Systems of Mechanics and Electrodynamics' which placed special emphasis, amongst other things, on Minkowski's then just published four-dimensional formulation of the special theory of relativity (previously he had coined the term 'Galilean transformations', since in use).

gained access to unpublished manuscripts by Bolzano and initiated new editions of his works. In 1914, the Society published, with him as editor, a new edition of the first volume of Bolzano's *Theory of Science*, and in 1920, the long-awaited new edition of Bolzano's *Paradoxes of the Infinite* – with annotations by none other than Hans Hahn.

Finally – and this is the fourth point of importance of Höfler for the first Vienna Circle – at least in the case of Hahn and Neurath, Höfler also was the author of the textbook of the obligatory instruction in philosophy – that is to say, in logic, epistemology and philosophy – they received as part of the curriculum for the upper two years in high school, prior to their *Matura*. This textbook, *Philosophische Grundlehren* (*Philosophical Propedeutics*) was a shortened version of the scholarly *Logik* which Höfler had published, as the cover indicates, 'with contributions by Alexius Meinong' in 1888. Without saying so explicity, Höfler's textbook, first published in 1890 with several editions up to 1906, embued its readers with the basic principles of Bolzano's logic, Brentano's descriptive psychology and even the first object–theoretical distinctions (content and object of representations), as well as with early conceptions of the deductive–nomological characer of scientific theories. Höfler's textbook thus continued the under-cover transmission of Bolzano's ideas begun by the textbook, which his own *Grundlehren* came gradually to replace, namely Zimmerman's *Philosophische Propädeutik*, published in 1852/1853. Zimmermann's textbook was written, as is known now but generally was unknown at the time, after Bolzano's own blueprint in accordance with his express request to repress his name in order to facilitate its wider use in the face of powerful clerical opposition.[15] The ruse worked brilliantly, as, I'd argue, even Höfler's own textbook still shows. (While Mach, who completed secondary school in 1855, most likely escaped Bolzano's underground influence, his Vienna Circle acolytes certainly did not.)

5 So much for Höfler as the link between the first Vienna Circle and the Austrian tradition. But what, you may ask, is the profit to be gained from a deepened understanding of the historicity, the historical location of Vienna Circle philosophy? Happily, this history, fascinating as it is already in its own terms, also has a philosophical point.

The activities of the Philosophical Society represent an aspect of the Austrian tradition that deserves attention in its own right: the scientific and philosophical culture of Habsburg Vienna. Of the great richness of that culture it was the philosophy of science that

[15] See Winter (1975).

Thomas E. Uebel

Hahn, Frank and Neurath focused on. The philosophy of physics as discussed in the Philosophical Society was their, as it were, philosophical modernity. Here the ideas of Mach were partially joined and partially opposed by those of Boltzmann and Höfler, providing a picture of early twentieth century philosophy of science in crisis. When we add to this that, as scientists interested in the foundations of their disciplines, Hahn, Frank and Neurath also experienced at first hand the foundational crises in their own disciplines – in mathematics, in physics and in social science – then one thing becomes obvious: the philosophical and scientific modernity, which the first Vienna Circle grew into, was, like what is called *Wiener Moderne* in the arts, characterised by a consciousness of crisis.[16]

That something like the scientific world-view was in crisis is something explicitly remarked upon in the contemporaneous writings of the French conventionalists Poincaré, Duhem and Rey and was noted as such not only in Frank's own retrospective accounts of the Vienna Circle, but already so by him and Hahn in recently rediscovered pre World War I reviews of their works.[17] Moreover, this consciousness of crisis was given clear expression by Felix Klein on an occasion which perfectly captures the intellectual ambience that characterised the first Circle's modernity and which I will come back to. But why is it so important that their modernity was a modernity in crisis? It underscores that, virtually from the start, Hahn, Frank and Neurath were not naïve positivists or simpleminded believers in scientific and social progress.

Once it is noted that their modernity was one of crisis, it should not be surprising anymore that on the occasion of Mach's death in 1917, Frank formulated the first Circle's understanding of the Enlightenment movement in the following striking terms. For Frank, an 'essential characteristic' of the enlightenment was its 'protest against the misuse of merely auxiliary concepts in general philosophical proofs'. Even a 'tragic feature' was discerned in the Enlightenment philosophy: 'It destroys the old system of concepts, but while it is constructing a new system, it is already laying the foundation for new misuse. For there is no theory without auxiliary concepts, and every such concept is necessarily misused in the course of time.' 'Hence', Frank concluded, 'in every period a new Enlightenment is required in order to abolish this misuse'. Mach himself had seen his role to be not to fight 'against the Enlightenment of the 18th century but rather to continue its work'.

[16] On this characteristic of the *Wiener Moderne* as different authors as Janik and Toulmin (1973), Schorske (1980) and Le Rider (1990) are agreed.

[17] See Frank (1949a) and Uebel (forthcoming), chapters 5–6.

(1917 [1949, pp. 73–78]). In this sense, it became the task of the first Vienna Circle in turn to study and criticise even Mach and what his theories had become – in the light of recent developments.

How in detail the devleopment of the first Circle's philosophy of science is to be understood from this perspective cannot be shown here, but it should be clear that their later appreciation of the need for reflexivity in the theory of science itself is rooted in their understanding of the enlightenment task, just as it may be already be suspected that their later constructivism is rooted in their early conventionalist sympathies. These sympathies in turn, of course, are owed in turn to the promise which conventionalism held for them who were deeply impressed by the central problem of the Viennese *philosophical* modernity, a problem which they made their own. And that problem was quite simply the question of precisely what was to take the place of Kant's *synthetic a priori*.

That, of course, was also the problem of which the later logical empiricism set out to give a definitive answer. Let me hasten to add therefore that I am not claiming that the first Vienna Circle already had to hand the answers for which the Vienna Circle proper, the Schlick Circle, is famous. What I am claiming is rather this. The first Vienna Circle developed the desiderata for a programme of research roughly like that of early logical empiricism. There is no need to lumber them with anticipations of later results, even though many a first step was already taken in the first Circle. But given simply such a programme for a programme, as it were, it makes perfect sense why Hahn should have expended the effort he did in recruiting Schlick, arguably the leading *bona fide* philosopher of science of his day in the German-speaking countries of Central Europe.[18]

Note also that the philosophical modernity of the first Vienna Circle was not just Viennese (Mach, Boltzmann, Höfler), but already international in orientation. I already noted (in fn. 14) Hahn's and Frank's connections to Göttingen, Neurath's to Berlin and Heidelberg and their shared enthusiasm for French conventionalism. We may add Frank's connections to Einstein first in Zurich and then in Prague (where he became Einstein's successor in 1912), and Hahn's long-standing admiration for Russell and his logicist programme. (Already in 1907, Hahn and Neurath planned a seminar on, besides Poincaré and Mach, Russell's *Principles of Mathematics*.) Clearly, it was a very rich brew that the first Circle was stirring up, and it became richer still. Thus note that the very contours of the problem–situation of the philosophy of science

[18] Given Hahn's roots in the Austrian tradition, it also makes sense of why the efforts of a Marburg Neokantian like Cassirer were less attractive for him.

Thomas E. Uebel

changed in the course of their own early work as physicists, mathematicians and social scientists. The develpments in set theory and the theory of relativity throughout the first two decades of the century, which to some degree Frank and Hahn actively participated in – to say nothing about social science – only sharpened the need for a new philosophy of science.

The basic problem, however, remained the same: to find an adequate *replacement* for Kant's *synthetic a priori* – not to repair it. That is the central Austrian theme that characterises their work from their time in the first to that in the left Vienna Circle.

6 To throw this theme into relief, let me take us back to the Philosophical Society of the University of Vienna, in particular the meeting on October 10, 1905. In several respects, it is enblematic for the distinctive historicity of the philosophy of Neurath Vienna Circle, that has been my topic here.

That evening Felix Klein, visiting from Göttingen, opened an evening of discussion under the title '*Grenzfragen der Mathematik und Philosophy*' (Questions on the Border of Mathematics and Philosophy) with some brief but incisive introductory remarks. Note first how Klein characterised the intellectual climate of the date:

> It is common to all the sciences in most recent times, that everything is called into doubt which previously was considered settled. Everything is in turmoil, mathematics included. I'd like to give expression to my wish that this development, which has come upon us by general necessity – no one individual is at fault or could claim responsibility for it, but it is in the nature of our times, that everywhere foundational questions stand in the forefront of our interest – I'd like to say then that it is my wish that this period will not end with universal scepticism but with a fresh effort to rebuild [*einem neuen Aufbau*]. (1906, p. 7).

In particular, Klein focussed on the foundational crisis in his own field and stressed that as regards mathematical definitions, even geometrical ones, *Anschauung*, intuition, no longer had any role to play. Hahn was amongst those present and contributed an example in support. Boltzmann, as was his custom, polemically sharpened Klein's own more modest conclusion as follows:

> I just can't understand how anybody can speak of proofs from intuition. When I read that Kant [sic], I just can't comprehend how any rational human being could write such things. Intuition does not prove anything at all. Intuition is merely the repetition

of that which we have perceived by our senses. That one should possess an intuition of space that goes beyond or comes before experiences, I just can't fathom; I have no idea what this is supposed to come to. (1906, pp. 8–9).

Whether Boltzmann understood Kant just right we need not consider; just savour his style and direction. Intuition no longer provided an epistemological court of appeal, but the importance of given forms of intuition was not neglected. Boltzmann was in the forefront of those who sought to replace the *synthetic a priori* by biologising it. Not unlike Mach in this respect and like Georg Simmel (who, however, may have thought of this as a repair), Boltzmann sought to explain the human constitutive contribution to cognition by means of evolutionary biology. Despite some early sympathies on the part of Neurath and due rather to the problematical psychologism with which Boltzmann flirted and which Hahn rejected – it flatly contradicted his logicist objectivism – the first Vienna Circle was to take a different path.

With the long-term trajectory of their thought pointing, as we saw, to the metatheoretical constructivism of the later Neurath (and Carnap), a view shared by Frank and prepared by Hahn, it becomes clear that instead of biologising the *synthetic a priori* they moved to socialise it. The Vienna Circle, as is well known, stripped the *a priori* of its apodicity, its *Denknotwendigkeit*, made it moveable, and then they replaced the seemingly substantial claims of the *synthetic a priori* either by analytical ones, insofar as *a priori* knowledge was still allowed, or recategorised them as emipirical hypotheses, insofar as synthetic claims were involved. Fully fledged, this view required a conception of tautology which was derived from Wittgenstein, of course. But compared to Boltzmann (and Simmel), already the first Vienna Circle historicised the *synthetic a priori* far more thoroughly by conventionalising the *a priori* determinations without which, they agreed, theoretical science would be impossible. (In the later Vienna Circle again it was Frank and Neurath who stressed the need for historical and sociological investigations of scientific practice.) Despite this difference of approach from Boltzmann, however, it is clear that they shared the basic problematic, the *Problemstellung* of the Austrian tradition.

7 One might wonder, of course, whether the identification of the Austrian philosophical tradition with anti-Kantianism is not somewhat shallow. Thus it could be pointed out that late nineteenth century German philosophy by no means accepted Kant's own rendition of critical philosophy as authoritative. This objection can be conceded without invalidating my point. It is precisely that

Thomas E. Uebel

Austrian philosophers did not try to think 'with Kant' in trying to correct or further develop his conceptions, but rather tried to do philosophy altogether differently, that distinguishes their tradition. Their anti-Kantian rhetoric betokens not only differences in presentational form but also in function (to the degree that intentions can fix any research programme).

Did the Austrian tradition then simply neglect Kant? Importantly, the answer is negative. Höfler's Kant commentary, for instance, expressly warned against the hubris that Kantian problems could be simply dismissed. Still, could it not be argued that they nevertheless neglected the study of Neokantianism of either the Marburg or the Southwestern school? This is harder to deny. With the exception of Neurath's critical reading of Rickert (most likely prompted by Weber's laudatory references) particularly the first Vienna Circle seems to have been little concerned with these thinkers – unlike Schlick who seriously studied the works of Cohen, Natorp and especially Cassirer. This fact may only seem to raise the stakes: was the first Vienna Circle, in virtue of their Austrian orientation, not simply behind the times philosophically?

Again the answer is negative. Recall first the immense influence the writings of the French conventionalists Poincaré, Duhem and Rey had on them. Thus already Frank's earliest philosophical essay of 1907 proposed to put conventions in place of the *synthetic a priori*. Secondly consider that also much Neokantian philosophy of science, especially that of Cassirer, was itself significantly influenced by the conventionalism of Poincaré and that under this influence it too jeopardised the *synthetic a priori* of old.[19] Then it becomes clear that the first Vienna Circle, through their own adoption of conventionalism, worked in parallel to the Neokantians – albeit with a different starting point. Whereas the Neokantians tried to fit conventionalism with Kant, the first Vienna Circle tried to fit conventionalism with empiricism.

None of this is to deny, of course, that there obtained mutual misunderstandings between the traditions of Neokantianism and the emerging logical empiricism. One partial exception here, of course, is Carnap whose early debts to the other tradition were much stronger still than Schlick's. In light of the impetus which the development of the perspective on scientific knowledge, developed in broadest outline already by the first Circle, gained from Carnap, we may consider his recruitment to the Schlick Circle especially fortunate and significant. But Carnap too, as noted, chose to distance himself from Neokantianism. Thus he could be seen to align him-

---

[19] See Richardson (1997).

self at least implicitly with the Austrian tradition at an advanced stage of its hybridisation.

To conclude. If German philosophy is widely understood to mean philosophy done in the German language, then of course even Neurath's Vienna Circle belongs to it. If it is more narrowly circumscribed as following in the tracks either of Kant or Hegel, however, Neurath's and Schlick's Vienna Circle do not so belong. Rather, they represent a particularly interesting late phase of the tradition of Austrian philosophy which since Bolzano saw itself in self-conscious opposition to Kant and German idealism. As it happens, Neurath saw in its international outlook a distinguishing feature of the Austrian tradition. Not surprisingly so, in exile both Frank and Neurath were keen to establish cooperation with leading representatives of American pragmatism like Dewey, a movement whose earlier teachings by William James were discussed but mostly summarily rejected by German philosophers in the first decade of this century.[20]

Bibliography

Ayer, A. J., ed., *Logical Positivism* (New York: Free Press, 1959).

Bell, D and A. Vossenkuhl, eds, *Science and Subjectivity*, (Berlin: Akademieverlag, 1992).

Blackmore, J., *Ludwig Boltzmann. His Later Life and Philosophy, 1900-1906*, vol II, (Dordrecht: Kluwer, 1995).

Boltzmann, L., 'Diskussionsbemerkung', *Wissenschaftliche Beilage zum 19. Jahresbericht der Philosophische Gesellschaft an der Universität zu Wien*, (Leizpig: Barth, 1906), pp. 8-10.

Bolzano, B., *Paradoxien des Unendlichen*, ed A. Höfler with annotations by Hahn. (Leipzig, Meiner: 1921).

Carnap, R., *Der logische Aufbau der Welt*, (Berlin: Bernary, 2nd ed Hamburg: Meiner, 1961,). trans. by R. A. George *The Logical Structure of the World* (Berkeley: University of California Press, 1967).

Carnap, R., *Logische Syntax der Sprache* (Vienna: Springer, 1934). rev. ed. trans. by A. Smeaton, *The Logical Syntax of Language*, (London: Kegan, Paul, Trench Teubner & Cie, 1937).

Carnap, R., H. Hahn and O. Neurath, *Wissenschaftliche Weltauffassung – Der Wiener Kreis*. Wolf, Vienna, Engl. in O. Neurath, *Empricism and Sociology*, ed. Marie Neurath and Robert S. Cohen, trans. P. Foulkes and M. Neurath (Dordrecht: Reidel 1973), pp. 299–318.

Cartwright, N. and J. Cat 'Unity on the Earthly Plane', in Cartwright, Cat, Fleck and Uebel (1996), pp. 167–252.

Cartwright, N., J. Cat, L. Fleck and T. E. Uebel, *Otto Neurath. Philosophy between Science and Politics*, (Cambridge University Press, 1996).

[20] On the early German pragmatism debate, see Dahms (1992).

Thomas E. Uebel

Coffa, A., *The Semantic Tradition from Kant to Carnap. To the Vienna Station*, (ed. L. Wessels), (Cambridge University Press, 1991).

Dahms, H.-J., 'Postivismus und Pragmatismus', in Bell and Vossenkuhl (1992), pp. 239–57.

Frank, P., 'Die Bedeutung der physikalischen Erkenntnistheorie Ernst Machs für das Geisteslebens unserer Zeit', *Die Naturwissenschaften* 5, trans. 'The importance for our times of Ernst Mach's Philosophy of Science' in Frank (1949b), pp. 61–79.

Frank, P., 'Historical Introduction' (1949a) in Frank (1949b), pp. 1–51.

Frank, P., *Modern Science and its Philosophy* (Cambridge, MA: Harvard University Press, (1949b).

Friedman, M., 'Epistemology in the *Aufbau*', *Synthese* **93**, (1992) pp. 15–57.

Gierre, R. and A. Richardson, eds., *Origins of Logal Empiricism* (Minneapolis: Univeristy of Minnesota Press, 1996).

Haller, Rudolf, 'Der erste Wiener Kreis', *Erkenntnis* 22, (1985a). trans. 'The First Vienna Circle', in Uebel (1991b), pp. 95–108.

Haller, Rudolf. 'Zur Historigraphie der österreichischen Philosophie', in J. Nyiri, ed., *Von Bolzano zu Wittgenstein, Zur Tradition der österreichischen Philosophie*, (Vienna: Hölder-Pichler-Tempsky, (1986), trans. 'On the Historiography of Austrian Philosophy' in Uebel (1991b), pp. 41–50.

Haller, Rudolf, *Neo-Positivismus. Eine historische Einführung in die Philosophie des Wiener Kreises* (Wissenschaftliche Buchgesellschaft, Darmstadt, 1993).

Höfler, A., *Grundlehren der Logik*, (Vienna: Tempsky, 1890).

Höfler, A., *Studien zur gegenwärtigen Philosophie der Mechanik. Als Nachwort zu: Kants Metaphysische Anfangsgründe der Wissenschaft*, (Leipzig: Pfeffer, 1990).

Höfler, A., 1899, ed., *Vorreden und Einleitungen zu Klassischen Werken der Mechanik: Galilei, Newton, D'Alembert, Lagrane. Kirchhoff, Hertz, Helmholtz* (Leipzig: Pfeffer, 1990)

Janik, A. and S. Toulmin, *Wittgenstein's Vienna*, (New York: Simon & Shuster, 1973).

Klein, F., 'Grenzfragen der Mathematik and Philosophie', *Wissenschaftliche Beilage zum 19. Jahresbericht der Philosophische Gesellschaft an der Universität zu Wien* (Leizpig: Barth, 1906), pp. 1–7, 10.

Le Rider, J., *Modernité viennoise et crises de l'identité* (Paris: Presses Universitaires de France, 1990).

Nemeth, E. and F. Stadler, ed., *Encyclopedia and Utopia. The Life and Work of Otto Neurath* (Dordrecht: Kluwer, 1996).

Neurath, O., '[Rezension] R. Carnap, *Der Logische Aufbau der Welt* und *Scheinprobleme der Philosphie*', *Der Kampf*, **21**, (1928) repr. in Neurath (1981), pp. 295–7.

Neurath, O., *Le developpement du Cercle de Vienne et l'avenir de l'Empiricisme logique*, (Paris: Hermann & Cie, 1936a). trans. 'Die Entwicklung des Wiener Kreises und die Zukunft des Logischen Empirismus', in Neurath (1981), pp. 673–703.

Otto Neurath, the Vienna Circle and the Austrian Tradition

Neurath, O., [Diskussionbemerkung], *Actes de 8e Congres Internationale de Philosophie, Prague 1934* (Prague: Orbis, 1936b).

Neurath, O., *Gesammelte philosophische und methodologische Schriften*, ed. by R. Haller and H. Rutte, (Vienna: Hölder-Pichler-Tempsky, 1981).

Reininger, R., *50 Jahre Philosophische Gesellschaft an der Universität Wien 1888–1938* (Vienna: Verlag der Philosophischen Gesellschaft an der Universität Wien, 1938).

Richardson, A., *Carnap's Construction of the World*, (Cambridge Univrsity Press, 1997).

Sarkar, S., ed., *Carnap: A Centenary Reappraisal, Synthese* **93**, (1992), nos. 1–2.

Schorske, C. E., *Fin-de Siècle Vienna. Politics and Culture*, (Cambridge University Press, 1980).

Spohn, W., ed., *Hans Reichenbach, Rudolf Carnap: A Centernary, Erkenntnis*, 35 (1991).

Stadler, F., ed., *Scientific Philosophy: Origins and Developments*, (Dordrecht: Kluwer, 1993).

Stadler, F., *Studien zum Weiner Kreis*, (Frankfurt: Suhrkamp, 1997).

Uebel, T. E., 'Neurath's Programme for Naturalistics Epistemology', *Studies in the History and Philosophy of Science*, 22 (1991a), 623–46.

Uebel, T. E., ed., *Rediscovering the Forgotten Vienna Circle*, (Dordrecht: Kluwer, 1991b).

Uebel, T. E. *Overcoming Logical Positivism from Within. The Emergence of Neurath's Naturalism in the Vienna Circle's Protocol Sentence Debate.* (Amsterdam-Atlanta, GA: Rodopi, 1992).

Uebel, T. E., 'On Neurath's Boat' (1996a), in Cartwright, Cat, Fleck, Uebel (1996), pp. 89–166.

Uebel, T. E., 'Normativity and Convention. On the Constructivist Element of Neurath's Naturalism' (1996b), in Nemeth and Stadler (1996), pp. 97–112.

Uebel, T. E., 'Anti-Foundationalism and the Vienna Circle's Revolution in Philosophy' (1996c), *British Journal for the Philosophy of Science*, 47, (1996) pp 415–40.

Uebel, T. E., *Vernunftkritik und Wissenschaft. Otto Neurath und der erste Wiener Kreis im Diskurs der Moderne*, (Vienna: Springer, forthcoming).

Winter, E., ed., *Robert Zimmerman's Philosophische Propädeutik und die Vorlagen aus der Wissenschaftslehre Bernard Bolzanos* (Wien: Verlag der Österreichischen Akademie der Wissenschaften, 1975).

Zolo, D., *Relfexive Epistemology. The Philosophical Legacy of Otto Neurath*, (Dordrecht: Kluwer, 1989).

Does the Nothing Noth?

MICHAEL INWOOD

In 1929 Heidegger gave his Freiburg inaugural lecture entitled 'What is Metaphysics?'[1] In it he announced: Das Nichts selbst nichtet, 'The Nothing itself noths (or 'nihilates', or 'nothings')[2]. This soon earned Heidegger fame as a purveyor of metaphysical nonsense. In his 1931 paper, 'Overcoming of Metaphysics through Logical Analysis of Language' Rudolf Carnap charged Heidegger with the offences of the whole metaphysical genre.[3] His sentence has the same grammatical form as the sentence 'The rain rains' – a sentence which Carnap, or at least his translator, regarded as a 'meaningful sentence of ordinary language'.[4] But this harmless guise conceals severe logical blemishes. Heidegger treats the indefinite pronoun 'nothing' as a noun, as the 'name or description of an entity'.[5] (When he says 'The nothing noths' he surely does not mean 'There is nothing that noths' or 'It is not the case that anything noths'.) He introduces the meaningless word 'to noth'.[6] He implies, and later affirms, the existence of the nothing, when the 'existence of this entity would be denied in its very definition'.[7] If all this were not enough, the sentence is meaningless, since it is neither analytic, nor contradictory, nor empirical[8]. It is metaphysics, and metaphysics seriously damages our spiritual health.

[1] 'Was ist Metaphysik?,' Reprinted in *Wegmarken* 2nd edn., (Frankfurt: Klostermann, 1978), pp. 103–21. 'What is Metaphysics?', trans. David Farrell Krell, in Martin Heidegger, *Basic Writings* 2nd edn., (London: Routledge, 1993), pp. 93–110. An earlier translation by R. F. C. Hull and Alan Crick appears in *Existence and Being*, by Martin Heidegger (London: Vision, 1949), pp. 355–80. Hull and Crick also translate the 'Nachwort zu: 'Was ist Metaphysik?' the 'Postscript' of 1943 (pp. 380–92). My page-references to 'What is Metaphysics?' are to *Wegmarken* and also to Krell's translation, though my own rendering often differs from his.

[2] *Wegmarken*, p. 113.

[3] Translated by Arthur Pap from 'Überwindung der Metaphysik durch logische Analyse der Sprache', *Erkenntnis*, 2 (1931), in *Heidegger and Modern Philosophy*, ed. Michael Murray (New Haven and London: Yale University Press, 1978), pp. 23–34.

[4] Murray, ed., p. 25.

[5] Ibid.

[6] Ibid., p. 24

[7] Ibid., p. 25

[8] Ibid., p. 30

Michael Inwood

One may doubt whether this case, the case of the nothing, is worth re-opening. After all, we know by now that Heidegger had some good ideas, ideas that anticipate, say, the later Wittgenstein and J. L. Austin. That is one side of Heidegger, his Dr. Jekyll. Why not interpret him charitably and forget about Mr Heidegger, who commits logical outrages in public places? But admirers of Dr. Jekyll may like to know why he occasionally lapses into Mr. Heidegger, why Mr. Heidegger says what he does, and what relationship, if any, his utterances have to those of Dr. Jekyll. Besides, Jekyll and Heidegger cannot be easily separated. They wrote books and lectures together. They co-authored 'What is Metaphysics?' and it bears the marks of both of them. Heidegger knew as well as Carnap that 'The Nothing noths' transgresses the canons of logically coherent discourse. He had had a sound neokantian training in logic. Nevertheless, he felt that he had to say it. Wittgenstein apparently shared this view. 'I can readily think what Heidegger means by Being and Dread', he said. 'Man has the impulse to run up against the limits of language. Think, for example, of the astonishment that anything exists. This astonishment cannot be expressed in the form of a question, and there is also no answer to it. Everything which we feel like saying can, *a priori*, only be nonsense'.[9] I ask then: What sort of nonsense, if any, does Heidegger talk about the nothing? and, What problem, if any, does he think that this nonsense solves?

1 The Sentence

I begin with another look at the sentence: 'The Nothing itself noths.' The first problem is 'the Nothing'. It is common enough for German philosophers to convert what is ordinarily a pronoun into a noun. Heidegger does so more often than most. In various texts he speaks of the I (das Ich), the self (das Selbst), the One or the They (das Man), the Nobody (das Niemand), the Something (das Etwas), and the Not (das Nicht). Such expressions often give rise to ambiguity. When a philosopher speaks of the I, for example, it is not always clear whether he means that we each have an I, or perhaps more than one – an ordinary I and a better I – or whether there is only one I for all of us. Still, that is no reason for rejecting the device as a whole. It is after all not confined to philosophers. We

---

[9] *Ludwig Wittgenstein und der Wiener Kreis: Gespräche, aufgezeichnet von Friedrich Waismann*, ed. B. F. McGuiness (Frankfurt: Blackwell, 1967), p. 68. The passage is translated by Michael Murray in 'On Heidegger on Being and Dread', in Murray, ed., Heidegger, pp. 80–3.

often say that a person is a nobody. If someone speaks of 'the nobody', it may be unclear whether he is referring to some particular nobody, or speaking in general about people who are nobodies, or referring to some such generalised anonymous Nobody, as that to which, as Heidegger claims in *Being and Time*, 'every Dasein has already surrendered itself in Being-among-one-another.'[10] In German *Nichts* can be used in the same way as 'nobody' – to describe something, usually a person, as a non-entity, a nobody. In this usage it has a plural *Nichtse*, nobodies, non-entities. Then there is *the* Nothing, the use of *Nichts* as a noun that has no plural – nothingness. Carnap thought this use illegitimate. Dr. Johnson, whose command of English was superior to Carnap's, did not. In discussing a poem, 'Upon Nothing', by John Wilmot, the Earl of Rochester, he wrote:

> *Nothing* must be considered as having not only a negative but a kind of positive signification; as I need not fear thieves, I have *nothing*, and *nothing* is a very powerful protector. In the first part of the sentence it is taken negatively; in the second it is taken positively, as an agent. ... *Nothing* can be a subject only in its positive sense, and such a sense is given it in the first line:
>
> Nothing, thou elder brother ev'n to Shade.
>
> ... The positive sense is generally preserved, with great skill, through the whole poem; though sometimes in a subordinate sense, the negative nothing is injudiciously mingled.'[11]

That is what Heidegger does: he injudiciously mingles different sense of 'nothing'. He starts off with the negative sense: the sciences consider beings – and nothing more. then he asks: 'What about this Nothing?' And finally: 'What about the Nothing?' That is the fully positive use of 'nothing'.[12]

But Heidegger does something else, which neither Wilmot nor Johnson did. He says that the nothing noths. He coins a new verb, *nichten*. He has two reasons for doing so. First, he regularly draws a distinction between something that is a being or entity (*Seiendes*) and something that, even though it is 'something', is not a being or entity.[13] For example, hammers, trees, people are entities, but the

---

[10] *Sein und Zeit*, 7th edn. (Tübingen: Niemeyer, 1953), p. 128; *Being and Time*, trans. John Macquarrie and Edward Robinson (Oxford: Blackwell, 1962), p. 166

[11] Samuel Johnson, *Lives of the English Poets*, vol. 1, (London: Dent, 1925), p. 130

[12] *Wegmarken*, pp. 105f; Krell, ed., pp. 95f.

[13] E.g. *Kant und das Problem der Metaphysik*; 5th edn. (Frankfurt: Klostermann, 1991), p. 122.

Michael Inwood

world in which they lie, time, and being itself are not entities, not something that is. It does not follow that they are nothing, or rather: they are nothing(s), but not what he sometimes calls a *nichtige Nichts*, a blank nothing.[14] Something that is not a being cannot, on Heidegger's view, be said to be, or to be such and such or a so and so. For to apply to it the verb 'to be' would imply that it is a being. Thus he often adopts, and sometimes coins, an appropriate verb for such things. For example, he does not say that the world (*die Welt*) is, but that *die Welt waltet*, the world reigns, wells, whirls, or, coining a verb, *die Welt weltet*, the world worlds.[15] The Nothing, Heidegger insists, is not a being or entity.[16] Hence we cannot say that it is, but we can say that it noths. We cannot interpret this as an implicitly existential claim, as, say, 'There is something, and that thing is the Nothing, and it noths.' For that would reintroduce the objectionable 'is'.[17] The nothing noths, and that is that. We should not, of course, think of the nothing as something that sometimes noths, but sometimes does not, and which does other things besides noth-ing. That would be to think of it as a being, distinct from its possible activities. The nothing essentially and constantly noths, just as the world essentially and constantly worlds.

Heidegger's second reason for saying that the nothing noths is this. He believes that if we are to speak of the Nothing, the Nothing must be given to us in experience. Since it is not a being, we cannot encounter it perceptually. Nor can we construct or define it in thought. For the concepts that we would have to employ to define the Nothing, denial (*Verneinung*) and negation or the Not (*das Nicht*), are made possible by, and are thus posterior to, the Nothing. Heidegger is trying to explain what makes our discourse, including our negative discourse, possible. He thus feels debarred from using it to capture the Nothing. But we do, he believes, encounter the Nothing in certain moods. Not all moods. Some of them, in particular what Heidegger calls 'authentic' or 'deep' boredom, reveal to us beings as a whole. Boredom disrupts our normal involvement with

[14] E.g., *Wegmarken*, p. 304.

[15] E.g., 'Vom Wesen des Grundes', in *Wegmarken*, p. 162: *Freiheit allein kann dem Dasein eine Welt walten und welten lassen. Welt ist nie, sondern weltet.* (Heidegger is also prepared to use 'bestehen' of non-beings such as time).

[16] *Wegmarken*, p. 114: Das Nichts ist weder ein Gegenstand noch ueberhaupt ein Seiendes.

[17] The German equivalent of 'there is …', *es gibt*, does not involve the verb 'to be', *sein*. Heidegger exploits this expression, and its literal meaning, 'it gives', when speaking about another 'non-entity', being (*das Sein*), but he does not use it in this context.

274

some particular range of entities – giving a lecture for example – and reduces everything, including oneself, to a 'curious indifference'.[18] Boredom reveals the whole, but it does not reveal the Nothing. Anxiety, *Angst*, reveals the Nothing as well as the whole. For in *Angst* beings, beings as a whole, do not simply become indifferent; they seem to slip or slither away, depriving one of all support. We say: '*ist es einem unheimlich*', 'One feels uncanny, it gives one the creeps'. It gives *one* the creeps, and not strictly *me* the creeps, for I too as a distinct individual am slithering away along with the rest.[19] This is our encounter with the Nothing. Sometimes when *Angst* strikes someone, and we ask them 'What's the matter?', they reply 'Oh, it was really nothing.' Yes, exactly, says Heidegger: 'the Nothing itself – as such – was there.'[20] But why say that the Nothing *noths*? Why not say, for example, that it annihilates? There is a respectable German verb, *vernichten*, meaning 'annihilate'. Why not say '*Das Nichts vernichtet?*' Because, says Heidegger, beings are not annihilated in Angst, leaving behind sheer nothingness. they are just slipping away; they do not disappear altogether.[21] So we are left with: *Das Nichts selbst nichtet*. Because of the affinity of *nichten* to *vernichten*, it is sometimes translated as 'nihilate'.[22] Since *vernichten* is transitive, *nichten* has a transitive flavour. But Heidegger never gives it an object in the accusative, and its affinity to other coinages, such as *welten*, suggests that it is intransitive. The nothing just noths as the world just worlds.

Heidegger's sentence is odd. Is it meaningless, as Carnap suggests? In two respects it is not. First, we can see quite well what is going on in the sentence itself. Its features are intelligibly related to other, more standard sentences and linguistic devices. Second, the sentence looks empirical. No doubt people do sometimes undergo the experience of *Angst* as Heidegger describes it. To say that the nothing noths is a not wholly inappropriate way of saying what happens to them. So to the question 'Does the Nothing noth?' we might reply: 'that is an odd way of putting it, but if you insist, then yes, sometimes at least the nothing does noth.' But that does not get to the bottom of the matter. We might agree that the nothing noths. But so what? Why does Heidegger make so much of it? What problem does it solve?

[18] *Wegmarken*, p. 110: 'eine merkwürdige Gleichgültigkeit'.
[19] *Wegmarken*, p. 111: Krell, ed., p. 101.
[20] *Wegmarken*, p. 112: In der Tat: das Nichts selbst – als solches – war da.
[21] *Wegmarken*, pp. 112f; Krell, ed., p. 102.
[22] E.g., *Basic Writings*, ed. D. F. Krell, p. 103.

Michael Inwood

II The problem

We are looking for a problem to be solved by the Nothing. But we find a surfeit of problems, all apparently solved, in part at least, by the nihilating of the Nothing. I list some of the problems that Heidegger raises in his lecture:

> 1 How do we manage to relate to beings as beings? I extract this from such remarks as the following: 'In the clear night of the Nothing of Angst the primordial openness of beings as such arises: that they are beings and not Nothing. ... The essence of the primordially nihilating Nothing lies in this, that it brings Da-sein for the first time before beings as such.'[23]
> 2 Why are we selves and why are we free? 'Without the primordial revelation of the Nothing, no selfhood and no freedom.'[24]
> 3 How do we, whether as scientists, metaphysicians, or ordinary humans manage to be aware of beings as a whole? This is implicit in such remarks as: 'Dasein's being held out into the Nothing on the basis of hidden Angst is the surpassing of beings as a whole: transcendence.'[25]
> 4 How is negation or denial possible? 'What testifies to the constant and widespread though distorted revelation of the nothing in our Dasein more compellingly than denial?[26]
> 5 Could God create the world out of nothing?[27]
> 6 Why do we ask the question 'Why?' Why do we ask why something is the case and look for reasons for it?[28]
> 7 What is the relationship between metaphysics and ordinary, everyday life?[29]
> 8 Why are there beings at all and not rather Nothing?[30]

This diversity of problems accords with Heidegger's view of metaphysics. One of its central features is, he says at the beginning of his lecture,[31] that 'every metaphysical question always encompasses the whole range of metaphysical problems. Every question is always the whole itself.' Consequently we expect Heidegger to raise a fair num-

[23] *Wegmarken*, pp. 113f; Krell., ed., p. 103.
[24] *Wegmarken*, p. 114; Krell, ed., p. 103: Ohne ursprüngliche Offenbarkeit des Nichts kein Selbstsein und keine Freiheit.
[25] *Wegmarken*, p. 117; Krell, ed., p. 106.
[26] *Wegmarken*, p. 115; Krell, ed., p. 104.
[27] *Wegmarken*, p. 118, Krell, ed., pp. 107f.
[28] *Wegmarken*, p. 120; Krell, ed., p. 109.
[29] *Wegmarken*, pp. 120f; Krell, ed., pp 109f.
[30] *Wegmarken*, p. 121; Krell, ed., p. 110.
[31] *Wegmarken*, p. 104; Krell, ed., p. 93

ber of problems, and we also expect the problems to be interconnected. For the moment I am concerned only with the problems and
their interconnexions, not with Heidegger's attempt to solve them.

I begin with the third question, 'How are we aware of beings as a
whole?' This is a constant refrain throughout the lecture. Human
beings, not just scientists and metaphysicians, are somehow aware,
however vaguely, of *das Seiende im Ganzen*, of beings as a whole,
even though they are themselves finite beings in the midst of other
beings.[32] In some lectures that he gave to students in the following
winter, 1929–30, Heidegger tried to explain it like this. He enters
the lecture room and notices that the black-board is in an unsuitable
position. He focuses on the blackboard and, if he says that it is
inconveniently placed, his utterance is about the black-board. But
the board can be ill-placed only in relation to the room as a whole.
He is therefore tacitly aware of the room as a whole, not in all the
detail of its contents, but in its general layout.[33] But isn't that just a
local whole? Must we be aware of beings as a whole, to notice this
about the black-board? Not exactly. The situation seems to be this.
The judgements we make about particular things call into play successively larger wholes, and there is no limit, short of beings as a
whole in the strict sense, to the extent of the whole in play. If, for
example, Heidegger says 'This is a good room to hold the lecture
in', he is tacitly calling into play the whole building, the building
that contains other rooms with which the present one is compared.
If he says 'I'm glad I teach at Freiburg', he calls into play the whole
German university system. And so on indefinitely.

This course of lectures – *The Basic Concepts of Metaphysics* – is
especially interesting because it contains a long discussion of animals, and compares them with human beings.[34] I say 'animals', but
apart from the odd reference to moles and dogs, Heidegger talks
mainly about insects. But that makes no difference for my purpose,
and presumably Heidegger's, namely to elucidate the nature of
human beings by contrast with creatures of a different type.
Heidegger's overall view of animals is that they are *weltarm*, world-
impoverished. They are not world-less, as stones are, but they are
not *weltbildend*, world-forming, as humans are.[35] This does not mean

[32] *Wegmarken*, p. 109: So aufgesplittert der Alltag erscheinen mag, er
behält immer noch das Seiende, wenngleich schattenhaft, in einer Einheit
des 'Ganzen'.

[33] *Die Grundbegriffe der Metaphysik: Welt – Endlichkeit – Einsamkeit*
(Gesamtausgabe, Bd. 29/30), ed. F.-W. von Herrmann (Frankfurt:
Klostermann 1983), pp. 498 ff.

[34] *Die Grundbegriffe der Metaphysik*, pp. 261–396.

[35] Ibid., pp. 261 ff.

Michael Inwood

that they have no access to beings other than themselves. A bee has access to the sun; the position of the sun guides it back to its hive. But a bee has no access to beings as a whole. According to Heidegger[36] if you present a bee with a bowl of honey, it drinks for a while, then flies away leaving the rest. We might say: the bee has noticed that there is too much honey for it to drink. But if you cut off the back of the bee's body, so that the honey runs out as soon as it drinks it, the bee will continue drinking indefinitely. So the bee does not notice in the former case that there is too much honey for it to absorb. The experiment suggests too that the bee is not aware of the situation as a whole. If someone were to perform a similar experiment on a person, draining off the food he ate so that he constantly felt hungry, he would after a while spot that something was amiss and take steps to repair his situation, not simply continue eating. But all this is lost on the bee. It is aware only of what triggers off its drives at the moment. It cannot, as Heidegger sometimes expresses it, let beings be,[37] be tacitly aware of them without being directly stimulated by them or doing something to or with them. But that is what is needed for awareness of a whole: letting beings be, apart form those beings that engage one's current attention. We generally neglect the whole because we are attending to some particular matter. But it is there all along even when we do not notice it. It becomes especially conspicuous, according to Heidegger, in moods such as deep boredom, when everything becomes indifferent.

I now turn to the first question. 'How do we manage to relate to beings as such?' Heidegger has said that a bee is not aware of beings as a whole and that it does not notice that a bowl of honey is too much for it to eat, that is, as Heidegger puts it, it is not aware of beings as such, as beings. Is there any connection between these two incapacities? Might there be a creature that is aware of beings as a whole, but not of beings as such? Or conversely, one that was aware of beings as such but not of beings as a whole? This second idea, that someone could focus on particular entities as such, but do so without any tacit awareness of a larger whole, is perhaps more plausible than the first. On Heidegger's account, several philosophers – Descartes, Husserl, etc – have viewed man in this way, concentrating on explicit attention and neglecting the implicit background. He presents an interesting argument against it at the end of these lectures.[38] If I am to be properly aware of something as actual, then I

[36] Ibid., p. 352.
[37] Ibid., p. 368: Seinlassen. On Seinlassen, see also Heidegger's *Einleitung in die Philosophie* (Gesamtausgabe, Bd. 27), ed. I. Saame and I. Samme-Speidel (Frankfurt: Klostermann, 1996), pp. 102ff.
[38] *Die Grundbegriffe der Metaphysik*, pp. 528ff.

must be aware, however implicitly, of possible alternatives. Not just logically possible alternatives, but genuinely possible alternatives. But to know these, I have to be aware of a larger whole, since what would have been possible at a given place and time does not depend only on what happens at that place and time. For example, it is logically possible that I should now be lecturing, uninterrupted, on Stonehenge. But in the context of this series of lectures that is not a genuine possibility. It is, or at least was, a genuine possibility that I should lecture on Hegel rather than Heidegger. But couldn't you still understand my lecture if you did not know about that possibility? Can't we appreciate actual beings without knowing, however hazily, about possible alternatives? To make it more plausible that we cannot, I take as the context my lecture itself. It is logically possible that I shall say, seriously and without quotation marks, 'And that concludes what I have to say about Stonehenge.' But it is not a realistic possibility given the lecture as a whole. But earlier I said: 'The Nothing, Heidegger insists, is not a being or entity.' It was a genuine possibility, not just a logical one, that I should have said instead: 'The Nothing, Heidegger insists, is a being or entity.' It seems to me plausible that you cannot really understand what a person says, as opposed to just hearing the words he utters, unless you are aware tacitly of what he realistically could have said instead, and you cannot be aware of that without an awareness of the larger whole, the context, in which he says it. Some such idea is at least a part of what Heidegger means when he says that if you are not aware of beings as a whole, then you cannot relate to beings as such.

I turn now to question 2: Why are we selves and why are we free? 'Without the primordial revelation of the Nothing', Heidegger said, 'no selfhood and no freedom'. Just before that he says: 'If in the ground of its essence Dasein did not transcend, which now means, if it did not in advance hold itself out into the Nothing, then it could never relate to beings, thus not even to itself.'[39] Here his argument seems to be: if we do not transcend, that is, if we do not transcend particular beings so as to be aware of beings as a whole, then we cannot be aware of beings as such. Since I myself am a being, then I cannot, in such a case, relate to, be aware of, myself as such. But selfhood involves awareness of, relation to, oneself. So in such a case I would not be a self. This seems clear enough. The bee that fails to notice that its back-end is missing is deficient in self-awareness and thus selfhood.[40]

[39] *Wegmarken*, p. 114; Krell, ed., p. 103

[40] Heidegger attributes a sort of Selbstheit to living organisms on the basis of their capacity for self-preservation, self-generation, self-management and self-renewal. He distinguishes them in these respects from machines (*Die Grundbegriffe der Metaphysik*, pp. 332, 339f.)

Michael Inwood

But what about freedom? How does that relate to the other questions Heidegger has raised? *The Basic Concepts of Metaphysics* contains an interesting argument that I summarise as follows.[41] When I am asked a question, say, 'Is so and so beautiful?' I can make up my own mind what I think about it, by weighing up pros and cons. Then I can decide whether to say 'She is' or 'She isn't' or 'Something in between'. As Heidegger puts it, 'the man who asserts in his talk must have in advance a *Spielraum*, free space or elbow-room, for the comparative to and fro of the "either-or", of truth or falsehood ...'[42] Only if I have this free space allowing me to compare my thought or assertion with the entity in question, and neither my judgement nor my assertion is directly and inevitably determined by it, can I be said to speak truly or falsely. Suppose, by contrast, that as I am asked this question, the woman enters the room; I am bedazzled and besotted by her; I see nothing but her and forget all my usual standards of assessment and points of comparison; I have no choice but to murmur 'Yes, she's beautiful'. My utterance just registers the effect that the object has on me. I cannot speak falsely, but nor can I really speak truly. I do not consider the object as an entity in its own right. I do not reflect on it, and decide whether, judged by appropriate criteria, it is beautiful or not. This is associated with the fact that I am wholly and exclusively absorbed by the object. I cannot compare it with other objects; they have departed from my field of vision. With appropriate qualifications this is what it is like to be an insect. Insects, and animals in general, are over the whole range of their behaviour, *benommen*, 'dazed' or 'benumbed'.[43] Usually we humans are not benumbed by the entities we interact with. We have free space. Thus we can relate to other entities as entities, not only in our utterances but in all our conduct.

This brings us to the fourth problem: How is negation or denial possible? In 'What is Metaphysics?' Heidegger asks: 'How is denial to produce the Not out of itself, when it can only deny if a deniable is already given to it? But how can something deniable and to be denied be noticed as something negative, unless all thinking as such already looks ahead to the Not?'[44] Here the question is not, as

[41] *Die Grundbegriffe der Metaphysik*, pp. 492 ff.

[42] Ibid., p. 493.

[43] Ibid., pp. 344ff. This is one reason why Heidegger insists that their behaviour is *Benehmen*, not, like that of humans, *Verhalten*. Another reason is that he associates *Verhalten* with being related to, or relating oneself to (*sich verhalten*), an entity conceived as distinct from oneself. Animals cannot do this, since they cannot be aware of beings as beings in their own right. (There is no warrant in ordinary German for differentiating *Benehmen* and *Verhalten* in this way).

[44] *Wegmarken*, p. 115; Krell, ed., p. 105

before, whether we are free to deny as well as to affirm, but whether such a thing as denial is possible at all. He seems to have two problems in mind. First, he feels that negativity is not in the world in the way that positivity is; the world contains beings, not non-beings. Negativity has to be supplied by us. If this is so, denial is more problematic than affirmation. But, secondly, he also thinks that if we cannot deny, then we cannot properly affirm. Negation and affirmation go together, and are equally problematic. To connect up this problem with the others, we might say something like this. Purely logical negativity is in the world independently of us. If something is hot, then it is not cold; if it is rough, it is not smooth. But this cannot account for our own denials and negations. A dog who is present at my lecture, hears the sounds I make and does not hear certain other sounds that I am not making. But it does not hear that I am not making these sounds. Our denials and negations begin with what is conspicuously not the case rather than with what is simply not the case. As Heidegger enters the room he does not notice that the black-board is not a pumpkin. Nor does he notice that it is not red but black. He notices that it is not in the right position. Not in the right position in relation to the room as a whole, not in the right position when it realistically could be in the right position. Noticing this presupposes tacit awareness of an indefinitely extensive whole. If we just concentrate on the black-board, excluding every other consideration from our consciousness, there is nothing conspicuously negative about it. It is hard even to see that it is not a pumpkin, if we are not to let pumpkins enter our thoughts.

We might think that Heidegger is unfair to dogs. A dog cannot disagree with what I say, nor can it really agree with me. But it is not clear that this has much to do with its awareness of wholes. Firstly, a human member of the audience might be drowsily listening to each sentence as it comes along, but not following the lecture as a whole. Then he too does not deny what I'm saying, and cannot really assent to it either. But if I suddenly say something outrageously false, such as 'This black-board is a pumpkin', then he wakes up with a start and thinks what I've said is false. Second, a dog can display something like what Heidegger calls 'nihilating conduct:'[45] it may growl if I stop speaking, bark if I begin to shout, or show distress, when its dinner does not arrive on time. Our superiority to the dog seems to consist as much, or more, in our ability to mark inconspicuous negativities, such as the

[45] *Wegmarken*, p. 116; Krell, ed., p. 105, where nihilating conduct (*nichtende Verhalten*) includes resistance, loathing, failure, prohibition and privation, as well as denial.

black-board not being a pumpkin, than in our ability to notice conspicuous ones. Since Heidegger does not, as far as I know, differentiate between dogs and insects, and since he does not explicitly discuss negation in his account of insects, I am not sure what he would have said about this, whether he would have granted to dogs a degree of whole-awareness and thus of world-formation, or whether he would have insisted that their drives are just triggered off by the stimulus of the moment, so that they do not really exhibit 'nihilating conduct'. The first objection is easier to deal with. In one sense the drowsy listener can deny the truth of what I said, 'This blackboard is a pumpkin'. But unless he has followed the lecture as a whole, or at least some of the preceding context, he is not in a position to disagree with me, since he will not know whether I asserted it or, as it happens, simply presented it as an example. In any case, in denying this proposition he is drawing on a mass of knowledge, about black-boards, pumpkins, and the meanings of words, derived from a wider context than this particular lecture.

I shall deal more briefly with the other questions Heidegger raises. Question 5 was 'Could God create the world out of nothing?' No, replies Heidegger, not if God is conceived as pure being, excluding all negation. For then he cannot relate to the nothing, he cannot be aware of it. It does not follow, of course, that Heidegger was an atheist. What follows is that he was not a Thomist. He was fully aware that Hegel's God involves negation, as does the God of such German mystics as Eckhart and Jakob Böhme. Some of them went so far as to say that God is nothing,[46] but they did not mean that, in the ordinary sense, he does not exist. Nor, in my view, does Heidegger.

Question 6 was 'Why do we ask why something is the case?' In terms of what we have said so far, there is an obvious answer to this. Our access to a more or less extensive whole enables us to consider realistically possible alternatives to what is actually the case. Thus we can ask: Why is this the case rather than some possible alternative? But Heidegger wants more than this. He says: 'Only if the strangeness of beings oppresses us do they arouse and evoke wonder. Only on the basis of wonder ... does the question 'Why?' arise.'[47] Because of this, he naturally goes on to raise, at the very end of his lecture, question 8, 'Why are there beings at all and not rather Nothing?' This, he says, is the basic question (*die*

---

[46] John D. Caputo, *The Mystical Element in Heidegger's Thought* (Athens: Ohio University Press, 1978), pp. 21f., 107.

[47] *Wegmarken*, p. 120; Krell, ed., p. 109

Grundfrage) of metaphysics.[48] He does not attempt to answer this question in any straightforward sense. But he thinks that it is crucial that we are able to ask this question, and that we regard beings as a whole as strange and contingent. If this were not so, we would not be able to ask 'Why?' questions at all. It is not obvious that this is so. Some 'Why?' questions arise naturally out of our practical interests and, while they presuppose an awareness of the whole, do not imply that we find beings as a whole strange or oppressive. 'Why is there no chalk?' 'Why is the blackboard out of place?' 'Is so-and-so trying to sabotage my lecture?' Other questions, especially those asked by scientists, presuppose a more than usual degree of wonder and perhaps of the strangeness of beings. Why, Darwin asked, do moths fly towards a candle, but not towards the moon?[49] This question is of no immediate practical relevance. But asking it need not surely commit one to asking, or in some sense presuppose that one has asked, 'Why is there anything at all rather than nothing?'

This brings us to question 7: What is the relation between metaphysics and everyday life? It is, Heidegger believes, very close. Metaphysics goes beyond beings, to ask what they are, why there are any, and so on. But in ordinary life we also go beyond beings, beyond to the world or to beings as a whole. If we did not we could not relate to beings at all. So metaphysics, going beyond, belongs to the nature of man. 'It is the basic happening in *Dasein*.'[50] When we emerge from this implicit, subterranean metaphysics to do explicit metaphysics, we do no more than realise our fundamental possibilities. These are Heidegger's problems. Some of them are quite good problems. Now I turn to the solution.

III The solution

Heidegger believes that all, or at least most, of these problems require for their solution a recognition of the fact that man or *Dasein* holds itself out into the nothing.[51] How is it possible for us

[48] Heidegger considers the question at length in *Einfuhrung in die Metaphysik* (Tübingen: Niemeyer 1953), pp. 1ff. He does not invariably describe it as the *Grundfrage*. In *Beiträge zur Philosophie* (*Vom Ereignis*) (Frankfurt: Klostermann 1989), p. 509, it is the *Übergangsfrage*, the transitional question between the *Leitfrage*, the guiding question, 'What are beings?' and the *Grundfrage*, 'What is the essence of being?' (*Nietzsche*, (I, Pfullingen: Neske, 1961), pp. 12f.)

[49] *Die Grundbegriffe der Metaphysik*, p. 366

[50] *Wegmarken*, p. 120; Krell, ed., p. 109

[51] Wenn das Dasein nur im Sichhineinhalten in das Nichts zu Seiendem sich verhalten, also existieren kann … (*Wegmarken*, p. 114; Krell, ed., p. 104)

to transcend to beings as a whole? How do we manage to deny things? It is because we hold ourselves out into the nothing. Must we therefore always hold ourselves out into the nothing? Must we always be in Angst? Here it is important to distinguish between three types of person: first, ordinary people, or everyday *Dasein*, that is, all of us for most of the time and some of us for all of the time; second, scientists, who examine beings as a whole; and third, metaphysicians, or rather, explicit metaphysicians, since everyone is in a way an implicit metaphysician. Each of these types go beyond beings to the whole, but they do so in different ways. A metaphysician might derive enlightenment from *Angst* if it were only fleeting and occasional. That beings as a whole sometimes seem to slip away from us might tell him, for example, that beings as a whole are contingent and that we can reasonably ask why there are any. Or that a human being is not simply a function of its environment, since otherwise there would be nothing left to feel *Ansgt* as beings slipped away. Or that the beings that surround us are more solid and reliable than they conceivably could be. The capacities of a metaphysician might, that is, be explained by occasional, fleeting *Angst*. But if *Angst*, being held out into the nothing, is to explain the capacities of everyday humans, it must be a more or less constant condition. So, on Heidegger's view, it is. It is there all the time, mostly obscured by everyday activity, but ready to pounce at the slightest provocation.[52] Why, if we are in constant implicit *Angst*, can we not induce explicit *Angst* at will, whenever we like? Because, Heidegger says, we are finite beings. Still, we can let that pass and assume that we are constantly held out into the nothing, in constant subdued *Angst*. Then the question is: How does that supposition help explain the capacities of everyday *Dasein*?

There is reason to doubt whether even Heidegger believed that it did. In *The Basic Concepts of Metaphysics*, he deals with these everyday capacities of ours, awareness of the whole, of beings as beings, and so on, without any essential use of the Nothing.[53] He explains them in terms of world-formation, and ultimately of world-projection.[54] There he makes do with boredom, which reveals the whole but not the nothing, and does not speak about *Angst*.

[52] *Wegmarken*, pp. 116f.; Krell, ed., p. 104.

[53] *Die Grundbegriffe der Metaphysik*, p. 433 discusses *die Hineingehaltenheit in das Nichts*. But here Heidegger is dealing with a misunderstanding of his previously expressed view, not making use of this view to account for our capacities.

[54] Ibid., pp. 526f.: Der Entwurf als Urstruktur des genannten Geschehens ist die Grundstruktur der Weltbildung.

Even in *Being and Time*, where *Angst* is important and the Nothing is said to be what *Angst* is about, it is not obvious that *das Nichts* has the same force as it does in 'What is Metaphysics?'. 'So if that in the face of which we have *Angst* turns out to be the Nothing, that is, the world as such, then that means: It is being-in-the world itself in the face of which Angst is anxious'.[55] Or again: 'In the dark there is in an emphatic way "nothing" to see, yet the world itself is *still* "there", and "there" *more obtrusively*.'[56] Here, we might think, what *Angst* is about is not the Nothing as such but the world. The world is a nothing, a non-entity, in contrast to the entities within it. But it is not *the* Nothing. There are other nothings, apart from the world: being, time, and so on. It is true that these nothings are not so clearly distinct from each other as beings are. They are, for a start, all dependent on *Dasein*, human being(s), in a way that other beings are not. The world in the face of which *Angst* occurs is then not sharply distinct from beings as a whole, or rather the whole as which, or in which, beings are.[57] If that is so, *Angst* in *Being and Time* is not very different from deep boredom in 'What is Metaphysics?' Nothingness is not essential to either. The world, the whole, is a nothing, only in the sense that it is not a being.

But it is not, I think, easy to eliminate the Nothing, or at least some sort of negativity, from Heidegger's account of the world. Explicit *Angst* reveals the world as such, and it does this because in some way or other beings within the world are negated, whether by slipping away, or by losing their significance and sinking into indifference. Correlative with the bare world, *Angst* reveals bare *Dasein*, not *Dasein* as a postman or *Dasein* as a philosopher, but *Dasein* stripped of its customary identity and its familiar moorings in intraworldly things. So nothingness comes in in two ways. Beings are in some way nihilated. And what is left is a nothing, not a blank nothing, but not a being: bare *Dasein* confronted by a bare world, being-in-the world as such without its usual accompaniments.

This is explicit *Angst*. Or explicit deep boredom. Heidegger does not, I suspect, establish that there is an essential difference between

[55] *Sein und Zeit*, p. 187; *Being and Time*, p. 232: Wenn sich demnach als das Wovor der Angst das Nichts, d.h. die Welt als solche herausstellt, dann besagt das: *Wovor die Angst sich ängstet ist das In-der-Welt-sein selbst*.

[56] *Sein und Zeit*, p. 189; *Being and Time*, p. 234: Im Dunkeln ist in einer betonten Weise 'nichts' zu sehen, obzwar gerade die Welt *noch* und *aufdringlicher* 'da' ist.

[57] The phrase 'beings as a whole' occurs only once in *Sein und Zeit*: die Ontologie des Alls des Seienden im Ganzen (p. 248; *Being and Time*, p. 292). Conversely, 'Welt' appears in 'What is Metaphysics?' only in the phrase *Bezug zur Welt* and in the compound *Weltbezug*, the scientist's 'relation to the world' (*Wegmarken*, pp. 104f.)

them. Why must *Angst* or boredom be our normal condition, albeit in an implicit form? Because, Heidegger believes, transcendence of beings is part of our normal condition. We do not let them get on top of us, we are not benumbed or dazzled by our immediate surroundings, we keep beings at a distance from us. We can do this only because we transcend beings and ascend to the whole, to the world in which they lie. All the time we are repelling, in a way negating, beings, and it is this that enables us to appreciate them as beings, to affirm them and negate them in the ordinary sense.

But here we need to look more closely at the notion of transcendence, and the equivalent expression, 'going beyond beings as a whole'.[58] Going beyond beings as a whole involves negating them. But in what sense do we go beyond beings as a whole? Heidegger begins with scientists and implies that they study beings as a whole.[59] Later, Heidegger is more inclined to assign this role to traditional metaphysics,[60] but for the moment we can assume that the sciences, or at least some scientists, talk about beings as a whole, saying, for example, that they all consist of energy. In a sense then they transcend beings as a whole. They need to do that to talk about them as a whole. Then there is the metaphysician. He talks not just about beings as a whole. He also talks about what the scientist is doing in talking about beings as a whole and how he manages to do it. He asks a question that scientists, in their capacity as scientists, do not ask: Why are there any beings and not rather nothing? In doing this he transcends beings as a whole in a way that the scientist does not. He may not be able to answer the question, but it is an intelligible question and the metaphysician is able to ask it. Whatever equipment is needed to ask this question cannot be denied to the metaphysician who asks it. Finally there is the ordinary person going about his everyday business. This involves transcendence of beings as well. But not transcendence to the whole of beings as such, just the ability to transcend any particular being to the local whole in which it lies, and the ability to transcend that local whole to a whole of the medium distance, and so on indefinitely.

Now, an objector might say, it may be that the metaphysician needs to undergo *Angst*, to experience a global nihilation of beings, if he is to do what he does, ask why there is anything at all, and so

[58] *Wegmarken*, p. 114: je schon über das Seiende im Ganzen hinaus; p. 117: das Übersteigen des Seienden im Ganzen: die Transzendenz; Hinausfragen über das Seiende; p. 120: Hinausgehen über das Seiende.

[59] *Wegmarken*, p. 105: Science is responsible for man's *Einbruch ... in das Ganze des Seienden*.

[60] E.g., in the 'Einleitung zu: "Was ist Metaphysik?"' that Heidegger published in 1949 (*Wegmarken*, pp. 361ff.)

on. But why does the scientist need it? Why does the ordinary person need it? Perhaps the scientist can make do with boredom, explicit or subterranean. That should be enough to enable him to talk about beings as a whole. He certainly needs negation. He needs to understand the supposition that not everything consists of energy or even that nothing does. He also needs perhaps to assign limits to his own enquiry. If someone asks: 'Well, do you think that unicorns consist of energy? Or God? Or angels?', he can reply: 'I'm only concerned with beings, nothing more.' To insist that this talk involves the Nothing, the global nihilation of beings as a whole, would be to succumb to that injudicious mingling of negative and positive 'nothings' against which Johnson warns us. Still, even if we insist that scientists, or some of them at least, need *Angst* and global nihilation, it is fairly obvious that everyday *Dasein* does not. In everyday life we rarely, if ever talk about beings as a whole. When we seem to do so, as when we say 'Everything is a mess' or 'You can buy anything in London' we don't literally mean 'everything' or 'anything' without exception. We do not transcend beings as a whole.

Heidegger has, I think, two replies to this. Scientists, metaphysicians and everyday people are not distinct breeds with different equipment. Almost everyone has some understanding of scientific and metaphysical questions. Almost everyone can understand religious claims, in particular about creation from nothing. Almost everyone, according to Heidegger, is prone to occasional *Angst*. There might perhaps in principle be creatures that have everyday dealings with beings, but are wholly incapable of metaphysical or even scientific reflexion. But we are not like that. So whatever nihilating and totalising powers are required for metaphysics must be attributed to humans as such. Heidegger agrees with Kant: Metaphysics is rooted in the nature of man, not just in the nature of metaphysicians.[61]

Secondly, the force that impels us to transcend to a local whole – boredom or *Angst* – cannot easily remain within its boundaries. In boredom, everything becomes indifferent; in *Angst* everything slips away. Not just what is far from us and unfamiliar, not just what is near to us and familiar, but everything. The distinction between the near and the far, the local and the global, is obliterated. Thus Heidegger might say that if anyone has the capacity to transcend to a local whole – this room, say, or this lecture – he must also have the capacity to go the whole way and transcend beings as a whole. Here

[61] Kant, *Critique of Pure Reason*, 2nd edn, p. 21. Cf. Heidegger, *Kant und das Problem der Metaphysik*, pp. 1ff.

Michael Inwood

we might ask: If transcendence or world-formation, to any degree, stems from a force that is intrinsically global and unrestricted, how can we stop at any point short of global nihilation? In the context of this lecture I could have said *this* about Heidegger or I could have said *that* about him. I could not have spoken about Stonehenge – except in the Pickwickian sense in which I am actually doing so. Or, looking at it from the point of view of my deliberation over possible alternatives, I can wonder whether to say *this* or *that* about Heidegger; it does not occur to me as a possibility to speak about Stonehenge. It is not, however, flatly impossible for me to speak about Stonehenge. But to consider that possibility I must transcend to a larger whole, one that takes in my eralier training and choices. I could have taken steps earlier to ensure that the alternatives now before me were whether to speak about Stonehenge or the Pyramids or even, if I were enough of a polymath, Heidegger. Here I have moved to the consideration of a wider whole than the first. And I could go further. The all-embracing whole, beings as a whole, is the limit to which these successively enlarged wholes tend. To consider beings as a whole is of little use in deciding what is realistically or practically possible. At that elevated level, anything is possible, or at least anything logically possible is possible. It may even be possible that there should be, or have been, nothing at all. But the question to Heidegger is this: If *Angst* or boredom is required to propel me to the consideration of a local whole, such as this lecture, what prevents it from propelling me further than I wish – to a wider whole in which I could have lectured on Stonehenge, or beyond that to beings as a whole? His answer is that there is a countervailing tendency – 'falling', *Verfallen*, induced, he sometimes implies, by Angst itself – that drives us back into the everyday 'world'[62] and its everyday concerns. Usually it drives us too far into the 'world', Heigegger believes. But it remains the case that we are all in principle capable of transcending beings as a whole. We are all implicit metaphysicians.

If we are all implicit metaphysicians, why should we ever engage in explicit metaphysics? Occasionally Heidegger suggests that, while hidden *Angst* makes possible our everyday involvements, there is nevertheless something disreputable about everydayness with its merely implicit *Angst*. The primordial nothing is distorted by our absorption in beings. 'The more we turn in our dealings towards beings, the less we let beings as such slip away and the more we turn away from the Nothing. But all the more surely we force our way into the public surface of *Dasein*.'[63] And at the end of the lec-

[62] The scare-quotes around 'world' here indicates that 'world' is used to denote worldly entities and affairs, and not in Heidegger's own special sense.

[63] *Wegmarken*, p. 115; Krell, ed., p. 104

ture it is clear that explicit metaphysics involves a personal liberation from the narrow confines of everyday life, not simply answers
to some interesting questions. It involves: 'first, making space for
beings as a whole; then, letting oneself go into the Nothing, i.e., getting free of the idols that everyone has and to which we are prone to
cringe.'[64] In *Being and Time*, *Angst* has a double role. Implicit, subdued *Angst* leads us to flee from the bare self and the bare world
that it implicitly reveals and to take refuge in intraworldly things
and concerns. Explicit *Angst* rips us away from such concerns by
bringing us face to face with the bare self and the bare world.[65]
When the enemy, *Angst*, is outside, he makes us cling to the familiar. When he bursts in, this disrupts the familiar. Later this idea led
Heidegger to duplicate *Angst*, and to speak, albeit with some dis-
comfiture, of '*Angst*' in the face of *Angst*, in contrast to readiness
for *Angst* or courage for essential *Angst*.[66] *Angst* still comes of its
own accord, but it depends on us whether we embrace or suppress
it. Heidegger avoids saying so explicitly, but he implies, that we
should embrace explicit *Angst* and let beings glide away. Not only
does the Nothing noth, but it should noth more intensely than it
does for most of us. Or at least it should noth explicitly as well as
implicitly. Why? Just so that we can do philosophy? In Heidegger's
case Yes. *Angst* clears the philosopher's head of idols. It is
Heidegger's substitute for Cartesian doubt or Husserl's *Epoche*. But
his claim that *Angst* is more intense in reserved people and in dar-
ing people than in busy people,[67] suggests that he has more than just
philosophers in mind. Perhaps soldiers too, or perhaps not. His
basic ideas is this: Human beings are usually involved in dealings
with entities in their environment. They have, however, the capacity to transcend their customary environment, to take stock of their
lives, and to decide how they are to be, in disregard of the idols
before which they normally cringe. This capacity enables us to

[64] *Wegmarken*, p. 121; Krell, ed., p. 110

[65] *Sein und Zeit*, pp. 184-91; *Being and Time*, pp. 228–35

[66] In the Nachwort zu: 'Was ist Metaphysik?', *Wegmarken*, p. 304; Hull
and Crick, p. 384: Eine Erfahrung des Seins als des Anderen zu allem
Seienden verschenkt die Angst, gesetzt, dass wir nicht aus 'Angst' vor der
Angst, d.h.in der blossen Ängstlichkeit der Furcht, vor der lautlosen
Stimme ausweichen, die uns in den Schrecken des Abgrundes stimmt.
Whenever Heidegger speaks of 'Angst' vor der Angst, the first occurrence
of 'Angst' is in scare-quotes.

[67] *Wegmarken*, p. 116; Krell, ed., p. 106: Ihr Atem zittert ständig durch
das Dasein: am wenigsten durch das 'ängstliche' und ünvernehmlich fur
das 'Ja Ja' und 'Nein Nein' des betriebsamen; am ehesten durch das ver-
haltene; am sichertsten durch das im Grunde verwegene Dasein.

Michael Inwood

engage with beings in the way we do, not benumbed by them as insects are, but regarding them as beings. But we need on occasion to exercise this capacity explicitly if we are not to descend too far into intraworldly beings and become too insect-like. The normal human condition is suspended somewhere between the *Angst*-less insect and the *Angst*-ridden angel. We need sometimes to ascend to angels to make sure that we do not become insects.[68] This too reminds me of Kant. It is structurally similar to Kant's view of morality. We need not constantly act from moral motives. We can do things for the fun of it. But we retain a capacity for moral stock-taking, which we must on occasion exercise if we are ever to act freely, even when we are doing something just for pleasure.[69] If the Nothing is to continue to noth implicitly and tacitly, then it must on occasion noth explicitly and intensely.

Philosophy, Heidegger later wrote, is not a system, not a finished edifice of thought. It is more like a quarry in which stone has been broken into various randomly situated blocks. The workers and tools that broke them are nowhere to be seen. It is hard to tell whether the blocks are self-contained shapes or supports for an invisible bridge.[70] Heidegger left some interesting shapes in the quarry and made some bold attempts to rearrange its contents. Did Carnap do him a deplorable injustice? Perhaps not. Mr. Heidegger was a showman. Many philosophers would enjoy being branded an arch-metaphysician, but Heidegger relished it more than most. May he long be remembered as the man who said the Nothing noths.

---

[68] Cf. *Beiträge zur Philosophie* (*Von Ereignis*), p. 399: Wird dann die Zeit der Götter um sein und der Rückfall in das blosse Leben weltarmer Wesen beginnen, denen die Erde nur noch als das Ausnutzbare geblieben? (Will the time of the gods then be over and the relapse begin into the mere life of world-impoverished creatures, for whom the earth remains no more than an exploitable resource?) Cf. p. 275: 'Is [technology] the historical way to the end, to the relapse of the last man, into the mechanised animal …?'

[69] In *Being and Time*, Heidegger's account of *Angst* is curiously similar to his account of conscience (*Sein und Zeit*, Division II, chapter 2). Both disclose bare *Dasein* in its thrownness (Geworfenheit). Both involve the Nothing. Both occur in two modes: in an implicit mode constantly and in an explicit mode occasionally. Both summon us to or prepare us for resoluteness. But conscience is not, like *Angst*, responsible for our flight from the self to intraworldly beings. After *Being and Time*, he shows no further interest in conscience.

[70] *Beiträge zur Philosophie*, p. 436. Cf. p. 421: Hier liegen die Blöcke eines Steinbruchs, in dem Urgestein gebrochen wird.

290

Reactionary Modernism

DAVID E. COOPER

I

'Reactionary modernism' is a term happily coined by the historian and sociologist Jeffrey Herf to refer to a current of German thought during the interwar years. It indicates the attempt to 'reconcil[e] the antimodernist, romantic and irrationalist ideas present in German nationalism' with that 'most obvious manifestation of means–ends rationality ... modern technology'.[1] Herf's paradigm examples of this current of thought are two best-selling writers of the period: Oswald Spengler, author of the massive domesday scenario *The Decline of the West* in 1917 and, fifteen years later, of *Man and Technics,* and Ernst Jünger, the now centenarian chronicler of the war in which he was a much-decorated hero, whose main theoretical work was *Der Arbeiter* in 1932. The label is also applied by Herf to such intellectual luminaries as the legal theorist and apologist for the Third Reich, Carl Schmitt, and more contentiously Martin Heidegger. At a less elevated level, reactionary modernism also permeated the writings of countless, now forgotten engineers, who were inspired at once by the new technology, Nietzschean images of Promethean *Übermenschen,* and an ethos of *völkisch* nationalism.

As befits his profession, Herf's primary concern is with the role of reactionary modernism in the aetiology of National Socialism. As befits mine, my aim is rather different: to locate reactionary modernism within post-Kantian German philosophy. I shall argue that it was a radical completion of tendencies that had their beginnings in Kant's own day. Acceptance of that conclusion requires an understanding of Spengler, Jünger *et al.* as being reactionary and modern in more philosophically charged senses of those terms than the essentially political and sociological ones intended by Herf. Such a view of them, moreover, will dissolve what he sees as the 'paradoxical' character of their attempt to wed rational technology and romantic hostility towards Enlightenment reason. First, however, let me fill out Herf's conception of reactionary modernism.

He is rightly concerned to dispel such familiar leftist perceptions of Nazism as either an ideology-less, purely opportunistic move-

[1] Jeffrey Herf, *Reactionary Modernism: Technology, Culture and Politics in Weimar and the Third Reich* (Cambridge University Press, 1984), p. 1.

ment, or as one inspired by a merely reactionary ideology, the product of a nostalgic rejection of modernity. Certainly, there were 'mere' reactionaries who played their part in the development of of German fascism – including Wagner's son-in-law, the racial theorist Houston Stewart Chamberlain, who regarded industrialisation as 'the most terrible catastrophe to have befallen mankind', productive of what the effetely conservative poet Stefan George called 'the ant-world'.[2] But the characteristic tenor of Nazi ideology was more authentically expressed by one of its main architects, Josef Goebbels, when referring to the movement's 'steely romanticism' and boasting that 'National Socialism understood how to take the soulless framework of technology and fill it with the rhythm and impulses of our time'.[3] Among its contemporary critics, it was not the Marxists, but Thomas Mann, who appreciated 'the really characteristic and dangerous aspect' of Nazism – its 'robust modernity ... combined with dreams of the past: a highly technological romanticism'.[4]

As Herf elaborates Mann's insight, the reactionary modernist ambition was to 'incorporate modern technology into ... German nationalism, without diminishing the latter's romantic and anti-rational aspects'. This was accomplished by incorporating it *'into* the symbolism and language of *Kultur* – community, blood, will, self ... race' and so *'out of* the realm of *Zivilization* – reason, intellect, internationalism, materialism, and finance'.[5] Instead of technology being viewed as the rational means towards material ends, it gets conceived as the *expression,* appropriate to modernity, of such romantically favoured forces as the *Geist* or 'soul' of a people, or its blind 'will to power'.

We shall come later to the details of the positions of, especially, Spengler and Jünger. It suffices for the moment to emphasize that – as talk of *Geist* or a 'will to power' indicates – such thinkers were self-consciously articulating metaphysical views endebted to ones advanced in the previous century of German philosophising. As for Heidegger, so for the reactionary modernists, technology was no mere socio–economic process, but something 'deeper' of which that visible process – in factory, shipyard or laboratory – was but a manifestation. As Schmitt put it, belief in technology is not in anything 'machine-like', but 'belief in an activistic metaphysics'.[6] Submitting

[2] Quoted in Michael E. Zimmermann, *Heidegger's Confrontation with Modernity: Technology, Politics and Art* (Bloomington: Indiana University Press, 1990), pp. 9 and 10.

[3] Ibid., p. 65.

[4] Quoted in Herf, *Reactionary Modernism*, p. 2.

[5] Ibid., p. 16.

[6] Ibid., p. 120.

to the technological 'logic' of our times, says Spengler, is to be 'in the silent service of Being'.[7] Let me then turn to the developments in post-Kantian thought of which, if I am right, the philosophical claims of the thinkers who concern us represent a radical completion.

II

Already in Kant's own lifetime, two central tenets of his Transcendental Idealism were coming under attack from some of his critical admirers, attacks which gathered momentum during the early decades of the nineteenth century. There was, first, rejection of his claim that, besides the empirically accessible world, there is a realm of noumena or things-in-themselves, whose way of appearing to us is the empirical world, but of which we can know next to nothing. Second there was increasing questioning of Kant's claim that it is in virtue of conformity with, or organisation by, a small set of eternal, universal *a priori* categories of thought that the world is accessible to experience.

Important implications were to be drawn from these attacks. First, if, as Kant held, the world must indeed conform with thought then, with the realm of things-in-themselves abolished, the only reality there is must be 'ideal', in the sense of being structured or 'constituted' by thought – if not by *our*, specifically *human* thought, then by Absolute Mind or *Geist*, in which we somehow participate. Second, with the abolition of things-in-themselves, a different account from Kant's of human freedom, and its relation to the realm of nature, is required: since it was Kant's view that it is as things-in-themselves, 'independent of the whole world of sense',[8] that we are free, not as empirical, natural beings. Third, once it was admitted that there are no eternal *a priori* categories to which the world must conform, the way was open to a *historicisation* of conceptual schemes, to a perception of their development from earlier ones of the frameworks which shape, at any given time, how the world may be experienced and articulated.

Such, in the broadest terms, were some of the implications drawn from rejection of central ingredients in Kant's position by Hegel or other Absolute Idealists inspired by him. As the nineteenth century grew older, more radical implications were to be drawn, so that

[7] Spengler, *The Decline of the West: Form and Actuality*, 2 vols (New York: Knopf, 1939), vol. II, p. 507

[8] Kant, *Critique of Practical Reason* (Indiana: Bobbs-Merrill, 1976), p. 162.

David E. Cooper

the distance from Kant's original vision becomes greater. We see this occurring especially in the writings of two pivotal figures in the ancestry of reactionary modernism, one an avowed neo-Kantian, the other someone whose critical engagement with Kant was greater than recent, fashionable treatment might suggest. I refer to Wilhelm Dilthey and Friedrich Nietzsche.

Nietzsche agreed with Kant and later idealists that the issue is not how we conform our minds to the world, but how the world conforms to our minds. But, for him, the idea that it is Mind or *Geist* that structures or 'constitutes' the world is both unnecessary and obfuscating, one still in hock to a conception of a 'true world' which deserves to be abolished along with that of things-in-themselves. Instead, we should frankly concede that it is humanly forged 'perspectives' which constitute the world – the only one there is – as we experience it. 'As if a world would still remain after one deducted the perspective!', he exclaims.[9] No sense, that is, can be attached to the idea of a world viewed from nowhere which could then be compared with our perspective on it.

Moreover, once the further idea is jettisoned that our perspective is constrained by *a priori* conditions of thought or understanding, we should be candid enough to concede that acceptance of it is due less to reflection and reason than to human interests and ambitions, to 'will' rather than to thought. Our perspective is not so much under 'cognitive command' as a response to 'eudaemonic *demand*'.[10] Thus even the so-called truths of logic are to be viewed pragmatically, not as articulations of *a priori* conditions of thought, but as belonging to a scheme which we cannot throw off, since it is necessary 'for the sake of the preservation of creatures like ourselves', with our kind of interests and aims, our way of embodying a 'will to power'.[11]

As for the attempt to salvage a notion of freedom of the will, once a noumenal realm distinct from the natural one has been abandoned, this too should be given up. This does not mean, for Nietzsche, that every concept of freedom must be rejected, but any viable one must be compatible with the human animal's inextricable enmeshment in the world's natural processes. Thus we might describe one person as freer than another if the former – a creative artist, say – is a more emphatic locus and exerciser of power than the latter, or if he better exhibits that recognition of the human con-

[9] Nietzsche, *The Will to Power* (New York: Vintage, 1968), §567.

[10] *Philosophy and Truth: Selections from Nietzsche's Notebooks of the Early 1970s* (New Jersey: Humanities, 1990), p. 93.

[11] *Beyond Good and Evil*, in *Basic Writings of Nietzsche* (New York: Modern Library, 1968), §11.

dition Nietzsche calls *amor fati* than the person who pathetically kicks against the pricks of nature's processes.

I noted that, for some critics of Kant, with the rejection of his *a priori* categories the way stood open to a historical treatment of the conceptual schemes employed to structure the world. This was not, however, a way taken by Nietzsche. While there is nothing *a priori* or universal in our perspectives, they are to be understood not as *Zeitgeiste* but as the products of physiology and psychology. The will to power gets manifested by different perspectives according to the kinds or 'breeds' of men adopting them. There is another respect, too, in which Nietzsche is closer to Kant himself than to those who 'historicised' the Master's position. For Kant, his own age of Enlightenment represented progress over earlier ones: human beings were becoming more rational in their assessment of their intellectual capacities and the limits to these. For Nietzsche, too, his own age – an increasingly scientifically minded one which was witnessing 'the death of God' – was also, in a sense, a more rational one than its predecessors. This was not because it was achieving an accurate delineation of 'the true world', but because it was dispelling those illusions, like that of God and 'the true world' itself, which had served for so long as comforting props for those 'weak', 'botched and bungled' people incapable of facing up to the nature of their condition. Nietzsche was as hostile as Kant to the romantic, *völkisch* position of those, like Herder in some of his writings, who forbad any comparison, on a scale of rationality, of different peoples or ages.

It was, above all others, Dilthey who developed the neo-Kantian conception of our organising schemes as historical episodes. For Dilthey, there is no such thing as '*the* human type' or the few 'physiological' types postulated by Nietzsche. 'The human type melts away in the process of history'.[12] 'The fundamental preconditions of knowledge' and experience are not timelessly inherent in the nature either of mind or of will: rather they are provided by 'Life', a 'historical whole ... of [an] Age', a complete 'conception of reality' and way of 'valuation'. This 'historical whole' constitutes a *Gestalt* in

[12] This and the following quotations from Dilthey come from many sources, including his *Gesammelte Schriften* (Leipzig: Teuber, 1923) and *Dilthey: Selected Writings*, ed. H. P. Rickman (Cambridge University Press, 1986). All of them are referenced in my '*Verstehen*, Holism and Fascism', in *Verstehen and Humane Understanding*, ed. A. O'Hear (Cambridge University Press, 1996). Let me repeat one point I made in that article: there are 'humane' and 'rationalistic' aspects of Dilthey's thought which sit uncomfortably alongside the 'historicist' aspects on which I am currently dwelling.

David E. Cooper

terms of which everything is interpreted and invested with the 'significance' it has as part of this whole.

Precisely because the 'Life' of an age is a total *Gestalt*, a 'self-enclosed horizon', no sense attaches to an ahistorical assessment of it. It cannot be 'cited before the tribunal of reason', since any criteria that a tribunal could employ would have to be drawn from *within* some 'closed horizon' of 'Life'. No sense either, therefore, can be made of rational progress. Since any criticism of an earlier age can only 'spring from the state of being-within-Life', it would be akin to criticism of one language, like French, for not being another, English say.

Unsurprisingly, Dilthey can make no room for the Kantian freedom supposedly enjoyed by autonomous individuals allegedly 'independent' of the empirical world. This is not, as for Nietzsche, because individuals are inextricably woven into natural processes, but because they are 'immersed in … woven into [the] common sphere' constituted by the cultural 'Life' of their age. An individual, Dilthey writes, is 'a point where webs of relationships' shaped by the 'historical whole' of the age 'intersect'. As 'expressions' of the prevailing 'Life' into which they are 'woven', individuals cannot gain that distance and independence from their historical situation which radical Kantian autonomy requires.

III

Writing of such Nazi ideologues as Alfred Rosenberg, Georg Lukács remarked that they 'completed th[e] journey which began with Nietzsche and Dilthey'.[13] The remark applies as much, I suggest, to our exemplary reactionary modernists, Spengler and Jünger. For what these authors did was to combine a Nietzschean metaphysics of the will to power with Dilthey's historicisation of 'Life', of the successive *Gestalts* which shape the conceptions and valuations available in a given culture. Nietzsche, they imply, was right to recognise the variety of perspectives that manifest people's will to power, but this variety does not so much register the existence of different, natural human kinds or 'breeds' as form an historical parade of different 'morphological' cultural kinds. Dilthey, correspondingly, was right to recognise the historical character of these 'Life-forms', but should not have concluded that this means the 'melting away' of 'the human type', for throughout the whole process human beings remain, in their essence, will to power. The

[13] Georg Lukács, *The Destruction of Reason* (London: Merlin, 1980), pp. 536f.

296

succeeding morphological forms are but different manifestations of that essence.

The combination of these Nietzschean and Diltheyan elements produced an explosive mixture, resulting in radical claims that could not have been reached on the basis of the elements taken separately. Taken together, they inspired a vision which was indeed a culmination of philosophical tendencies which began with the abandonment of central tenets of Kant's position. Before I bring into relief the main features of the reactionary modernists' radicalisation of Nietzsche and Dilthey, it will be useful to have brief overviews of Spengler and Jünger's closely related visions. Since neither author develops his vision systematically or with much regard for consistency, these overviews reflect a degree of regimentation on my part.

Spengler's ambition in *The Decline of the West* is to outline a 'morphology of world-history'. Like earlier or rival accounts of history and man's relation to the world, Spengler regards his own as a 'myth', but as being none the worse for that and, indeed, as superior to these other accounts. According to his own 'myth', world-history is 'the marvellous waxing and waning of organic [or morphological] forms' which obey an inexorable 'logic of time'. These 'forms' are whole 'cultures', the ingredients of which – mathematics and religion, say, or art and science – are organically connected 'expression– forms' given their 'stamp' by the whole.[14] The latest 'form' has its origins in medieval Germany and is referred to by Spengler as 'Faustian' culture, a Promethean endeavour to master the world both in thought and action and whose most recent manifestation is scientifically informed technology and industrialisation.

Many readers at the time understood Spengler's book to be accusing technology of responsibility for the decline referred to in its title. But this was never his intention, as he makes clear in the later *Man and Technics*. Industrial technology has indeed been responsible for ills and, in his view, is subject to a fairly imminent doom: but it has represented 'the victory ... of technical thought' in a 'pitiless no-quarter battle of the will to power', a will never more emphatically embodied than in the 'energy' of 'Faustian man'.[15] In Spengler's account, there is, predictably, little or no room for the free, rational and autonomous individual of Enlightenment and Kantian philosophy. All of us, to recall Spengler's remark, are caught up 'in the silent service of Being', the inexorable rolling on of succeeding 'forms' each of which 'stamps' those who live within

[14] Spengler, *Decline of the West*, Vol. 1, pp. 41, 22, 6 and 21.
[15] Spengler, *Man and Technics: A Contribution to the Philosophy of Life* (London: Allen & Unwin, 1932), pp. 77 and 16.

it. Nor are rationality and autonomy any kind of ideals. Despite the reference to 'the victory of technical thought', it is central to Spengler's vision that technology is not to be construed, *pace* Max Weber, as the rational adoption of means in order to satisfy individual wants. Rather it is embraced by 'Faustian man' as an expression of his will to power, as an attempt to 'enslave and harness [Nature's] very forces', without concern for its utilitarian pay-off. Technology, he says, is the way of the 'Vikings of the blood', not the 'Vikings of the mind'.[16]

Ernst Jünger recorded how he was thoroughly 'familiar with [the] appeal' of Spengler's magnum opus.[17] Like the older man, he argued that history has 'a destiny of forms for its content', *Gestalts* which, in their philosophical articulation, are 'myths', and which 'stamp' every aspect of the cultures in which they prevail.[18] His interest, however, was less in earlier historical 'forms' than in the one prevailing in our modern age of technology, the 'form of the worker', as he calls it.

Jünger's vision was shaped by his experience in the trenches of the First World War, one he describes in *Storms of Steel* and other works as being at once a theatre of horror and of beauty, a hell yet a place where, in 'masculine camaraderie', men fully realise themselves, and – more pertinently – a context in which men were both 'totally mobilised', robotic cogs in battles dominated by machinery and heroes of Homeric proportions. If Spengler's 'Faustian men' sound like 'beasts of prey' who happen to have taken a degree in engineering, Jünger's heroes are at once 'bee[s] and titan[s]', 'cybernetic storm troops'.[19] The 'worker' of whom he writes in his long essay of that name is not the man in the cloth-cap, but the equivalent in an age of technological industry of the soldier in a mechanised war.

'Hardened', 'steely' and 'chiseled', the worker is the 'type (*Typus*)' of the age, who bears the 'stamp' of the prevailing *Gestalt* under 'the compulsion of iron lawlikeness'. As a creature of technology, characterised as the 'mobilisation of the world through the *Gestalt* of the worker', the 'mobilisation of matter', this worker enjoys no freedom or autonomy. Indeed, he is not really a 'person or individual' at all, but rather a cypher, a symbol of the form which a 'metaphysical' will to power has taken in our times – times which Jünger incidentally, unlike Spengler, thought are here to stay.[20]

[16] Ibid., pp. 84 and 10ff.
[17] Quoted in Thomas Nevin, *Ernst Jünger and Germany: Into the Abyss 1914–1945* (London: Constable, 1997), p. 79.
[18] Ernst Jünger, *Der Arbeiter*, in *Essays II* (Stuttgart: Klett, 1964), p. 42.
[19] Nevin, *Ernst Jünger*, pp. 135 and 140.
[20] Ernst Jünger, *Der Arbeiter*, pp. 159, 164 and 42.

Although standardly described as fascist figures on the 'right', neither Spengler nor Jünger accepted the many invitations, from Goebbels and others, to join the NSDAP, and Jünger at least counted among his friends and fellow thinkers so called 'national bolsheviks' like Ernst Niekisch. (Further evidence, were it needed, for the waywardness of the Marxist understanding of Nazism, and for the uselessness of the 'Left' versus 'Right' dualism, is the enthusiasm for – indeed, envy of – the directed Soviet economy displayed not only by Niekisch and Jünger, but by leading Nazis, such as Goebbels and, perhaps, Hitler himself.) Certainly Spengler and Jünger were both enemies of bourgeois capitalism and its accompanying political ideology of liberal democracy. The collapse of Weimar democracy, proclaimed Jünger, will be our 'greatest day of festivity'.[21] Not especially interested in the detailed political arrangements appropriate to the 'form' of the worker, he seems to have favoured a dictatorship of men equipped to put the 'stamp' of the age on the masses they control. Spengler, more mildly, advocated an authoritarian brand of Prussian state socialism.

Some of the two men's objections to liberal democracy were of a relatively practical type. Thus, like Carl Schmitt, Jünger was convinced that states which manifested a will to power in the form of technological domination were inevitably poised for war, preparation for which democratic governments are very poorly equipped. But their objections were also, and more importantly, at a spiritual level, so to speak. They and Schmitt all agreed that liberalism, with its individualistic ethic, served only to produce alienated citizens without a sense of integration into the larger collective culture.[22] Moreover, the liberal bourgeoisie entirely misunderstood the character of industrial technology, seeing in it only a means for the satisfaction of individual, material wants – something to utilise rather than immerse oneself in, and if necessary sacrifice oneself to, as the authentically modern mode of human self-expression.

IV

These overviews make plain, I hope, the blend of Nietzsche's metaphysics and Dilthey's historicism – as popularly construed, at any

[21] Quoted in Hermann Glaser, *Spiesser-Ideologie von der Zerstörung des deutschen Geistes im 19. und 20. Jahrhundert* (Freiburg: Rombach, 1964), p. 99.
[22] For Schmitt's views, see his *Political Romanticism* (Cambridge, MA: MIT Press, 1986) and Paul Gottfried, *Carl Schmitt* (London: Claridge, 1990).

David E. Cooper

rate – which constitute the reactionary modernist vision. Each 'historical whole' or Diltheyan *Gestalt,* including the latest technological 'form' of 'Faustian man' or the 'worker', is a manifestation, appropriate to its age, of the essential nature of human beings, their will to power. I want now to focus on how the blend of those two ingredients produced more extreme results than anything the individual views of Nietzsche and Dilthey could themselves yield.

One such result is an *irrationalism* indicated, for example, by invidious comparisons between 'Vikings' of the blood and of the mind respectively, by speaking of 'fate' or 'destiny' governing the 'waxing and waning' of 'forms', and – most significant, perhaps – by references to the organising ideas, the conceptions and valuations, belonging to these 'forms' as 'myths' or mere 'symbols'. 'There are no eternal truths', wrote Spengler, only 'life-symbols', including such 'deep myths' as science and mathematics.[23]

Clearly we have come a long way from the much earlier criticisms of Kant's *a priori* categories outlined above. That the ideas which organise experience do not incorporate *a priori* 'eternal truths' hardly implies, just like that, that they are only 'myths' or 'symbols'. Nietzsche, it is true, spoke of our organising schemes as 'perspectives', intending thereby that they neither depict 'the true world' nor reflect necessary constraints on the very possibility of thought and experience. And Dilthey explicitly denied that the 'historical whole' and its *idées mères* may be assessed for their rationality or lack of it. But neither of these thinkers were *irrationalists,* and neither spoke of science, maths *et al.* as belonging to the realm of myth. Thinking within the constraints of logic and scientific methodology, Nietzsche argues, may not be necessary for the very possibility of experience: but, at least since 'the death of God', we can see it to be necessary for the effective exercise of the will to power and for the maximum 'preservation of creatures like ourselves'. For Dilthey, there is a 'deep coherence' between rational enquiry and Life: whatever the prevailing *Gestalt* or 'Life-form', the pursuit of empirical knowledge and of certainty increases the level of our 'Life-activity'.[24]

What effects the shift to the irrationalist predilections of Spengler and Jünger is an explosive mixture of Nietzschean and Diltheyan themes. Nietzsche's respect for rational enquiry rests on the assumption that all human beings are, more or less, 'creatures

[23] Spengler, *The Decline of the West*, vol. I, pp. 41 and 427. I discuss Spengler and Jünger's mythopoeia in my 'Modern Mythology: The Case of Reactionary Modernism', *History of the Human Sciences*, 9, 1996.

[24] Dilthey, *The Essence of Philosophy* (Chapel Hill, NC: University of North Carolina Press, 1954), p. 36

like ourselves', with constant 'physiological' needs which logic, science *et al.* serve. That case, as the reactionary modernists see it, is punctured once the Diltheyan thought is absorbed that 'the human type melts away in the process of history'. There can then be no guarantee that what serves one 'Life-form', one age, serves another: better, then, to regard the *idées mères* of an age as myths or symbols that suit. So, as Jünger put it, one age will have its 'spiritual' 'expressive symbols', another its 'technical' ones.[25] As for Dilthey's claim that the 'Life-activity' of any age is enhanced by rational enquiry, this exaggerates the degree to which the coherence of any *Gestalt* is a matter of shared belief, and underestimates, therefore, its debt to the prevailing 'stamp' given to it by an inexorable and blind will to power. In short, the individual cases for reason offered by Nietzsche and Dilthey cancel one another out.

A second result of the blending of Nietzschean and Diltheyan themes is the extreme anti-individualism and hostility to the idea of freedom registered by talk, once more, of fate or destiny, but especially of the way people are 'stamped' by the *Gestalt* of an age. Jünger's rhetoric here is particularly extreme. I have already recorded his view that the worker is so thoroughly 'stamped' by the technological *Gestalt* as no longer to be 'a person or individual'. Elsewhere he writes of this *Gestalt* as a 'destiny' which is 'independent of circumstances' over which men and women have control, subject as they are to 'the new order as the will to total mobilisation'.[26] Everybody, he writes, is 'inscribed' in a 'raging process'.[27]

Once more we have travelled a long distance from the criticisms, more than a century earlier, of Kant's notion of the free, autonomous person, one which required his distinction between empirical and noumenal selves. That we are not denizens of a 'suprasensory' realm hardly entails, just like that, that we are without freedom and autonomy at all. Nor was this a conclusion that those later, more radical critics, Nietzsche and Dilthey, could embrace without qualification. For Nietzsche, there was no contracausal free will: but he explicitly allows for a viable notion of freedom in terms of individual power. The more power exerted, the more 'resistance' offered against other centres of power, the more 'effects' produced, the greater is the freedom a person may be said to possess. Nietzsche's idea of the *Übermensch* is that of someone who possesses it to an exemplary degree. Dilthey, too, may have spoken of the 'Individual as a point where webs of relationships

[25] Jünger, *Der Arbeiter*, p. 170.
[26] Jünger, *Der Arbeiter*, pp. 89 and 50.
[27] 'Total mobilization', in *The Heidegger Controversy: A Critical Reader*, R. Wolin ed., (Cambridge, MA: MIT Press, 1993), p. 128.

intersect' and as 'immersed in the common sphere', but this was no blanket denial of individuality or freedom. For him, people are constrained, not by 'raging processes' and 'forces', but by the limited range of meaningful actions and ideas available to them in a given culture. They are 'immersed' rather as one may be immersed in the language one speaks, with all that this implies by way of limitations on what one can meaningfully say.

What enables the shift to the reactionary modernists' extreme denials of individuality and freedom is, once again, an explosive mixture of Nietzsche and Dilthey. Nietzsche's loci or centres of power, including human beings, are individuals – or better, perhaps, the individual, atomic events of which things and persons are, in a somewhat Humean manner, 'bundles'. Collective entities, like states or societies, can only exert power in a derivative way, as functions of their individual parts. What the rhetoric of Spengler and Jünger displays is the result of superimposing on the doctrine of the will to power the Diltheyan conception of cultural, 'historical wholes'. According to the resulting rhetoric, the real, basic loci or centres of the will to power are *Gestalts*, the cultures which 'stamp' their character on so-called individuals. Or matters can be put the other way round: the reactionary modernist vision results from superimposing a doctrine of the will to power on Dilthey's theory of *Gestalts*. For Dilthey himself, we saw, the primary sense in which a *Gestalt* constrains people is that of limiting the range of meanings available to them. If, instead, each *Gestalt* is thought of as the expression and locus of an underlying, blind will to power, the primary constraints imposed take on a different aspect, so that people may now indeed be described as subject to a 'raging process' or as 'inscribed' by a *Gestalt* which is the medium of a will independent of individual control.

V

It is in the light of this 'collectivisation' of the will to power, I suggest, that the reactionary modernists' enthusiastic embrace of technology is to be understood. Their claim, briefly, was that the will to power finds its most complete and authentic expression in technology's total mobilisation of matter by 'Faustian man' or the worker. It was Heidegger who appreciated that Spengler and Jünger, in somewhat different ways, 'achieve what all the Nietzsche literature was not able to achieve so far, namely, to communicate an experience of being ... as the will to power'.[28] While the centres or loci of this

[28] Heidegger, *The Question of Being* (New Haven: College & University Press, 1956), p. 43. This article discusses Jünger's 1950 essay *Über die Linie*, in which he critically revisits the themes of *Der Arbeiter*.

will were regarded as individuals, it was possible to retain vestiges of a romantic vision of the will to power as something paradigmatically manifested by particular men, creative artists, say, following a 'gospel of self-overcoming'. But when those centres are construed as whole cultures or *Gestalts,* the measure of the will to power's expression will be the weight of the 'stamp' that a *Gestalt* is able to impress upon the age and the people who live in it.

By that measure, the *Gestalt* of the 'worker' wins hand down. It is not simply that, in the technological age, there is *total* mobilisation, so that all aspects of life, including its supposedly 'private' ones, are caught up in, and bear the 'stamp' of, the technological imperative. More importantly, perhaps, as Heidegger was to put it, technology 'drives out every other possibility of revealing'.[29] Here he is following Jünger and Schmitt in understanding by technology not the processes visible in factory or coalmine, but the 'metaphysic' or interpretation of the world behind those processes. And his point, like theirs, is that technology has a power possessed by no earlier 'way of revealing' – a religiously informed one, say – to achieve hegemony: to the degree, indeed, that it gets forgotten that other ways of revealing were ever available.

There is another respect, according to Heidegger, in which the reactionary modernists were right to see in modern technology the ultimate expression of the will to power. Spengler, Jünger and Schmitt, I noted, all emphasised the distance between their understanding of technology and that of Weber and others who regarded it as the instrument of means–end rationality. For the former trio, the technological enterprise is without purpose beyond itself, a sheer manifestation of will. And this, for Heidegger, captures a point which escaped Nietzsche himself that the will we see at work in the human world is less a will to power – to something that might, in principle, be finally achieved – but 'the unconditional will to will'.[30] Technology owes its grip upon men and women, not so much because it brings with it power over nature so as to satisfy their needs, but because it opens up ever greater opportunities and vistas for the exercise of will. Previous manifestations of the will to power have been in hock to the illusion of there being ends or purposes to be striven for. In the technological era, the honest among us can at last recognise that the only real object of the will is itself, the endless expansion of its domain of activity.

I have argued that reactionary modernism should be regarded as the extreme culmination of lines of thought that began with rejec-

[29] Heidegger, *The Question Concerning Technology (and other essays)* (New York: Harper & Row, 1977), p. 27.
[30] Heidegger, *The Question of Being,* p. 37.

David E. Cooper

tion of central tenets of Kant's position and continued through Nietzsche's doctrine of the will to power and Dilthey's historicist, cultural holism. If I am right, there is nothing of the 'paradox' that Herf purports to find in the combination of reactionism and modernism exhibited by Spengler, Jünger and others. They are, one might say, two sides of the same coin. The political reactionism of these writers was the product in part of a deeper reactionism, the invocation of notions like myth, destiny, will, which Enlightenment thought had presumed to replace by the explanatory categories familiar from nineteenth- and twentieth-century social theory. Through invoking those notions, the reactionary modernists were also able to see their own age as modern in more than the obvious sense, a technological age in which the driving force of history, a will evident in the 'waxing and waning' of cultural forms, is realised or completely expressed as never before. Hence, since this will is also the essence of human being, it is an age to which, were there any choice in the matter, the people who live in it should feel obliged to conform.

Adorno on Disenchantment: The Scepticism of Enlightened Reason

JAY BERNSTEIN

T. W. Adorno's and Max Horkheimer's *Dialectic of Enlightenment* is fifty years old. Its disconcerting darkness now seems so bound to the time of its writing, one may well wonder if we have anything to learn from it. Are its main lines of argument relevant to our social and philosophical world? Are the losses it records losses we can still recognise as our own?

Let me begin my re-evaluation indirectly, by citing a passage from Adorno's *Minima Moralia*, a book of aphoristic fragments whose composition overlapped in part with the writing of *Dialectic of Enlightenment*. The subtitle of *Minima Moralia* is *Reflections from Damaged Life*; one can thus consider its fragmentary form a consequence of the fact that our ethical life is somehow damaged, damaged in such a way that the traditional work of the philosopher, teaching what the good life for man should be, is no longer possible – a thesis which has become part of our present philosophical culture through the writings of Alasdair MacIntyre and Bernard Williams.[1] Adorno's take on this situation is significantly different from theirs. Speaking of the man who 'conforms his reactions to social reality', rather than myopically attuning them to private existence, Adorno says:

> Where civilisation as self-preservation does not force on him civilisation as humanity, he gives free rein to his fury against the latter, and refutes his own ideology of home, family and community. It is this that is combated by micrological myopia. It detects in the formless familiarity and slackness a mere pretext for violence, a show of being nice in order to be nasty to our heart's desire. It subjects the intimate sphere to critical scrutiny because *intimacies estrange, violate the imponderably delicate aura of the other which is his condition as subject. Only by the recognition of distance in our neighbour is strangeness alleviated: accepted into consciousness.* The presumption of undiminished nearness present from the first, however, the flat denial of strangeness, does the

[1] Alasdair MacIntyre, *After Virtue* (Notre Dame: University of Notre Dame Press, 1981); Bernard Williams, *Ethics and the Limits of Philosophy* (London: Fontana Press/Collins, 1985).

other supreme wrong, virtually negates him as a particular human being and therefore the humanity in him, 'counts him in', incorporates him in the inventory of property. Wherever immediateness posits and entrenches itself, the bad mediateness of society [as self-preservation only] is insidiously asserted. The cause of immediacy is now espoused only by the most circumspect reflection. This is tested on the smallest scale.[2]

For now civilisation as self-preservation can still force on individuals the rules and regularities of civilisation as humanity, permitting the further (Marxian and/or Nietzschean) suggestion that perhaps the force of moral humanity has always been held in place by its consonance with civilisation as self-preservation, that what we think of as morality has been in league with, underwritten and supported by, the human pursuit of instrumental ends. So long as the two civilisations harmonised, then the espousal of humanity aided the ends of the individual and no decision between the two was necessary; they are 'two' civilisations only in retrospect. Only when the two civilisations are sundered can it appear, as it did to Hobbes, that the goods of humanity are themselves illusory existences until understood as instruments for furthering individual self-interest.

What Adorno's approach intends to reveal, or, better, to insinuate, is the categorial inadequacy of the naturalistic and instrumental framework in the newly won immediacies of the intimate sphere. The intimacies that estrange are, finally, the intimacies of Hobbesian man, natural man, at home. These 'violated' intimacies rehearse the inversion whereby, for example, one loves for the sake of personal gratification, egoistically, and thereby betrays and forfeits the good of love. In opposition to the claims of immediate feelings, desires, wants, and needs Adorno asserts, almost as a counterpoint and with apparently nothing but the justness of its rhetorical dissonance to support him, the *claim* of distance: the 'other's delicate aura' which is his 'condition as subject'. What is this imponderability? Is it essential or only contingent? And why employ a term like 'aura' in this context? Is it meant to adumbrate the return of a religious outlook? Above all, why claim that this aura is the individual's 'condition' as subject?

The contrast Adorno is drawing out in this passage is a familiar one: it is the distinction between seeing and treating another as an end in him- or herself, and treating him or her as a means, a piece of property. But at least here Adorno is giving this familiar Kantian distinction a perceptual or experiential or phenomenological slant:

[2] *Minima Moralia: Reflections from Damaged Life*, translated by E.F.N. Jephcott (London: NLB, 1974), p. 182; emphasis mine.

the other's condition of being an end is given through her aura. Without being here able to even begin elaborating Adorno's understanding of aura, I can none the less note that even Kantians draw on some version of it when attempting to explicate deontological reasons for action. For example, Christine Korsgaard comments: 'It is the particular badness of treating someone as a means that explains the badness of deontological reasons. It is the horribleness of looking into a pair of human eyes, while treating their owner like a piece of furniture or tool.'[3] How are we to make intelligible to ourselves the precise 'horribleness' of looking into a pair of human eyes and yet treating their owner as a thing to be used? What sort of 'looking' is this? And those eyes, they are looking back at us and yet, somehow, are not seen, they are ignored, crushed in their plea or defiance, their vulnerability and reproach. For Adorno, this exchange of looks, of seeing and not seeing, of being seen and disregarding that seeing, is very near the centre of the intelligibility of ethical life; unless the 'horribleness' of this scene can be or become intelligible (in principle) the ethical as such will be lost to us.

As Adorno conceives of it, our world is riven with the horribleness of this scene; the same deformations to social practice that generate the aporiai of ethical life that are tracked throughout *Minima Moralia* simultaneously infect our experience of others: their aura decays, the look they return is unseen, or even worse, their eyes no longer look back at us because they no longer possess any moral uniqueness. (The epitome of the absence of aura, the place of its utter vanquishment, is for Adorno Auschwitz.) The moral substance of individuals has disappeared with the transformations of the practices that supported and gave point to it. In the terms of the development of reason Adorno and Horkheimer offer in *Dialectic of Enlightenment*, this can be stated as the thesis that the perceptual experience of others, the experience of their aura, as a consequence of the rationalisation of our dominant institutions became, at best and for as long as they last, deontological reasons, that is, it became the reflective question of rules or the constraints on rules for treating others as ends in themselves. Which is not to claim that whatever was or may be significant in perceiving the aura of another is a matter of simple or direct perception, a raw experience beyond all conceptualisation, rules, or norms. Aura could not decay, evaporate, or wither if that were the case. The disenchantment of the world, its rationalisation, among other consequences, drains persons and things of their auratic particularity and thereby transforms questions of value *into reflective ones* concerning the character and status of rules (reasons) for action.

[3] Christine M. Korsgaard, *Creating the Kingdom of Ends* (Cambridge University Press, 1996), p. 297.

Jay Bernstein

In *Dialectic of Enlightenment* Adorno and Horkheimer provide a genealogy of modern enlightened reason that seeks to demonstrate, first, that it is through and through a form of instrumental reason, and, secondly, that this formation of reason now structures the dominant practices of social life. This work thus provides Adorno and Horkheimer's version of the Weberian account of the disenchantment of the world through intellectualism, and modern society's becoming an 'iron cage'. Since the writing of *Dialectic of Enlightenment* partially overlaps the writing of *Minima Moralia*, it is reasonable to assume that the theoretical framework of the former structures the aporetic account of ethical life in the latter. The 'dialectic of enlightenment', which at least in one of its construals refers to the rationalisation of reason, is thus responsible for the destruction of auratic individuality.

In this essay I want to examine the focal argument of *Dialectic of Enlightenment*, namely, that enlightened reason is instrumental and instrumental reason is inherently negative and critical, and therefore sceptical; and further, finally, that the precise character of that scepticism converges all too well with the disappearance of auratic individuality. In forwarding these claims, I will need to concede that the conceptual resources deployed by Adorno and Horkheimer are not sufficient for their purposes. However, I will want to suggest that the argument does possess a prima facie plausibility, and its inadequacies are those of incompleteness – a working with too large a brush – rather than straightforward falsity.

My paper will have three main parts: first, an inventory of the elements of enlightened or rationalised reason; second, an account of the conceptual underpinning of those elements; and, finally, a demonstration that the underpinning makes enlightened reason necessarily sceptical and irrational.

I Disenchantment, rationalism, universalism, and self-sufficiency

> Liberation from superstition is called *enlightenment* ...
> it must be very difficult to preserve or instil in someone's way
> of thinking (especially the public's) that merely negative element
> which constitutes enlightenment proper. (Kant)

The process of disintegration implied by Adorno's account of the decay of aura projects an historical movement from ethical life lived in terms of a complex of practices expressive of a conception of the good life for man to its being supported by some anchoring first principles ideally susceptible to *a priori* theoretical legitimation. For

Adorno the relation between these two ideal type ethical situations is one of cause and effect: the disintegration of pre-modern *Sittlichkeit* engenders theoretical reflection in search of *a priori* foundations, which search itself then contributes to the further disintegration of ethical life and a further rationalising of reason. If once it was the case that rational reflection on ethical life meant its codification or harmonisation with some privileged, canonical texts, it has since become the attempt to ground *a priori* or found the moral point of view, to give it pertinence and significance apart from the contingencies of communal practice. Modern moral rationalism transforms ethical reflection into moral theory.

Historically, three pressures converged to make the search for rational foundations for morality necessary and intelligible. The first pressure was the explosive emergence of natural science. Its mathematical, quantitative depiction of the world challenged the view that ethical predicates could be descriptive. Once it was conceded, for example, that colour predicates (as exemplars of secondary qualities) do not refer to anything that is mimetically like red sensory impressions and that the look of the visible is in fact a product of the action of invisible particles on our sensory apparatus, then there could be no hope that predicates like 'cruel' or 'generous' referred to real properties of worldly events like actions. Secondly, and directly continuous with this, there developed the privilege of reason-giving or theoretical justification itself. If the truth of canonical texts could be challenged by a theoretical physics resting on axiomatic first principles, there was no reason to believe the truth-claims on moral issues of canonical texts (and the traditionalist practices they supported) were any firmer. It thus became urgent to supply non-conventionally or non-traditionally backed reasons for the existence of any moral norm or practice, and ideally to propound a conception of moral truths and moral reasoning that would operate on analogy with mathematical or logical reasoning. Finally, the growth of religious, economic, and political individualism within a world in which the first two pressures were already operative stripped the last remnants of legitimacy from the belief that social roles constituted the moral substance of persons. When this new individualism was harnessed with the new rationalism of moral theory, it generated, with the backing of previous Christian thought, a demand for universalism as the 'flip-side' of individualism.[4]

[4] 'The idealising supposition of a universalistic form of life, in which everyone can take up the perspective of everyone else and can count on reciprocal recognition by everybody, makes it possible for indivduated beings to exist within a community – individualism as the flip-side of universalism.' Jürgen Habermas, *Postmetaphysical Thinking: Philosophical Essays*, translated by William Mark Hohengarten (Oxford: Polity Press, 1992), p. 186.

Jay Bernstein

Disenchantment (of the natural world), *rationalism* (the demand for theoretical justification) as the rationalisation of reason, and *universalism* as the flip-side of *individualism* converge to instigate the belief that morality could be salvaged only by *a priori* argumentation since, clearly, no socially constituted or factual evidence could be shown to be legitimate against these characterisations of the world and demands on reflection.[5]

So, for example, a contemporary moral philosopher, Jürgen Habermas, potently condenses the experience of the historical collapse of ethical life into moral reflection and theory into the image of the phase of adolescence concentrated into a single moment of time in which the adolescent adopts, for the first time, a hypothetical attitude 'towards the normative contexts of his life-world which enables him to see through everything unmercifully'. Under his unmerciful gaze, the world he has unproblematically inhabited is 'suddenly deracinated, stripped of its natural validity',[6] it becomes a disenchanted world. If this adolescent is to avoid returning to the prejudices of the community he must reconstruct his world by distinguishing between norms that are factually held from those that deserve to be held. Ultimately, Habermas argues, he will come to recognise that there remains *only* the idealised procedures of rational argumentation itself (Habermas' intersubjective and communicational version of Kant's formula of universal law) that can be rationally and motivationally satisfying. Rationalism is thus the necessary and ideal response to the experience of disenchantment.

When measured against the moral actions of everyday life, the change of attitude which discourse ethics with respect to the procedure it singles out (i.e. the transition to argument) retains something unnatural; it signifies a break with the naivety of spontaneously held validity claims upon whose intersubjective recognition the communicative practice of everyday life depends. This unnaturalness is like an echo of that developmental catastrophe which the devaluation of the world of tradition signifies histori-

[5] This is a massively idealising account of the emergence of moral modernity since it ignores the sceptical and naturalistic responses to the identified pressures. For one version of this complex story see Stephen Darwall, *The British Moralists and the Internal 'Ought' 1640–1740* (Cambridge University Press, 1995).

[6] Jürgen Habermas, *Moral Consciousness and Communicative Action*, translated by Christian Lenhardt and Shierry Weber Nicholsen (Cambridge, MA: MIT Press, 1990), pp. 126–7. In concentrating enlightenment into the phase of adolescence, Habermas is picking up Kant's statement that 'Enlightenment is mankind's exit from its self-incurred immaturity.'

cally – and which is what prompts us to attempt *a reconstruction on a higher plane.*[7]

Habermas' adolescent discovers that the only thing that is reliable is rational argumentation itself just as the Kantian agent discovers that the only thing rationally reliable is the procedure for maxim testing. But by making unperturable reliability central, the adolescent finds himself cut-off from the contingencies that constituted the possibilities of ethical experience for him and those around him. 'Reconstruction on a higher plane' is precisely the movement from experience into theory; in conceiving of reflection as argumentation governed by *a priori* rules both arguer and norms lose their cultural-historical place, the urgencies of the present and the weight of

---

[7] Ibid.; italics mine. Habermas' theory possesses two aspects: a conception of the pragmatic presuppositions of communicative interaction, and an associated moral principle. Consensual speech acts, he contends, rest on a background consensus which is formed from the implicit mutual recognition of four validity claims: (i) that what is said be linguistically intelligible and comprehensible; (ii) that the propositional content or the existential presuppositions of what is said be true; (iii) that the speaker be truthful (honest or sincere) in what she says; (iv) that what the speaker says (and hence does) is right or appropriate in the light of existing norms and values. Habermas' universalisation principle (U), is meant to provide a rule for the impartial testing of norms for their moral worthiness. It states that a norm is valid only if: 'All affected can accept the consequences and the side effects its general observation can be anticipated to have for the satisfaction of everyone's interests (and these consequences are preferred to those of known alternative possibilities)' (p. 65).
It is not to the point to here rehearse in detail objections to Habermas' proposal; for this see my *Recovering Ethical Life: Jürgen Habermas and the Future of Critical Theory* (London: Routledge, 1995), and Albrecht Wellmer, 'Ethics and Dialogue: Elements of Moral Judgement in Kant and Discourse Ethics', in his *The Persistence of Modernity*, translated by David Midgley (Oxford: Polity Press, 1991), pp. 113–256. Three objections, all of which circulate around the problem of rationalised reason and its abstraction from the concreteness of ethical experience, are worth mentioning at this juncture. First, Habermas makes an error that Kant also makes, namely, conflating norms of rationality (which are norms for argumentation in Habermas' case) with moral norms. As Wellmer nicely states the point, 'obligations to rationality are concerned with arguments regardless of who voices them, whereas moral obligations are concerned with people regardless of their arguments' (p. 185; and see also p. 187). Secondly, Habermas is unable to close the gap between norms that have been found intersubjectively valid and those that are true. Thirdly, by its attention to the validity of norms, discourse ethics conceives of normative validity as independent from application, and thereby displaces ethical knowledge from knowledge had *through* ethical concepts to knowledge *about* ethical concepts.

memory: 'discourse generalises, abstracts, and stretches the presuppositions of context-bound communicative actions by extending their range to include competent subjects beyond the provincial limits of their own particular form of life'.[8] As Habermas thus concedes, because rationalised moral theory de-contextualises, it inevitably demotivates as well.

Finally, the consequence of the interaction of sceptical disenchantment, the rationalism of reconstructing morality on a higher plane, and universalism is the production of the isolated individual, on the one hand, and, on the other, the discovery that there '*are no shared structures preceding the individual except the universals of language use*',[9] just as there are no moral norms preceding the Kantian moral subject except those of reason itself. Hence, the combination of disenchantment, rationalism, and universalism entail that enlightened reason be autonomous and self-sufficient. On this account, the critical gaze of the enlightenment subject marks a movement from a complexity of beliefs binding subjects to one another and their objects to reason itself; the only stable objects for rationalised, enlightened reason are its own norms and procedures. Hence, under the 'moralising gaze' of the rationalised moral subject the ethical totality loses its 'quality of naïve acceptance, and the normative power of the factual [is] weakened'.[10] We should include within the scope of the normative power of the factual the eyes, now deadened, of the once auratic individual.

The identification of disenchantment, rationalism as the form of the rationalisation of reason, universalism, and self-sufficiency as fundamental elements of and ingredients in the evolution of modern moral thought is meant to be a relatively benign and neutral characterisation. Habermas, for one, grants them. Adorno and Horkheimer's *Dialectic of Enlightenment* can be conceived of as possessing two interlocking analytical motives: first, to explain the profound inner unity of these elements of enlightened reason through the elaboration of their joint conceptual presuppositions; and, secondly, to demonstrate how those same conceptual presuppositions explain the dual character of enlightened thought as simultaneously progressive and disintegrating. As stated this second claim is ambiguous since even Kant is content to characterise enlightenment as critical and negative, as a work of 'desecration'.[11]

[8] *Moral Consciousness and Communicative Action*, p. 202.

[9] Ibid., p. 203; emphasis mine.

[10] Ibid., p. 108.

[11] Rüdiger Bittner, 'What is Enlightenment?' in James Schmidt (ed.), *What is Enlightenment? Eighteenth-Century Answers and Twentieth-Century Questions* (London: University of California Press, 1996), p. 352.

Calling enlightened thought disintegrating involves a stronger thesis, namely, that the formation of reason that eventuates from the process of enlightenment is partly constituted by the negativity from which it evolves; which is to claim that enlightened reason is intrinsically sceptical. Enlightened reason cannot shake off or eliminate from itself the negativity that permits it to accomplish its fundamental tasks of disenchantment, desecration, rationalisation, and universalisation.

II The principle of immanence

If this characterisation of enlightened reason is accurate, then in the first instance what is required is a critical explanation of why the process of enlightenment produces a rationalisation of reason that leads it to claiming self-sufficiency, and why self-sufficient reason is sceptical. Notoriously, Adorno and Horkheimer claim that enlightened reason is instrumental reason, the constituting action of which is abstraction and the consequent identifying and subsuming of different particulars under some common universal (concept or law), and that the sceptical negativity of instrumental reason is carried through by its work of abstraction and subsumption. It would be perverse in the extreme to flatly assert that instrumental rationality is intrinsically sceptical; nor is this what Adorno and Horkheimer say. Rather, they claim that enlightened reason and rationality as a whole are only instrumental, and that the scepticism of instrumental rationality only occurs when it claims to be and/or becomes total and self-sufficient. And while this thesis might sound anodyne, it is not since the claim to totality and self-sufficiency is not accidental but rather a consequence of the essential negativity of instrumental reason; enlightening critique necessarily includes other formations of reason amongst its critical targets. Rationalisation is necessarily the rationalisation of reason; rationalised reason is sceptical, and because sceptical thereby irrational. If it is the self-sufficiency of instrumental reason that renders it sceptical, and the claim to self-sufficiency intrinsic to its movement, form of claiming, and formation, then this would explain how and why our highest value, critical reason, devaluates itself.

It is tempting to read *Dialectic of Enlightenment* as telling a counter-history to the progressive, demythologising philosophy of history provided by writers like Kant and Habermas. And there are passages of *Dialectic of Enlightenment* that sound as if it were proposing such a regressive philosophy of history.

Jay Bernstein

Mythology itself set off the unending process of enlightenment in which ever and again, with the inevitability of necessity, every specific theoretic view succumbs to destructive criticism that it is only belief, until even the very notion of spirit, of truth and, indeed, enlightenment itself have become animistic magic. The principle of fateful necessity which brings low the heroes of myth and derives as a logical consequence from the pronouncement of the oracles, does not merely, when refined to the stringency of formal logic, rule in every rationalistic system of Western philosophy, but itself dominates the series of systems which begins with the hierarchy of gods and, in a permanent twilight of the idols, hands down an identical content: anger against insufficient righteousness. Just as myths already realise enlightenment, so enlightenment with every step becomes more deeply engulfed in mythology. It receives all matter from myths, in order to destroy them; and even as judge it comes under the mythic curse. (DoE, 11–12)[12]

This passage does not represent a turn to the philosophy of history in order to unseat an intransigent abstract rationalism. Rather, the historical endpoints inscribed in it are dictated by the enlightenment conception of reason itself: it opposes myth. What appears as a developmental history to Habermas and Kant is thus dependent upon a structural or conceptual dualism: enlightenment versus myth. The mythic dominated origin of culture and civilisation is a posit of enlightenment rationality itself (DoE, 8). This posit raises a wholly *conceptual* question: what are the logical parameters of myth and enlightenment which could explain how the project of overcoming myth, a project that in its self-conscious form is uniquely modern (however much anticipated by Greek philosophy), could eventuate in the nihilistic present? That we should conceive of this conceptual issue historically, as a process of overcoming, is demanded by enlightened reason, whose modern hegemony indeed comes to create the very process it projects on to the historical past. It is the coming-to-be of an historical necessity as project and process postulated by enlightenment philosophies of history, from Bacon and Kant to Marx, that Adorno and Horkheimer are seeking to undo, not by the substitution of a regressive history in place of a progressive one, but by dismantling the conceptual dualism of

[12] All references in the body of this essay to 'DoE' are to: Max Horkheimer and Theodor W. Adorno, *Dialectic of Enlightenment*, translated by John Cumming (London: Allen Lane, 1973). For the sake of accuracy, I have routinely modified Cumming's translation.

enlightenment and myth, and thereby the idea of history it grounds.[13]

It is because enlightenment has so demonstrably failed to realise its fundamental aims and ideas that Adorno and Horkheimer turn in the third sentence of the text to its actual 'programme': enlightenment understands itself as progressive demythologisation, 'the disenchantment of the world. [T]he dissolution of myths and the ruin of fancy through knowledge' (DoE, 3). Myths as conceived of by enlightenment are a function of anthropomorphism – the projection on to nature of what is merely subjective. Because some mythic claims really were illusory and were a function uncontrolled and naïve anthropomorphism, the programmatic and methodological negativity of enlightenment is not groundless. None the less, it is this programme, so defined, that is the critical object of Adorno and Horkheimer's analysis; there has been a mismatch between the aims and ideals of enlightenment, and its method of progressive demythologisation. Progressive demythologisation has yielded disenchantment but not liberation. *Dialectic of Enlightenment* rejects the conceptual dualism of enlightenment and myth upon which the project of progressive demythologisation relies: 'already myth is enlightenment, and: enlightenment reverts to mythology' (DoE, xvi). The 'already' and the 'reverts' indicate that myth and enlightenment are being speculatively identified: myth contains a central moment of enlightenment and therefore is not its opposite; and

[13] In pursuing this project they were patently following the lead of Walter Benjamin's 'Theses on the Concept of History', which had insisted that 'there is no document of civilisation which is not at the same time a document of barbarism' (*Illuminations*, p. 258) and that by reifying the entwined process of civilisation and barbarism into a progressive philosophy of history the barbarism of civilisation is ideologically legitimated – it is part of the cost of progress – permitting the process it signifies to continue unabated. Again, the entwinement of civilisation and barbarism is not a thesis an enlightenment thinker need deny; nor that the costs of progress should be remembered. Benjamin's contention can only have force if he can demonstrate that barbarism is not an accidental accretion but intrinsic. But how could barbarism be intrinsic to reason? For Benjamin the answer to this question is that progressive philosophies of history, in virtue of conceiving of history in wholly teleological terms, must regard each present as only a means to the posited end, and thus can deny it significance in itself. And while this is pointed against historicism and strongly teleological theories, it does not touch the breadth of modern, enlightened rationality. Horkheimer and Adorno translate Benjamin's thesis into a narrower conceptual thesis; in place of barbarism they put instrumentality and scepticism. It is the effects of these features of enlightened reason which explain the entwinement of civilisation and barbarism.

Jay Bernstein

enlightenment, in reifying itself against myth, falls prey to a fundamentally mythic principle.

The constitutive principle of mythic thought is the *principle of immanence*: 'the explanation of every event as repetition' (DoE, 12). It is the principle of immanence – what Adorno will later call 'identity thinking' – that is the join between myth and enlightenment; equally, it is the hinge connecting rationality and instrumentality. The principle of immanence turns on a series of familiar platitudes: an item (object, event, property, etc.) is neither known nor explained by giving it a proper name; rather, an empirical item is recognised , and so cognised, only when it is classified in some way, when it is shown, via subsumption, to share characteristics or features with other items. Analogously, and by extension, an event is explained if it can be shown to fall within the ambit of a known pattern of occurrence, if it falls within the ambit of a known rule or is deducible from (subsumable by) a known law. What holds for empirical items equally holds for the concepts, rules, and laws that classify and explain them: they become cognised, rationalised, when subsumed under or shown to be deducible from higher-level concepts, rules, or laws.

The work of classification, subsumption, explanation, deduction each permit the item in question to be detached from its immediate sensory impact on the cognising subject: classification and explanation negate immediacy and thereby objectify experience. Only when an item is objectified, detached from the subjective states which its presence gives rise to, can it be manipulated and controlled. Conceptualisation accomplishes the minimum of objectification necessary for cognition. But since many, if not most ordinary empirical concepts classify objects (properties and events) merely in accordance with their phenomenological appearance to subjects, not all empirical concepts are robustly objective or permit manipulation and control. Hence, minimal conceptualisation or subsumption is insufficient for the sort of objectivity necessary to defeat the operation of anthropomorphic projection. What is truly objective, out there, must be what can be maximally or ideally detached from the attitudinal effects it produces. But a subject matter is most compellingly detachable from the attitudinal effects to which it gives rise if 'citing the kinds of states of affairs with which it deals is potentially contributive to the explanation of things *other than,* or *other than via,* our being in attitudinal states which take such states of affairs as object'.[14] Although the idea of strong objectivity as involv-

[14] Crispin Wright, *Truth and Objectivity* (London: Harvard University Press, 1992), p. 196. What makes an explanation good, Wright is contending, is its possessing 'a wide cosmological role'. Wright contends, plausibly enough, that moral facts are unable to play a wide cosmological role (pp. 197–8).

ing a 'wider range of intelligible and legitimate uses of the relevant' subject matter cited than its role in explaining the state of a subject does not restrict such objectivity to either explanatory contexts or, within those 'discourses dealing with causally active states of affairs', explanatory contexts dealing with causally active states of affairs are, arguably, paradigm cases of such objectivity.[15]

Disenchantment is the extirpation of what is subjective, or, as expressed in a formulation I will come back to, 'the extirpation of animism' (DoE, 5). Disenchantment progresses through the operation of the two dominant, albeit logically distinct, features of the platitudinous principle of immanence: reiterability and instrumentality. If an item is cognised by being subsumed under a concept, rule, or law, that concept, rule, or law is further cognised by being subsumed under a more general concept, rule, or law. Cognition is subsumption, subsumption is necessarily reiterable, and reiteration occurs through cognitive ascent from concrete to abstract, from particular to universal, from what is relatively universal to what is more universal. If subsumption is a necessary condition for objectification, and objectification a necessary condition for manipulation, then what provides for greater objectivity, a further detachment from subjectivity, ideally provides for greater control and manipulability.

Here are some indicative passages from Horkheimer and Adorno elaborating the principle of immanence as reiterative subsumption and instrumentality.

> There is no difference between the totemic animal, the dreams of the ghost-seer, and the absolute idea. On the road to modern science, men renounce any claim to meaning. They substitute formula for concept, rule and probability for cause. (DoE, 5)
> ... the Enlightenment recognises as being and event only what can be grasped in unity: its ideal is the system from which all and everything follows. The rationalist and empiricist versions do not differ on that. Even though the individual schools may interpret the axioms differently, the structure of scientific unity has always been the same. ... The multiplicity of forms is reduced to position and arrangement, history to fact, things to matter. (DoE, 7)
> To the Enlightenment, that which does not reduce to numbers, and ultimately to the one, becomes illusion; modern positivism writes it off as literature. Unity is the slogan from Parmenides to Russell. The destruction of gods and qualities alike is insisted upon. (DoE, 7–8)

The platitudes of the principle of immanence – subsumption, reit-

[15] Ibid., p. 198.

erability, and instrumentality – are sufficient to explain the disenchantment of the world and its ramified consequences for even the most minimal forms of anthropomorphism. Since subsumption on its own is logically compatible with anthropomorphism, the negativity of the principle of immanence must be accomplished through the co-operation of reiteration and instrumentality. Logically, reiteration, the cognitive ascent to more embracing forms of unification, is the methodological activation of the normative element of subsumption: if collection of the diverse under the one objectifies the diverse, then higher-level acts of unification are more objective. We realise or make actual the normative presupposition of subsumption through reiteration. What provides for objectivity is rational; hence, cognitive ascent is intrinsically rational. In fact, however, by itself reiteration will not put an end to anthropomorphism; gods can be principles of unity just as well as laws or theories, and the positing of ever-more abstract gods was certainly intended as an effort at an anti-anthropomorphic rationalisation of experience. Since gods can be and usually are causally active explainers, then what causally explains plausibly can be regarded as a component of the principle of reiteration itself, part of what gives reiteration its cognitive bite. Instrumentality shifts the idea of causal explanation from the wholly contemplative, which still lets the gods in, to the interventionist; only those ascents that provide for increased predictive power and potential control over natural events truly escape from the anthropomorphic web. Thus the reiterative operation of subsumptive thinking generates an emphatic pull toward rationalisation, universalism, and the self-sufficiency of reason which becomes fully or properly disenchanting only when reiteration is harnessed to instrumentality. The platitudes of the principle of immanence are thus sufficient to explain how disenchantment, rationalisation, universalism, and self-sufficiency becomes constitutive features of enlightened reason.[16]

[16] It follows from the argument of this section that Adorno and Horkheimer do not equate instrumental reason with means–ends reasoning. Rather instrumental reason is defined in terms of the principle of immanence; hence, for them formal logic would count as instrumental reasoning. The justification for employing the notion of instrumental reason to cover whatever falls under the principle of immanence is that the latter is conceived of as the rational expression of the drive for self-preservation, and that drive is the original motive for adopting it. It is thus the genealogical origin of the principle of immanence that reveals its functional or instrumental character. Equally, although it is not a matter I will take up here, because the principle of immanence is grounded in the drive for self-preservation its domination over other (potential) forms of rationality is thought by Adorno and Horkheimer as the domination of nature over culture.

III Enlightenment depends on myth

For Adorno and Horkheimer enlightenment refers not to an historical epoch but to 'a series of related intellectual and practical operations which are presented as demythologising, secularising, or disenchanting some mythical, religious or magical representation of the world'.[17] Their identification of the principle of immanence with instrumental reasoning is intended as an *explanation* of one of the cognitive achievements of mythic thought – how myths helped conquer fear by giving terrifying events an intelligible structure as recurring events within a cyclically structured natural world; thereby providing for a potential linkage between enlightenment and myth: 'Myth intended report, naming, the narration of the beginning; but also presentation, confirmation, explanation ...' (DoE, 8). Myth is indifferently or indiscriminately authoritative narration and instrumental knowledge. To say myth indifferently contained these two aspects is to suggest that they were not clearly differentiated within mythic telling; hence the modern question whether myth and ritual were proto-science, or 'religious' representations enabling the acknowledgement of what could not be controlled presses for a cognitive discrimination wholly extrinsic to myth. The syntax of myth appears to use as an interweaving of narration and explanation, meaning and cause, and since there are no grounds short of enlightened reason's own sharp, evaluative discrimination of the cognitive difference and worth of the two, it must be presumed that myth contains both. Further, because the mythic world was cyclical and ahistorical in character, the principle of myth as a whole was the principle of immanence – even mythic narration cognised events as repetitions of older events. While myth was always more than this principle, in being authoritative narration, it was the principle of immanence that was picked up and exploited by enlightenment. Yet that development would not have occurred without the modern conceptual dualism between myth and enlightenment – identificatory or subsumptive thinking was not, after all, exhaustive of mythic conceptuality.

Enlightenment defines itself in opposition to myth, which is to claim that enlightenment is, in accordance with its own original understanding, *essentially critique*, without a positive content of its own and receiving 'all its matter' from myth.[18] *The sceptical premise of enlightenment is its constitution as the abstract (because indefinite)*

[17] Simon Jarvis, *Adorno: A Critical Introduction* (Oxford: Polity Press, 1998), p. 24.
[18] This definition is defended by Bittner in his 'What is Enlightenment?', *op cit*. The proximate origin of Adorno and

negation of myth. While in the first instance enlightenment took the basic principle of myth to be anthropomorphism, 'the projection onto nature of the subjective' (DoE, 6), since neither the notion of projection nor that of subjective was defined, then neither was myth; hence there existed no natural terminus to critique short of the principles of reason and critique making it possible. What began with the critique of religion and the removal of the gods is carried through in the disappearance of values and secondary qualities (DoE, 8). But that is too mild a statement. If what counts *as* projection and *as* subjective are not defined, and if enlightenment is critique, then in the final analysis, at the end of the negative process, the process of negation, the human itself, and hence truth and enlightenment themselves, cannot be protected from coming to be regarded as also myths and projections.

Trivially, reiterative cognitive ascent and sceptical critique are the same process looked at from different angles. Sceptical critique, in seeing in each objective configuration something still too subjective, still too bound to the subjective affects to which gives rise to, seeks items with a wider cosmological role, and in seeking for items with a wider cosmological role it performs the operations of reiterative cognitive ascent. The final picture of a disenchanted world is projected by the presupposition that the human is a projecting animal caught in the mirror of itself, hence the 'true' world is a world without the human, the human becoming only a distorting perspective on a world wholly and forever independent of it. The perfection of enlightenment scepticism is, exactly, one which surmounts the human and leaves it behind, a perspectival take on a world without perspective, a view from nowhere (which, of course, cannot be a 'view' at all).[19]

Enlightenment and myth contain, at least, a double signification. Enlightenment is (i) positively, the overcoming of fear and the establishment of sovereignty; and (ii) methodologically and formally, a negativity with respect to all contents. (ii) is the means for real-

---

[19] See Thomas Nagel, *The View from Nowhere* (Oxford University Press, 1986), chapter 5.

Horkheimer's characterisation of enlightenment as critique and pure negativity is the Enlightenment chapter of Hegel's *Phenomenology of Spirit*, translated by A.V. Miller (Oxford: Clarendon Press, 1977), especially pp. 328–49, where 'pure insight', relentless negativity, opposes itself to 'pure faith', blind trust (p. 334). Trust here is blind because Enlightenment can only affirm itself, reason affirm itself, through its lack of trust. Proleptically, trust can be regarded as a figure for what rationalised reason excises from itself.

ising (i). Myth is hence (i) substantively, the dogmatic (because mimetic) and subsumptive (cyclical) presentation (narration) of content; and (ii) formally, that content itself, the indeterminate object of critique. Myth in sense (i) is already enlightenment in sense (i); while enlightenment in sense (ii) reverts to myth in sense (i). Enlightenment so reverts because it has no space for myth in sense (ii): all presumptive content is a projection. What is to count as myth at any juncture is defined formally as what remains outside the reach of progressive negation. It is for this reason that 'the very notions of spirit, of truth, and, indeed, enlightenment itself become animistic magic', mere beliefs, more anthropomorphic illusions; or, in a similar vein, enlightenment 'treats its own idea of human rights exactly as it does the old [Platonic] universals' (DoE, 6). It is not, of course, the negativity of enlightenment which is its reversion to myth, but the dogmatic consequence of reiterative cognitive ascent: 'The world as a gigantic analytic judgement, the only one left over from all the dreams of science, is of the same mold as the cosmic myth which associated the cycle of spring and autumn with the kidnapping of Persephone' (DoE, 27). Hence the conclusion: 'The absorption of factuality, whether in legendary prehistory or into mathematical formalism ... makes the new appear as the predetermined, which is accordingly old' (ibid.). Reiterative cognitive ascent, as requiring explanation through items with a wide cosmological role, necessarily entails weakening the normative power of the factual.

The dialectical entwinement of enlightenment and myth is dependent upon their mutual formation because mutual dependency in sense (ii) of each: critique is always of an indeterminate content. Enlightenment as the pure light of reason, whose purity is constituted through its negative self-definition, and hence in its constitution through the practice of abstract negation, needs and *depends* upon myth in sense (ii) as the material condition of its processive self-affirmation. Structurally, enlightenment instrumentalises the object of critique for the sake of its own self-possession and self-affirmation: each successful critical encounter further legitimates enlightenment's scepticism and rationalism. Because myth (ii) material remains material-to-be-negated, indeterminate stuff for the light of reason to shine upon, then the progressive marriage of enlightenment and myth is the dissolution of both: enlightenment into abstract, self-sufficient reason and myth into a meaningless world – events and practices as only instances of natural law. Reiterative cognitive ascent and disenchantment as demythologisation are, again, the same effort of reason seen from competing perspectives; from the perspective of reiterative cognitive ascent, enlightenment reverts to mythic stasis, e.g., the laws of pure reason,

Jay Bernstein

the universals of language use, the method and/or laws of natural science; from the perspective of progressive demythologisation the negativity of reason overtakes all the objects it forms along the way, including itself. Reiterative cognitive ascent progresses toward the self-sufficiency of reason in relation to any content; while sceptical demythologisation progresses toward the autonomy of the will, pure will, will to power. It is the claim to self-sufficiency of reason or will in relation to any content, the inability of enlightened reason to avow its material conditions of operation, that demonstrate that its *scepticism* is equally a form of *irrationality*.

The contention that rationalised reason is intrinsically sceptical – because without an intrinsic end or purpose, and reflectively bound to dissolving its own meaning and worth – does go some of the way toward de-legitimating 'the modern version of independent theoretical curiosity, utility, self-knowledge, progress in research, and so on'.[20] However, the charge of scepticism by itself could, conceivably, leave enlightened reason in the aporetic predicament which Nietzsche and Weber, for instance, placed it, that is, as truly and rightfully being all the reason there is or could be and yet being self-stultifying in its operation. In giving their account of the formation of the self-sufficiency of instrumental reason through the course of its critical endeavours, Adorno and Horkheimer thus continually underline the *dependence* of critique on the objects it seeks to desecrate. If the objects of critique are in some weighty sense a condition of critique that reason cannot avow – they are only occasions for self-affirmation – then enlightened reason is not self-sufficient in the manner it presumes. Enlightenment *depends* on myth, it depends upon the entire range of anthropomorphisms (appearing objects, images, language, social practices, history, and tradition) for the possibility of enacting it sceptical reflections. Without material to negate, there can be no enlightenment; if this is neutral as an historical thesis, it is performatively self-defeating as a characterisation of reason as a whole. *If rationalised reason is constituted essentially by the principle of immanence, then it cannot avow its conditionality.* Enlightened reason's intrinsic claim to independence and self-sufficiency rationally prohibits its from acknowledging its dependency on its objects. The 'dialectic' of enlightenment is a dialectic of claimed independence and disavowed dependence; and thus in the same way in which in Hegel's version of the dialectic of independence and dependence the

[20] The phrase here is from Robert Pippin's critical account of what Hans Blumenberg was attempting to legitimate in his *The Legitimacy of the Modern Age* (Cambridge, MA: MIT Press, 1983): 'Blumenberg and the Modernity Problem', in *Idealism as Modernism: Hegelian Variations* (Cambridge University Press, 1997), p. 283.

master, through and in virtue of his claim to absolute independence, becomes the slave of the slave, so in Adorno and Horkheimer's rationality version of this dialectic enlightenment 'reverts' to myth, to mythic stasis, to the historical inertia of the master.

In brief, the dynamic of rationalisation that Horkheimer and Adorno uncover operates in the following way: some beliefs are discovered to be wholly anthropomorphic, mere projections. Adopting the platitudinous principles of immanence is discovered to be the most effective tool in combating naïve anthropomorphism. As we become increasingly aware of the claims of the principle of immanence, it becomes rational to adopt them as principles of reason in general; which in its turn enables enlightenment to become a generalised critical practice opposing *all* anthropomorphism. Because no beliefs can withstand the dissolvent rationality of enlightened criticism, enlightenment is forced to regard itself as self-sufficient, and as thus incapable of regarding any material conditions as intrinsic to it. In the end we are left with only pure reason (*Wille*) or pure will (*Willkür*).

What makes this argument less than fully satisfactory is its generality: What material *exactly* is it that rationalised reason cannot avow? What are the material conditions of its operation that rationalised reason cannot acknowledge? And what makes Adorno and Horkheimer believe that the material conditions of reason are *intrinsic* to it? There is a looseness of fit in their argument between, on the one hand, the demonstration of the self-defeating nature of reflective rationalisation, and, on the other, the panoply of objects they cite as its defeated victim: anthropomorphic nature, immediacy, tradition, history, particular objects, etc. In the eventual formation of reason Adorno proposes the role of each of these items will require vindication; but if the argument concerning the constitutive dependency of enlightened reason is to be effective, then Adorno and Horkheimer will need to show how reason cannot simply avow but must *contain* these dependent moments as elements of itself. It is the lack of such a demonstration that can make the argumentative strategy of the book appear to contain the *petitio principii* that they admit to in the 'Introduction' (DoE, xiii). If the destructive element of enlightened reason is its relentless negativity, and the critique of enlightenment requires the activation of that same power of reflective negation (DoE, 194–5), then critique is self-stultifying – something which the critics of *Dialectic of Enlightenment* have been eager to insist upon.[21] To state the same point another way: the demon-

---

[21] Jürgen Habermas, *The Philosophical Discourse of Modernity*, translated by Frederick Lawrence (Oxford: Polity Press, 1987), p. 119; and Steven Vogel, *Against Nature: The Concept of Nature in Critical Theory* (Albany, NY: State University of New York Press, 1996), pp. 66–71.

stration that, broadly speaking, some of the objects dissolved in the course of enlightened progress are material conditions for that progress occurring does not, by itself, transform the abstract negations of enlightened reason into the hoped for determinate negations of dialectical reason (DoE, 27). If this diagnosis is correct, then the argument of *Dialectic of Enlightenment* is not false or self-defeating, but simply incomplete.

None the less, however benighted about itself, however irrational and untrue, enlightenment thought is necessarily 'stronger', logically and critically, than whatever might oppose it.[22] We will fail to understand the modern hegemony of enlightened reason and its continuing appeal unless we can comprehend it as actually logically stronger and critically more powerful than any competitor. Enlightened reason possesses the strength of a dogmatic scepticism that shapes itself as the whole of reason. Because what opposes it is either myth, dogma, or argument, it cannot lose.

> Every spiritual resistance [enlightenment] encounters serves merely to increase its strength. Which means that enlightenment still recognises itself even in myths. Whatever myths the resistance may appeal to, by virtue of the fact that they become arguments in the process of opposition, they acknowledge the principle of dissolvent rationality [*zersetzenden Rationalität*] for which they reproach enlightenment. Enlightenment is totalitarian. (DoE, 6)

Enlightenment's rationalised scepticism, scepticism rationalised as reason, secures an abstract, determinate syntax – universalisation, the procedures of communicative rationality, deductive formalism, pure logic, the methodologism of positivistic science – against all, essentially indeterminate semantic claims, say, the kinds of claims that emerge in narrative. Because the latter can only *claim* by giving themselves a syntactic, argumentative shape, then the claims of syntactical reason will always trump what seeks to oppose it – which is what Adorno and Horkheimer meant by the claim that enlightenment is 'anger against insufficient righteousness': no contingent semantic claim is true enough. The trumping power of enlightened reason is 'dissolvent' because it forces claims to declare themselves,

[22] Again, Bittner's 'What is Enlightenment?' draws this conclusion: 'to call superstition what enlightenment fights against is to imply that in any case its opponent is wrong ... Yes, enlightenment is always right against its opponent ...' (p. 351). What Bittner fails to consider in his defence of enlightenment as critique is the formation of reason, the rationalisation of reason, that is a consequence of that practice.

show their righteousness, in syntactic terms alone.[23] In this respect, Habermas's concession that the advance of procedural reason has meant a 'weakening' of the factual is an understatement: 'In myths everything that happens must atone for having happened. And so it is with enlightenment: the fact becomes null and void, and might as well not have happened' (DoE, 12). How can the fact *matter* if, for example, moral sense and meaning is exhausted by its fitness for either universal legislation or rational communicative consensus? Fitness and consensus trump.

It is the weakening of the factual, making its moral meaning dependent upon rules and reasons that derive from reason's own rationalised self-understanding, that vanquishes auratic individuality from *sight*. From here it does not seem untoward to claim that the unmerciful gaze of Habermas' adolescent is just an expression of rationalised reason. Adorno and Horkheimer offer Sade's Juliette as the sceptical fate of the moral reason that takes itself to be truly enlightened. She is a rational demythologiser, bent on employing reason to demonstrate that what has been superstitiously believed is empty, and what has been reviled only superstition. In demythologising the taboo against extreme forms of sexual behaviour she takes seriously the decay of aura that eventuates if one regards others only as aids or obstacles to one's own ends. If Sade's thought-experiments go beyond the organisation of bodies and pleasures, it does so only on the basis of a wholly demythologised conception of others which leads to a scepticism about even instrumental rationality: how much is its validity premised upon the desire for stable conditions for the pursuit of ends, and thus upon risk averseness? Is not the requirement to acknowledge and believe in reason or logic as superstitious as belief in religious commandments and taboos? Because rationalised reason cannot answer these questions without turning against its own principles, attempting to circumscribe and curtail their field of operation, it becomes a short step to the Nietzschean admonition to live dangerously and obey no law except that which one prescribes for oneself (DoE, 99).

[23] In general, the issue of the priority of the abstract over the concrete can be phrased in terms of whether formal logic, it laws are determining for rationality or whether they are dependent upon, simply 'make explicit', the patterns of *material inference* implicit in everyday practices. Adorno's conception of the priority of material inference structures is implicit in his accounts of, for example, essay as opposed to the system, his own 'fragmentary' form of writing, and his notion of constellations. For an analytic defence of the priority of material inference, see Robert B. Brandom, *Making It Explicit: Reasoning, Representing, and Discursive Commitment* (London: Harvard University Press, 1994).

Jay Bernstein

Conclusion

Adorno and Horkheimer contend that what initially appear as two distinct and benign aspects of modern reason are the same reason seen from two different perspectives: enlightening reason which seeks to overcome all myth, where myth is extensionally equivalent to anthropomorphism; and instrumental reason as constituted by the two features of the principle of immanence, subsumptive reiterability, and instrumentality. The operation of enlightening reason initially occurs by means of instrumental reason (myth is already enlightenment), and the hegemony and self-sufficiency of instrumental reason is a consequence of the on-going process of disenchantment (enlightenment reverts to myth). The idea of strong objectivity as involving the priority of items with a wide cosmological role, I claimed, was a perfect exemplar of the convergence between overcoming anthropomorphism, on the one hand, and instrumental reason, on the other. But this convergence should be unsettling since it provides for an unequivocal extirpation of anthropomorphism, of animism.

Adorno's epithet to 'Part One' of *Minima Moralia* is 'Life does not live'. In *Dialectic of Enlightenment*, Adorno and Horkheimer comment: 'The *ratio* [viz., instrumental reason] that supplants mimesis is not simply its counterpart. It is itself mimesis: mimesis of what is dead. The subjective spirit which abolishes animation from nature, can master this inanimate nature only by imitating its rigidity, and abolishing its own animism in turn' (DoE, 57). These passages point to a constellation of issues which our talk of disenchantment, subsumptive reiterability, instrumentality, and the like passes over, namely, that no doubt incoherently but emphatically the distinction between living and non-living is structuring and orienting Adorno's theorising. Adorno's scepticism about moral theory and modern moral reason does not derive from his desire to disparage the attempt to provide rules of reasoning that would tell us what counts as treating a person as a means, a dead thing, and what counts as treating them as an end in themselves, it is that in so far as we think that distinction is *constituted* by those second-order rules and reasons, then the very thing at issue, that it is a living being before us, is necessarily discounted – necessarily because in thinking in this way we are 'abolishing our own animism in turn'.

Again, if paradigmatically the search for objectivity involves searching for items with a wide cosmological role, then objectivity is purchased at the price of eliminating from the repertoire of items that explain our affective states those which are irreducibly anthropocentric. Hence the search for items with the widest possible cosmological role inevitably comes to involve a rational mimesis of what is dead because only items belonging to non-anthropomorphic nature can have a wide cosmological role. The reason which operates with only explanatory natural laws ranging over quantifiable processes or its own abstract principles of organisation internalises the lifelessness of its non-anthropomorphic objects; enlightenment assimilates the animate to the inanimate. Because he believes that rationalised reason has become hegemonic for us, Adorno always approaches the question of living/non-living indirectly, by means of circumspect reflection. Although Adorno does believe that the rationalisation of modern society – bureaucratisation, capital exchange, technology, etc. – tendentially deform social practices so that they are non-responsive to the living/non-living distinction,[24] it is not that which makes his writing so disconcerting. It is rather his overly acute sense that any *direct attempt* to register the normative and rational weight of that distinction, the normative weight of that factual distinction, would necessarily fall short of what for now counts as a good reason; and that any indirect account of the distinction, like the very ones offered in *Dialectic of Enlightenment*, betray the phenomena. This is the aporetic space of all his philosophising: no matter how reflective and self-critical, rationalised reason extirpates what it wants to salvage, and any direct approach to the phenomena betrays what reason has become.

Above, I claimed that part of what goes wrong with the argument of *Dialectic of Enlightenment* is that it fails to show precisely what items are being depended upon by rationalised reason which make it irrational. Arguments claiming that rationalised reason disavows material conditions of operation have become legion, from hermeneutical defences of authority and tradition through post-positivistic philosophies of science which embed scientific reason in the practices of a scientific community. Adorno is travelling along a similar path as these philosophies, and much of what they want to insist upon he would be sympathetic to. However, the stakes in these forms of argument vary as the analysis of rationalised reason varies. In making the destruction of auratic individuality central, and tying the question of auratic individuality to, on the one hand, the ratio-

[24] For Adorno the prime example of this is in the operation of capital exchanges where 'living labour' is converted into 'labour time'. And while this is readily transparent, I am here contending that less transparently enlightened moral theory imposes an analogous abstraction. This, I would want to argue, is at the heart of the debate between 'internalism' and 'externalism' in moral philosophy. I attempt to prosecute this claim in my *Adorno: Disenchantment and Ethics* (Cambridge University Press, forthcoming).

nalised distinction between treating persons as means and treating them as ends in themselves, and, on the other, to the living/non-living distinction, my intention has been to *focus*, to begin to make precise where we must look for a contentful dependency that is in principle capable of both demonstrating *the* irrationality of rationalised reason, and by inference what ethically is most in need of saving. If living and non-living is the correct level to examine the independence and dependence of reason, if that distinction is the most emphatic one in which the factual must be accorded normative power, then the focus of a philosophy honouring it must begin where the whole process of subsumptive reiterability and instrumentality begin: simple acts of perceptual awareness. For Adorno, the medium of perceptual awareness is the concept; hence the whole question of the independence and dependence of reason became for him a question of concept and object, concept and intuition. *Negative Dialectics* is the interrogation of the dependency of the rationalised concept on its rationalised object, the non-identical. And there is at least one prima facie reason to believe that this is a sound strategy, namely, our concession earlier that everyday conceptualisation and judgement, minimal subsumption, was both objectifying *and* anthropomorphic since most ordinary empirical concepts track and/or are sensitive to, depend on, the way things phenomenologically appear to subjects. Empirical concepts in this sense would appear to possess rational constraints that are quite different in kind to the constraints on scientific explanation and theory; there would appear to be a sense of cognition and knowing at stake in everyday empirical encounters that is unlike what knowing and cognition are in science. And arguably, we cannot leave this level of cognition behind. Hence, if reiterative ascent can thus be shown to be incommensurable with standard empirical judgements and ordinary language, if scientific rationality is discontinuous and incommensurable with the rationality of everyday judgements and language, then the normative force of anthropomorphic nature might be salvageable. Whether or not *Negative Dialectics* fulfils the promissory note of *Dialectic of Enlightenment* must here remain moot. What is beyond doubt is that the interrogation of reason in Adorno and Horkheimer's minor classic continues to raise questions that are fundamental to philosophy in all its aspects.

Habermas, Science and Modernity

FRIEDEL WEINERT

The work of Jürgen Habermas has been described as eclectic. It is also prolific. Fortunately for his readers the prolificacy and eclecticism of the author are mitigated by the recurrence of his themes. These concern the emergence and nature of modern occidental society, both from a sociological and philosophical perspective. On a more philosophical level, there is also a strong plea for a paradigm change. The philosophy of the consciousness made the lone subject, in search of knowledge, face the external world. The dialogic philosophy of Habermas sees interlocutors engaged in dialogue about the material, social and internal world and their many aspects. Furthermore, there are many fruitful sidelines: the nature of language, the personality structure of the individual, socialisation and the status of the social sciences. All these various strands are woven into a coherent model of the nature of western civilisation. In the recombination of the contributory constituents, derived from American pragmatism, German Idealism, Hermeneutics, Marxism, the Frankfurt School of Sociology and Systems Theory, lies the originality and breadth of his work.

For reasons to be elucidated, it is appropriate to characterise the Habermas account as a *hypothetical model*. This model gives a hypothetical representation of the structure of modernity. It attempts to characterise its constituents and how they may be related. An essential part of occidental thinking is scientific rationality. Key figures in the history of occidental science – Descartes, Galileo, Kepler, Newton and Boyle – worked out a new type of explanation, mechanical in essence, of the natural world. This resulted in the image of the cosmos as clockwork. In Habermas's model of modernity, science, too, occupies a central role but there is serious doubt whether Habermas's view of occidental science is adequate. It seems that Habermas does not fully appreciate its role in the shaping of the occidental way of thinking.

According to Habermas we still live in the age of modernity. He rigorously rejects the view that the present century has suffered a serious postmodernist deflation and entered the age of relativism. The ills of the present-day society are not due to the resignation of reason but to the encroachment of the imperatives of bureaucratic

A reference to a page number in square brackets refers to the English translation of the work cited.

Friedel Weinert

and economic systems on the lifeworld. Thus Habermas's model strives to offer an explanation of the structural defects of occidental societies. There are, however, rival explanations, as for instance Giddens's institutional analysis of modernity. There are also features of modernity, which the Habermas model ignores. Habermas is tempted to call the body of his thought a *theory*. A theory of society would have to negotiate between these alternatives and state which features of modernity are primary and which ones are only secondary and could therefore be regarded as negligible. The explanations should be testable. Views on modernity are in a flux and there is not even a general agreement whether we live in a modern or postmodern age. But the essential elements of the Habermas model are clear. They give us a certain characterisation of modernity. From this platform other concerns arise: the role of science in the shaping of occidental thinking and the debate about modernism and postmodernism.

1 A model of modernity

The most characteristic feature of the Habermas model of modernity is its duality of structure. Viewed from an internal position, society appears as a lifeworld (*Lebenswelt*); seen from an external position, society appears as a network of interlocking functional systems. But this is more than a convenient framework for analysis. Both components lay claim to a reality of their own; both exhibit different structural elements. The dual components of society are required by Habermas to achieve his aim: a theory of the pathologies of modernity.[1] If modern societies suffer from structural defects, which are experienced as pathological symptoms in the lifeworld, these structural inadequacies are themselves the result of the historical evolution of Western societies. A further feature of the Habermas model is therefore an evolutionary explanation, inspired by the work of Max Weber, of both the 'signature' and 'sting' of modernity, i.e., the departmentalisation and differentiation of societal systems.[2] The central idea is that the evolution of Western societies has been one-sided, resulting in a structure, which causes damage in the lifeworld. The Habermas model claims to be able both to describe and to explain the symptoms of malfunctioning and even to suggest remedies.

The differentiation of society into systems and the lifeworld is introduced to increase the adequacy of the model of society. There

[1] J. Habermas, 'Dialektik der Rationalisierung', in *Die Neue Unübersichtlichkeit* (Frankfurt: Suhrkamp, 1985), p. 171.
[2] Ibid., p. 204.

are features in highly differentiated societies, which cannot be accounted for by the purely functional systems theory. Accordingly, Habermas assigns different functions to the dual aspects of his model of society to capture the hitherto neglected features. There are also relations between the systems and the lifeworld for which an account needs to be given.

Important societal systems in the Habermas model are the economic and the bureaucratic system. A number of characteristics are ascribed to them, which distinguish them sharply from the lifeworld aspect of the model.

First, they possess their own type of rationality – *instrumental* or *purposive rationality*. In this type of rationality the end is given (for instance: profit maximisation) and the agent's rationality consists exclusively in finding the most appropriate means of achieving this end. Means–end rationality (*Zweckrationalität*) plays an important part in economic models as an idealisation of how rational agents operate in the market. These too are hypothetical models: the economic agents are treated *as if* they were perfectly rational in their choice of the appropriate means to attain the pre-given end. Agents operating in these systems pursue *strategic* action: they seek to interfere in the objective world in an effort to realise their aims. This type of means–end rationality has had a distinguished career in the social sciences. Weber analysed it as the distinctive type of rationality, which emerged in the recent history of occidental societies. Horkheimer and Adorno branded it as a destructive force, which had annihilated the ideals of freedom and autonomy, cherished by the Enlightenment. Habermas has inherited the negative view of means–end rationality, suggested by Adorno and Horkheimer. Not only do the economic and administrative system practise this type of rationality, the so-called value sphere of science has developed its own brand of cognitive-instrumental rationality. In his model instrumental rationality in either form is said to exercise a damaging effect on the lifeworld.

Second, societal systems depend on *system integration*, which must be distinguished from the social integration sought in the lifeworld. The function of the system is stability and the management of complexity. Its individual units must be co-ordinated in such a way that this stability is maintained. There is no rational consensus amongst individuals to co-ordinate their actions. The system provides *steering mechanisms* to achieve the systemic integration of the consequences of individual actions.[3]

[3] J. Habermas, *Theorie des kommunikativen Handelns*, II (Frankfurt: Suhrkamp, 1981), pp. 179, 226; *The Theory of Communicative Action*, II (Cambridge: Polity Press, 1987), pp. [117], [150f]; *Legitimationsprobleme*

Third, functional systems like the economy and bureaucracy are run via the use of particular media, *money* and *power*, which reduce complexity and provide mechanisms for the co-ordination of action *at the expense* of a communicative consensus.[4]

The differentiation of modern occidental society into subsystems has also caused the separation of three important *value spheres* from the lifeworld and their sedimentation into independent domains: *science* and *technology*, *law* and *morality*, *art*. As they are largely in the hands of academics and other professionals, they grow by their own inner logic. This specialisation gives rise to ideals of rationality, characteristic of the particular domains.[5] Weber explained the emergence of these spheres as the result of the rationalisation and secularisation of traditional worldviews. The existence of these value spheres has led to the absorption of knowledge into elitist expert cultures, again with potentially damaging effects on the lifeworld.[6]

The lifeworld (*Lebenswelt*) has three structural components to which correspond three functions: culture or cultural patterns whose function is cultural reproduction, society or legitimate orders whose function is social integration (solidarity) and personality structures whose function is socialisation.

I use the term *culture* for the stock of knowledge from which participants in communication supply themselves with interpretations as they come to an understanding about something in the world. I use the term *society* for the legitimate orders through which participants regulate their memberships in social groups and thereby secure solidarity. By *personality* I understand the competencies that make a subject capable of speaking and acting,

---

[4] J. Habermas, *Theorie*, II, pp. 391–4 [261–3].
[5] J. Habermas, *Theorie des kommunikativen Handelns*, I (Frankfurt: Suhrkamp, 1981), pp. 324–31; *The Theory of Communicative Action*, I (Boston: Beacon Press, 1984), pp. [237–42]. The types of rationality involved are cognitive-instrumental rationality (science), moral-practical rationality (law and morality) and aesthetic-practical rationality (art), but cognitive-instrumental rationality is, according to Habermas, the dominant type of rationality in occidental societies.
[6] *Theorie*, II, pp. 488ff [332ff].

---

im Spätkapitalismus (Frankfurt: Suhrkamp, 1973), p. 14; *Legitimation Crisis* (London: Heinemann Educational, 1976), p. [4]; *Zur Rekonstruktion des Historischen Materialismus* (Frankfurt: Suhrkamp, 1976), p. 114; *Der philosophische Diskurs der Moderne* (Frankfurt: Suhrkamp 1985), p. 421; *The Philosophical Discourse of Modernity* (Cambridge: Polity Press, 1987), p. [363].

that put him in a position to take part in processes of reaching understanding and thereby to assert his own identity.[7]

The lifeworld is quite generally a resource on which culture, society and personality draw to fulfil their functions. The lifeworld serves as a background, the elements of which are suspended from doubt at any one time and which provide the participants in the lifeworld with symbolic meaning.[8]

The dual aspect of the Habermas model is emphasised by the contrasting characteristics, which separate the lifeworld from the societal subsystems.

First, the lifeworld has its own kind of rationality, which Habermas dubs *communicative rationality*. The type of action associated with this kind of rationality is *consensus-oriented* action. A major vehicle to achieve consensus and understanding is language and linguistic competence. The introduction of the concept of communicative rationality marks a significant departure from Weber's analysis of the rationalisation of occidental societies for several reasons. On the one hand, it widens the notion of rationality beyond instrumental rationality to include other types of rationality associated with morality and art. This enlargement allows Habermas to postulate the existence of inherent rational structures in everyday discourse in the lifeworld. The idea of rational speech is already embedded in the structure of linguistic action.[9] This point can be elaborated by noting Habermas's distinction between three formal world concepts: an *objective* world of material things and their interrelations, a *social* world of interacting social agents and actors and its normative structure and a *subjective* world of inner mental states and their behavioural influence. About each of these worlds an individual can make validity claims, which can be evaluated, accepted or rejected in discourse. The validity criterion in the objective world is the *propositional truth* of an assertion about a segment of the material world, in the social world it is the *normative rightness* of the speech act with respect to existing norms and values and in the subjective world it is the *subjective truthfulness* of the intentional expression.[10] The widening of the concept of rationality permits

[7] Ibid., p. 209 [138] and J. Habermas, *Nachmetaphysisches Denken* (Frankfurt: Suhrkamp, 1988), pp. 95ff.

[8] J. Habermas, *Nachmetaphysisches Denken*, p. 99; *Die Neue Unübersichtlichkeit*, p. 186; *Diskurs der Moderne*, pp. 365, 378f, 397f [313, 325f, 343f].

[9] J. Habermas, *Rekonstruktion*, p. 339.

[10] J. Habermas, *Rekonstruktion*, p. 11; this book is partly translated as *Communication and the Evolution of Society* (London: Heinemann Educational, 1979); the corresponding reference to this translation is on p.

Habermas on the other hand to defend a modified version of the 'unity of reason' thesis of German Idealism against all forms of postmodern relativism. And finally, it allows him to proclaim the thesis both against Weber and against all postmodern, relativist thinkers that modern, occidental societies have cultivated only a selective type of rationality. Thus modern occidental societies have not fully exhausted the rationality potential which lies dormant in their very structures.[11]

Second, Habermas emphasises that the lifeworld seeks a form of integration, which is different from that of the subsystems – the social integration established in the lifeworld is *solidarity*.

Third, media like *money* and *power* are incapable of delivering the symbolic meaning and the cultural reproduction, which is the main function of the lifeworld. 'Money and power can neither purchase nor enforce solidarity and meaning.'[12] To achieve this end, language and consensus are the main vehicles. The penetration of the lifeworld by media, which guarantee the functioning of subsystems, is seen by Habermas as a major threat to the integrity of the lifeworld. The importance of consensus-oriented action in the lifeworld, which relies heavily on symbolic meaning for the assessment of validity claims, has rendered the lifeworld in modern societies reflexive. This *reflexivity* of a cultural tradition implies an awareness that it is one amongst other cultural traditions and the ability to question the basic assumptions on which it is built.

The differentiation of the subsystems and the value spheres is one aspect of the rationalisation of modern societies. The other aspect is that the lifeworld itself has been rationalised as manifested in some formal features. Apart from the reflexivity of cultural traditions, there is a generalisation of norms and values and a differentiation into three formal world concepts with concomitant validity claims. There should also be feedback mechanisms between the value spheres (science, art, and morality) and the lifeworld and socialisation patterns should be in place, which are conducive to the formation of autonomous individuals.[13]

[11] *Theorie*, I, pp. 202, 306, 320 [140, 221, 232f].

[12] *Diskurs*, p. 421 (this is my own translation which I prefer to the 'official' one which is to be found in the English translation of *Diskurs*, p. [363]; *Theorie*, II, p. 391 [261].

[13] *Theorie*, I, p. 109 [71]; *Neue Unübersichtlichkeit*, pp. 183, 236, 252. The reflexivity of modern societies has also been stressed by A. Giddens, *Consequences of Modernity* (Cambridge: Polity Press, 1990), pp. 36ff, 144, 152f.

[97]; *Theorie*, I, pp. 99–113 [63–74]. Habermas is aware (*Theorie*, I, p. 154 [103f]) that especially the concepts of normative rightness and subjective truthfulness are not as straightforward as that of propositional truth.

The structural components

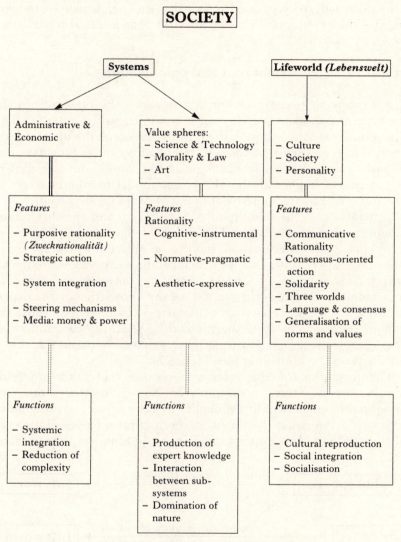

Figure 1. A Model of Modernity

The dual aspect of the Habermas model of modernity brings to the fore the *structural* components of the model (see Figure 1). But the model cannot come to life as long as no driving mechanism is built into it. A driving force is provided by a consideration of the interrelations and interactions between the functional subsystems, the value systems and the lifeworld. By injecting this dynamism into

335

the model, Habermas attempts to explain the peculiar pathologies of modernity. The model also sets up constraints to prevent a typically postmodern consequence, i.e., that the 'juggernaut of modernity' (Giddens) plunges into the abyss of total cultural relativism.

2 Cultural impoverishment and colonisation

There exists an uneasy relationship between the lifeworld on the one hand and the functional systems and value spheres on the other. The *paradox* is that although the rationalisation of the lifeworld has enabled the emergence of these different subsystems, they have had by and large a negative feedback on the lifeworld. But it is part of the normative aspect of the Habermas model to suggest ways in which the tide of the negative influences could be stemmed.

Consider, first, the value spheres (science, art and morality). Each sphere constructs its own edifice of knowledge according to rationality and truth criteria which tend to be inherent to the sphere in question. Expert cultures arise which produce expert knowledge for expert consumption. A divide opens up between the everyday knowledge of the lifeworld and the arcane knowledge of the expert cultures. The elitist separation of the expert cultures may cause the *cultural impoverishment* of the lifeworld. Whether this happens or not depends on the modalities of the exchange between the expert cultures and the lifeworld[14] (see Figure 2).

The formation of the value spheres has had other worrying effects on Western societies. It has narrowed the rich Enlightenment concept of rationality to a cognitive–instrumentalist skeleton, presumably dominant in the natural sciences. This one-sided paradigm of rationality stresses the domination of nature and

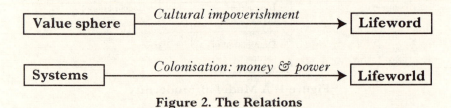

Figure 2. The Relations

[14] J. Habermas, *Theorie*, I, pp. 328–9 [240–1]; *Theorie*, II, p. 488 [331]. The qualification concerning the modalities of exchange is made in *Diskurs der Moderne*, p. 394 [340]. The emergence of autonomous expert fields entails problems of mediation, as Habermas explains in 'Questions and Counterquestions', in R.J. Bernstein ed., *Habermas and Modernity* (Cambridge: Polity Press, 1985), p. 209.

the production of technologically exploitable knowledge.[15] Habermas recommends a three-pronged therapy, which could repair the damage. The fixation on the cognitive–instrumental rationality of the natural sciences must be broken; the expert cultures must communicate with each other; and the cognitive potential developed by the expert cultures must be fed back into the life-world and made available to the social subsystems.[16] This would repair some of the structural defects, from which modern societies suffer and presumably avoid the pathologies in the lifeworld. A potential for reason and consensus is already inherent in everyday communication. This means that the members of a social community can adopt a critical attitude towards validity claims which are made by another member either with respect to the objective world (truth assertions), with respect to the social world (normative rightness) and the subjective world (subjective truthfulness). Thus, reason and validity are built into everyday communication – a dimension of rationality, which the fixation on purposive–instrumental rationality had left dormant.

Consider, secondly, the relation of economic and administrative subsystems to the lifeworld. These systems function by the employment of the complexity-reducing media *money* and *power*. But to analyse the whole of society in terms of functional systems as proponents of the systems theory of society (Talcott Parsons and Niklas Luhmann) have done, is to ignore the demands of the lifeworld. In particular, it leads to a misunderstanding of the needs of social integration and communicative rationality. Solidarity and meaning in the lifeworld cannot be installed by the use of the media money and power. Money and power are *steering mechanisms* and their malfunction leads to disturbances in the *material* reproduction of society. The lifeworld, however, functions by the use of *communicative means* and breakdowns in communication lead to failures in the *symbolic* reproduction of the lifeworld.[17]

Just as the existence of the three value spheres has the potentially damaging effect of cultural impoverishment on the lifeworld, so the existence of functional subsystems threatens the lifeworld with instrumentalisation. This is Habermas's well-known thesis of the *colonisation* of the lifeworld by the imperatives of systemic rationalisation[18]

---

[15] J. Habermas, *Neue Unübersichtlichkeit*, p. 136; *Theorie*, I, pp. 102, 113, 328 [66, 74, 240].

[16] J. Habermas, 'Questions and Counterquestions', in *Habermas and Modernity*, pp. 209, 197; *Theorie*, I, pp. 328–9 [240–1].

[17] *Theorie*, II, pp. 293, 391–419, 421 [196, 261–82, 283].

[18] See R.J. Bernstein, 'Introduction', in *Habermas and Modernity*, p. 23; *Theorie*, II, pp. 470f, 483 [318f, 327].

(see Figure 2). It is the most important consequence of the dual conception of the model of modernity, since it raises the *explanatory* claim that the interference of the economic and administrative subsystems in the lifeworld can account for the pathologies of the modern world. The colonisation of the lifeworld by the imperatives of the subsystems means, according to Habermas, that the media, characteristic of these systems, interfere in the symbolic reproduction of the lifeworld, i.e., the cultural reproduction, the social integration and the socialisation of the individual. The symbolic reproduction of the lifeworld depends on the medium of communicative action. Pathologies arise when steering mechanisms like money and power spill over into the lifeworld. By way of illustration this happens when interpersonal relations are redefined in consumer terms and when ordinary life situations are bureaucratised.[19]

More importantly, Habermas claims that certain recent phenomena in society should count as a confirmation of his colonisation thesis. He interprets the appearance of new social conflicts – clustering around problems like the quality of life, equality between men and women, personal fulfilment and human rights issues – as well as tendencies towards juridification (*Verrechtlichung*) and experiences of the loss of freedom and meaning as supporting evidence of the thesis.[20] In this sense, his model claims to be explanatory. Observable phenomena, like new social conflicts, are explained as the result of an underlying tension in the lifeworld. The colonisation of the lifeworld is the quasi-causal mechanism, which brings about the pathologies of the modern world. There is no doubt some truth in the observation of increasing bureaucratisation and monetarisation. However, the plausibility of this explanatory claim is lessened by the scientific status of the explanatory mechanism. There are genuine difficulties in devising tests for this claim. Firstly, it must be assumed that the pathologies of the modern world are objective, interpersonal phenomena about which a certain consensus exists between social scientists. Secondly, inferences in the social sciences from observable data to underlying quasi-causal mechanisms notoriously suffer from a failure to exclude spurious correlations. Thirdly, if the pathologies are caused by the intrusion of the media of *power* and *money* into the symbolic reproduction of the lifeworld, this causal mechanism should be independently testable. At least, alternative explanations should be excluded. Fourthly, the model was expressly constructed to accommodate the pathologies of modernity, which makes it look perilously *ad hoc*.

[19] J. Habermas, *Neue Unübersichtlichkeit*, pp. 189, 195; also Giddens, 'Reason without Revolution?', in *Habermas and Modernity*, p. 110.

[20] *Theorie*, II, pp. 215, 471ff, 523ff, 575ff [143, 318ff, 356ff, 391ff].

The model is constructed in such a way that the pathologies necessarily follow from it. The pathologies can then not be used as *supportive* evidence for the model. The pathologies are in agreement with the model but do not confirm it. The model would have to have some independently testable consequences in the social world in order to achieve confirmation. Or at least, if the model has been inductively constructed, as seems to be the case here, the 'evidence' of pathologies would have to raise the credibility of the Habermas model and lower the credibility of some rival model, which also attempts to 'explain' these pathologies. It is therefore premature on the part of Habermas to claim evidential support for his model as long as these outstanding issues have not been clarified.

This is a good reason to withhold the title 'theory' from Habermas's account and to grant it no more than the status of a *hypothetical model*. The explanation of the pathologies of the modern world, *insofar* as they are agreed phenomena, in terms of the uncoupling of system and lifeworld is one of several possible explanations. This does not render the model useless. It may still have *empirical adequacy*. It makes sense of the new social conflicts and it provides a *possible* account of the genesis of the pathologies of modernity. It may satisfy Weber's postulate of adequate causation. It gives an account of the emergence of pathologies in modernity *as if* modern societies were strictly split into the lifeworld and subsystems. But there are reasons to doubt the neatness of this model. This can be brought to light by a consideration of the nature of science and reflexivity. If some of the relations between the expert cultures and the lifeworld are built into the model, the strict duality of the model seems to disappear.

3 Science and reflexivity

The most striking criticism, which Habermas levels at Weber, is that the latter has failed to see the one-sided nature of the process of Western rationalisation. Weber succumbed to the fixation on the instrumentality of scientific reason and failed to see the selectivity of capitalist rationalisation with its emphasis on purposive rationality (*Zweckrationalität*). With his dualistic model, Habermas wants to capture the potential for rationality in the lifeworld. Adorno and Horkheimer, too, overemphasised the means–end type rationality and failed to see the *rational contents* embedded in cultural modernity: (a) the theoretical dynamism and self-reflexivity of the sciences which drives them beyond the mere production of technologically exploitable knowledge; (b) the universalistic foundations of

Friedel Weinert

law and morality which have been incorporated into social institutions and (c) the liberating force of aesthetic experiences.[21] An important consequence of the rationalisation and differentiation of modern lifeworlds, which Habermas has stressed throughout his writings, is the *reflexivity* of modernity.[22] By this he means that appeals to ultimate authorities and metaphysical principles have increasingly been replaced by rational deliberations about the formal conditions of the acceptability of arguments. Thus, Habermas's writings allude to features, in particular the theoretical dynamism of science and the reflexivity of modern life forms, which have not been explicitly incorporated into his model of modernity. Hypothetical or *as if* models are open to the introduction of new parameters, which should bring the model representation closer to the system it is supposed to model. If some of these factors are included in the Habermas model its duality of structure, I suggest, begins to be blurred.

Science In his criticism of Adorno and Horkheimer, Habermas stresses the self-reflexivity and theoretical dynamism of modern science. But he does little to delineate the consequences of this insight for his dualistic model. He views science predominantly as an instrumental enterprise, which produces means for the domination of nature.[23] Thus he fails to see the implications of scientific knowledge for the *understanding* of the modern world. The narrowing of the modern concept of rationality to the cognitive–instrumental production of technologically exploitable knowledge is, according to Habermas, the heritage of the scientific revolution of the seventeenth century. According to this understanding, science renounces any attempt of an interpretation of nature.[24] Against this *instrumentalist* view of science, it is imperative to observe that the greatest scientists have always sought to stress the philosophical implications of great scientific discoveries, including implications for the self-understanding of humankind. The most common examples are the Copernican Revolution, the Darwinian Revolution

[21] *Diskurs der Moderne*, pp. 138, 364f [113, 312f]; J. Habermas, *Die Moderne – ein unvollendetes Projekt* (Leipzig: Reclam, 1990), p. 41.

[22] *Die Neue Unübersichtlichkeit*, pp. 183, 236; *Rekonstruktion*, pp. 277f [184f]; *Diskurs der Moderne*, p. 10 [2] and Giddens, *Consequences of Modernity*, pp. 151ff.

[23] *Zur Logik der Sozialwissenschaften* (Frankfurt: Surhkamp, 1970), pp. 85f, 93f; *On the Logic of the Social Sciences* (Cambridge, MA: MIT Press, 1988), pp. [12f, 18f].

[24] *Theorie*, II, p. 584 [397f].

and even the Freudian Revolution.[25] In such contributions, scientists, prompted by the most recent discoveries in their respective fields, provide both philosophical interpretations of science as a cognitive enterprise and physical interpretations of scientific theories as explanations of the natural world. In both these ways they contribute to the understanding of science and the natural world. The heartbeat of science is at its most philosophical rhythm when major conceptual revisions or revolutions are afoot. Then, scientists feel the need to go beyond the mathematical equations in order to reach a level of *understanding* which assigns some physical meaning to the mathematical comprehension of the natural world. What is interesting in this process from a philosophical point of view is that empirical facts filter through to the level of conceptualisation and bring about changes in the way the world is conceptualised. 'Old notions are discarded by new experiences.'[26] The common territory between science and philosophy lies in this interaction between facts and concepts. In re-interpreting the world *in the light of new experiences* the scientist becomes an active participant in the shaping of human views about the surrounding world. In the face of a confusing amount of new evidence at the level of atomic phenomena, Planck, for instance, called for a comprehensive physical worldview. This is the role of the *philosopher-scientist* of which scientists are fully aware:

> History has shown that science has played a leading part in the development of human thought.[27]

Concepts like *understanding* and *meaning* are usually associated with particular aspects of the Social Sciences. Social life produces and

[25] It should be noted that there are serious doubts about the *scientific* status of the Freudian model of the mind. Habermas re-interprets Freud in terms of his theory of communicative action; see *Erkenntnis und Interesse* (Frankfurt: Suhrkamp, 1973), pp. 262–332; *Knowledge and Human Interests* (London: Heinemann, [2]1978), pp. [214–45]; *Theorie*, II, pp. 152, 570f [99, 388f]; *Die Neue Unübersichtlichkeit*, pp. 214, 230.

[26] M. Born, *Natural Philosophy of Cause and Chance* (Oxford, 1949), p. 75. This idea has been expressed by other physicists, c.f. W. Heisenberg, *Gesammelte Werke*, Abteilung C, Vol. I (Munich: Piper, 1984), pp. 29, 40; A.S. Eddington, *The Philosophy of Physical Science* (Cambridge, 1939), p. 33; P. Langevin, *La Physique Depuis 20 Ans* (Paris, 1923), pp. 301–3; and E. Cassirer, *Determinismus und Indeterminismus in der modernen Physik* (Darmstadt, 1977), p. 273.

[27] Born, *Natural Philosophy*, p. 2; cf. M. Planck, *Vorträge und Erinnerungen* (Darmstadt, 1975), p. 53; A. Eddington, *The Philosophy of Physical Science* (Cambridge University Press, 1939), p. 8; J. Jeans, *Physics and Philosophy* (Cambridge University Press, 1943), p. 2.

reproduces symbolic meaning and the social scientist needs to acquire an understanding of the inherent symbolic meaning in social life by adopting the viewpoint of a passive participant. In the natural sciences *understanding* may mean several related things: (a) in one sense it may mean the assignment of representable physical mechanisms and causal processes to the formal, mathematical aspects of physical theories as they may be expressed in scientific laws.[28] The formalism of statistical mechanics, for instance, is given an interpretation in the kinetic model of gases. Newton made a clear distinction between knowledge of the regularities discovered by the quantitative analysis of observed phenomena and the causes, which might produce them. He provided understanding of different classes of observable phenomena by a corpuscular theory of light, a theory of gravitation and the notions of absolute time and space, fully aware of the theoretical nature of such postulations. Thus, there is a need to assign an underlying physical structure to the detectable phenomena in terms of which the measurable processes can be interpreted. For Planck understanding had a slightly different sense (b): it was not the discovery of the quantum of action, expressed in the constant *h*, but the assignment of a physical meaning to this constant which was the 'theoretically most difficult problem'. Planck interpreted the quantum of action – which he had introduced into his distribution law for blackbody radiation – not as a fictitious entity but as a real physical constant.[29] This interpretation led to a radical revision of the physical worldview and to a rethinking of fundamental notions – like causality and determinism, particles and waves – with which scientists described the natural world. For Heisenberg (c), understanding in physics meant the ability of the physicist to relinquish old concepts in new areas of experience and to develop new concepts which were more adequate to deal with the new experiences.[30]

It is sometimes affirmed that although the metaphysical principles of science can change they 'are *assumed* to be true indepen-

[28] See J. T. Cushing, 'Quantum Theory and Explanatory Discourse', *Philosophy of Science*, **58** (1991), pp. 337–58 and H. J. Folse, 'Ontological constraints and understanding quantum phenomena', *Dialectica*, **50**, (1996), pp. 121–36.

[29] See Planck, *Vorträge*, pp. 29, 129, 131.

[30] 'Philosophische Probleme in der Theorie der Elementarteilchen' (1967), in W. Heisenberg, *Gesammelte Werke* C/Vol. II (Munich, 1984), pp. 410–22; 'The Concept of Understanding in Theoretical Physics' (1969), in: W. Heisenberg, *Gesammelte Werke* C/Vol. III (Munich, 1985), pp. 335–8.

dently of any *scientific* experience'.[31] The present considerations suggest the contrary: Specific scientific discoveries can lead to a reshaping of some of the fundamental notions with which scientists explain the natural world. By implication this means that no scientific experience prior to the discovery had led to a questioning of these fundamental notions. Hence the status of these notions changes as a function of scientific experience. Fundamental, even metaphysical notions of science have undergone changes as a direct result of scientific discoveries. More specifically, fundamental scientific discoveries had an immediate impact on the way scientists interpreted the structure of the natural world by reference to such fundamental notions as *time* and *space*, *causality* and *determinism*. The classical concepts of time and space required an urgent review as a result of the experimental implications of the special theory of relativity. In his seminal paper *'Zur Elektrodynamik bewegter Körper'* (1905, §4) Einstein predicted that clocks placed at the equator of the earth would run more slowly, by a quantifiable amount, than identical clocks placed at the poles. The classical notions of causality and determinism came under scrutiny after the first experimental successes of quantum theory. Often these two notions are used interchangeably.[32] This identification of strict causality with determinism is a feature of classical physics eternalised in Laplace's spirit. However, a central conceptual change, which occurred as a result of experimental evidence from quantum mechanics – the phenomenon of radioactivity, the need for quantum discontinuity and the experience of spontaneous emissions and absorptions – was the separation of these two notions. Central figures like Planck and Born came to hold that causality and indeterminism were compatible.[33]

Habermas quite rightly stresses that philosophy must heed the results of the natural and social sciences. But this relationship also works in the opposite direction. Science has had and continues to have impact on philosophy and on how the world around us is to be interpreted. In this specific sense, Habermas is mistaken to assert that science no longer interprets nature. The awareness of great sci-

---

[31] C. Dilworth, *The Metaphysics of Science* (Dordrecht: Kluwer, 1996), p. 71. E.A. Burtt's classic study *The Metaphysical Foundations of Modern Science* (1924) discusses the philosophical underpinning of the scientific thinking of Copernicus, Galileo, Newton and others without reference to any of the empirical discoveries associated with these scientists.

[32] See R. Penrose, *The Emperor's New Mind* (London, 1990), pp. 273–8; H. Pagels, *The Cosmic Code* (London, 1994), p. 75; L. de Broglie, *Matter and Light* (Dover, 1939), p. 227.

[33] Planck, *Vorträge*, p. 292; Born, *Natural Philosophy*, pp. 101–2.

entists of the philosophical implications of their discoveries reveals the theoretical dynamism and self-reflexivity, which Habermas attributes to science in his criticism of Adorno and Horkheimer. This awareness takes our understanding of scientific rationality far beyond the instrumental understanding which Habermas, in much of his work, proclaims. As the above examples show, there is an inevitable interaction between science and philosophy and through it an impact on everyday knowledge which Habermas would like to see realised.[34]

This suggests that everyday knowledge and communicative rationality do not constitute a separate category, threatened by cultural impoverishment, but that scientific and communicative rationality are the same in their formal structure, although their specific manifestations differ due to their different contents. Once it is recognised that science is not driven exclusively by cognitive technical interests, communicative rationality can be found at work in the natural sciences. Communicative rationality is concern with argument – that is, to make reasons support a conclusion and the evaluation of validity claims. Habermas is at pains to distinguish the mere social acceptability of ideas from their reason-induced validity. A conclusion reached through valid reasoning is binding on anyone who accepts the premises of the argument. There is a striking example of this form of reasoning in science. It is the *argument by exclusion*. Consider the question of the origin of β-radioactivity (consisting of electrons). Isotopes are chemical elements, which occupy the same place in the periodic table but differ in their radioactive behaviour. Isotopes can emit β-rays which differ in their velocities. But isotopes have identical chemical properties so that their electronic configurations must be identical. This identity of electronic configurations excludes the possibility that the β-radiation originates from this configuration. By exclusion, the seat of the expulsion of the β-particles must be the nucleus. Thus argued Bohr.[35] This is only one type of argument used in science but it carries the logical compulsion which is characteristic of rational argumentation. Arguments by exclusion also play a prominent part in other areas of life, as the work of Sherlock Holmes testifies.

It can be concluded, then, that rational argument and explanatory reasoning are formally the same in both science and everyday

[34] *Theorie* I, pp. 328f [240]; cf. Th. McCarthy, 'Reflections on Rationalisation' in the *Theory* of *Communicative Action,* in *Habermas and Modernity,* pp. 176–7. A.C. Crombie, *Styles of Scientific Reasoning in the European Tradition,* Vol. II (London: Duckworth, 1994), pp. 1198–9.

[35] See A. Pais, *Niel's Bohr's Times* (Oxford University Press, 1991), p. 151.

practice. Even aesthetic and moral concerns can be found at the heart of science. Habermas does not seem to notice these dimensions because he approaches science from the external point of view of a system in which individual scientists only appear as agents. If, however, an internal viewpoint is adopted, according to which science becomes a community of researchers, then the narrowing of reason to one validity aspect for each value sphere becomes questionable. In the Habermas model an intermeshing of the validity dimensions only exists for the participants of the lifeworld.[36] This can be extended to the community of scientists. They do, in fact, adopt differential attitudes towards the objective, the social and the subjective world. Apart from the question of the propositional truth of factual statements, scientists have often debated the *norms* of scientific research, have taken instrumentalist or realist attitudes towards the *ends* of science and have made appeals to the *simplicity* of scientific theories as a criterion of acceptance. Darwin, for instance, defended his theory of natural selection by pointing out that it simplified the explanation of numerous, hitherto unrelated facts. This is not to deny that a cognitive–instrumental aspect of science exists. But if *means–end* reasoning can be found in science, it also occupies a firm place in everyday practice, as every rational consumer is only too well aware. One difference, which Habermas constructs between the subsystems, the value sphere of science and the lifeworld seems to crumble. There is another line of argument, which suggests the same conclusion.

Reflexivity Although Habermas emphasises that reflexivity is a central feature of modernity, he does not seem to see that the recognition of reflexivity poses a threat to the neatness of his model. For if there are institutional mechanisms, which permit a feedback of expert knowledge claims into the lifeworld – Habermas states this as a necessary condition for a non-selective pattern of rationalisation[37] – then the duality of the model would again be broken. Not only would the same types of rationality be present in all types of discourse, the lifeworld would not be threatened by cultural impoverishment from this corner. Knowledge would flow from the expert cultures to the lifeworld and from the lifeworld to the expert cultures. One such institutional mechanism is education. In particular it is the role of philosophy to provide a critical analysis of the value

[36] See J. Habermas, 'Questions and Counterquestions', in *Habermas and Modernity*, p. 196 and *Theorie*, II, pp. 584ff [397ff].

[37] *Theorie*, I, p. 328 [240]; see also *Habermas and Modernity*, pp. 102, 177, 207.

spheres of science, morality, art and society. Another institutional mechanism resides in the popularisation of scientific findings to keep lay people in touch with developments in the expert cultures. Scientists have written numerous popular accounts to explain the implications of quantum theory and relativity theory for the understanding of the natural world. Yet another institutional mechanism resides in the reflexivity of modernity. Reflexivity is quite generally the ability of human beings to question the fundamental assumptions on which their actions and thought systems are based. It is one of the characteristics of the modern age that this reflexivity has been generalised and institutionalised. *Everyone* and *everything* is subject to reasonable doubt and critical questions. No knowledge claim is more than *conjecture*. No knowledge claim is free from possible refutations. But there is also reflexivity in a more sociological sense: 'The reflexivity of modern social life consists in the fact that social practices are constantly examined and reformed in the light of incoming information about those very practices, thus constitutively altering their character.'[38] Thus there is a 'dialectical interplay' between the subsystems, the value sphere and the lifeworld *and* there is a process of constant reappropriation of expert knowledge on the level of everyday practice. This reappropriation is especially affected by the 'circularity' and ready accessibility of social science knowledge. But if the above considerations of the impact of scientific discoveries on the everyday view of the surrounding world are correct, everyday knowledge and rationality will remain open to corrective insertions from the world of science. The installation of the *mechanical worldview* in everyday thinking, which is the result of the work of generations of scientists from Copernicus to Newton, is one example of how science has affected the lifeworld. The replacement of theological accounts of the origin of species and *homo sapiens* by Darwin's evolutionary explanation is another example. Because of the inaccessibility of scientific knowledge, two outstanding conceptual revisions of twentieth century physics still await their incorporation into the lay knowledge of the lifeworld: the conceptual change from determinism to indeterminism brought about by the empirical findings of quantum mechanics; and the revision of the notions of space and time to a notion of space-time which Einstein's special and general theory of relativity have engendered. 'Indeterminism' and 'space-time' may one day be as familiar notions as 'evolution' and 'Copernicanism' are today.

It is only fair to observe that Habermas himself has acknowledged many of these above-mentioned features. But the one-sided-

[38] Giddens, *Consequences of Modernity*, p. 38 and pp. 144–54.

ness of his view on science, despite occasional remarks to the contrary, and his philosophical commitment to the Enlightenment project of global, ends-comprising reason have lead him to the construction of a dualistic model of modernity which prevents him from drawing the consequences of these insights for his model. One of the functions of the lifeworld is its cultural reproduction. The history of Copernicanism, Darwinism and Freudianism show that the lifeworld was both affected by these revolutions in thought and that it incorporated the new views associated with these revolutions after sometimes violent opposition. The message of each of these revolutions – the loss of centrality, the loss of rational design and the loss of ego transparency – was at first experienced as a massive offence to the established self-understanding of the place of humans in the cosmos, in the order of nature and the range of reason. But in each case the lifeworld eventually adapted its map of knowledge to these new views. That humans are not placed at the very centre of the universe, are not the result of a special act of

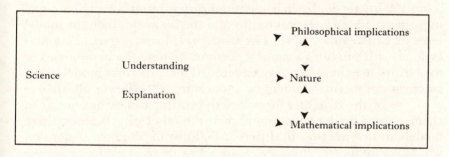

Figure 3. Alternative Views of the Relations

347

creation and are not as transparent to reason as the Enlightenment had imagined, became part of the cultural background knowledge which the lifeworld, according to the Habermas model, provides. Rather than pushing the lifeworld, metaphorically speaking, out on a limbo, where it is plagued by colonisation and cultural impoverishment, the lifeworld seems to dovetail with the value sphere and the subsystems. The presence of communicative rationality in both science and the lifeworld, the interplay between the expert systems and the lifeworld and the appropriation of expert knowledge in everyday knowledge are good reasons to doubt the neat separation of society into subsystems and lifeworld with their own structural components (see Figure 3).

This does not mean that Habermas's observations about modernity lack credibility. It is the ascription of the underlying structure, which is open to criticism. The model splits society into several components, with their distinctive structural characteristics, which then struggle to uphold relations between them. If colonisation and cultural impoverishment are questionable mechanisms and if there is no reason to doubt that communicative rationality is of equal importance in science, philosophy and the lifeworld, then the model loses its explanatory value. The model retains its *empirical adequacy* for it still provides a *possible* account of how the pathologies of modernity may have been engendered. The Habermas model is one amongst competing models of modernity all offering alternative accounts of the structure of twentieth century society but none can claim greater evidential support than the other can. Besides, these models draw attention to different features of Western society on whose meaning they disagree. Some offer these as evidence for the presence, others for the absence of postmodernity. Two of these features deserve attention:

> Personal freedom and the imperative to make choices under a lack of moral or societal constraints is interpreted by one author as the hallmark of Western societies at the end of this century and as evidence of the arrival of the postmodern world.[39] Habermas, however, sees the freedom of individuals under threat from excessive bureaucratisation and cultural impoverishment. And he interprets the observable features of postcapitalist societies as evidence, not of the arrival of postmodernity, but of the unfinished nature of the project of modernity.

The appearance of public clocks on churches and town halls all over Europe after the invention of the mechanical clock (*circa*

---

[39] Z. Bauman, *Postmodernity and its Discontents* (Oxford: Polity Press, 1996).

1271) has been interpreted as a symbol of urban modernisation.[40] The invention and diffusion of watches amplified this trend. But the invention of the mechanical clock was embedded in a much larger intellectual movement towards the linear, progressive notion of time which is characteristic of occidental societies. The growing need for precision since the thirteenth century and the universalisation of civil time since the end of the nineteenth century have generated profound socio-economic changes in the subsystems and the lifeworld.[41] The philosophical notion of the linearity and progression of time has left an enduring effect on Western societies. There is no mention of the connection of temporalisation with modernisation in the Habermas model. It is certainly one of the most compelling examples of the penetration of the lifeworld by the invention of technical devices and the development of fundamental temporal notions in the expert cultures. Part of the rationalisation of the everyday world is its temporalisation. But the regularisation of everyday life through the clock clearly satisfies neither the criteria for cultural impoverishment nor the colonisation thesis. The clock has led to a cultural enrichment, which has not only improved the rational conduct of life but has also inspired many works of art.[42] But its domineering presence has also been experienced, especially towards the end of the last century, as a restriction of personal freedom. The clock at first seems to have colonised the lifeworld, since its misuse at the hands of factory owners can be interpreted as an abuse of power. But once workers came into the possession of wristwatches to read their own worktime, the abuse of power could be effectively checked. The Habermas model does not seem to be incompatible with the inclusion of temporal aspects as a symbol of modernity. Yet the very ubiquity of temporalisation across subsystems,

[40] D.S. Landes, *Revolution in Time* (Harvard University Press, 1983), p. 325; G. Dohrn-van Rossum, *Die Geschichte der Stunde* (Munich: Carl Hanser Verlag, 1992), pp. 150, 163, 251.

[41] See H. Nowotny, *Eigenzeit* (Frankfurt: Suhrkamp, 1989); N. Elias, *Über die Zeit* (Frankfurt: Suhrkamp, 1988); A. Giddens, *Consequences of Modernity*, pp. 14ff relates the dynamism of modernity, amongst other factors, to 'the separation of time and space and their recombination in forms which permit the precise time-space "zoning" of social life'. The classic sources for the impact of time awareness on social structures are E. Thompson, 'Time, work-discipline and industrial capitalism', in *Past & Present*, **38** (1967), pp. 56–97 and Jacques Le Goff, 'Le temps du travail dans la "crise" du XIVe siècle: du temps médiéval au temps moderne', in *Pour un Autre Moyen Age* (Paris: Gallimard, 1977), pp. 66–79.

[42] A famous example is Dali's picture *The Persistence of Memory* (1931).

Friedel Weinert

expert cultures and the lifeworld in modern societies, and indeed the globe, resists its subsumption under either of the structural components of the model.

Several reasons have been advanced against the neat duality of the Habermas model. It has been suggested that the inclusion into his model of the very factors, which Habermas himself mentions, throws doubts on the neat structural characterisation of the model's components. Doubts have also been expressed about the explanatory value of the mechanisms, which are intended to ensure the dynamism of the model. Yet a loss of explanatory value does not destroy the usefulness of the Habermas account, if it is understood as a *hypothetical model*. It proves its empirical adequacy by making sense of at least *some* prominent features of modernity. Its structural aspect of the validity claims allows a definite stance in the postmodernist debate. In addition, it gives rise to some noteworthy reflections on the role of philosophy in a modern, scientific world.

4 Modernity and postmodernity

Habermas regards modernity as an unfinished project and consequently rejects the view that the age of postmodernity has arrived.[43] He characterises postmodernity as the view that the end of the twentieth century has distanced itself from the conceptual horizon of Western rationalism.[44] The latter comprises both the association of occidental rationalism with unified, comprehensive worldviews (either in science or philosophy) and the unity of rationality through various types of discourse. The postmodern age is supposed to herald the end of unified reason and the emergence of a plurality of divergent language games. In science, postmodern thinkers claim, the aim of truth has given way to the technological application of scientific results.

Against the thesis of the onset of postmodernity, Habermas not only defends the project of modernity; he also upholds the conceptual and cognitive superiority of modern civilisations. This is a sociological, not an evaluative thesis. Modern civilisations display a much greater degree of differentiation and reflexivity than traditional civilisations with their mythological worldviews. A rational

[43] *Die Neue Unübersichtlichkeit*, p. 145.

[44] *Diskurs der Moderne*, p. 11 [3]; see also A. Wellmer, 'On the Dialectic of Modernism and Postmodenism', in *Praxis International*, **4** (October, 1984), pp. 337–62. An expanded version of this essay has recently been published in A. Wellmer, *The Persistence of Modernity* (Cambridge: Polity Press, 1991), pp. 36–94.

350

solution of problems has a higher chance of success in the modern, differentiated world. The *fundamental thesis* is that the rationality of worldviews is a measure of the core concepts, which are at the disposal of individuals for the interpretation of their respective worlds.[45] A society, which is mainly in possession of qualitative concepts – for instance for the indication of time or temperature – has, by such a thesis, less rational potential than a society, which is in possession of quantitative concepts for time and temperature measurements. For the availability of the latter not only increases the precision with which statements about time and temperature are made, they also enable their users to pass more objective judgements, the accuracy of which can be rationally debated.

Mythological worldviews are closed in a dual sense: a) there is no differentiation between fundamental attitudes towards the objective world, the social world and the subjective world (with which different validity claims are associated); b) mythological worldviews are not reflexive – they do not identify themselves as worldviews, that is as cultural traditions amongst others which have symbolic meanings, refer to different aspects of the world, are associated with different validity claims and are therefore subject to criticism and revision. However, modern worldviews are characterised by openness, the degree of which can be measured in terms of (a) the differentiation of three formal world concepts (objective, social, subjective worlds); (b) the specialisation of domains of inquiry into science, morality and art and (c) the differentiation into validity claims under which these fields of inquiry operate (the propositional truth of a factual assertion; the normative rightness of a speech act with respect to existing norms and values and the subjective truthfulness of the intentional expression and finally (d) the reflexivity of the worldview and the degree to which it is seen as a cultural tradition.[46]

The thesis that the differentiation of areas of discourse reveals a general evolution towards an expansion of rationality has been labelled Habermas's most questionable claim.[47] It is questionable if it is interpreted as a *substantive* thesis to the effect that the sum total of concrete rational acts has increased over the last three hundred years. As a substantive thesis, it would even be wrong about traditional worldviews, since the lack of conceptual differentiation is compatible with numerous rational attitudes in traditional societies. It becomes less questionable if it is read as a *formal* thesis: The

---

[45] *Theorie* I, p. 75(ff) [45(ff)].
[46] *Theorie* I, pp. 85, 99, 109f [52f, 64, 71f].
[47] A. Giddens, 'Reason without Revolution?', in *Habermas and Modernity*, p. 100. This claim is discussed most explicitly in *Rekonstruktion*, pp. 34–5, 152–7, 162, 278, 330 [119f, 138–42, 148, 184f].

potential for rational problem solving is increased, if conceptual and institutional differentiation evolves in a society, which caters for a more objective and intersubjective engagement with problems and their solutions.

There is evidence in Habermas's work for the interpretation of the thesis of the expansion of rationality as a formal rather than a substantive claim. This evidence can be found in his rejection of the inherent relativism of all postmodernist thinking. The postulation of a plurality of language games entails a renunciation of *external* evaluations of the validity of particular language games. Against such relativist strategies, Habermas employs the idea of the unity of reason in the diversity of its voices.[48] First, a distinction imposes itself between what is rationally valid and what is socially acceptable. This distinction creates room for the improvement of conceptual schemes. In the history of science, conceptual schemes like Geocentrism and the Great Chain of Being functioned as socially acceptable views but under the weight of evidence turned out to be rationally invalid. Heliocentrism and evolutionary biology developed as alternative, improved views which both had to overcome the threshold of social acceptability. Second, if this distinction is heeded, then both the possibility of the conceptual improvement of the worldviews of respective cultures and their empirical confirmation as the essential criterion of validity can be envisaged. In all criticism of relativism, the distinction between the conceptualisation (as the reference) used in the description and explanation of the natural and social world and this world itself (as the referent of the conceptualisation) is absolutely essential. It is true, of course, that humans have no unconceptualised access to their surrounding world, but it does not follow from this truth that our conceptual systems predetermine the way in which we see the world. In fact, the material world offers a number of resistances to false attempts at explaining it. To express this distinction between the reference and the referent, Habermas introduces the concept of *situational reason* which is both context-dependent in that it relies on language categories to express propositions about the world and context-independent in that the validity claims, made for propositions and norms, transcend the local contexts set by the language barriers in which these claims are cast.[49] Therefore knowledge claims can become universal and can be universally assessed for their *cognitive adequacy*. Cognitive adequacy – a function of the true statements, which are possible

[48] *Nachmetaphysisches Denken*, chapter 7; *Postmetaphysical Thinking* (Cambridge: Polity Press, 1992), chapter 6.

[49] Habermas, Nach meta-physiches Denken, p. 179 [139]; *Theorie* I, pp. 93, 88 [58f, 55].

within a conceptual scheme – is a major reason why worldviews evolve and replace each other. Both the Copernican and the Darwinian views were cognitively more adequate than their predecessors.

In an age of widespread relativism, Habermas reaffirms the universality of reason and rationality. The Kantian problem of the unity of reason still faces us today.[50] This problem redefines the position of philosophy with respect to the specialised sciences. As Habermas sees the modern world in the grip of cognitive-instrumental rationality, muted aspects of rationality in morality and art need to be revitalised. Philosophy must clarify the concept of communicative rationality and lose the fixation on the natural sciences.[51] But doubts have already been entertained concerning the ubiquitous identification of scientific reason with cognitive-instrumental rationality in Habermas's work. The very nature of scientific rationality, with its concern for the cognitive adequacy of theories and models, harbours philosophical presuppositions, implications and validity concerns far beyond means-end considerations. Even though aesthetic considerations seem to play a minor part in the work of scientists, appeals to mathematical beauty and theoretical simplicity are considered to be important values in theory choice. Calls for the moral responsibility of scientists have multiplied since the explosion of the first A-bomb and the first genetic manipulations in the early 70s. Thus, the differentiation into three formal world concepts with associated validity claims, which the Habermas model sees intermeshed only in the communicative rationality of the lifeworld, also exists in the value systems. These dimensions can only be ignored at the expense of a serious misrepresentation of science.

Moral concerns even begin to penetrate into the economic subsystem, as testified by the growing moral awareness in business, which supposedly is governed by strict means-end rationality. Habermas's own general characterisation of communicative rationality as a disposition of social agents to acquire and use knowledge and the more specific *procedural* conception of rationality as the ability to evaluate validity claims also capture the essence of scientific rationality. The tripartite division of rationality into the cognitive–instrumental (science), the normative-pragmatic (morality) and the aesthetic-expressive (art)[52] and its separation from the lifeworld is an artefact of the model. In view of the inherent philosophical and moral dimensions

[50] *Die neue Unübersichtlichkeit*, p. 136.

[51] Habermas, 'Questions and Counterquestions', in *Habermas and Modernity*, pp. 196–7.

[52] *Diskurs der Moderne*, p. 366 [314ff]; *Theorie*, I, pp. 25ff [8ff]; *Nachmetaphysisches Denken*, chapter I [I]; *Rekonstruktion*, p. 34 [119f].

Friedel Weinert

of scientific knowledge, of which scientists are aware, it is difficult to agree with Habermas's judgement that 'rationality shrinks to a purely formal concept insofar as the rationality of the contents evaporates into the validity of the results'.[53]

Such a view of science will not help in the new task which Habermas reserves for philosophy: to mediate between the expert cultures and the lifeworld.[54] A co-operation between science and philosophy requires of the philosopher an acquaintance with some of the expert knowledge in the area of expertise – be it science, law, art or society – whose mediation is sought. But more importantly, it imposes important *constraints* on the philosophical claims, which can justifiably be made about some expert area, like physics or sociology. In his identification of scientific rationality with cognitive-instrumental rationality, Habermas himself falls short of such a desideratum. Communicative rationality is not restricted to the lifeworld but a feature of many expert cultures. Great science of any kind has philosophical implications, which affect not only the expert cultures but also the lay public at large. Against the rapid torrent of specialisation, philosophy is engaged in the rational reconstruction of some of the fundamental assumptions *and* implications, which are buried in the welter of empirical and theoretical knowledge. Habermas's work is concerned with the reconstruction of the rational basis of modern societies and not with any expert science in particular. His work re-evaluates the *Lebenswelt* more than the subsystems. Differentiation is the key to the possibility of rationality. Habermas stresses the importance of upholding relations between the subsystems, the value sphere and the lifeworld. Some consequences of a fleshing out of such relations for the Habermas model have been discussed. The insistence on links between its components prevents his model of society from breaking up into myriad, non-interacting cells of activity. Unrelated plurality of societal cells only breeds relativism, which is the hallmark of postmodern interpretations of the modern age. Reason hums in many voices but its unity is preserved in the recognition of the difference between socially acceptable and cognitively valid views. The institutionalised doubt and the reflexivity, which characterise modern societies, do therefore not imply the cognitive levelling of all claims to knowledge. The appraisal of validity claims will always involve the assessment of the strength of support, which a conclusion can muster from its premises. As long as the distinction between what is socially

[53] *Nachmetaphysisches Denken*, p. 42; I have slightly amended the English translation on p. [35].
[54] *Nachmetaphysisches Denken*, p. 46 [38]; *Neue Unübersichtlichkeit*, p. 208.

acceptable and what is cognitively valid does not collapse and the cognitive adequacy of our theories remains open to criticism, so that conditions in the lifeworld can benefit from improvements in knowledge, Habermas must be right that modernity is still an unfinished project.

German Philosophy Today: Between Idealism, Romanticism, and Pragmatism

ANDREW BOWIE

1 History and philosophy

In his essay *On the History of Religion and Philosophy in Germany*, of 1834, Heinrich Heine suggested to his French audience that the German propensity for 'metaphysical abstractions' had led many people to condemn philosophy for its failure to have a practical effect, Germany having only had its revolution in thought, while France had its in reality. Heine, albeit somewhat ironically, refuses to join those who condemn philosophy: 'German philosophy is an important matter, which concerns the whole of humanity, and only the last grandchildren will be able to judge whether we should be blamed or praised for working out our philosophy before our revolution.'[1] He then makes the following prognosis:

> the German revolution will not be more mild and more gentle because it was preceded by Kantian critique, Fichtean transcendental idealism and even philosophy of nature. Revolutionary forces have developed via these doctrines which are just waiting for the day when they can break out and fill the world with horror and admiration. ... Don't smile at my advice, the advice of a dreamer who warns you about Kantians, Fichteans and philosophers of nature. Don't smile at the fantast who expects the same revolution in the realm of appearance as took place in the realm of spirit. ... A play will be performed in Germany in comparison with which the French Revolution could appear just as a harmless idyll (ibid., pp. 616–17).

What exactly is meant by these assertions is open to interpretation, but it is clear that Heine regards Kant and German Idealism, for all his criticisms of them, as a resource in the modern fight against established religion and illegitimate political authority. From our perspective, though, these remarks can also seem rather disturbing, despite what Heine may have intended. In the light of the perceived

---

[1] Heinrich Heine, *Sämtliche Werke in Drei Bändern* (Essen: Phaidon, n.d.) pp. 615–16.

Andrew Bowie

failure of German Idealism Marx will soon demand that philosophers stop interpreting the world and begin changing it, much in the way Heine predicts. But then one remembers the story of Martin Heidegger, turning up during the student movement in 1970 to give the *laudatio* at Hans-Georg Gadamer's seventieth birthday celebration, who disarmed the threat of accusations about his Nazism by citing Marx's thesis on Feuerbach and conceding that Gadamer's view of philosophy as interpretation might have been a better idea after all. Clearly, the uneasy relationship between philosophy and praxis in Germany requires particularly close scrutiny.

Judging by its reception in Britain for much of this century, the perceived dangers of, if not always Kantian, then certainly Fichtean, Schellingian, and – remembering Popper – Hegelian ideas have excluded them from any serious philosophical consideration. The course of German history after 1933 only served to speed what had been initiated by Russell's and others' attacks on 'British Idealism', and indigenous philosophers like Heidegger made their own contribution by their disgraceful political interventions. German philosophy has, as Heine's remarks suggest, often been very explicitly connected to history and politics in a way which has not until very recently been the case for British philosophy in particular. At a time when Germany is less than a decade on from re-unification one might therefore have expected philosophy once again to have moved decisively on to the political stage. A feature of the re-unification of Germany has, though, been the *lack* of sustained engagement in the political events on the part of many West German philosophers. Although responses to re-unification have been forthcoming from Jürgen Habermas, the Munich philosopher Dieter Henrich and others, an attempt to look at 'German philosophy today' in terms of recent history is, as yet, unlikely to produce observations of philosophical value. The interesting fact here is that there is a marked contrast between the insistence on socio-political *engagement* of 1968 onwards – in which the illusory hopes for revolutionary political change were really an indirect response to an increasingly prosperous West Germany's failure to come to terms with its Nazi past, rather than the result of actual revolutionary conditions in the present – and the disengagement that has followed a real political change which is still viewed with suspicion by many on the Left. Ironically, the actual effects on *philosophy* of 1968 and after were, despite the failures in other respects, quite radical.[2] The

[2] It should not be forgotten, though, how much the development of West German democracy owes to the opening up of certain aspects of political debate by the anti-authoritarian ideas of the Student Movement.

358

post-war institutional dominance of Heidegger and of existential philosophy was broken by an insistence on investigation of the socio-political implications of philosophy, and this led to the renewed influence of Frankfurt School Critical Theory, to a productive questioning of the traditions of German philosophy, and, eventually, by a more indirect route, to a growth of interest in analytical philosophy.

Just how complex the relationships between philosophy and history can be is suggested in the recent assertion by Dieter Henrich (himself no radical), in relation to the topic of 'Philosophy in One Germany', that it would be very mistaken for thinkers in the former GDR now to reject Marx as a philosopher.[3] Given the widespread dismissal of Heidegger in post-1968 Germany, because of his Nazism, and, more recently, of Marx, because of the events of the late 1980s, Henrich's assertion that 'The real productive effects of philosophical theories are ... almost always long-term effects which arise via a series of mediating instances' (ibid., p. 191) is a more appropriate response to the history of philosophy than the desire to keep up with philosophical fashion evident in the unreflective wholesale adoption of post-structuralism, or, for that matter, of analytical philosophy, in certain quarters in Germany.[4] When asked about the effects of the French Revolution on modern history Chou En Lai replied that it was 'too soon to tell'. The fact is that it is also still too soon to tell what the effects of German Idealist and Romantic ideas have been and will be, which leads me to my main theme.

My title of 'German philosophy today' refers not only to philosophy now being done in Germany, but also to how the history of German philosophy plays a role in philosophy today. It would, of course, be impossible to deal with all the contemporary approaches to philosophy in German intellectual life: the list of approaches would anyway not necessarily differ much, apart from very considerable differences in the relative numbers of people engaged in each

[3] Dieter Henrich, *Nach dem Ende der Teilung. Über Identitäten und Intellektualität in Deutschland* (Frankfurt: Suhrkamp, 1993), p. 203.
[4] For the reflective response to post-structuralism, see Manfred Frank, *Was Ist Neostrukturalismus?* (Frankfurt: Suhrkamp, 1984)/*What is Neostructuralism?*, trans. Sabine Wilke, Richard Gray, (Minneapolis: University of Minnesota Press, 1989); for Habermas' less sensitive response, see *Der philosophische Diskurs der Moderne* (Frankfurt: Suhrkamp, 1985)/ *The Philosophical Discourse of Modernity*, trans. Frederick Lawrence (Cambridge: Polity Press, 1987); for a differentiated recent view see Wolfgang Welsch, *Vernunft. Die zeitgenössiche Vernunftkritik und das Konzept der transversalen Vernunft* (Frankfurt: Suhrkamp, 1996).

Andrew Bowie

approach, from the equivalent list in America.[5] What interests me here is *why* certain aspects of the modern German philosophical tradition have succeeded in surviving both the announcement of their demise, and, indeed, their actual demise as the focus of debate during parts of the intervening period.[6] Looking at this issue will lead to a perspective from which our philosophical self-image may become rather clearer.

2 Science, metaphysics and subjectivity

As in most of the Western world, philosophers both in Germany and in this country are increasingly being forced by the pressures of political and economic reality to ask what they do is actually for. However, *this* demand for praxis tends to come from a rather different quarter. The demand is not only a contingent one, brought about by crudely instrumental government policies of the kind which tend in this country to be answered with another course on applied ethics: such government policies are themselves in part a result of perhaps the most inescapable feature of modernity. In 1964 Heidegger declared that: 'The development of the sciences is at the same time their separation from philosophy and the establishment of their independence. This process belongs to the end/completion *Vollendung*) of philosophy.'[7] The theme of the 'end of philosophy', as Heidegger acknowledges, takes one back to the Utopian view of the relationship of philosophy to praxis adumbrated by Heine and developed by the Young Hegelians, Marx, and others after the death of Hegel. At that time the practical realisation of the aims of philosophy, which was regarded as the expression of human self-legislation, was supposed eventually to obviate the need for philosophy altogether – an idea which is these days echoed in

[5] What *would* tend to differ is the number of philosophers happy to work in relation both to the German and the analytical traditions, such as Rüdiger Bubner, Wolfram Hogrebe, Albrecht Wellmer and some of the philosophers discussed below.

[6] My most glaring omission is that I do not discuss the work of Gadamer, who relies almost exclusively on the tradition I am considering, in any detail. Gadamer's influence has been so widespread that it is not feasible to give an adequate account of it here: it has been well documented in English anyway. As will soon become apparent, my main theme is essentially a version of what is expressed by the title of Gadamer's *Truth and Method*, though my development of that theme is quite different from Gadamer's.

[7] Martin Heidegger, *Zur Sache des Denkens* (Tübingen: Niemeyer, 1988) p. 63.

360

certain versions of pragmatism. The idea of the end of philosophy also, though, takes one forwards in a very different direction. Heidegger foresaw essential links between the end/completion of philosophy and what has become the conception of thinking as information processing, which informs theories of cognitive science and evolutionary epistemology. For Heidegger the question implicit in the idea of the 'end of philosophy', *both* in the past *and* in the present, concerns the relationship of 'metaphysics' to subjectivity, and here we encounter a crucial apparent paradox.

Attempts to reduce theories of subjectivity to theories of information-processing – the brain as 'super computer', with mental states as states of the software, etc. – would appear to aim at the final 'subversion' of the self-conscious subject, via the revelation that the subject's cognitive processes can be digitally reproduced and are ultimately the same processes as can be shown to occur in other systems in nature. Heidegger thinks such claims are the result of what is already implicit in the link between Descartes' claim to establish foundational certainty for philosophy in the *cogito* and his idea that we should be 'lord and master of nature'. The link comes about because in modernity 'philosophy becomes the empirical science of man, of everything that for man can become the experiencable object of his technology' (ibid., pp. 63–6). As such – and this is the essential point of the argument – the rise of the idea that consciousness can be explained in the same terms as the rest of nature is regarded as *itself* the product of the subject's growing control of nature which characterises modernity. From Descartes, to Hegel's claim that 'the substance is subject', to Husserl's search for the 'principle of all principles', Heidegger maintains, the 'concern (*Sache*) of philosophy ... is subjectivity' (ibid., p. 70). As I have shown elsewhere, Heidegger's story is simply mistaken in historical terms, because it ignores thinkers in his own tradition who had already made many of the same points as he did.[8] Despite this, the questions that result from his way of formulating the vital issue should not be ignored. Hegel's 'absolute knowledge' or Husserl's 'definitive evidence' are supposed, Heidegger contends, to constitute the subject's own true description of itself, which would guarantee that the truth it generates could not be sceptically undermined by questions about the reliability of its origins. Heidegger connects this – idealist – view of subjectivity to what is inherent in the *materialist* scientific account of the world which he links to the cul-

[8] See Andrew Bowie, *Schelling and Modern European Philosophy* (London: Routledge, 1993), and 'Rethinking the History of the Subject: Jacobi, Schelling and Heidegger', ed. Simon Critchley and Peter Dews, *Deconstructive Subjectivities* (Albany: SUNY Press, 1996), pp. 105–26.

Andrew Bowie

mination of Western philosophy manifest in Nietzsche's 'Will to Power'. The point of *both* the idealist *and* the materialist views for Heidegger is that they assume a final, articulable ground, either in the self-certainty of the subject, or in a physicalist reduction of that subject to its material ground.

Heidegger argues that this link between apparently opposed positions can make us 'aware that something is hiding which it can no longer be philosophy's concern to think' (ibid., p. 71) – 'philosophy' now being defined exclusively as the enterprise that would found itself in the power of the subject. This leads Heidegger himself to questionable reflections on a different – non-'philosophical' – kind of 'thinking', apparent in poets like Hölderlin, which receptively 'listens to the sendings of being', rather than spontaneously imposing its frameworks on nature. In this emphatic form Heidegger's destruction of metaphysics just reproduces a different – and potentially dangerous – version of the problems involved in what he wants to leave behind: the question of who decides when the words of being are being spoken does not differ greatly from the question of how the subject can be its own absolute authority. What matters in the present context is that the interesting aspect of Heidegger's move against foundationalism was already prefigured in F. H. Jacobi's critiques, in the 1780s and 1790s, of Spinoza, Kant and Fichte, whom Jacobi linked together as foundationalists from the perspective of what he termed his own '*Unphilosophie*' in a very similar manner to the way Heidegger links idealism and materialism. This leads Jacobi to reject the *cogito* as the foundation of philosophy, insisting that 'I am not a *Cartesian*. I begin like the Orientals (*Morgenländer*) in their conjugations with the third, not with the first person, and I believe that one simply should not put the *Sum* after the *Cogito*'.[9] Jacobi's move against philosophical foundationalism has been shown to be one of the main elements in the development of the Romantic philosophy to be considered below, which is, I want to claim, now becoming one of the most important contributions of German philosophy to philosophy today.[10]

[9] Heinrich Scholz, ed., *Die Hauptschriften zum Pantheismusstreit zwischen Jacobi und Mendelssohn* (Berlin: Reuther and Reichard, 1916), p. 52. The idea of inverting the *cogito*, which is still too often credited to Kierkegaard (who got it from Schelling, who got it from Jacobi), would seem to stem from J. G. Hamann, who proposed it in a letter to Jacobi in 1785: see Manfred Frank '*Unendliche Annäherung*'. *Die Anfänge der philosophischen Frühromantik* (Frankfurt: Suhrkamp, 1997), p. 676.
[10] See Andrew Bowie, *From Romanticism to Critical Theory. The Philosophy of German Literary Theory* (London: Routledge, 1997), and

One way of suggesting why Heidegger's approach cannot just be dismissed is to reflect that if, since Kant, much of modern philosophy has been concerned with the conditions of the possibility of knowledge, which are to be grounded in the activity of the subject, this neither explains what makes subjectivity itself possible, nor, unless one accepts an account of absolute idealism of the kind I shall discuss in a moment, does it explain why, once there is subjectivity, it encounters a world which is intelligible to it. If the subject is, as Heidegger puts it, the 'ray of light', the ray cannot itself 'create the clearing, the opening' (ibid., p. 73) which establishes the space for truth beyond its own contingent and fallible beliefs. There is, in these terms, as Jacobi already argued, an inevitable circularity involved in any claim to establish cognitive foundations, whether from an idealist or a materialist perspective. The cognitive scientist, for example, presupposes that what is subjective can be rendered objective, by coming to know itself as based on the kind of causally based information processing that is carried out by computers. Such a claim, however, cannot be warranted by cognitive science itself, because cognitive science necessarily relies on the ungroundable judgement that this presupposition is the true basis of thought for it to constitute its object as the appropriate object of scientific investigation in the first place. Henrich makes the obvious (Kantian) objection to cognitive science's claims to philosophical status as follows: 'Theories are conceived for domains of objects (*Sachbereiche*), without being able to be inferred from those domains. They connect facts (*Gegebenheiten*) and regularities, which can be observed or documented, in systems which themselves cannot in any way be discovered.'[11] The simple Kantian question for the foundationalist cognitive scientist is: what can cause something that is supposed to be an exclusively causal system to apprehend itself *as* causal in the first place? As Henrich puts it, in a formulation which offers an indication of an important alternative conception to Heidegger's of what 'metaphysics' might be: 'cognition of the real can never completely integrate itself into its conception of the whole of reality' (ibid., p. 166).

Reflections upon what is apparent in the deficiencies of cognitive science's account of 'mind and world' were very much part of the

---

[11] Dieter Henrich, *Fluchtlinien. Philosophische Essays* (Frankfurt: Suhrkamp, 1982), p. 81.

'Romanticism and Technology' in *Radical Philosophy* 72, 1995 pp. 5–16. Jacobi presents his arguments in the name of theology, but their effects went well beyond theology. Jacobi was, incidentally, a significant philosophical influence on Hölderlin.

work at the end of the eighteenth and beginning of the nineteenth century of (among many others) Fichte, Jacobi, Schelling, the 'early Romantics', Novalis and Friedrich Schlegel, and Schleiermacher – as we shall see, the case of Hegel is more complex. The further point is that responses to what is implied by Heidegger's account of metaphysics play a substantial role in philosophy both in Germany and in parts of the English-speaking world today. One of the major achievements of the German philosophy of the last thirty or so years, notably in the work of Henrich,[12] and of the Tübingen philosopher Manfred Frank,[13] has been the revelation of the depth and complexity involved in the story Heidegger tells in too reductive a manner. Furthermore, such historical research does not just consist of a 'rational reconstruction' of past arguments which echo the arguments of contemporary philosophy, but seeks rather to develop the potential of past theories which may not have become manifest during their initial reception.[14].

As is well known, certain factors in Kant's critical philosophy have always troubled subsequent philosophers. One is the account of how the spontaneity of the subject is both what makes the world given in receptivity an object of knowledge rather than the empiricist's inarticulate mass of impressions, and the basis of practical

[12] E.g., in *Fichtes ursprüngliche Einsicht* (Frankfurt: Klostermann, 1967), English translation in ed. D. Christensen, *Contemporary German Philosophy*, Vol. 1 (University Park, Pa: Pennsylvania University Press, 1982), *Selbstverhältnisse* (Stuttgart: Reclam, 1982), *Konstellationen. Probleme und Debatten am Ursprung der idealistischen Philosophie (1789–95)* (Stuttgart: Klett-Cotta, 1991), *Der Grund im Bewußtsein. Untersuchungen zu Hölderlins Denken (1794–5)* (Stuttgart: Klett-Cotta, 1992).

[13] E.g., in *Der unendliche Mangel an Sein* (Frankfurt: Suhrkamp, 1975), *Eine Einführung in Schellings Philosophie* (Frankfurt am Main: Suhrkamp, 1985), *Einführung in die frühromantische Ästhetik* (Frankfurt: Suhrkamp, 1989), *Das Problem 'Zeit' in der deutschen Romantik* (Paderborn, Munich, Vienna, Zürich: Schöningh 1990), and, most importantly, '*Unendliche Annäherung*'.

[14] See Henrich, *Nach dem Ende der Teilung*, p. 1993. The other alternative here is the stultifying historicism exemplified by Frederick Beiser and some German researchers, which, for all its valuable contributions to knowledge of the history of philosophy, rigidly restricts the arguments of the past to their contexts of emergence. Beiser bizarrely thinks one should investigate the history of philosophy in this manner because revelation of the potential of past arguments for the present will supposedly be unlikely to be valid for more than a few years. Despite Beiser's claims to the contrary, this really is Ranke's view of history from what turns out to be the point of view of eternity (see *Bulletin of the Hegel Society of Great Britain*, 34, Autumn/Winter 1996).

self-determination; another is Kant's insistence that the role of the subject in cognition separates the subject from nature 'in itself', because the subject can only know nature as nature appears to it. The central questions in early German Idealism follow from these aspects of Kant: what relationship does the spontaneity of the subject have to the activity of the rest of nature, and how can we know about this? Furthermore, how does nature 'in itself' give rise to appearances in the subject at all, if it is topically separate from what we can know about it? In other words, as Jacobi asked in 1787, how do noumena 'cause' phenomena, if the category of 'cause' is only applicable to what the spontaneity of the subject brings about by linking intuitions via the schema of temporal succession?[15]

3 The grounds of modern philosophy

The recent growth of interest in such questions in Anglo-American philosophy results from a variety of factors. When cognitive scientists start to claim they can give physicalist answers to German Idealist questions, philosophers are, as we just saw, likely to ask whether they are not forgetting Kantian and Fichtean objections to the idea that the activity of thought could explain itself as an object like any other. Fichte asserts that 'the mistake of all realism [by which he means roughly what we would term 'physicalism'], is that it regards the I just as a not-I, and therefore does not explain the transition from not-I to I'.[16] One does not have to accept Fichte's own idealist account of the I to be able to accept the initial point: contemporary realists like Frank Farrell also insist, along with Hilary Putnam, John McDowell and others, that 'intentional directedness toward the world is not something that can be added on after we have given a causal account of intentional states nonintentionally described'[17] The reappearance of post-Kantian questions also becomes likely when the effects of the technical application of certain forms of scientific knowledge to nature become increasingly catastrophic for nature as a whole, thereby occasioning questions, of the kind raised by Schelling, Heidegger, Adorno and others about just what science and nature really are. The central questions here derive from the ways in which the mind-world question is framed. At the risk of appearing to follow Wagner's procedure in the com-

[15] Friedrich Heinrich Jacobi, *David Hume über den Glauben oder Idealismus und Realismus ein Gespräch* (Breslau: Gottl. Löwe, 1787), p. 224.
[16] *Fichtes Werke I* (Berlin: de Gruyter, 1971), p. 211.
[17] Frank B. Farrell, *Subjectivity, Realism and Postmodernism* (Cambridge University Press, 1996), p. 62.

position of the *Ring* I need, before getting to contemporary debates, to pursue certain central aspects of the philosophical history presupposed in those debates, some of which is still unfamiliar to many Anglo-Saxon philosophers.

According to Kant the world of nature is only intelligible because of the ability of subjects spontaneously to *take* things to be in certain ways, including law-bound ways, rather than receive them wholly passively. Consequently, if nature *qua* object of knowledge is, as Kant insisted, only that which is 'conditioned' by necessary laws, the genesis of what could come to know those laws and spontaneously effect changes in the world of appearance becomes inaccessible to our knowledge. Hegel encapsulated Fichte's response, in the *Wissenschaftslehre* of 1794, to Kant's dualism by his assertion in 1801 that Fichte's arguments had led to a 'subjective subject–object', a knowable world of nature that *appears* to individual subjects in the form of resistant deterministically constituted objects but is in fact generated by the absolute spontaneity (the 'absolute I'), of which their individual self-generating activity of thought (the 'relative I') is a part. Hegel also suggested that Schelling, by insisting on the need to understand how the self-conscious subject could emerge from nature, had posited a further 'objective subject–object', which was required to establish the bridge between mind and nature, nature itself being, at different levels and to different degrees, inherently self-determining.[18] The aim of German Idealism was to articulate the relationship between mind and nature as a relationship between two ultimately identical aspects of a totality, the Absolute, thus overcoming the split between idealism and materialism. The real difficulty was that overcoming this split always seems to have to take place by subordinating one side to the other. Fichte's problem was the status of nature, which became merely the object of practical reason, leaving him open to Schelling's prophetically ecological accusation that he had made nature into something just to be kicked around. Schelling's problem was the relationship of his philosophy of nature to the transcendental philosophy required if one was not to fall back into pre-Kantian Spinozist 'dogmatism'. Either way, 'nature in itself' has somehow to involve a 'subjective' aspect if an implausible dualism is to be avoided. How, though, could this aspect of nature in itself be described from the philosophical vantage point of finite individual subjects? Could those subjects' ideas of the totality become constitutive, as Hegel would try to show, or did they have to remain merely regulative, as Kant

[18] G. W. F. Hegel, *Differenz des Fichteschen und Schellingschen Systems der Philosophie* (Stuttgart: Reclam, 1982).

had insisted, and as the Romantics also came to argue? From Kant's initial epistemological viewpoint, a move – which also tempted Kant himself – is therefore made towards ontological considerations about how nature could come to 'intuit' itself at all in our thinking. Whether the latter position merely represents a regression to a pre-Kantian stance has, as we shall see, been a bone of contention ever since it surfaced in interpretations of aspects of Kant's *Critique of Judgement*.[19]

The central issue here arises from Kant's conception of the 'imagination' in the first *Critique*, which shifts uneasily between spontaneity and receptivity, thereby leaving wide open the question of his idealism or realism. The importance of the refusal to elimi-nate the role of spontaneity in epistemology has recently been high-lighted once more by McDowell's *Mind and World*, which directs an attenuated version of Fichte's position (and its development in Hegel) against cognitive science's reductionist physicalism. The decisive problem is what *sort* of spontaneous activity is involved in the 'productive imagination', the locus of the schemata which make concepts sensuous.[20] In order to explain his conviction that an apparently wholly objective nature must be the result of something inherently subjective if it is to come to the point of knowing itself, Fichte argues that the 'I cannot be conscious of its activity in the production of what is intuited' (*Fichtes Werke I*, p. 230) – otherwise there would be an endless regress of being conscious of being con-scious, etc. – so individual subjects can only be conscious of the *results* of its unconscious activity – appearing objective nature – via the cognitive faculty of understanding. Although, for Fichte, the foundational spontaneity is what allows transcendental philosophy to ground itself, by making receptivity (the 'not-I') simply a reduced form of spontaneity ('the absolute I'),[21] the idea that the spontaneity is 'unconscious' – and thereby leads to our sense of an external world – constitutes one of the key initial moves towards

---

[19] See Robert B. Pippin, 'Avoiding German Idealism', in *Idealism as Modernism* (Cambridge University Press, 1996), pp. 129–53, and the argu-ments below.

[20] See Andrew Bowie, 'John McDowell's *Mind and World*, and Early Romantic Epistemology', *Revue internationale de philosophie*, 50, (197) 3/1996, pp. 515–54, which questions McDowell's version of the question via his failure to consider the issue of schematism as it appears in the tra-dition from Kant to Heidegger.

[21] Frank terms this position '*Produktionsidealismus*'. Jacobi and others argued that this was essentially a version of Spinozism, in which the sub-stance was re-named as the absolute I (see Bowie, *From Romanticism to Critical Theory*, chapter 1).

what will become a highly influential structure in modern German philosophy.

In this structure a prior 'active' ground of some kind (and here lie several tales) splits itself into a subjective and an objective world. The Berlin philosopher Herbert Schnädelbach has suggested a division with regard to this structure, between the 'speculative idealism' of Fichte, early Schelling and Hegel, and the 'speculative naturalism' of Schopenhauer, Marx and Horkheimer and Adorno.[22] The thinkers who do not share Fichte's idealist faith that the ground is in principle accessible to thought belong in the latter category.[23] For Fichte the ethical task of philosophy is to make nature – undeveloped spontaneity – accord with the articulated spontaneity of reason. At a time when he was also in contact with Novalis and Schlegel, Schelling – who tends to move between the 'idealists' and the 'naturalists' at differing times – sees the ground in his 1800 *System of Transcendental Idealism* as 'unconscious productivity' which is, following hints from Kant's third *Critique* about beauty as the possible means of access to the 'supersensuous substrate' where nature and freedom are reconciled, only accessible to us in aesthetic production and reception. In his middle philosophy Schelling moves against idealism by characterising the basis of the subject – object relationship as an '*Ungrund*' (unground), which is the inexplicable active source both of a manifest world and of human freedom to do both good and evil.[24] In the wake of Schelling, Schopenhauer removes any residual sense that a rational account of the ground is possible, terming the ground the 'Will', and he is followed in this by Nietzsche, who sees it initially as Dionysus,[25] and then in terms of the 'Will to Power'. Nietzsche's conception of the notion of the will is, for the later Heidegger, the culmination of seeing being in terms of subjectivity which begins with Descartes. Even Heidegger himself, who sees the 'ontological' disclosure of 'being' as the inexplicable prior ground of 'ontic' explanation, can be said to follow part of this tradition.

Habermas claims in relation to the tradition in question, as he interprets it in Nietzsche, Heidegger and Derrida, that 'Whenever

[22] Herbert Schnädelbach, *Vernunft und Geschichte* (Frankfurt: Suhrkamp, 1987), pp. 159–61.

[23] Fichte himself eventually renounced this faith.

[24] On the stages of Schelling's philosophy, see Bowie, *Schelling*. Heidegger owes much to these ideas, as is apparent in Martin Heidegger, *Schellings Abhandlung Über das Wesen der menschlichen Freiheit*, (Tübingen: Niemeyer, 1971).

[25] This conception of Dionysus derives, without acknowledgement, from Friedrich Schlegel and Schelling.

the One is thought of as absolute negativity, as withdrawal and absence, as resistance against all propositional articulation (*Rede*), the ground (*Grund*) of rationality reveals itself as an abyss (*Abgrund*) of the irrational'.[26] Given the suspicions which any kind of putative irrationalism not unnaturally provoke in post-Nazi Germany, it is hardly surprising that Habermas thinks this structure must now be left behind. However, the question which forms the focus of some of the most significant debates in German philosophy today is whether the resources of this admittedly questionable tradition are as exhausted and invalidated as Habermas assumes, via his conviction that attention to what cannot be propositionally articulated is likely to lead to unaccountable claims based on 'intuition'.

The leading role in the modern German controversy over the ground of philosophy is generally attributed to Hegel, who is still too often interpreted as simply having overcome the failures of his idealist and Romantic predecessors, and thus as having obviated their potential 'irrationalism'. Hegel, whose basic conception is echoed in Habermas' rejection of the idea of 'the One ... as absolute negativity', and, as we shall see, in other aspects of Habermas' work, maintains that accounts of the prior ground of the subject–object relationship involve an intuitive 'immediacy'. Such accounts therefore either presuppose the unbounded nature of the subject's spontaneity in an invalid manner, or give no way of understanding how the supposed unity of mind and world could ever become explicable: this would seem to Hegel to contradict the modern success in finding post-traditional ways of organising society and discovering the laws of nature. The subject is, for Hegel, only able to articulate its founding role at the *end* of the system, as the 'mediated' 'substance which is subject', when it understands its feeling of limitation at the beginning to be the 'immediate' ground of its ultimately unlimited nature. Hegel's Absolute is, then, in Henrich's useful phrase, 'the finite to the extent to which the finite is nothing at all but negative relation to itself' (Henrich, *Selbstverhältnisse*, p. 160). Without the 'negative' relationship between finite moments – of the kind that results from conflicting assertions, one of which must be wrong – there would be no progress in knowledge, and thus no sense in which finitude can be overcome by philosophical insight into the necessary limitations of

[26] Jürgen Habermas, *Nachmetaphysisches Denken* (Frankfurt: Suhrkamp, 1988), p. 160/*Postmetaphysical Thinking*, trans. William Mark Hohengarten, (Cambridge MA: MIT Press 1992). On the link between Schelling, Nietzsche and Derrida (and Rorty), see Bowie, *Schelling*, chapter 4.

Andrew Bowie

everything particular. Instead of leading either to an idealist system grounded on immediate self-certainty, like Fichte's, or to a sceptical sense that we never have any certainty that our thought is in contact with being, Hegel thinks the *failure* of any particular thought to become immediately identical with its object, which results from the particular always requiring further 'mediating' relationships to other particulars beyond itself to be determinate, is the motor which drives us towards the 'absolute Idea'. The coherence theory via which the system is constructed will therefore become a correspondence theory when the system is completed.

Such a version of Hegelianism can be seen as idealist megalomania, the system of the 'stomach become spirit', as T. W. Adorno put it, in a phrase which sums up the basic argument of the critiques of Hegelianism and other idealisms that begin, even before Hegel develops his system, in early Romanticism, and are explicitly applied to Hegel by Schelling from the 1820s onwards. However, more modest Hegelianisms, of the kind developed by Klaus Hartmann, Robert Pippin, John McDowell or even, to some extent, Richard Rorty, as well as other pragmatist-influenced contemporary defenders of Hegel in Germany, would maintain that all Hegel really meant is that the question of the meaning of being is obviated by the fact that our puzzlement about being is a result of the failure to see that 'being' is merely the empty notion of a Quinean something looking for its value. The notion can be filled when we realise that it is only when we concretely engage in determination of being that it means anything at all – 'no entity without identity.' Otherwise it is the irrational One, which would have to be reached in 'intuition', and would therefore be conceptually inaccessible. In this view the 'absolute Idea' simply stands for the claim that the actual process of knowledge can be left to the specific sciences, which fill out the system's integrated classification of the spontaneous forms thinking has taken on in the history of its real encounters with the world. This is a seductive vision, because it apparently obviates 'metaphysical' worries,[27] and comes to terms with what works with huge success anyway. In Hartmann's terms Hegel offers a 'theory of categories or of such determinations of the real as permit of reconstruction and are thus borne out as categories' (in MacIntyre, *Hegel*, p. 104). As such, Hegel has been the next port of call for analytical philosophers, like McDowell, who have realised that the post-Kantian dilemmas are very much still with us, but who invoke absolute idealism in order to prevent mind and world becoming dis-

[27] Hartmann offers a 'non-metaphysical' reading of Hegel in ed. A. MacIntyre, *Hegel. A Collection of Critical Essays* (Notre Dame, London: University of Notre Dame Press, 1972) p. 101–24

connected. Lurking in even these attenuated versions of the Hegelian position, however, is Heidegger's suspicion that philosophy will, despite all, culminate in natural science, because the problem of 'being', which is the prior real condition of any science, has been conjured away by being 'subjectivised'.

The problem which Hegel shares with any version of absolute idealism was already foreseen in the Romantic critiques of Fichte and other post-Kantian foundationalists in the middle 1790s by Novalis, Schlegel and others, and was suggested in Henrich's formulation, cited above, that 'cognition of the real can never completely integrate itself into its conception of the whole of reality'. In a 'reflexive' conception of mind and world like Hegel's the subject must in principle be able to make itself fully transparent to itself *via* its relations to the world, which therefore reflect back to it its own essential truth. This is, of course, one way of seeing the project of cognitive science: knowledge of the causal functioning of the world is supposed to tell us what mind really is.[28] The fact is, though, that the articulated unity of mind and world that Hegel regards as possible at the end of the system's explication of their relationship requires a *prior* unity which he seeks to exclude by his insistence that being itself is empty until it is determined in the 'reflexive' process of mediation. However, if this prior ground did not already have immediate (non-reflexive) access to itself *as* itself there could be no way in which what is fully articulated at the end could *re*-cognise itself – i.e. know itself *again* – as the same as what was there at the beginning. How would one know when the end had been achieved, unless it can be known to mirror, as the 'other of itself', what one began with? This means that what is at the end (i.e., the philosopher building the system) must presuppose an unexplained, immediate access to being at the beginning, in precisely the manner Hegel must avoid if he is to establish that philosophy can exhaustively articulate the structure of the Absolute.[29]

If this prior ground is in fact irredeemably resistant to being subsumed under a concept that would identify it, and if consciousness 'exists' in a way nothing we subsequently come to know about the world can finally explain – because consciousness' 'reflexive' knowledge of itself, and its determinate knowledge of the world, are both

---

[28] This does not mean that I think Hegel or his successors would subscribe for a moment to this materialist conception, just that the structures in question are notably similar, because they rely on one side reflecting to the other what it really is.

[29] See Dieter Henrich, *Hegel im Kontext* (Frankfurt: Suhrkamp, 1971) for the classic account of the problem with Hegel's 'logic of reflection', where this problem becomes apparent.

dependent on a pre-reflexive existential continuity – absolute idealism becomes impossible. In this – Romantic – view, being, the
immediate, real ground, is not of the same order as the reflexive,
cognitive ground which ensues from it.[30] As Frank points out –
which will also be important for the arguments about self-consciousness to be considered in a moment – this means that 'Just as
[reflexive] self-*relationship* must be explained from out of the undi-
vided unity of a pre-reflexive *self*, analogously, the [reflexive] relation of a subject to a predicate in a judgement [which constitutes the
cognitive form of access to the changing world of determinate
knowledge] must be explained via the simple unity of the absolute
position or existence [the 'real ground']' (Frank, '*Unendliche
Annäherung*', p. 672).[31] The real ground, which cannot be dissolved
into determinate knowledge, ensures that a revised judgement can
be predicated both of the same world, and, in the case of self-
knowledge, of the same self, as a preceding, now false, judgement.
One therefore either presupposes, as Hegel in fact does, the cognitive answer to what being really is, or one cannot claim to have given
an exhaustive account of the relationship of mind and world. I shall
return to some implications of this rather difficult issue later.

Assuming such objections to absolute idealism are valid, what is
at stake now is suggested in Habermas' comment that, despite all
the intervening philosophical developments, 'There is nothing for
it: we are philosophically still contemporaries of the Young
Hegelians' (Habermas, *Nachmetaphysisches Denken*, p. 277), because
their 'arguments reclaim the finitude of spirit against the self-relat-
ed-totalising thinking of the dialectic' (ibid., p. 47). Habermas takes
this to be the 'post-metaphysical' situation,[32] to which he wishes to
respond by a change in philosophical paradigm, from a tradition
based, as we saw, on the attempt to establish the ground of subjec-

---

[30] See ed. and trans. Andrew Bowie, *F. W. J. von Schelling: 'On the
History of Modern Philosophy'* (Cambridge University Press, 1994); Frank,
Der unendliche Mangel; Bowie, *Schelling*, 'The Actuality of Schelling's
Hegel-Critique', in *Bulletin of the Hegel Society of Great Britian* 21–2,
1990, pp. 19–29, 'The Schellingian Alternative' in 'Symposium on Bowie:
Schelling contra Hegel' issue of the *Bulletin of the Hegel Society of Great
Britain* 30, Autumn/winter 1994, pp. 23–42, and 'John McDowell's *Mind
and World*'.

[31] This follows from Kant's argument against the ontological proof, that
'being is not a real predicate': Hegel, one should remember, defends the
ontological proof.

[32] As Schnädelbach has suggested, the term is unfortunate: he suggests
'post-idealist', though even that also involves problems, given the unresolved disputes over the notion of 'realism'.

tivity, to a paradigm based on intersubjectivity, in which 'communicative action' is fundamental. Habermas' route to this conception is highly complex, but it is also based on a problematic account of the significance of the history I have been outlining. The reasons for 'linguistic turns' in philosophy are not always as straightforward as Habermas sometimes suggests, and Hegelianism cannot be escaped as readily as Young Hegelians might wish. This has led to one of the defining debates in contemporary German philosophy, in which the claims of idealism, Romanticism and pragmatism compete in instructive ways. In order to understand this debate another historical point must now be addressed, albeit one which turns out to involve some of the same issues as we have just been investigating.

4 The return of hermeneutics

It might appear as though I have so far wilfully ignored the dimension of modern German philosophy represented by the founders of analytical philosophy, such as Frege and Carnap, whose work began seriously to be taken up again after the War, particularly via the influence from the 1960s onwards of Ernst Tugendhat,[33] Karl-Otto Apel,[34] and others. This influence was decisive for the development of Habermas' critical relationship to the tradition I have been outlining, and has now also, despite its predominantly positive effects, led to there being departments in Germany as dogmatically analytical in their orientation as the vast majority are in Britain or America. However, the 'linguistic turn' in German philosophy cannot, as it can in the English-speaking world, be seen as a result of the interventions of Frege, Russell, or the early Wittgenstein. The hermeneutic turn in German philosophy, which is already de facto a 'linguistic turn', is a product of the early Romantic philosophy which plays an until recently largely ignored or misunderstood role in the story I have been outlining, and was fully developed by Schleiermacher from 1805 until his death in 1834.[35] The importance

[33] E.g., *Einführung in die sprachanalytische Philosophie* (Frankfurt: Suhrkamp, 1975)/*Traditional and Analytical Philosophy*, trans. P.A. Gorner (Cambridge University Press, 1982), *Selbstbewußtsein und Selbstbestimmung* (Frankfurt MA: Suhrkamp, 1979)/*Self-Consciousness and Self-Determination*, trans. Paul Stern, (Cambridge, MA: MIT Press, 1986), *Philosophische Aufsätze* (Frankfurt: Suhrkamp, 1992).

[34] E.g., *Transformation der Philosophie* (Frankfurt: Suhrkamp, 1973). Apel was also important for his introduction of the work of C. S. Peirce into the German debate: see K.-O. Apel, *Der Denkweg von Charles S. Peirce* (Frankfurt: Suhrkamp, 1975).

Andrew Bowie

of hermeneutics in Schleiermacher's thought results from arguments against Hegelian and other idealisms which exemplify the Romantic tendency in German philosophy. Frank sees 'philosophical Romanticism' – the position we have just considered, that questions the Hegelian 'reflexive' paradigm – as leading to the idea that 'the transcendence of being in relation to consciousness forces philosophy on to the path of an endless progression on which being is at no time exhausted by being adequately grasped in consciousness and so presents itself in never ending interpretation' (Frank, '*Unendliche Annäherung*', p. 729). The Romantic concept of the subject is accordingly summed up in Novalis' suggestion from his critique of Fichte of 1795–1796 that 'Consciousness is a being outside being in being', which requires a 'Theory of ... not-being in being, in order to let being be there for itself *in a certain manner*'.[36] This means, of course, that being cannot ever be said to be present in an absolute manner, and that our sense of being is itself generated by the failure of 'reflection' to grasp the totality of one's being in relation to the being of the world. I will return to some consequences that ensue from this idea a bit later, but first we need to see how it might relate to the linguistic turn.

It is now fairly clear that the foundational project of an analytical philosophy of language no longer promises what its originators intended. A recent account of the history of the philosophy of language suggests that 'To study the philosophy of language is to see that there is progress in philosophy', and then offers what is in fact a startlingly Hegelian account of the moves from what one might see as the 'immediacy' of concern (1) with the word (early Wittgenstein and Russell), to (2) with the (observation) sentence (logical positivism), to (3) with language as a whole (speech act theory), to (4) with a 'mediated' holism which no longer sees language and the world as separate (Quine, Davidson – these days one could hopefully even begin to add the early Heidegger and Gadamer).[37] This is indeed progress, but it is rather less obviously global progress when it emerges that the end of the story was already present in some detail in Schleiermacher's hermeneutics.

[35] I take Schleiermacher as the central figure because, unlike Hamann, Herder, Wilhelm von Humboldt and the other Romantics, he was already fully aware of all the dimensions of language – i.e., the semiotic, the semantic, the pragmatic and the 'world-disclosive' – which have become central to contemporary philosophical debate.

[36] Novalis. *Band 2 Das philosophisch-theoretische Werk*, ed. Hans-Joachim Mähl, (Munich Vienna: Hanser, 1978), p. 100.

[37] John V. Canfield, ed., *Philosophy of Meaning, Knowledge and Value in the Twentieth Century* (London: Routledge, 1997), p. 35.

374

Thus Schleiermacher: (1) 'in its single appearance the word is isolated; its determinacy does not result from itself but from its surroundings';[38] (2) 'The proposition (*Satz*) as a unit is also the smallest thing that can be understood or misunderstood' (ibid., p. 98) (a thought which he connects with the idea of a 'speech act' (ibid., p. 89)); (3) 'if one considers language as emerging from each act of speaking, it cannot ... be subjected to calculation' (ibid., p. 80); (4) 'If we ... assume that the utterance is a moment of a life, then I must seek out the whole context and ask how the individual is moved to make the utterance (occasion) and to what following moment the utterance was directed (purpose)' (ibid., p. 89) – such interpretation is an 'endless task'. Obviously I am not taking account here of the massive and unquestionable advances in logic and in the resources for examining the structure of language that accompanied the emergence of the analytical philosophy of language, but it is evident that Schleiermacher reveals facts about language and interpretation which have only fairly recently begun to become part of mainstream English-language philosophy.[39]

The (admittedly reductive) outline of the history of the twentieth century analytical philosophy of language just cited suggests that a large part of that history was determined by the attempt to find a grounding connection between language and the world, in which the aim was to exclude psychology and epistemology from semantics, on the assumption that the subject could not be the ground of intersubjective meanings.[40] However, the way this attempt was carried out in fact initiated a linguistic re-run of some of the problems of grounding in German Idealism. Whether it was Russell's 'propositions', Carnap's 'observation statements', Schlick's 'constatations', or whatever, such positions invalidly take some initial language-world relationship to be self-legitimating –

[38] F. D. E. Schleiermacher, *Hermeneutik und Kritik*, ed. Manfred Frank, (Frankfurt: Suhrkamp, 1977), p. 106. By the time this essay appears there will be an English translation and edition by Andrew Bowie of *Hermeneutik und Kritik*, in '*Hermeneutics and Criticism*' and Other Texts (Cambridge University Press, 1998).

[39] See Andrew Bowie, 'The Meaning of the Hermeneutic Tradition in Contemporary Philosophy', in ed. A. O'Hear, '*Verstehen' and Humane Understanding*, Royal Institute of Philosophy Lectures (Cambridge University Press, 1997) pp. 121–44.

[40] These moves are in fact generally associated with a suspicion of Kant, and are historically linked to Jacobi and the Romantics in ways which have yet to be explored in detail: see J. Alberto Coffa, *The Semantic Tradition from Kant to Carnap* (Cambridge University Press, 1991); Andrew Bowie, 'The Romantic Connection: Neurath, the Frankfurt School, and Heidegger' (forthcoming).

the verification criterion cannot itself, for example, be verified – or end in a regress in which one statement has to be justified by another, without it ever being clear what justifies the first statement, unless one assumes that its initial 'immediacy' is somehow irreducibly given. The net result is invariably that giving a complete analytical explanation of what people do when they understand a statement becomes impossible: the statement of the conditions under which the original statement can be held true leads to the need to analyse the conditions of the statement of the conditions, and so on. Friedrich Schlegel had already suggested in 1796, as part of the Romantic critique of idealism, that 'There are no basic propositions (*Grundsätze*) which would universally be appropriate accompanists and leaders to the truth. Even the most dangerous [basic propositions] can be justified for certain stages and for the development of the mind and even the most secure and best can lead into an abyss of errors',[41] and he is followed in this – which suggests the questionable nature of most accounts of the history of the linguistic turn – by Otto Neurath: 'We have no magic oracle at our disposal with whose help we can separate dangerous expressions from the less dangerous expressions'.[42] Furthermore, the 'world-disclosing' dimension of language, which is the focus of the Romantic tradition that was revived in part by Heidegger and Gadamer (and is present in the more Romantic side of the later Wittgenstein), is often excluded as 'meaningless', in the name of attempting to establish how it is that language refers to the system of what Putnam ironically terms 'All The Objects There Are'.[43]

Even the most obvious, and still popular, referential relationship takes us back to German Idealism. As Frank has suggested (Frank, '*Unendliche Annäherung*', p. 89; see also Bowie, *From Romanticism to Critical Theory*, Chapter 3), the causal theory of reference – where there is supposed to be 'a causally determined relation holding between mental representations and objects in the world'[44] – raises all the problems that were already present in the question of how Kant's things in themselves could cause appearances, which Jacobi used against any philosophical claim to be able to ground knowledge. How can a world–object cause a meaning, given that meanings relate to states of affairs in which things are *understood* as

[41] Friedrich Schlegel, *Philosophische Lehrjahre* (1796–1828) (*Kritische Friedrich Schlegel Ausgabe* vol. 18) (Munich, Paderborn, Vienna: Ferdinand Schöningh, 1963) p. 518.

[42] Otto Neurath, *Gesammelte philosophische und methodologische Schriften. Band 2* (Vienna: Hölder-Pichler-Tempsky, 1981), p. 924.

[43] Hilary Putnam, *Representation and Reality* (Cambridge, MA, London, 1989), p. 120.

[44] Jerry Fodor, cited in J. E. Malpas, *Donald Davidson and the Mirror of Meaning* (Cambridge University Press, 1992), p. 65.

being *in a certain manner*, not to the bare existence of objects? Schleiermacher was already fully aware of the problem: 'at different times the same organic affection [where causality plays a role] leads to completely different concepts. The perception of an emerald will at one time be for me a schema of a certain green, then of a certain crystallisation, finally of a certain stone'.[45] There evidently are causal events, which are often identifiable, taking place between world objects and my organism, but these are so particular and so varied that they could never be said to generate iterable and communicable meanings: the problem of the relationship between spontaneity and receptivity just resurfaces here in another form.[46] This problem is apparent even in the challenging non-reductive contemporary realism of a Frank Farrell, who, when it comes to the crunch, always has recourse to the unexplained active metaphor of the world generating beliefs in us (see, e.g., Farrell, *Subjectivity*, p. 254).

The hermeneutic tradition inaugurated by Schleiermacher, then, like the recent work of Putnam, and other pragmatically oriented thinkers, sees no appropriate way of finally answering 'the' question of reference, if 'the' question is meaningful at all. The conditions of understanding are simply too varied ever to be able to establish one foundational kind of referential relationship. In Schleiermacher's terms we can *neither* wholly isolate the world, including language, from what our minds spontaneously contribute to it, *nor* can we wholly isolate our minds from their receptive involvement with the world. Already for Schleiermacher (and for his friend Schlegel), then, there is no foundational point from which to proceed, so 'we must be satisfied with arbitrary beginnings in all areas of knowledge' (Schleiermacher, *Hermeneutik und Kritik*, p. 149; see Bowie 'The Meaning of the Hermeneutic Tradition').[47] It is precisely the contingency inherent in the transcendence of being in relation to consciousness that gives rise to Schleiermacher's view of hermeneutics, and which has also led to 'the interpretive turn' becoming so central to contemporary philosophical discussion.[48]

[45] F. D. E. Schleiermacher, *Dialektik (1814–15). Einleitung zur Dialektik (1833)* (Hamburg: Meiner, 1988), p. 39. Tugendhat makes this point very clear in *Einführung in die sprachanalytische Philosophie*.

[46] As I show in 'John McDowell's *Mind and World*', the key issue here is the adoption of Kant's notion of schematism, which is intended as the bridge between spontaneity and receptivity, for the theory of language.

[47] The same point was repeatedly made by Friedrich Schlegel in the 1790s, and by Novalis.

[48] See David Hiley, James Bohman, and Richard Shusterman, eds., *The Interpretive Turn* (Cornell University Press, 1991).

Andrew Bowie

5 Paradigm shifts

Given Habermas' attachment to an – admittedly pragmatised – interpretation of the analytical linguistic turn,[49] I want now to show why certain aspects of Romantic ideas, of the kind both adopted and initiated by Schleiermacher, have been used to put in doubt whether Habermas' desire for a *wholesale* change of philosophical paradigm to the paradigm of communication is likely to succeed. This will depend on the conception of the subject in the competing theories and will tell us something, both about the role of the linguistic turn in contemporary philosophy and about German philosophy's relations to its past. Habermas' move to the paradigm of communication is a speech–act oriented version of the linguistic turn, which, in certain respects, shares Heidegger's view of modern philosophy's failure to ground philosophy in an account of the subject. Habermas adopts aspects of (among others) Kant, Hegel, George Herbert Mead and of Tugendhat's formal semantics, in order to argue that: 'everything which deserves the name subjectivity … owes itself to the unyieldingly individuating compulsion of the linguistic medium of processes of learning' (Habermas, *Nachmetaphysisches* Denken, p. 34) which is constituted in subjects' public articulations of 'criticisable' cognitive, ethical and aesthetic validity claims.

Habermas' core move is evident in his remarks on Ernst Cassirer's linguistic neo-Kantianism: 'with the semiotic turn not only the point of reference of one objective world, but also the transcendental subject beyond this world is lost. As soon as the transcendental capacities are transferred to differing symbolic systems the transcendental subject loses its place beyond the empirical world … and is drawn into the process of history';[50] in short, 'world-constituting capacities are transferred from transcendental subjectivity to grammatical structures' (Habermas, *Nachmetaphysisches Denken*, p. 15). It is therefore only in communicative action that the validity of a world-view can be established, because the new kind of rationality 'can no longer guarantee an *antecedent* unity in the multiplicity of appearances' (ibid., p. 43) of the kind Kant claimed, albeit without succeeding in explaining how, was provided by the 'I

---

[49] He gives an excellent summary of his interpretation of the linguistic turn in Habermas, *Faktizität und Geltung* (Frankfurt: Suhrkamp, 1992), pp. 24–45/*Between Facts and Norms*, trans. W. Rehg (Cambridge: Polity Press, 1996).

[50] Jürgen Habermas, *Vom sinnlichen Eindruck zum symbolischen Ausdruck* (Frankfurt: Suhrkamp, 1997), p. 33. The point is, incidentally, much the same as that made by Derrida against Husserl's conception of the transcendental subject in *La voix et le phénomène*.

think that must be able to accompany all my representations'. For Habermas this view of rationality results in an important and productive emphasis on the ethical and normative aspects of communication: if validity can only result via public consensus, because there are no foundational epistemological means of access to the world, that consensus must be able to be seen as free of coercion if its rationality is to be vouchsafed.[51] Judged by its pragmatic effects, Habermas' theory has often been signally successful, having made a substantial and positive contribution to the theory and practice of many humanities and social science subjects, to legal theory, and even, at times, to the standard of political debate in Germany.

Habermas arrives at his theory partly as a way of escaping the consequences of the position espoused at the end of the War by his mentors in the 'first generation' of the Frankfurt School, Max Horkheimer and T. W. Adorno, in *Dialectic of Enlightenment* (1947). This book's proximity to the neo-Nietzscheanism of post-structuralism and its Schellingian articulation of criticisms of the effects of modern technology on nature have made it a focus of much recent discussion in Germany (see, e.g., Habermas, *Der philosophische Diskurs*; Welsch, *Vernunft*). The underlying issue here is the 'reflexivity' of reason that we have been explicitly and implicitly considering all along. Modernity is regarded by Habermas as 'self-legislating', because the legitimacy of reason can only be established by reason itself, which is constituted in communicative action. What, though, if the 'unconscious' dimension in the structure adumbrated by Fichte cannot be conceived of in rational terms, as one part of the tradition beginning with Schelling came to assert? *Dialectic of Enlightenment* takes this possibility to its extreme by suggesting, in the light of the disasters of modern history, that the 'instrumental reason' driving modern technology is itself driven merely by the subject's Hobbesian instinct for self-preservation. Consequently, 'enlightenment falls back into mythology', because the 'subordination of everything natural to the arrogant subject finally culminates in precisely the dominance of the blindly objective, of the natural'.[52] As we saw, one of Schelling's Romantic-influenced attempts to establish the ground of the world's intelligibility was to suggest that art, because it is neither produced solely by the following of rules, nor merely instrumental, offers a – still rational – way of coming to terms with this ground. For the authors of

[51] As I suggest in *From Romanticism to Critical Theory*, chapter 5, the ethical dimension was also central, albeit in a somewhat different manner, to Schleiermacher.

[52] Max Horkheimer and T.W. Adorno, *Dialektik der Aufklärung. Philosophische Fragmente* (Frankfurt: Fischer, 1971), pp. 3–5.

Andrew Bowie

Dialectic of Enlightenment even art has largely ceased to be a metaphor for the reconciliation of necessity and freedom. Instead, all but the most advanced and recalcitrant art has itself become subject to instrumental reason by being made into a commodity for the 'culture industry'. There is, as such, no location available from which a new kind of philosophically legitimated rationality could develop. Habermas justifiably regards this universal verdict on modernity as obscuring the advances which modernity has also brought about, because it reduces reason, which can be both instrumental and communicative, solely to the former, and so leads Horkheimer and Adorno to a position not very far from the later Heidegger's notion of the 'subjectification of being' in Western metaphysics. More importantly, in the present context, Habermas sees this verdict as a result of the 'paradigm of subject philosophy', which renders insoluble the problems to which it gives rise.[53] Anyone who does not accept the need for the move to intersubjectivity is therefore supposed to be trapped in the old aporias of 'metaphysics', which relies on 'cognitive reason finding itself once again in the rationally structured world' (Habermas, *Nachmetaphysisches Denken*, p. 42), or, when this fails – because 'self-reflection must make something into an object which, as the spontaneous source of all subjectivity, withdraws itself altogether from the form of objectivity' (Habermas, *Der philosophische Diskurs*, p. 433) – on an 'irrationalist' appeal to an inaccessible origin.

Given the problematic link between philosophy and praxis we began with, one has to be wary of invoking the past to question Habermas' view, but certain features of it have rightly been questioned in terms of the tradition we have been examining. Most evident at first sight is the reification involved in Habermas' – probably Gadamer-derived – metaphor of language, rather than the transcendental subject, as the locus of world-constitution.[54] Whereas,

[53] Unlike Heidegger, though, the authors of *Dialectic of Enlightenment* still intended to contribute to new forms of rationality, not just to claim it was inherently bound to domination. Adorno later developed a conception not always so far from that of Habermas: see Bowie, *From Romanticism to Critical Theory*, chapter 9. Habermas tends to concentrate too exclusively on Adorno's claims that only radical modern art, such as the work of Kafka, Beckett or Schönberg, can retain a sense of what a new rationality would be, via its resistance to existing ways of making sense in modernity. Adorno's *Negative Dialectics*, though, offers more interesting perspectives for a workable theory of critical rationality than Habermas' account would suggest: see, e.g., Schnädelbach, *Vernunft und Geschichte*.

[54] Gadamer himself adopts such metaphors from the later Heidegger: cf. his remark that 'The "subject" of the experience of art, that which remains and persists, is not the subjectivity of the person who experiences it, but

380

since Kant, the very notion of the subject requires spontaneity, grammatical structures can only be said to direct activity, not to constitute the activity itself: the refusal to acknowledge this threatens to lead to a reified linguistic idealism, in which the transcendentalised structures of language are themselves the determining factor, rather than one aspect of a more complex process of world-constitution. Schnädelbach suggests regarding 'the transcendental as a whole as the *competence* of empirical human beings to *follow* certain rules and principles in thinking, cognition and action'.[55] Even then, however, the actual interpretation of real communicative acts cannot be reduced to analysis of the rules which are part of what makes them possible, as Schleiermacher showed when he insisted on the need for 'technical' interpretation to complement rule-bound 'grammatical' interpretation. He did so because, as Kant already realised, knowing which rule to follow in interpretation cannot, on pain of a regress, itself be the result of a rule. This means that interpretation of cognitive claims also requires (albeit to a lesser degree) an aspect of the same kind of non rule-bound judgement as is required for something to be seen as a work of art (see Bowie, *From Romanticism to Critical Theory*, chapter 5). Habermas' claim that the world is essentially constituted by already existing forms of communicative action into which we are socialised by learning the rules basically relies, then, as Frank suggests, on the mistaken assumption that what are evidently necessary conditions of world-constitution are also sufficient conditions.

Inverting philosophical positions often has the effect of producing much the same problem in another form. Habermas, like Gadamer, sometimes merely transfers the attributes of spontaneity into the language which individual subjects acquire via receptivity. The assertion that 'language reveals itself to speaking subjects as something prior and objective, as the forming structure of conditions of possibility' (Habermas, *Nachmetaphysisches Denken*, p. 51) hardly differs in this respect form Heidegger's claim that 'Language speaks. Man speaks to the extent to which he corresponds to lan-

---

[55] Herbert Schnädelbach, *Zur Rehabilitierung des animal rationale* (Frankfurt: Suhrkamp, 1992), p. 289

---

the work of art itself' (Gadamer, *Wahrheit und Methode* (Tübingen: J. C. B. Mohr, 1975, p. 98/*Truth and Method*, revised translation by Joel Weinsheimer and Donald G. Marshall (New York: Seabury Press, 1989)), which suggests the reification which recurs in his thought. Gadamer is insistent, like Hegel in his account of '*Sittlichkeit*', that we can never free ourselves of 'prejudices' in whose genesis we play no role and to which we are subject by the very fact of being in a social world at all.

guage'.[56] the Romantic tradition, on the other hand, avoids this Heideggerian reification, but still gives a central role to language. In his *Ethics* Schleiermacher, who first made properly explicit the ways in which language took over *some* of the functions attributed to transcendental subjectivity,[57] asserted that: 'If language appears to come to [the child] first as receptivity, this only refers to the particular language which surrounds it; spontaneity with regard to being able to speak at all is simultaneous with that language.'[58] The question is, once again, what role one should attribute to subjective spontaneity: the significance of the linguistic turn looks different, depending upon the answer one gives to this question.

Given the fact that in actual language use we very often are effectively 'spoken' by what we have learned to do in already familiar social contexts, Habermas' position points to an ineliminable dimension of communicative action, albeit one which can also begin to sound like 'ideology': how much do the existing resources of language in a social context enable and how much do they obscure and constrain, and who decides which is the case? In his earlier work, *Knowledge and Human Interests*,[59] the ways in which a particular society or social group could involve 'systematically distorted communication' had been a central concern, but Gadamer's argument that 'prejudice', in the sense of unthematised background norms and knowledge, is ineliminably built into all communication in real societies made Habermas aware that the location from which to judge what is distorted is more problematic than he had realised, because there cannot be a meta-perspective outside communication in real contexts (such a perspective would involve precisely the metaphysics he wishes to avoid). He consequently tried to restore a critical perspective that could establish the 'ideological' nature of some forms of communication via the counterfactual postulate of the 'ideal speech situation', in which communication would not be distorted by power, because the participants would acknowledge an orientation towards the truth beyond their particular interests that is supposedly inherent in communicative action itself. However, despite these developments, Habermas does not take adequate

[56] Martin Heidegger, *Unterwegs zur Sprache*, (Pfullingen: Neske 1959), pp. 32–3.

[57] A suggestion first made by Hamann in 1784: see Andrew Bowie, *Aesthetics and Subjectivity: from Kant to Nietzsche* (Manchester University Press, 1993) chapter 6.

[58] Friedrich Schleiermacher, *Ethik (1812–13)*, (Hamburg: Meiner, 1990) p. 66.

[59] *Erkenntnis und Interesse* (Frankfurt: Suhrkamp, 1973), *Knowledge and Human Interests*, trans. J. J. Shapiro (London: Heinemann, 1978).

account of the spontaneous dimension of language use on the part of individual subjects, which cannot be attributed to language itself without getting involved in questionable metaphorical contortions.[60]

6 The limits of the semantic turn

The debate on these questions was focused by Henrich's contention that Habermas' paradigm shift could not be successfully accomplished, because it ignored a crucial dimension of the history of arguments about self-consciousness.[61] For the essential move in his paradigm shift Habermas relies on Tugendhat's claim that the problem of self-consciousness can be semantically dissolved by an analysis of the status of first, second, and third person propositions.[62] If these can be mutually converted into each other 'idealist' problems of self-consciousness, apparent in the need to give an account of the self-ascription of psychological predicates – and an account of 'qualia', though that is not the main issue here – will be obviated by the demonstration that the first person propositions required to establish self-ascription do not in fact have a different status from other propositions. Self-consciousness will therefore be inherently propositional, and so will be accessible in the same intersubjective terms as any other aspect of the world. To be myself in Tugendhat's terms, then, entails knowledge on my part that another person could use any of my first person ascriptions in the second or third person and the proposition would still refer to me.[63]

[60] See Manfred Frank, *Stil in der Philosophie* (Stuttgart: Reclam 1992), 'Wider den apriorischen Intersubjektivismus', ed. Micha Brumlik and Hauke Brunkhorst, *Gemeinschaft und Gerechtigkeit* (Frankfurt: Fischer, 1993), pp. 273–89, and *The Subject and the Text. Essays in Literary Theory and Philosophy*, ed. Andrew Bowie, (Cambridge University Press, 1997).

[61] For more detail on the debate see Peter Dews' outstanding account in *The Limits of Disenchantment* (London, New York: Verso, 1995), chapter 8. The main texts are Habermas, *Nachmetaphysisches Denken*; Tugendhat, *Selbstbewußtsein und Selbstbestimmung* (Frankfurt: Suhrkamp, 1979); Henrich, *Konzepte* (Frankfurt: Suhrkamp, 1987), 'Noch einmal in Zirkeln. Eine Kritik von Ernst Tugendhats semantischer Erklärung von Selbstbewußtsein', ed. Clemens Bellut and Ulrich Müller-Scholl, *Mensch und Moderne* (Würzburg: Königshausen und Neumann, 1989), pp. 93–102; and Frank, 'Subjektivität und Intersubjektivität', in *Selbstbewußtsein und Selbsterkenntnis* (Stuttgart: Reclam, 1991), pp. 410–77.

[62] The positions of Habermas and Tugendhat differ in certain respects, which would require some complex differentiations. All that concerns me here is the way in which they both rely on semantic premises for their arguments about self-consciousness, and share the same crucial fault.

[63] This is in fact a version of Strawson's arguments about personhood, in which my identity is established via the means for discriminating a spatio-temporal object.

Significantly, Tugendhat's position can be construed as a kind of linguistic Hegelianism: in the same way as, for Hegel, I can only be myself via the structure of self-recognition in the other, which is the basic structure of *Geist*, in the semantic model language takes over the role of *Geist* by being the medium via which I individuate myself from other world objects, including other subjects. Henrich already identified the implicit problem with this kind of position in the 1960s, using an argument from Fichte (see Henrich, *Fichtes ursprüngliche Einsicht*; Bowie, *Aesthetics and Subjectivity*, chapter 3),[64] and Frank has shown how the main objection to such positions informs the Romantic strand of post-Kantian thought in ways which are still relevant for contemporary philosophy. The underlying question here is what, apart from my own *prior* acquaintance with what it is for me to be a locus of understanding, could 'cause' me in the first place to judge that a material event occasioned by a physical object in the world is a linguistic sign produced by another subject?[65] The objections to Tugendhat and Habermas that ensue from such questions point to a division in modern German philosophy which Henrich thinks is decisive for whether there can be a 'consistent analytical philosophy of language' (cit. in Frank, *Selbstbewußtsein*, p. 435).

The initial arguments here should further elucidate the problem with Hegelian absolute idealism which we examined earlier. Attempts to give an externalist account of self-consciousness end up in a circle, which could only be avoided if one denied the existence of self-consciousness altogether and adopted a kind of radical behaviourism which both Habermas and Tugendhat wholly reject. The circle arises because an externalist theory of self-consciousness could only explain what is in question by *presupposing* it in a non-externalist manner. Novalis condenses this problem into a simple question: 'Can I look for a schema [i.e., a means of applying a con-

[64] Henrich, unlike Frank, would not directly associate himself with early Romantic philosophy, preferring to see Hölderlin as the key figure, and he still thinks that it may be possible to work out a viable version of Hegelianism. Despite this, I would maintain that the Romantics are very close indeed to the ideas Henrich outlines in *Fluchtlinien* and elsewhere.

[65] See Frank, *Selbstbewußtsein und Selbsterkenntnis*, and his demonstration in '*Unendliche Annäherung*', pp. 804–6, that Novalis, via Fichte's account of the genesis of intersubjectivity in the *Grundlage des Naturrechts*, already identified the reification which renders the semantic model of self-consciousness unworkable. In *Kampf um Anerkennung* (Frankfurt: Suhrkamp, 1994)/*The Struggle for Recognition* (Cambridge: Polity Press, 1995) Habermas' successor in Frankfurt, Axel Honneth, does not, despite his many insights into the problem of intersubjective recognition in social philosophy, even consider the problem at issue here.

cept to an intuition] for myself, if I am that which schematises? (Novalis, *Das philosophisch-theoretische Werk*, p. 162). Frank illustrates the basic argument with the metaphor of a mirror, in which the mirror image in the world can be construed as the proposition about myself in the second or third person. How can I identify myself as *myself* in a mirror without *already* 'knowing' myself in a non-objective manner?[66] Identifications of objects are inherently fallible and prepositional, but when Ernst Mach fails to see *himself* as the 'shabby pedagogue' reflected in the mirror at the end of the tram, he is – *qua* first person – at that moment still infallibly and immediately aware that he is seeing somebody, even though he fails to identify himself in a proposition *qua* external spatio-temporal object. This awareness therefore involves a kind of knowledge which cannot be perceptual and inferential. What is required in an adequate theory of self-consciousness, and communication, then, is a way of distinguishing what one must be familiar with to understand what it *means* for a self-conscious individual to say 'I', from what is required for the noise 'I' to be produced via a rule or mechanism. In common with many contemporary philosophers, Habermas does not have a convincing way of explaining this. Rorty, who exemplifies the problem most clearly, contends that a concept is just 'the regular use of a mark or noise',[67] The exorbitant weight which falls on the notion of 'use' in this assertion is occasioned by Rorty's reductionist approach to subjectivity: does he think he should use the noises 'self-conscious subject' for his computer when it 'uses' the noise 'I' in voice mode? Frank sums up the main contention against the semantic view as follows: 'the knowledge which is attributed to the "I"-sayer from the "he" perspective is something different and something more than the command of the rule of the convertibility of the deictic expressions' (*Subjektivität und Intersubjektivität*', p. 446). Henrich insists in relation to this conception that it is not, as German Idealism had hoped, that one can deduce 'basic logical forms or the ways of founding science and metaphysics or the basic norms of action' from self-consciousness, but that these aspects of thought 'lose their meaning and their proper use and the basis of their legitimation if self-conscious beings cannot be presupposed by them' (Henrich, *Konzepte*, p. 31).

[66] If to 'know' is to identify by classifying with a predicate, this kind of 'knowledge' cannot, strictly, be termed knowledge. What Frank is pointing to are facts like my certainty of having an indeterminate feeling of malaise before I come to know – assent to the proposition that – I am clinically depressed.
[67] Richard Rorty, *Essays on Heidegger and Others. Philosophical Papers Volume Two* (Cambridge University Press, 1991), p. 126.

Andrew Bowie

This may seem a rather abstruse point to make against the impressive edifice of Habermasian theory, and it is important not to exaggerate the distance, particularly of Frank, from the emancipatory aims of that theory.[68] Furthermore, it is not that I think for a moment that Habermas' attempt to establish a communicative theory of rationality is mistaken as a whole: the undesirable alternatives are basically either dogmatic theology or scientism. My questions are directed at the consequences of his preparedness to jettison too much of the German philosophical tradition in the name of an analytical linguistic turn which is now turning out to be more than questionable. Henrich's and Frank's objections reveal an important, specifically philosophical, tension that results when the communicative paradigm is confronted with the tradition it claims to have left behind. Two factors are immediately significant in the present context. The first is the relationship of the structure of the problem for Tugendhat and Habermas to the structure of the problem entailed by Hegel's system: in both, what is supposed to *result* from a reflexive structure of self-recognition in the other has to rely on something prior which cannot be reflexive, because the reflexive relationship depends upon it to be intelligible at all; the second is that Heidegger's reasons for saying good-bye to 'philosophy', or 'Western metaphysics' cease to apply if these arguments are correct. Both issues relate to the rejection of the idea that the spontaneity of the self-conscious individual should play a grounding 'metaphysical' role in philosophy, which is echoed in the semantic tradition.[69] The point of the Romantic position is, though, that the subject could *not*, as it was supposed to in the early Fichte, play this grounding role, but that it was not therefore reducible to something else that could be established as playing that role. The real problem is to explain how it is that individual subjects can become able to understand, to come to terms with, and to change their relationships to the admittedly often all but overwhelming constraints – including the constraints both of language and of their own social identity formed in social interaction – with which they are confronted.

If one does not *become* self-conscious, as Habermas' theory (in the wake of Hegel) claims one does, via socialisation into communicative action, individual self-consciousness cannot be reduced to a theory that explains the phenomenon of self-consciousness in the

[68] In *Die Grenzen der Verständigung. Ein Geistergespräch zwischen Lyotard und Habermas* (Frankfurt: Suhrkamp, 1988) Frank expressly adopts key aspects of Habermas' theory against Lyotard.

[69] Tugendhat studied with Heidegger early in his career before turning to analytical philosophy.

386

same way as it would a world object. Henrich therefore insists, in line with the Romantic conception, that the perspective of the subject and the perspective of the person are not reducible to each other: 'that [each individual] is precisely this person must be experienced as contingent from the perspective of their subjectivity' (Henrich, *Fluchtlinien*, p. 21); consequently, 'We understand ourselves equally primordially as one [person] among others', in the realm in which concepts are what makes the world intelligible, and 'as the One [subject] opposed to the whole world' (ibid., p. 138), where they are not. The two ways of understanding do not harmonise, and this is the source of philosophical questions with which everyone in modernity is faced if they ponder their own existence.

The idea of the divergence between subject and person is not merely a piece of metaphysical nostalgia: it offers, for example, a way of understanding the new significance of aesthetic production and reception in modernity. The very need for novel, non-conceptual means of articulating individual being in the world relates to a specifically modern sense that concepts (or established language games) may be adequate to the person, but are not finally adequate to the subject. The correlate of this need is the need for ways of revealing how being itself is, as Heidegger will maintain, both disclosed and obscured by any articulation of what there is. In modernity it is, significantly, the non-conceptual art of music which often comes to be regarded as revealing ways of being, both of the subject and of the world, which can be obscured by an increasingly science- and technology-dominated society.[70] Frank cites Jacobi's remark in his letters on Spinoza of 1789 that 'We only have a feeling, even of our own existence, not a concept,'[71] and comments 'for we do not know of ourselves (and know *that* we exist) by attributing an entity to a class of entities (what would the concept be which classified the experience of being a self?)' (Frank, *Unendliche Annäherung*, p. 688). There is, then, in these terms, a link, which informs the rise of hermeneutics, of philosophical aesthetics, and the history of modern art, between the being of the subject which transcends the relationship between itself as subject and what it knows of itself as its own object, and being, which transcends whatever we predicate of it.

[70] See Andrew Bowie, 'Adorno, Heidegger and the Meaning of Music', in *Thesis 11* (forthcoming). It is notable, of course, how important music is for the later Wittgenstein.
[71] F. H. Jacobi, *Über die Lehre des Spinoza in Briefen an den Herrn Moses Mendelssohn* (Breslau: Loewe, 1789), p. 420.

Schleiermacher sums up the basic ontological claim as follows:

> as thinkers we are only in the single act [of thought]; but as beings we are the unity of all single acts and moments. Progression is only the transition from one [reflexive] moment to the next. This therefore takes place through our being, the living unity of the succession of the acts of thought. The transcendent basis of thought, in which the principles of linkage are contained, is nothing but our own transcendent basis as thinking being . ... *The transcendent basis must now indeed be the same basis of the being which affects us as of the being which is our own activity*.[72]

Schleiermacher's conception of art relies precisely on the need to take account of the pre-reflexive 'feeling' of our existence that transcends particular acts of thought – Novalis usefully explains the pre-reflexive immediacy of 'feeling' by his remark that 'feeling cannot feel itself' (Novalis, *Das philosophische-theoretische Werk*, p. 18). Schleiermacher terms this feeling 'immediate self-consciousness', in which 'the single life [i.e., the subject, in Henrich's sense] expresses itself in its difference',[73] so that 'in lyric poetry, where it is a question of expressing the movement of immediate self-consciousness [=feeling], the thought is itself really only a means of presentation [rather than a proposition that has claims to validity]' (Schleiermacher, *Hermeneutik*, p. 138). In this way the non-propositional aspect of self-consciousness is not relegated to mystical inarticulacy, as Habermas sometimes suggests, but is instead seen as the basis of the need for, and production of, non-conceptual forms of articulation.

7 The future of metaphysics

There are further important dimensions to these issues. In the Romantic conception the being of nature and the being of the subject are linked in a way which means nature cannot be reduced to what the natural sciences – which can only ever be constituted in 'single acts' of thought (i.e., in propositions) – can tell us about it. Adorno sums up the essence of the Romantic view of the self and nature when he states that 'We are really no longer ourselves a piece

[72] *Friedrich Schleiermachers Dialektik*, ed. R. Odebrecht, (Leipzig, 1942), pp. 274–5. The 'transcendent basis' is where Schleiermacher locates God, but this does not affect the philosophical point: he arrived at this position not least via his engagement with Jacobi.

[73] Friedrich Schleiermacher, *Vorlesungen über die Ästhetik*, ed. Carl Lommatzsch, (Berlin, New York: de Gruyter, 1974), p. 76.

of nature at the moment when we notice, when we recognise that we are a piece of nature', so that 'what transcends nature is nature which has become aware of itself'.[74] Without this realisation 'external' nature just becomes the object of instrumental reason, which no longer seeks to understand its own activity as part of a whole which transcends particularistic knowledge. The strange fact is that if, as evolutionary epistemology and other scientistically oriented theories want to insist, human beings are to be seen purely naturalistically, they ought to conclude, as Schelling did, that nature, far from being reducible to determinism, must *inherently* involve what can move beyond determinism and develop reflexive self-determination.

Habermas' own Kantian suspicion of questions about nature's relationship to subjectivity leads him to underplay such perspectives, although as Peter Dews points out, he comes close to them in remarks such as the following: 'It is true that the timebombs of a ruthlessly exploited nature are quietly yet stubbornly ticking away. But while outer nature broods in its way on revenge for the mutilations we have inflicted on it, nature within *us* also raises its voice.'[75] He suspects such questions on the grounds that, as Dews suggests, any normative claims that ensue from the link between nature and the subject 'which are presumed to have metaphysical backing could be used to override the democratic consensus of the members of a society' (Dews, *The Limits of Disenchantment*, pp. 161–2). Communicative consensus here takes on the role of Kant's transcendental subject, which also has no access to nature in itself. Such putatively Kantian assumptions can admittedly disarm reductive physicalism, or irrationalist ecological theories, but they also surrender any sense that philosophy might still have ways of asking meaningful questions about nature which could not be answered by a 'nomothetic' scientific theory. The really difficult problem, therefore, is the problem, already apparent in German Idealism, of what to make of the distinction between what may be revealed in philosophical engagements with the relationship between nature and subjectivity, and the consequences that may be drawn from these engagements for action within the public sphere. Habermas' suspicions that Romantic ideas may either rely on pre-Kantian dogmatism or involve 'an abdication of problem-solving philosophical thinking before the poetic power of language, litera-

---

[74] T. W. Adorno, *Probleme der Moralphilosopie* (1963) (Frankfurt: Suhrkamp, 1996), p. 154–5.

[75] Jürgen Habermas, *Vergangenheit als Zukunft* (Zürich: Pendo, 1991), p. 125, quoted in Dews, *The Limits of Disenchantment*, p. 165. It should be remembered that Habermas wrote his Ph.D. on Schelling.

Andrew Bowie

ture and art',[76] are, in this respect, as much historical as specifically philosophical. By orienting his approach to what can be publicly validated he wishes to avoid the worst features of what was exemplified by Heidegger's claims to a new kind of 'listening to the words of being', which suggested that the language of public argument is merely 'the language of metaphysics'. In the process, though, Habermas diminishes the role of those forms of world-disclosure which *are* important because of their resistance to being converted into discursivity or into scientifically verifiable theories. As the case of Schelling shows, it was the attempt to develop a philosophy of nature whose role was not just to give epistemological grounding to the natural sciences that first opened up the possibility of a viable ecological conception in which nature could not be reduced to what science may eventually tell us. Particular branches of the sciences cannot, on pain of vicious circularity, be used to explain their own existence.[77]

Habermas' doubts about Romantic conceptions rely on the notionally Kantian assumption that the establishing of three separate spheres of cognitive, ethical and aesthetic validity is the main positive result of what Max Weber termed the 'disenchantment' characteristic of modernity. The problem is that this assumption leads back once again to Heidegger's question of what philosophy's role could now be, given the indubitable success of the 'ontic' sciences in obviating so many of its former tasks, and given the fact that legislation *within* these supposed spheres is hardly the task of philosophy itself. Habermas' response is to maintain that philosophy today might 'at least help to set in motion again the frozen interplay between the cognitive–instrumental, the moral–practical and the aesthetic–expressive, which is like a mobile that has become stubbornly entangled.'[78] He does not, though, give a convincing explanation of what would allow this – Romantic – interplay to begin again. The aim is obviously to find new forms of orientation which would re-integrate these differing spheres of modernity, rather than allowing means–ends rationality to dominate. But this aim necessarily leads towards ideas that *contradict* the notion that

[76] Jürgen Habermas, *Texte und Kontexte* (Frankfurt: Suhrkamp, 1991) p. 90.
[77] This is most obvious in evolutionary theories, which have to explain themselves as the result of evolutionary adaptation. See Bowie, *Schelling*, chapter 2. This does not make such theories false, but it does mean they cannot be self-grounding.
[78] Jürgen Habermas, *Moralbewußtsein und kommunikatives Handeln* (Frankfurt: Suhrkamp, 1983), p. 26/*Moral Consciousness and Communicative Action*, trans. C. Lenhardt and S. Weber (Cambridge: Polity Press, 1992).

390

they constitute separate spheres in the first place. It is for this reason that any interrelation of the spheres requires a revaluation of resources from aesthetics, which cannot be reduced to the merely expressive function Habermas often attributes to it. Indeed, Kant himself came to argue that the very possibility, not only of a shared social life, but also of knowledge – and, given his argument, language itself – depends on the central focus of the aesthetic, the imagination.[79] He claims in the *Critique of Judgement* that a 'common sense' of the kind 'required for the universal communicability of a feeling' is 'the necessary condition of the universal communicability of our cognition', because without postulating such a common sense there is no way of even beginning to understand how spontaneity and receptivity could interact in a way that produces intersubjectively accessible knowledge.[80] Kant even uses a musical analogy to argue this, talking of the 'tuning/attunement' (*Stimmung*) of the cognitive powers, which is differently 'proportioned', depending on the object in question, and which 'can only be determined by feeling (not by concepts)' (ibid.).

It was, once again, Schleiermacher who first worked out in detail some of the methodological consequences for modern philosophy of what is implied by such ideas. Although the fact of immediate self-consciousness means we 'cannot know whether the other person hears or sees as we do' (*Friedrich Schleiermachers Dialektik*, p. 371), we have to postulate, in the manner of Kant's 'common sense' – thus in a way which cannot be conceptually analysed – that knowledge is constituted in the same way in everyone for there to be anything that can count as knowledge at all. The key relationship is between receptivity, which can never be proved to be the same in others and which anyway involves radically different 'input' for each individual and each culture, and spontaneity, which must be *assumed* to structure receptivity in the same ways, despite these differences. Whether what spontaneity produces is *in fact* the same, however, must be established by 'exchange of consciousness ... this presupposes a mediating term, a universal and shared system of designation' (ibid., p. 372), namely language (on this see Bowie, Introduction to '*Hermeneutics and Criticism*'). This might appear to lead directly back to Habermas and to his procedural conception of

[79] This aspect of Kant is what led Schelling and Schleiermacher to see 'schematism', which links spontaneity and receptivity, as the basis of the ability to use a finite number of relatively fixed signifiers for an infinite number of ways of articulating the world. See Bowie, *From Romanticism to Critical Theory*, chapter 2.

[80] Immanuel Kant, *Kritik der Urteilskraft* (Frankfurt: Suhrkamp, 1977), p. B66. This issue is excellently dealt with in Welsch, *Vernunft*, pp. 490–5.

Andrew Bowie

the self and language. Schleiermacher, though, does not think self-consciousness comes into being via 'the unyieldingly individuating compulsion of the linguistic medium of processes of learning' (Habermas, cited above), which makes the interpretation of the other less dependent on rules than Habermas would like to make it. For Schleiermacher, as we saw, interpretation is an 'endless task', which ultimately relies on the non-rule-bound *art* of 'technical interpretation'. His arguments about the nature of individual self-consciousness mean that 'semantic symmetry', the identity of the sense of a word from the 'I' and the 'you' or 's/he' perspective, can only be a postulate that is tested in real communication, not a methodological foundation.[81] As Frank contends:

> We must come to agreement with each other as individuals, but not although, but rather *because* we cannot build on a system of agreement which is agreed in advance. If this were not the case the conception of truth as intersubjective consensus would lose its meaning: it would no longer be a specifically post-metaphysical alternative to the classical–ontological [representational] theory of truth (Frank, *Stil in der Philosophie*, p. 83).

Habermas agrees that semantic symmetry can only be a necessary counterfactual assumption (Habermas, *Faktizität und Geltung*, p. 35), but he does not give a convincing account of why it is no more than that. Were he to do so, the limitations of the semantic turn in relation such questions would rapidly become apparent.

It is the aesthetic moment required for a plausible account of cognition that leads Putnam to assert, against Habermas, that 'interpretation, in the very wide sense of the term, and value are involved in our notions of rationality in every area.'[82] The division of the spheres of rationality may in some respects be a real fact in the institutional functioning of modern societies, but there is no philosophical reason to think they can be anything but heuristically separated – *unless*, as Habermas sometimes tends to do, one presupposes that his model of the physical sciences is the model for rationality as a whole. Putnam argues, in line with the Romantic conception, that, rather than there being a philosophically viable account of reason

---

[81] Schleiermacher is also aware of the principle danger of a consensus theory, as he makes clear in the assertion that 'even incorrect thought can become common to all' (ibid., p. 374). On the problems with the concept of semantic symmetry, see Manfred Frank, *Die Unhintergehbarkeit von Individualität. Reflexionen über Subjekt, Person und Individuum aus Anlaß ihrer 'postmodernen' Toterklärung*, (Frankfurt: Suhrkamp, 1986).

[82] Hilary Putnam, *Realism and Reason. Philosophical Papers*, vol. 3 (Cambridge University Press, 1983), p. 300.

that can be based on the primacy of the methods of physics, 'rationality in the "nomothetic" sciences is just as vague and just as impossible to formalize as "Verstehen"' (ibid., p. 299). There is always an indeterminate number of possible theories that can cover any series of regularised observations, even though informed 'aesthetic', non rule-bound judgement (which Kant termed 'reflective judgement') will tell us that virtually none of them is a candidate for rational acceptability.

The underlying problem is that the sort of 'Hegelian' problems revealed by the Romantic paradigm tend to recur in Habermas. It is unclear, for example, both to which sphere the theory of communicative action itself belongs, and what could ground the theory's role as *arbiter* of the division of the spheres. The arguments required to ground the theory rely on the sort of differentiations we undoubtedly do make in the course of validity-oriented communication between truth, normative rightness, and subjective veracity, but what enables the differentiations to be recognised as *constitutively* valid in the theory, without already presupposing the truth of the theory of communicative action itself? The uneasy Kantian relationship between the empirical and the transcendental reappears here in another form. We may, furthermore, often judge in a manner said to belong to one of the spheres in order to achieve something in another sphere, for example when biologists employ metaphors to arrive at a new conception.[83] Given that some of the most significant philosophical conflicts arise precisely in relation to the distribution of competencies between spheres, one cannot ground from within a sphere a judgement that some kind of utterance or performance belongs to a particular sphere. From one aesthetic point of view, for example, certain kinds of psychology of music are not about music at all, because what makes something music is not apparent either in the analysis of the acoustic elements or in the measurable responses of the hearer; on the other hand, the psychologist can argue that, given the impossibility of final consensus over what music is, her project is at least grounded in accessible evidence. Where, in terms of Habermas' theory, is the meta-rule located which decides which sphere of competence is appropriate in a disputed case?[84]

[83] See, e.g., Ludwik Fleck, *Entstehung und Entwicklung einer wissenschaftlichen Tatsache* (Frankfurt: Suhrkamp, 1980).

[84] Jean-François Lyotard, *Le différend* (Paris: Minuit, 1983) stylises this question into a completely implausible theory of the incommensurability of kinds of discourse. My claim is that Habermas' version of the division of the spheres intensifies the problems inherent in any fundamental disagreement, which are actually better negotiable if one does not attempt to

Andrew Bowie

Habermas' theory, which has been distinguished by a progressive attenuation of its more emphatically transcendental claims over the years, ultimately rests on a 'massive background consensus' in the 'lifeworld' which he sees, following Husserl, in terms of the 'pre-predicative and pre-categorial' foundation of everyday meanings (Habermas, *Faktizität und Geltung*, p. 38). This would appear to suggest that Habermas acknowledges Heidegger's view, derived from Romantic aesthetics,[85] that without prior, pre-predicative 'ontological' world-disclosure, which allows something to be understood as something at all, the 'ontic' sciences could not even get off the ground. Habermas claims, though, following Tugendhat's main (semantic) objection to Heidegger,[86] that this background knowledge of the 'lifeworld' is not knowledge at all the strict sense' (ibid., p. 39), because it is not fallible and open to debate as to its assertability. Habermas himself sees truth as 'a validity claim which we connect with a statement by asserting it',[87] towards which one can take up a 'Yes/No position' ('*Ja/Nein Stellungnahme*'),[88] but his insistence on a strict distinction between the 'discursive cashing-in of validity-claims', and what has always already happened in understanding in the lifeworld threatens the pragmatic credentials of his theory. Putnam has pointed out that Rorty's analogous separation of 'human thought into speech within "criterion governed language games" and speech "outside" language games' introduces an essentially metaphysical distinction between kinds of language, which

[85] Heidegger would not have seen it in these terms, but see Bowie, *From Romanticism to Critical Theory* for the demonstration of the continuity of Romantic ideas with the workable aspects of Heidegger.

[86] Ernst Tugendhat, *Der Wahrheitsbegriff bei Husserl und Heidegger* (Berlin: de Gruyter, 1970). Tugendhat argues for a radical difference between the world-disclosure inherent in any kind of meaning and the notion of a claim to validity that can be responded to negatively or positively by its recipient.

[87] Jürgen Habermas, *Vorstudien und Ergänzungen zur Theorie des kommunikativen Handelns* (Frankfurt: Suhrkamp, 1984), p. 129

[88] As Wolfram Hogrebe notes in *Ahnung und Erkenntnis* (Frankfurt: Suhrkamp, 1996), p. 29, the concept of '*Stellungnahme*' is a metaphor, and the status of 'taking up a position' in this manner 'is ontologically no less problematic than representations and intentions' which Tugendhat and Habermas try to obviate with the metaphor. Where is the 'position' in question actually located?

divide spheres of validity from the outset. On this issue, see also Manfred Frank, *Das Sagbare und das Unsagbare. Studien zur deutsch-französischen Hermeneutik und Texttheorie*, Erweiterte Neuausgabe, (Frankfurt: Suhrkamp, 1989), pp. 590–607.

neither Rorty nor Habermas ought to countenance.[89] Following the Romantics, Frank argues that propositional truth which can be assessed as to its assertability 'is founded in truth-*qua*-comprehensibility' (Frank, *Stil in der Philosophie*, p. 73). We cannot give a definitive description of truth, of the kind demanded by formal semantics, because we always already rely upon it *qua* comprehensibility – i.e., on some prior immediate sense or 'feeling', of the kind invoked by Kant and Jacobi, of what it means for something to be true at all – to describe or understand anything, including, of course, a semantic theory of truth or the claim that truth is a validity claim.[90] Habermas actually seems to accept something like this view, but then seeks to restrict its application via Tugendhat's semantics. As Nelson Goodman has shown, though, in the wake of Wittgenstein, worlds – including in the sciences – are made 'by what is exemplified and expressed – by what is shown as well as by what is said', so that 'knowing cannot be exclusively or even primarily a matter of determining what is [semantically] true'. 'Rightness', for example of a literally false metaphor that solves a problem, is often more significant in our actual dealings with the world than propositional truth, and it is, furthermore, open to being accepted or rejected.[91]

If validity is not to be limited to what can be propositionally asserted, and the notional spheres of rationality are to be brought into what is indeed an urgently needed new interplay, philosophy *must*, then, use resources from aesthetics in a manner which Habermas' approach tends to underplay or preclude. The questions raised by aesthetics in German philosophy since Kant both offer ways of questioning whether there is a more than heuristic separation between notional kinds of validity, and sustain an orientation towards the idea of a whole which is not reducible to specific discourses, of the kind involved, for example, in ecological questions concerning the place of self-conscious life in nature. Such questions are often only possible in metaphorical form, but that does not mean that they cannot offer vital insights that other discourses obscure.

These are, of course, metaphysical issues, but they do not, unless one ontologises Kant's suggestion of the link between cognition and aesthetics, entail that metaphysics is, as Habermas insists, a ground-

---

[89] Hilary Putnam, *Pragmatism* (Oxford: Blackwell, 1995), p. 64.

[90] This is, I presume, why Davidson thinks truth is indefinable, and assumes an 'intuitive grasp we have of the concept' (Donald Davidson, *Inquiries into Truth and Interpretation* (Oxford University Press 1984), p. 267).

[91] Nelson Goodman, *Ways of Worldmaking* (Indianapolis: Hackett 1978), pp. 18–21. I am not concerned here with the validity of the rest of Goodman's position.

Andrew Bowie

ing ontological or epistemological discipline: it was, after all, worries about the kind of grounding available to modern philosophy that led Kant and the Romantics to aesthetics in the first place. Indeed, the questions just posed suggest that Habermas' own theory may, because of its residual scientism, itself sometimes fall under the category of the 'metaphysics' he wishes to leave behind. The point of the Romantic position is that it involves what Schnädelbach terms 'negative metaphysics', 'the warranted reminder that discourse does not have complete control of the true and the good: that there is something here which cannot be anticipated by a method, but which must show itself and be experienced' (Schnädelbach, *Vernunft und Geschichte*, pp. 171–172). He associates this sort of metaphysics with precisely those ideas which Habermas associates with irrationality: Kant's 'thing in itself', Wittgenstein's 'the mystical', Adorno's 'non-identity', and Heidegger's 'being', to which, I would contend, one should add the Romantic notion of 'being'.[92]

Schnädelbach, like Henrich, sees the specific role of modern philosophy, which prevents it being either a foundation for, or subsumable into the natural sciences, as 'thinking orientation', which thematises 'what already precedes and lies at the base of our thematisations in thinking, cognition and action' (Schnädelbach, *Zur Rehabilitierung des* animal rationale, p. 131). The key to what distinguishes philosophy, then, is that 'it takes place in the medium of saying I or saying we', *not* in the third person:

> Philosophy is the articulation in thought of our theoretical *and* practical relationship to ourselves, which indeed participates in a relationship to the world, but does not disclose itself – as scientism maintains – via that relationship: Rather we can only, on the contrary, elucidate and understand our relations to the world by beginning with our relationship to ourselves ... The perspective of the first person ... is the *only* locus of a possible rehabilitation of philosophy after the end of metaphysics and idealism (ibid., p. 320).

Schnädelbach, like Habermas, often refers suspiciously to 'Romanticism', as though it belonged to the irrationalism he wishes to counter in his defence of negative metaphysics, but the point he makes here is already central to Novalis' critique of Fichte. Novalis

---

[92] See Andrew Bowie, 'Non-Identity: The German Romantics, Schelling and Adorno', in ed. T. Rajan, D. Clark, *Intersections: Nineteenth Century Philosophy and Contemporary Theory* (Albany: SUNY Press, 1995), pp. 243–60.

both decentres the subject, as Schnädelbach demands (ibid.), and establishes its primacy as the concern of philosophy in the manner of Henrich's distinction between subject and person: 'I is basically nothing – Everything has to be *given* to it – But it is to it alone that something can be given and the given only becomes something via the I' (Novalis, *Das philosophisch-theoretische Werk*, p. 185). It is very clear that the consequences Novalis draws from such reflections do not correspond to the received picture of Romantic philosophy:[93] 'Humankind cannot reach any higher than to see what knowledge is appropriate for its particular stage – for the duration and constitution of its life – and to see that it does not pathologically favour the drive for knowledge – that it leaves it in harmony with its other powers and dispositions' (ibid., p. 793). At this point a Romantic tradition which has generally been ignored or regarded as a mystical flight form the pressures of modernity turns out to be a significant precursor of the suspicion of foundational philosophy and scientism that is characteristic of the best American pragmatism.

Putnam has recently claimed that 'what is publicly verifiable (or even what is intersubjectively "warrantably assertable") is not all of what any human being or any culture can live by' (Putnam, *Pragmatism*, p. 75), adding elsewhere, in relation to the survival of bad metaphysics in significant parts of the analytical tradition, that 'Grown men and women arguing about whether the number three "really exists" is a ludicrous spectacle' (ibid., p. 44). He sees the task of contemporary philosophy as therefore lying in 'criticism of culture' (ibid.), rather than in futile attempts exhaustively to describe the relationship between the supposedly 'ready-made' world and the symbols that represent that world. In the same vein, Henrich cites the example of the neurophysiologist who, in a classic example of the philosophical questions raised by the separation of the spheres, 'leaves his laboratory, in which consciousness and emotions are just complexes of firing neurones, to return to the circle of the family he loves'. Henrich asks whether, in view of the undoubted success of natural science, the only 'unity of understanding' left to us is to give up on the idea that we could ever 'hold together a world in thinking' (Henrich, *Fluchtlinien*, p. 60), as scientistically oriented philosophy has now done. As I have suggested, if the attempt to hold together a world in thinking that informed the best German

[93] There are sometimes elements of the received picture in Novalis (and Schlegel), but the real direction of their thought is the one I have outlined. Much of the received picture depends anyway on misinterpretation of the Romantics' use of key terms like 'feeling', and 'longing', which generally have quite strict epistemological meanings.

philosophy since Kant is renounced, it indeed becomes increasingly unclear what is left for philosophy to do that will not be better done by the specific sciences. Forgetfulness of some of the resources available in the German tradition for confronting this situation seems to me the danger lurking in Habermas' otherwise uniquely far-sighted attempt at a communicative theory of rationality and modernity.

What is implicit in the image of the neurophysiologist was, significantly, already evident in Jacobi's anxiety that a narrow concern with the results of the natural sciences would lead to what he termed 'nihilism', because it would forget that the 'the greatest achievement of the researcher is to disclose (*enthüllen*) and to reveal (*offenbaren*) existence (*Daseyn*) … Explanation is a means for him, a path to the goal, the proximate, but not the final purpose' (in Heinrich Scholz, ed., *Die Hauptschriften zum Pantheismusstreit*, p. 90). If philosophy is not about goals beyond mere explanation we may indeed have reached the end of philosophy. At the moment a large part, particularly of the Anglo-American philosophical world, appears happy to conspire with this situation. It is one of the ironies of the history of philosophy that parts of a German tradition, which for at least the last hundred years have been simply forgotten or largely dismissed in the English-speaking world, have now come to be more in touch with the possibility of the future health of philosophy and human culture than much of the philosophy which is so prepared to condemn that tradition for its failure to relate to the real world.

The Career of Aesthetics in German Thinking

MARTIN SEEL

In German philosophy of the last 250 years, aesthetics has played a leading part. Any arbitrary list of great names contains mainly authors who either have written classical texts on aesthetics or are strongly influenced by aesthetic reflection, for instance, Kant, Hegel, Schelling, Schopenhauer, Marx, Nietzsche, Dilthey, Heidegger, Wittgenstein, Gadamer, and Adorno – the few exceptions being Husserl and Frege. It is not by chance that Frege is one of the founding fathers of modern Anglo-Saxon philosophy, where, generally speaking, aesthetics has had only marginal influence. That is not an insignificant difference. The wildest dreams of one tradition were focused on logic, those of the other on aesthetics.

At any rate, the hopes placed by German thinking in aesthetics were enormous. Aesthetics was to be at times the better ethics, at other times the better epistemology, and at still other times simply the best philosophy. Since Kant's days, however, sceptical voices have been heard repeatedly that have wanted to transfer aesthetics back to the modest state of a subdiscipline; but they have not succeeded in doing so. Aesthetics up until today continues to be one of the great temptations of German philosophy (and not solely of German philosophy, if we think of the later Michel Foucault or the later Nelson Goodman).

Careers can go up or down. The career of aesthetics in German thinking has gone in both directions. If the highest demands raised by aesthetics since Romanticism are taken seriously, then we have to say that its history has been an uninterrupted *fall*. If, on the other hand, aesthetics is liberated from all messianic missions within and without philosophy, then the history of German aesthetics can be written as the history of a continual *rise*: as its development into an independent and indispensable mode of philosophising.

In what follows I shall attempt to recount this *second* history. Instead of telling a story of fatal regressions, which could be done quite easily, I shall be telling a story of vital progressions. Its plot will be how aesthetics gradually gained autonomy *vis-à-vis* epistemology and ethics. Nevertheless, the seven very short stories from the history of modern aesthetics that I shall submit will have to take some rather drastic shortcuts. But that is unavoidably so whenever we are to tell how everything turned out well in the end.

Seven short stories

Baumgarten

It all began with a radical step. Alexander Gottlieb Baumgarten's *Aesthetica* (1750–1758), which gave the new discipline its name, presents itself as a new, hitherto neglected form of epistemology.[1] This is concerned not solely with the beautiful objects of nature or art but, much more generally, with a special faculty of perception. Baumgarten gave it the title 'sensuous knowledge' (*cognitio sensitiva*). In contrast to clear and distinct conceptual knowledge, sensuous knowledge is a *cognitio confusa* – as Baumgarten says in reference to Leibniz. This is however intended as the opposite not of the *clarity* but of the *distinctness* of propositional knowledge. Knowing something aesthetically possesses a conciseness completely different from knowing it scientifically. The two kinds of knowledge maintain a relation of complementarity. It follows for Baumgarten that 'complete' knowledge can be achieved only through scientific *and* aesthetic thinking. Each mode of reflection beholds the given in an essentially different manner.[2]

According to Baumgarten, aesthetic knowledge is specialised in perceiving complex phenomena; not to analyse them in their composition but to make them present in their intuitive [*anschaulich*] density. Here, something is not determined *as something*, rather it is apprehended in the repleteness of its features. The goal of this knowledge is not the universal (which is grasped by classification and generalisation) but the consideration of the particular. *To come to know the particular in its particularity* – that is the real accomplishment of *cognitio sensitiva,* which is something no science will ever be able to achieve.

In the case of art, this requires a particular capability in presentation; everything it presents is presented with an appreciation for the particularity both of the presentation itself and of what is presented. In principle, however, the 'lower' knowledge faculty – as

[1] A. G. Baumgarten, *Theoretische Ästhetik*, trans. and ed. H. R. Schweizer (Hamburg: Meiner, 1983).

[2] Reflections on this complementarity in Baumgarten are analysed by B. Scheer, *Einführung in die philosophische Ästhetik* (Darmstadt: Primus, 1997); along these lines are the arguments advanced by G. Gabriel, *Zwischen Logik und Literatur. Erkenntnisformen von Dichtung, Philosophie und Wissenschaft* (Stuttgart: Metzler, 1991).

Baumgarten also calls sensuous knowledge within the scheme of traditional divisions – is not dependent upon the medium of art. It can come into operation at any time and in any place – through a sensuous comprehension that lingers [*verweilen*] with a thing or a situation in the individuality of its appearing.

Kant

But is it really appropriate to call this perception in every case a *knowing?* Can, therefore, aesthetics be grasped correctly as a sub-species of epistemology? 'No' is the response that Immanuel Kant gives in the first part of his *Critique of Judgment* (1787). Nevertheless, he attaches great importance to the fact that all the *powers* of knowledge are involved in aesthetic perception. But, he adds, what matters in aesthetic perception is not an acquisition of knowledge. The powers of knowledge are not required here for knowledge – that is the kernel of the numerous paradoxical expressions with which Kant characterises the aesthetic attitude.

Being capable of cognitive [*erkennend*] determination, the subject of aesthetic intuition refrains from determining cognitively. It does not determine the object of its perception in terms of particular features. Rather, the subject perceives the object in the unpresentable repleteness of its features. For instance, when intuiting a beautiful flower – at the beginning of his aesthetics, Kant considers primarily objects of nature – it is a matter of keeping 'the cognitive powers engaged [in their occupation] without any further aim. We *linger* in our contemplation of the beautiful, because this contemplation reinforces and reproduces itself.'[3] In contrast to *theoretical* contemplation, *aesthetic* contemplation is not concerned with certain insights that are to be gained by turning towards the object. The object is not to be conceptualised, no more than it is to be directed to a certain practical purpose. Without being reduced to this or that determination, the object is perceived solely *in the presence of its appearing*.

This line of thought provides a plausible initial conception of aesthetics. More resolutely than Baumgarten, Kant ties the analysis of the aesthetic object to an analysis of the perception of this object (and the analysis of this perception to the analysis of the judgments that recount the exercise of this perception). Aesthetic object and aesthetic perception are acknowledged as interdependent concepts. The aesthetic object is the object of a genuine form of perception that is concerned not with its object's fixated *appearance* [*Erscheinung*] but with its process of *appearing* [*Erscheinen*].

[3] Immanuel Kant, *Critique of Judgment*, trans. Werner S. Pluhar (Indianapolis: Hackett, 1987), §12, p. 68.

Martin Seel

Admittedly, this distinction between product and process – between objects having this or that *appearance* and objects in their momentary *appearing* – is not drawn by Kant himself. However, it captures the core of the difference between theoretical and aesthetic modes of comprehension introduced by Kant in the *Critique of Judgment*. The process of aesthetic appearing intended here is by no means just a subjective appearing in the sense of a mere 'looking like' or 'seeming like' (as, for instance, when I say, 'There seems to be a cat on the mat'). Rather, it is a particular *givenness* [*Gegebensein*] of phenomena that can be apprehended intersubjectively. (Otherwise, Kant argues, aesthetic judgments would not be possible.) Aesthetic appearing can be followed by anyone who, first, possesses the appropriate sensuous and cognitive faculties and who, second, is willing to be attentive to the full sensuous presence of an object, while forgoing cognitive or practical results.[4]

This theory of aesthetic appearing developed by Kant generates, together with a minimal concept of aesthetic perception, a minimal concept of the aesthetic object. The aesthetic object is an object in the process of its appearing, aesthetic perception is attentiveness to this appearing.

Although this is nothing more than a minimal starting point, it is nevertheless a point of intersection at which the domains of aesthetics, epistemology, and ethics – separated initially by Kant – are internally connected. Moreover, this intersection, as it is delineated in Kant's text on aesthetics, has retained a central place in German philosophy ever since. As Kant shows, we are in a particular way *free* when engaged in aesthetic perception – free from the constraints of conceptual knowledge, free from the reckoning of instrumental action, free as well from the conflict between duty and inclination. In the aesthetic state we are free from the compulsion to determine ourselves and the world. This negative freedom, however, has a positive side according to Kant. In the play of aesthetic perception we are free to experience the *determinableness* of ourselves and the world. Wherever the real presents itself in a repleteness and changeability that cannot be grasped but can nonetheless be affirmed, there we experience a scope for the possibilities of knowing and acting that is always already presupposed in theoretical and practical orientations. For that reason, Kant sees the expe-

[4] That is, the 'full presence' of a sensuously perceivable phenomenon is not open to cognitive access; it cannot be reduced to the empirical *constitution* of an object of the sensory world; it is a givenness of the object that cannot be described as the composition of this object. The relation of complementarity between aesthetic and conceptual knowledge that Baumgarten envisioned is thereby annulled.

rience of the beautiful (and the sublime) as an exercise of the most advanced capabilities of the human being. The richness of the real that is released in aesthetic contemplation is experienced as a pleasurable confirmation of the extensive determinableness of reality by the human mind.

Hegel

A minimal concept of the aesthetic object such as we find it developed in the first part of the *Critique of Judgment* can nevertheless be nothing more than a beginning for a plausible aesthetics. The basic concept of appearing, for instance, does not yet say anything about the particular aesthetic constitution of the objects of *art*. Any aesthetics that deserves the name, however, has to prove itself ultimately in the most complex of all aesthetic phenomena. That is the reason why Georg Wilhelm Friedrich Hegel defined aesthetics in his lectures (held in the 1820s) simply as a 'philosophy of art'.

That art essentially has to do with appearing is self-evident for Hegel. The work of art is, as Hegel once remarked succinctly, 'an appearance that means something'.[5] However, in contrast to other signs about which one could say the same, the meaning of an artwork is tied to the particular sensuous execution of the individual work. Like the simple object of nature, the work of art appears in its individual form; but in the case of the latter this is a matter of an *articulated* or, even better, an *articulating process of appearing*. In art the *sheer* appearing of the aesthetic object is transformed into an object of *meaning*. However, what artworks intimate in the process of their appearing cannot be detached from their execution. It is only accessible to an interpretive perception that pursues, in sensitive attentiveness, the constellations and correspondences of the sculptured, gestured, visual, or acoustic appearance of the work. The content of the works is interwoven with the configuration of the artistic materials. Thus, artworks are not just indescribable *events* in the empirical layout of world, but at once an inexhaustible *expression* of the human *spirit*. The work of art presents its own process of appearing in order to allow forms of human world encounter to appear. In this way, it makes possible an intuitive *self-encounter* on the part of the human spirit.

In Hegel's view, then, artworks are always media of aesthetic *knowledge*. What Baumgarten claimed for all forms of aesthetic perception, this applies to the perception of artworks. They can be perceived as *artworks* only if they are perceived cognitively in a specific

[5] G. W. F. Hegel, *Hegel's Introduction to Aesthetics,* trans. T. M. Knox, intro. Charles Karelis (Oxford: Oxford University Press, 1979), p. 19.

manner. According to Hegel, art in classical antiquity was the highest medium of knowledge, only to be then surpassed first by religion and then by philosophy.[6] In the present, however, Hegel says with provocative coolness and sobriety (and here little has changed since the beginning of the nineteenth century), art is just one *among other* forms of knowledge – a form of knowledge, moreover, that has increasingly distanced itself from its traditional function of being knowledge of the *absolute*. It is only for the art of *his time,* then, that Hegel becomes the theorist of an *autonomous* art in a strict sense. This is no longer the representation of 'eternal powers' that determine the lives of all people; it becomes a presentation of historical perspectives and life forms, an exemplary externalisation of subjective worlds, closely tied to a heightened self-presentation of artistic material and artistic procedures.[7] Even in modern times, however, art (together with philosophy and religion) remains for Hegel one of the three successors of classical *theories*. It participates in the process of making present the basic constitution of the real. There is also an eminent ethical heritage connected to this theoretical heritage of aesthetic practice. The 'thinking contemplation' of art is for Hegel an indispensable dimension of a life liberated from confinement in everyday life, just as the philosophical *theories* were for Plato and Aristotle.

Schopenhauer

Arthur Schopenhauer established this connection between aesthetic, theoretical, and ethical practice much more closely. The danger of an *integrative* aesthetics, which assumes not only points of contact and overlap but also a *convergence* of theoretical, ethical, and aesthetic orientations, can be studied here in an exemplary manner. To be sure, the entire German tradition of aesthetics is very exposed to this danger. But whereas the other authors I am dealing with here can be read as having ultimately escaped this danger, this possibility of a redeeming interpretation does not apply to Schopenhauer. In his *opus magnum The World as Will and Representation,* first published in 1818, Schopenhauer supports and amplifies the view defended by Kant and Hegel that aesthetic per-

[6] Philosophical theories from Schelling to Adorno have tried repeatedly to reverse this order of precedence. Such reversals, however, merely reproduce the compulsion to establish an order of *precedence,* where only *one constellation* of forms of world interpretation can prevail.

[7] From the revelation of the absolute to the self-contemplation of cultural worlds – that is the course taken by the history of art (and of our dealings with art) in Hegel.

ception enables distance both to conceptual knowledge and to teleological action. His basic thesis is, however, that the subject of aesthetic intuition *abandons* the world of empirical appearances in favour of a contemplation of Platonic 'ideas'.

According to Schopenhauer, the contemplation of a mountain stream is directed not at the flowing, gushing, sprinkling of this individual stream but at the universal *idea* of a stream: at the unrestrained downward rush of a fluid material. Individual appearance is not that with which aesthetic perception is really concerned; it is simply the unavoidable external occasion for aesthetic perception. Hence, contemplation of an artwork is devoted not actually to the simultaneously sense-catching [*sinnenfällig*] and articulating presence of the particular work but to the possibility of transforming oneself during contemplation into a 'pure will-less, painless, timeless subject of knowledge' that exposes the world of everyday life and mundane striving as illusion.[8] For Schopenhauer, the aim of aesthetic perception is not a transformed *encounter* with, but a cognitive *overcoming* of the empirical world. This is the world in which the principle of causality drafted by human understanding [*Verstand*] prevails, and it is also the world in which we are herded about without any prospect of fulfilling our desires. By being able to expose this world in aesthetic contemplation as an illusion – albeit an unavoidable one – the subject of this insight is not only in a privileged *knowledge* position but also in a privileged *ethical* position. It experiences moments of a 'deliverance from will' and a liberating 'resignation' *vis-à-vis* the striving for worldly goods. The subject succeeds in overcoming all illusions about what is real and what is really important.

Aesthetic, theoretical, and ethical attentiveness are thus traced back to one source. Aesthetic perception is interpreted as the avenue to optimum knowledge and action, as the acquisition of an ultimate view of things. Schopenhauer's aesthetics, however, pays a high price for this reduction. It blinds itself to the individual process of appearing of aesthetic objects. Aesthetic objects of nature and of art are degraded to 'means of facilitating'[9] the acquisition of theoretical and ethical insight. Aesthetic respect for the particular is forced to betray individual appearances – to 'forget … all individuality'.[10] Instead of offering an alternative access to the phenomenal world, Schopenhauer's aesthetics preaches a radical exit from this world.

[8] Arthur Schopenhauer, *The World as Will and Representation*, vol. I, trans. E. F. J. Payne (New York: Dover Publications, 1969), p. 17 (italics in original).

[9] Ibid., p. 195.

[10] Ibid., p. 197.

Martin Seel

Nietzsche

Nevertheless Schopenhauer may not be excluded, if the history of German aesthetics is to be told with the prospect of a happy end. For without Schopenhauer there would be no Nietzsche (and without at least one bad guy there could not be a good story). In his book on *The Birth of Tragedy* (1872), Nietzsche puts Schopenhauer's sense-hostile aesthetics on its feet again. For Nietzsche too, the experience of art means a radical rupture of the natural attitude. However, it comprises not an *ascent* to objective spirit or to pure ideas but a *decent* into an amorphous clamor [*Rauschen*] devoid of ideas.

Proceeding from the example of music, Nietzsche describes the constitution of artworks as an interplay of Apolline construction and Dionysiac destruction. The work of art creates a complex sensuous and mental order out of the chaotic process of nature; to that extent it is a construct of illusion. In contrast to other cultural artifacts, however, the work of art discloses its own chaotic origins. In the play of its forms, it lures the observer into the process of an unformed reality. In so doing, the subject of aesthetic perception, as Nietzsche says, 'suddenly loses his way amidst the cognitive forms of appearance'.[11] It (the subject) encounters a process of appearing that cannot be classified in any order of appearances.

In diametrical opposition to Schopenhauer, the distance to the interpreted world that is torn open by the Dionysiac energy of artworks is, for Nietzsche, not a going beyond the world of appearances but rather a radical losing of oneself in this world. Here, the empirical world changes its guise completely. It appears no longer in a continuum of reliable features but in a movement of permanently dwindling forms. Without the construction of an artwork and without the competence of subjects capable of knowledge, though, this state could not come about. Without the presupposition of established culture, it would not be possible to step out of the confines of convention. It is only within a cosmos of meanings, as Nietzsche knows, that we can depart from the cosmos of meanings. It is only within a context of meanings which remain within reach that this departure can be experienced as an ecstatic moment.

Nietzsche changes the position of aesthetics reached by Kant and Hegel in three respects. Firstly, he corrects Kant's assumption on the reason for aesthetic delight. It is not the *determinableness* – and thus the ultimate controllability – but rather the *indeterminableness* and ultimate uncontrollability of the real that is the source of aes-

[11] Friedrich Nietzsche, *The Birth of Tragedy*, trans. Shaun Whiteside, ed. Michael Tanner (Harmondsworth: Penguin, 1993), p. 16.

thetic pleasure. In the aesthetic state we overcome our belief in the possibility and the point of any complete determination of the given. Aesthetic pleasure is guided by an interest in the unknown.[12] Accordingly, playful self-discovery in free aesthetic contemplation has as its complement an ecstatic self-abnegation.

Secondly, Nietzsche provides a reason – one going beyond Kant – as to why aesthetic perception does indeed have a great affinity to knowledge but must not be apprehended from beginning to end as knowledge. In experiencing many artworks – and sublime nature too we live through phases of an acoustic or visual rapture, of a happening without anything recognisable happening, something that can be followed sensuously but not cognitively apprehended. Sensitive perception here goes beyond the limits of cognitive consciousness. Extreme consciousness, it turns out, does not have to be cognitive consciousness at the same time; the intensity of perception and that of knowledge can diverge.

From this follows, thirdly, an altered conception of art. The integration of form and content, already fragile in Hegel, is abandoned by Nietzsche. Artworks do continue to be regarded as sign objects that obtain their meaning from their individual form; this form, however, is now understood as a *process* that again and again transforms all meanings back into an asemantic appearing.

Heidegger

In Martin Heidegger's and Theodor W. Adorno's theories of art – the last two stops in my story – this motif has wide-reaching consequences. Thus, in his article 'The Origin of the Work of Art' (written in 1936 but not published in German until 1952) Heidegger sees the work of art caught in an irresolvable 'conflict' between meaningful and non-meaningful elements. The meaningful appearances of and within the work of art are based on appearings – such as tone, colour, sound, and the sheer gesture of words – that tend to make those meanings disappear. But they disappear only to reappear over and over again – as meanings within a cultural 'world' that is grounded on an asemantic, ungraspable, impenetrable 'earth'. For Heidegger, this process of appearing and disappearing in great works of art is at once an event of far-reaching historical depth. The trans-

[12] There is an element of this position already in Kant when he says of the work of art that it displays aesthetic ideas that are not fully graspable in terms of understanding; whereas in Kant it is the richness and power of the human mind that is demonstrated here, for Nietzsche it is the limits of every intellectual effort (the arbitrariness and one-sidedness of all of its constructions) that is celebrated in artistic experience.

gression of cultural horizons of meaning is what transpires in the appearing of artworks. Anyone who experiences this in a work of art participates immediately in the changes brought about by the work of art; it offers the prospect of cultural worlds that it itself opens. In this way, there occurs an appearing of meaning contexts that evade objectivising appropriation. Thus, the work of art makes it possible to experience all determining knowledge and all instrumental disposability [*Verfügen*] as relying on presuppositions that cannot be determined conceptually or technologically. That is why the work of art in the modern technological world is, for Heidegger, evidence of the radical nondisposability [*Unverfügbarkeit*] of the human situation.

Adorno

It is no great step from here to Theodor W. Adorno's incomplete *Aesthetic Theory* from 1970. For Adorno, the work of art is an object of articulation that is in a permanent state of suspension. As such, it puts up resistance to the petrified living conditions of the present; it tries to bring chaos to a compulsive social order.[13] Doing this, it relies on an irritating appearing that calls for a sensitive interpretation that wishes 'to use concepts to unseal the non-conceptual, without making it their equal'.[14] Adorno understands the work of art not as an empirical appearance in the sense of a complex sensory datum but as an 'appearance' in the sense of a reality that remains ungraspable as reality. 'Artworks become appearances, in the pregnant sense of the term – that is, as the appearance of an other – when the accent falls on the unreality of their own reality.'[15] They relate to the rest of reality as an 'apparition', that is, like a religious or hallucinogenic vision in which something is suddenly present and then in the same instant no longer there.[16] In this way, the appearing of an artwork differs radically from all phenomena that can be

[13] Theodor W. Adorno, *Aesthetic Theory*, ed. G. Adorno and Rolf Tiedemann, trans. Robert Hullot-Kentor (Minneapolis: University of Minnesota Press, 1997), pp. 93f.

[14] Theodor W. Adorno, *Negative Dialectics*, trans. E. B. Ashton (London: Routledge & Kegan Paul, 1973), p. 10. [Translator's note: Translation altered slightly.]

[15] *Adorno, Aesthetic Theory*, p. 79.

[16] 'Fireworks [being prototypical for artworks] are apparition kat exochen: They appear empirically yet are liberated from the burden of the empirical, which is the obligation of duration; they are a sign from heaven yet artifactual, an ominous warning, a script that flashes up, vanishes, and indeed cannot be read for its meaning.' Ibid., p. 81.

apprehended in knowledge and action; it is irreal in relation to what is otherwise known and acknowledged as real. 'In each genuine art-work', we read in Adorno, 'something appears that does not exist'.[17]

Since this sounds somewhat mysterious, an example may be help-ful. The painting *Who's afraid of red yellow and blue IV* by Barnett Newman is 274 x 603 cm; the huge canvas does not have a frame. On the left we see a large red space, on the right a large yellow one; in the middle there is a much narrower blue strip that is approxi-mately 60 cm wide. The paint has been applied homogeneously throughout. Pure colours, symmetrical arrangements − the whole painting rebels against such an apparently well-tempered and well-balanced composition. It is above all the vast colour zones that gen-erate a distinct imbalance. Whereas the red stands out aggressively, the yellow recedes from the beholder. This arrangement, which appears askew to a lingering perception, is further shaped by the different demarcations of the two large colour spaces to the blue in the middle. The blue overlaps the neighbouring red just a little, whereas it itself is covered minimally by the yellow surface. The aggressive red is restrained by the blue, the soft yellow, on the other hand, remains unbound. What could act like a balance between the colours' various spatial effects serves only to intensify the boldness of the red and the restraint of the yellow field. In this manner, the painting generates doubt in its own form, but that's not all: it also generates doubt in all so-called pure and controlled artistic forms. It is a piece of anticompositional and antipurist painting. It breaks the form in which the beholder encounters it at first glance.

'In each genuine artwork something appears that does not exist.' In this work of art there appears a rebellion of colour against the coercion of balanced design. This cannot be seen in the natural atti-tude. What this attitude sees is just a red, yellow, and blue surface, a piece of technically good painting, nothing more. Nor can a sim-ple *aesthetic* perception notice anything of the excesses of this painting. Such a perception could regard it as a pleasant wall deco-ration: 'A really attractive modern painting, at last.' 'Quite the opposite!' the art critic will exclaim: 'What you see is the instant in which pure form changes to pure chaos. This is the wildest painting I have ever seen!'

In each accomplished artwork something appears that exists only there, where it is really perceived as a work of art. Of course, this appearing is based on the appearances that are also accessible to a non-aesthetic and nonartistic attitude. However, it cannot be reduced to those. It emerges with a certain kind of perception of artistic constructions, one that triggers a non-representable play of

[17] Ibid., p. 82.

Martin Seel

articulation in them.

The work of art – this is Adorno's plausible contention, which refers back to Baumgarten and Kant no less than to Nietzsche and Heidegger – reveals to its beholder that reality is richer than all of the appearances we can fix in the language of conceptual knowledge. It unfolds the difference between determinable appearance and indeterminable appearing; it celebrates the fact that reality is not just given to us as a collection of facts. 'Beauty demands, perhaps, the slavish imitation of what is indeterminable in things', Adorno quotes more than once from Paul Valdry's *Rhumbs*.[18] Consideration of this indeterminable is not only of great theoretical but also of great ethical significance to Adorno. It opens a 'freedom to the object', which is a condition of real freedom among subjects.[19] For Adorno, art thus becomes the sign indicating that the world has not been comprehended if it is known only conceptually; that the world has not been appropriated if it is appropriated only technically; that individual and social freedom have not been attained if they are guaranteed merely as a license to make profit; in a word, that we do not really encounter the reality of our lives if we encounter it merely in a spirit of mastery.

Toward an aesthetics of appearing

This is the end of my rough history of aesthetics, being composed of a series of short stories. It could be continued with many other names – and would nevertheless remain a very artificial history. For it is constructed as the prehistory to an aesthetics of appearing, which does not yet exist. What do exist, however, are the many tracks leading to such an aesthetics, some of which I have traced here. I would like to close this sketch with a systematic synopsis that might explain as well as *justify* why German philosophy has accorded aesthetics such a powerful position.

To apprehend something in the process of its appearing for the sake of its appearing – that is the starting and end point of all aesthetic perception. Of course, aesthetic perception frequently goes way beyond such elementary lingering apprehension. Above all the perception of artworks necessarily includes a cognitive and interpretive attentiveness. However, the aim of this knowledge and interpretation is to remain with the articulating appearing of artworks. In reference to Hegel, Nietzsche, Heidegger and Adorno I have said

[18] Ibid., p. 72 and Theodor W. Adorno, 'Valérys Windstriche', in *Noten zur Literatur*, I (Frankfurt: Suhrkamp, 1989), p. 200.

[19] Adorno, *Negative Dialectics*, p. 28.

a number of things about the value of this encounter. Hence, in conclusion, I would like to focus again on the meaning of aesthetic perception *in general*.

In all aesthetic perception – that is the unbroken thread in aesthetic theory from Baumgarten to Adorno (and beyond) – there occurs an affirmation of the conceptually and practically *indeterminable;* it is – as we could say with Paul Valéry – a sensitive consideration of what is indeterminable in things. It wants to leave its objects not as they *are* but as they *appear* individually to our senses. This lingering with the appearing of things, however, is also a lingering of the perceiving ones with themselves – with the present of their own lives. Aesthetic attentiveness to what happens in the external world is always an attentiveness to ourselves too: to the moment here and now. In addition, aesthetic attentiveness to the *objects of art* is frequently an attentiveness to situations in which we do not find ourselves and perhaps never will: to a moment now and never.

This aesthetic self-intuition has a relation of irresolvable tension to other forms of self-consciousness. As an intuiting consciousness of the factual or possible presence of our being, it differs (in various kinds and degrees) from all consciousness of *who we are* over an extended period of time, and *who we want to be* over such a period. In the course of aesthetic experience we suspend this knowledge in order to be outside the continuity of our lives for a while. Aesthetic interest – or, if we want to follow Kant's choice of words, particular aesthetic disinterest – is grounded on the desire to be perceptually aware of the presence of ones own being.

To live in full consciousness of one's own life is, therefore, impossible without various kinds of aesthetic awareness. Aesthetic awareness – in the middle of a city, in the solitude of a park, in perceiving or performing art – is an essential feature of self-consciousness, but it is essentially a *particular* one. It is not an awareness of facts or duties or life plans, it is an awareness of the here and now of one's own life. It is given only in the intense perception of a present situation's processes of appearing. These changing appearings remind us at once of the finiteness of this and every presence, as much as they remind us of the pleasures of such finiteness. (Without finiteness there would be no play of appearances. That is the intriguing argument of Valéry's Socrates in his dialogue on architecture and music.)[20]

Heidegger once told philosophers that they should not be forgetful of Being [*seinsvergessen*] (whatever that Being might be).

[20] Paul Valéry, 'Eupalinos', in *Eupalinos. L'âme et la danse. Dialogue de l'arbre* (Paris: Gallimard, 1944).

Martin Seel

Aesthetics – including Heidegger's own philosophy of art – tells another story: we should not be forgetful of appearance [*erscheinungsvergessen*]; we should not forget to sense where we are here and now. This aesthetic sense makes it possible to see the uncontrollable presence of our own being not as a lack of meaning or Being but as an opportunity to perceive ourselves.

As I said at the outset, aesthetics in Germany has developed into an independent and indispensable discipline in philosophy. Aesthetics is *an independent* part of philosophy because it is concerned with a relation to the world that cannot be traced back to theoretical or ethical approaches. Aesthetics is *indispensable* for other philosophical disciplines – and thus for philosophising itself – because it is concerned with aspects of the world and life that have to be considered by other disciplines, without them being able to deal with these aspects adequately.

From the perspective of *theoretical* philosophy, aesthetics makes an indispensable contribution because it uncovers a dimension of reality that evades knowledge but is nevertheless an aspect of knowable reality. Lingering with what is appearing makes it possible to experience reality as being richer than everything that can be known about it by means of propositional determination. Aesthetics reveals a limit of all theoretical world comprehension – a limit to which epistemology and the philosophy of mind must not close their eyes.

From the perspective of *practical* philosophy, aesthetics makes an indispensable contribution because it is concerned with a particular ability for human life, one that discloses the presence of one's own being as an end in itself. Since aesthetic world encounter represents an excellent possibility for human life, it may not be neglected, neither by an ethics of the good life nor by an ethics of moral respect. It is a part of those life forms that should be both sought after in one's own interest and protected by moral norms.

All this, to be sure, is not to say that aesthetics is the regal discipline of philosophy. Nor is it to say that aesthetic practice is the point of all knowing and living. The quality of the aesthetic moment does not overrule the importance of truth or of moral or juridical law, just as the latter must not overrule openness to aesthetic awareness. All I want to say is that aesthetic awareness is one of the points without which everything else would have less point. This, I believe, has been the true message of German aesthetics since the days of Baumgarten and Kant.

Translated by John Farrell

Hermeneutic and Analytic Philosophy. Two Complementary Versions of the Linguistic Turn?

JÜRGEN HABERMAS

In a series of lectures on German philosophy 'since Kant', the names of Fichte, Schelling, and Hegel and their critical reference to Kant are, of course, a must.[1] No less a must, though, would seem to be Wilhelm von Humboldt, a philosopher and linguist who, together with Herder and Hamann, formed the alliterating triumvirate of a romanticist critique of Kant.[2] The response, within the discipline, to transcendental philosophy from this side was, in contrast to the idealistic mainstream, long in the coming but, in the end, rich in consequences. It was Heidegger who, looking back at Humboldt, and informed by the Humboldtian tradition of linguistics,[3] first recognised the paradigmatic character of hermeneutics as continued by Dilthey. At about the same time, Wittgenstein, in turn, discovered a new philosophical paradigm in Gottlob Frege's logical semantics. What later was called the 'linguistic turn' thus came about in a hermeneutic and an analytic version.

My interest here is to see how these two relate to each other. I will look upon it, however, from a special angle. The tension between Critical Rationalism and Critical Theory which, in the early 1960s, vented itself in the polemics between Popper and Adorno, concealed another opposition with political as well as philosophical connotations. After the end of World War II, hermeneutics, having been continued without interruption during Nazism, was confronted with the currents of an analytical theory of science and a critical social theory, both returning from emigration. This tension was in

---

[1] This text formed the basis of a lecture delivered as the conclusion of a series of lectures organised by the Royal Institute of Philosophy at London, between October 1997 and March 1998.

[2] Ch. Taylor, 'Theories of Meaning' in *Philosophical Papers*, vol. I, ed. Ch. Taylor (Cambridge, 1985) pp. 248–92.

[3] On the influence of linguists such as J. Lohmann and L. Weisgerber on Heidegger, see K. O. Apel, 'Der philosophische Wahrheitsbegriff als Voraussetzung einer inhaltlich orientierten Sprachwissenschaft,' in *Transformation der Philosophie*, vol. I, ed. K. O. Apel (Frankfurt, 1973), pp. 106–37

Jürgen Habermas

the minds of a generation who had taken up their studies after the war under the unbroken influence of Dilthey, Husserl, and Heidegger, and then faced the powerful continuation of this tradition through Gadamer and other students of Heidegger. In any case, it is the constellation defined by Gadamer, Adorno, and Popper which explains the opposite directions of that kind of an immanent critique of hermeneutics which I will outline on the basis of the work of my colleague and friend, Karl-Otto Apel. The self-critical development of the hermeneutics approach into a kind of transcendental or, as I would prefer to say, formal pragmatics would not have been possible without the reception of impulses and insights from the analytic tradition. The traditions of hermeneutics and analytic philosophy as I see them, today, are complementary rather than competing.

In a first step, I will elucidate the philosophical significance of Humboldt's linguistic theory (I). This will be the background for pointing out the coincidences of the two versions of the linguistic turn as performed, respectively, by Wittgenstein and Heidegger. As it is, the paradigm-shift from mentalist to linguistic philosophy, carried out in two very different ways, surprisingly results in the same priority of an 'a priori of meaning' over the representation of facts (II). It is in response to this devaluation of the cognitive dimension of language that in my generation the attempt was made to re-establish the universalist tendencies of Humboldt's philosophy of language.[4] Departing from Humboldt's critique of Kant, Apel once again summoned up, against Wittgenstein's contextualism of language games, against Heidegger's idealism of linguistic world disclosure, and against Gadamer's rehabilitation of prejudice, a pragmatically transformed Kant[5] (III).

I

Humboldt distinguishes three functions of language: the cognitive function of forming thoughts and representing facts; the expressive function of manifesting emotions and arousing feelings; finally, the communicative function of talking, of raising objections, or coming to an agreement. The interaction between these functions presents itself differently depending on whether it is seen from the semantic

[4] See my reply to Charles Taylor in *Kommunikatives Handeln,* (eds) A. Honneth, H. Joas, (Frankfurt, 1986), pp. 328–37.

[5] K. O. Apel, 'Wittgenstein und Heidegger', in *Der Löwe spricht … und wir können ihn nicht, verstehen,* (eds) B. McGuiness, J. Habermas *et al.,* (Frankfurt, 1991), pp. 27–68.

point of view of how linguistic content is organised, or from the pragmatic point of view of communication between the speakers. Humboldt's semantic analysis is concerned with the linguistic world view; pragmatic analysis focuses on discourse. On the one side, he explores the cognitive function of language in its relation to the expressive features of the mentality and lifeform of a people while, on the other side, he analyses the same function in the context of an exchange of questions, answers and objections. The tension between particularistic world disclosure and universalistic bent of fact-stating discourse is pervasive in the hermeneutic tradition as a whole. Because both Heidegger and Gadamer proposed a one-sided solution for this tension, they became a challenge for part of my generation. But let us first turn to Humboldt's transcendental conception of language.

1 The romanticist conception of 'nation' is the point of reference for the world-making character of language: 'Man thinks, feels, lives in language alone, and has to be formed by it in the first place'[6]. Humboldt conceives languages as 'organs of the peculiar ways of thinking and feeling of nations'[7]. The lexicon and syntax of a language shape the totality of concepts and ways of apprehension by which, in some kind of pre-understanding, a space is articulated for everything the members of the community may come upon in the world. For the nation it has shaped, each language articulates a certain 'view' of the world as a whole.

Between the 'construction' and 'inner form' of a language and a certain 'view' of the world, Humboldt establishes an 'undissoluble connection'. The horizon of meanings projected in advance by a certain language '[is] equal to the extensions of the world': 'Each language draws a circle around the nation to which it belongs, a circle the leaving of which is possible only to the extent of one's moving, at the same time, into the circle of another language.'[8] Thus, the formula of language being the 'formative organ of thought' must be seen in the transcendental sense of spontaneous world-constitution. Through the semantics of the world view, a language simultaneously structures the form of life of the linguistic community, there being, in any case, mutual mirroring between the two. This transcendental conception of language – which includes culture and

[6] W. v. Humboltd, 'Über den Nationalcharakter der Sprachen', in *Werke*, III, ed. A. Flitner and K. Giel, p. 77.
[7] Humboldt, 'Über den Einfluss des verschiedenen Charakters der Sprachen auf Literatur und Geistesbildung', *Werke*, III, p. 26.
[8] Humboldt, 'Über die Verschiedenheiten der menschlichen Sprachbaus', *Werke*, III, pp. 224f.

cognition – is at odds with the four fundamental premises of the philosophy of language prevailing from Plato to Locke and Condillac.

A holistic conception of language is, first, incompatible with a theory which holds that the meaning of complex sentences is composed of the meanings of its building blocks, that is, individual words or elementary sentences. According to Humboldt's conception, individual words gain their meaning through the context of the sentences they help construct; sentences, through the interrelations of the text they help form; and kinds of text, through the subdivision of the vocabulary of a language. Second, the idea of a linguistically articulated world view structuring the form of life of a community is incompatible with the traditional preference for the cognitive function of language. Language is no longer primarily seen as a means of representing objects or facts, but as the medium for shaping a people's spirit. Third, a transcendental concept of language is incompatible with the dominating instrumentalistic view of language and communication according to which signs are attached, so to speak, to pre-linguistically formed ideas, concepts, and judgements in order to facilitate cognitive operations and to communicate beliefs or intentions to other persons. Finally, this priority of meaning over intention corresponds to the priority of the social character of language over the idiolects of individual speakers. A language is never the private property of an individual speaker, but generates intersubjectively shared meanings, embodied in expressions, cultural objects, and social practices: 'Phenomenologically, every language evolves as something social only, and man understands himself only through his having tested the understandability of his words on others.'[9]

2 As a medium of the objective spirit, language transcends the subjective mind, enjoying a peculiar autonomy from it. As an illustration of this objectivity not only of linguistic expression, but of every symbolic expression, Humboldt refers to the shaping power we experience in the process of learning a language. The power of tradition, 'the mass of what is brought to us by means of whole epochs and nations', is objective in affecting later generations.[10] On the other hand, Humboldt elaborates an expressivist model of language use. Between the objectivity of the rules governing a language, and the subjectivity of speakers manifest in their performance, there is an interplay: 'It is in its being subjectively effected and dependent that language is objectively effecting and indepen-

---

[9] Ibid., p. 196.
[10] Humboldt, 'Über den Nationalcharakter', *Werke*, III, p. 68.

dent. For nowhere, not even in writing, has it a fixed abode. Its dead part, so to speak, must again and again be reproduced in thought, as living in speech or understanding.'[11] But what is brought to bear on this circular process of language, which is 'ergon' and 'energia' at the same time, is not only the feeling and mentality of subjects, but also what they come to experience in the world, in confrontation with reality. The objectivity of the world, however, is made up of a stuff different from that of the 'objectivity' of language forms 'which undeniably give the mind a certain coast and impose upon it a certain constraint.'[12] Different languages may produce different world views, but the world itself appears one and the same to all speakers.

The idea, however, of the 'objective world' 'appearing' as an identical world to members of different linguistic communities presents some difficulties. Though language as such is tuned to the 'production of objective thought' and fulfils the cognitive function of the representation of facts, these facts can be described only within the horizon of a specific linguistic world view. For what is expressed in the grammatically fixed 'categorisation' of objects is the specific 'view' of 'multifaced objects' and, insofar, something subjective, the cast of mind and peculiar character of a linguistic community. The cognitive and the expressive functions of language can only be fulfilled simultaneously.[13] How, then, is it possible that despite the differences of collectively shared linguistic perspectives members of different linguistic communities look at the same world or, in any case, at a world appearing as objective to them? This question of the commensurability of linguistic world views was already discussed in the early nineteenth century.

If we conceive the world-making character of a natural language in a strictly transcendental sense, that is, as constituting the world of possible objects of experience, the world views inscribed in different languages must claim a validity which, for the linguistic communities concerned, is *a priori* necessary.[14] But this premise would mean, as is already pointed out by Hamann in his 'Metacritique' of

[11] Humboldt, 'Über die Verschiedenheit des menschlichen Sprachbaus und ihren Einfluss auf die geistige Entwicklung des Menschengeschlects', *Werke*, III, p. 438.

[12] 'Sprachcharakter und Literatur', *Werke*, III, p. 30.

[13] This is supposed to be true also for the representation of perceivable objects: 'The expressions for sensual objects are equivalent insofar as the same object is thought of in all of them, but since they express the specific way of representing it, their meaning, too, diverges in this respect.' *Werke*, III, p. 21.

[14] For the following, see C. Lafont, *Sprache und Welterschließung*, (Frankfurt, 1994), Einleitung, pp 113–28.

Kant's 'Critique of Pure Reason', that the *a priori* of meaning inherent in linguistic world views, being plural, must loose the universal validity of a transcendental *a priori*. Rather, the pre-understanding of the world as a whole, as structured by an individual language, is '*a priori* contingent and indifferent, but *a posteriori* necessary and indispensable'.[15] Humboldt evidently means to forego this obvious consequence. Notwithstanding certain misleading phrasings[16], he does not see the linguistic world view as a semantically closed universe from which speakers might escape only in order to be converted to another world view.

In this respect, Humboldt is no more troubled by the particularism of the linguistically disclosed world of a nation than by the peculiar character of its form of life, because he does not examine the cognitive function of language only from a semantic point of view. He relies on a division of labour between the semantics of linguistic world views and the formal pragmatics of dialogue – 'of a dialogue where there is true exchange of ideas and feelings'. It is the role of pragmatics to work out the universalistic aspects of communication. Semantics, it is true, discovers language as being the formative organ of thought: the interpenetration of language and reality is such as to preclude any immediate access for the knowing subject. Reality – the totality of objects of possible descriptions – is always already 'absorbed' into a specific horizon of meanings and, in Humboldt's words, 'assimilated to' one's own language. But from the pragmatic point of view of the 'living use of speech', a countertendency to semantic particularism becomes apparent. In dialogue, which 'can be seen as the core of language'[17], participants want to understand each other and, at the same time, to reach an agreement about something. And this also holds for communication across the borders of different linguistic communities.

Humboldt addresses translation as the extreme case that illuminates the normal problem of interpretation. In doing so, he strongly emphasises both of its aspects: the resistance which linguistic differences offer to the effort of translating the utterances of one language into another, and the fact that this resistance can be over-

[15] J. G. Hamann, 'Metakritik. Über den Purismus der Vernunft' (1784), in *Schriften zur Sprache*, ed. J. G. Hamann (Frankfurt 1967), p. 226.

[16] Humboldt, 'Über das vergleichende Sprachstudium', *Werke*, III, pp. 20f: 'For what remains to be conquered is, essentially, always what is objective, and if man approaches it on the subjective path of a peculiar language, his second effort is to re-isolate what is subjective, if only by exchanging one linguistic subjectivity for another, and to re-abstract from it what is objective in as pure a state as possible'.

[17] *Werke*, III, p. 81.

come: 'the experience of translations from highly different languages ... shows that any series of ideas can be expressed, be it with widely differing degrees of success, in any one of them.'[18] Indeed, the hermeneutic tradition has never substantially doubted the possibility of translating the utterances of one language into all other languages; the only question was how to explain the almost transcendental fact that any semantic distance can be bridged: 'Lucid recognition of difference requires (from the interpreter) a third term, that is, unimpaired and simultaneous consciousness of the forms of one's own and of the foreign language.'

Humboldt postulates a 'superior point of view' from which the interpreter 'assimilates what is foreign, and is assimilated to it.'[19] Thus, the encounter of strangers learning to understand each other over the linguistic distances takes place, from the start, in formal anticipation of such a 'third' point of view. This point of view, however, must be adopted with regard to the same objects upon which an agreement is to be reached.[20] There is an interpenetration of the communicative use and the cognitive function of language insofar as in order to be able to understand the foreign language, both sides must, from their own point of view, share the assumption of, and refer to, the point of convergence of an objective world. To the extent that strangers can dispute controversial views of what they take to be 'the same' state of affairs (or know how to explain, if necessary, why reasonable disagreements are expected to persist), they will find a common language and learn to understand each other. Linguistic expressions can be understood only when people know the specific conditions in which they could be used to reach an agreement on something in the world. A shared view of reality as a 'territory half-way between' the 'world views' of different languages is a necessary condition for meaningful dialogues to come about at all. For the participants, the concept of reality is connoted with the regulative idea of a 'sum total of all that is knowable'.

This internal relation between understanding linguistic expressions and knowing how to use them for reaching an agreement about something in the world explains why Humboldt attaches a cognitivist promise to the communicative function of language. In discourse a world view is supposed to prove itself against the opposition of others in a way that brings about, with the progressive

[18] W. v. Humboldt, 'Über das vergleichende Sprachstudium', *Werke*, III, p. 12.
[19] Humboldt, 'Über die Verschiedenheit des menschlichen Sprachbaus', *Werke*, III, p. 156.
[20] This is why C. Lafont (1994), in her discussion of Heidegger, emphasises the problematic of reference.

decentration of individual perspectives, the enlargement – and progressive overlapping – of the meaning horizons of all participants. This expectation, however, is well-founded only if the form of dialogue and the pragmatic presuppositions of discourse can be shown to include a critical potential capable of affecting and shifting the horizon of a linguistically disclosed world itself.

Humboldt tries to furnish this proof by analysing the system of personal pronouns present in all languages. He distinguishes from the Ego-Id relation of the observer the interpersonal Ego-Alter-relation that is constitutive for the attitude of a speaker performing a speech act. Each can decide for himself whether to choose the expressive attitude of a first person revealing his or her subjective experiences or ideas, or the objectivating attitude of a third person perceiving and describing his or her environment. But the attitude of a speaker towards a second person to whom he is addressing his utterance is dependent on a complementary attitude of another who is supposed – but cannot be made – to conform. By conceding the role of the speaker to the first person, the addressee must consent to being himself addressed in the attitude of the second person. In discourse, both sides can enter this relationship only on a mutual basis. One person concedes the performative role of the speaker to another one only with the reservation that roles be exchanged, thus ensuring the communicative freedom of response for both of them.

In the use of personal pronouns, Humboldt detects an 'inalterable dualism' grounded in the speech situation itself: 'All speech is tuned to address and response'.[21] From this dialectical structure, a public space emerges, conferring actual 'social existence' to the intersubjectively shared lifeworld. This intersubjectivity of communication, generated by dialogue, is at the same time a necessary condition for the objectivity of thinking: 'Even thinking is essentially accompanied by a propensity to social existence, man is yearning ... even for the sole purpose of thinking, for an Alter corresponding to the Ego; a concept seems to him to attain its definiteness and certainty only by its being reflected in the faculty of thought of someone else.' The objectivity of one's own judgement is established only when 'the representing subject really sees the thought outside of himself, which is possible only in another representing and thinking being. But between one faculty of thought and

[21] Ibid., p. 201; also see Humboldt, 'Über den Dualis', *Werke*, III, p. 139: 'Nor can language achieve reality by the efforts of the individual, it can do so only socially, only by a new attempt following the attempt that was hazarded. The world, therefore, must attain its essence and language its enlargement, in someone who is listening and responding.'

another, there is no mediation but language[22]. The second person's reply to the utterance of a speaker not only facilitates, in case of an affirmative answer, social integration, but also implies, in view of possible objections, the critical power of confirmation and refutation. We learn from the world by learning from each other.

It was not, however, along the lines of a theory of argumentation that Humboldt proceeded with his investigation of the pragmatic interplay of the cognitive and the communicative functions of language. Choosing instead the hermeneutic guideline of 'mutual understanding of strange speech', he discusses the moral implications of an exchange between competing world views and cultures. As the horizon of one's own understanding of the world is enlarged, one's value orientations, too, are subject to relativisation: 'If there is an idea which is obvious, and progressively enlarging its validity, in all of history ... it is the idea of humanity, the endeavour of bringing down the frontiers which all kinds of prejudice and biased views erect between people, and of treating humanity as a whole, regardless of religion, nation, and colour, as one big tribe of closely related brothers.[23] Humboldt not only establishes an internal relation between understanding and discourse. In the practice of discourse he sees, more generally, the working of a cognitive dynamics which, when dealing with purely descriptive questions, contributes to the decentration of a linguistic world view and, through the extension of horizons, fosters universalistic perspectives even in questions of morality. This humanistic nexus of hermeneutic open-mindedness and egalitarian morality is lost in Dilthey's and Heidegger's historicism. Later on, it will take a critique of philosophical hermeneutics to bring it back.

II

Emerging in Humboldt there are the outlines of an architectonics of a philosophy of language which up to this day remains the point of reference for a pragmatic transformation of Kant's philosophy. Let me summarise.

From a semantic viewpoint, Humboldt has developed the transcendental concept of the 'world-making' spontaneity of language in two directions. Language is constitutive both on the level of the cognitive patterns of a linguistic community and on the level of its cultural and social practices. Concerning cognition, language is rel-

[22] Ibid., pp. 138f.
[23] Humboldt, 'Über die Verschiedenheiten des menschlichen Sprachbaus', *Werke*, III, pp. 147f.

Jürgen Habermas

evant insofar as it articulates a pre-understanding of the world as a whole, which is intersubjectively shared by the linguistic community. This world view is the resource of shared patterns of interpretation. Inconspicuously pointing out relevant perspectives and shaping prejudices, it creates the unproblematical background, or frame, for interpretations of what possibly happens in the world. At the same time, concerning the practices, language shapes the character and form of life of a nation. This linguistically structured lifeworld forms a background for everyday communication and marks the points of contact between linguistic theory and social theory.[24] The achievements of language as the formative organ of thought will later be analysed by Heidegger as linguistic 'world-disclosure'; this, however, must be distinguished from the 'constitution' of contexts for situations of action and communication.

From a pragmatic viewpoint, Humbolt discusses the general structure of discourse. These formal features shed light on the participants' roles, attitudes, and interpersonal relations. Participants address their utterances to second persons, expecting to be understood and to get a reply. The content of discourse is differentiated in view of whether the participants want to communicate about events in the objective world or about normative claims and value orientations of social and cultural life. For Humboldt, rational discourse in which claims and reasons are exchanged is obviously capable of transcending the limits of particular world views. These suggestions are, however, not limited to the domain of intercultural communication. The mutual understanding of other cultures and forms of life, and reciprocal learning among strangers serve to overcome prejudices. For Humboldt, the decentering of peculiar meaning horizons is more generally bound up with the advancement of universalistic value orientations. But this horizontal approximation and overlapping of different interpretative perspectives does not yet explain how facts can be apprehended in the vertical dimension of reference to the objective world, and how knowledge is improved by the controversy about statements of facts. The absence of a convincing analysis of the representational function of language, that is, of the prerequisites for the reference and truth of propositions, will remain the Archilles heel of the entire hermeneutic tradition.

This deficiency reflects an estrangement of rhetoric and grammar from logic that set in with Renaissance humanism. Humboldt particularly shares the distrust of the abstraction of the proposition from speech act and speech context: 'As long as logical analysis is

[24] J. Habermas, *Theorie des kommunikativen Handelns*, Vol. I (Frankfurt, 1981) pp. 182–229.

422

concerned with thinking only, instead of the grammatical analysis of speech, there is no need for the second person. ... What is representing, then, has only to be distinguished form what is represented, not from a receiving and re-acting person.'[25]

This is exactly what formal semantics in focusing on the representational function of language does. This research tradition was initiated by a mathematician and logicist, Gottlob Frege, not himself involved with the tradition of Humboldt, Schleiermacher, Droysen, and Dilthey. In spite of his interesting observations on the illocutionary force that only the act of assertion confers to the proposition, Frege essentially confined himself to the logical analysis of propositions. In formal semantics, the communicative dimension of language which, for Humboldt, was the locus of communicative rationality, is exempted from logical analysis and left to empirical approaches. This neglect of a formal pragmatics the outlines of which at least emerge in Humboldt's philosophy, however, applies to Heidegger as well as to Frege. Heidegger took up only one of the lines of Humboldt's philosophy of language, the semantic one. Starting out from the linguistic function of world-disclosure, rather than from the representational function, he focuses on the semantic analysis of conceptual structures inherent in what Humboldt had called 'innere Sprachform'.

Thus, both analytic and hermeneutics philosophy, while approaching language from opposite starting points, confined themselves to semantic aspects: to the relation of sentence and fact, on the one hand, to the conceptional articulation of the world inscribed in language as a whole, on the other. Both sides use different means: the instruments of logic, on the one hand, the methods of content-oriented linguistics, on the other. Still, the abstraction is the same in both, the holistic approach of content semantics and the elementaristic approach of formal semantics. Neither of them expects from the pragmatic features of speech any essential contribution to the rationality of communication. Humboldt, by contrast, had elaborated a categorical frame providing for three analytic levels. The first level is concerned with the world-forming character of speech, the second, with the pragmatic structure of speech and communication, the third, with the representation of facts. Hermeneutic and analytic approaches are respectively located on the first or on the third analytic level. Both are committed, in their specific way, to the priority of semantics over pragmatics. They therefore face the same problem of how to revoke the initial abstraction without causing any undue reduction. Let me briefly account for their gains and losses, as compared to Humboldt.

[25] Humboldt, *Werke*, III, pp. 202f.

Jürgen Habermas

1 Humboldt was aware of the fact that we understand a linguistic expression if we know the conditions in which we can use it for the purposes of reaching an agreement about something in the world. It was Frege, though, who explained this internal relation of meaning and validity on the level of simple assertoric sentences. He starts out from sentences as the smallest linguistic units that can be true or false. Thus, 'truth' can serve as the basic semantic concept for explaining the meaning of linguistic expressions. The meaning of a sentence is exactly determined by the conditions under which the sentence is true (or which 'make it true'). Ludwig Wittgenstein, like Frege, conceives the sentence as an expression of its truth conditions: 'To understand a proposition means to know what is the case if it is true.'[26] This opening move leads to a series of interesting consequences. If sentences only have a definite meaning because they are the only form in which a state of affairs or a complete thought can be expressed, the meaning of individual words must be measured by their contribution to the constructions of true sentences. But as the same words may serve as building blocks for quite different sentences, this 'context principle' seems to suggest that all the expressions of a language are interconnected by a complex network of semantic threads. Such a holistic conception, however, would jeopardise the semantic determination of individual sentences. Frege, therefore, at the same time defends a 'composition principle' according to which the meaning of a complex expression is composed of the meanings of its elements. The corresponding idea in Wittgenstein's *Tractatus* is that a logically transparent language fulfilling the exclusive function of representing facts must be constructed, in a truth-functional way, of elementary sentences.

Another consequence arising from the priority of sentence over word (or of judgement over concept) is the rejection of the traditional view of linguistic symbols as being essentially names for objects. Frege, in his analysis of simple predicative sentences, relies on the model of mathematical functions. This enables him to explain the combination of two different acts, predication of properties, on the one hand, reference to objects to which properties are attributed, on the other. And just as predication must not be assimilated to reference, predicates or concepts must not be assimilated to names. 'Meaning' must not be confused with 'reference', nor propositional content with the reference to the object about which something is said. Only under this condition, different and perhaps contradictory propositions about the same object can be made and, as such, compared. If we were not capable of recognising the identity

[26] L. Wittgenstein, *Tractatus logico-philosophicus* (London, 1974), pp. 40–42.

of the same object under different descriptions, there could be neither gain of knowledge nor revision of languages, nor an extension of the worlds they semantically 'disclose'.

Frege's concepts of 'meaning', 'reference', and 'truth' are generally acknowledged as defining the range of a multi-faceted ongoing discussion on the representative function of language and its relations to the objective world. The later Frege, though, found it difficult, as can be seen from the highly problematical construction of his doctrine of an independent domain of 'thoughts', to locate language within the coordinates of facts, thoughts, and the formation of judgments in the human mind. At the same time as Husserl, he had put forward a convincing critique of contemporary psychologism; but only in Wittgenstein's turn to a transcendental conception of language, the embodiment of 'thoughts expelled from consciousness' in the medium of language was taken seriously.[27] Wittgenstein ascribes the character of world-constitution to a logically transparent, fact-stating universal language. The limits of language 'are the limits of my world', while the propositions of logical semantics guide us to see the 'infrastructure of the world'. The categories of understanding which for Kant constitute the objects of possible experience are replaced by the logical form of the elementary sentence: 'To give the essence of a proposition means to give the essence of all description, and thus the essence of the world.'[28] With this step, Wittgenstein ratifies the linguistic turn initiated by Frege.

The logical analysis of language gains its philosophical significance only by replacing the paradigm of consciousness by the paradigm of language, thus revolutionising mentalist foundations. For Russell or Carnap, the method of explaining forms of thought by way of a logical analysis of forms of language is still bound up with conventional empiricist epistemology. This methodologically limited understanding of the linguistic turn[29] is far from being a challenge to the mentalist paradigm. Only Wittgenstein touched the very premises of mentalism by his assumption that the form of the assertoric sentence determines the structure of possible facts. He

---

[27] M. Dummett, *Ursprünge der analytischen Philosophie* (Frankfurt, 1988) chapter 4, pp. 32–44.

[28] *Tractatus* 5.4711.

[29] This is meant by Dummett when he claims that the philosophers of the Vienna Circle, in contrast to Frege and Wittgenstein, were not interested in a philosophy of language 'for its own sake', but because this 'arsenal' could furnish weapons 'for their battle in other domains of philosophy': M. Dummett, 'Ist analytische Philosophie systematisch?, *Wahrheit*, ed. M. Dummett (Stuttgart, 1982), p. 195.

Jürgen Habermas

later, and for good reasons, abandoned this conception of a universal, fact-stating language. The world-forming character of this Tractatus-language, however, is retained even as its transcendental spontaneity is transposed from the dimension of representation to the dimension of linguistic practice.

Wittgenstein criticises mentalism in detail only after replacing the ideal language by many language games which are constitutive of as many forms of life. It is through Wittgenstein, therefore, that Frege's intuitive distinction between '*Gedanken*' and '*Vorstellungen*' is given an unequivocal interpretation. We cannot 'experience' the meaning of a sentence because understanding is not a mental episode, but depends on rule following: 'Vergleiche: Wann haben deine Schmerzen nachgelassen?' und Wann hast Du aufgehört, das Wort zu verstehen?'[30] Knowing how to use a criterion is a practical skill – just as one 'knows' how to play chequers – but neither a mental state nor a psychical property.

2 Heidegger takes a different approach, but comes to a similar critique of mentalism. Without as much as a glance at the philosophy of language, he first elaborates an 'existential analytic' of man, while taking up and integrating perspectives from both Dilthey and Husserl. These impulses explain why his investigation which starts from a different angle ends up converging with Humboldt's view that 'there is world only where there is language'.

According to Dilthey, the historical humanities of the nineteenth century are supposed to distinguish themselves from science by a method of interpretation that they have developed from the informal art of reading. Their purpose is not the nomological explanation of empirical events but the interpretation of meanings embodied in all kinds of symbolic utterances, cultural traditions, and social institutions. This allegedly scientific operation of 'Verstehen', or understanding, is taken, by Heidegger, out of its methodological context and radicalised to constitute the basic feature of human existence. The original task of man is to understand his world, and himself in this world: 'In every understanding of world, existence is understood with it, and vice versa.'[31] *Being and Time* is supposed to analyse this vague pre-understanding of self and world.

Heidegger replaces the phenomenological model of describing perceptions of objects by the hermeneutic model of the interpreta-

---

[30] Wittgenstein, *Philosophische Untersuchungen*, vol. I, p. 356; see the interpretations of part II of the P. U. in *Wittgenstein über die Seele*, E. v. Savigny, O. R. Scholz, eds, (Frankfurt 1995).

[31] M. Heidegger, *Being and Time* (Oxford, 1980), p. 194.

tion of texts, but retains the design of Husserl's 'transcendental phenomenology': 'the meaning of phenomenological description as method lies in interpretation'.[32] The perspective of the observer in which objects are perceived is replaced by the perspective of an interpreter trying to catch the meaning of utterances and forms of life. Such a phenomenology with a hermeneutic turn is, however, not primarily concerned with the manifest content of an utterance, but with the tacit and context-giving features of its performance. Already Husserl had analysed the pre-predicative stratum of the concomitant horizons of perceived objects as 'ein assoziativ strukturiertes Feld passiver Vorgegebenheiten', characterising the world of subjective experience as the 'universalen Glaunbensboden der Erfahrung'.[33] Heidegger benefits from differentiated phenomenological descriptions of such background phenomena in his analysis of reference-complexes as are disclosed to human actors in their practical dealings with things and events of their familiar environment. He investigates the articulation of the pre-understanding of the world as mirrored in such everyday projects, expectations, and anticipations in the horizon of which we only face something as something. The phenomenon of this 'fore-structure of understanding' is Heidegger's point of convergence with Humboldt's transcendental conception of language.[34] But in contrast to Humboldt, he jumps to the conclusion that the linguistic world view enjoys an 'a priori of meaning' – a conclusion of considerable philosophical impact.

For instance, by ascribing the quality of 'blue' to the car in which the expected guests at last arrive, we determine this car 'as' blue. This 'predicative as' is distinguished, by Heidegger, from an 'hermeneutic as' which depends on categories of a preceding, but implicit, apprehension of the world as a whole. In certain practical respects, our world is grammatically divided into different types of bodies that move and can be moved, into which we knock, which appear in a different light at night or by day, etc. The strategic move, then, which permits Heidegger to prejudge all the rest is the subordination of the 'predicative as' under the 'hermeneutic as' of a tacit conceptual organisation of the whole of beings. It follows that we can ascribe or deny specific properties to specific objects only after they have been made available to us within the conceptual coordinates of a linguistically disclosed world, that is, 'given' to us as objects which are already implicitly interpreted and, in rele-

---

[32] Heidegger, *Being and Time*, p. 61.
[33] E. Husserl, *Erfahrung und Urteil* (Hamburg, 1948), §§6–10, §15ff.
[34] See C. Lafont, *Sprache und Welterschliessung*, first part.

Jürgen Habermas

vant respects, categorised. With this *a priori* classification of types of objects, a particular language per se preempts any specific inquiry as to which properties may be here and now predicated of which entities. All the speaker himself may 'discover' within this inescapable semantic network is which of the linguistically projected possibilities of truth is realised in the actual case.

For Heidegger, the fact that a predicate is ascribed to an object, as well as the truth of the corresponding predicative sentence is a derivative phenomenon that depends on a prior world disclosure which is a linguistic 'happening of truth'. With this notion of 'Wahrheitsgeschehen', the universalistic meaning of truth is relinquished. An ontological 'truth', changing with the mode of world disclosure, no longer appears in the singular of the 'one and indivisible truth'. Rather, the 'manifestation' of specific types of objects is determined by a transcendental 'event' of linguistic world disclosure, which in itself is neither true nor false, but just 'happens'.

This priority of the 'hermeneutic as' over the 'predicative as' marks the crucial difference from a truth-conditional view. The latter also, to be sure, holds that the meaning of linguistic expressions determines the possibilities of the truth and falsity of sentences. But this does not amount to the claim that on the semantic level, there is an irrevocable pre-determination or lasting precedence of which properties might be ascribed to which categories of objects. As long as we separate the predication of properties from the reference to objects, and as long as we are able to recognise the same objects under different descriptions, there is a possibility of learning – of enlarging our knowledge of the world with the possibility of a consequential revision of our linguistic knowledge.

Philosophical hermeneutics is not aware of the cognitive function of language having a right of its own. Heidegger precludes any interaction of linguistic knowledge and knowledge of the world. He does not allow for the possibility that the meaning of a vocabulary is affected by the results of learning processes within the world, because for him, the semantics of linguistic world views takes unlimited precedence over the pragmatics of communication. In contrast to Humboldt, he transfers the locus of control from the achievements of the participants in discourse to the higher-order events of linguistic world disclosure. Speakers are prisoners in the house of their language, and it is language that speaks through their mouths.[35] Authentic discourse is nothing but a statement of being; that is also why hearing takes precedence over speaking: 'Speaking is of itself a listening. Speaking is listening to the language that we

[35] For Heidegger's critique of Humboldt, see C. Lafont, *The Linguistic Turn in Hermeneutics*, (forthcoming), Chapter III.

speak ... We do not merely speak the language – we speak by way of it.'[36]

Wittgenstein, though less mystifying, came to a similar conclusion. The pragmatic turn from truth semantics to a use theory of meaning – and from the one universal fact-stating language to the many grammars of language games – means not only a detranscendentalisation of language. At the same time, Wittgenstein's descriptive approach to the actual language use levels off the cognitive dimension of language. Once the truth conditions which one has to know in order to make the right use of assertoric sentences are read off from the customary practice of language, there is no longer a clear-cut difference between the validity of an utterance and its social acceptance – what we are entitled to is assimilated to what we are merely accustomed to. By transferring the world forming spontaneity to the diversity of historical language games and forms of life, Wittgenstein confirms the primacy of the *a priori* of meaning over the representation of facts: 'All testing, all confirmation and disconformation of a hypothesis takes place already within a system. And this system is not a more or less arbitrary and doubtful point of departure for all our arguments: no it belongs to the essence of what we call an argument.'[37] Just as Heidegger, Wittgenstein relies on the background of an understanding of the world which, in itself, is not capable of being true or false, but pre-determines the standards for the truth and falsity of propositions.

III

The history of theoretical philosophy in the second half of our century can very roughly be said to be characterised by two major currents. On the one hand, there is a synopsis of the two heroes, Wittgenstein and Heidegger. The higher-level historicism of language games and epochal world disclosures is the common source of inspiration for a post-empiricist theory of science, a neopragmatist linguistic philosophy, and the post-structuralist critique of reason.[38] On the other hand, there continues from Russell and Carnap onwards an empiricist analysis of language with a purely methodological understanding of the linguistic turn, a stand that has gained world-wide predominance with Quine and Davidson. Davidson

[36] M. Heidegger, *On the Way to Language* (New York, 1982), pp. 126f.
[37] L. Wittgenstein, *On Certainty* (Oxford, 1974), p. 16 (para. 105)
[38] J. Habermas, 'Coping with contingencies', *Debating the State of Philosophy*, eds. J. Niznik, J. T. Sanders (eds) (Westport, 1996), pp. 1–24.

Jürgen Habermas

assimilates, from the start, the understanding of a linguistic expression to the theoretical interpretation of observational data[39], and ends up with a nominalistic conception of language that gives precedence to the passing idiolect of each person over the symbolically embodied and intersubjectively shared social universe of meaning.[40] With this move language loses the status of being part of the objective mind that Humboldt had attributed to it.

In the present context, however, I am interested in a third current characterised by positions as diverse as those of Putnam, Dummett, or Apel. These authors have in common that they take the linguistic turn seriously, in the sense of a change of paradigm, without paying the price of the culturalist assimilation of being true to taking for true. This implies a characteristic double front: against the half-hearted linguistic analysis that only tackles by new means the old problems of Kant and Hume,[41] on the one hand; and, on the other hand, against a semantic particularism which is hostile to the enlightenment and ignores the rational self-understanding of linguistic creatures on whom reasons are binding.[42]

This double thrust already characterises Karl-Otto Apel's thesis dating from the late 1950s. Objecting to an intentionalist conception of meaning as well as to an instrumentalistic conception of communication, he calls to mind Humboldt's insight 'that every world understanding pre-supposes ... also (!) a synthetic a priori of meaning (not necessarily in the form of complete sentences, but certainly in the form of construction plans for sentences, categories, concepts, even of word-meanings).'[43] On the other hand, Apel is wary of isolating the function of linguistic world disclosure from the cognitive function of the representation of facts and of giving meaning priority over validity. He postulates, instead, a 'relation of mutual pre-supposition' and 'interpenetration' between a particularistic 'projection of meaning' and a 'universalist design for knowledge'. His reference is to Kant's architectonics of reasons and understanding. Corresponding to 'reason' as the faculty of world-generating ideas, is the semantic *a priori* of the linguistic world view which is settled in

---

[39] D. Davidson, *Wahrheit und Interpretation* (Frankfurt, 1990).

[40] D. Davidson, 'Eine hübsche Unordnung von Epitaphen' *Die Wahrheit der Interpretation*, ed. G. Picard; and J. Schulte (Frankfurt, 1990), pp. 203–227; for a critical comment, see M. Dummett, *Ursprünge*, pp 248–78

[41] R. Rorty, *Der Spiegel der Natur* (Frankfurt, 1981), p. 287.

[42] R. Brandom, *Making it Explicit* (Cambridge, MA., 1994), p. 5: 'We are the ones on whom reasons are binding, who are subject to the peculiar force of the better reason'.

[43] K. O. Apel, *Die Idee der Sprache in der Tradition des Humanismus von Dante bis Vico* (Bonn, 1963), p. 27.

the life of a society, but only through understanding, that is, by being incorporated in successfully functioning practices. While a 'poietical-ly' projected meaning preempts specific forms of apprehension, this advance, inversely, depends on a confirmation by successful 'prac-tice'.[44] Thus, the problem of the 'mediation' of meaning and practice is unequivocally stated; what remains unclear is how it functions.

For Michael Dummett, the problem is the same, while the back-ground is completely different – lacking any reference to the Humboldtian tradition. Dummett joins Wittgenstein in admitting that language games project intersubjectively shared horizons of meaning and shape cultural forms of life. Languages, being public institutions, interpenetrate with the existing practices of a linguis-tic community. But in opposition to Wittgenstein's use theory of meaning, which takes the critical spur out of the truth conditions, thus denying the cognitive dimension of language any right of its own, Dummett puts forward an epistemic truth semantics. If the sentence is an expression of its truth conditions we must, in order to understand it, be able to *grasp* the conditions under which the sentence is true – and not just know the observable circumstances indicative of the speakers' habit of taking it for true. The know-ledge of truth conditions depends on the knowing the sort of rea-sons that explain whether and why they are met. Because of this internal relation between the truth-conditions of a proposition and the kind of reasons which might justify a corresponding truth claim, the practice of justification, that is, the game of argumentation, gains a particular significance also for Dummett.

The fact-stating mode of speech not only involves making and rejecting assertions, but also justifying or refuting them: 'Accepting or rejecting a statement made by another, checking whether it was war-ranted, and evaluating circumstances as warranting or not warranting an assertion made at once or subsequently – all these are activities which demand to be described in any full account of the practice of using language: they are all components of that practice. A statement's satisfying the condition for it to be true, is certainly not in itself a fea-ture of its use. The question at issue is whether there is nevertheless a need to appeal to it in a characterisation of linguistic practice.'[45] For Dummett, too, the formal pragmatics of that linguistic game in which the participants give and ask for reasons is the basis of a theory of meaning as opposed to the ad hoc character of a merely descriptive linguistic phenomenology. The same intention is the source of Karl Otto Apel's idea of a transcendental pragmatics.

[44] Ibid. p. 38.
[45] M. Dummett, 'Language and Communication', *The Seas of Language*, ed. M. Dummett (Oxford, 1993), p. 182.

Jürgen Habermas

1 In Germany, the state of argumentation, after World War II, was a particular one, since what had to be achieved in the first place was the re-appropriation of an interrupted analytic tradition.[46] In this endeavour, Apel was one of the first to discover, from a hermeneutic viewpoint, the convergences between the positions of Heidegger and Wittgenstein.[47] Any meta-critical reply to Heidegger's critique of reason, however, involved also, if not primarily, a critical examination of philosophical hermeneutics in its current form, marked by Hans Georg Gadamer's more recent work, *Wahrheit und Methode* (1960).

Gadamer's approach to his analysis of the understanding of meaning is not, as was Heidegger's, the semantic one of linguistic world disclosure, but the pragmatic one of communication between author and interpreter. Like Collingwood, he examines the practice of the interpretation of canonical texts along the lines of a 'logic of question and answer'. 'Dialogue' is seen as the model for an exchange between interlocutors reaching an agreement about something in the world. In dialogue, there is an interpenetration between the intersubjectivity of a shared lifeworld, actually rooted in the reciprocity and exchangeability of the perspectives of first and second persons, and, on the other hand, the reference to something in the objective world. As Humboldt had already stressed, there is a dimension of representation inherent in communication. And this dimension establishes an internal relation between the meaning of what is said and its possible truth. Otherwise Humboldt would not have been able to postulate the hermeneutic extension of the horizons of mutual understanding at the same time, with the hope of an ever wider agreement.

At first glance, it would seem that Gadamer rehabilitates, along with the communicative dimension of language, the universalist promise of reason. He too claims that in the attempt to understand each other, the initially distant horizons of understanding tend to converge and, finally, overlap. And this dynamic of mutual understanding follows, as Gadamer is well aware of, from the logic of a progressive agreement about facts. Gadamer's conclusion is nevertheless widely different from that of Humboldt. As with Heidegger, the dimension for possible reference and representation which guides the process of understanding is supposed to be delimited by a pre-established consensus within shared traditions. Why even this

[46] K. O Apel, 'Die Entfaltung der sprachanalytischen' Philosophie und das Problem der "Geisteswissenschaften", in Apel (1964), vol. II, pp. 28–95.
[47] K. O. Apel, 'Wittgenstein und Heidegger' (1962), in Apel (1973), pp. 225–275.

hermeneutics with its what is after all a pragmatic approach takes an 'ontological turn'[48] will be understood when we examine the motives of the whole enterprise.

Gadamer elaborates his hermeneutics in response to what was on his contemporaries' mind since Nietzsche's *Second Untimely Treatise*, that is, the 'problem of Historicism'. Gadamer means to stand up against the objectivism of the humanities which, as he sees them, isolate the great historical traditions from their context, confine them to the museum, deprive them of their intrinsic potential of stimulation and, thus, neutralise them as a 'formative power'. His orientation, therefore, is to the example of the hermeneutic appropriation of classical works – literary, artistic, religious and, more generally, all dogmatic works, for instance legal texts. With regard to the lasting impact of classical works, the reflexion on the situation of the interpreter may produce the insight which, for Gadamer, is crucial. The pre-understanding with which the interpreter approaches the text is, whether he likes it or not, pervaded and shaped by the effective history of the text itself.

This explains, first, why the process of interpretation – that is, revision of the pre-understanding through confrontation with the text, and progressive specification of it in a virtual dialogue with the author – is possible only on the basis of a shared context of tradition prior, in encompassing them, to both sides. Because the interpreter is thus inserted in tradition, the interpretation of an exemplary text consists, secondly, in the application of a received superior knowledge to the actual situation. The hermeneutic work may thus continue a tradition without immobilising it by reflexion, nor impairing its binding character. The essentially conservative task of hermeneutics thus consists in promoting the ethical self-understanding of an inherited community. Therefore, the method of the humanities or, as things stand, of any attempt to assimilate interpretations to scientific propositions is, thirdly, based on a misconception. Any hermeneutic ascertainment of the living core of a tradition depends on an unproblematic background consent. And in this, it is once more the pre-understanding of self and world of one's own linguistic community that is articulated. Hence, the contrast between 'truth' and 'method'. Any procedure which is to warrant the truth of propositions would only obstruct the revealing truth of tradition.

Gadamer reduces the ancient hermeneutics principle of understanding an author better than he understands himself to under-

---

[48] H. G. Gadamer, *Wahrheit und Methode*, Tübingen 1960, Part Three

Jürgen Habermas

standing him in so many different ways. Apel, in contrast, stresses that hermeneutics, as a scientific discipline, may not relinquish
the goal and standards of 'better understanding'. Conditions necessary for understanding cannot even be explicated without, at
the same time, raising 'the methodologically pertinent question of
the validity of competing interpretations'. If the normative concept of truth is not to be revoked in favour of a happening of
world disclosure, 'all interpretation remains bound to the reflexion on its validity'.⁴⁹ Apel proposes to explain the commensurability of different linguistic world views in terms of pragmatic
universals. He is guided by a simple idea: the linguistic knowledge that makes our coping practices possible is in turn, if only in
an indirect way, also tested by the success of being implemented
in those practices.⁵⁰

2 Around the transition from the fifties to the sixties, the intellectual constellation suggested discussing the cognitive dimension of
language from the aspect both of scientific knowledge and of
enlightenment. Enlightenment differs from science in its reflexive
reference to the subject of knowledge; it 'is not primarily progress
of knowledge, but loss of naiveté.⁵¹ Against an anti-scientistic
Gadamer, one could, with Popper, refer to the testimony of the
learning processes of empirical science: wasn't there still a cumula-
tive growth of knowledge? And against the traditionalistic
Gadamer, one could, with Adorno, proceed along the line of a
critique of ideology: wasn't there, imposing itself along with the
effective history of a prevailing tradition, the hidden power of
repression, which destroyed the very conditions of unconstrained
communication? Moreover, since Gadamer had elaborated his ideas
in the context of methodology, the critique could develop in the

⁴⁹ K. O. Apel (1973), vol. I, p. 49.
⁵⁰ Apel (1973), vol. II, p. 352: 'Die Möglichkeit einer Vorprägung des
subjektiven Sinnverständnisses impliziert die umgekehrte Möglichkeit
einer Umstrukturierung der semantischen Komponente lebender'
Sprachen durch die pragmatisch erfolgreiche Sinnverständigung in der
Ebene der Sprachverwendung.' Since I share and support this critique of
the hypostization of world-disclosure from the very start, I disagree with
the tenor of the second chapter of C. Lafont, *The Linguistic Turn in
Hermeneutics*. The problem of reference that we indeed neglected provides just one of those many objection that I actually have been putting
foreward; cf. J. Habermas, *Nach Metaphysisthes* Denken, Ffu, 1988, 50ff.,
55f., 103f., 175ff.; idem, *Der philosophische Diskurs der Moderne*, Ffm.
1986, 240ff.
⁵¹ E. Martens and H. Schnädelbach, *Philosophie* (Hamburg, 1985), p. 32.

434

shape of a controversy over 'Explanation and Understanding'.[52] Both lines of argumentation, the critique of science and of ideology, later converged in a theory of knowledge and human interests which, however, has in the meantime been passed over by the philosophical discussion.[53]

In the present context, this attempt is interesting only in as much as it suggests the outlines of a transcendental hermeneutics or formal pragmatics. Two distinctions were important for coping with the pluralism of allegedly incommensurable world views. Apel first distinguishes from the semantic *a priori* of different languages and linguistic world views the pragmatic constitution of larger domains of inquiry. A domain of observable states and events is structured by necessary conditions for instrumental interventions, while the domain of symbolic objects and meaningful expressions immediately mirrors the infrastructure of communication and interaction. Thus, general structures of action take the role of a pragmatic *a priori* for 'objects of possible experience', whether they are accessible to perception or interpretation. From this *a priori* of experience, Apel distinguishes, second, an *a priori* of argumentation in the form of the general pragmatic presuppositions of rational discourse in which truth claims are checked. In contrast to Kant, Apel thus separates the constitution of object domains from the check of validity claims by distinguishing the pragmatic conditions for the objectivity of possible experiences from the communicative conditions for the discursive redemption of truth claims.[54]

In this context, Apel comes up with general pragmatic presuppositions of any cooperative search for the truth. He is inspired by Peirce's model of an unlimited communication community where investigators justify their fallible assumptions to one another with the purpose of reaching an agreement (principally always open to revision) by discursive means, that is, by the refutation of objections (possible at any time). This idea not only gives support to a dis-

[52] J. Habermas, *Zur Logik der Sozialwissenschaften* (1967), (Frankfurt, 1982), pp. 271–305. K. O. Apel *et al.*, *Hemeneutik und Ideologiekritik* (Frankfurt, 1971). Subsequent to the work, published at the same time, of G. H. von Wright, *Explanation and Understanding* (London, 1971), the controversy was continued and extended to analytic contributions: K. O. Apel, J. Mannichen, R. Tuomela, eds., *Neue Versuche über Erklären und Verstehen* (Frankfurt, 1978)

[53] K. O. Apel, 'Szientistik, Hermeneutik, Ideologiekritik' (1968), in Apel (1973), vol. II, pp. 96–127; J. Habermas, *Erkenntnis and Interesse* (Frankfurt, 1968).

[54] J. Habermas, 'Nachwort', *Erkenntnis und Interesse*, ed. J. Habermas (Frankfurt, 1973), pp. 382–401.

course conception of truth,[55] but encourages a discourse ethics that develops an intersubjectivist reading of Kant's categorical imperative. While Gadamer basically conceives of hermeneutic understanding in the Aristotelian sense, that is, as the promotion of an ethical self-understanding of a community constituted by shared traditions, Apel puts forward a Kantian conception of morality which is orientated to questions of justice. For Apel, language, having taken the systematic place of the – pragmatically transformed – 'Bewußtsein überhaupt', is the necessary condition 'of the possibility as well as validity of understanding and self understanding and therefore, at the same time, of conceptual analysis, objective knowledge, and intentional action'.[56]

This comprehensive program is, it is true, still inspired by a hermeneutic concept of language; what is still lacking, except for a reception of Peircian semiotics, is the very core of a theory of language – a 'theory of meaning', if this expression is used in the sense of the analytic tradition. The starting point of a methodological dispute over the role and the scope of the 'operation called understanding' explains why Apel began elaborating his program in terms of epistemology and then reverted to moral theory.[57]

But in the context of a social theory based on the complementary concepts of communicative action and lifeworld,[58] this deficiency of a theory of language in the analytical sense became obvious.[59] With regard to this desideratum of a theory of meaning, however, two basic decisions had already been reached: the uncoupling of the formal pragmatics of communication from the particularistic implications of the semantics of linguistic world disclosure, one the one hand; and the differentiation between the levels of rational discourses and of action, as well as a further distinction between propositional truth and moral rightness, on the other. I will conclude by at least mentioning three basic assumptions of this formal pragmatic theory of meaning, indicating how significant results of analytic philosophy have been assimilated and elaborated from a hermeneutic point of view.

[55] J. Habermas, 'Wahrheitstheorien' (1972), in *Vorstudien und Ergänzungen zur Theorie des kommunikativen Handelns,* J. Habermas, (Frankfurt, 1983), pp. 127–83.

[56] Apel, (1973), 333.

[57] K. O. Apel, 'Das Apriori der Kommunikationsgesellschaft und die Grundlagen der Ethik', in K. O. Apel (1973), vol. II. pp. 358–436; K. O. Apel, *Diskurs und Verantwortung* (Frankfurt, 1988).

[58] J. Habermas, *Theorie des kommunikativen Handelns* (Frankfurt, 1981).

[59] See my introduction to the new edition of J. Habermas, *Logik der Sozialwissenschaften* (Frankfurt, 1982), pp. 7–11.

(i) The theory of speech acts proposed by Austin and Searle[60] is a suitable frame for situating some thoughts of Dummett's theory of meaning[61] in a theory of communicative action.[62] First, an observation concerning the internal relation of meaning and validity. We understand a sentence if we know how to justify its truth, as well as the action-relevant consequences incurred in case of our accepting it as true.[63] This conception already provides the design for the critical reaction of a hearer to a speaker performing a speech act and claiming validity for its content. The hearer will understand the expression if he knows, on the one hand, the kind of reasons in the light of which this validity claim deserves intersubjective recognition and, on the other hand, the action-relevant consequences incurred with the acceptance of the validity claim.[64] The internal relation between the meaning of an expression and the conditions of its rational acceptability follows from a pragmatic conception of understanding and communication according to which the illocutionary success of a speech act is assessed in terms of the conditions for the Yes/No positions taken towards validity claims which are open to criticism.

(ii) Communication aiming at agreement is per se of a discursive nature; it is, at the same time, intrinsically differentiated in the levels of discourse and action. For communicative action, validity claims are naively put up and, before the background of a shared lifeworld, more or less taken for granted. As soon as they become a problem, and are made the topic of a controversy, the participants pass (in however elementary a way) from action to another form of communication, that is, to a practice of argumentation,

[60] J. R. Searle, *Speech Acts* (Cambridge, 1969); J. R. Searle, *Expression and Meaning* (Cambridge 1979); for a critique of Searle's intentionalism, see K. O. Apel, 'Is Intentionality more than Linguist Meaning?' in *John Searle and his Critics*, E. Lepore, R. von Gulick eds, (Oxford, 1991), pp. 31–56; J. Habermas, 'Comments on J. Searle: Meaning, Communication, and Representation', pp. 17–30.

[61] M. Dummett, 'What is a Theory of Meaning? II,' in Dummett (1993), pp. 34–93.

[62] J. Habermas, vol. I (1983), pp. 369–452; vol. 2 (1983) pp. 182–205.

[63] M. Dummett, 'Language and Truth', in Dummett (1993), p. 142: 'What we have been considering are two alternative ways of explaining the meanings of sentences of a language: in terms of how we establish them as true; and in terms of what is involved in accepting them as true ... they are complementary in that both are needed to give an account of the practice of speaking the language.'

[64] See the theory of language of R. Brandom (1994), based on the complementary relation of inferential semantics and formal pragmatics.

willing to convince each other of their views and to learn from each other. Under the changed communicative presuppositions of such a rational discourse[65], beliefs which up to this point were part of an unproblematic background are examined as to their validity. In the process, descriptive propositions about something in the objective world are differentiated from normative propositions about legitimate expectations within the social world.

The linguistically structured lifeworld forms, more or less behind the back of the participants, the context of dialogue and provides a source of communicative content. This *lifeworld* has to be distinguished from the formal presupposition of an *objective* as well as a *social* world, which is made by speakers and actors themselves in their linguistic reference to the world or, more generally, in coping with the world. What once was conceived, in an epistemological perspective, as the constitution of two objects domains, is now, in formal pragmatics, sublimated to a presupposition of purely formal reference-systems, or 'worlds'. The presupposition of an 'objective' as well as a shared 'social' world is just the grammatical reference system for everything that speaker and actor can ever encounter in the world. These frames lack any content beyond the conditions necessary for reference either to possible objects or to possible interpersonal relations – objects about which we state facts in an objectivating attitude, or relations the binding character of which we claim in a performative attitude.

(iii) The question remains how the pragmatic universals that are constitutive for communicative action, rational discourse, and the world relations of propositions can disrupt the ethnocentrism of linguistic world views and linguistically structured forms of life. As we have seen with Gadamer, the communicative dimension of language does not per se possess a universalist potential. As learning processes are always starting from a particularistic context of meaning, their results can change the limits of this linguistically disclosed world only if world-knowledge is not just depending on linguistic knowledge, but actually gains the power to revise it. This power of revision is explained by the discursive processing of the action-related experiences, that is, disappointing experiences, we make in our attempts to cope with an objective world presupposed as identical and independent, on the one hand, and in our interactive dealings with members of a social world presupposed as shared, on the other.[66] Experiences that

[65] Habermas (1981), vol. 1, pp. 44–71.
[66] J. Habermas, 'Rortys pragmatische Wende', *Deutsche Zeitschrift für Philosophie* (1996) pp. 715–741.

indicate the collapse of routine practices can initiate a revision of assumptions and normative expectations and, in the end, even affect linguistic knowledge itself.

The performative failure to cope with the world – be it because of the resistance of a reality that refuses to go along, or because of a conflict with a strange, and normatively dissonant, form of life – is hard to deny. In this regard, the distinction between discourse and action comes to the fore in a different way, that is, not as an intra-linguistic difference between levels of communication, but as a difference between language and non-linguistic (yet propositionally structured) action. Once validity claims are routed out of the contexts of interventions or social interactions, they are addressed, checked and, if need be, revised in discourse. In order to learn from the world and to improve empirical beliefs, the hypothetical attitude of the participants in discourse requires the complement of abductive imagination; whereas for learning from each other, the context-transcending dynamics built into the very form of rational discourse has an immediate significance. The decentering of one's own perspective expected from participants in discourse promotes, in cases of action conflict, the mutual extension of competing horizons of value orientations which is required if, by the generalisation of values, mutual agreement on shared norms is to be reached.

4 In this formal-pragmatic approach, the concept of language is developed from a notion of discourse where participants raise, with their utterances, claims that can be criticised. Validity claims which can be backed by reasons are of two kinds: we claim truth for assertions about things and events in the objective world, and rightness for propositions about normative expectations and interpersonal relations which, at eye level, so to speak, are part of a social world that is accessible in a performative attitude only. The cognitive function of language attains a relative independence from the function of world disclosure in both domains, coping with external reality and socio-moral learning. That is the reason why a theory of communicative action grounded in this conception of language may link up with a materialistic social theory.

So far, I have not yet mentioned the most salient physiognomical difference between the hermeneutic and the analytic tradition. Since the issues of an analytic philosophy of language are more or less an inheritance from epistemology, it lacks a certain sensibility for the looser and larger issues of a diagnostics of the age. Since Hegel, the philosophical discourse of modernity has, therefore,

Jürgen Habermas

been the domain of a so-called continental philosophy. In this context, the confrontation of analytic and continental currents, otherwise obsolete, still in a way makes sense.[67] With Wittgenstein, even his reflections on the *zeitgeist* – his anti-scientistic sentiment, his criticism of science and technology, his scepticism about progress, his disgust with sociology, the contrast of 'culture' and 'civilisation', the devaluation of 'talent' and cleverness in contrast to 'genius', in short: the ready-mades of a 'German ideology' which distinguish him, to his disadvantage, from his teacher, Bertrand Russell[68] – still are of a rather private and more ornamental nature and, in any case, do not affect the structure of his inimitable philosophical world.

With Heidegger, in contrast, critique of culture is a pervasive feature of his philosophy as a whole. The author of *Being and Time*, in the grand posture of a critic of his time, already brings together Aristotle and Kierkegaard, pre-Kantian metaphysics and post-Kantian ethics. In his later work, the widely received critique of science and technology and of the totalitarian features of the age as a whole is inspired by a convincing deconstruction of Cartesianism and a discussion of Nietzsche. Heidegger thus takes up issues which had already been discussed, in a similar critical vein though in a different manner, by Max Weber and Georg Lukacs. Conducting his analysis of the present by means of a critique of metaphysics, Heidegger furnishes the idealistic counterpart to the materialist critique of objectification. In the present context, though, I would like to stress the homogenising and at the same time fateful character of Heidegger's diagnosis of the destiny of modernity. This diagnosis itself – self-empowered subjectivity practising an all round objectification – is not novel. Heidegger's specific contribution is that he stylises the phenomena of self-preservation running wild to make up an irruption of destiny in profane history. He indeed conceives them as the fateful symptoms of a world-view that, taking hold of modernity, flattens out and overpowers all differences.

'Technology' takes on features of a '*Seinsgeschick*' because the critique of metaphysics by means of which Heidegger wants to oppose the prevailing philosophy of the subject is grounded in the conception of linguistic world-disclosure. Once we steer clear of this hypostatisation of the linguistic function of world-disclosure, a more differentiated view of modernity emerges. Indeed, as soon as we admit that there is a dialectics of world-disclosure and learning processes within the world, the monolithic and fateful character of a world view prejudging all and everything falls apart. At the same

[67] See the protest of Michael Dummett (1988), pp 7f.
[68] L. Wittgenstein, *Vermischte Bemerkungen* (Frankfurt, 1977).

time, the diagnosis itself is deprived of its sheerly idealistic character, for the pathologies of modernity can then no longer be attributed to the semantics of an inescapably deforming pre-understanding of the world. This is what a last look back on Humboldt may
teach us.

Humboldt himself, to be sure, has not in any significant way contributed to a critique of modernity. What he sees, though, are the
dysfunctional consequences of linguistic communication being
blocked as a mechanism of social integration. Communicative
action fosters individuation and social integration at the same time.[69]
Language 'associates by individuation', thus saving the communicatively associated subjects 'from degeneration through isolation'.[70] From this point of view, characteristical social pathologies
may be explained as disruptions of a communicatively mediated
social integration. Since the issue, then, is the analysis of patterns
of systematically distorted communication, philosophy can no
longer solve the problem on its own. While Heidegger carries diag-
noses his time one-handedly, Humboldt's philosophy of language
suggests a division of labour with a social theory. While a lifeworld
which is reproduced though communicative action provides a
resource of social solidarity, this solidarity is at the same time always
in danger of being overpowered and even destroyed by those two
further mechanisms, markets and bureaucracies, through which
modern societies are integrated.[71] From this perspective, modernity
is threatened not by a monotonous and providential *Seinsgeschlick* as
vague as it is sinister, but by systemic and, above all, economic
imperatives consuming the lifeworld resources of social solidarity.

[69] J. Habermas, 'Individuierung durch Vergesellschaftung', in
Nachmetaphysisches Denken, J. Habermas, (Frankfurt, 1988), pp. 187.
[70] W. v. Humboldt, Über die Verschiedenheiten des menschliechen
Sprachbaus, *Werke*, vol. III, pp. 160f.
[71] Habermas (1981), vol. 1, pp. 485–8.

Index of Names

Index of Names